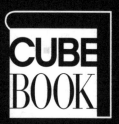

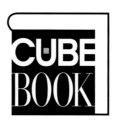

CUBE
BOOK

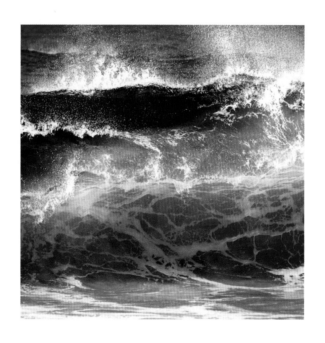

THE SEA

WHITE STAR PUBLISHERS

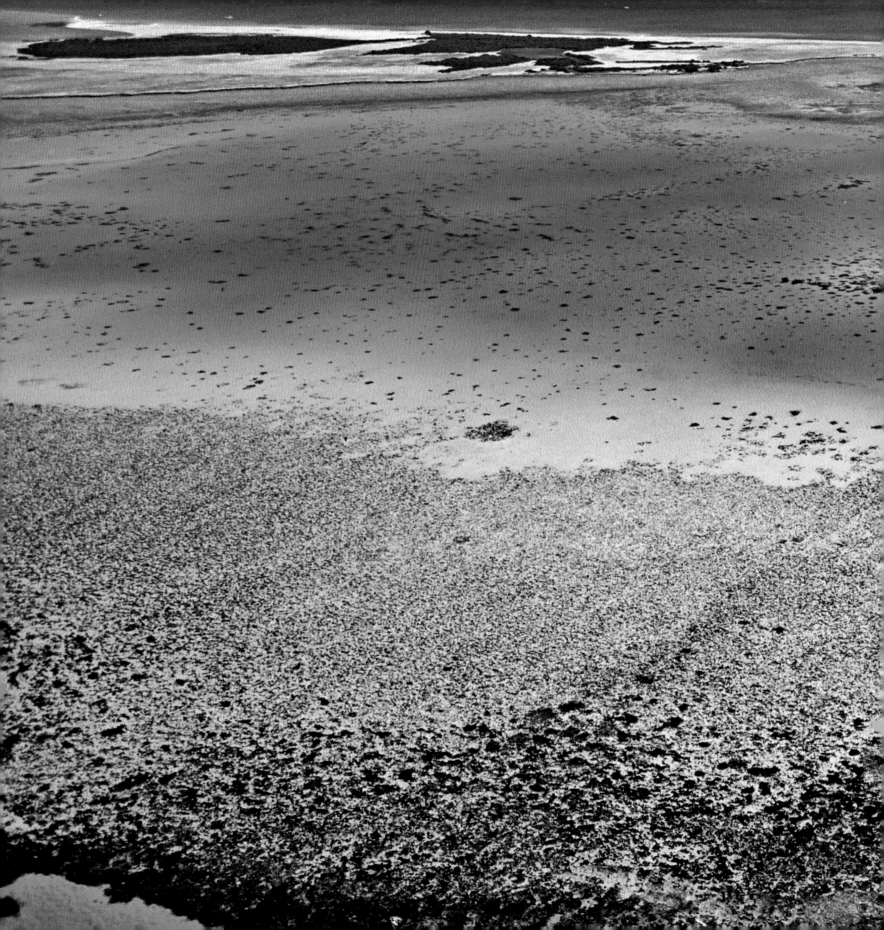

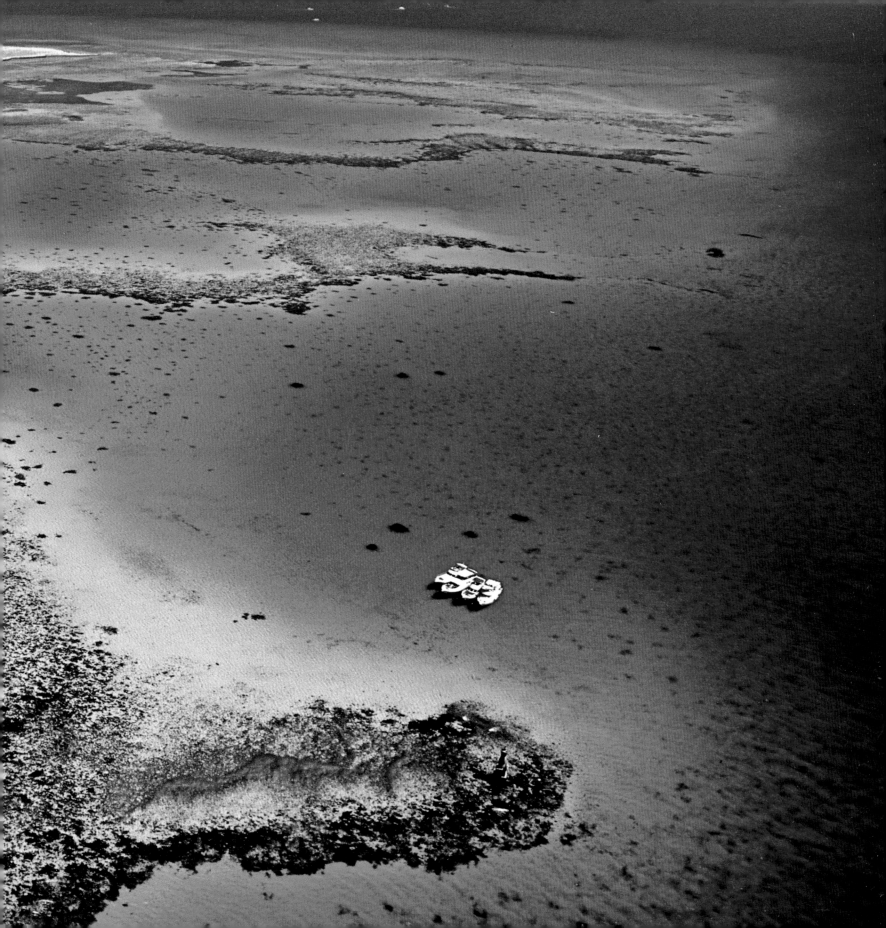

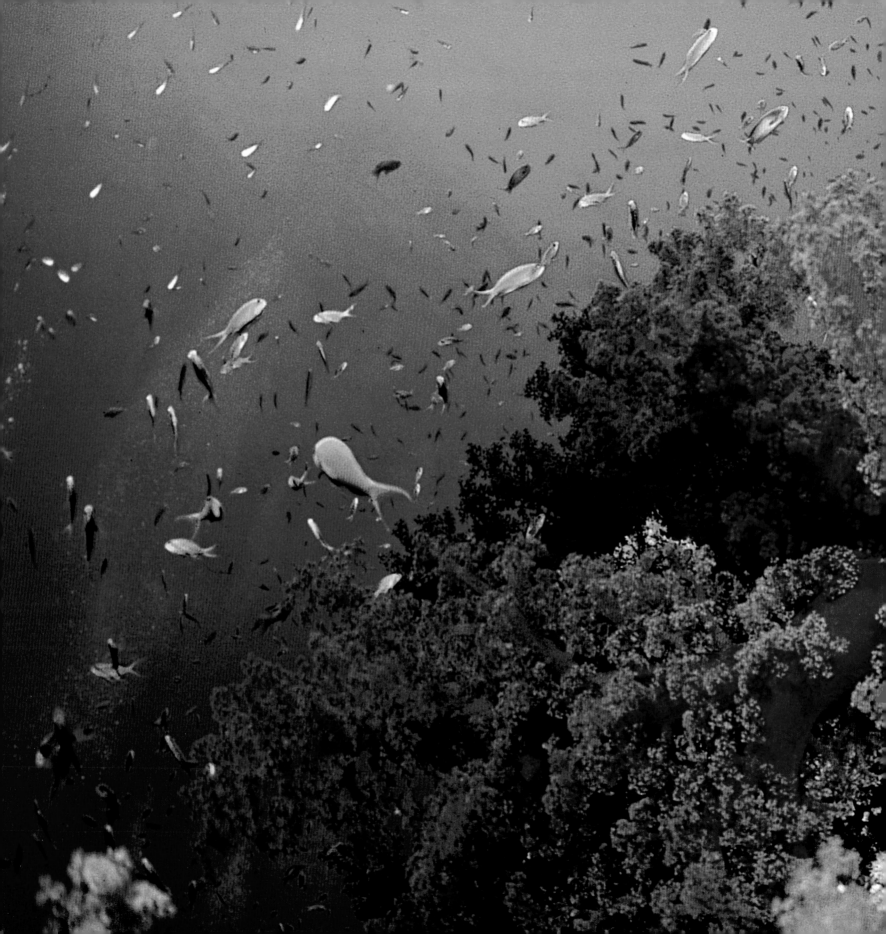

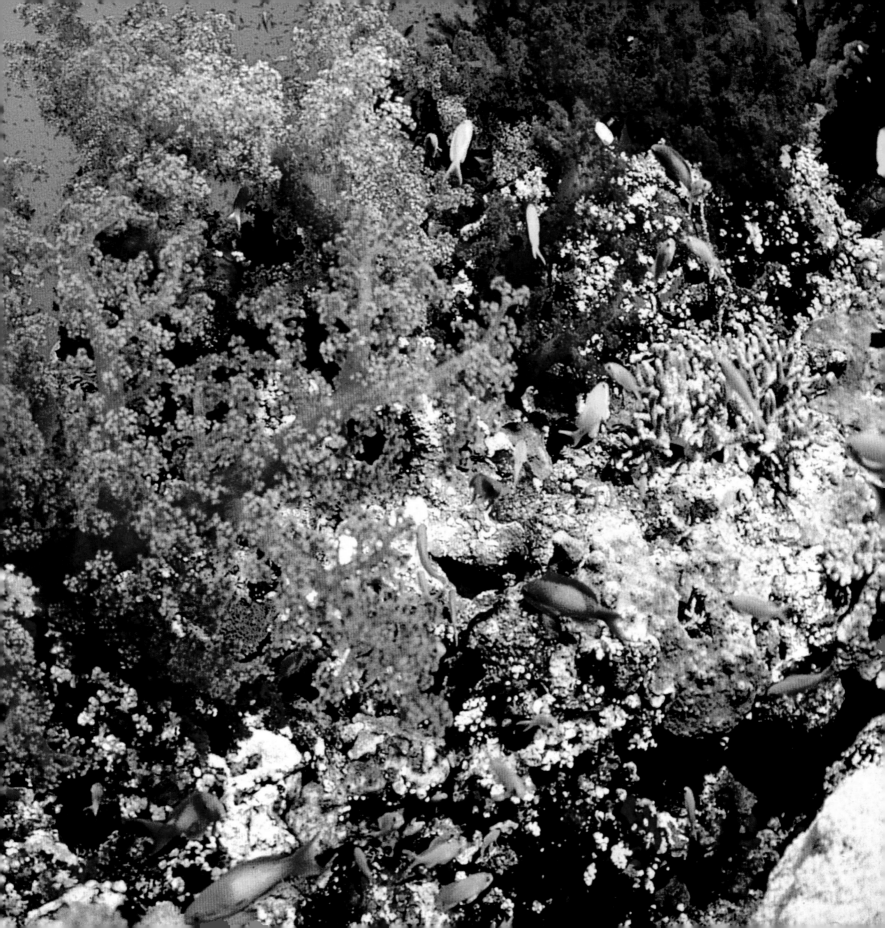

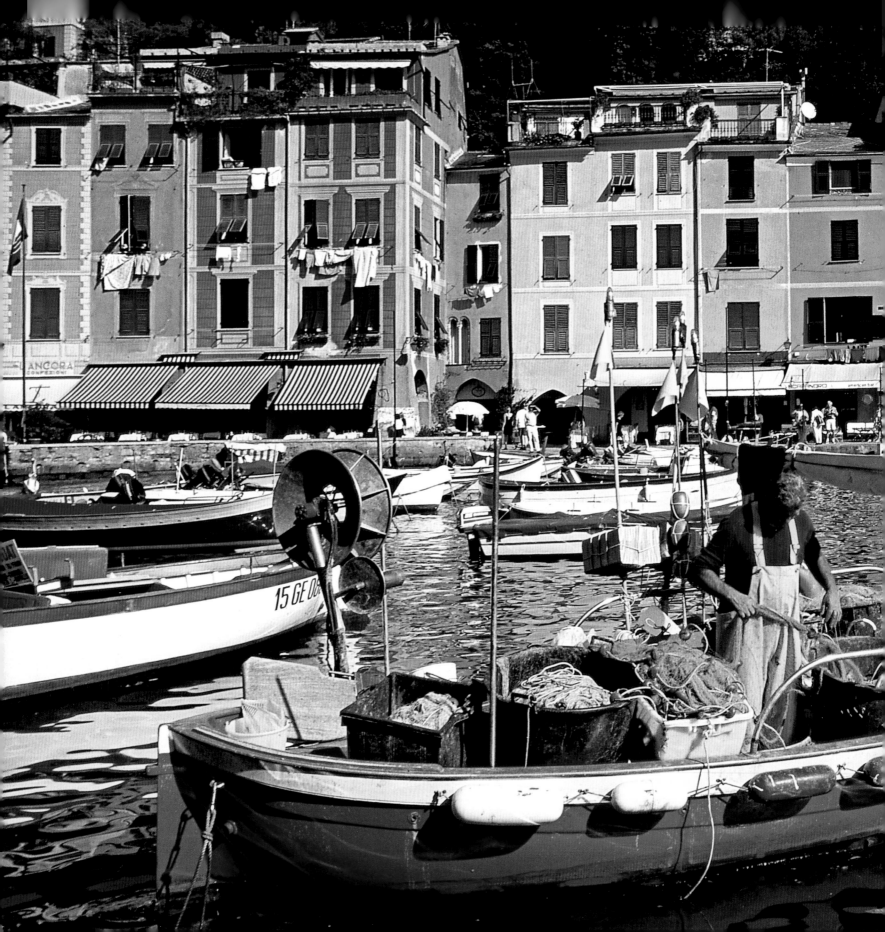

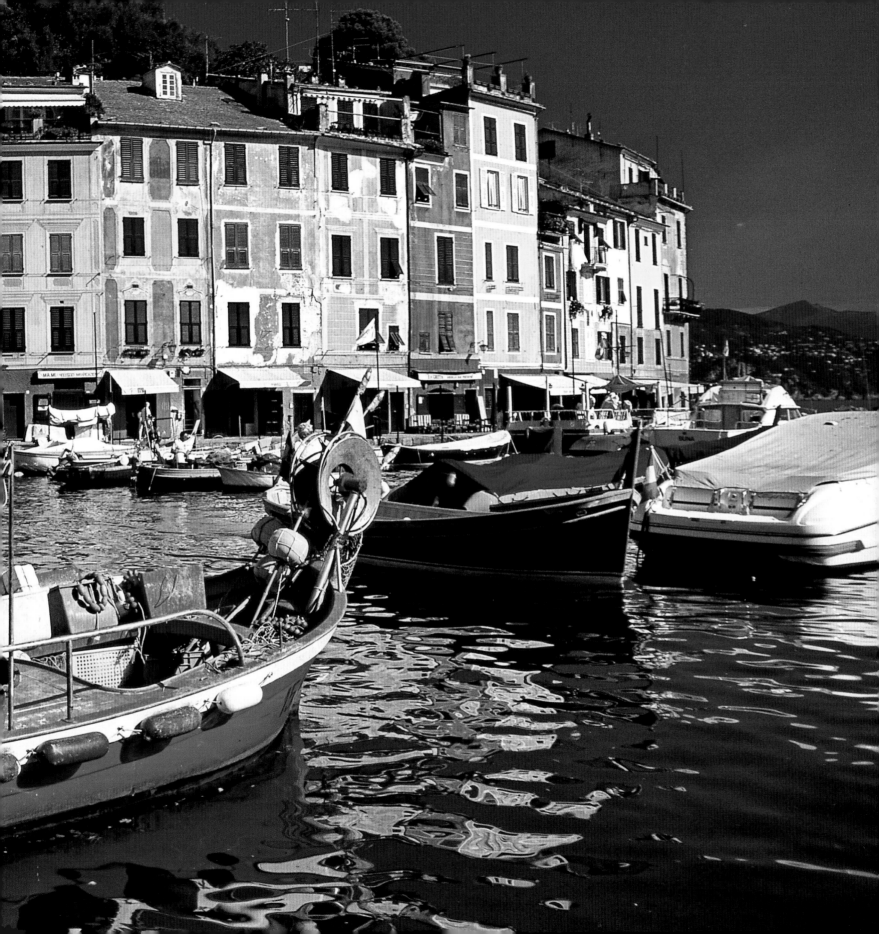

TEXTS BY

GAETANO CAFIERO

NORA L. DEANS

GIANNI GUADALUPI

THIERRY JIGOUREL

CORNELIA LAUF

CARLO MARINCOVICH

GIULIO MELEGARI

ANGELO MOJETTA

COLIN MONTEATH

ALESSANDRA SENSINI

GIOVANNI SOLDINI

project manager and editorial director
VALERIA MANFERTO DE FABIANIS

graphic design
CLARA ZANOTTI

graphic layout
CLARA ZANOTTI
PATRIZIA BALOCCO LOVISETTI

editorial coordination
ALBERTO BERTOLAZZI
CLAUDIA ZANERA
MARIA VALERIA URBANI GRECCHI

translation
TIMOTHY STROUD

© 2003 WHITE STAR S.P.A.
VIA CANDIDO SASSONE, 22-24
13100 VERCELLI - ITALY
WWW.WHITESTAR.IT
REVISED EDITION IN 2005

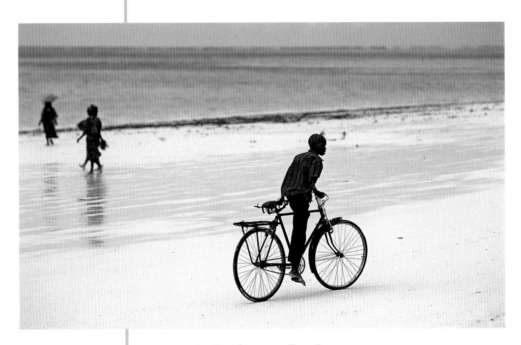

• Indian Ocean - Zanzibar

ISBN 10: 88-544-0125-0
ISBN 13: 978-88-544-0125-9
REPRINTS:
2 3 4 5 6 09 08 07 06

Printed in Thailand
Color separation: Fotomec, Turin, Italy

CONTENTS

THE SEA

1 ● Atlantic Ocean, Portugal - The Algarve.

2-3 ● Red Sea, Egypt - Hurghada.

4-5 ● Red Sea, Egypt - The coral reef.

6-7 ● Mediterranean Sea, Italy - Portofino.

11 ● Pacific Ocean, French Polynesia - Bora Bora lagoon

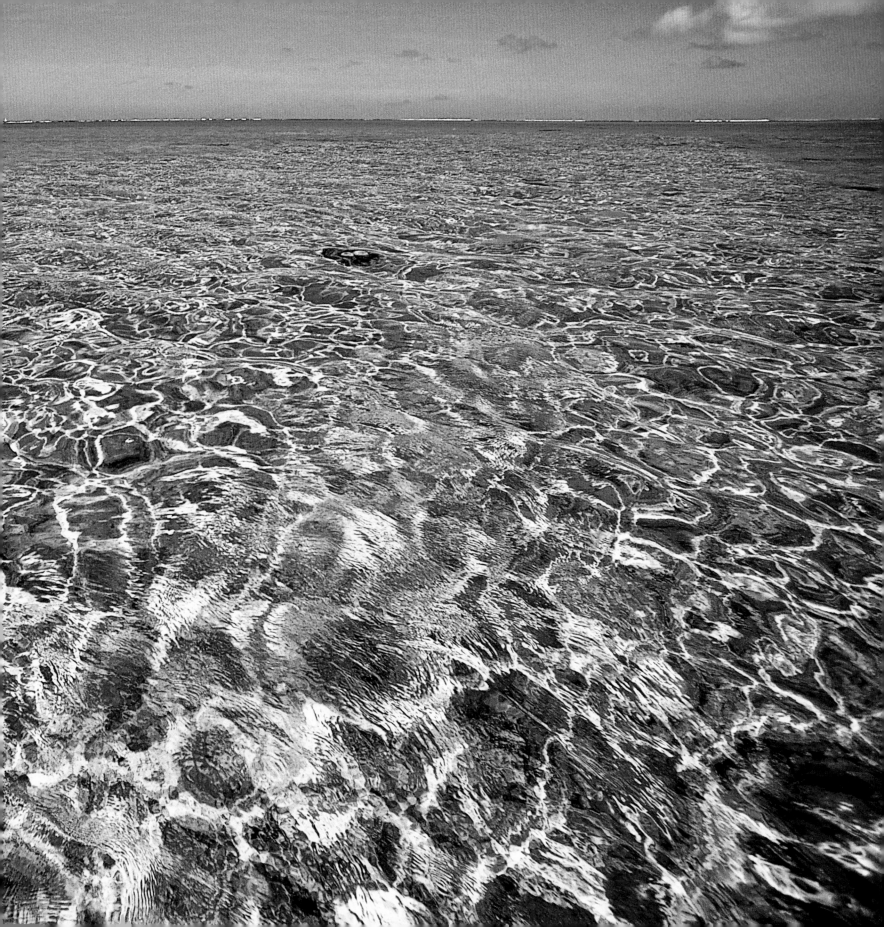

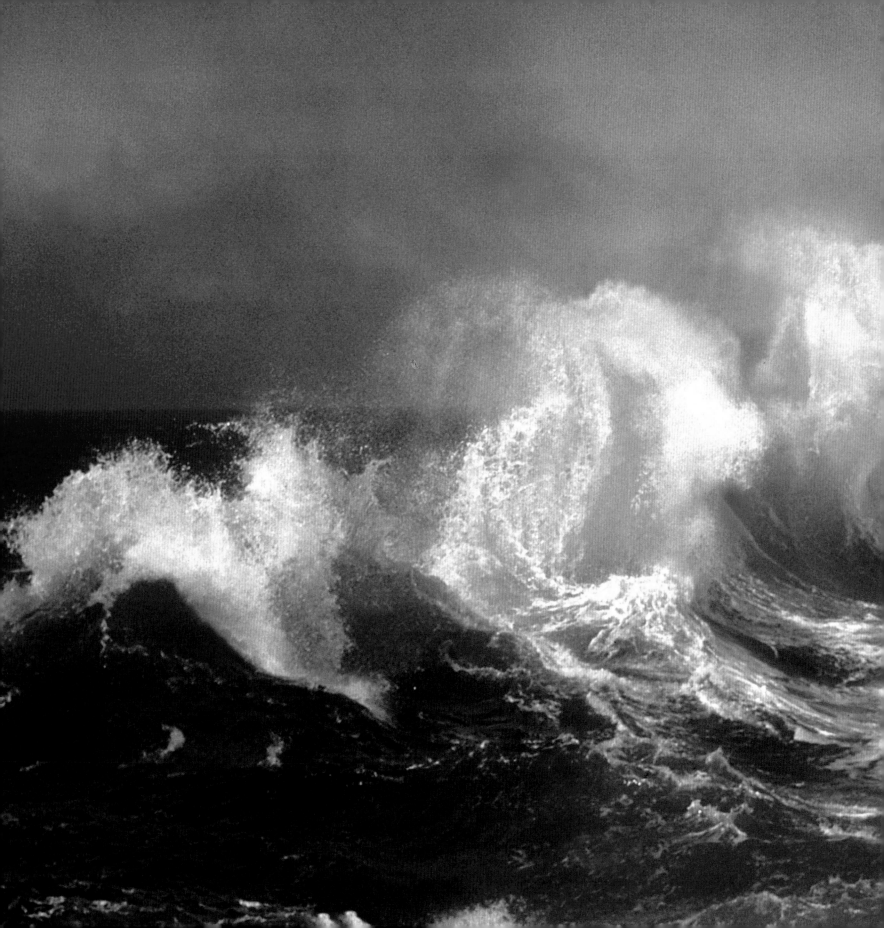

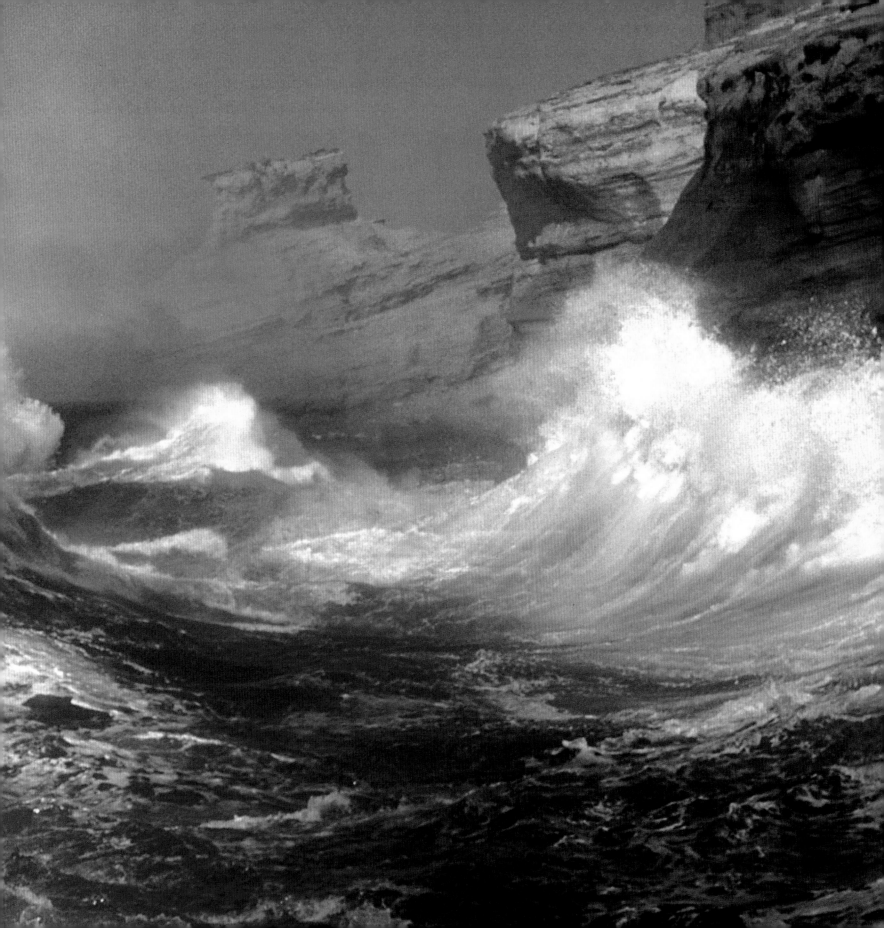

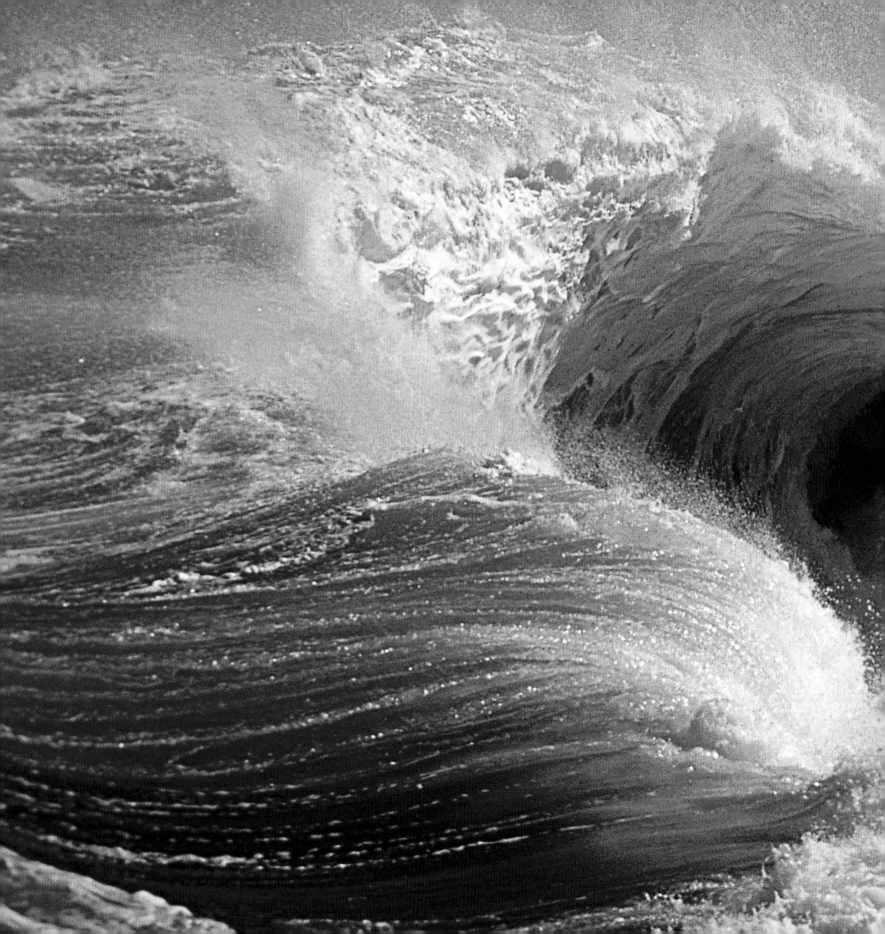

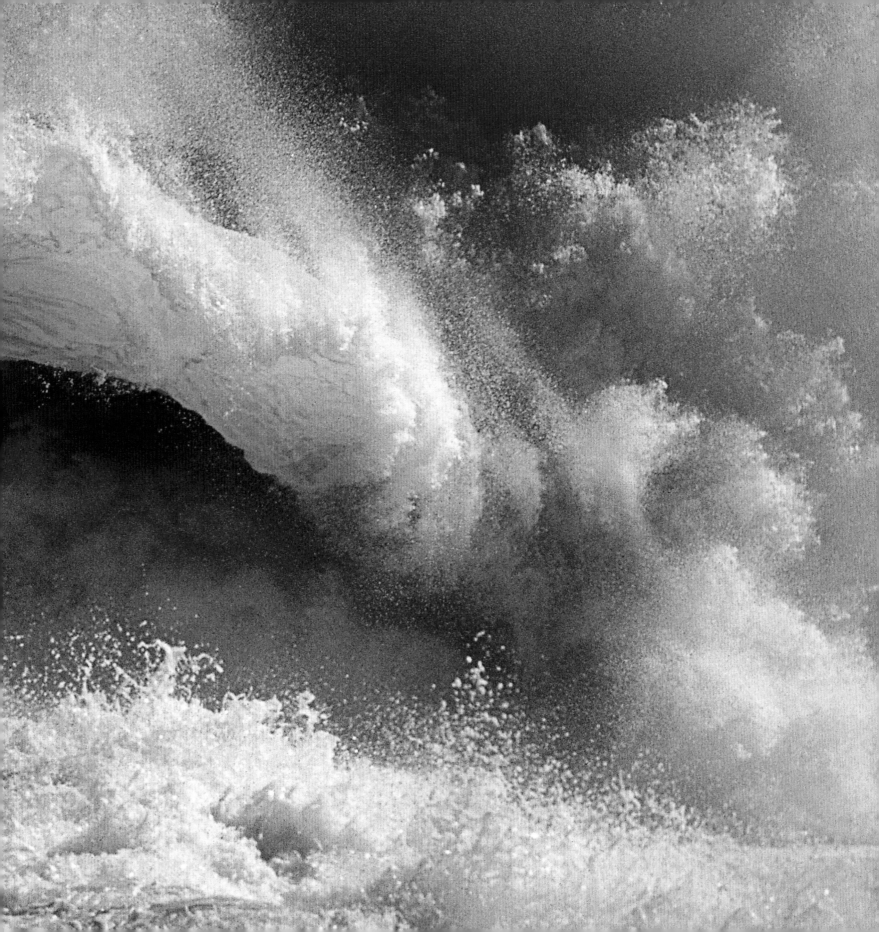

Introduction

by Gaetano Cafiero

IN ALL THE WORLD'S WRITTEN LANGUAGES THE WORD

'EARTH' IS USED TO DEFINE THE WHOLE OF OUR PLANET, NOT JUST

TERRA FIRMA, OR LAND. THIS MIGHT BE CONSIDERED CONTRADIC-

TORY: WATER COVERS BY FAR THE GREATEST SURFACE AREA OF

THE PLANET, AND THE CONTINENTS AND ISLANDS INHABITED BY

MAN, THE ANIMALS, AND THE PLANTS THAT BREATHE AIR ARE

KNOWN AS 'LANDS ABOVE SEA LEVEL.' PERHAPS THIS HAS HAP-

PENED BECAUSE MAN HAS DISCOVERED THE TRUTH ONLY RECENT-

LY: UNTIL FIVE CENTURIES AGO, AT THE TIME OF CHRISTOPHER

COLUMBUS, MAN'S UNDERSTANDING OF THE SIZE AND PHYSICAL

12-13 ● Pacific Ocean, California (USA) - Rollers at Big Sur.

14-15 ● Pacific Ocean, Hawaii (USA) - Waves on the coast of Oahu.

17 ● Caribbean Sea, Florida (USA) - Bathing hut with wharf at Key Biscayne.

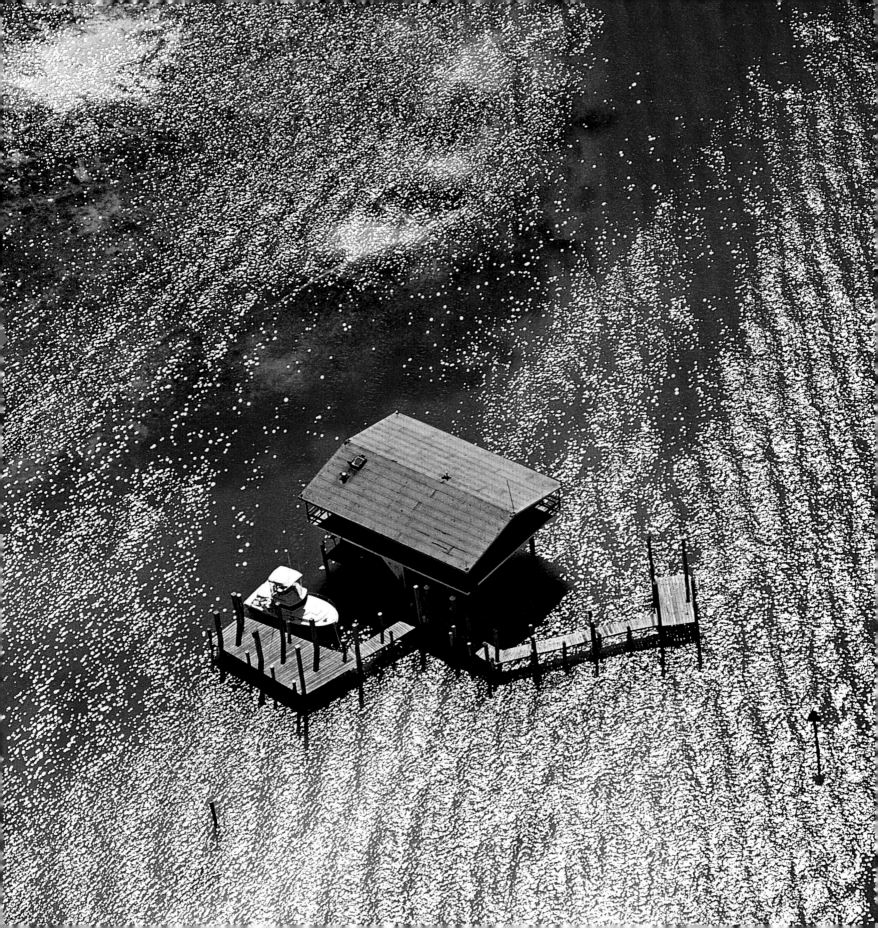

Introduction

REALITY OF THE LAND AND SEA WERE VERY APPROXIMATE AND OFTEN INCORRECT. SINCE THEN, CONTINUAL RESEARCH HAS BROUGHT INCREASINGLY PRECISE UNDERSTANDING OF THE ORIGIN, COMPOSITION, AND PHYSICAL AND DYNAMIC PROPERTIES OF THE HEAVENLY BODY WE INHABIT. BUT THERE ARE STILL MANY MYSTERIES TO BE UNVEILED. THE OCEAN IS THE ALEMBIC IN WHICH LIFE ORIGINATED. THOUGH DISPLAYING THE SIGNS – LIKE THE SOIL AND THE AIR – OF MAN'S USE AND CUSTOMS, IT STILL RETAINS MANY OF ITS ORIGINAL CHARACTERISTICS. IN THE LAST TWO CENTURIES, THE PLANET'S HUMAN POPULATION HAS MULTIPLIED BY FIVE, AND HUMAN PRESENCE IS ESTABLISHED ON MOST OF WHAT

Introduction

WAS NOT SO LONG AGO WILDERNESS: FORESTS, DESERTS, STEPPES AND EVEN TUNDRA HAVE CEDED SPACE TO CITIES, FARMS AND FACTORIES. SHIPS, SOME LARGER EVEN THAN TYPICAL SEA-SIDE VILLAGES, HAVE CROSSED EVERY POSSIBLE SEA ROUTE ON THEIR VOYAGES BETWEEN THE CONTINENTS; AND YET THE IMMENSE BLUE EXPANSE REMAINS THE WILDEST OF WILD REGIONS, FOR THE MOST PART UNTAMED AND INTACT. SINCE THE START OF HIS ADVENTURE ON EARTH, MAN'S RELATIONSHIP WITH THE SEA HAS BECOME INCREASINGLY COMPLEX. THE SEA REPRESENTS LIFE AND DEATH: ANCIENT PEOPLES ASSOCIATED IT WITH THE GODS OF CREATION; INDUSTRIAL MAN APPRECIATES ITS INEXHAUSTIBLE

Introduction

RESOURCES; WHILE THE INTELLECTUAL, SCIENTIST, AND POET ATTEMPT TO REVEAL THE SECRET OF THE INTIMATE, SPIRITUAL, AND CULTURAL BOND OF MAN WITH THE LIQUID WORLD THAT SURROUNDS HIM. THE INVENTION OF EQUIPMENT THAT ALLOWS MAN TO BREATHE UNDERWATER HAS LED TO THE EXPLORATION OF THE DEPTHS, BEYOND THE MYSTERIOUS DIVIDE REPRESENTED BY THE SURFACE. AND THUS BEGAN THE ERA THAT WILL LEAD TO THE CONQUEST OF WHAT HAS BEEN CALLED 'INNER SPACE,' I.E., THE SPACE THAT EXISTS INSIDE THE PLANET, ANALOGOUS IN MYSTERY AND FASCINATION TO THAT OF OUTER SPACE.

21 ● Pacific Ocean, Tonga - Island in Vavau Archipelago.

22-23 ● Pacific Ocean, California (USA) - Wave breaking over a surfer.

24-25 ● Pacific Ocean, French Polynesia - Marquesas Islands.

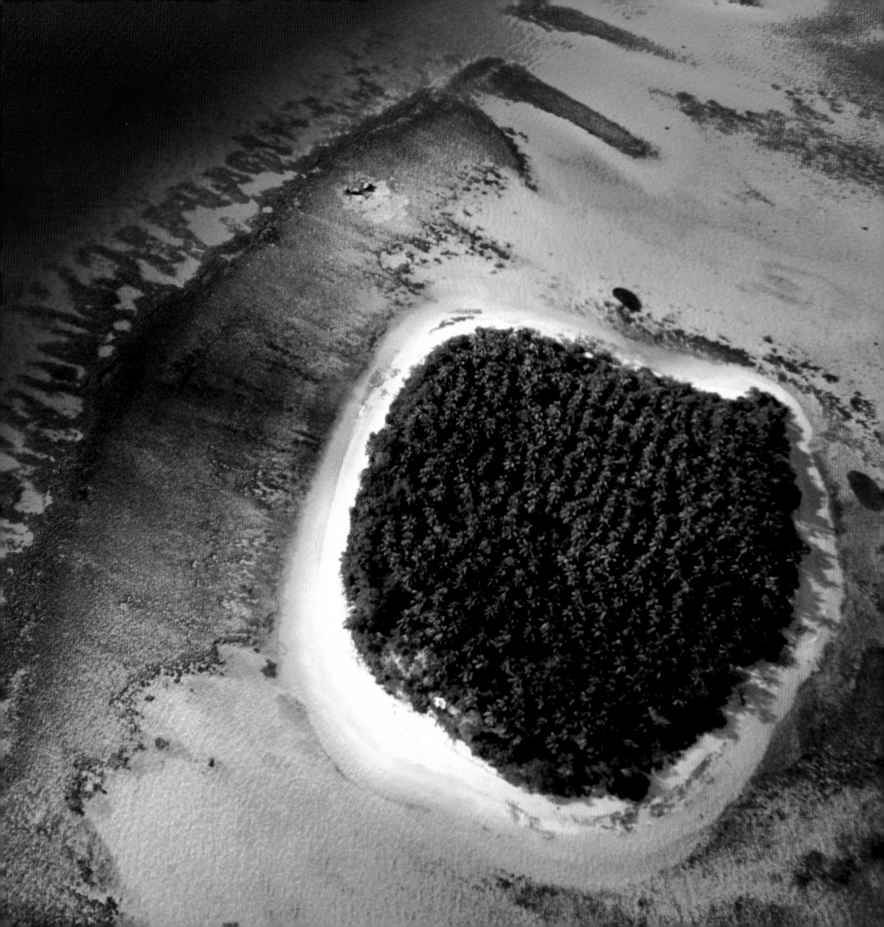

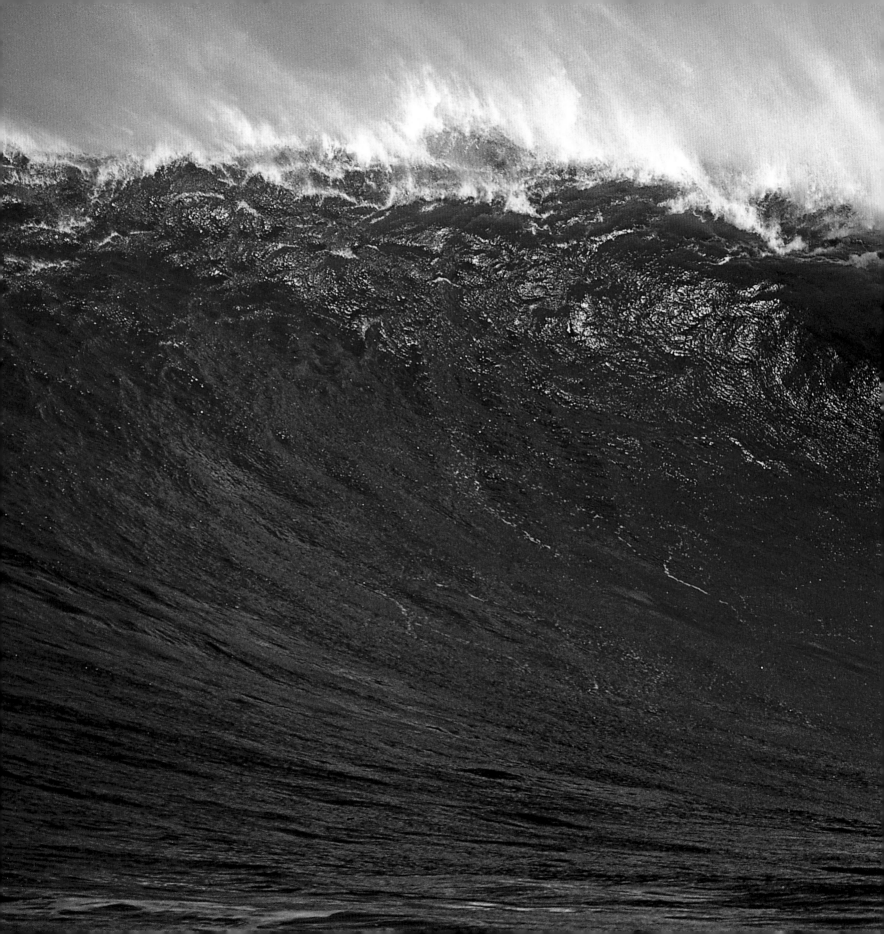

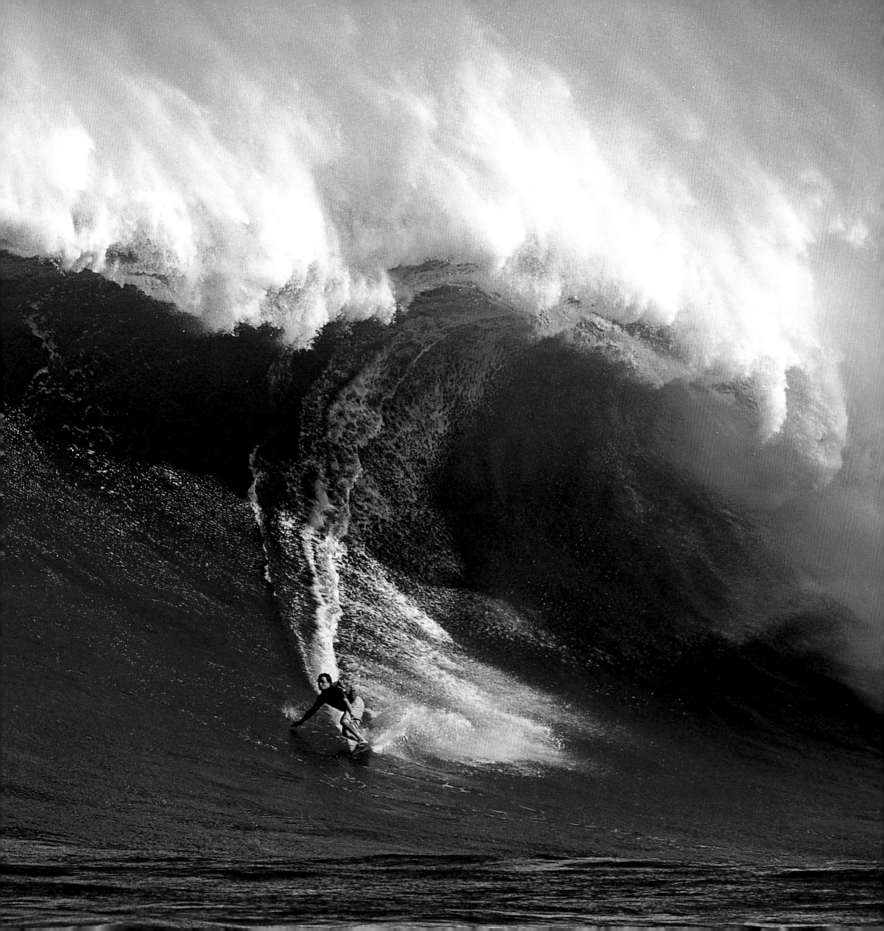

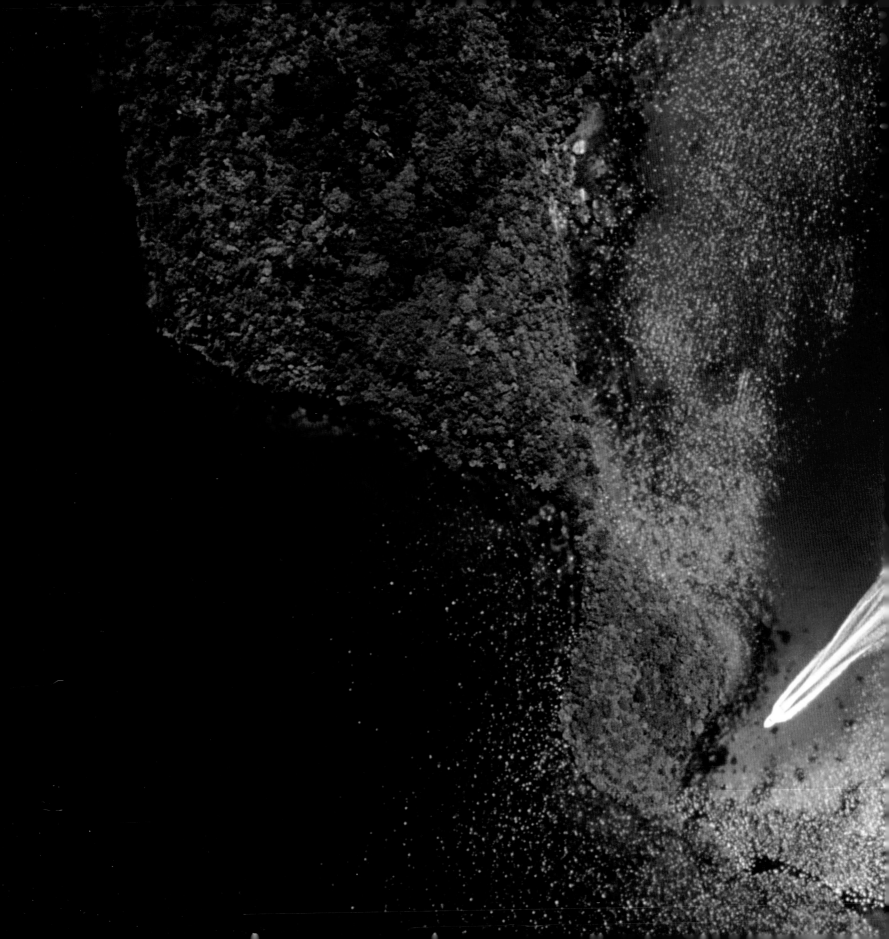

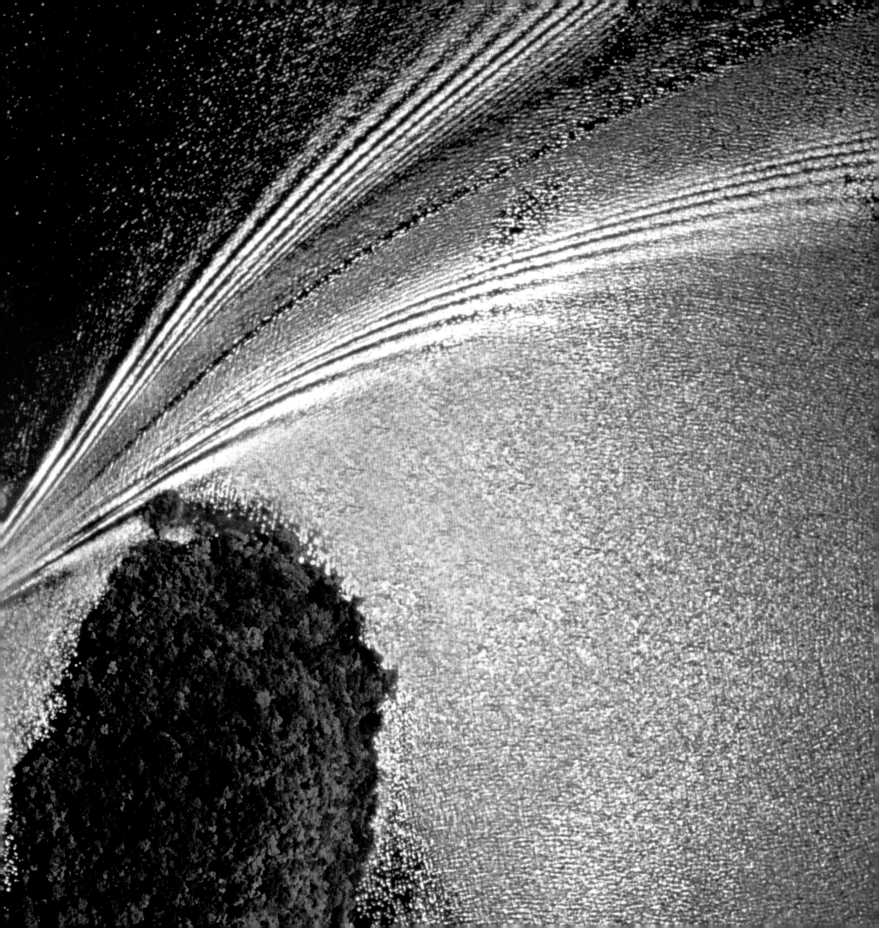

PICTURES from SPACE

GIULIO MELEGARI

Pacific Ocean – Storm south of Alaska.

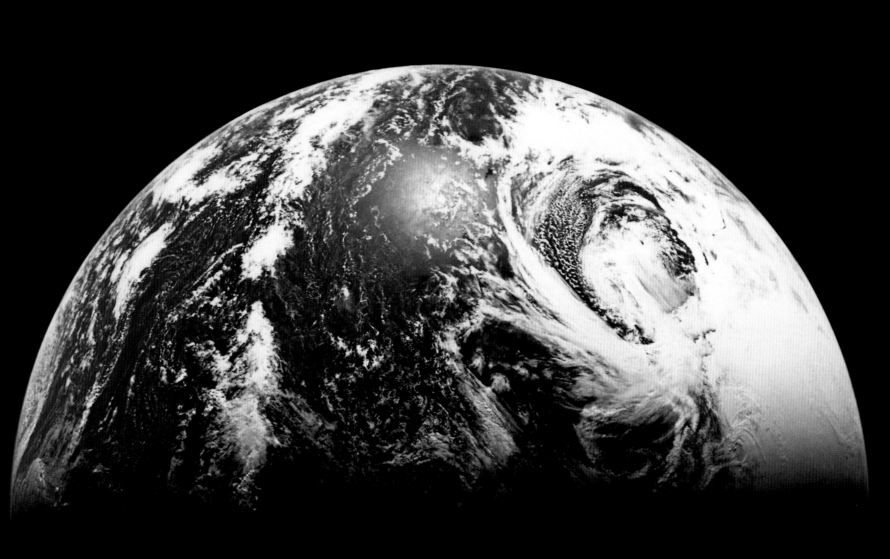

INTRODUCTION Pictures from Space

"ON THE THIRD DAY OF CREATION, GOD SAID 'LET THE WATERS UNDER THE HEAVEN BE GATHERED TOGETHER UNTO ONE PLACE, AND LET THE DRY LAND APPEAR: AND IT WAS SO. AND GOD CALLED THE DRY LAND EARTH; AND THE GATHERING TOGETHER OF THE WATERS CALLED HE SEAS: AND GOD SAW THAT IT WAS GOOD.' (GENESIS, 1, 9–10) THE FIRST GLOBAL VIEW OF OUR PLANET IS FOUND IN THE BIBLE. SEVEN TENTHS OF THE PLANET'S SURFACE ARE COVERED BY WATER AND FOR EACH SQUARE METER OF SOIL THERE ARE ALMOST TWO AND A HALF IN WHICH WE CAN SWIM OR BATHE. WATER DOMINATES OUR LIFE AND THE LIVES OF ALL OTHER ANIMAL FORMS, YET THE FIRST PHOTOGRAPHS TAKEN FROM SPACE AND SENT BACK

INTRODUCTION Pictures from Space

TO EARTH SIMPLY AMAZED US: BENEATH THE CLOUDS IMMENSE

SHEETS OF WATER, AT TIMES LIGHT BLUE, AT OTHERS DARK BLUE OR

EVEN GOLD, COVER THE GLOBE, SEPARATE THE CONTINENTS, AND

SURROUND ISLANDS. THE COLORS CHANGE WITH THE DIFFERENT

DEPTHS AND DEGREES OF REFLECTION OF THE WATER, AND THUS

DIFFERENTIATE THE VARIOUS OCEANS AND SEAS: THE LIGHTEST IS

THE MEDITERRANEAN, THE DARKEST THE ATLANTIC, THE GREENEST

THE PACIFIC, WITH ITS THOUSANDS OF ISLANDS AND ATOLLS OF

VARYING SIZE. THE DEEPEST TRENCHES ALONG THE EASTERN

COASTLINE OF ASIA, WHICH DESCEND TO UNIMAGINABLE DEPTHS

BETWEEN JAPAN AND THE PHILIPPINES, SHOW UP ON THE PHOTO-

Pictures from Space

Introduction

GRAPHS AS BLACK. THEN THERE IS THE LIGHT. THAT REFLECTED BY

THE NORTH AND SOUTH POLES IS ALMOST METALLIC, WHEREAS THE

LIGHT THAT BOUNCES OFF THE MOST ENCLOSED SEAS IS WARM IN

COLOR. AND FINALLY, THE CLOUDS: THEY ACCUMULATE AND THICK-

EN IN THE LATITUDES WHERE THE AIR MASSES MEET, DANCING LIKE

BALLERINAS ABOVE THE SURFACE OF THE SEAS; IN THE MORE CEN-

TRAL BANDS OF THE EARTH THEY ARE WHIRLED INTO SPIRALS AND

VORTICES BY THE FAST-MOVING WINDS BENEATH. CLOUDS ARE THE

MOST DRAMATIC INDICATION OF THE PLANET'S BREATH AND FORM A

KALEIDOSCOPE IN PERENNIAL TRANSFORMATION THAT CAN ONLY BE

OBSERVED BY THE UNBLINKING EYE OF SATELLITES.

● Atlantic Ocean - Abnormal waves out in the ocean.

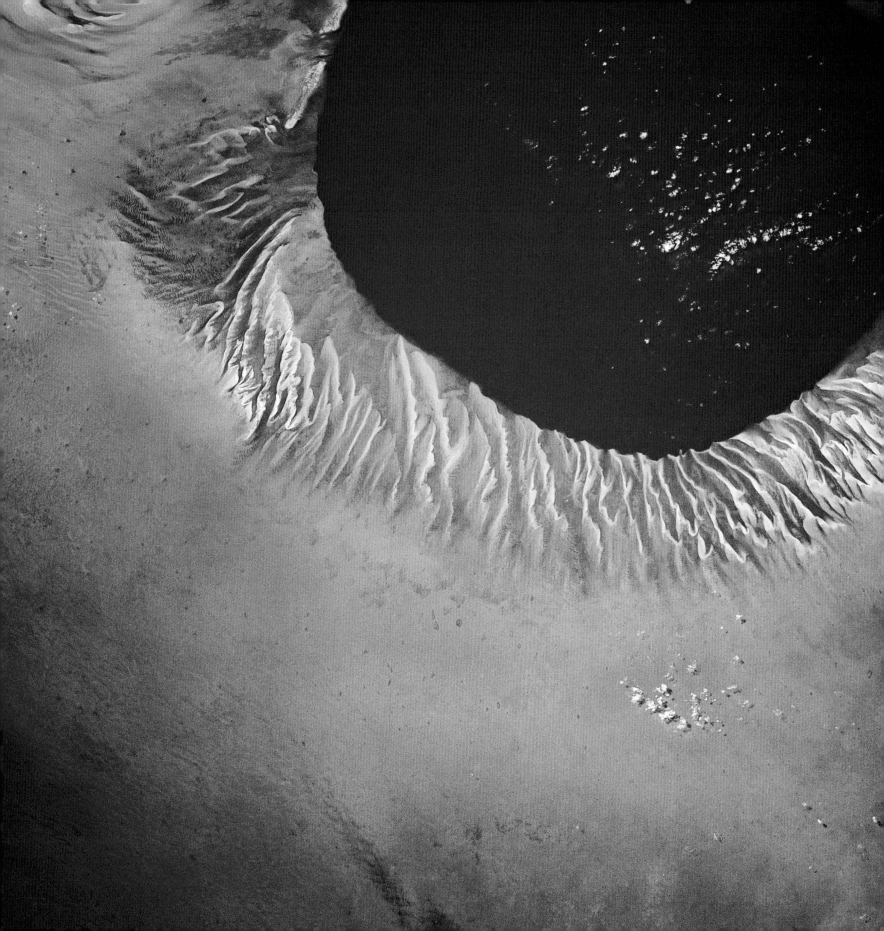

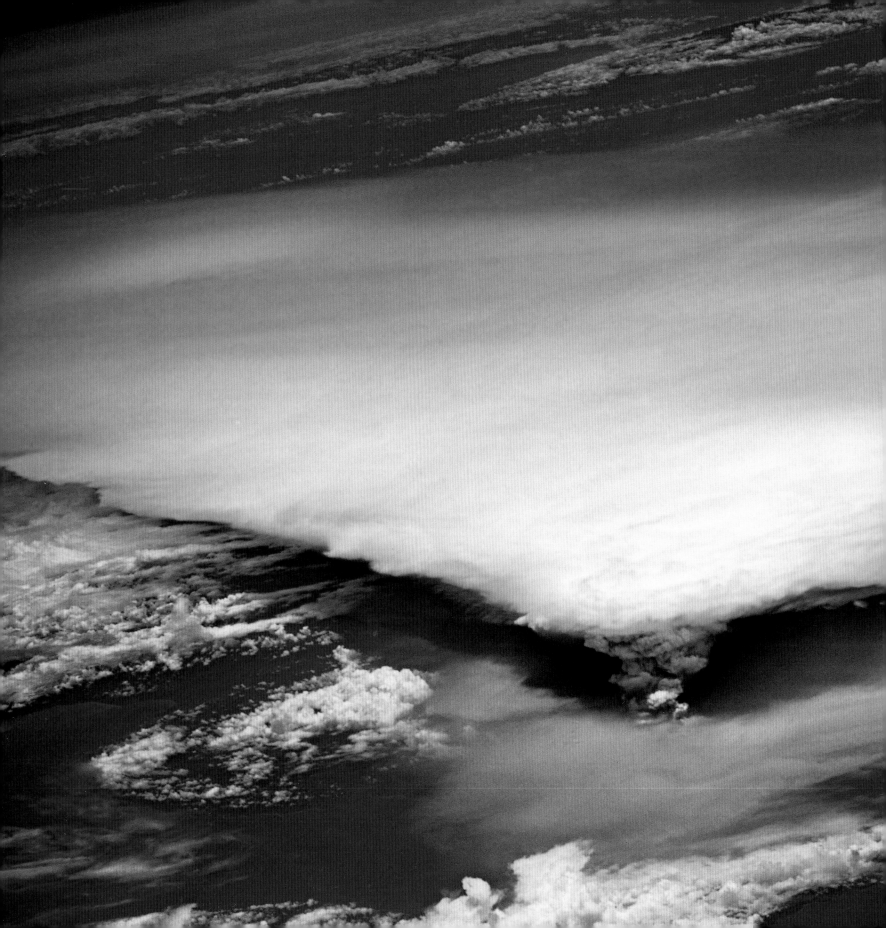

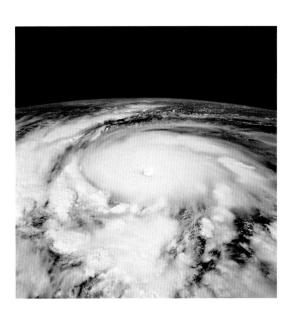

32-33 ● Pacific Ocean, New Guinea
- Eruption of Mount Rabaul.

33 ● Atlantic Ocean - Subtropical cyclone.

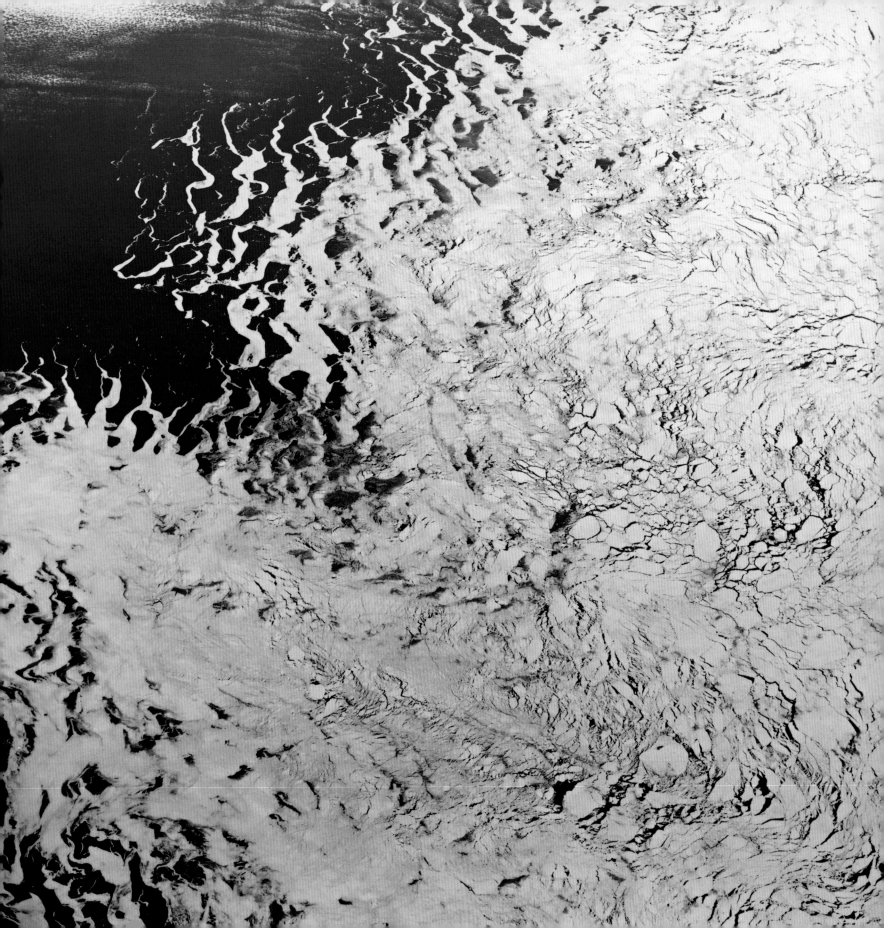

Lands of ice

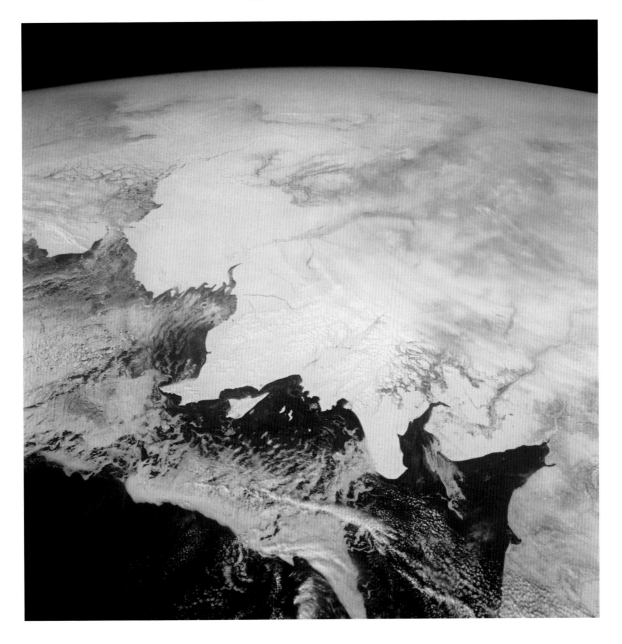

34 ● Atlantic Ocean - West coast of the Antarctic.

35 ● Bering Sea - West Alaska and the Bering Strait.

The Tropics

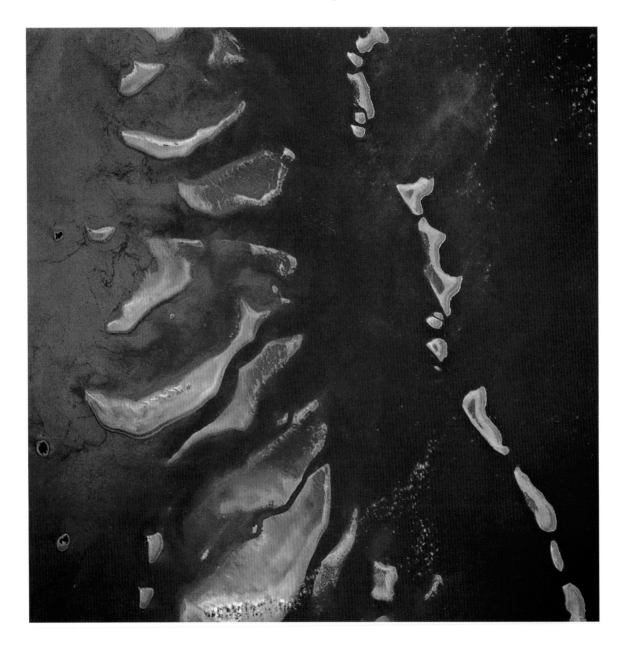

36 ● Pacific Ocean, Australia - Great Barrier Reef.

37 ● Pacific Ocean - Australia, Disappointment Reach.

38-39 ● Caribbean Sea - Cuba, the Florida Keys (top left)
and Andros Island in the Bahamas (right).

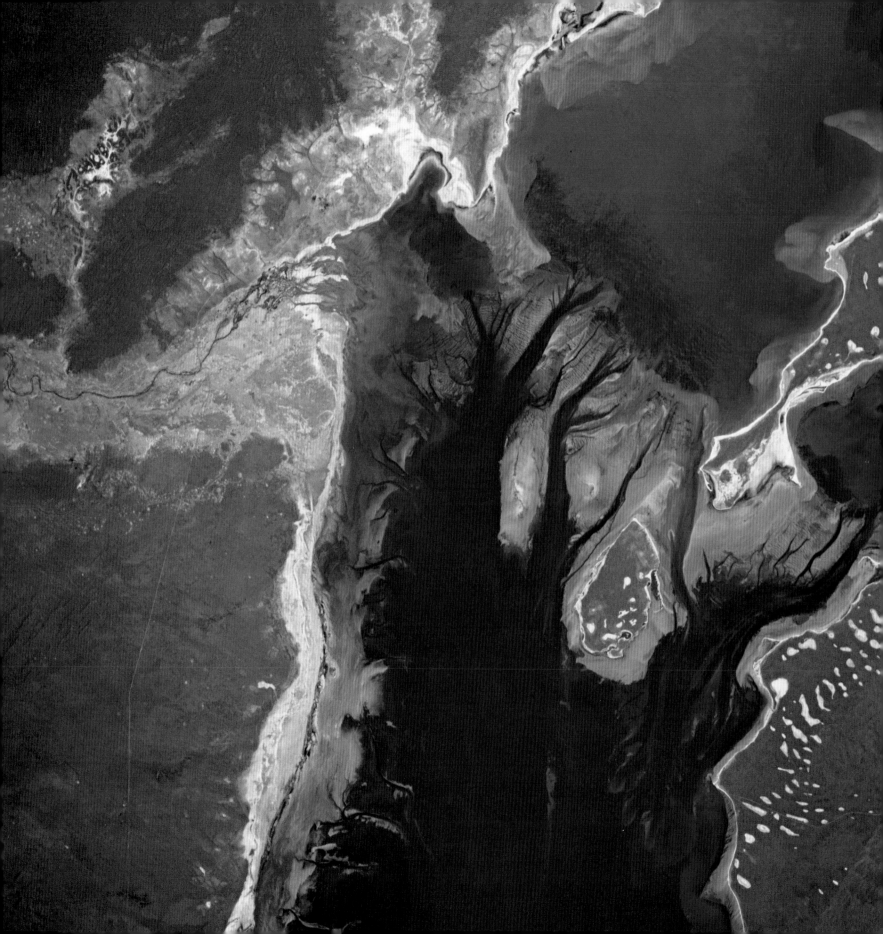

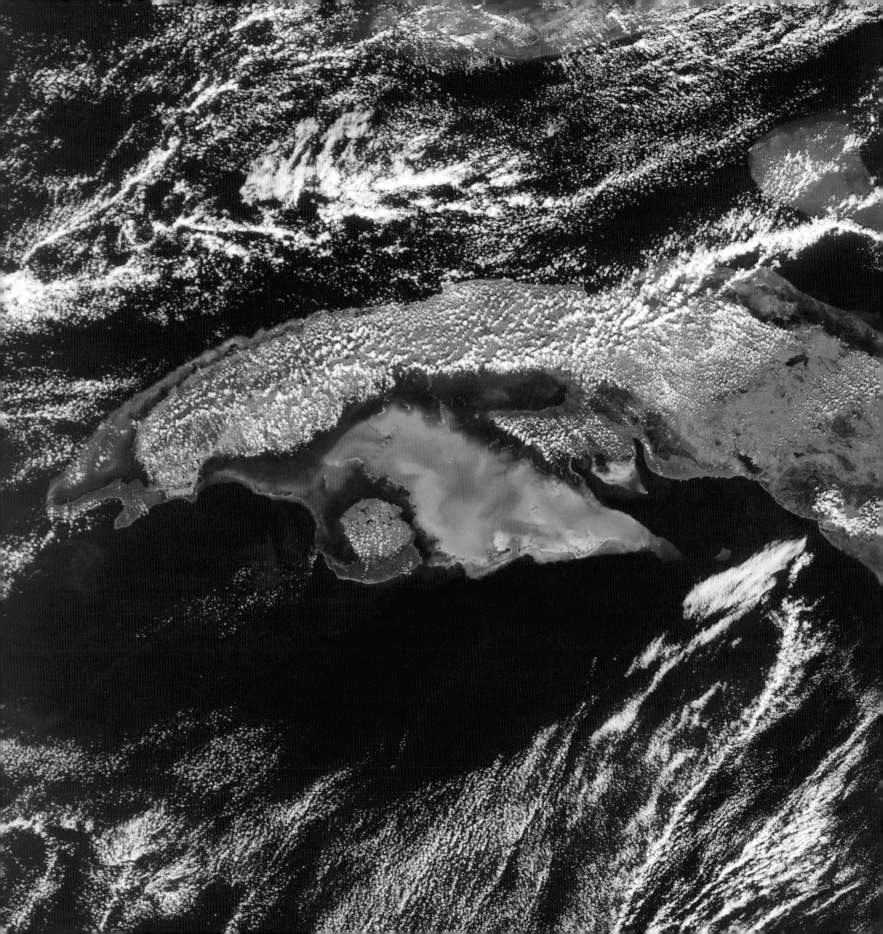

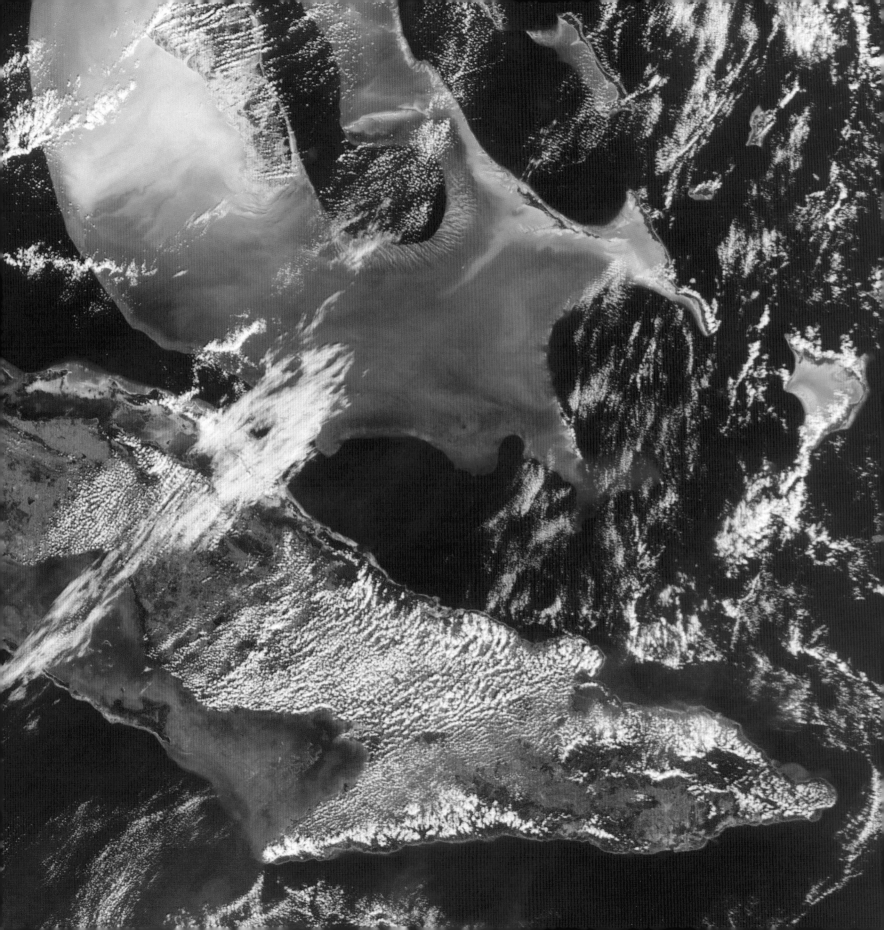

Mare Nostrum

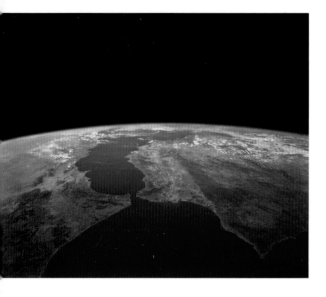

40 ● Mediterranean Sea
- Strait of Gibraltar.

40-41 ● Mediterranean Sea
- South Italy and Sicily.

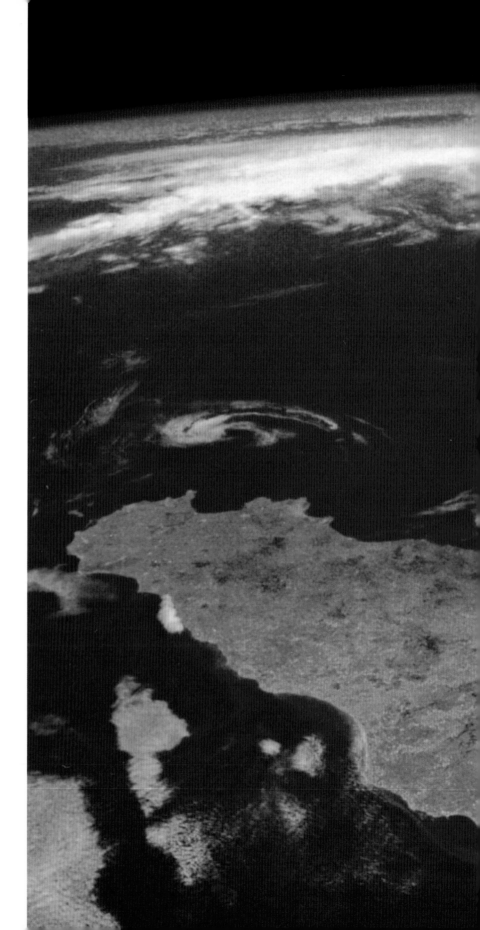

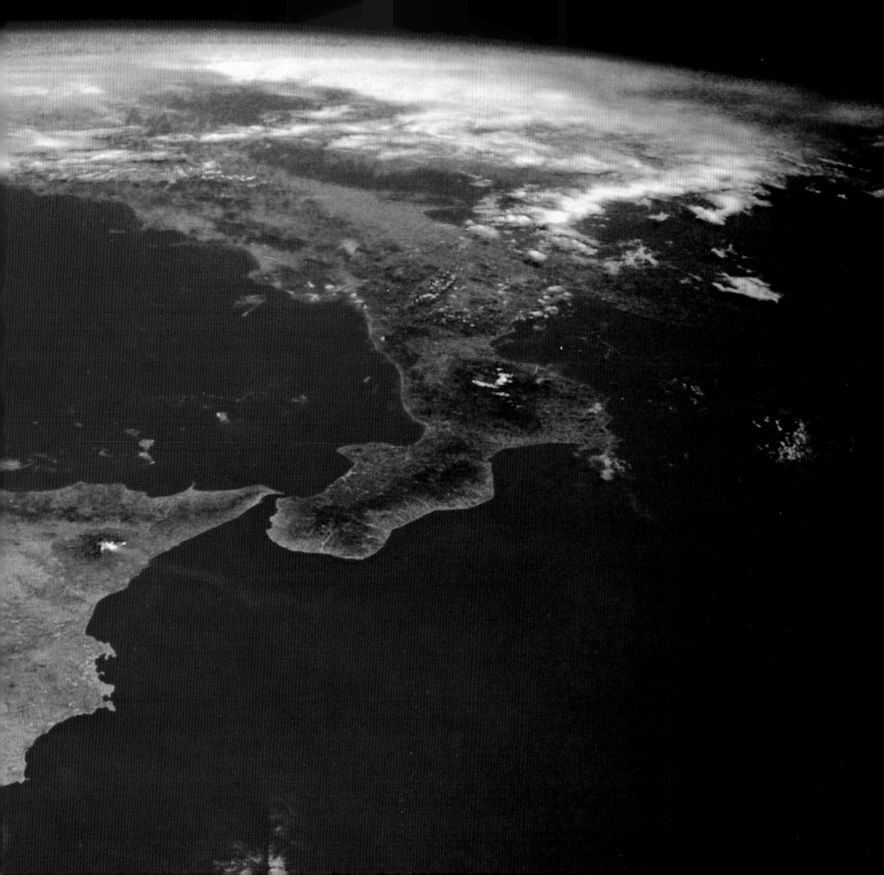

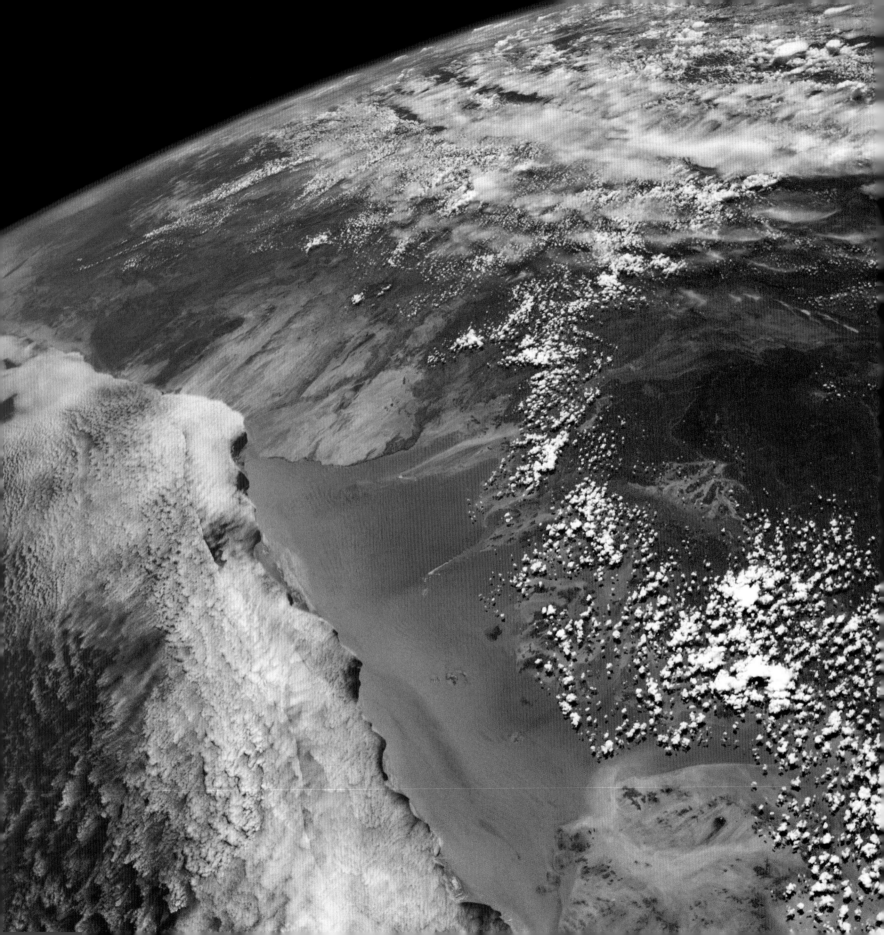

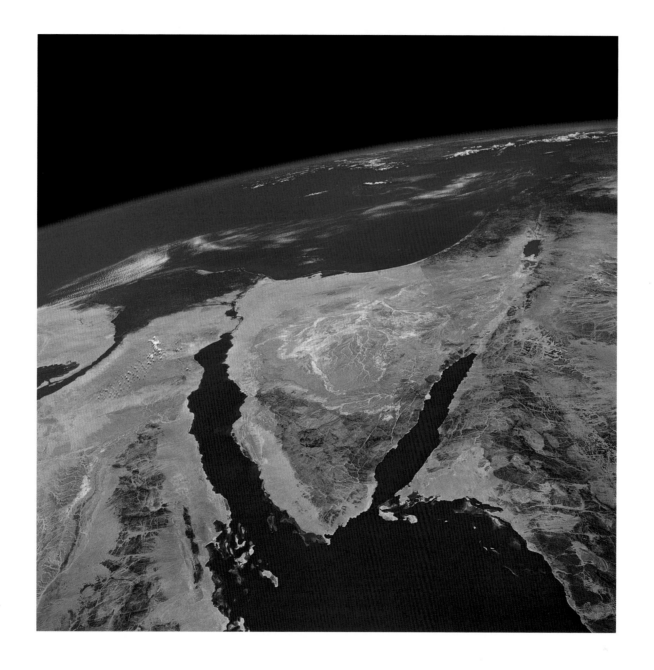

42 ● Atlantic Ocean - Africa, coast of Namibia.

43 ● Red Sea - Coast of Egypt, Sinai peninsula and part of the Arabian peninsula.

44-45 ● Southern hemisphere - Africa, Arabian peninsula and the Indian Ocean.

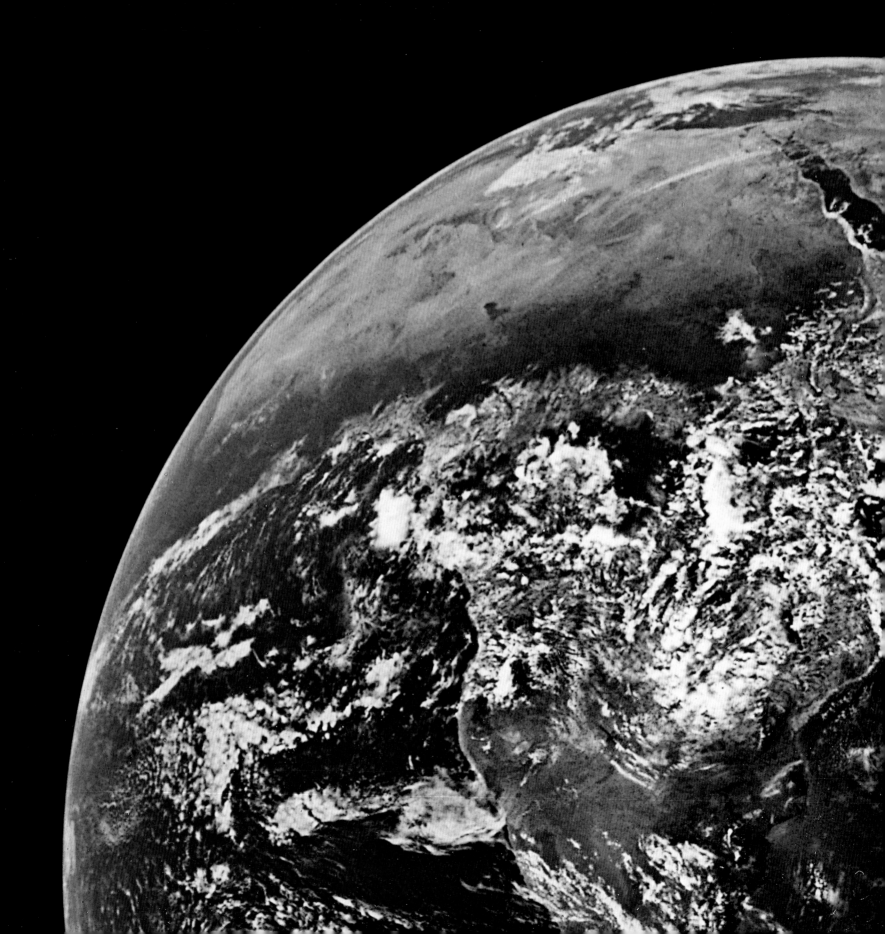

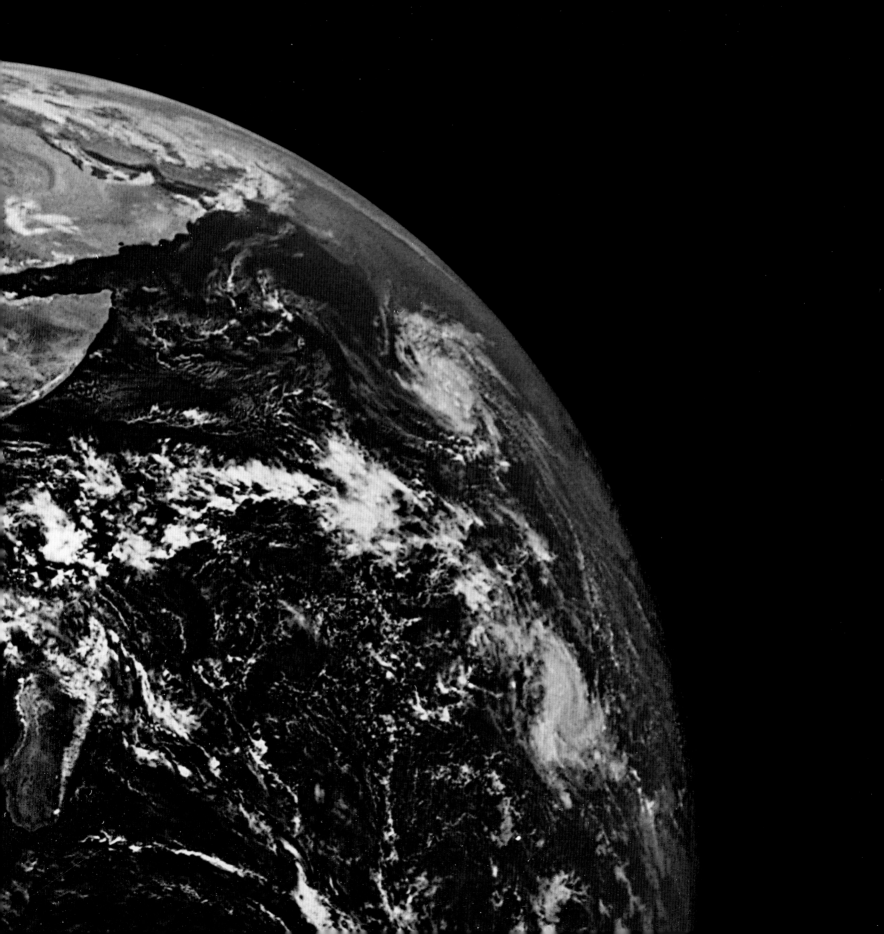

COASTS and SHORELINES

GIANNI GUADALUPI

Indian Ocean, Ladigue (Seychelles) - Anse Source d'Argent.

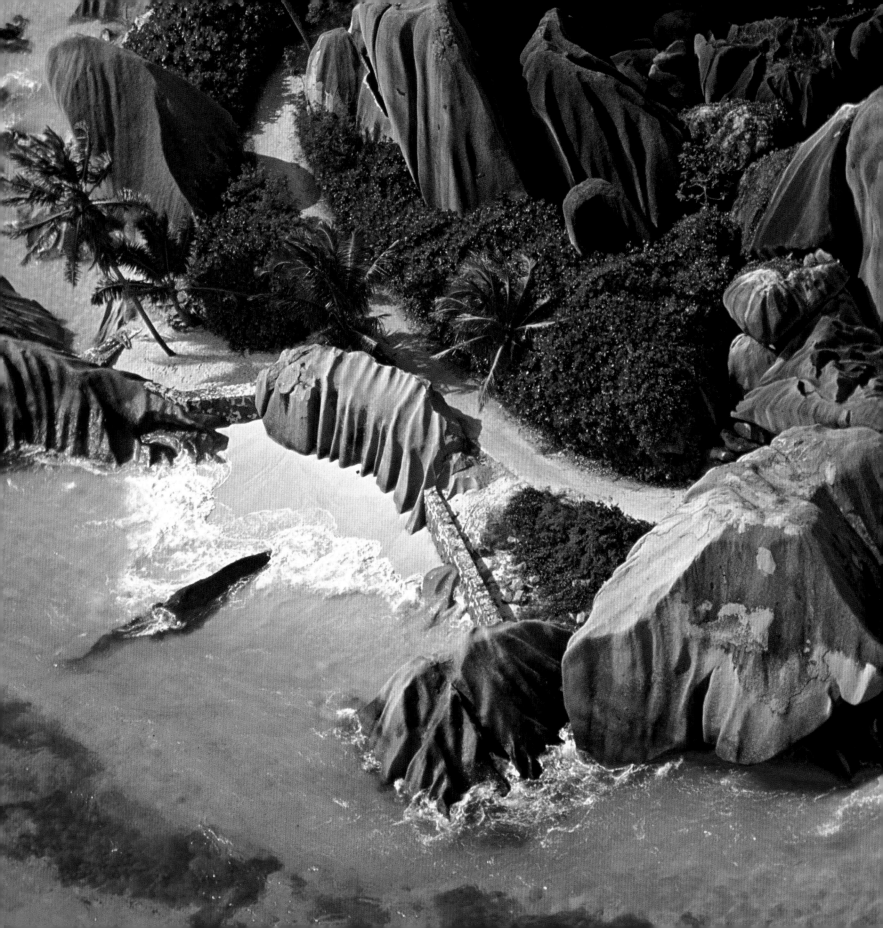

INTRODUCTION Coasts and Shorelines

THE SEA CREATES AND THE SEA DESTROYS, OR RATHER,
IT CHANGES, TRANSFORMS AND DEVOURS. WITH INCESSANT
PATIENCE, IT HAS TOILED FOR MILLENNIA AS THE UNTIRING SCULP-
TOR OF THE DRY WORLD, MODELING *TERRA FIRMA* AS IT PLEASES.
IT HAMMERS, DIGS, CRUMBLES, CHIPS AND DISINTEGRATES UNTIL
IT REDUCES ROCK TO SAND, CARVES OUT FJORDS, RAISES CLIFFS,
SHAPES PROMONTORIES AND PENINSULAS, AND SPREADS COATS
OF GRAVEL AND SANDSTONE ALONG COASTLINES. LIKE A LAND-
SCAPE ARCHITECT EMBELLISHING A PARK, THE SEA ARRANGES
WRECKS ALONG ITS COASTLINES, WASHED BY CURRENTS AND
TIDES, AND SWEPT BY THE WIND. THESE REMAINS OF SHIPS THAT

INTRODUCTION Coasts and Shorelines

HAVE BEEN THROWN BACK ON LAND ARE AN ETERNAL WARNING

NOT TO FORGET THE POWER OF THE SEA. WHEN MEN RESPECTED

THE SEA AND FEARED ITS SECRETS, IT WAS INHABITED BY THE

STRANGEST CREATURES: MERMAIDS THAT ABDUCTED HANDSOME

SAILORS, THE WHALE THAT SWALLOWED JONAH, AND THE MON-

STER THAT DEVOURED ANDROMEDA. AT TIMES THE GODS

ORDERED IT TO CRASH AGAINST THE CITIES OF MEN THAT HAD

SINNED, TO WASH AWAY THEIR EVERY LAST TRACE TO LEAVE THE

SHORES AS CLEAN AND PURE AS THE SEA ITSELF. CATASTROPHES

OF THIS NATURE HAVE BEEN HANDED DOWN THROUGH THE GEN-

ERATIONS IN LEGEND OR IN THE PAGES OF HISTORY BOOKS. THUS,

Coasts and Shorelines

Introduction

IN BRITTANY, PERISHED THE RICH CITY OF YS, OF WHICH EVERY SO

OFTEN THE SUBMERGED BELL-TOWERS ARE HEARD TO RING; AND

IN CORNWALL THE GREAT LYONESSE, WHOSE TREES STILL GROW

ON THE BOTTOM OF THE SEA. AND BEAUTIFUL VINETA, NEAR

RAGEN, WAS ALSO DESTROYED, ITS DROWNED INHABITANTS WAN-

DERING AMONG THEIR UNDERWATER HOUSES, UNAWARE THEY

ARE DEAD, LIKE FIRES THAT HAVE BEEN PUT OUT. YEAR AFTER

YEAR, CENTURY AFTER CENTURY, THE SEA EATS AWAY AT THE

LAND, AND ONE DAY OCEAN WILL REGAIN ITS ABSOLUTE DOMINION

OVER THE WORLD.

51 ● Mediterranean Sea, Budelli, Sardinia (Italy) - Spiaggia Rosa.

52-53 ● Mediterranean Sea, Balearic Islands (Spain) - Minorca.

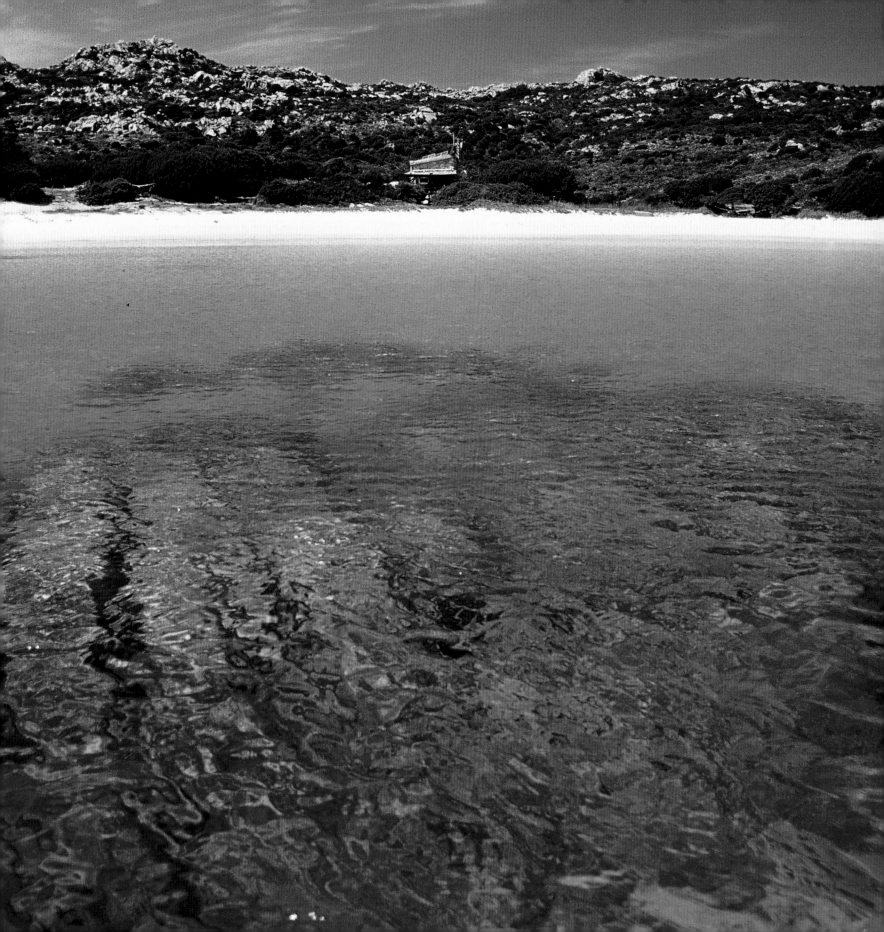

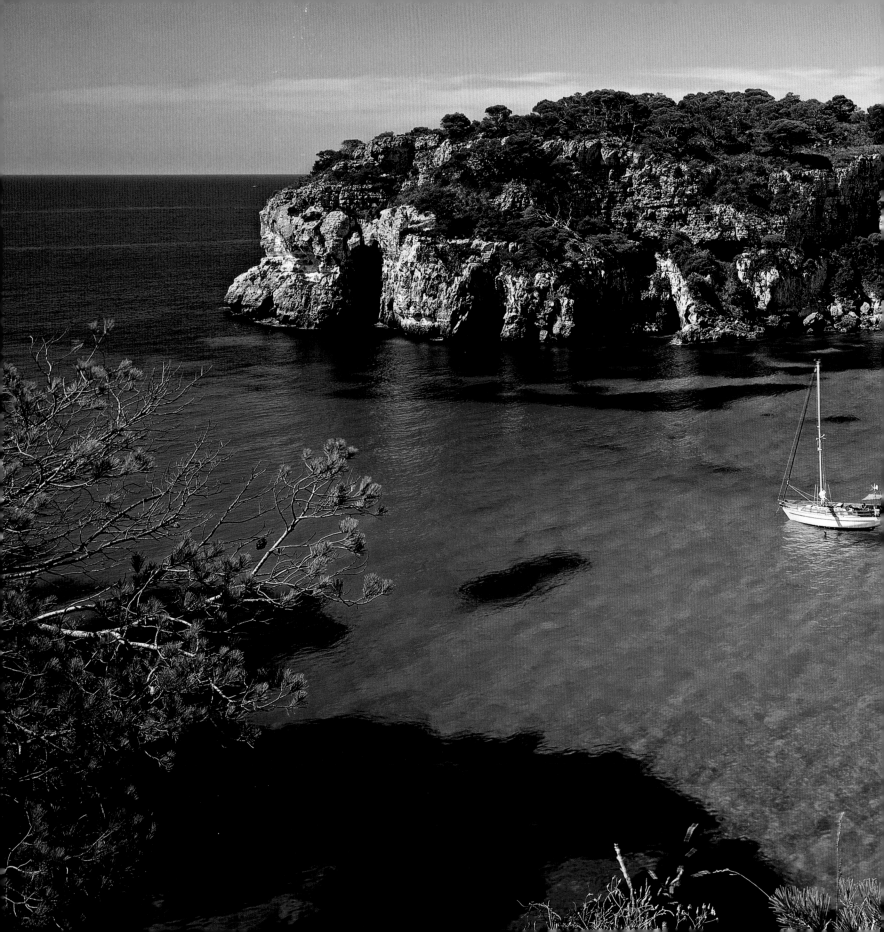

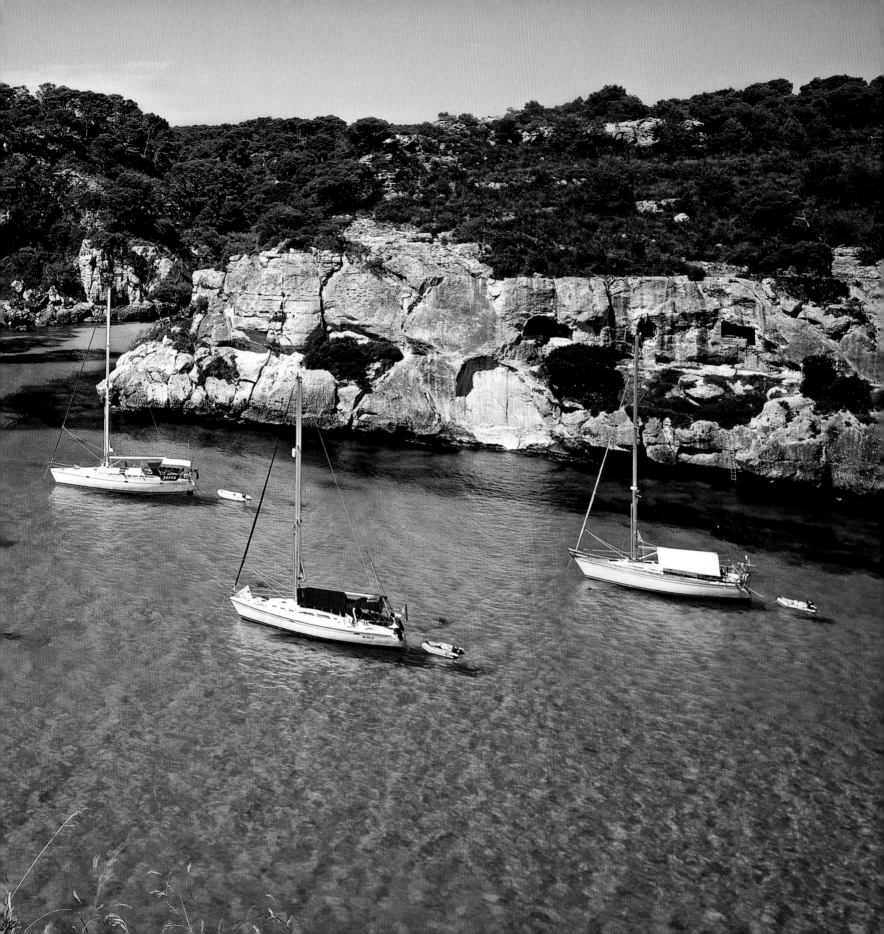

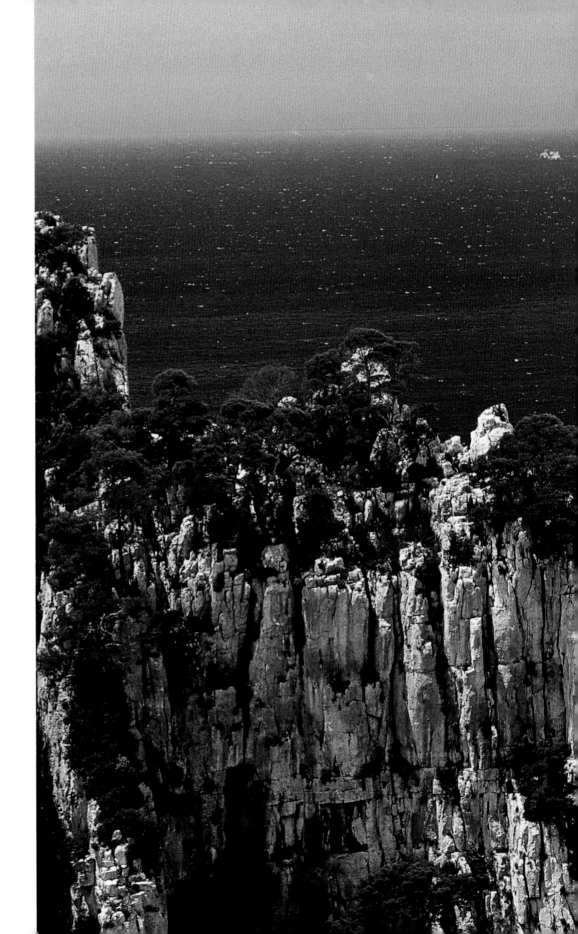

Mediterranean Sea,
Provence (France)
- Les Calanques.

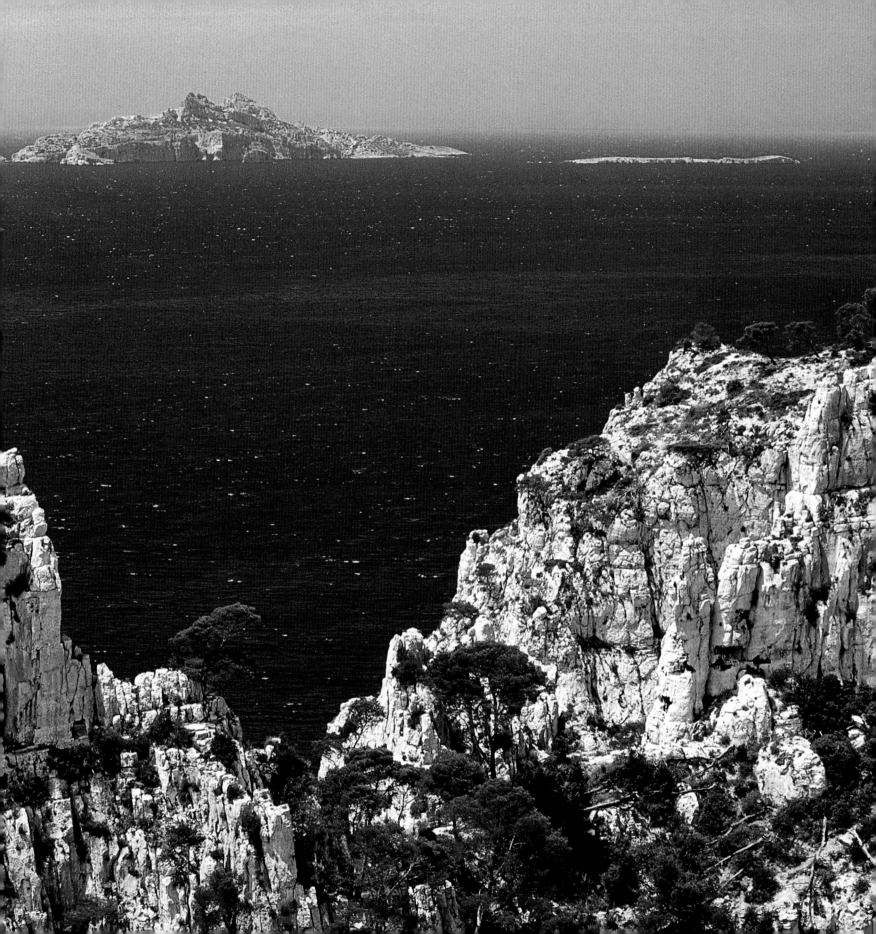

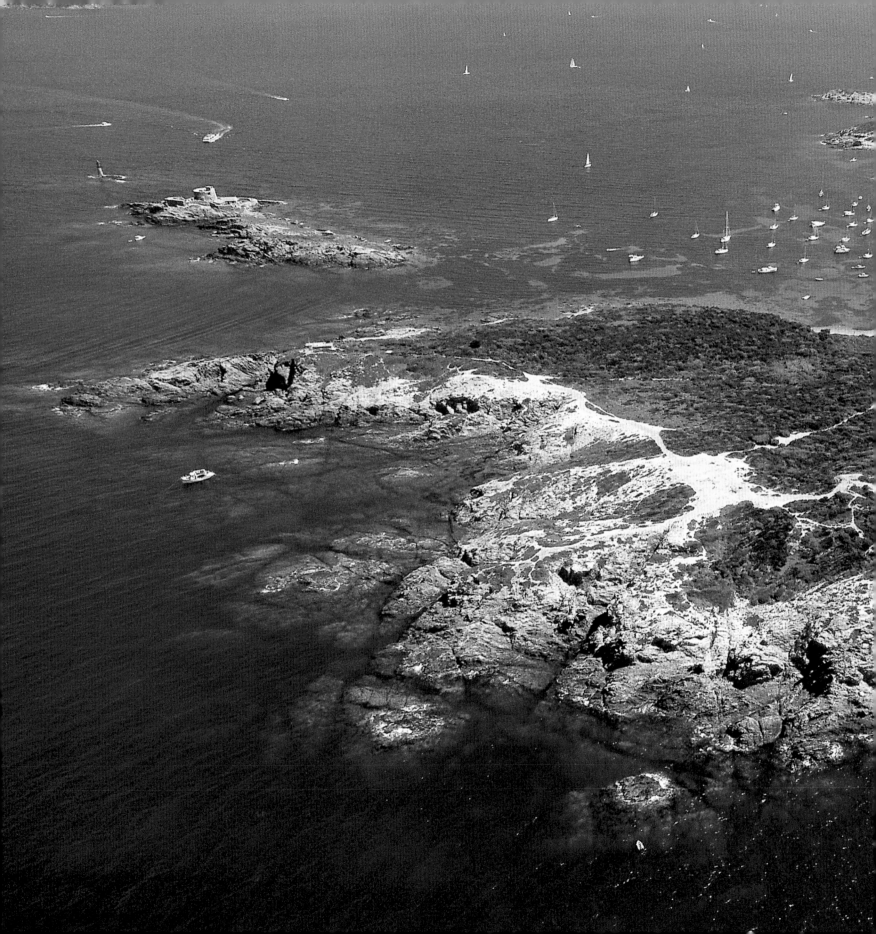

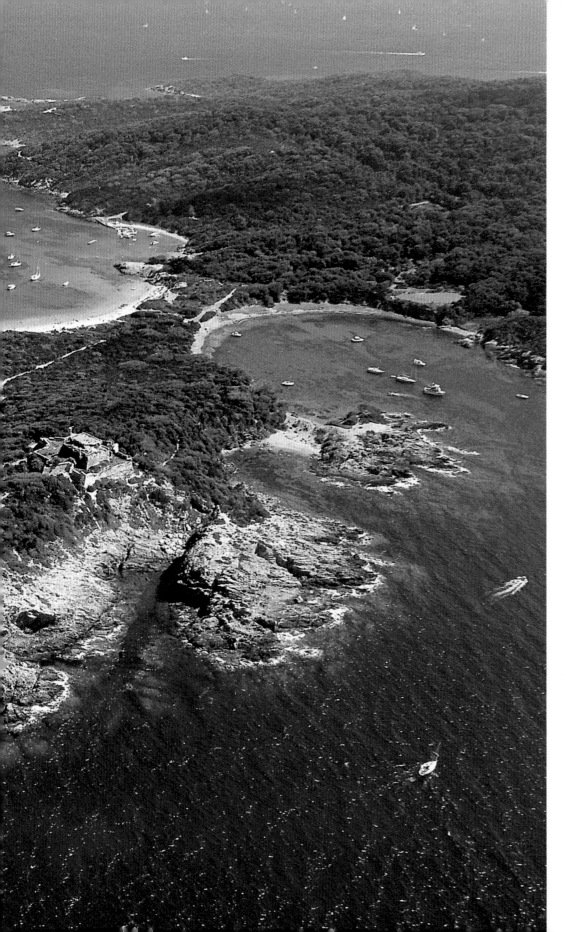

● Mediterranean Sea,
Provence (France) -
Porquerolles.

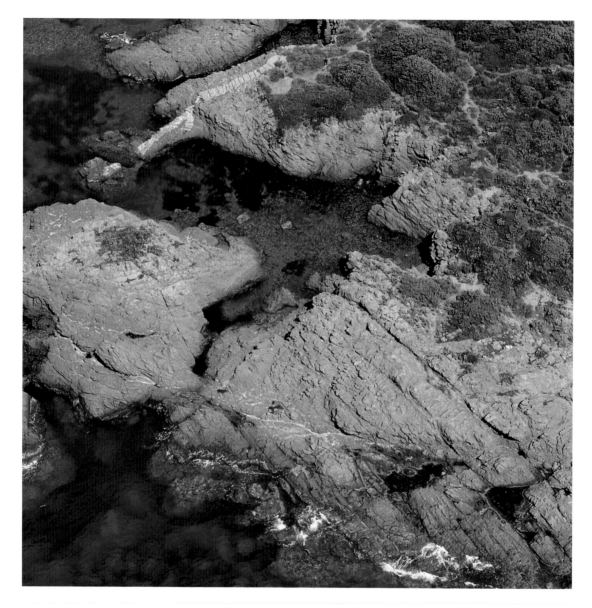

58 ● Mediterranean Sea, Provence (France) - Estérel, the coast near Saint Raphaël.

59 ● Mediterranean Sea, Corsica (France) - Cap Rosso.

60-61 ● Mediterranean Sea, Corsica (France) - Les Calanches.

62-63 ● Mediterranean Sea, Liguria (Italy) - Promontory of Portofino.

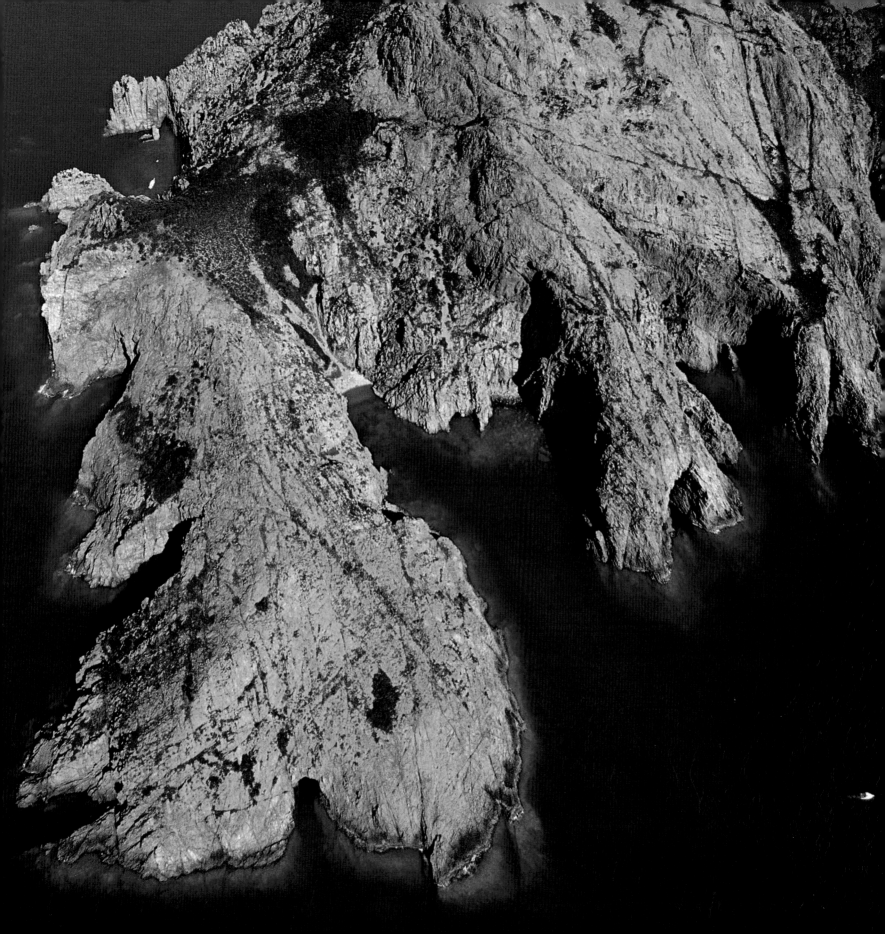

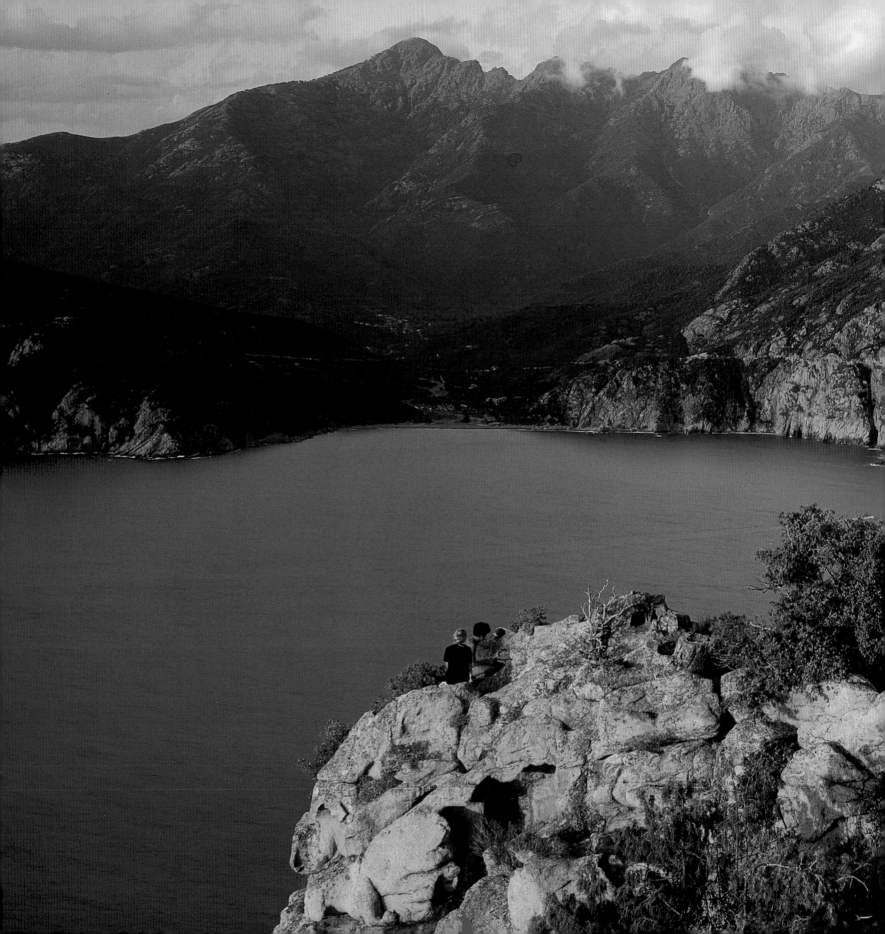

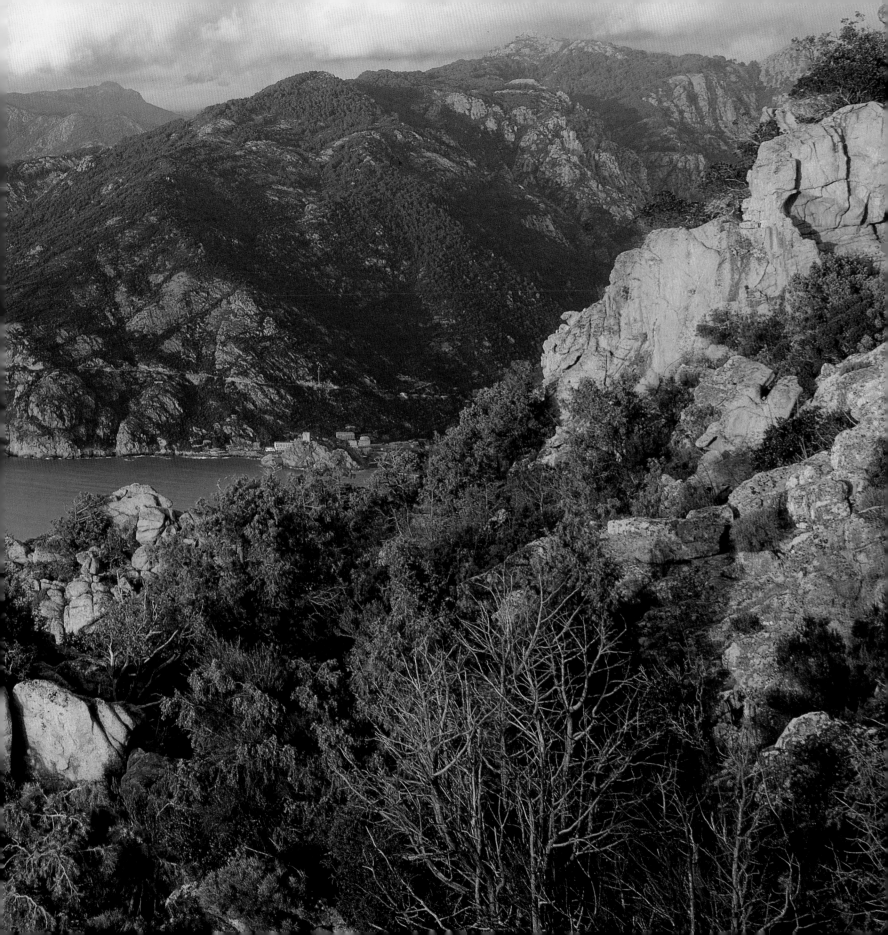

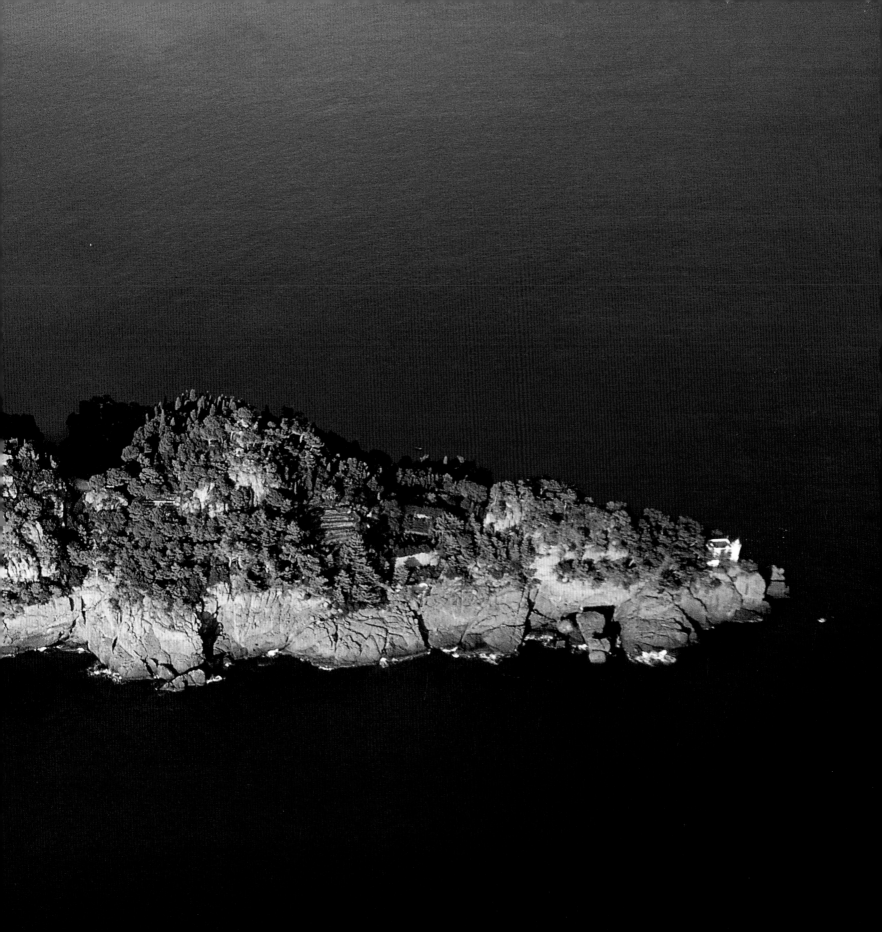

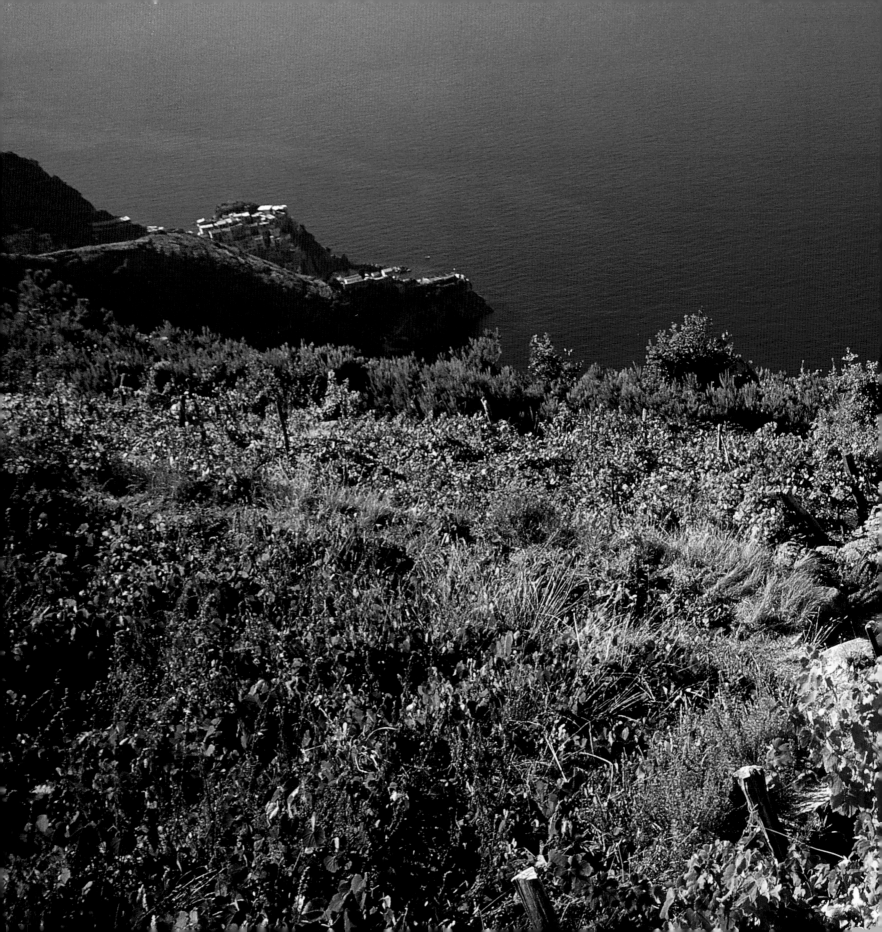

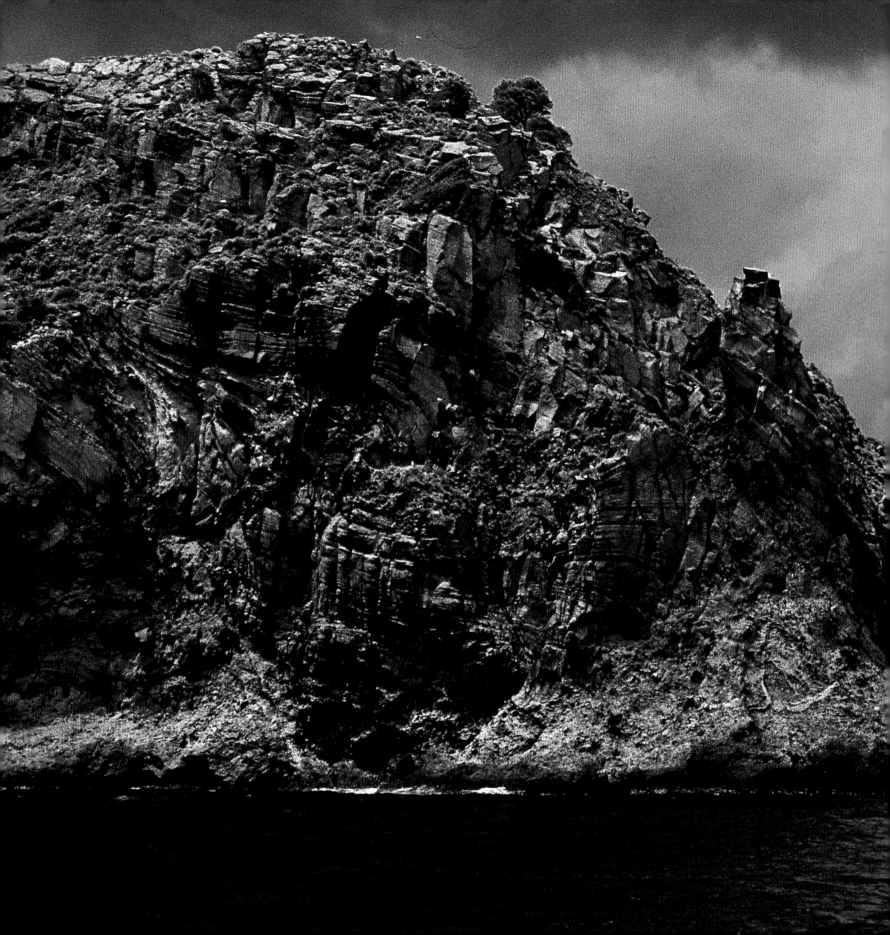

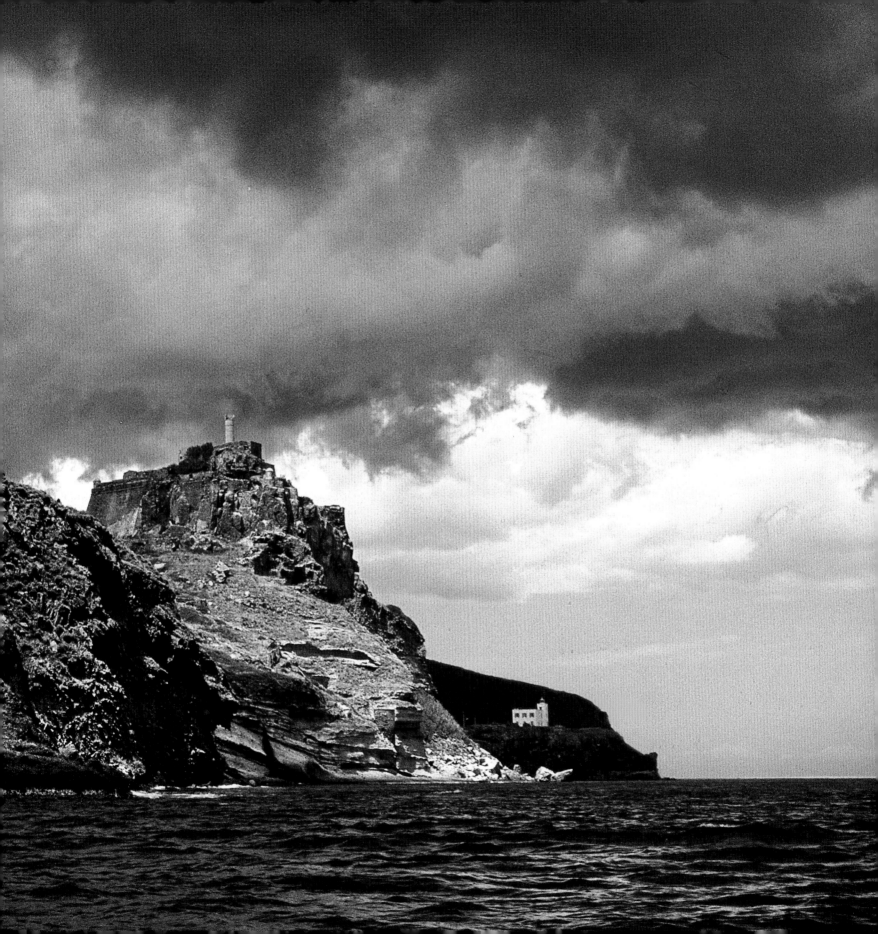

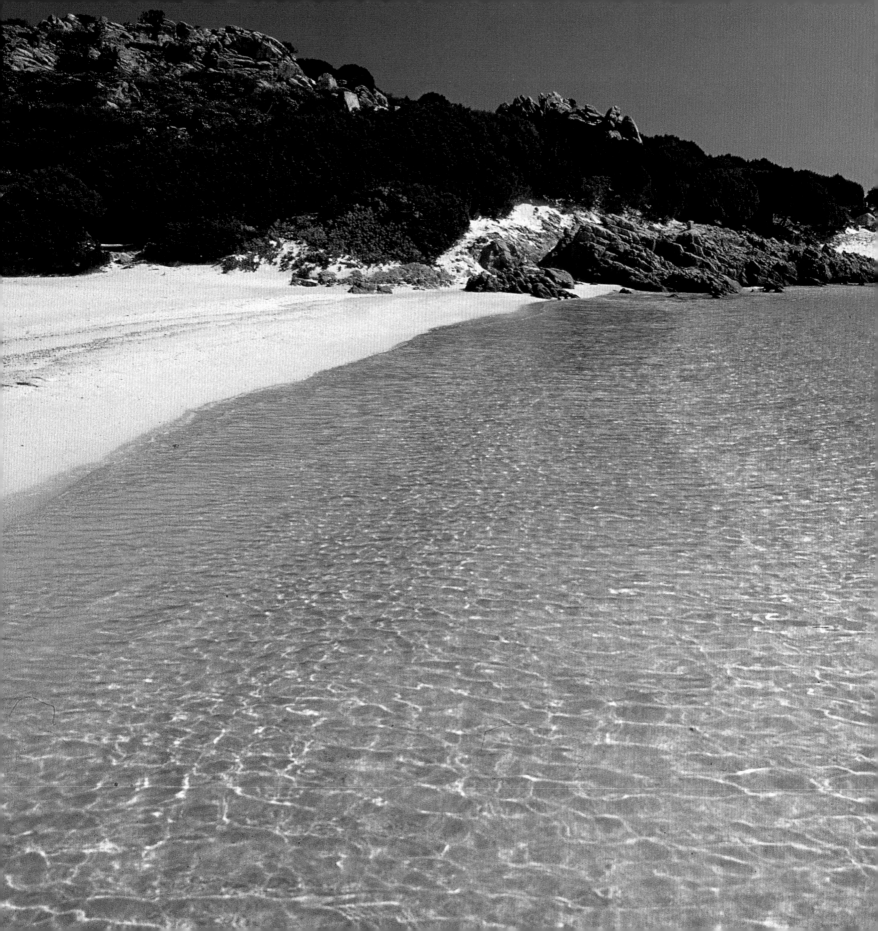

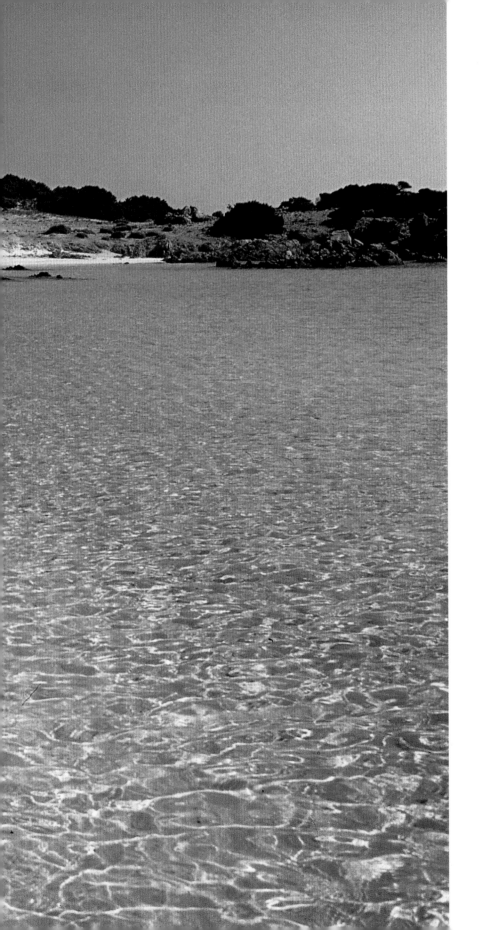

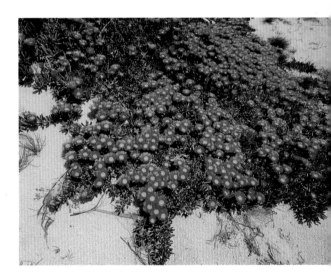

64-65 ● Mediterranean Sea, Cinque Terre, Liguria (Italy) - Manarola.

66-67 ● Mediterranean Sea, Tuscany (Italy) - Capraia.

68-69 and 69 ● Mediterranean Sea, Budelli, Sardinia (Italy) - Spiaggia Rosa.

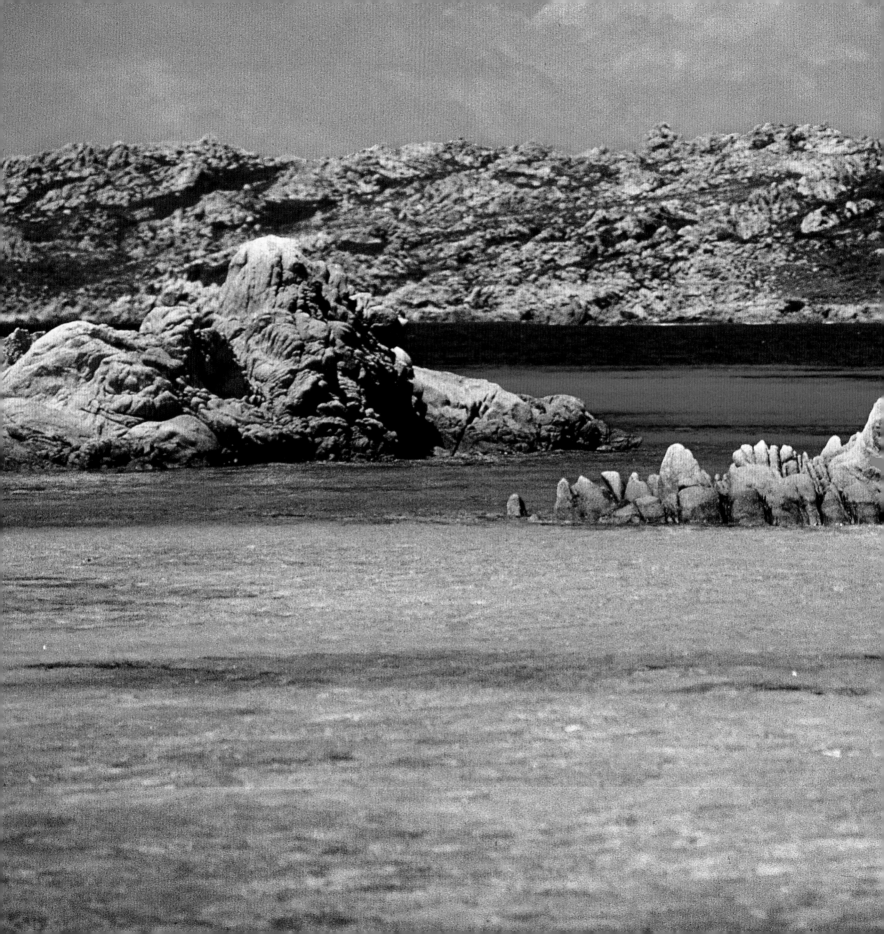

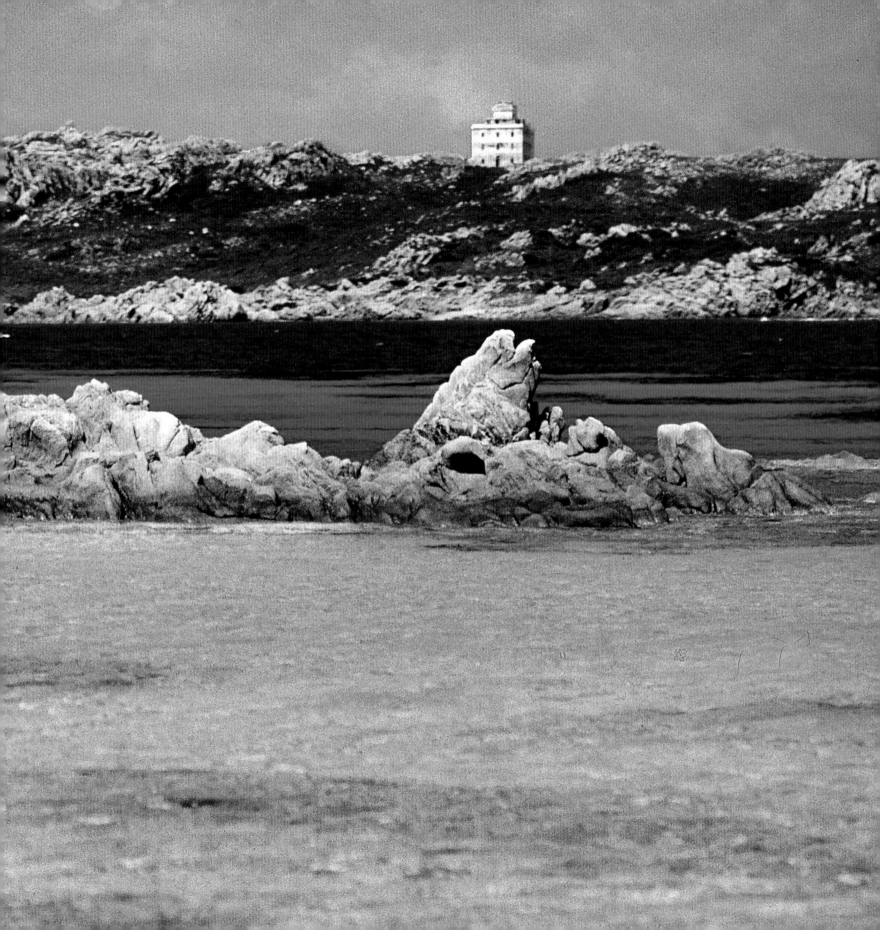

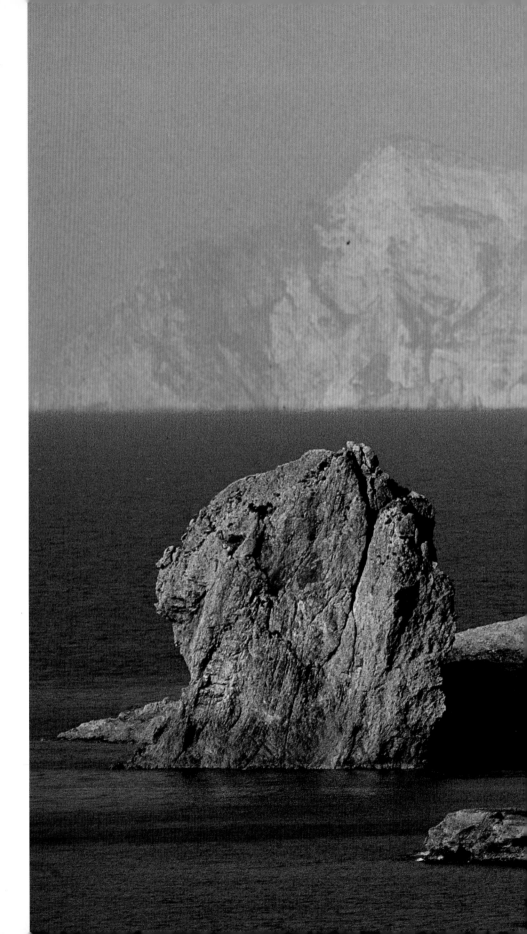

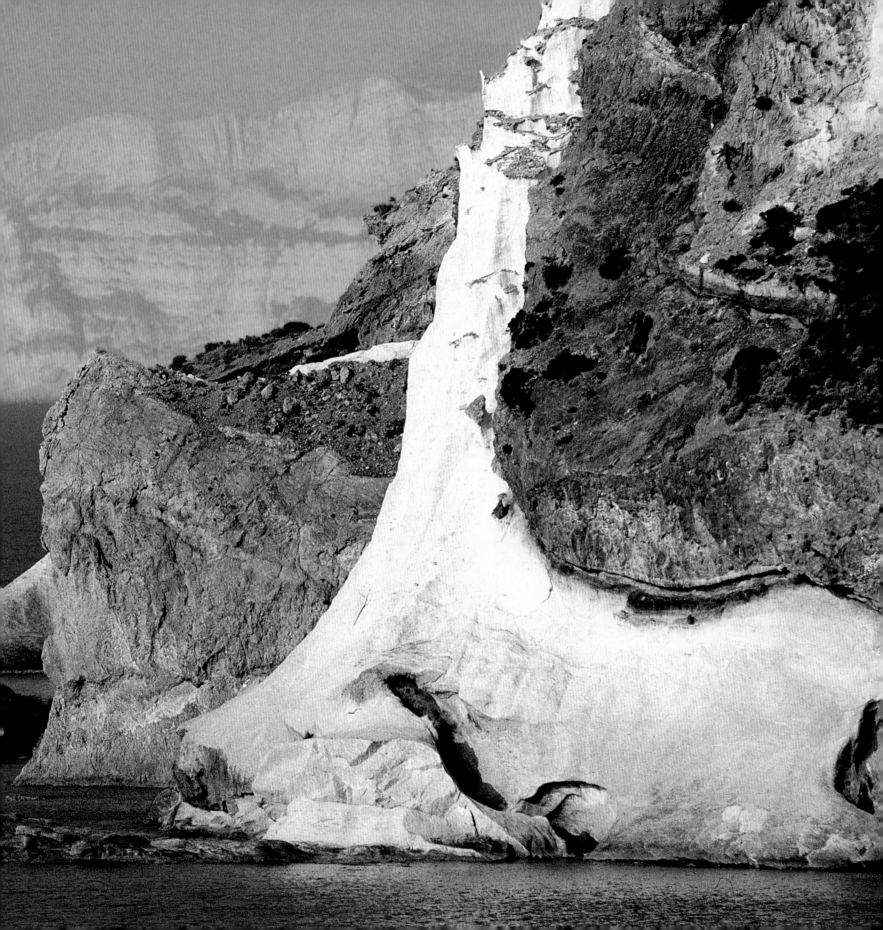

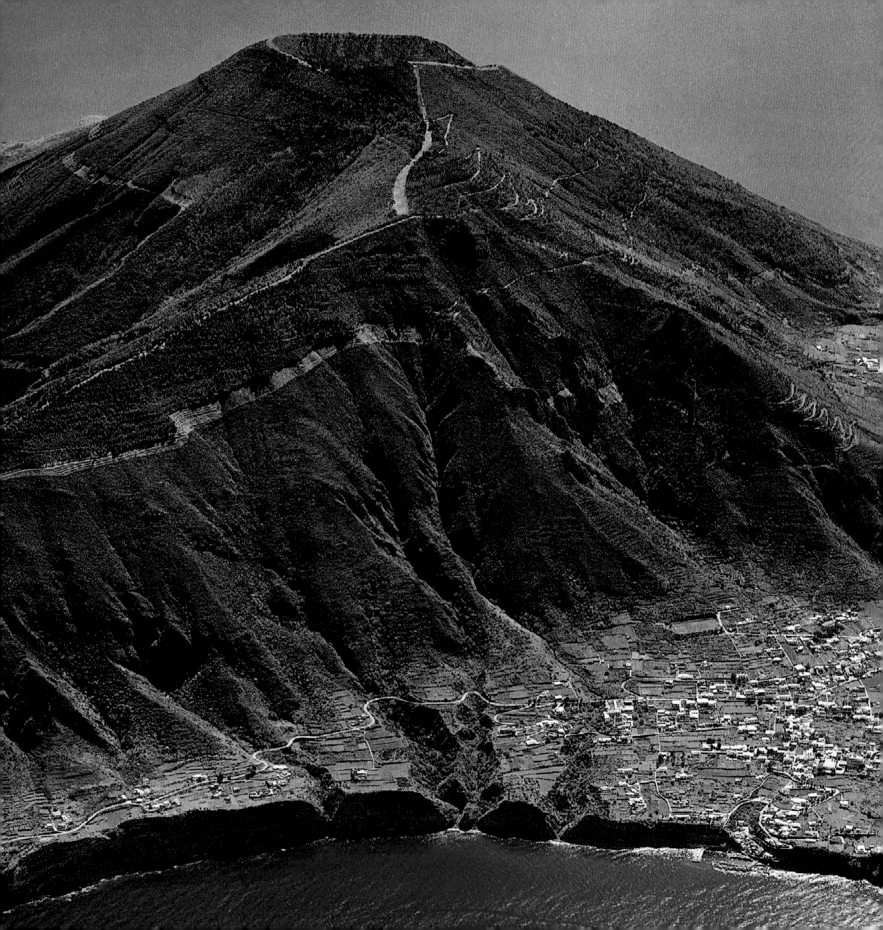

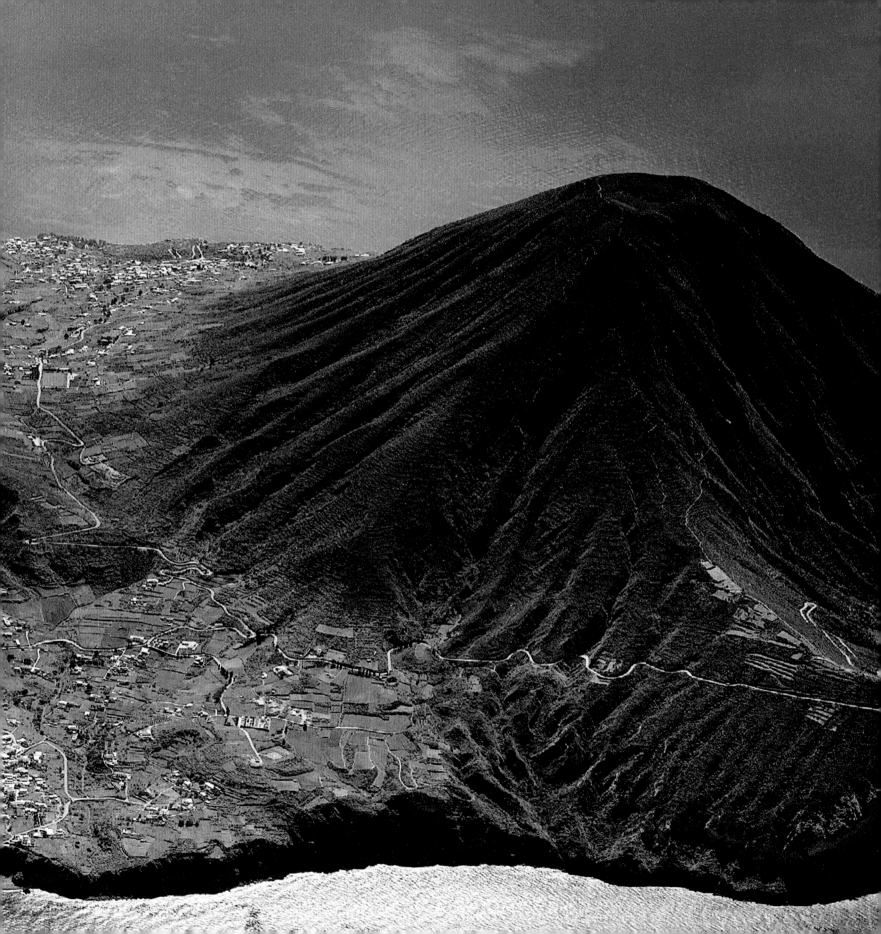

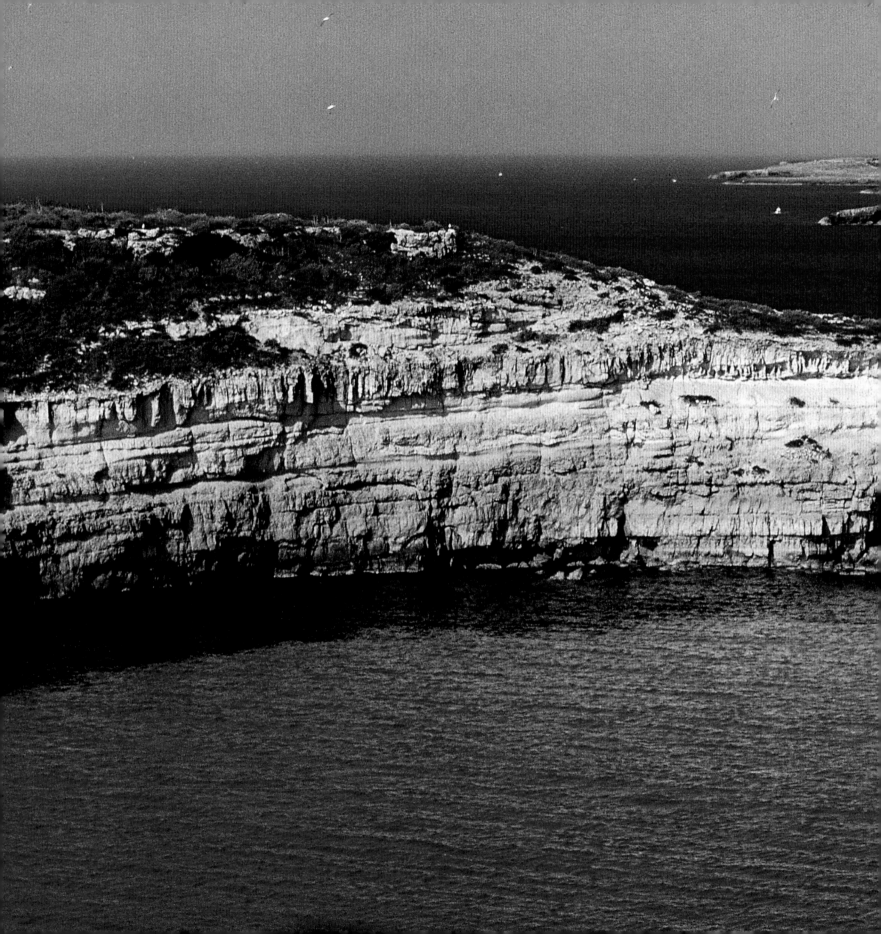

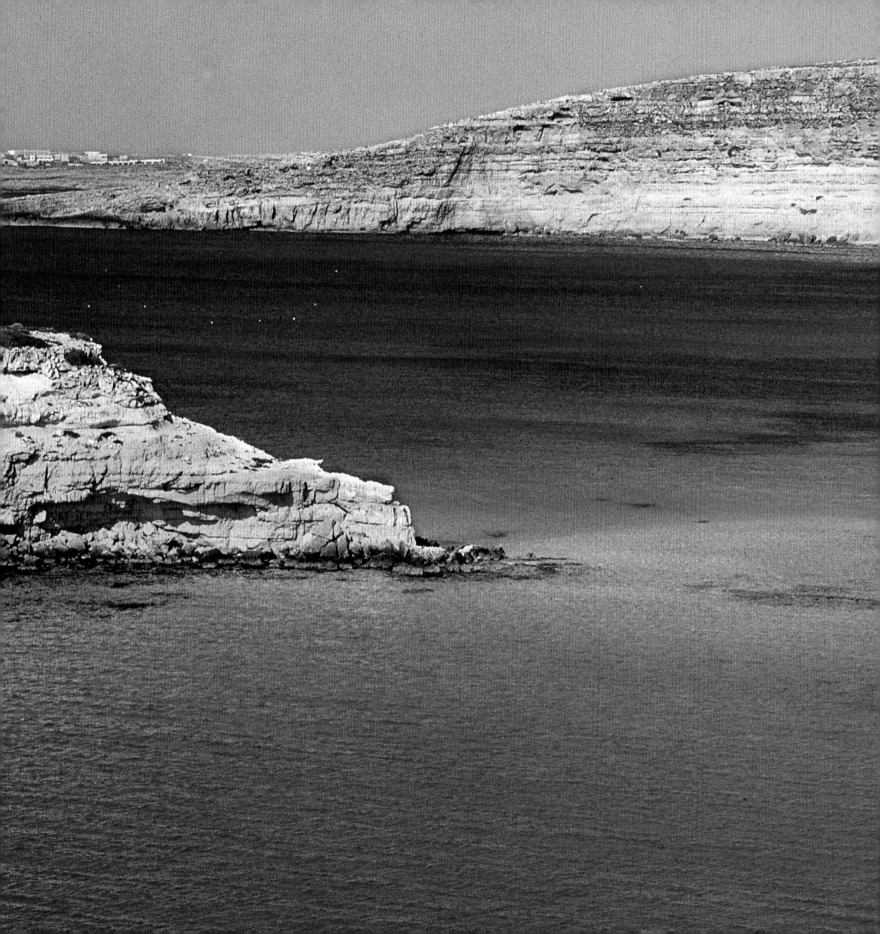

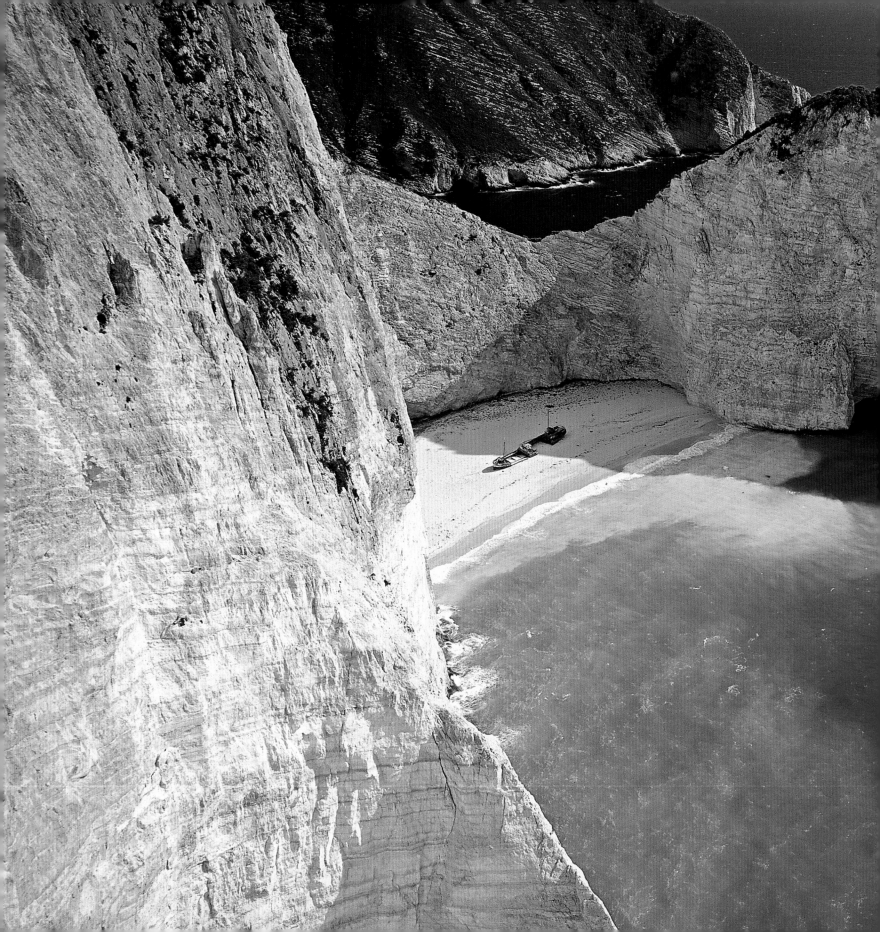

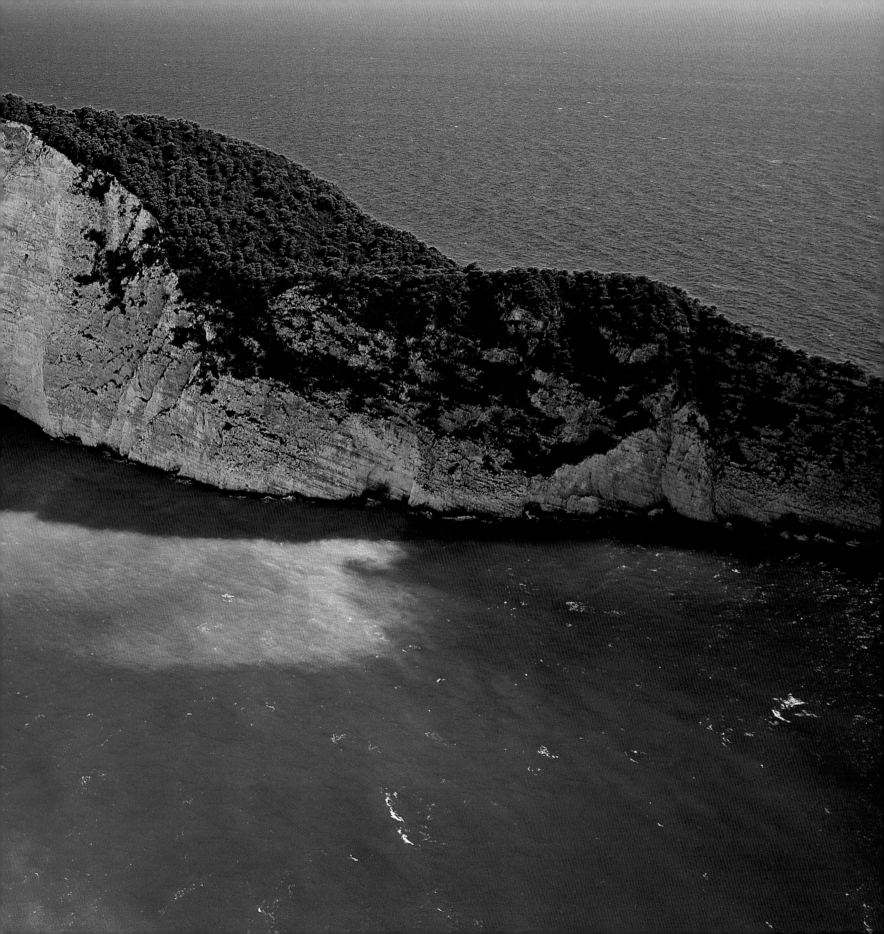

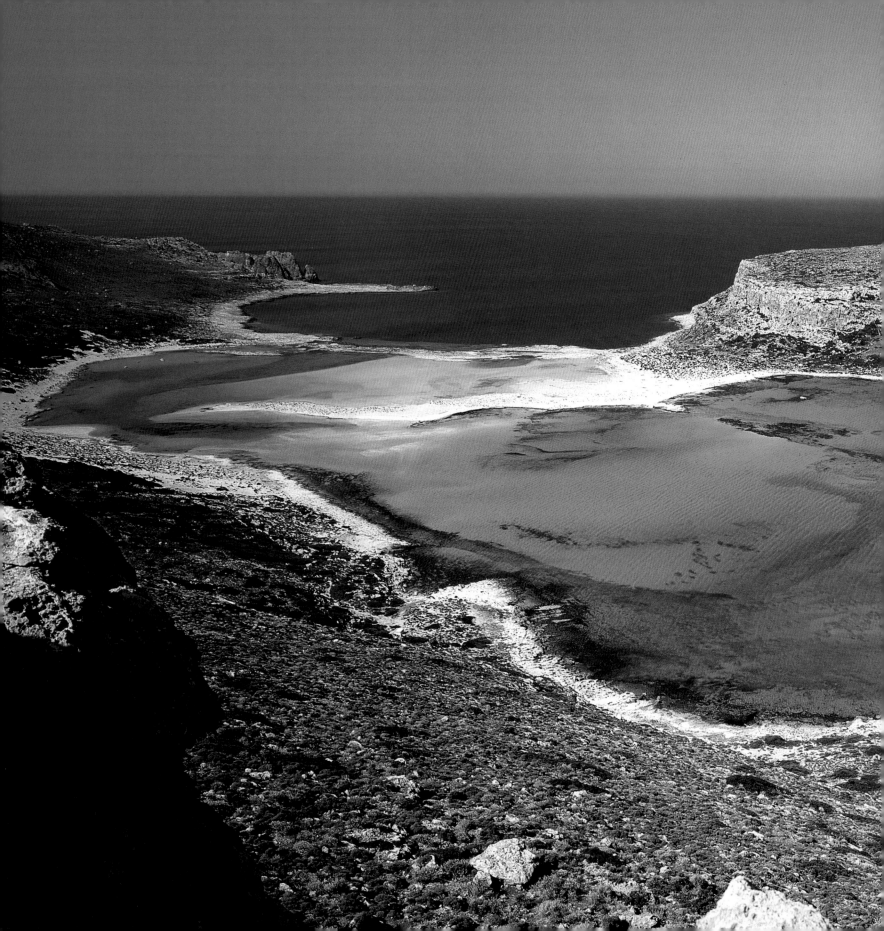

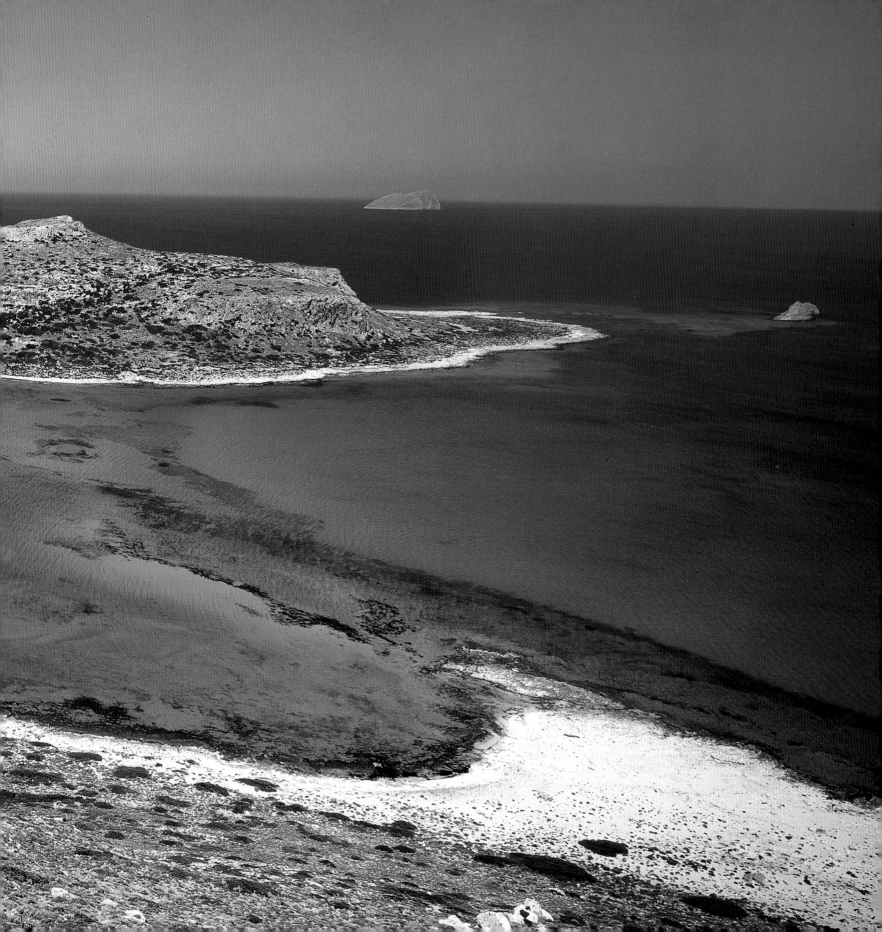

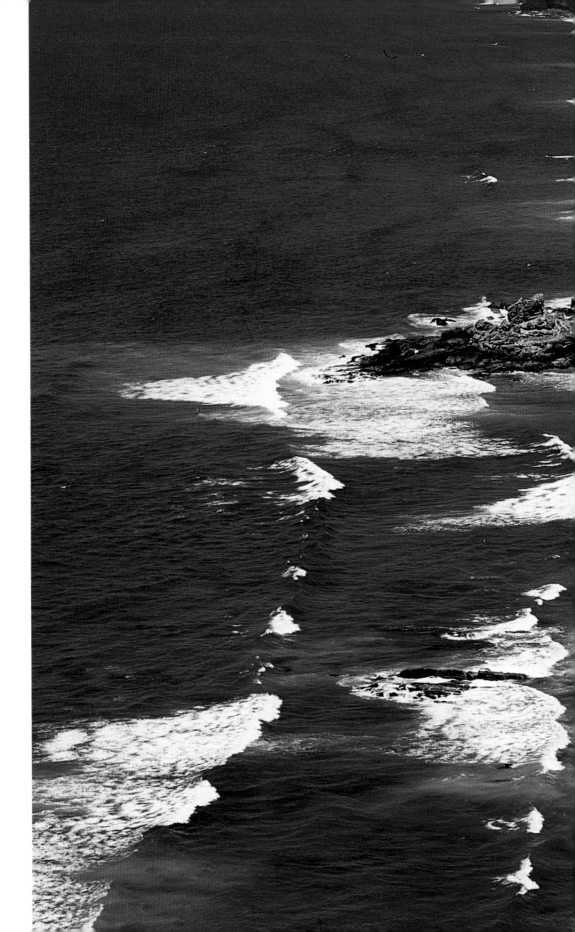

78-79 ● Ionian Sea,
Greece - Zakynthos.

80-81 ●
Mediterranean Sea,
Crete (Greece) - Bay
of Balos.

82-83 ● Atlantic
Ocean, The Algarve
(Portugal) - Coast
near Sagres.

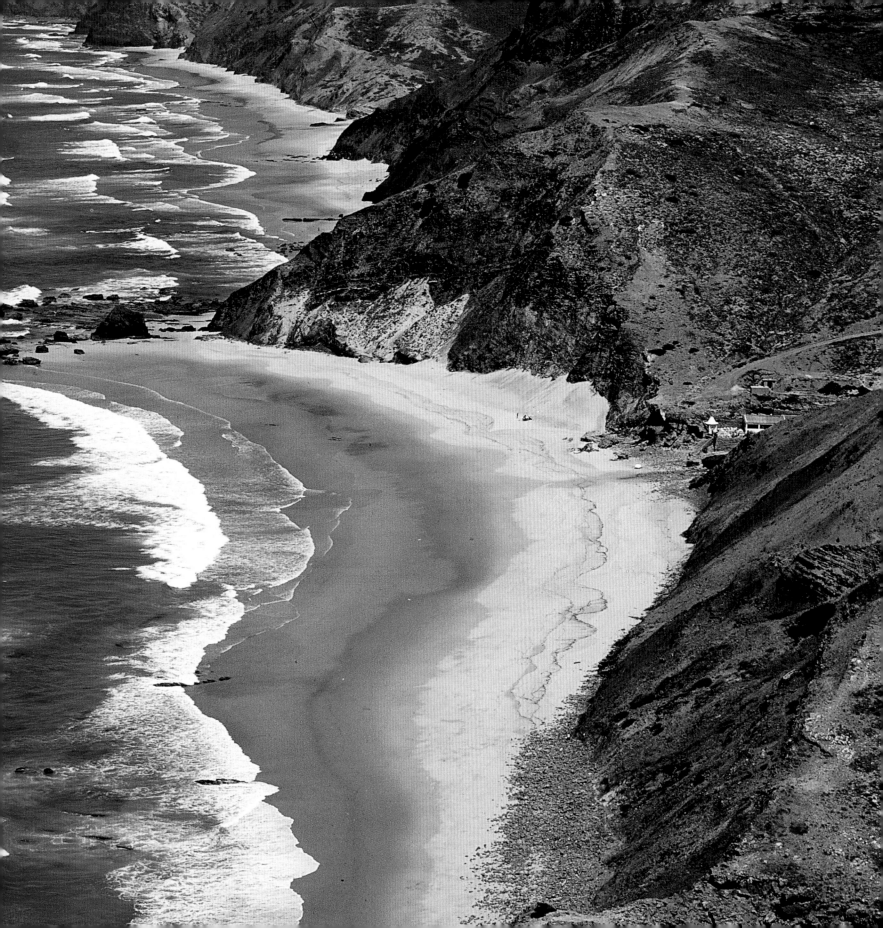

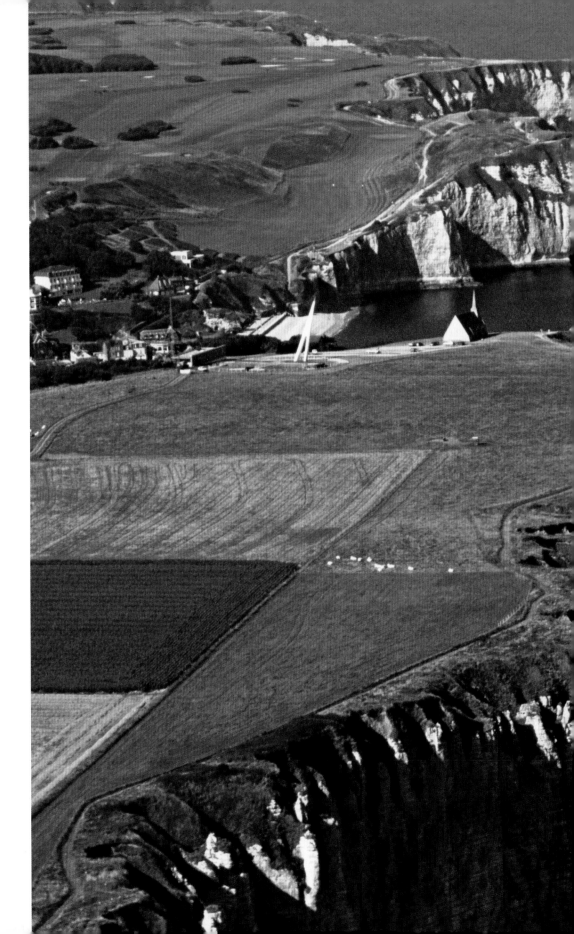

English Channel, France
- Côte d'Albâtre.

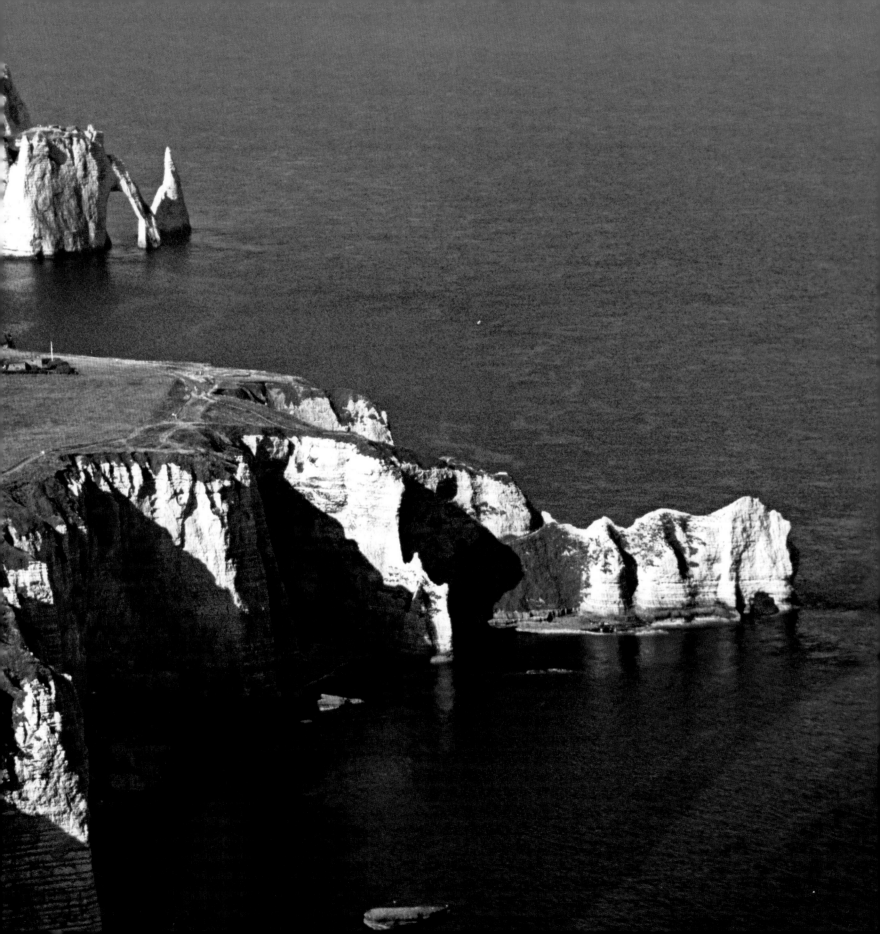

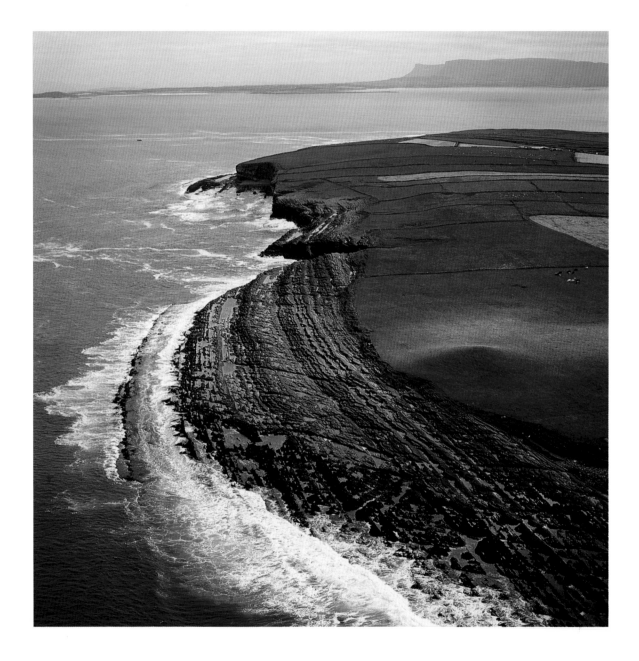

86 ● Atlantic Ocean, Sligo Bay (Ireland) - Benbulben.

87 ● Atlantic Ocean, Donegal (Ireland) - Donegal Bay.

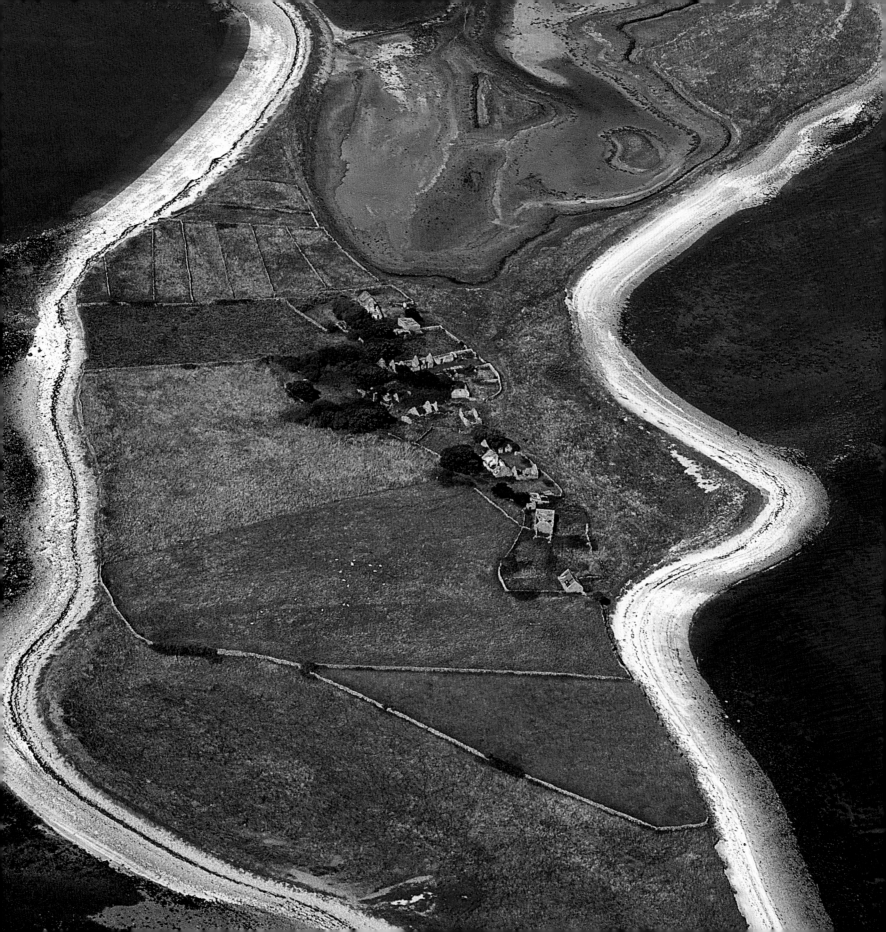

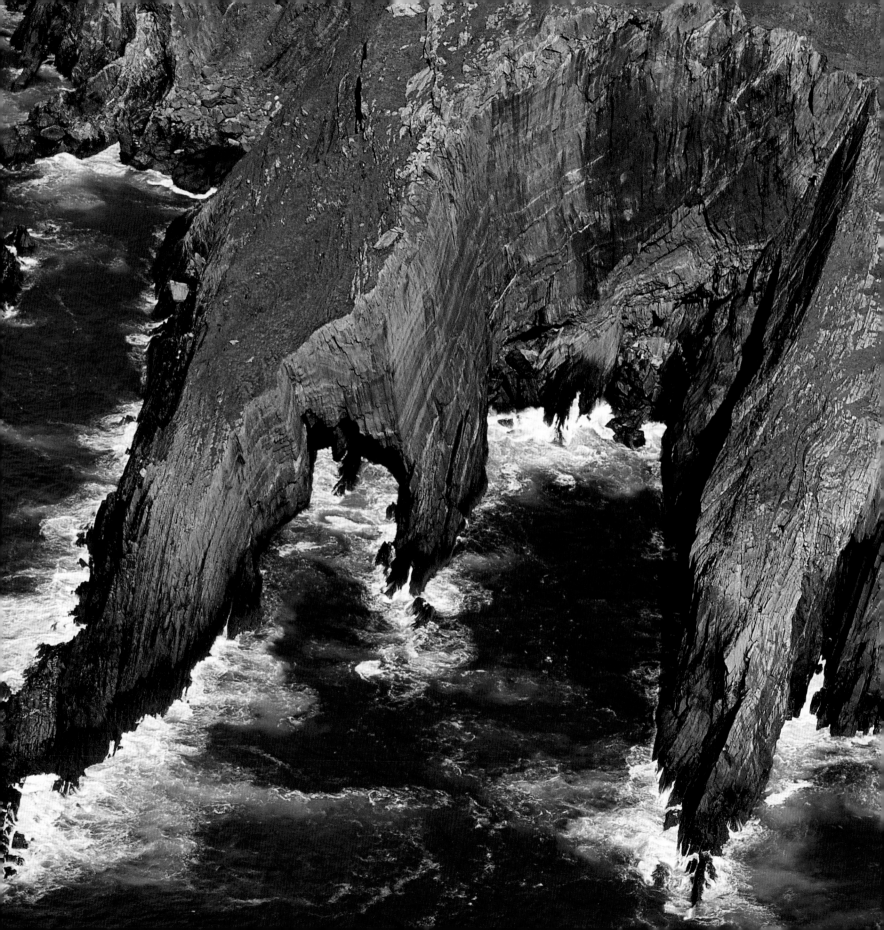

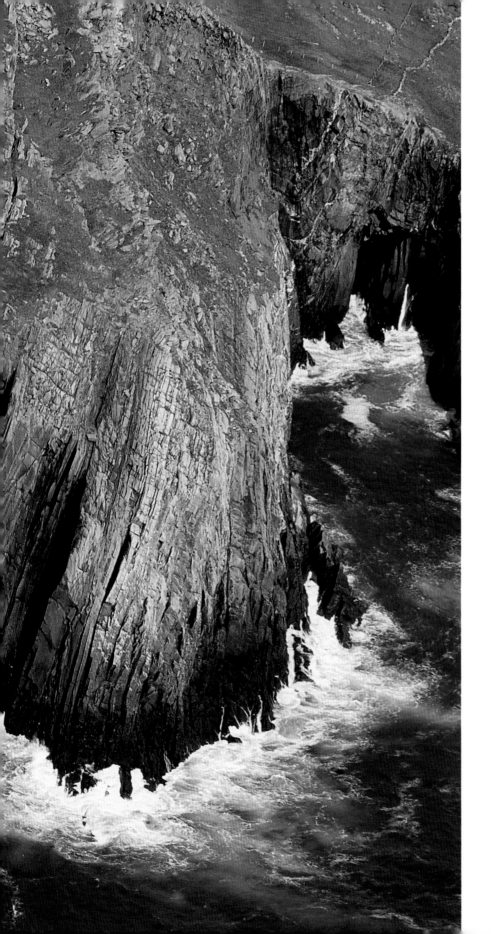

"THE SEA VENTED ALL ITS RAGE AND SEEMED TO SEEK REVENGE... IN THOSE DAYS THE SOUTH-WEST WIND WAILED, THE CHOPPY, PEAKED WAVES OF THE INLET FOUGHT FURIOUS DUELS TO BE THE FIRST TO CRASH ONTO THE SHEER CLIFFS FARTHER WEST."

From DREAMS BY THE SEA
by Björn Larsson

88-89 ● Atlantic Ocean, Cork (Ireland) - Mizen Head.

90-91 ● Atlantic Ocean, Isle of Skye (Scotland) - Neist Point.

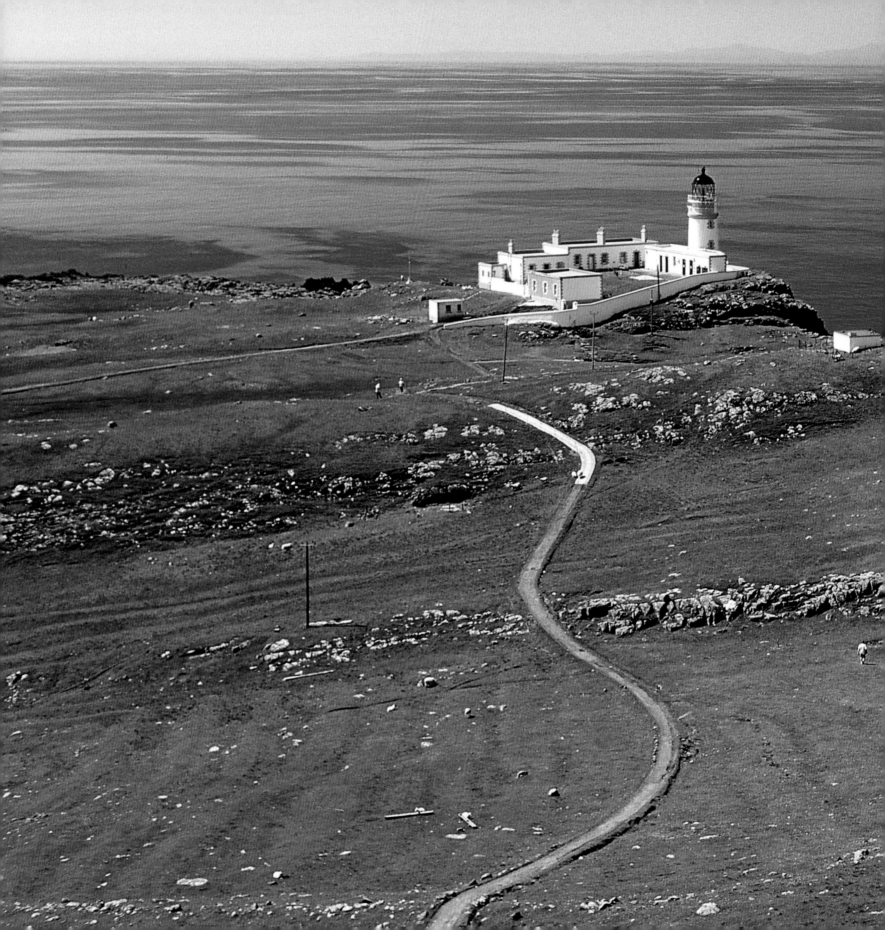

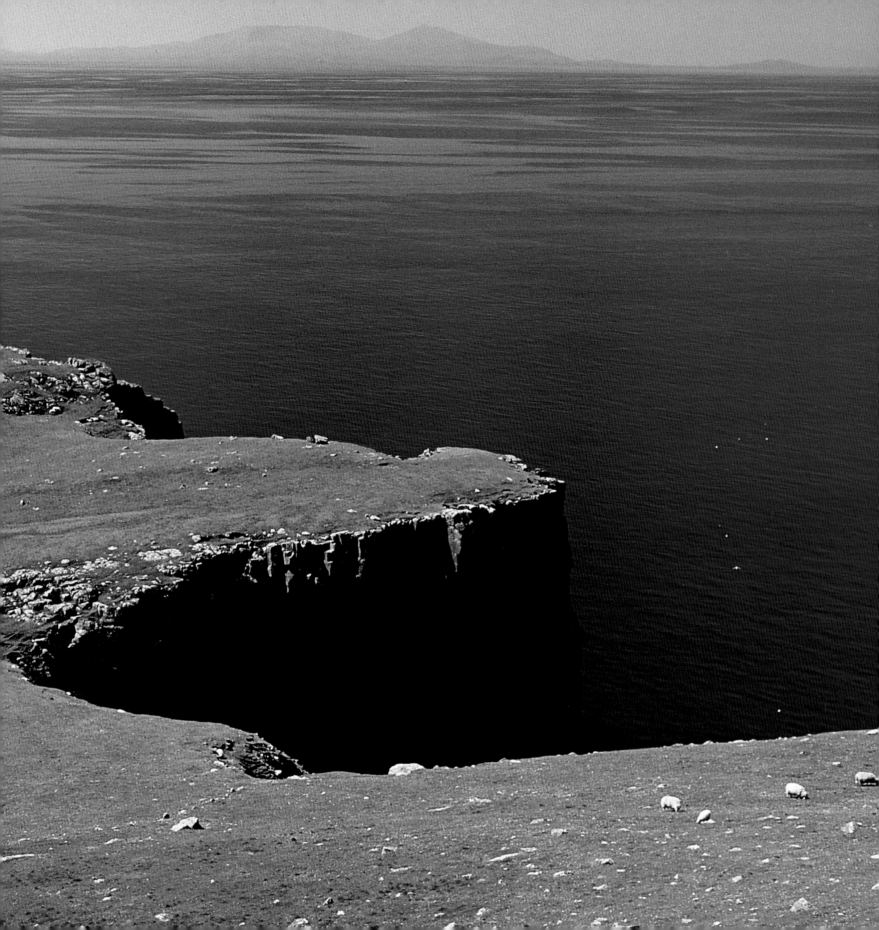

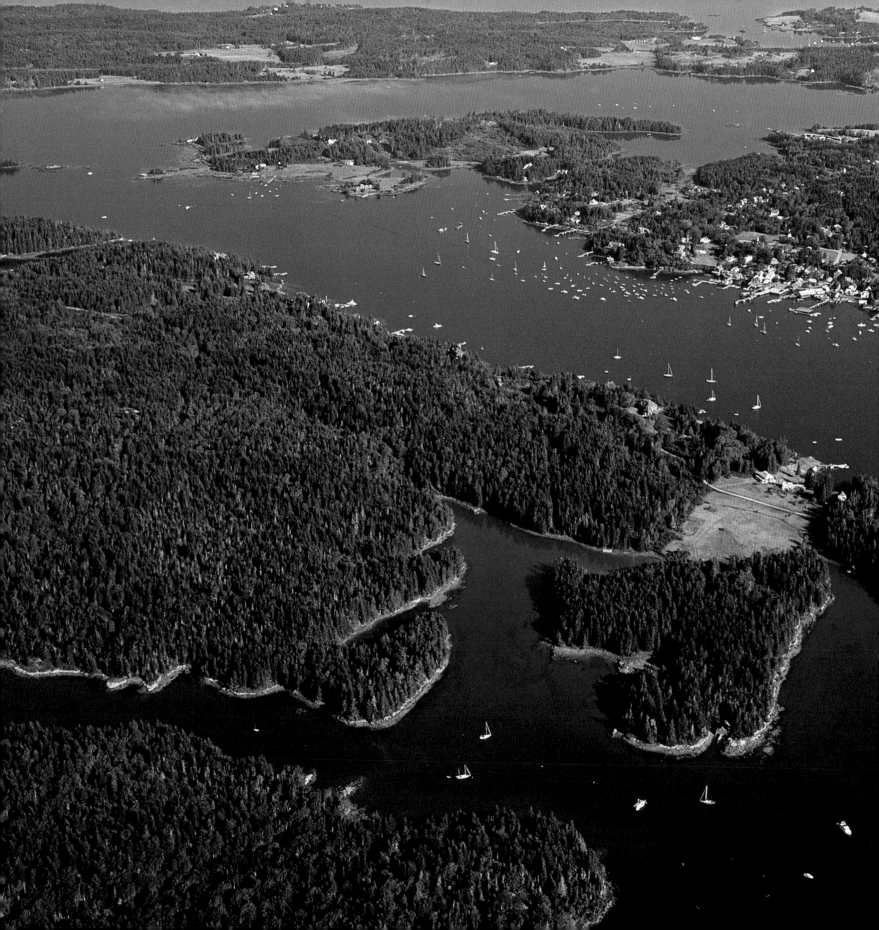

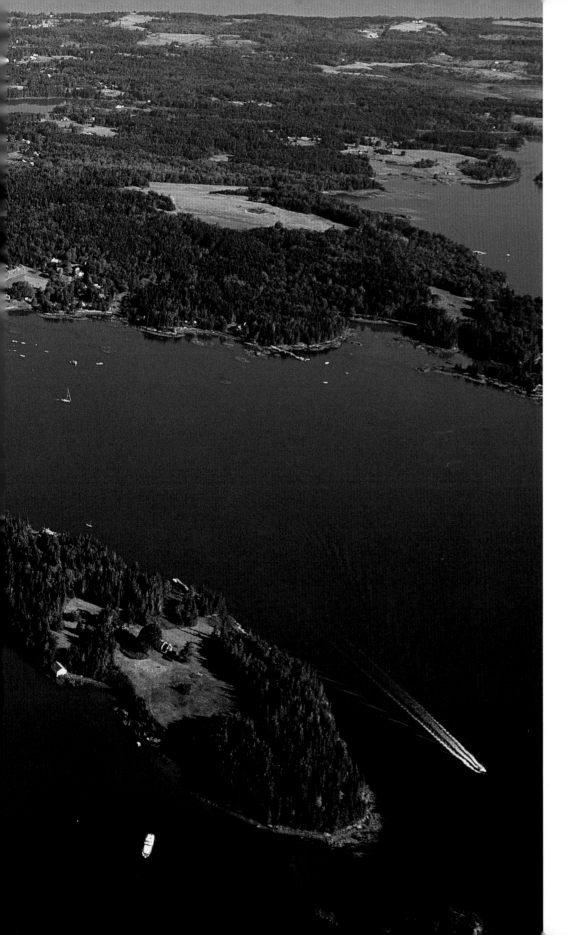

92-93 ● Atlantic Ocean, Maine (USA) - Acadia National Park.

94-95 ● Atlantic Ocean, Florida (USA) - Everglades National Park.

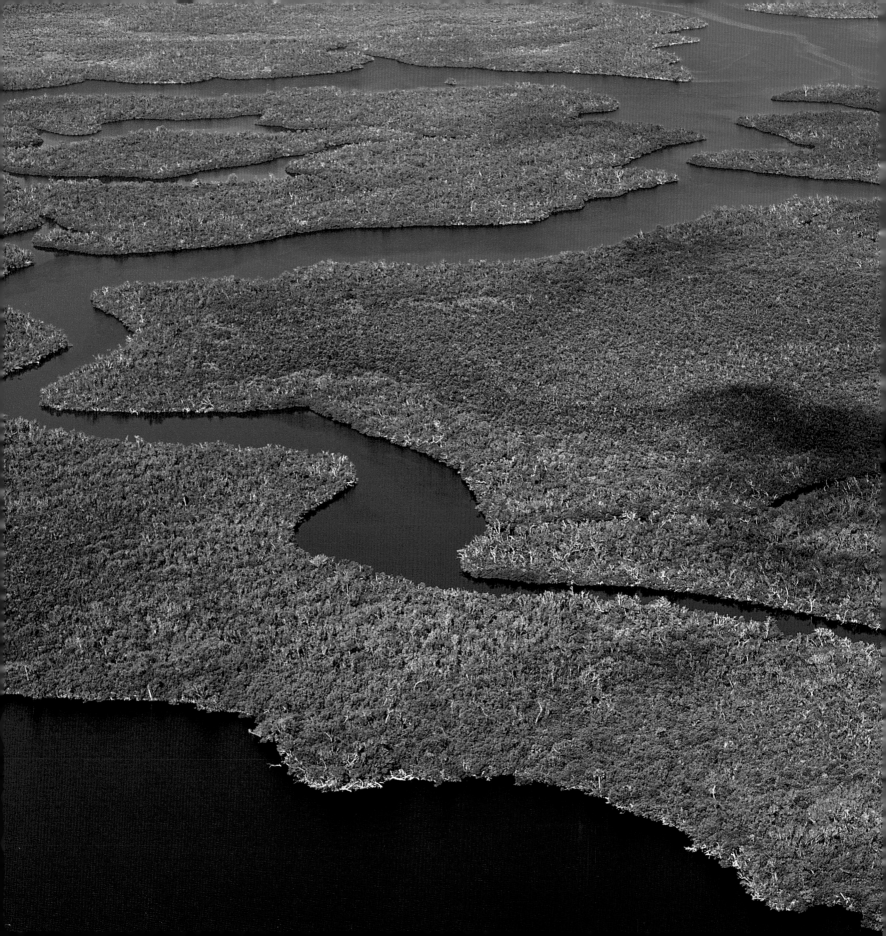

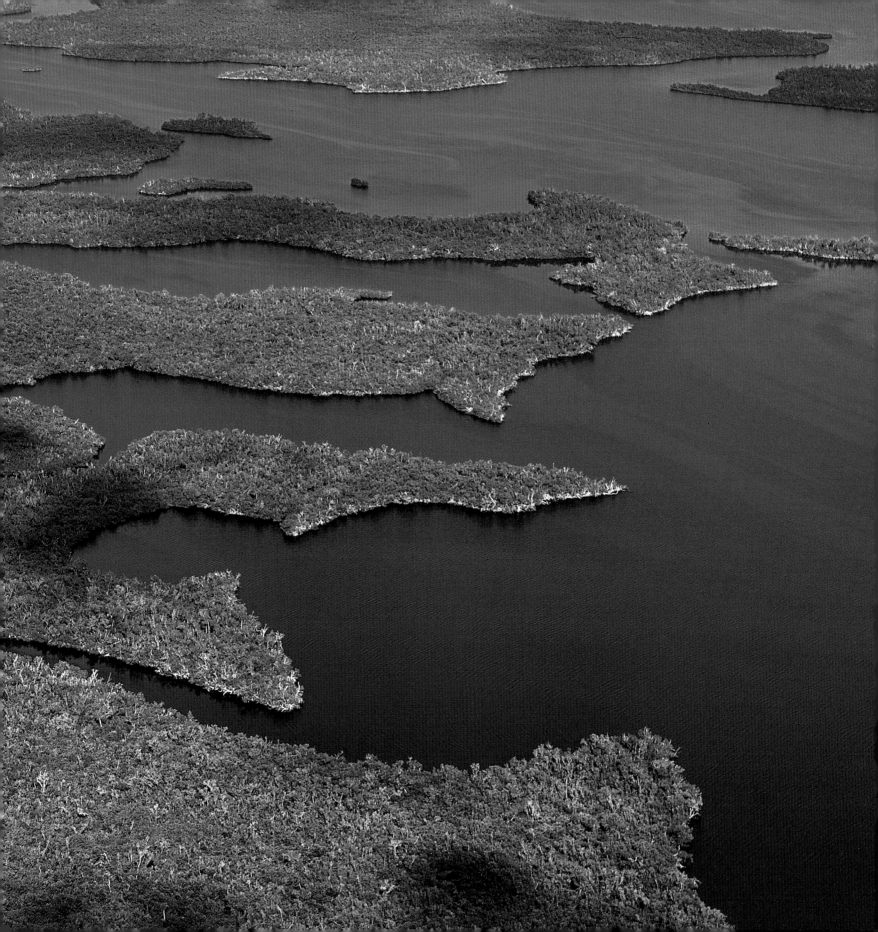

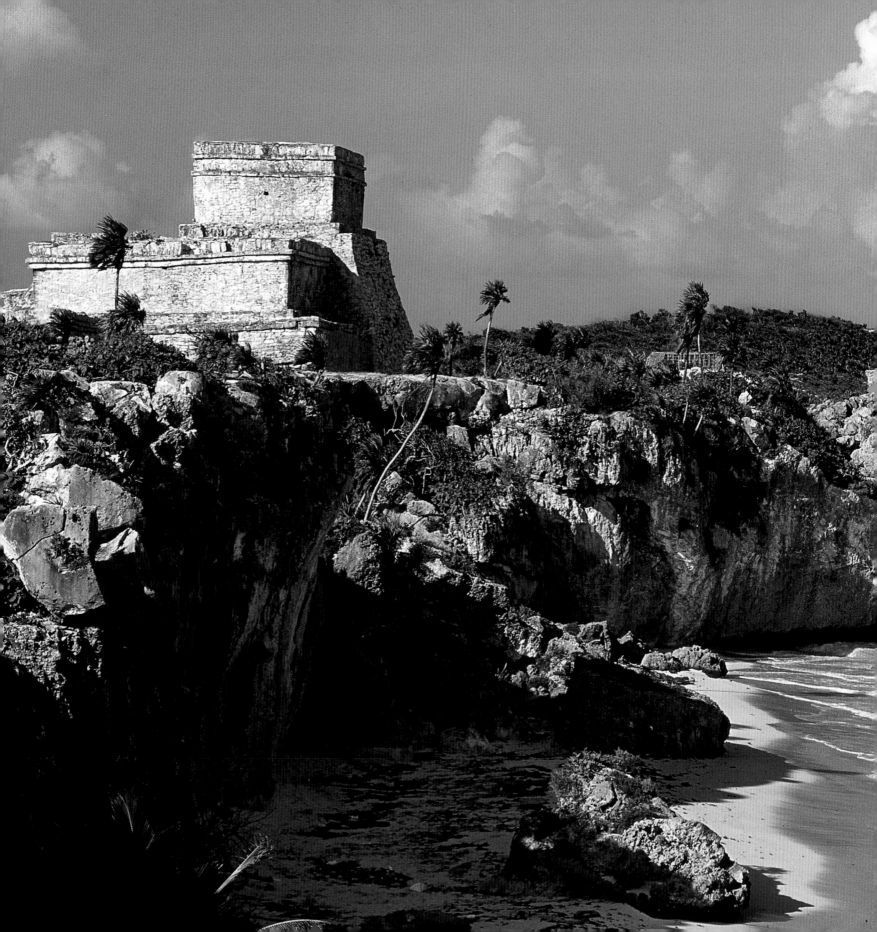

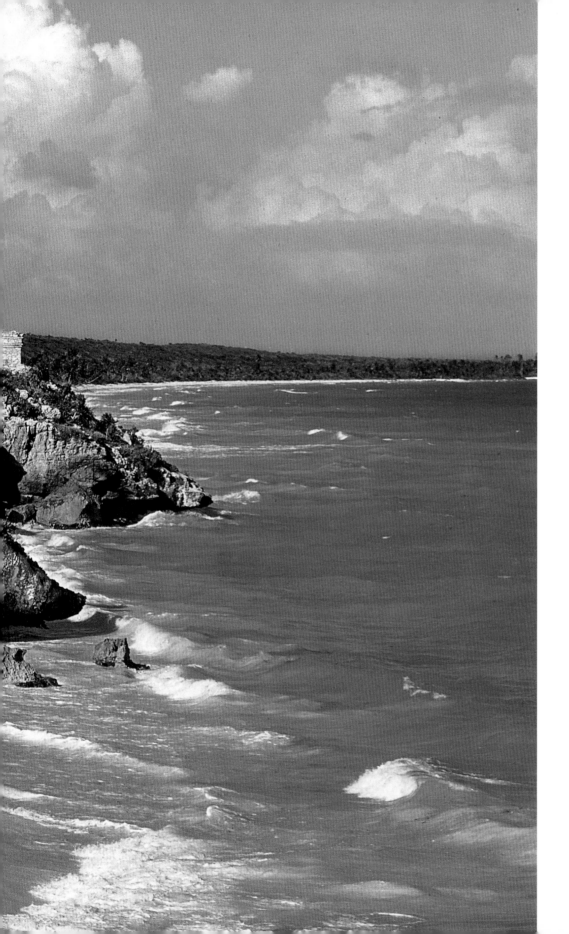

Gulf of Mexico,
Quintana Roo (Mexico)
- El Castillo at Tulum.

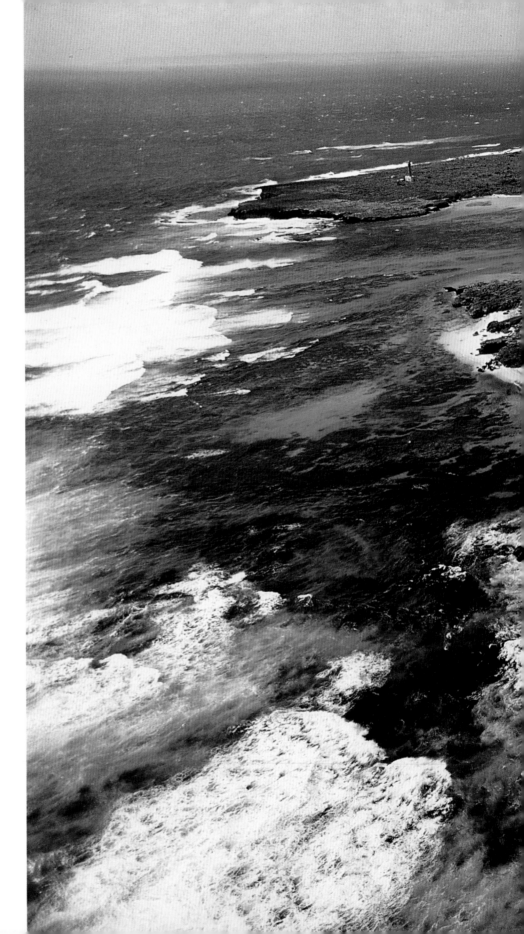

98-99 • Caribbean Sea,
Guadalupa - Pointe des
Chateaux.

100-101 • Caribbean
Sea, Cayo Coco (Cuba).

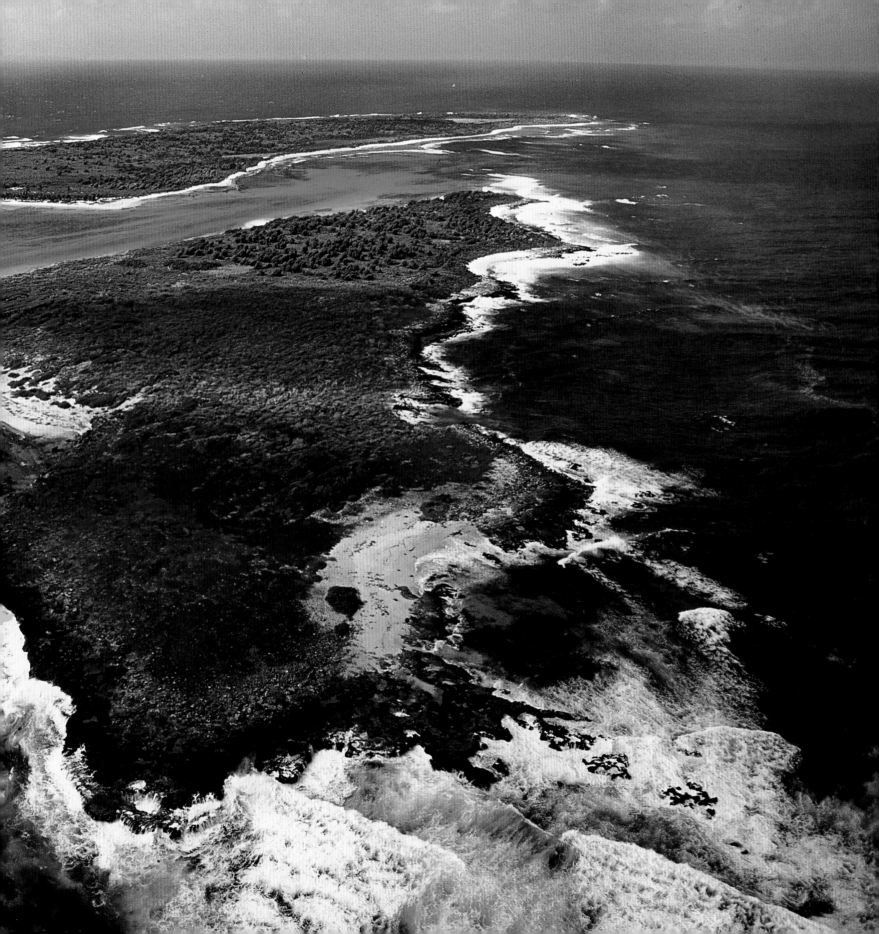

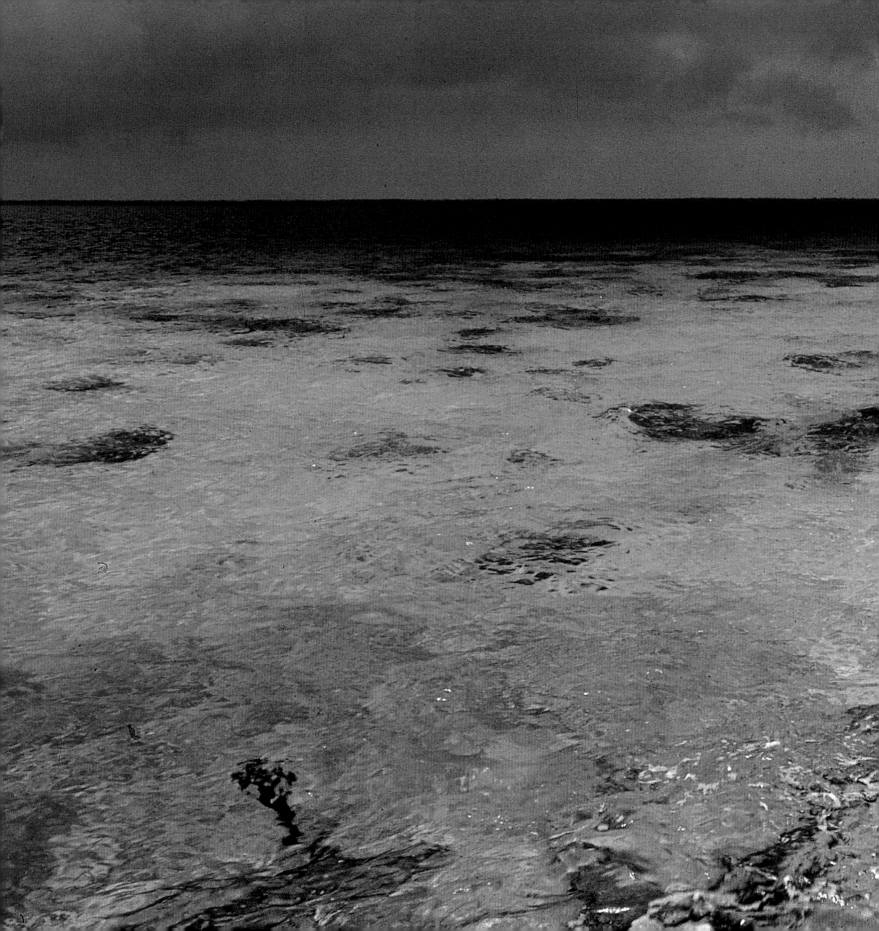

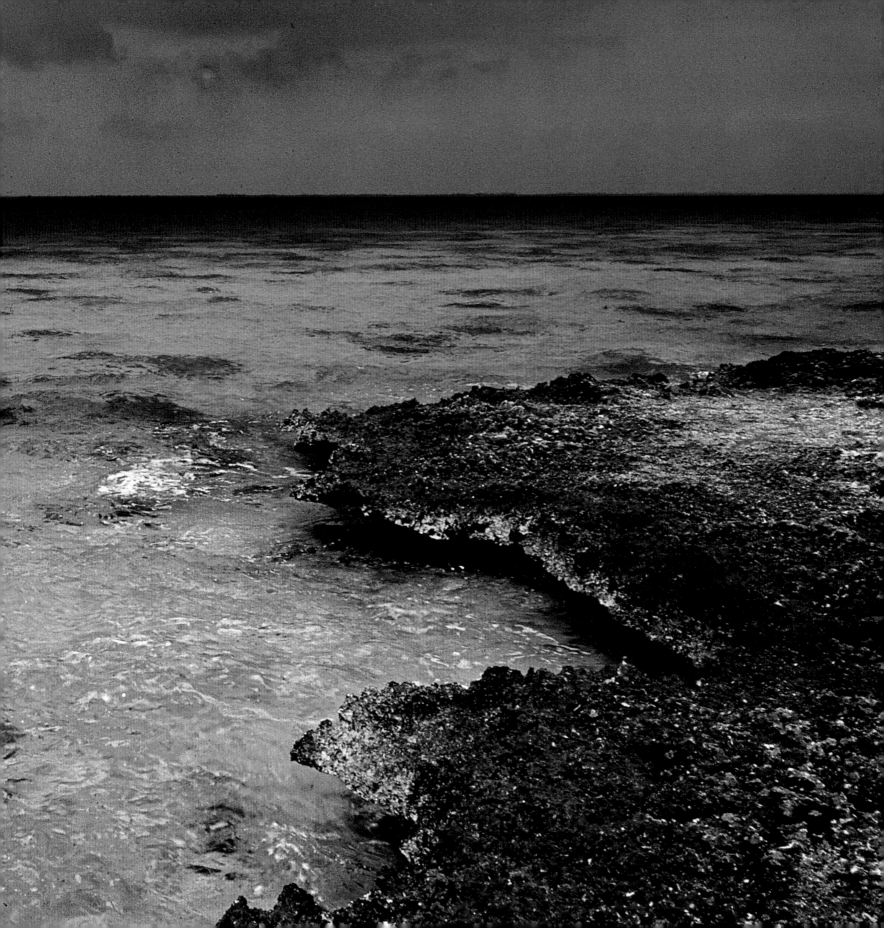

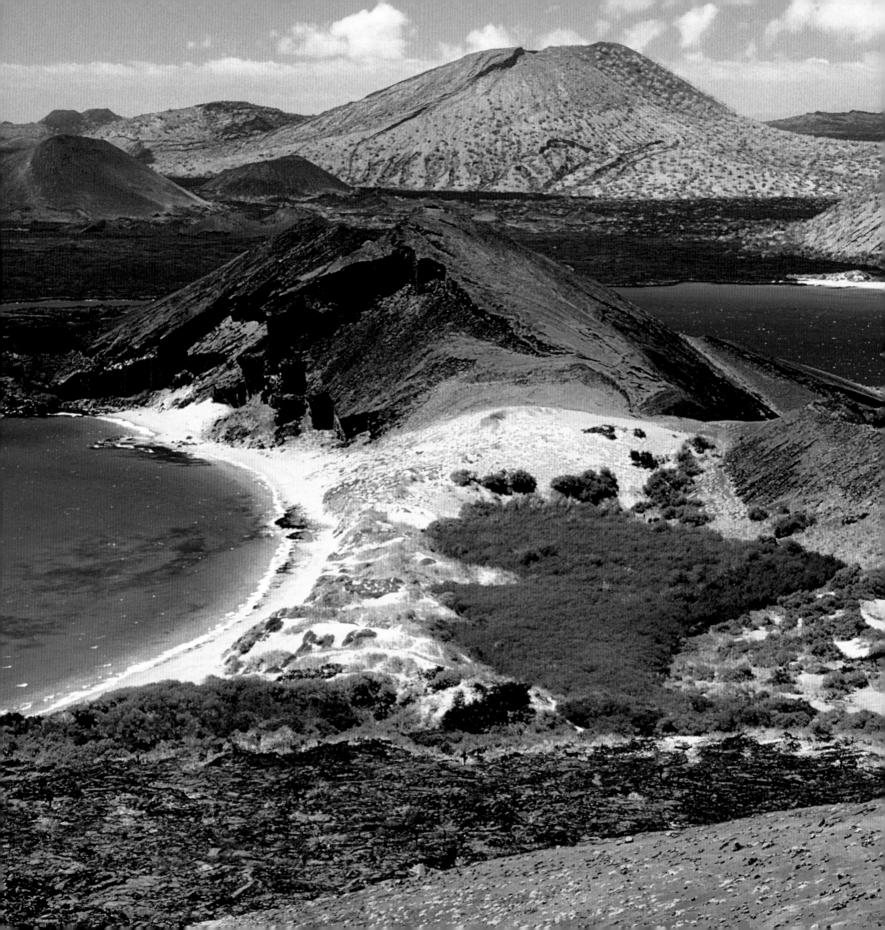

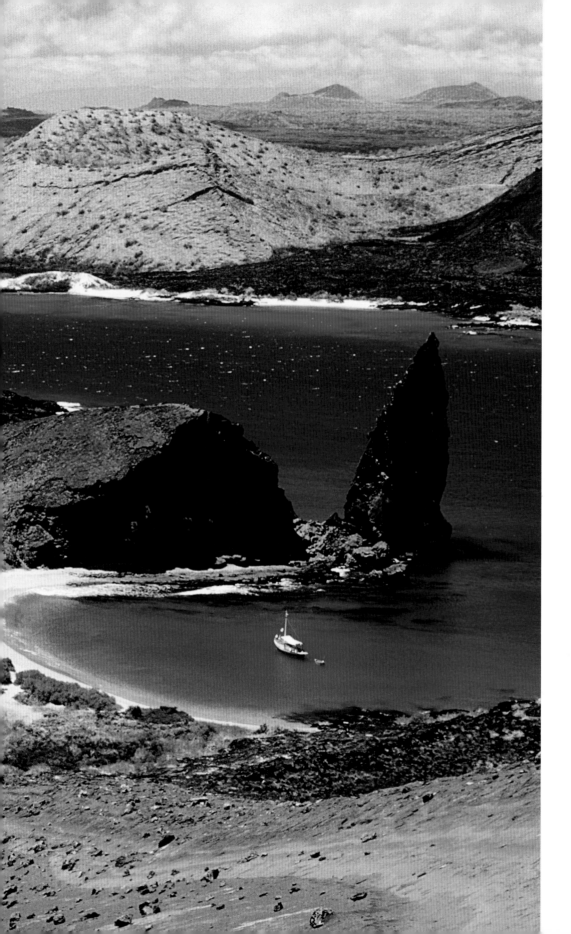

Pacific Ocean, Gálapagos (Ecuador) - Bartholomé and San Salvador islands.

Pacific Ocean,
Galapagos (Ecuador) -
Caldera di Cerro Azul on
Isabela Island.

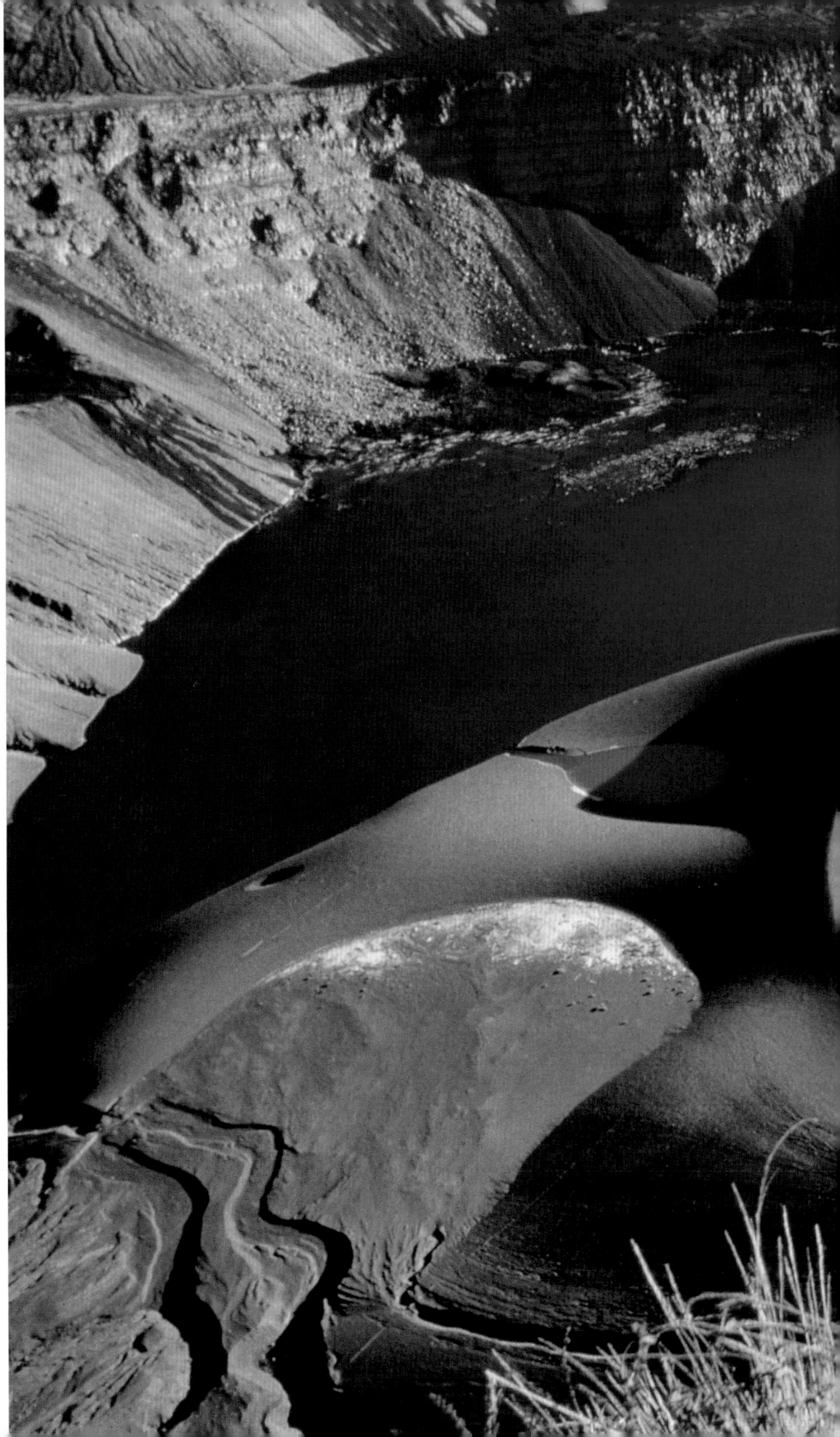

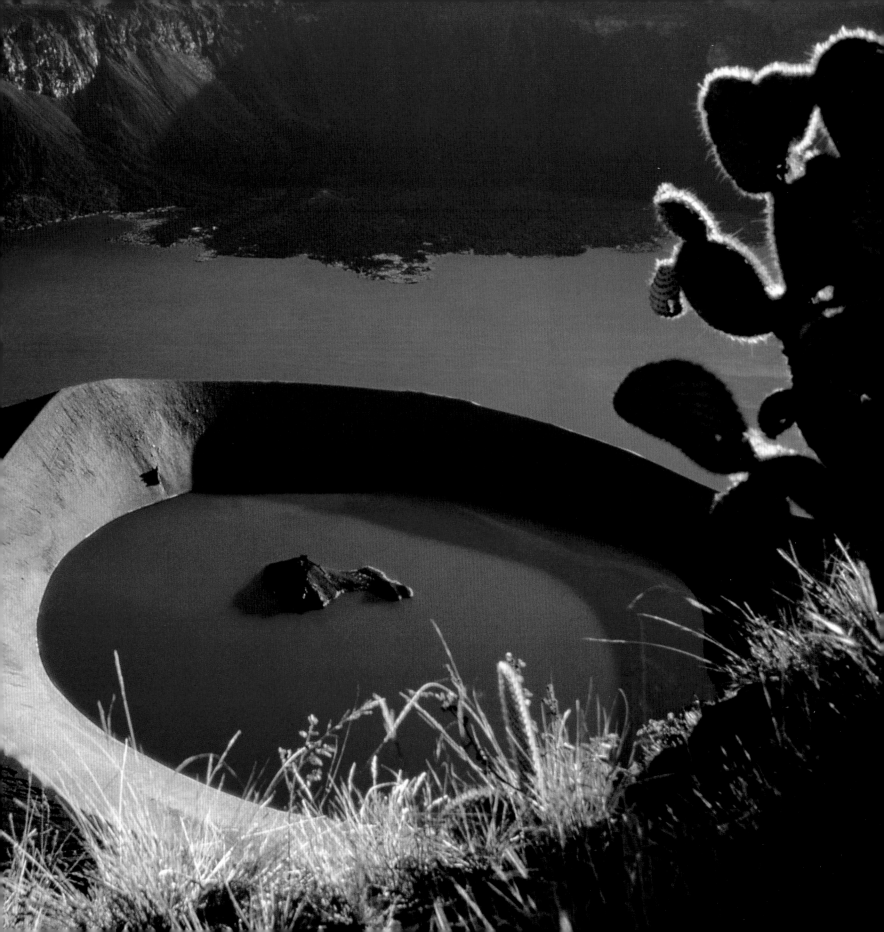

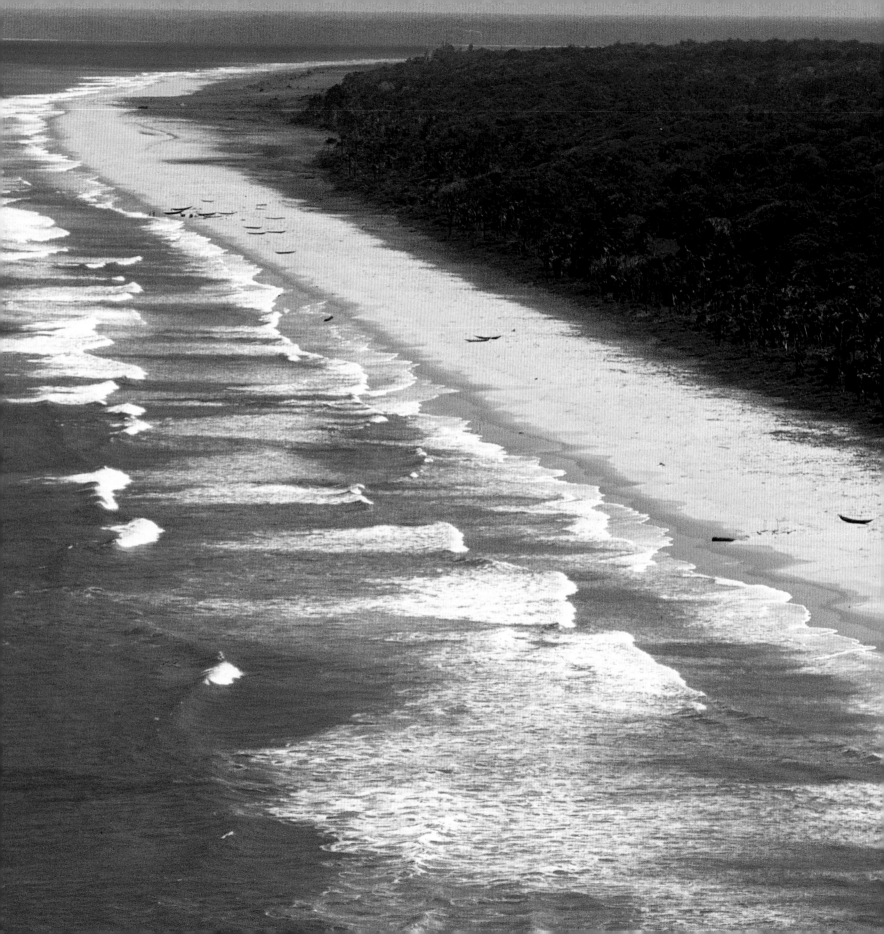

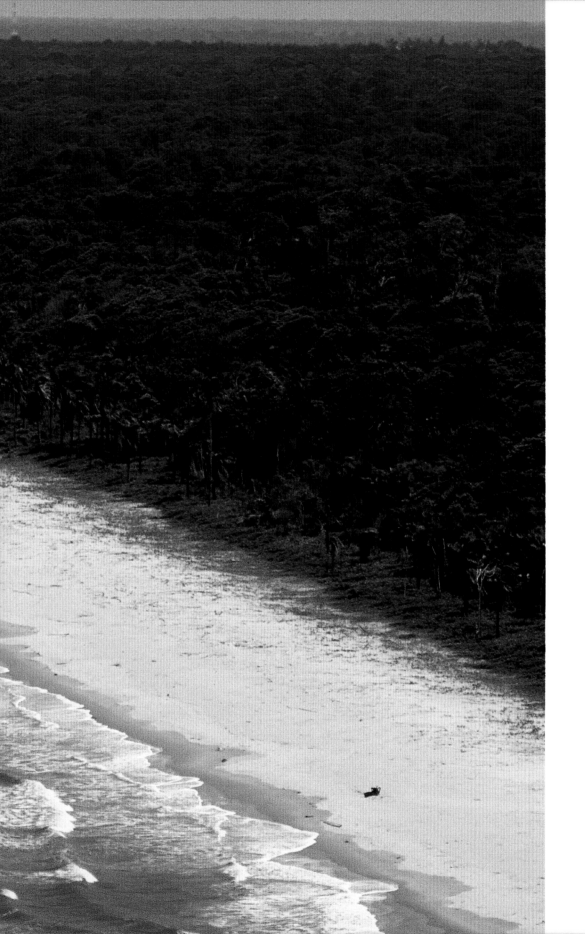

Atlantic Ocean, Nigeria -
Coast near the Niger delta.

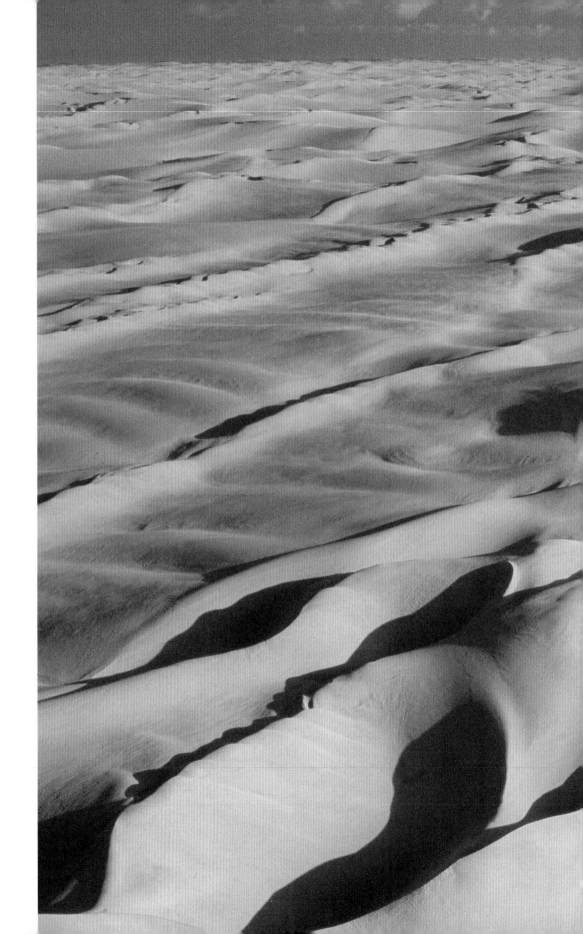

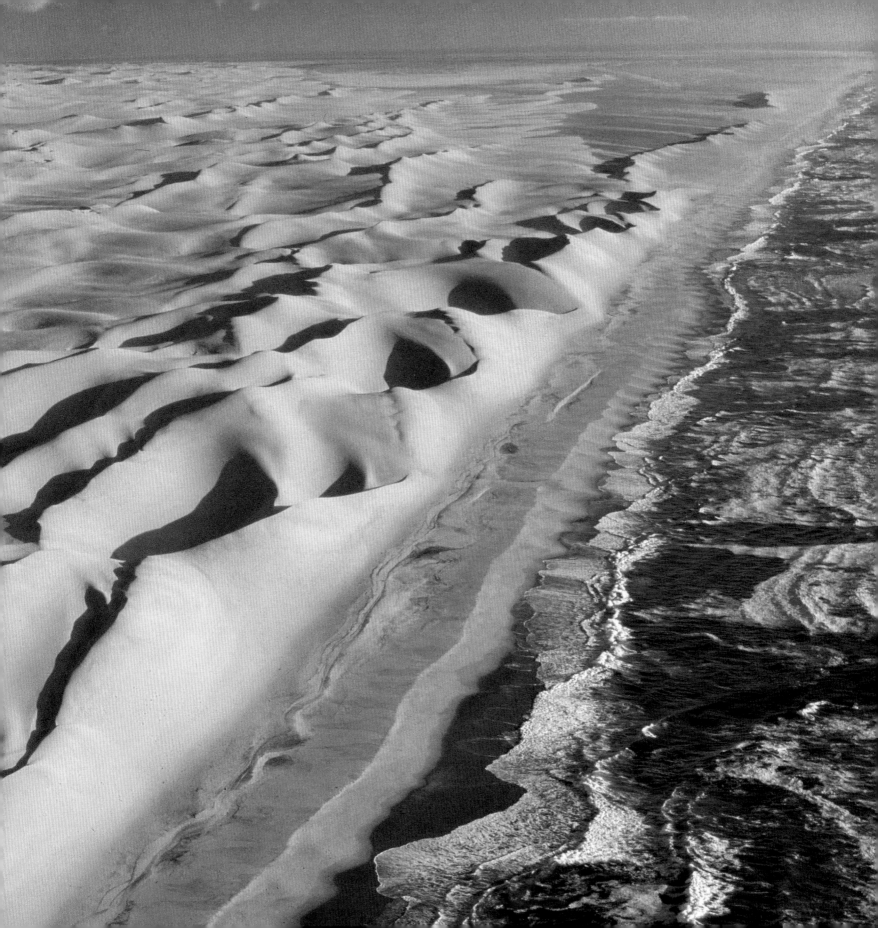

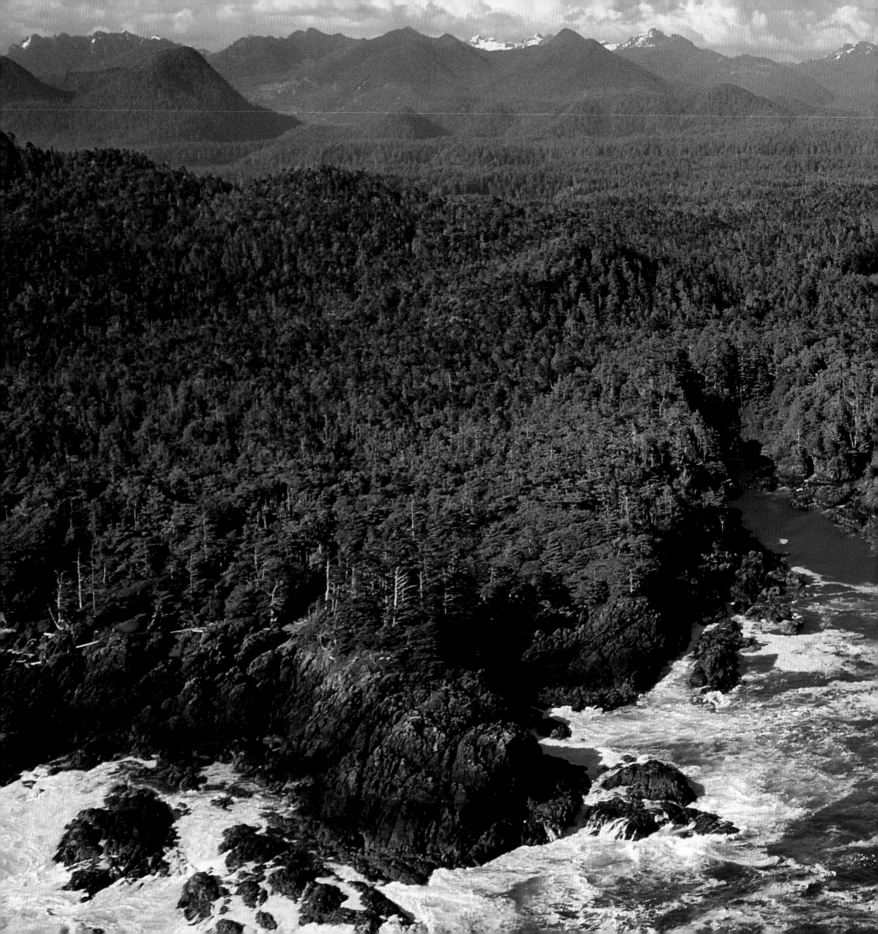

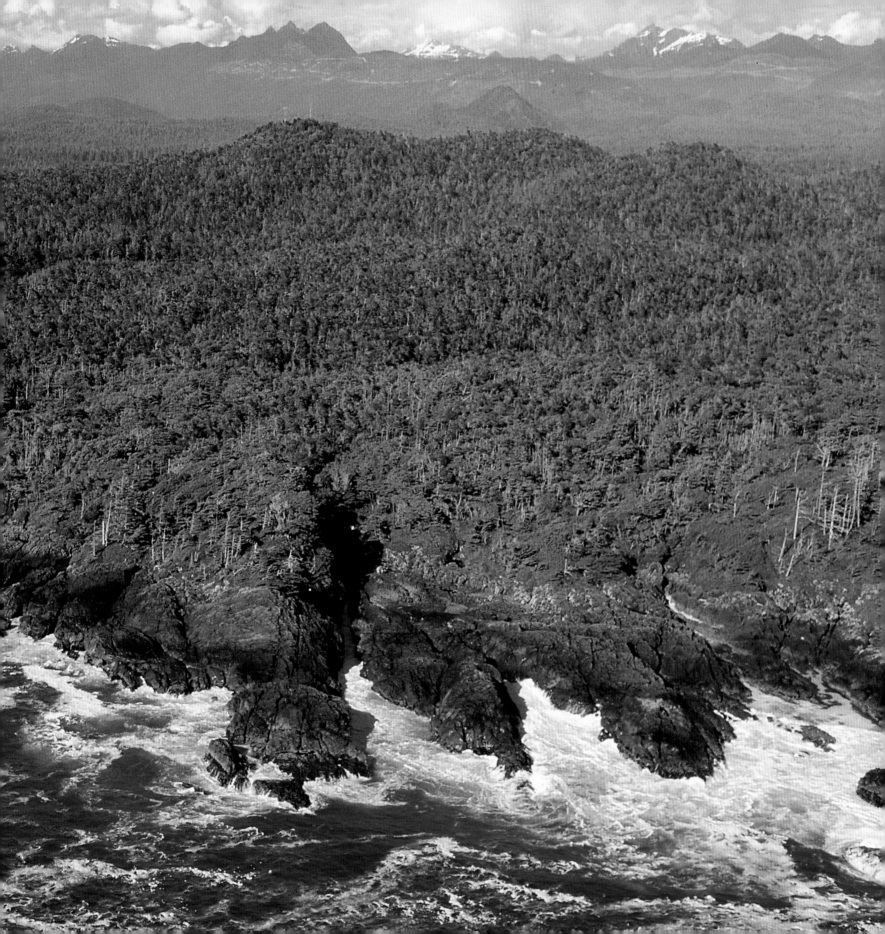

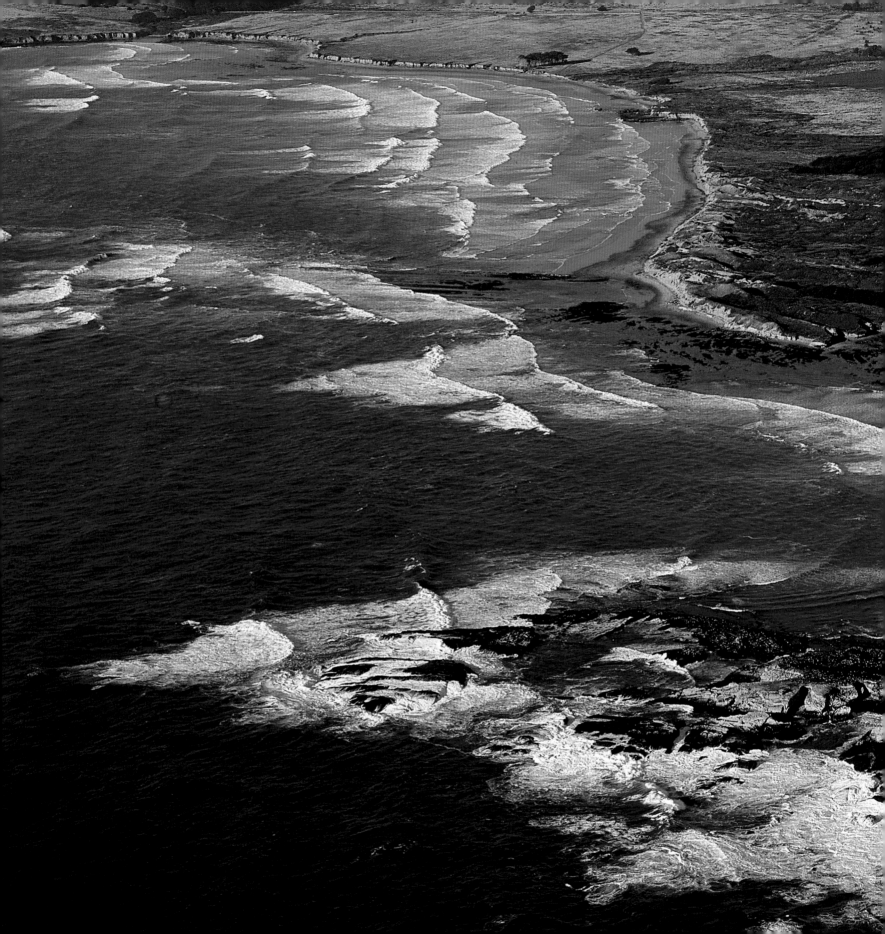

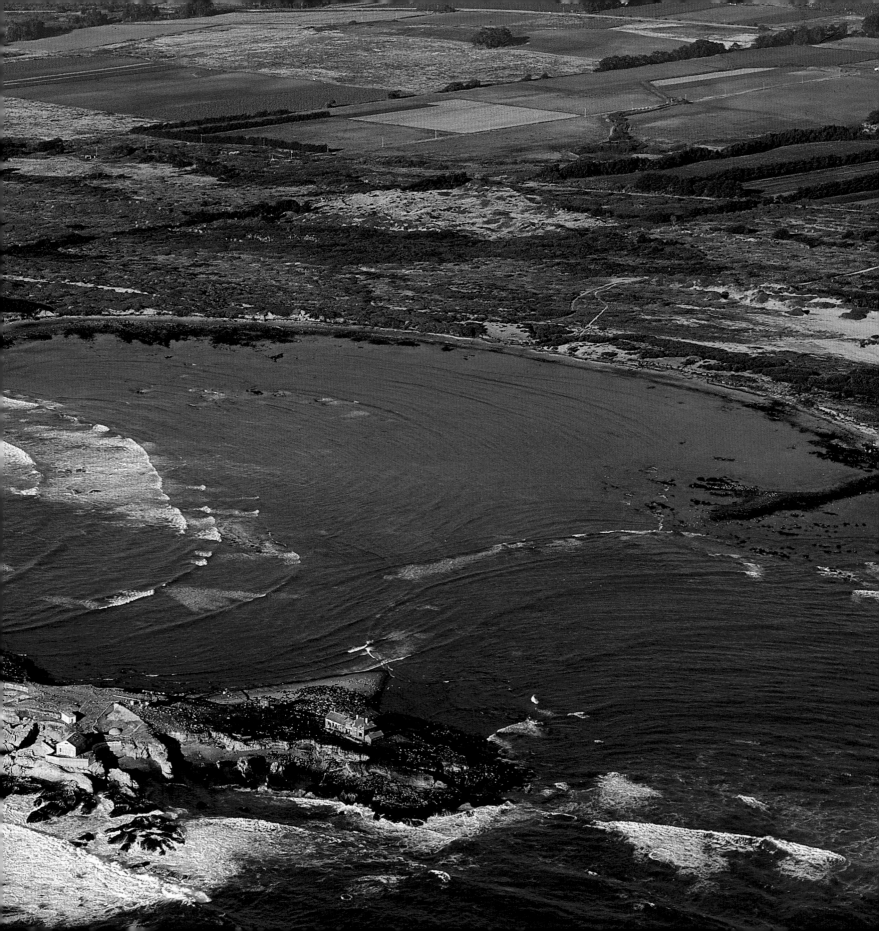

"ORANGE, GOLD, AND GREEN SPARKLED ON THE OCEAN...THE WATER FLICKERED WITH OTHERWORLDLY FIRES. THE SILENCE FRAMED THAT MAGICAL VISION, A SILENCE...THAT MADE MEN FEEL THEY WERE DEAF, THEIR SENSES ENRAPTURED BY THAT MARVELLOUS SCENE."

from THE BURNING SHORE
by Wilbur Smith

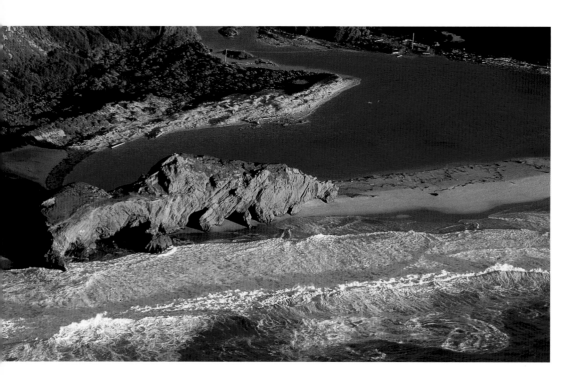

Pacific Ocean, California (USA) - Big Sur.

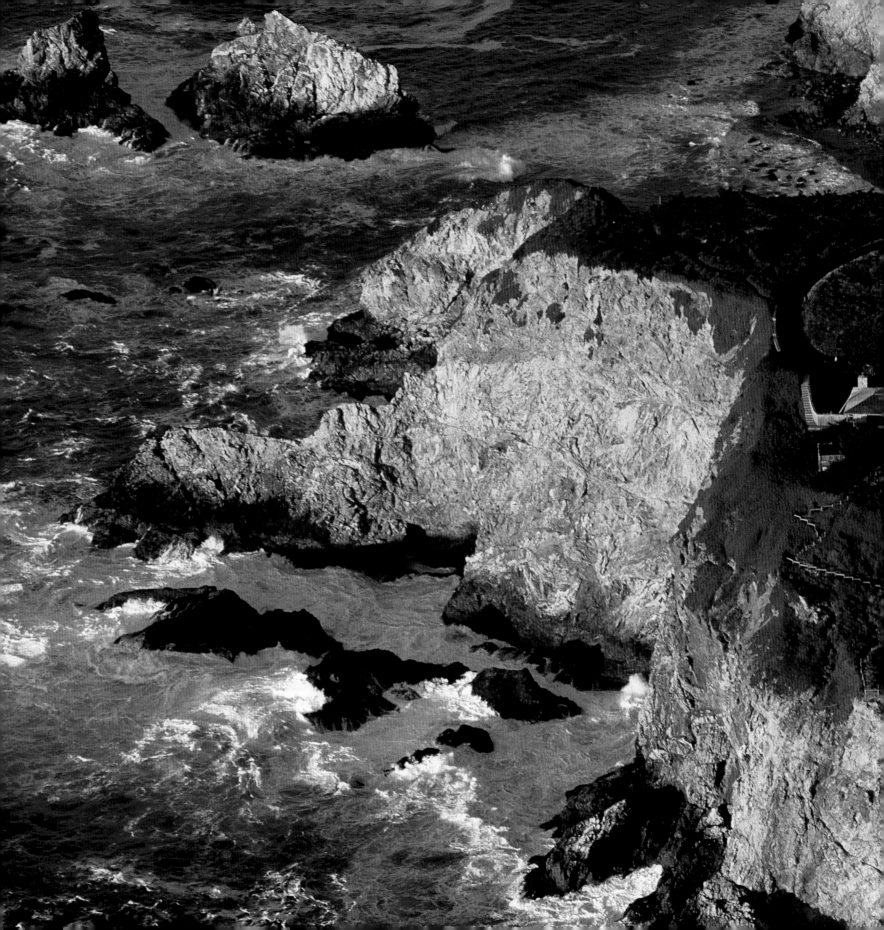

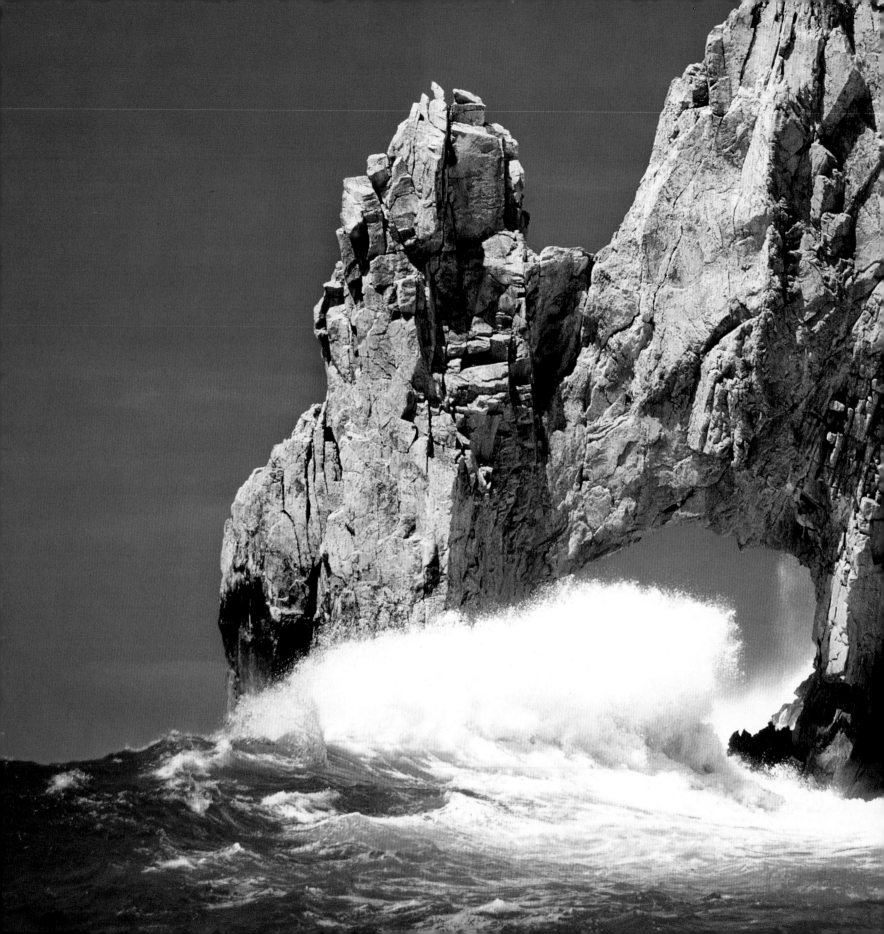

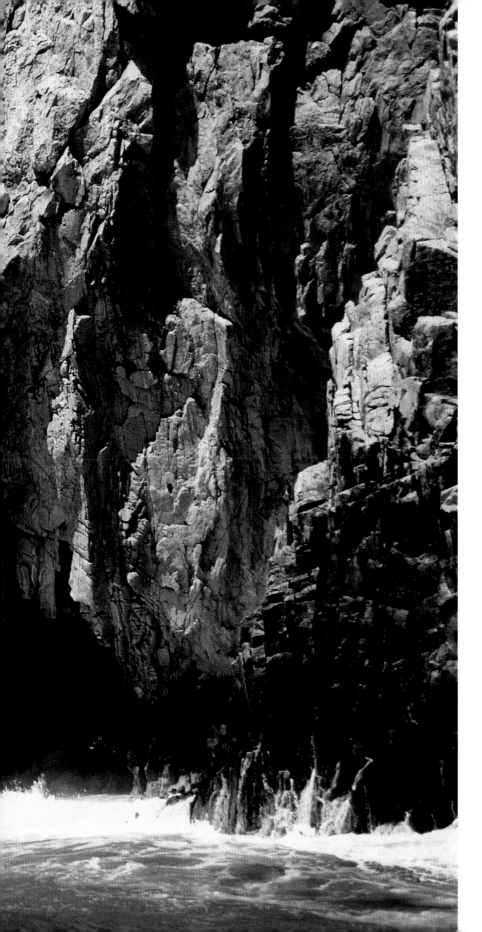

116-117 ● Pacific Ocean,
Baja California (Mexico)
- Cabo San Lucas.

118-119 ● Pacific Ocean, Hawaii
(USA) - Na Pali.

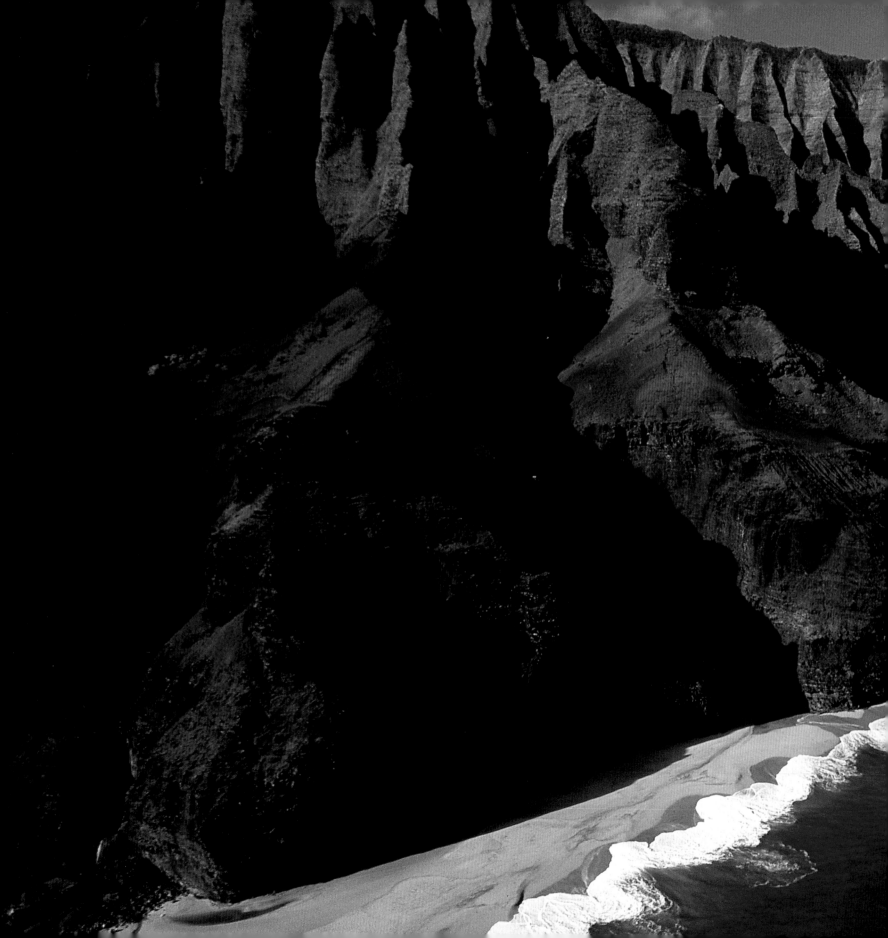

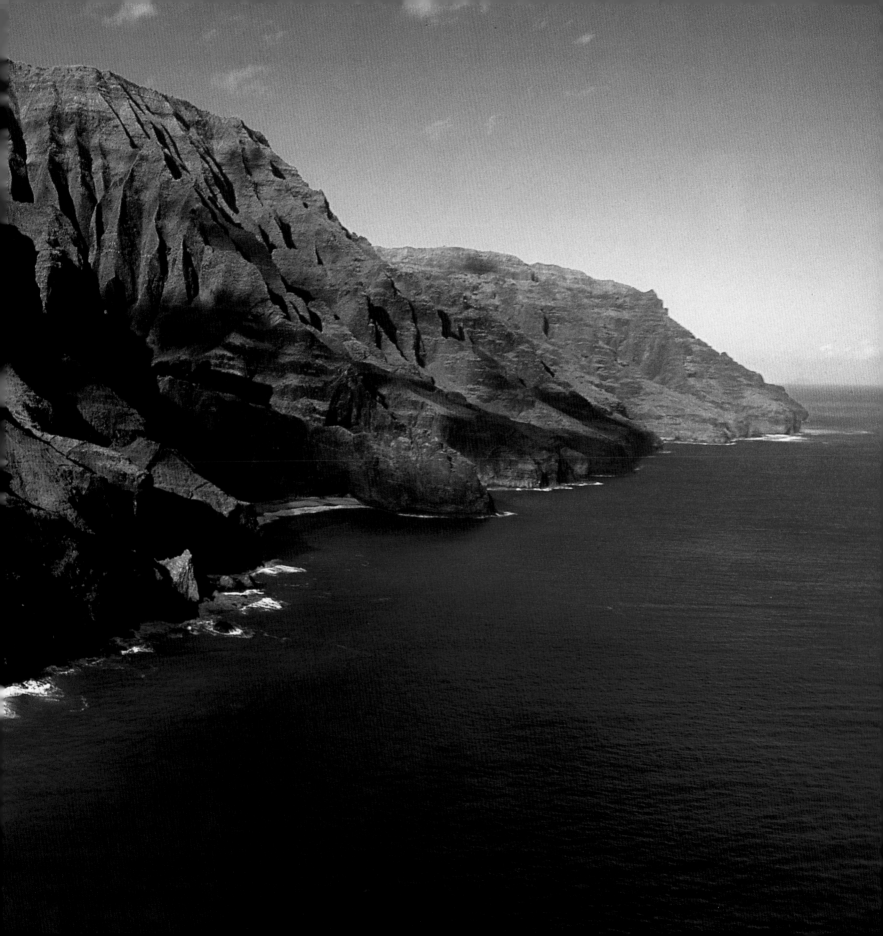

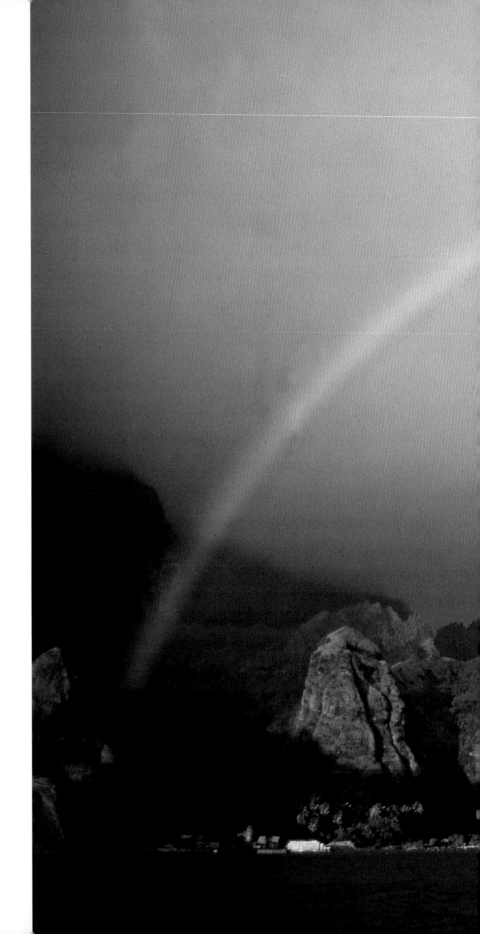

The islands
of the rainbow

Pacific Ocean, Marquesas Islands
(French Polynesia) - Bay of the
Virgins on Fatu Hiva.

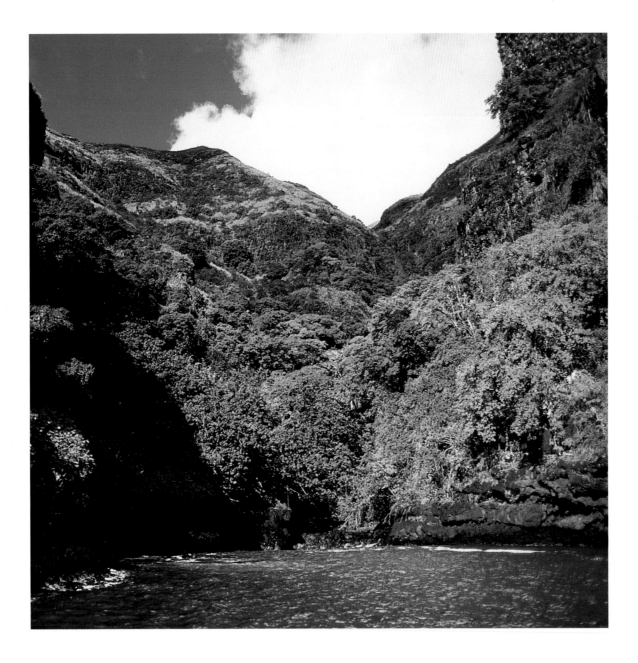

122 and 123 ● Pacific Ocean, Marquesas Islands (French Polynesia) - Fatu Hiva.

124-125 ● Pacific Ocean, Tuamotu Islands (French Polynesia) - Tikehau.

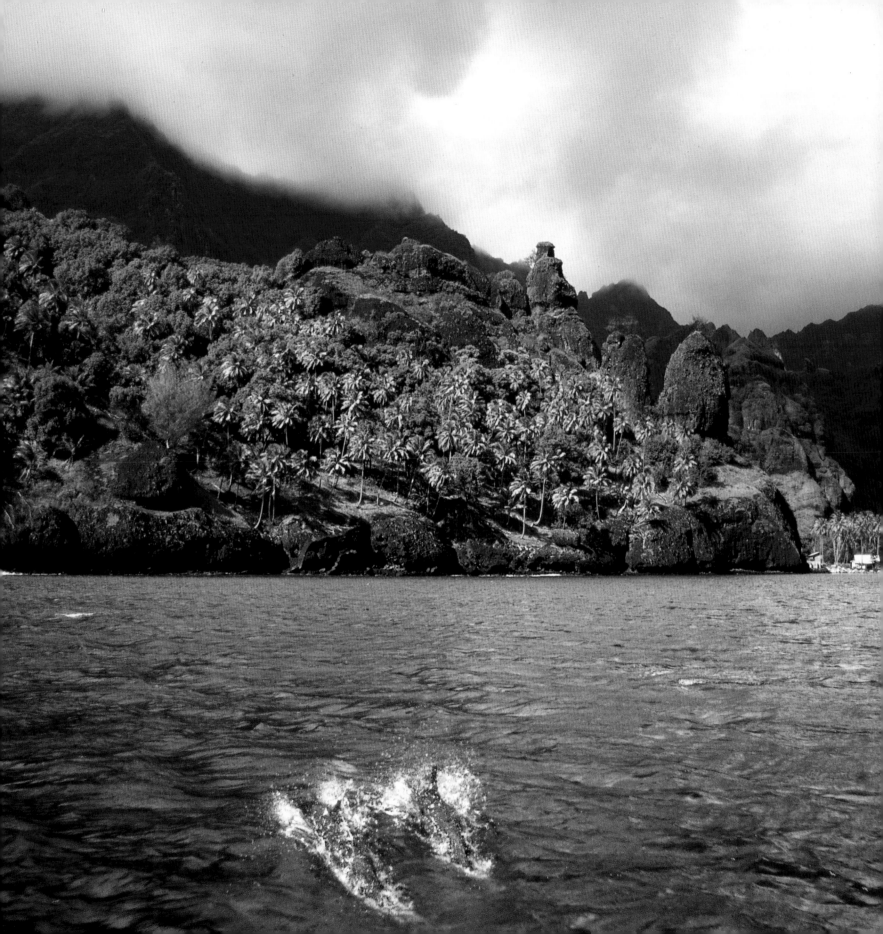

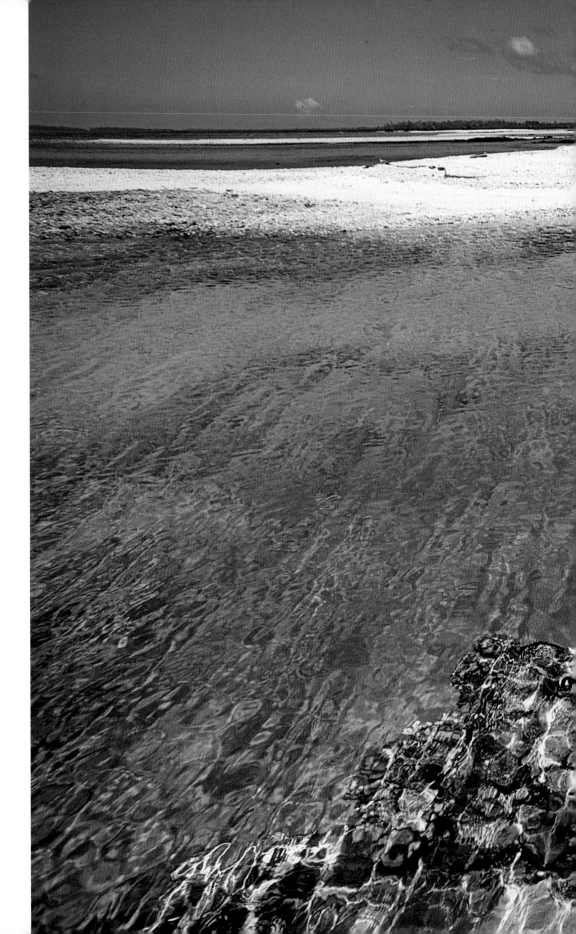

Crystal waters

- Pacific Ocean, Tuamotu Islands (French Polynesia) - Rangiroa.

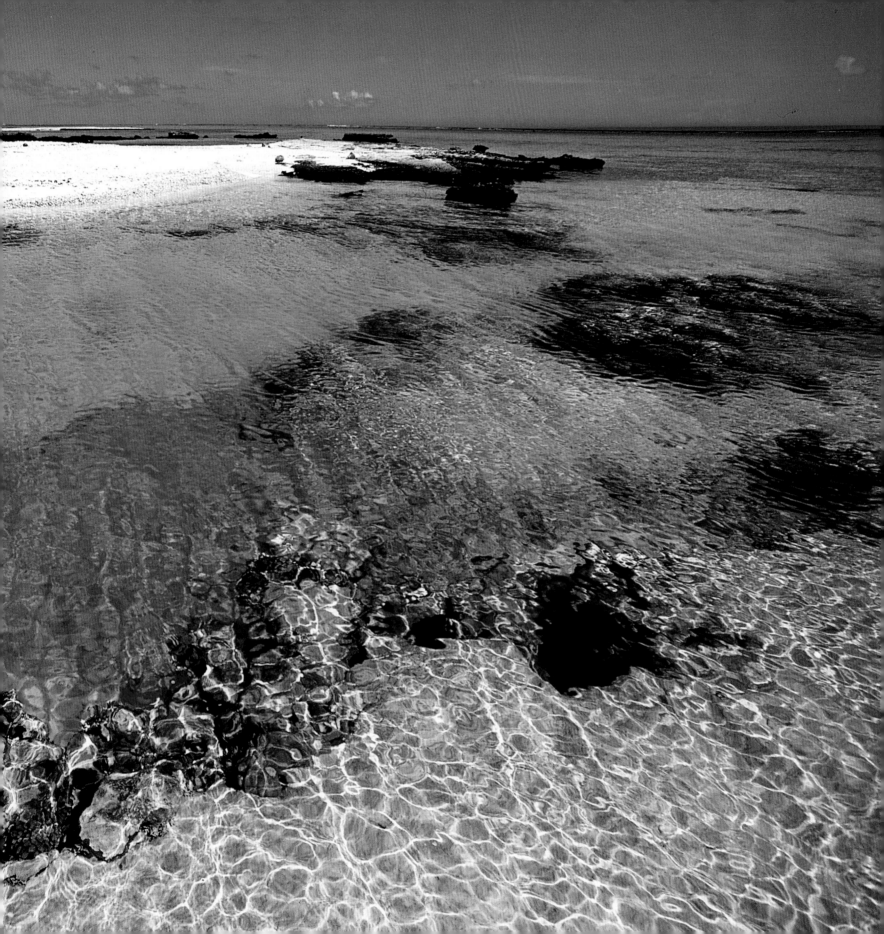

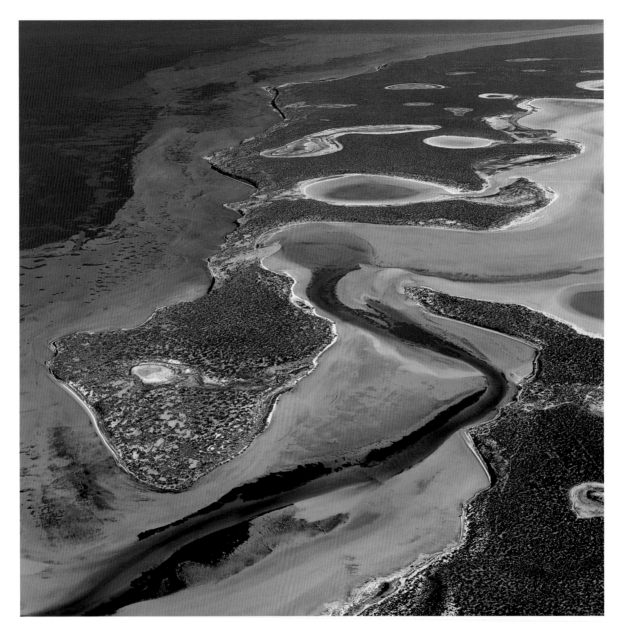

128 and 129 ● Indian Ocean, Peron National Park (Australia) - Big Lagoon in Shark Bay.

130-131 ● Indian Ocean, Kimberley (Australia) - Gantheaume Point, near Broome.

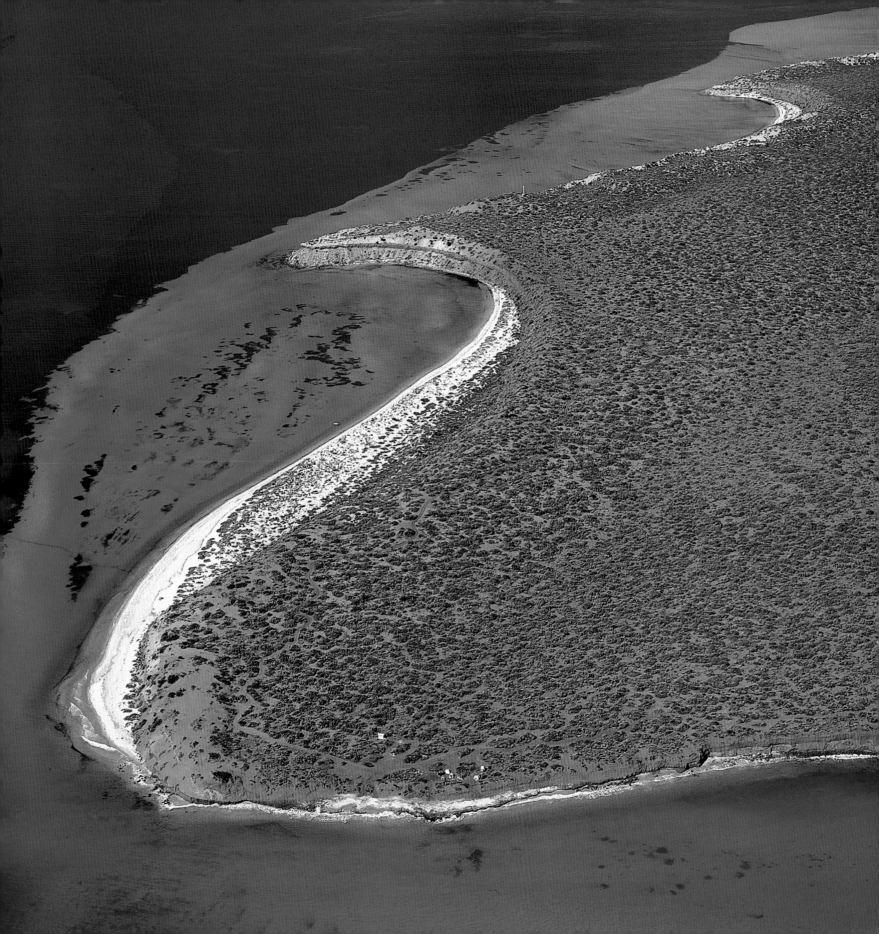

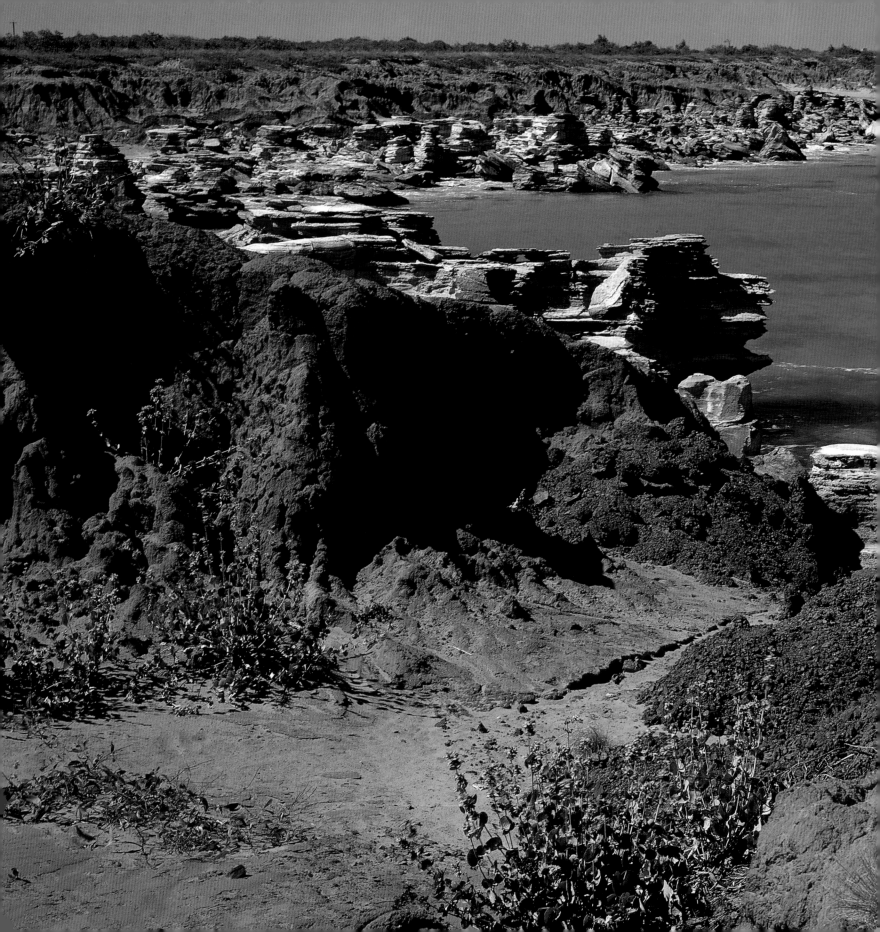

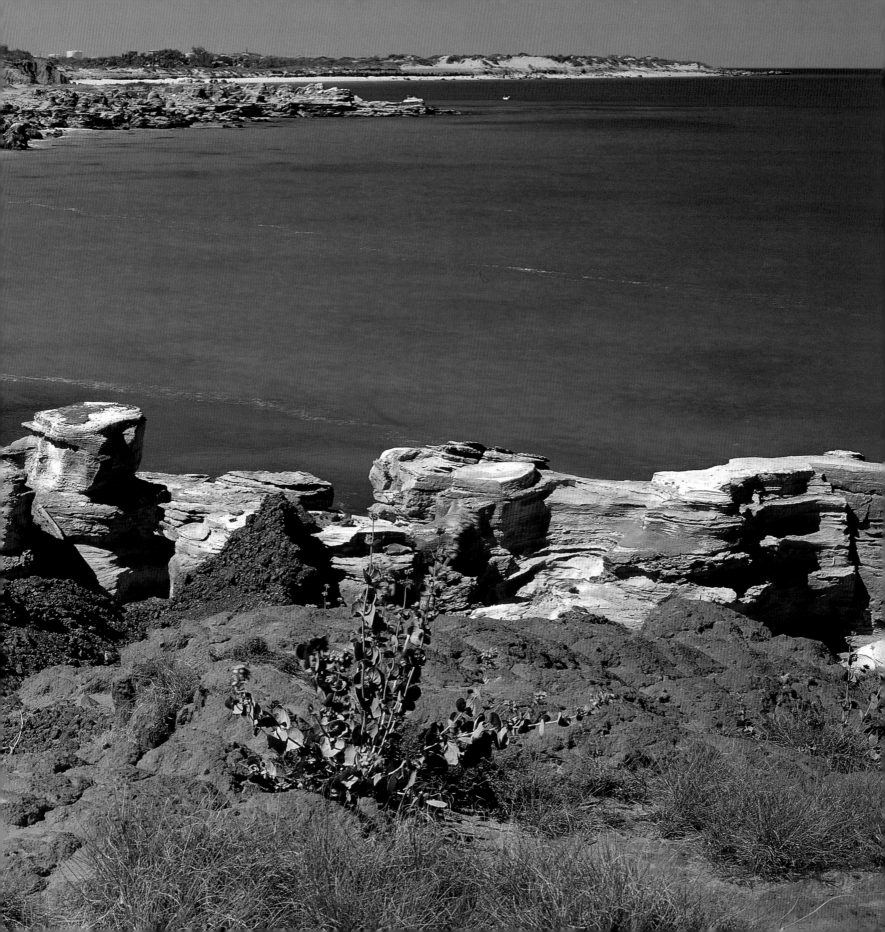

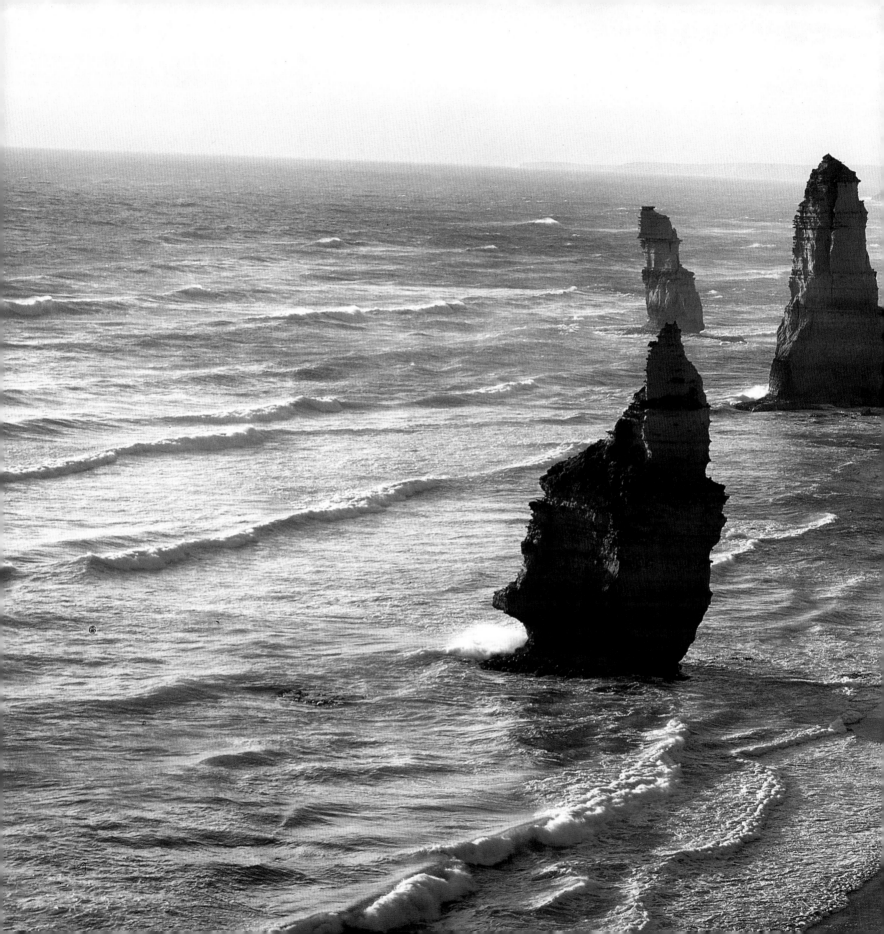

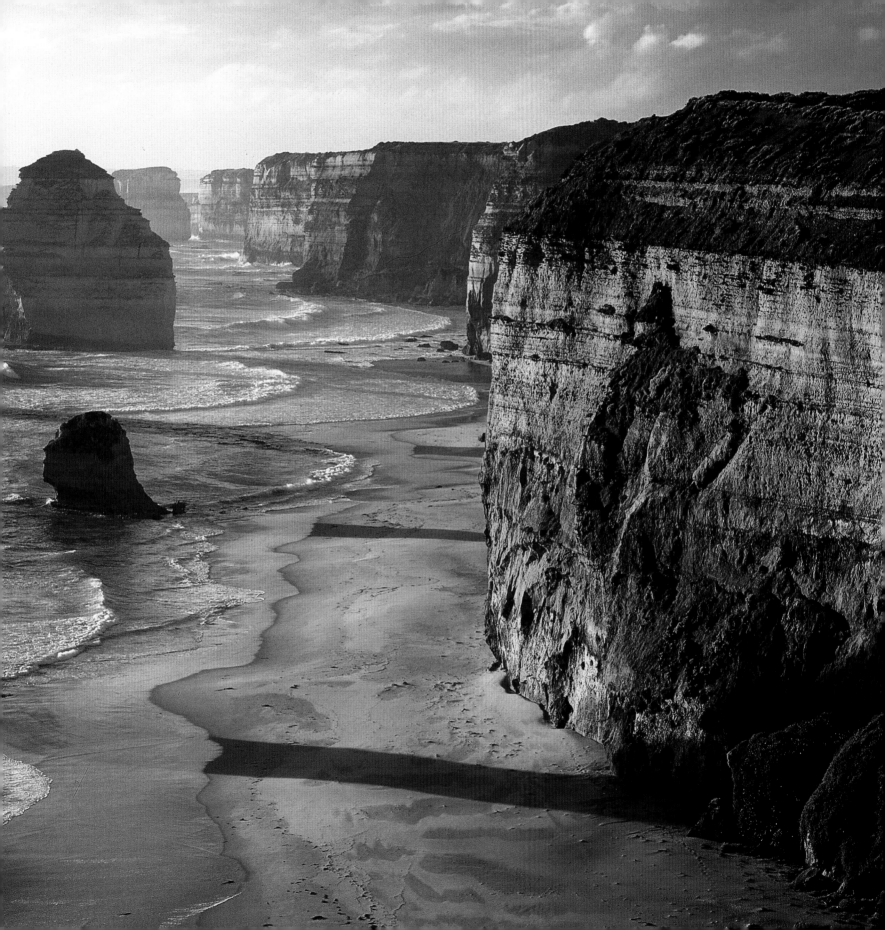

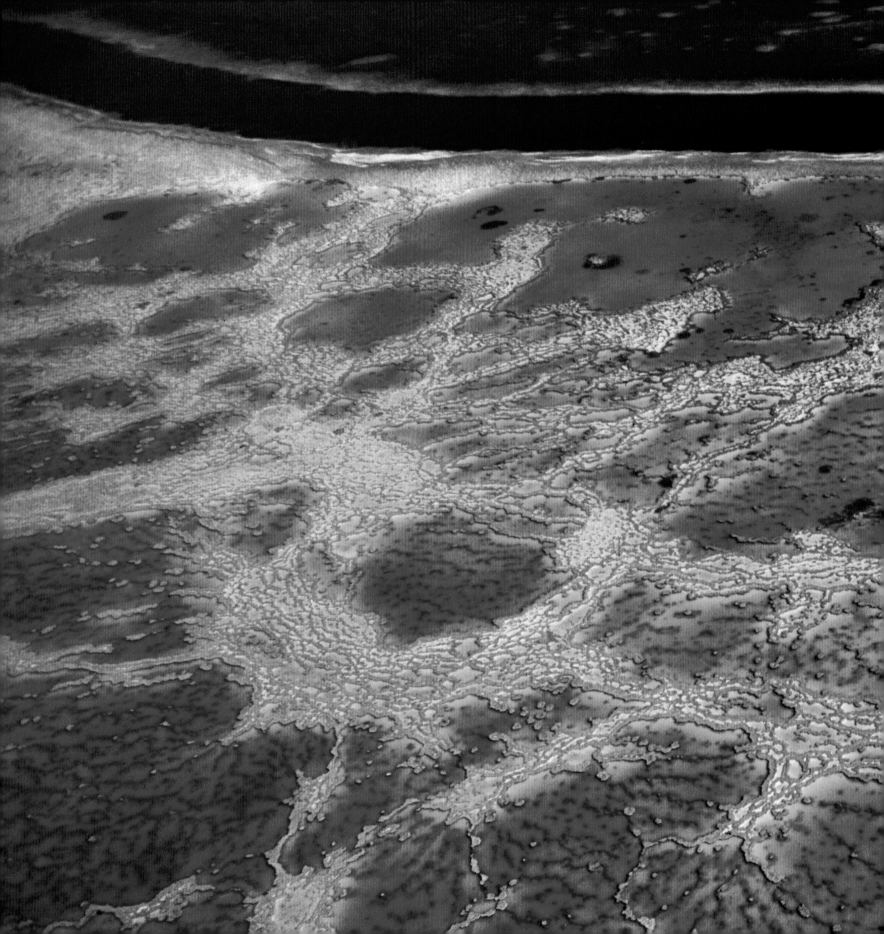

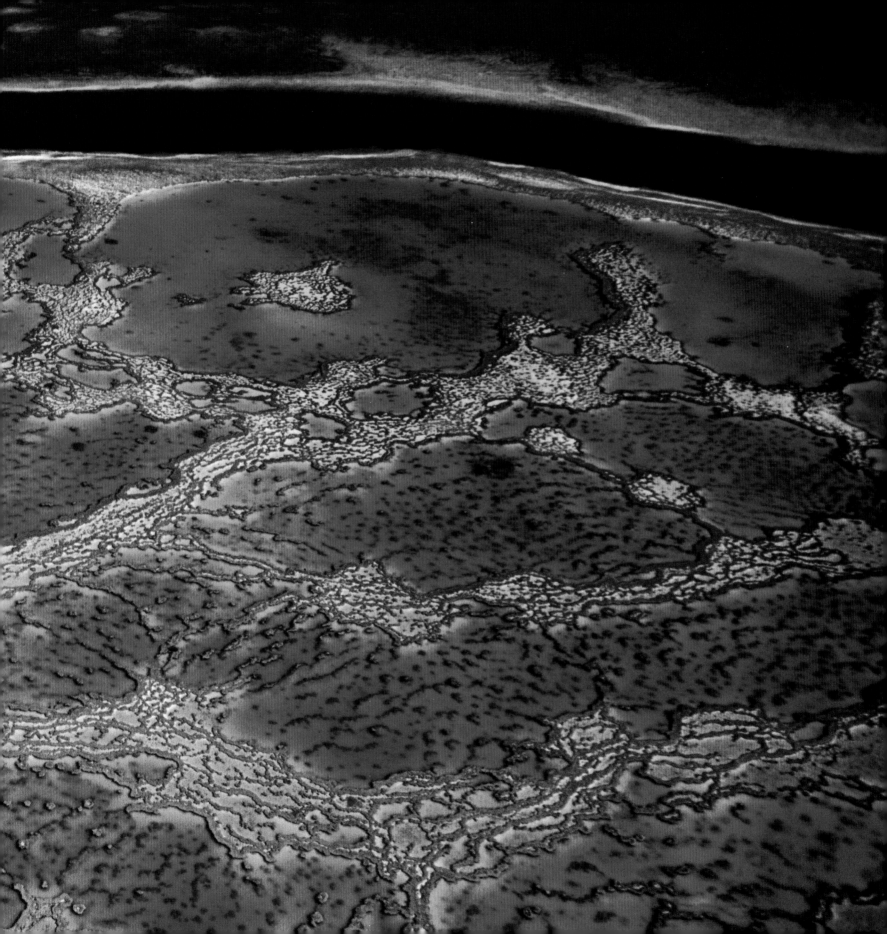

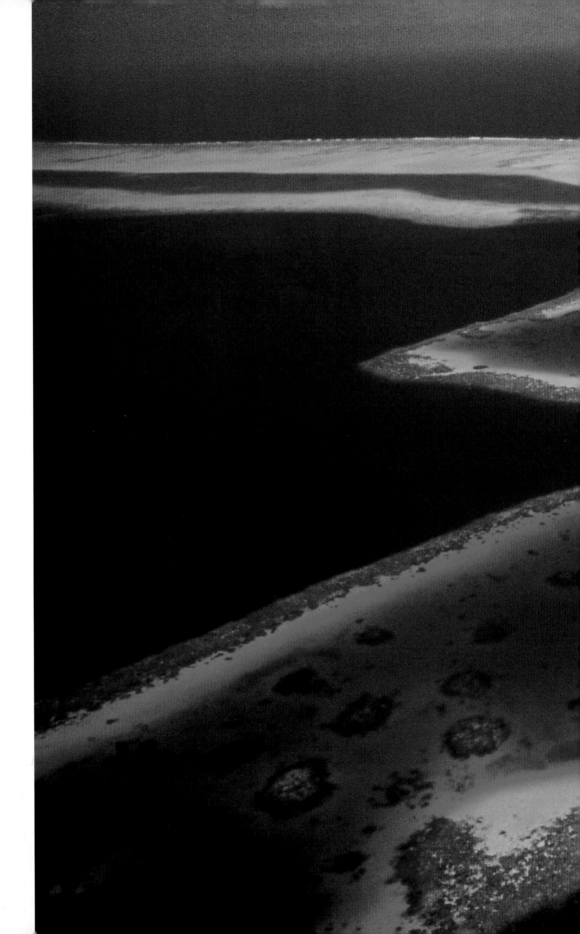

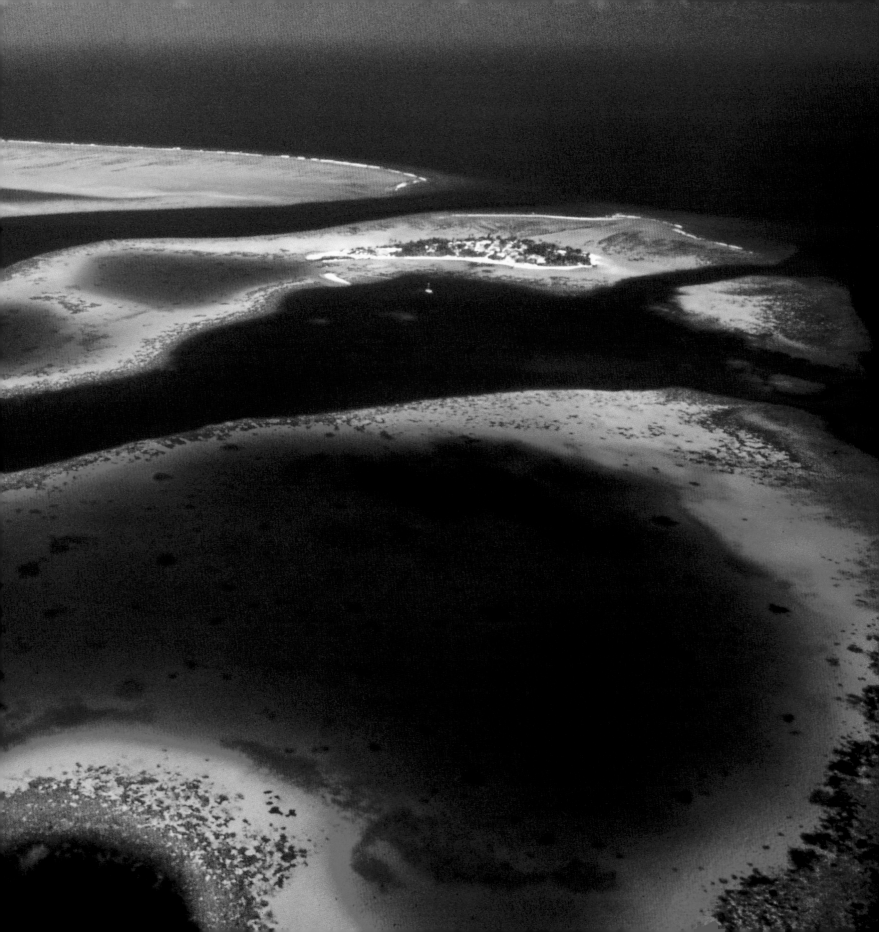

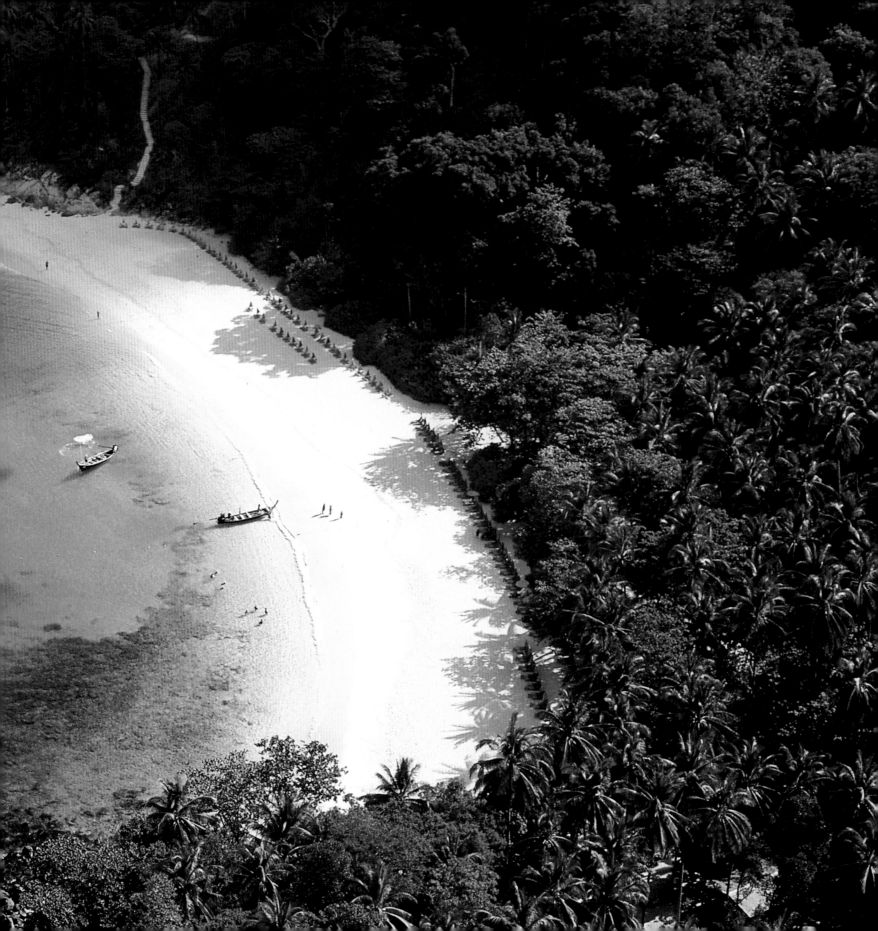

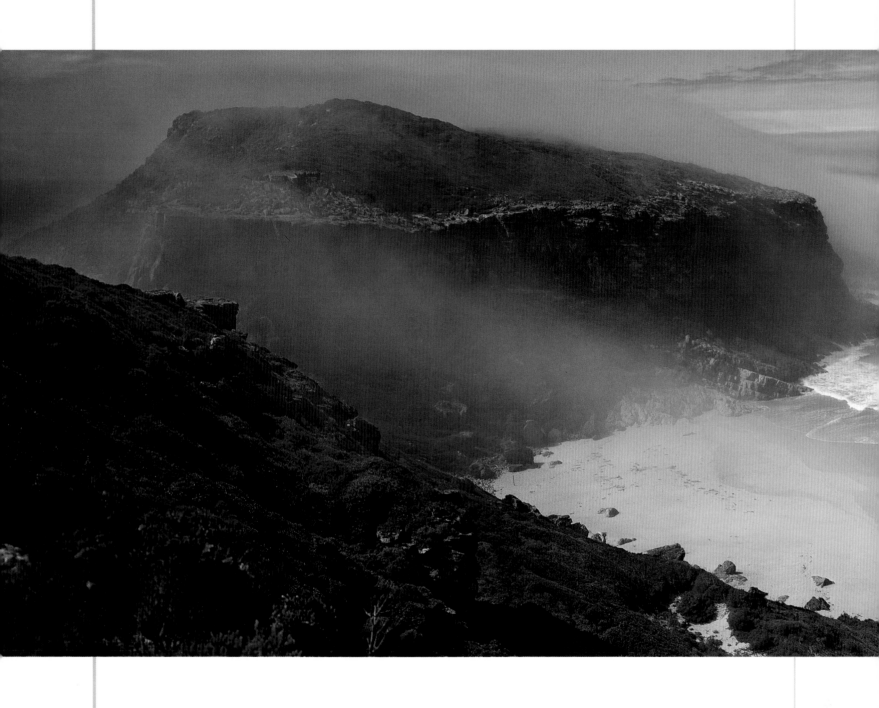

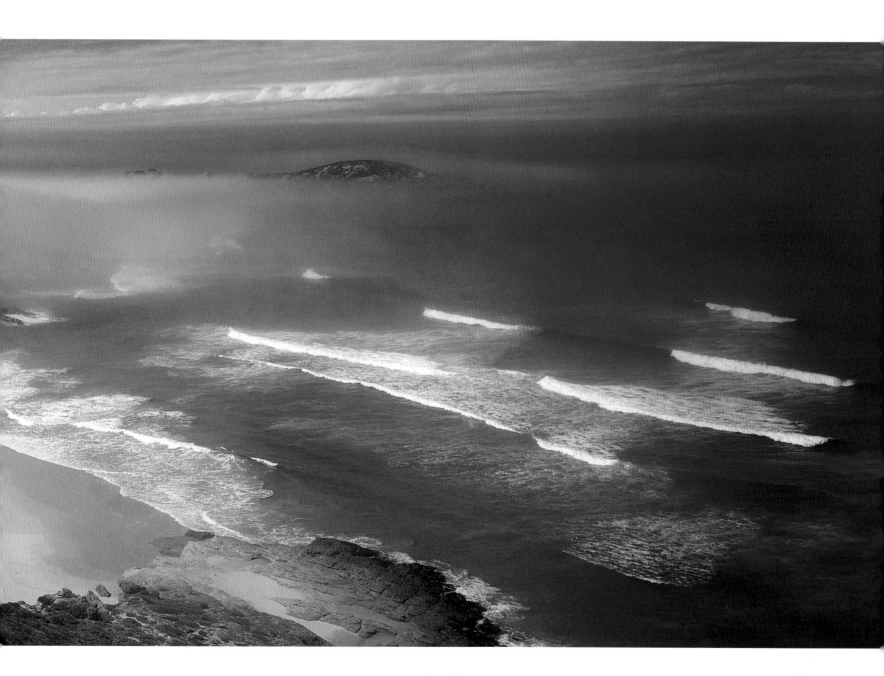

140-141 ● Indian Ocean, Southern Karroo (South Africa) - Pletterberg Bay.

142-143 ● Indian Ocean, Tanzania – Coast south of Dar es Salaam.

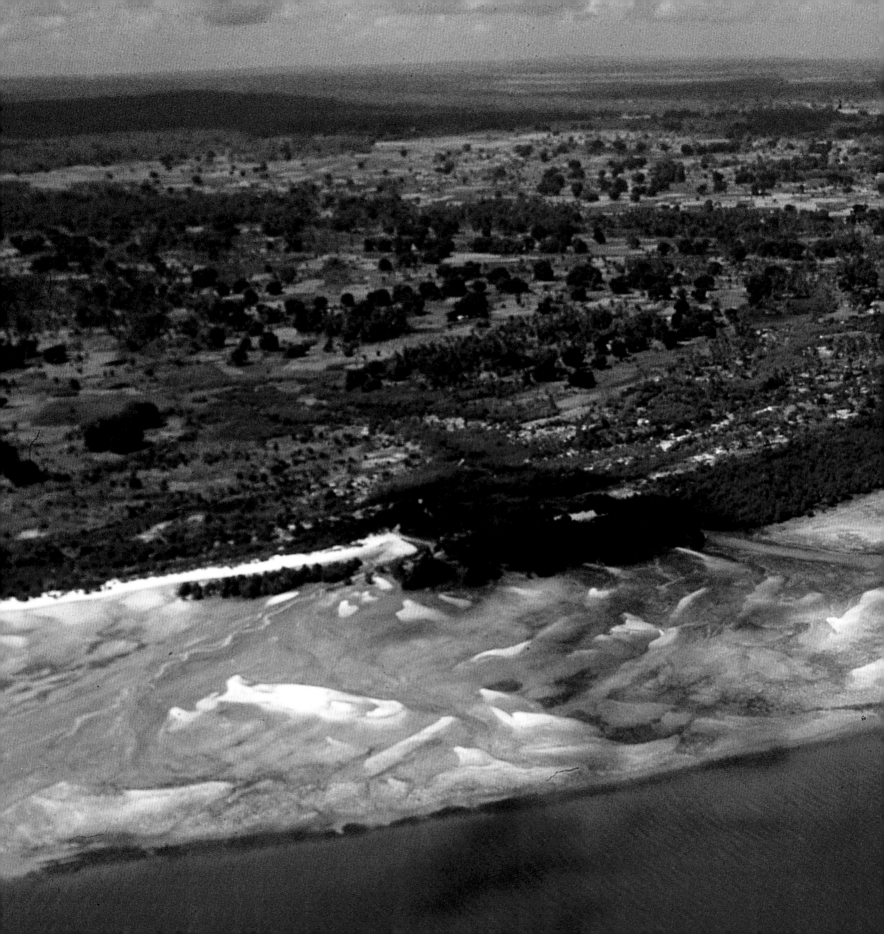

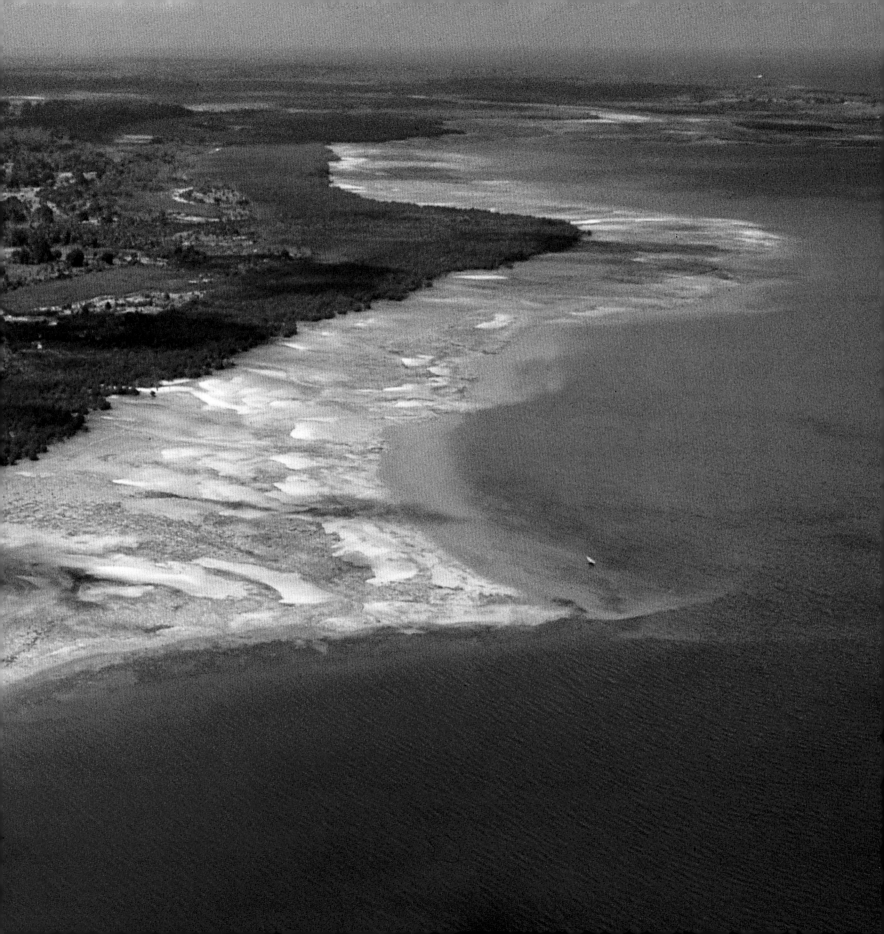

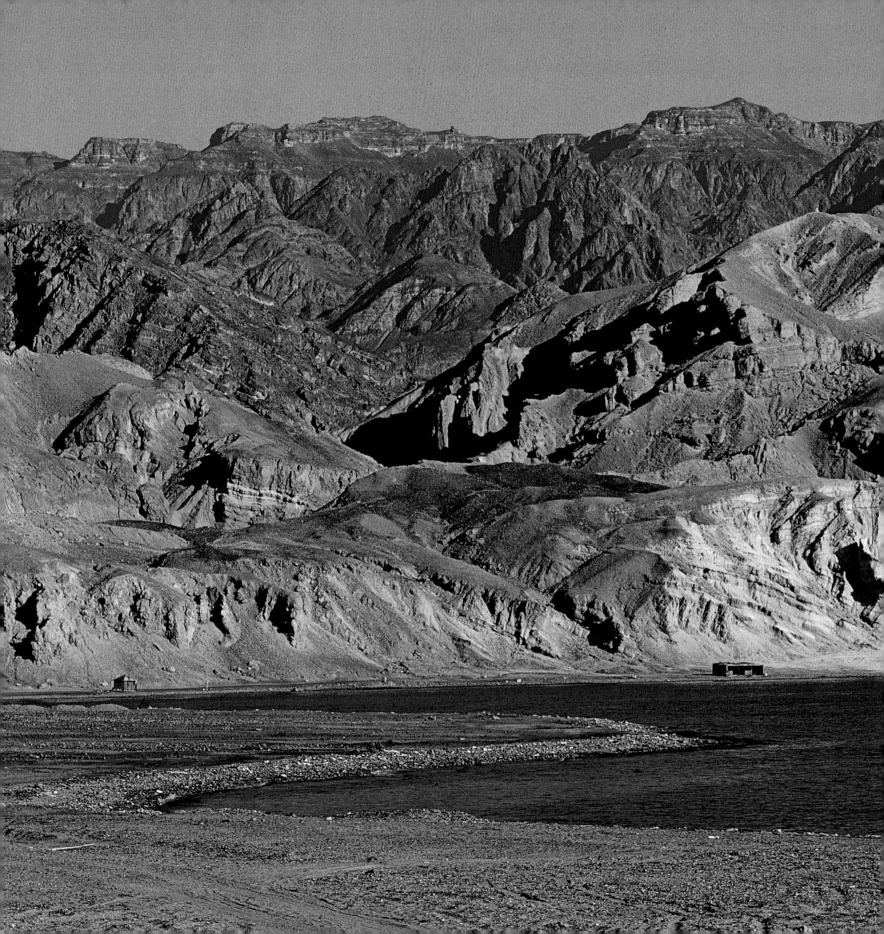

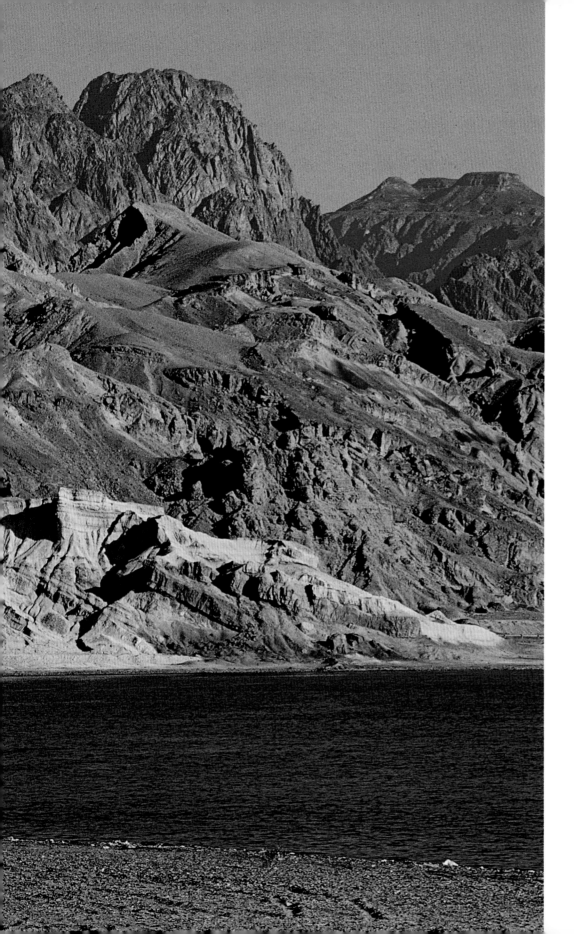

● Red Sea, Sinai (Egypt) -
Coast near Taba.

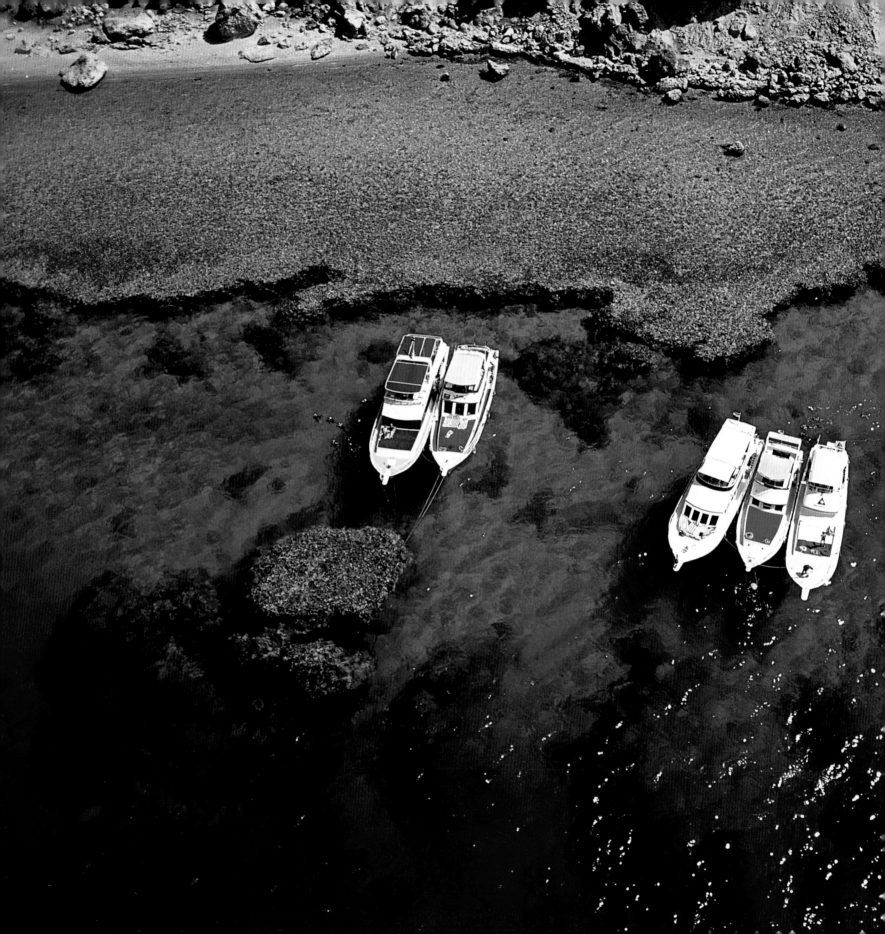

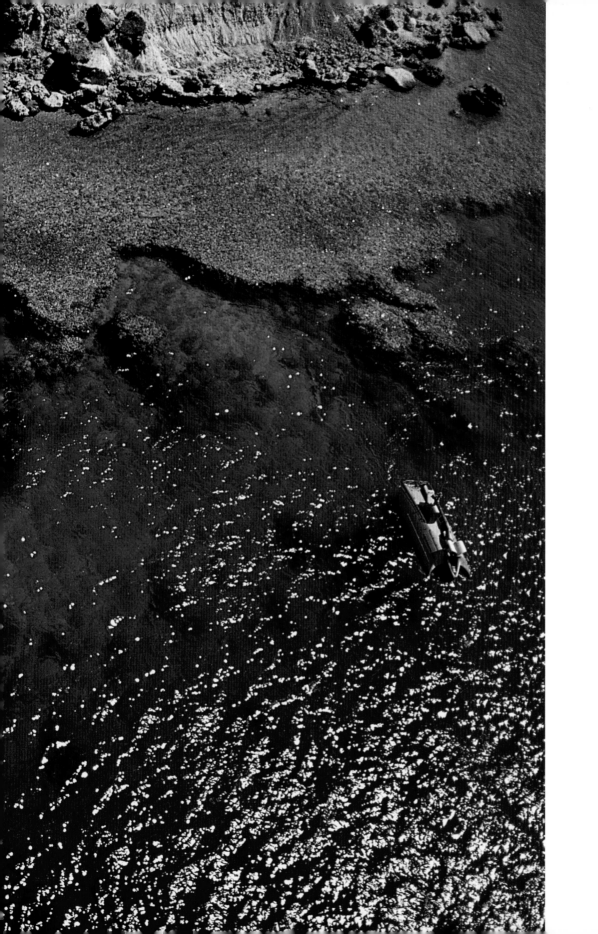

● Red Sea, Sinai
(Egypt) - Coast near
Sharm el-Sheikh.

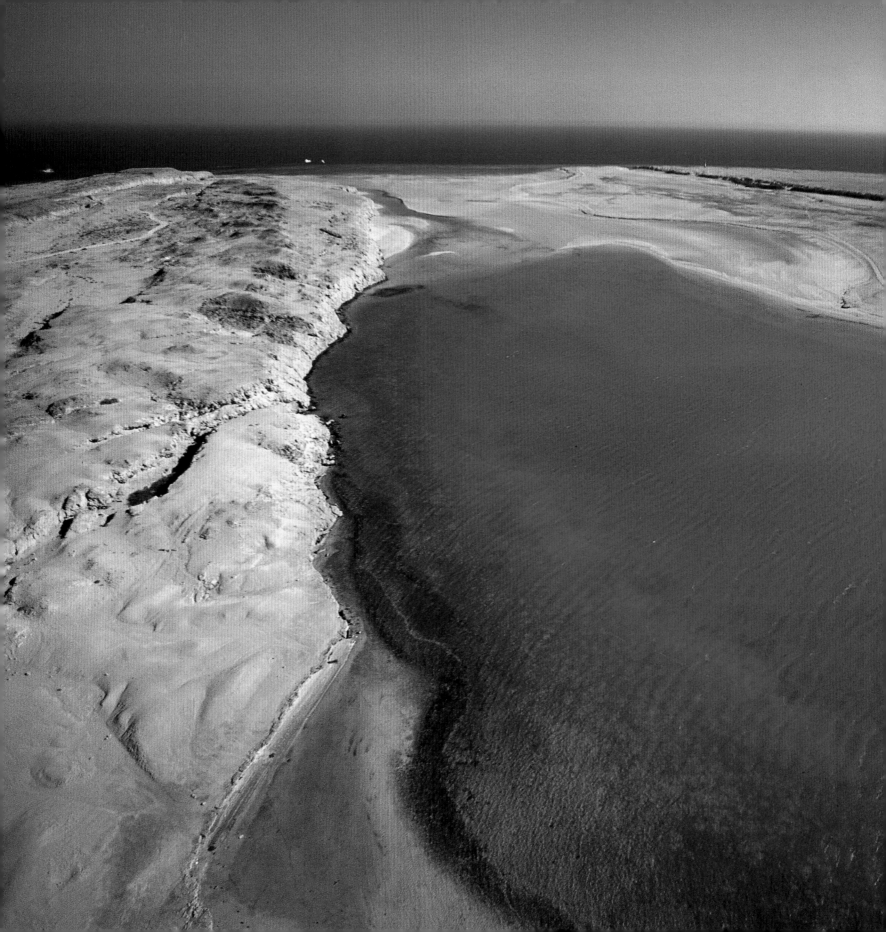

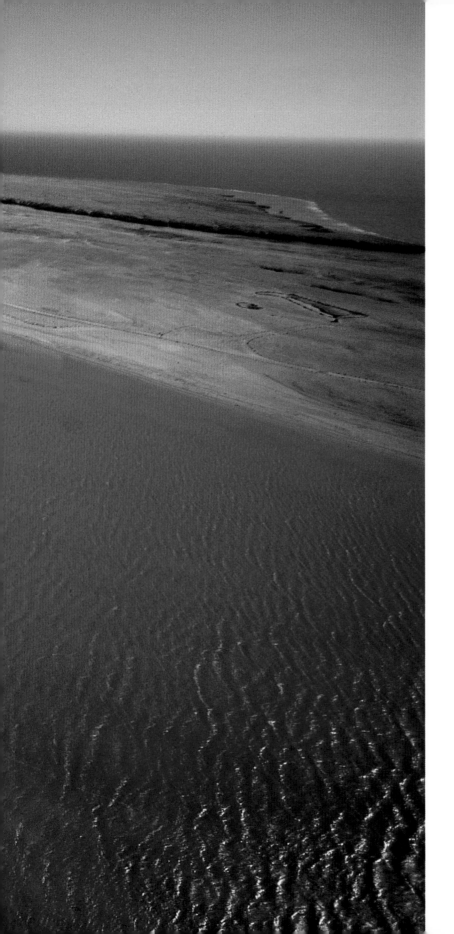

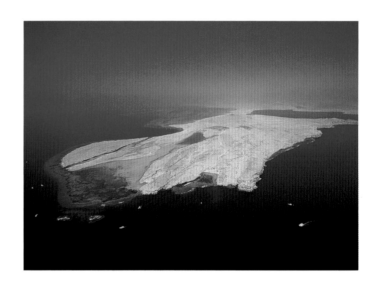

148-149 and 149 ● Red Sea, Sinai (Egypt)
- Ras Mohammed.

150-151 ● Red Sea, Egypt - Tiran.

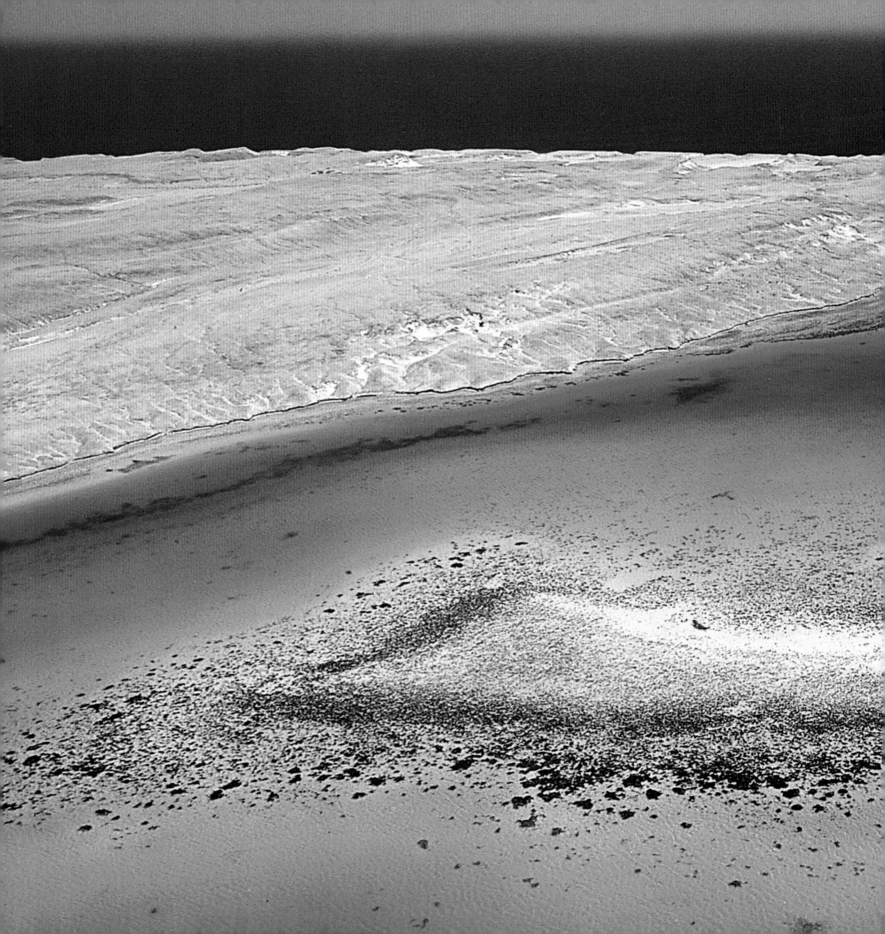

PEARLS in the BLUE

GIANNI GUADALUPI

● Pacific Ocean, Queensland (Australia) - Capricorn Group.

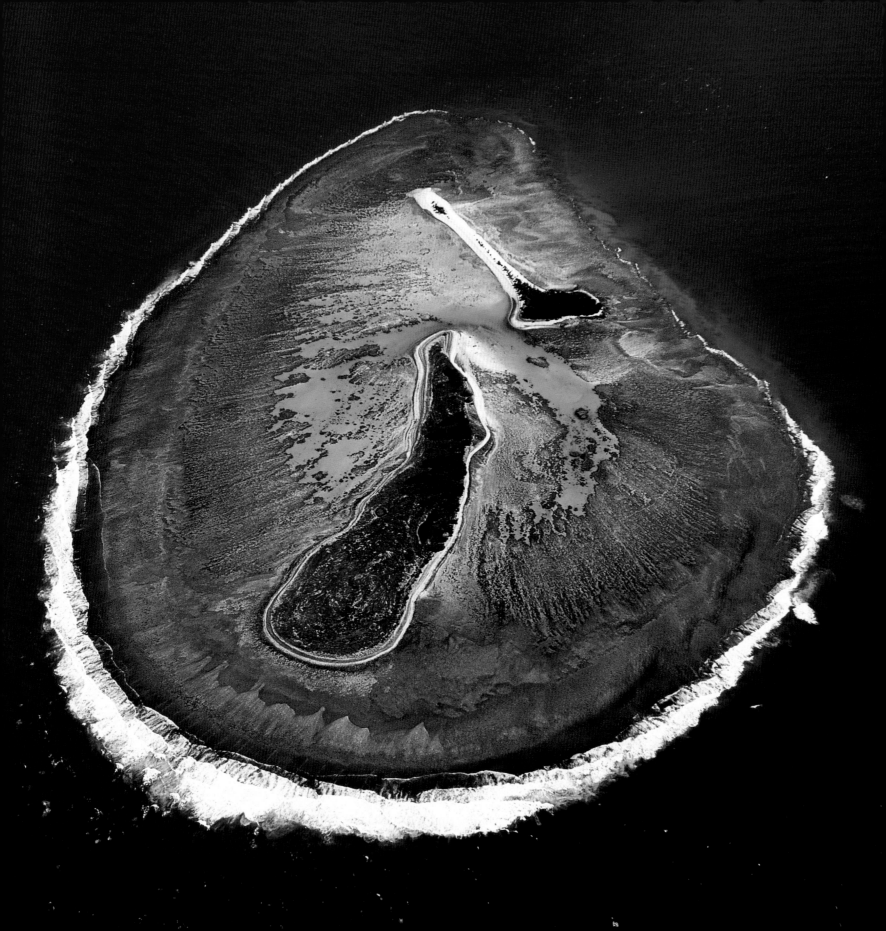

INTRODUCTION Pearls in the Blue

FACING THE MYSTERY OF THE SEA, THAT INFINITE LIVING

EXPANSE WHICH THE EXPOUNDERS OF ANCIENT MYTHS IDENTIFIED AS

THE SOURCE OF LIFE AND THE MATERNAL WOMB OF THE WORLD, THE

GEOGRAPHERS OF PAST ERAS CATALOGED THE WONDERS AND MIRAGES

OF EXISTENCE, TOGETHER WITH THE UNINSPIRING REALITIES OF ACTUAL

LIFE. THEY RECORDED DISTANT, DREAMED OF ISLANDS THAT RINGED

REMOTE LANDS WHOSE INSULARITY PERMITTED THE CREATION OF

UNIQUE FORMS OF NATURE, AND WHOSE ISOLATION HELPED TO HIDE

THEM FROM DISCOVERY. THESE THEREFORE REMAINED THE BLESSED

ISLANDS, THE LUCKY ISLANDS, THE HESPERIDES: SMALL AND INSIGNIFI-

CANT, THEY REMAINED IMMERSED IN ETERNAL HAPPINESS AND ENJOYED

INTRODUCTION Pearls in the Blue

UNCHANGING YOUTHFULNESS. THUS, ANCHORED TO THE BOTTOM OF

THE SEA BY IMMENSE GILDED BRONZE PILLARS, THEY AWAITED THE

ARRIVAL OF BOATS RUNNING FROM UNEXPECTED STORMS. UNHEEDING,

THEY AWAITED THE EVOLUTION OF BELIEFS AND RELIGIONS, AND LIVED

THROUGH THE ARRIVALS OF NEPTUNE-WORSHIPING GREEKS, ASTARTE-

WORSHIPING PHOENICIANS, THE KNIGHTS OF THE ROUND TABLE IN

SEARCH OF THEIR LOST KING ARTHUR, IRISH MONKS LED BY SAINTS IN

SEARCH OF PARADISE ON EARTH, AND VIKINGS VOYAGING TO SUNNIER

CLIMES. THEN, WHEN THE SAILORS BECAME TOO NUMEROUS FOR THE

ISLANDS TO SUPPORT, THE ISLANDS THEMSELVES DISAPPEARED FROM

THE MAPS AND HID IN THE PAGES OF BOOKS WRITTEN BY IMAGINATIVE

Pearls in the Blue

Introduction

SPIRITS WHERE THEY CONTINUED TO STIMULATE THE UNSHACKLED

DREAMS OF THEIR READERS. THEY CHANGED THEIR NATURE AND GAVE

THEMSELVES UP TO ADVENTURE, ATTRACTING SHIPWRECKED SAILORS

LIKE ROBINSON CRUSOE, PIRATES PLANNING TO BURY STOLEN TREASURE,

MAD SCIENTISTS LIKE DOCTOR MOREAU, AND MINUSCULE OR GIGANTIC

PEOPLES LIKE LILLIPUTIANS OR BROBDINGNAGIANS. TODAY, TIRED AFTER

SEVERAL MILLENNIA OF A FABLED EXISTENCE, THEY HAVE RESIGNED

THEMSELVES TO A PROSAIC EXISTENCE, SPARINGLY EXERCISING THEIR

INSULAR ATTRACTIONS TO DRAW CHARTER PLANES FILLED WITH HOLIDAY-

MAKERS COME DOWN TO FROLIC ON THEIR PALM-LINED BEACHES.

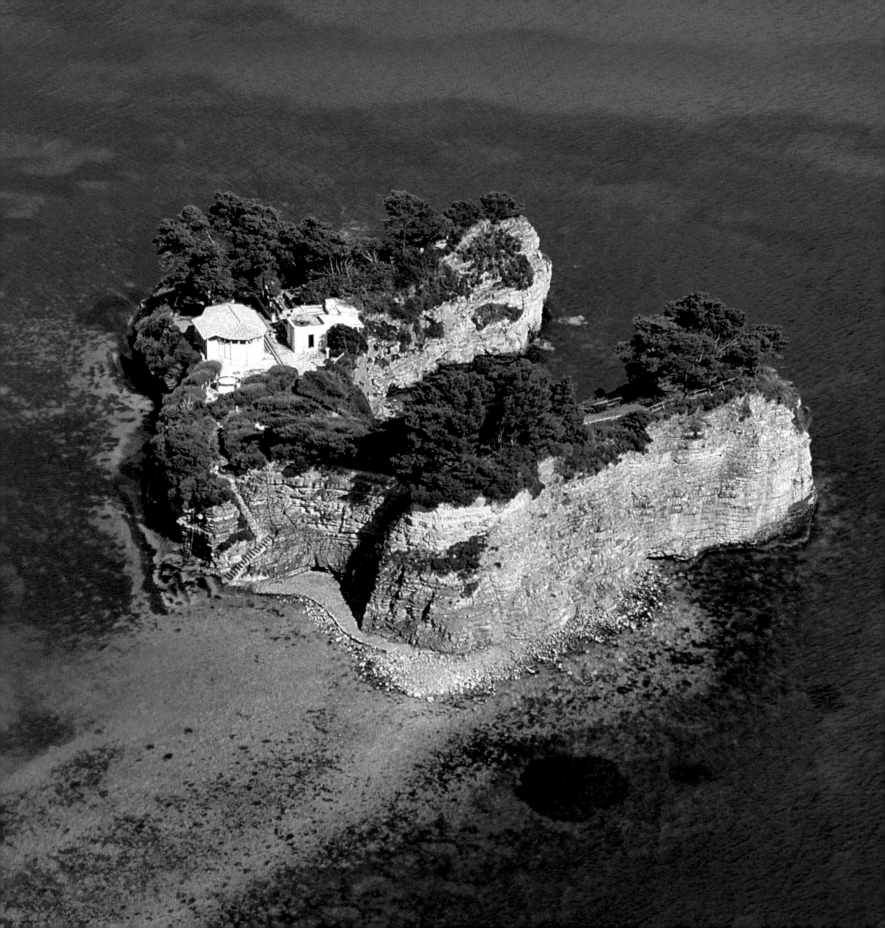

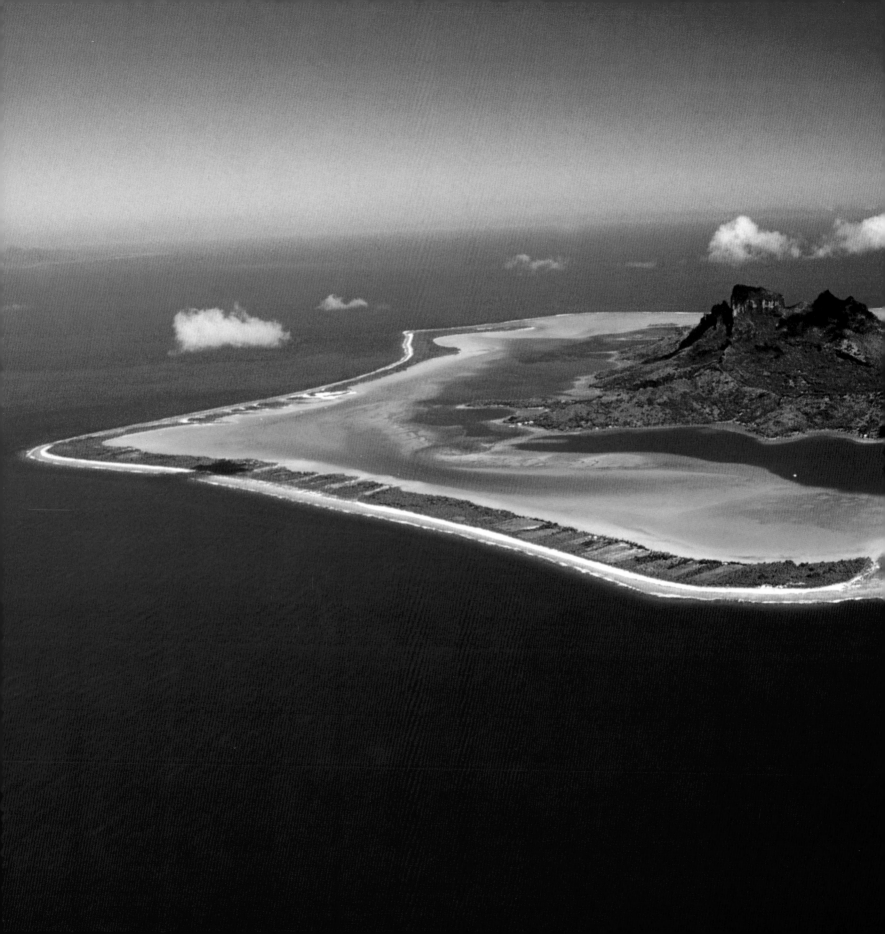

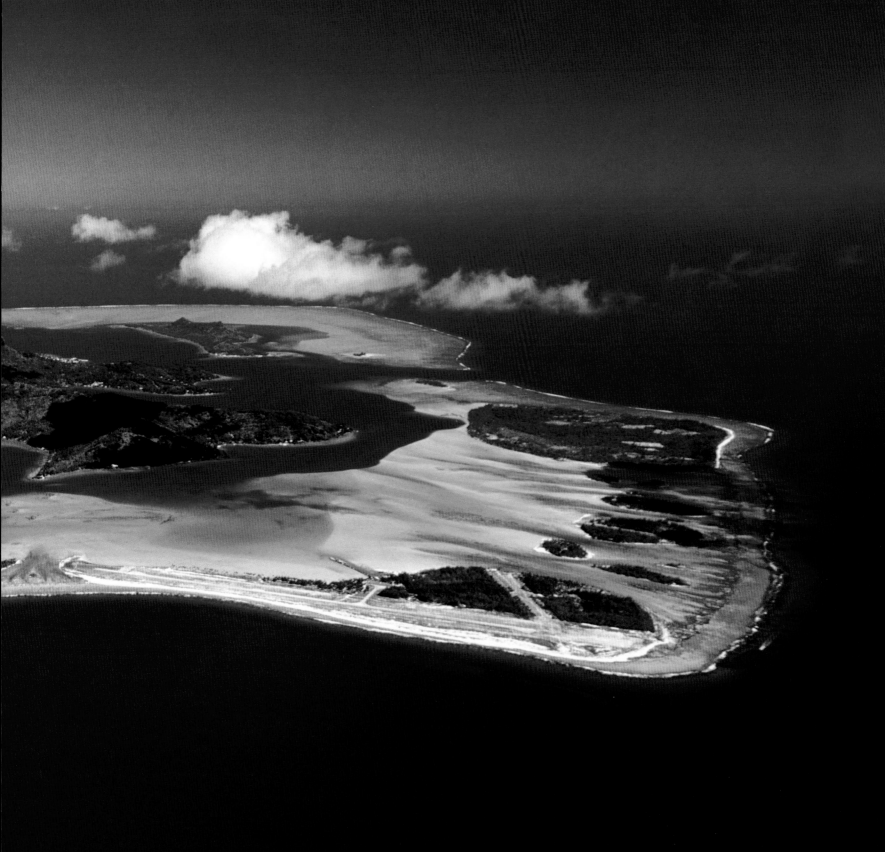

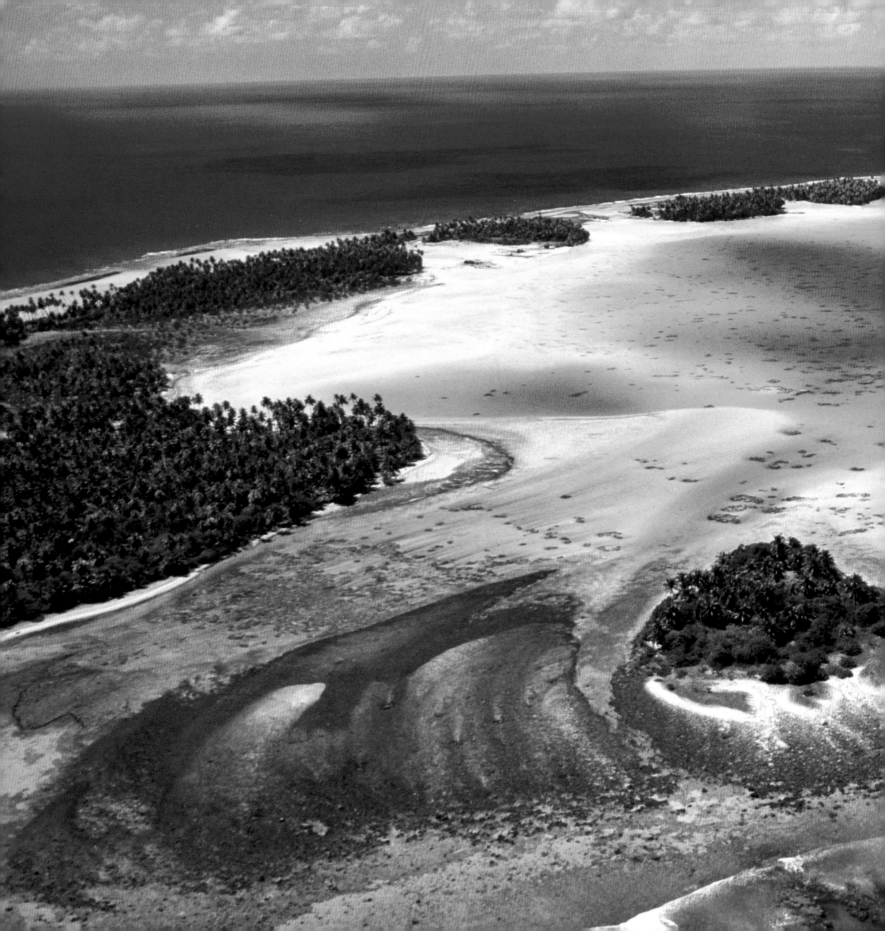

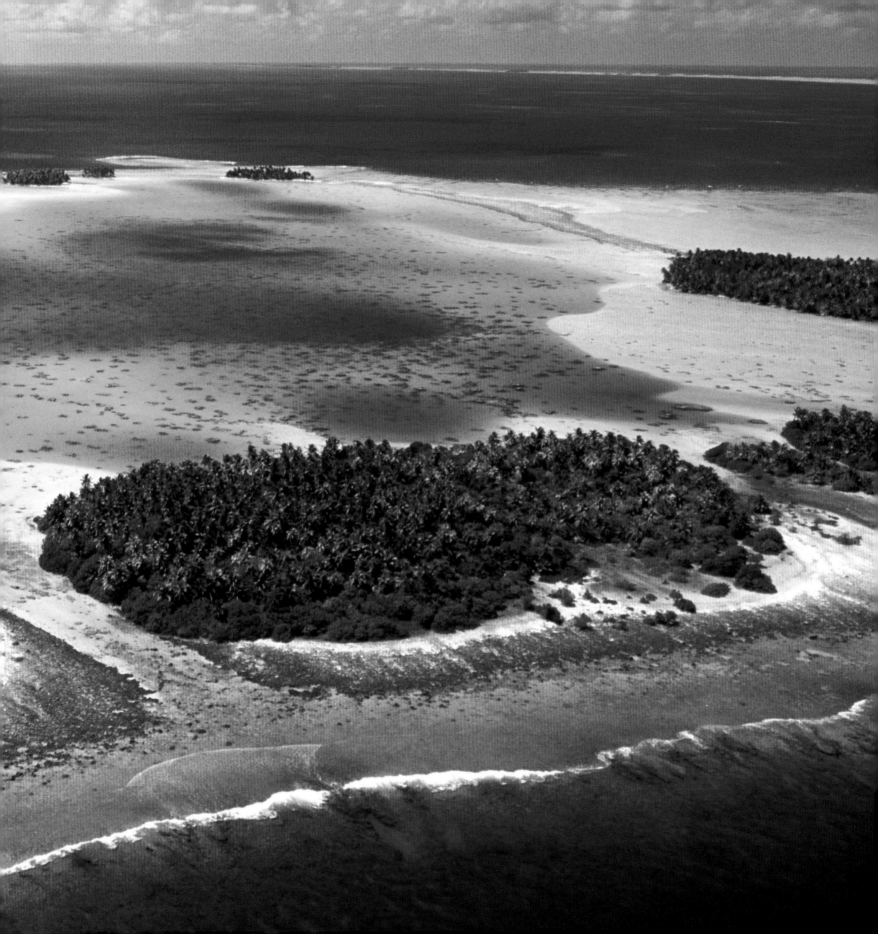

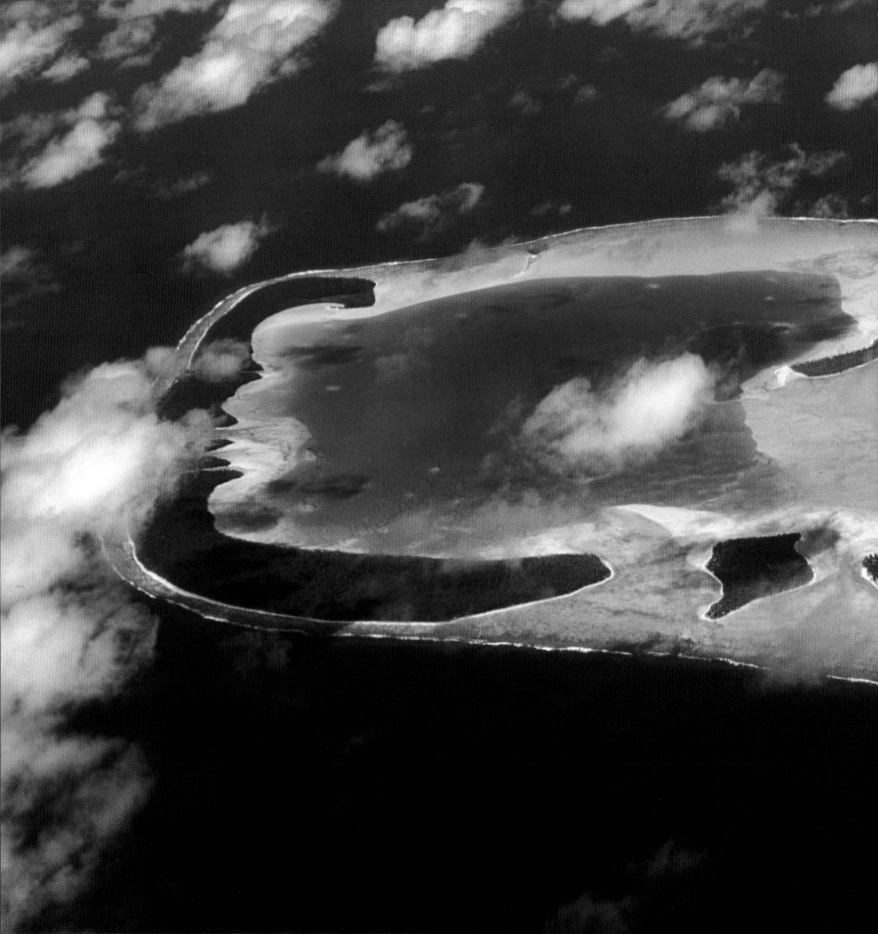

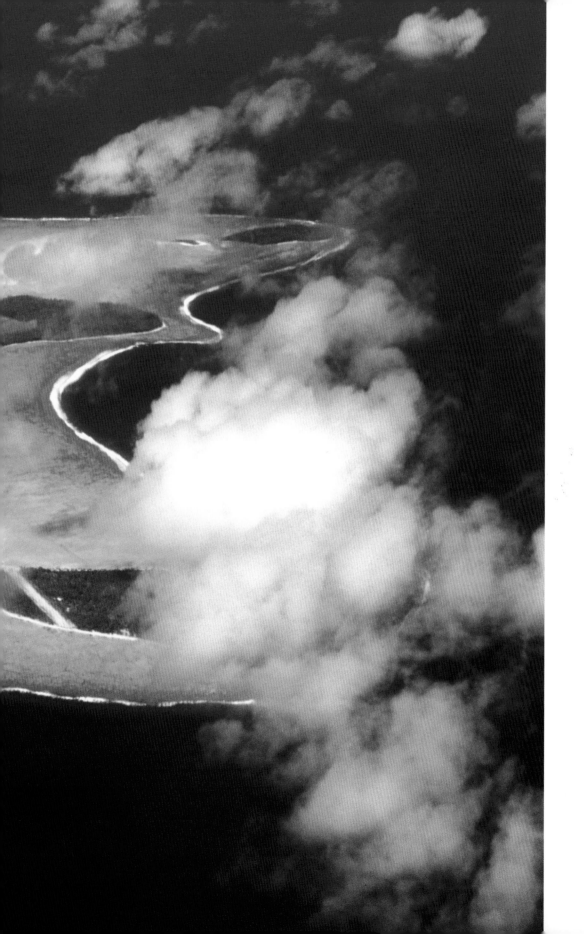

Jewels in the Pacific

162-163 ● Pacific Ocean, French Polynesia - Tetiaroa.

164-165 ● Pacific Ocean, Hawaii (USA) - Molokini.

166-167 ● Pacific Ocean, Micronesia - Palau.

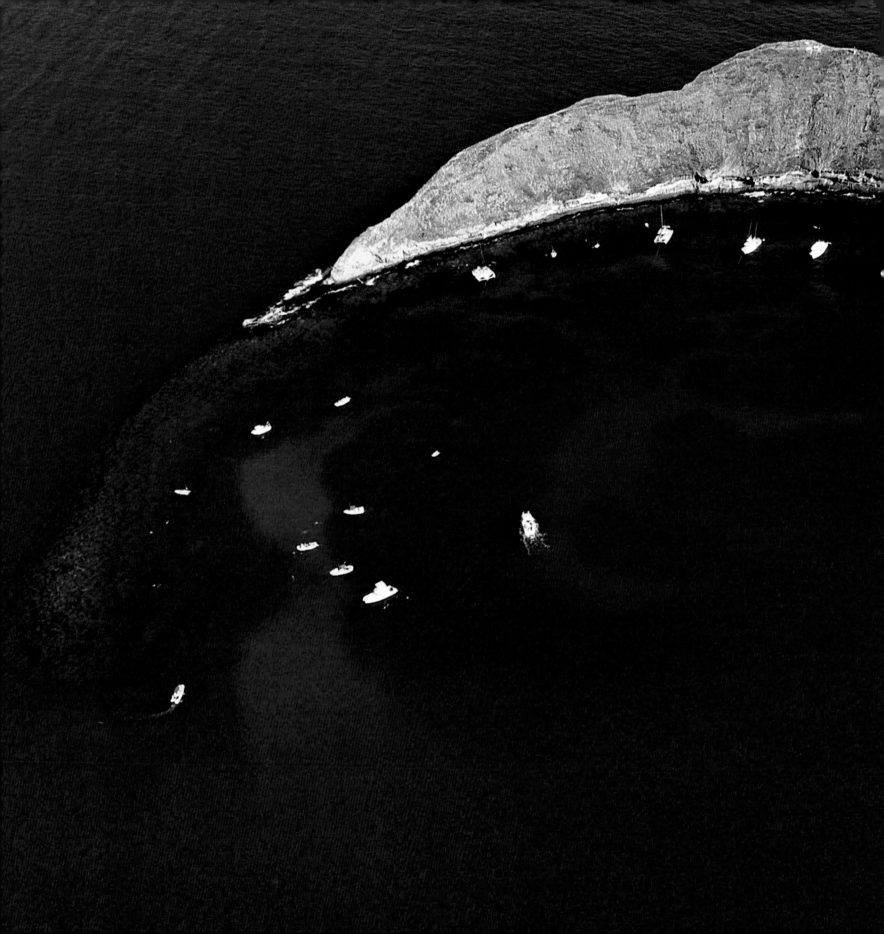

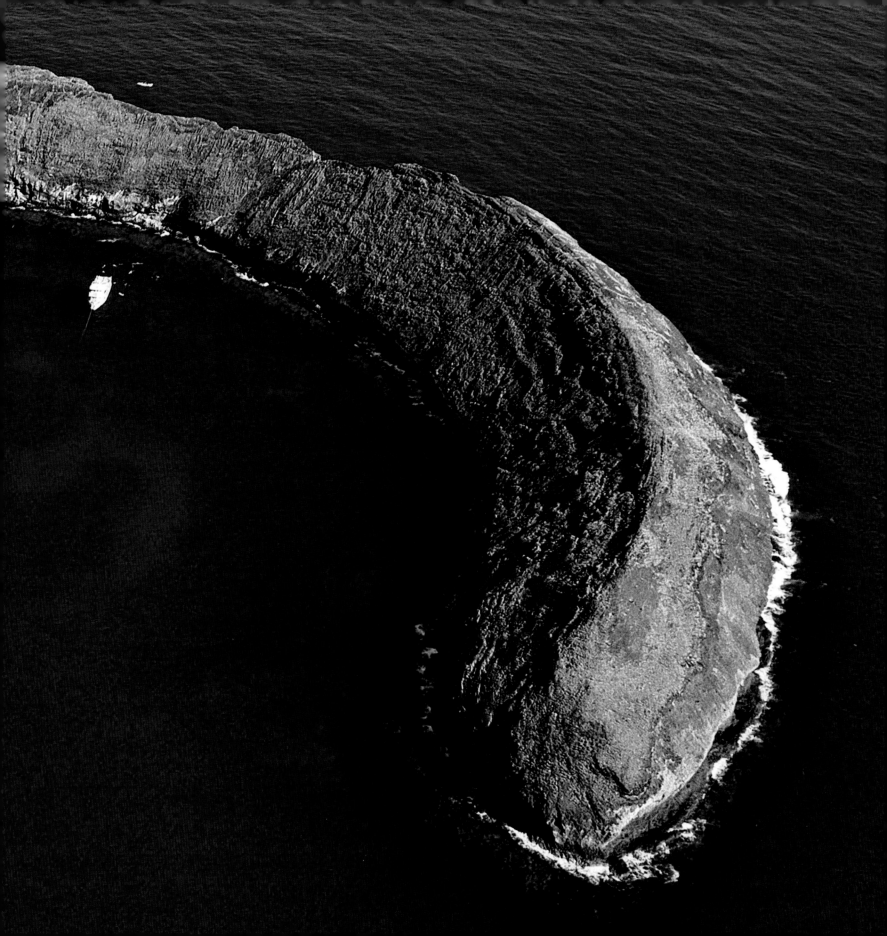

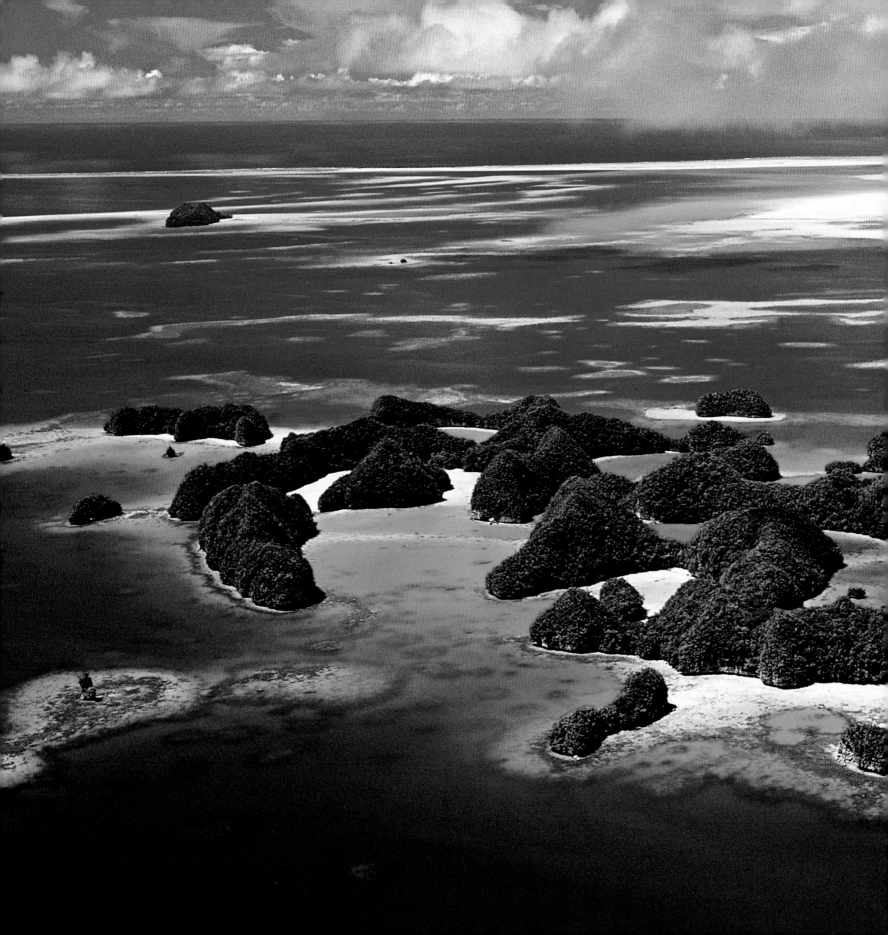

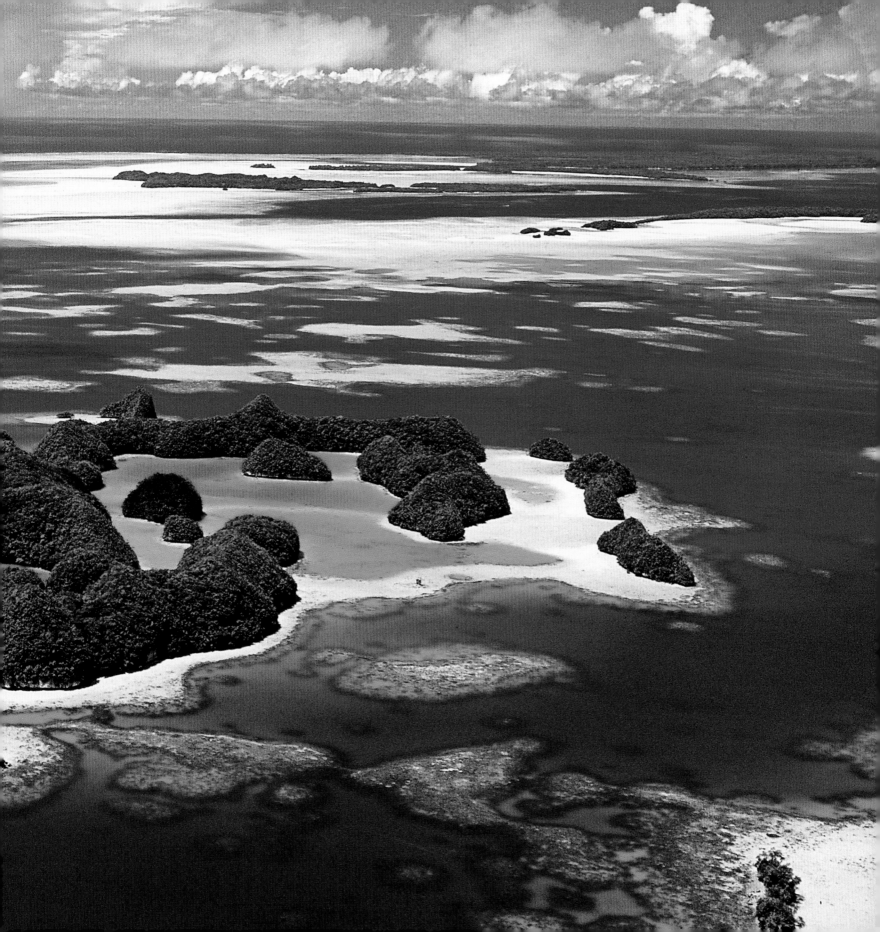

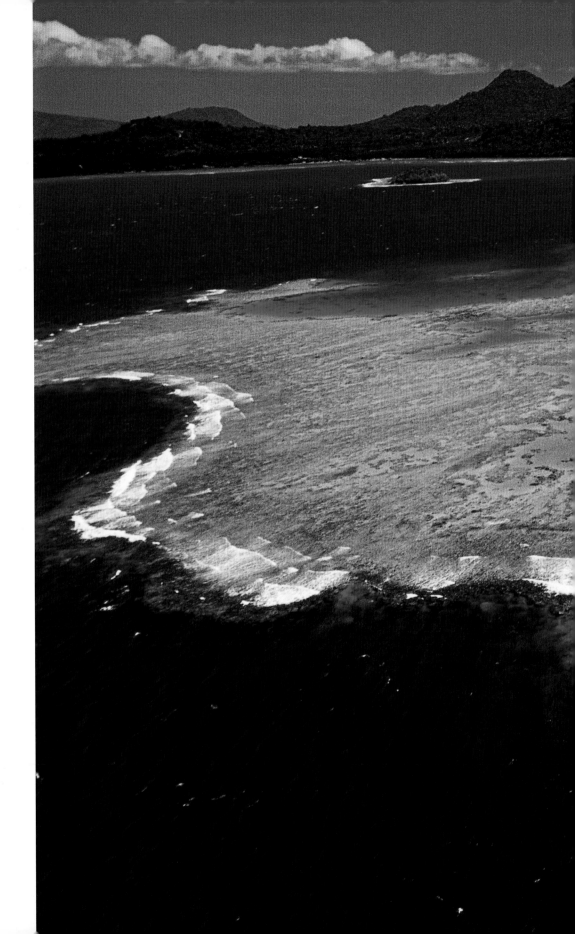

168-169 ● Pacific Ocean, Papua New Guinea - Bismarck archipelago.

170-171 ● Indian Ocean, Thailand - Phi Phi Leh.

172-173 ● Pacific Ocean, Kuril Islands (Russia) - Paramushir.

174-175 ● Indian Ocean, Maldive Islands - Atolls.

176-177 ● Red Sea, Gobal Strait (Egypt) - Coral islands near Ras Gemsa.

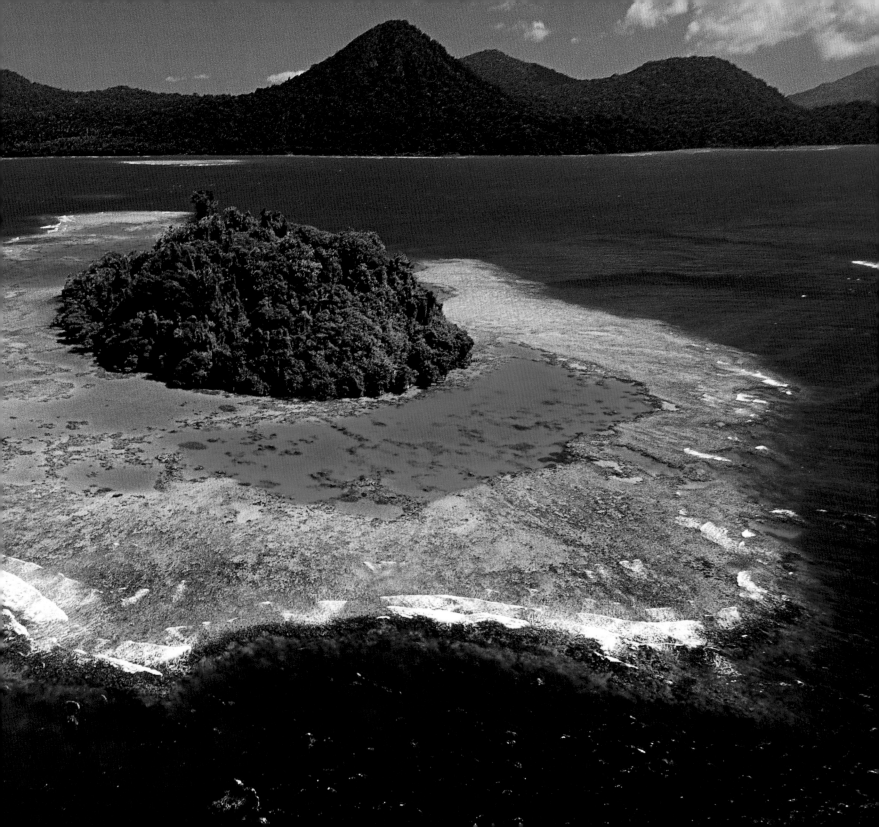

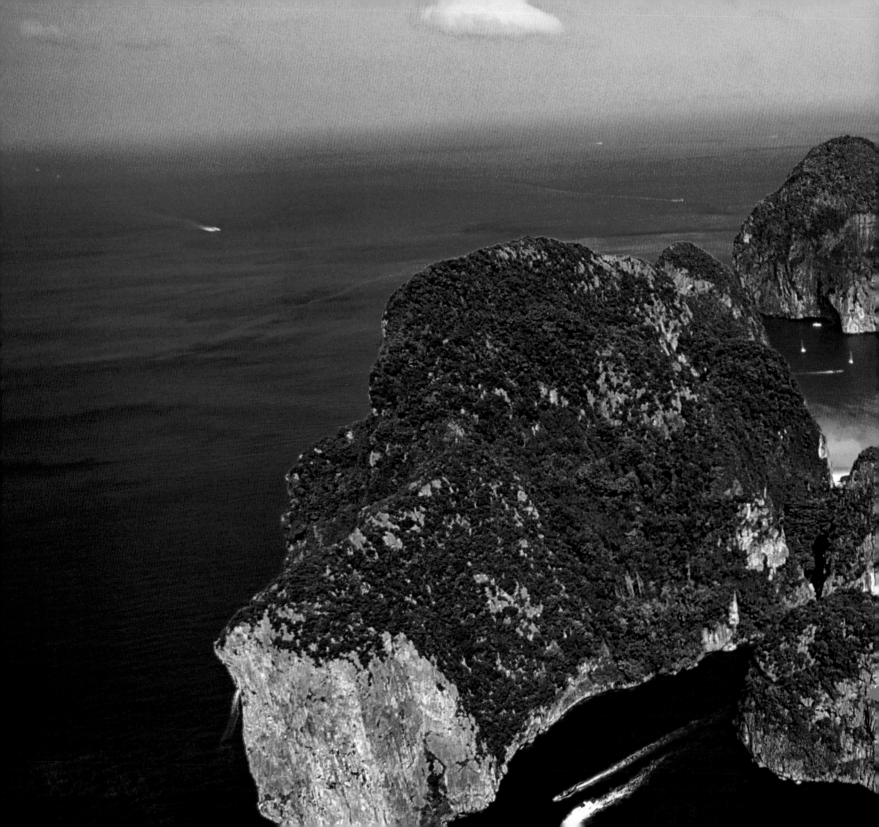

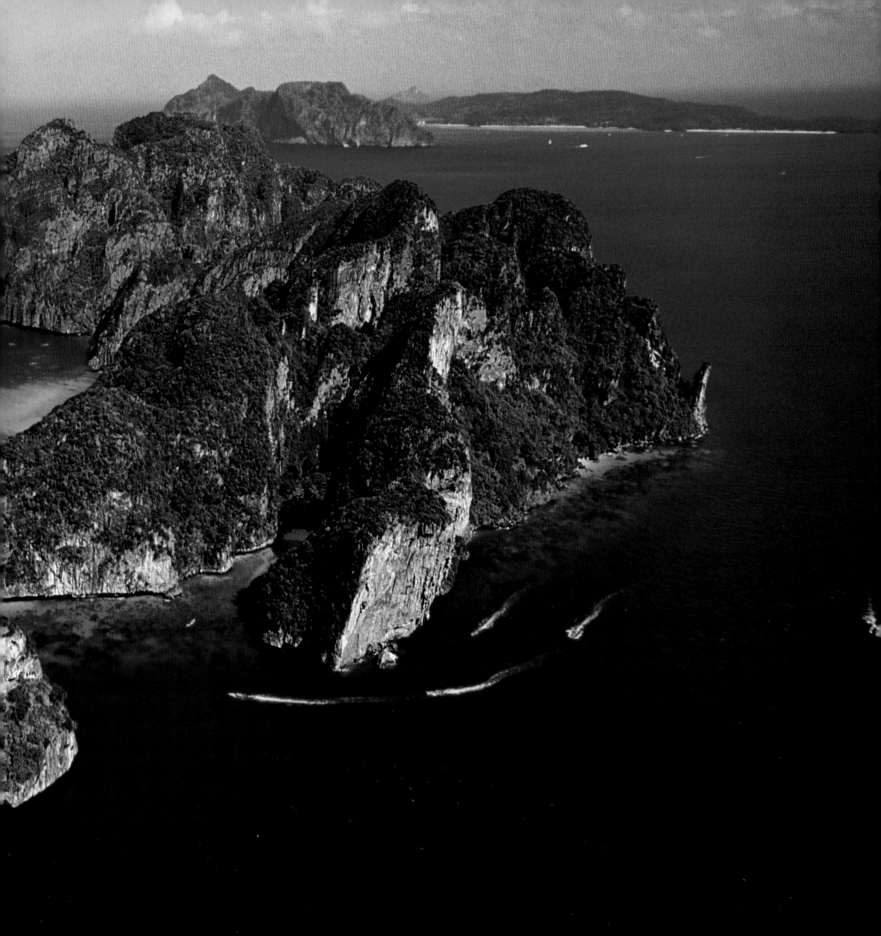

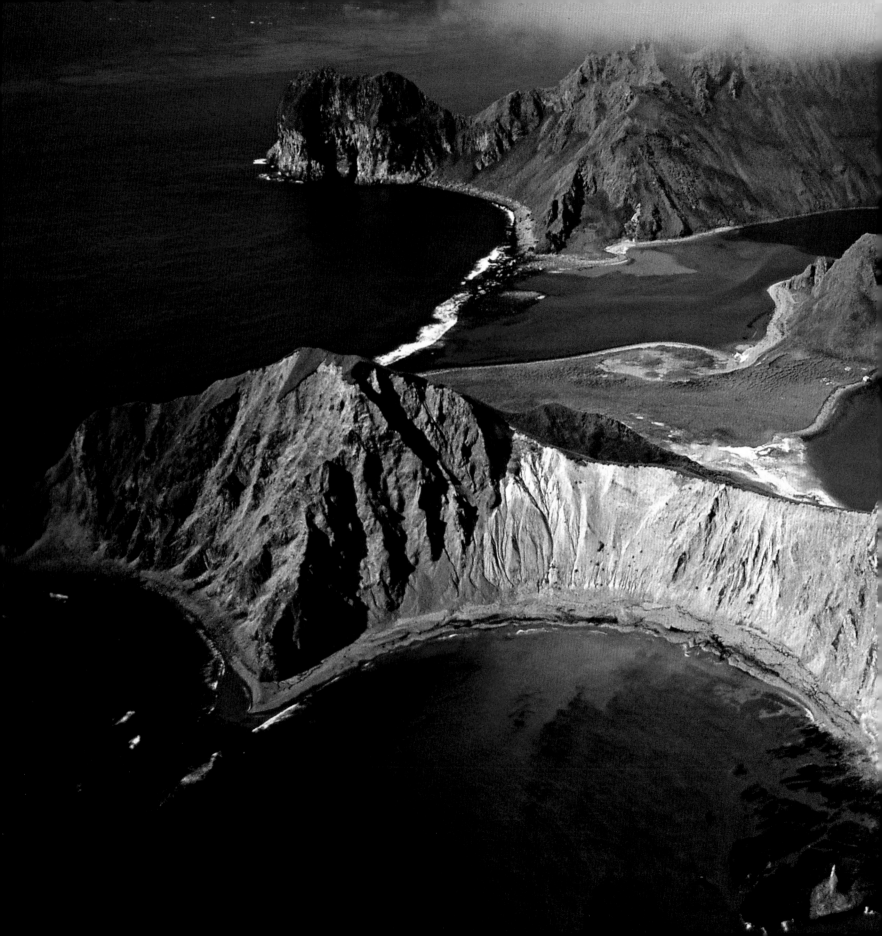

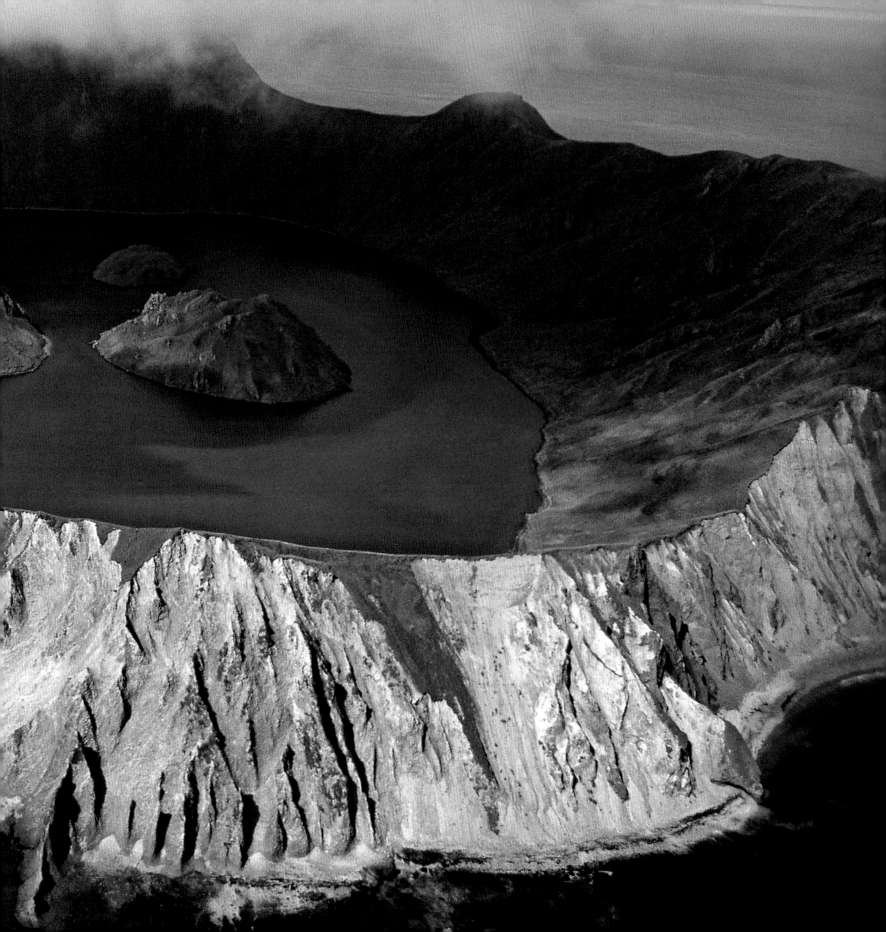

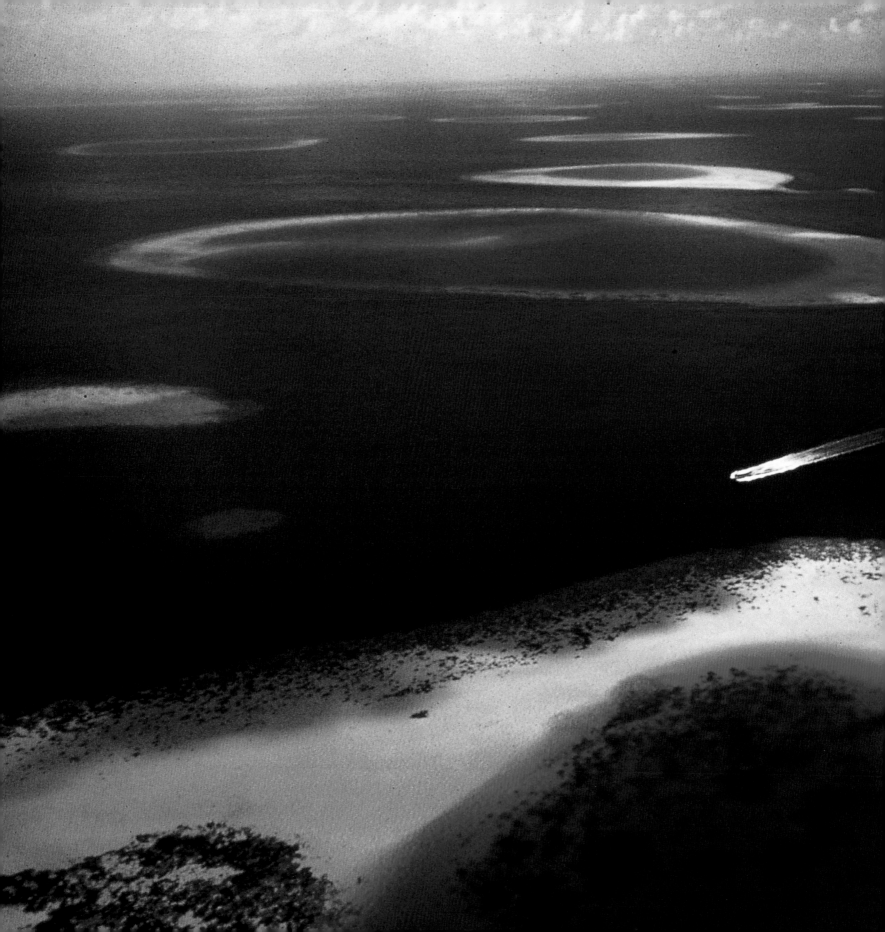

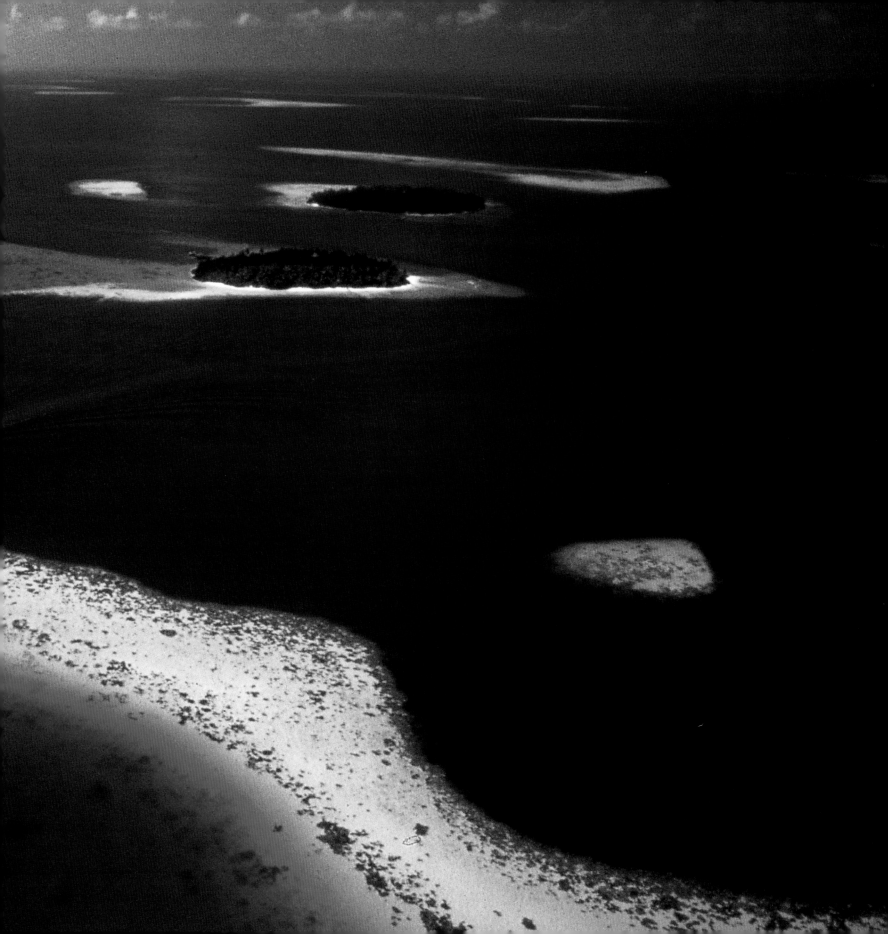

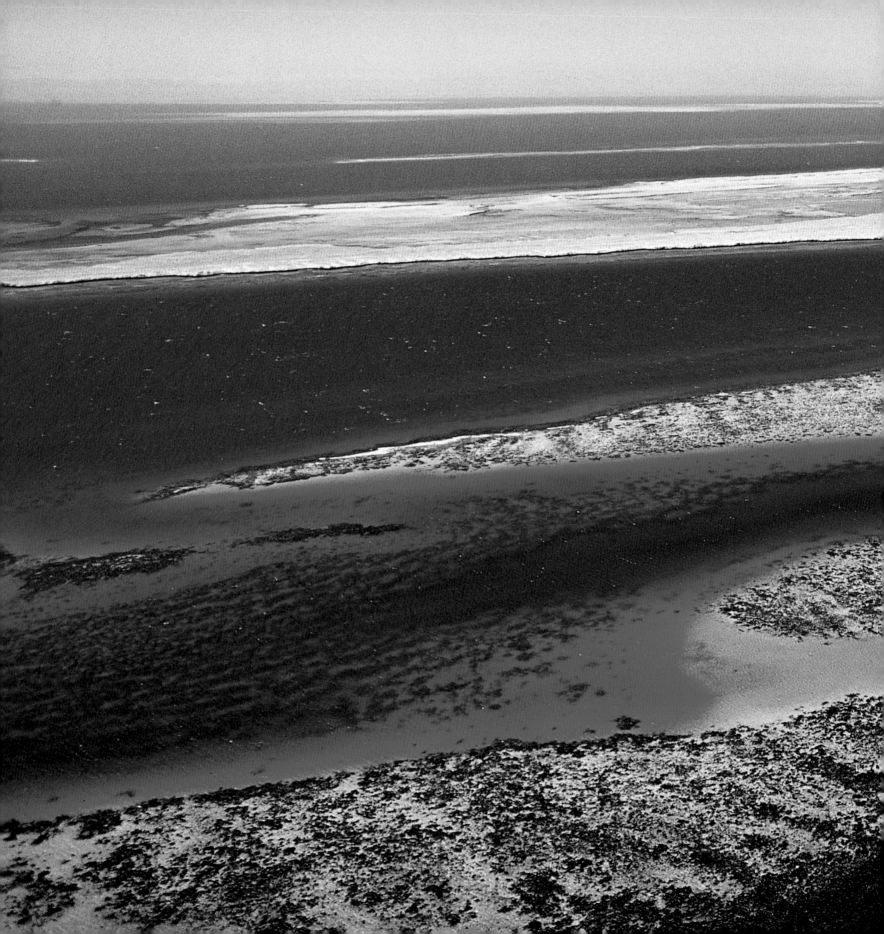

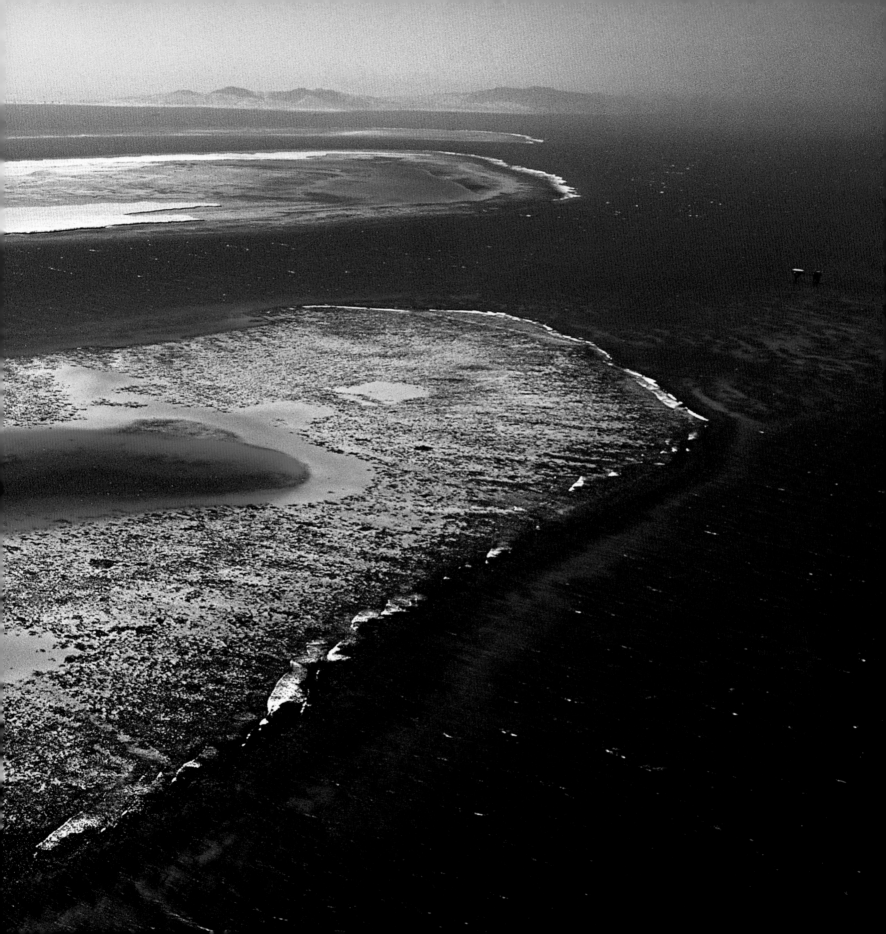

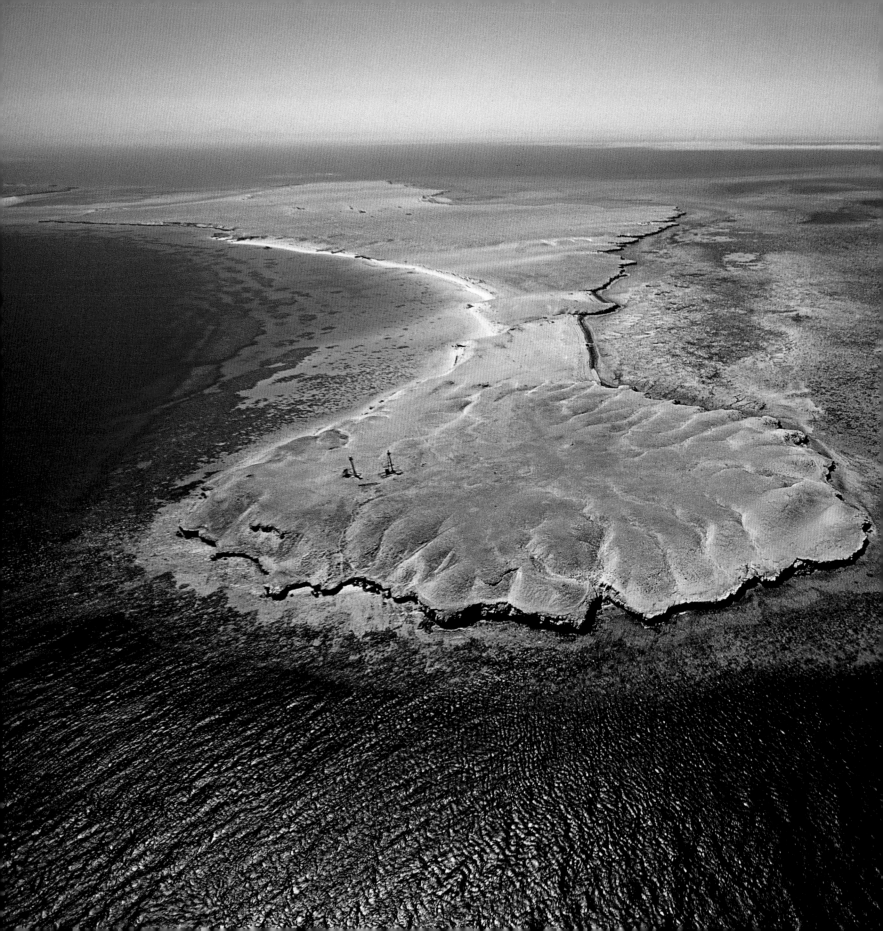

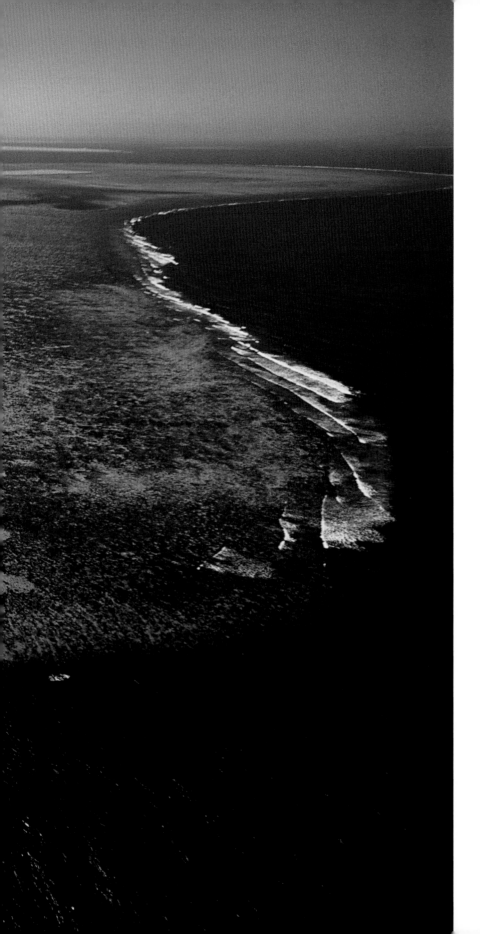

"ALONE, ALONE, ALL, ALL ALONE, ALONE ON A WIDE, WIDE SEA!"

from THE RIME
OF THE ANCIENT MARINER
by Samuel Taylor Coleridge

● Red Sea, Egypt - Southern tip of
the island of Tiran.

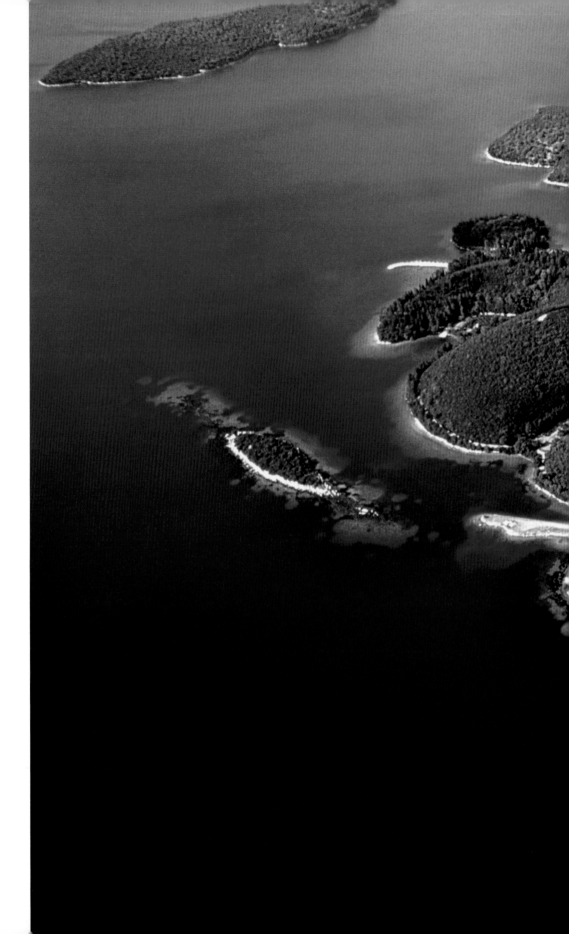

The Paradise
of the Onassis'

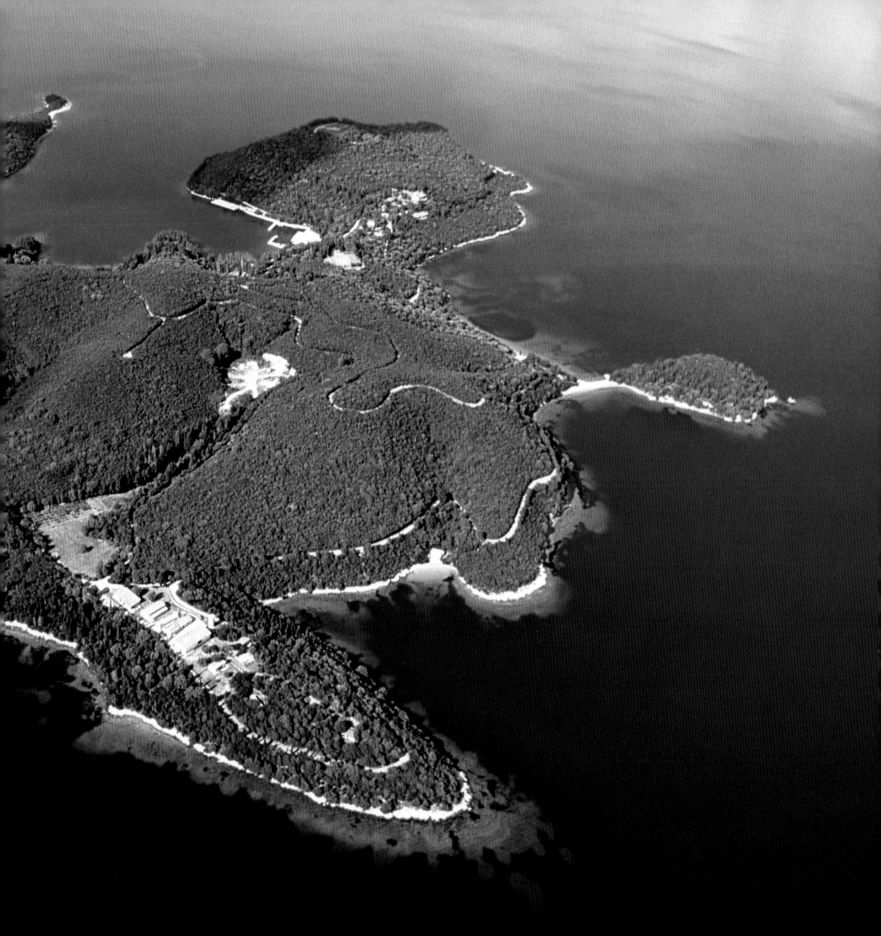

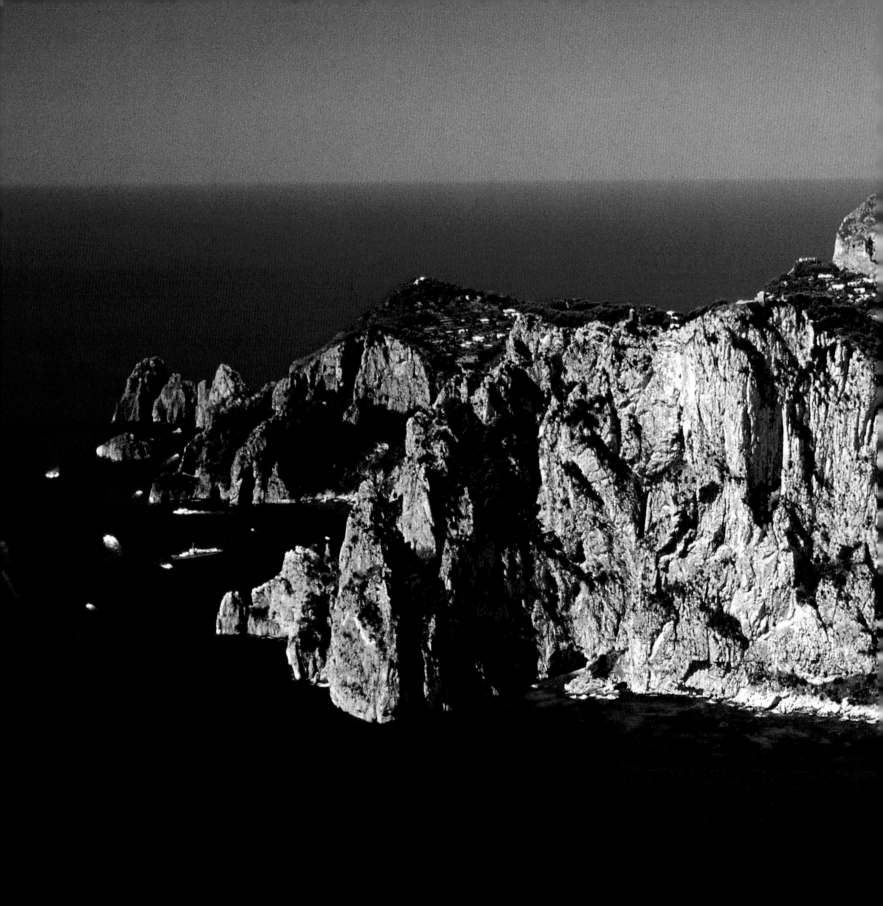

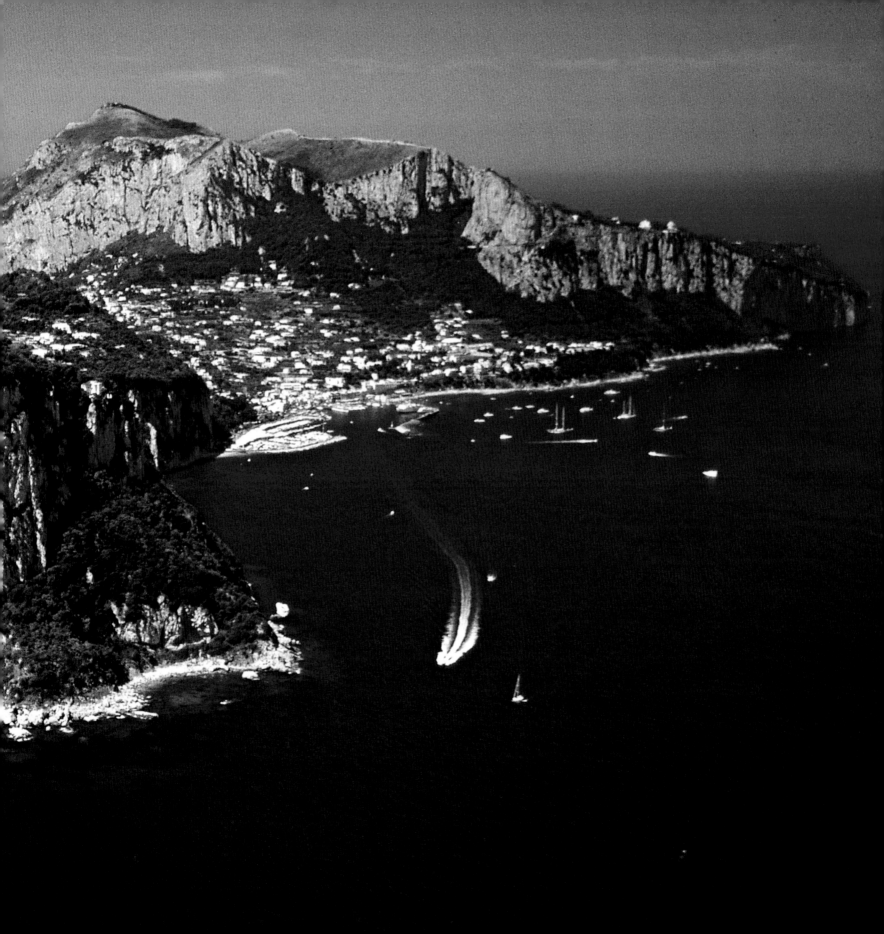

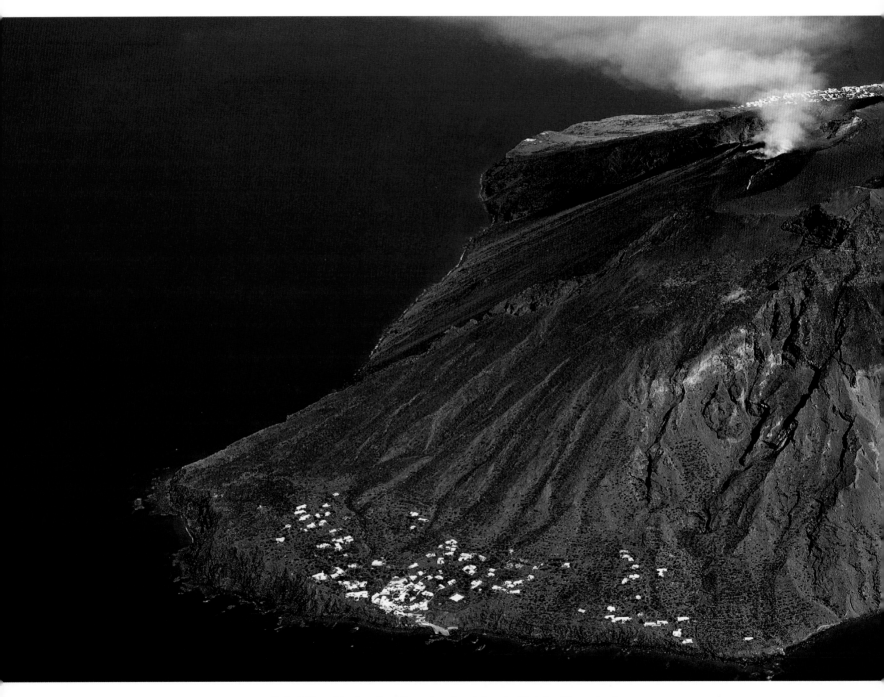

184-185 ● Tyrrhenian Sea, Aeolian Islands (Italy) - Stromboli.

186-187 ● Mediterranean Sea, Sardinia (Italy) - Mortorio.

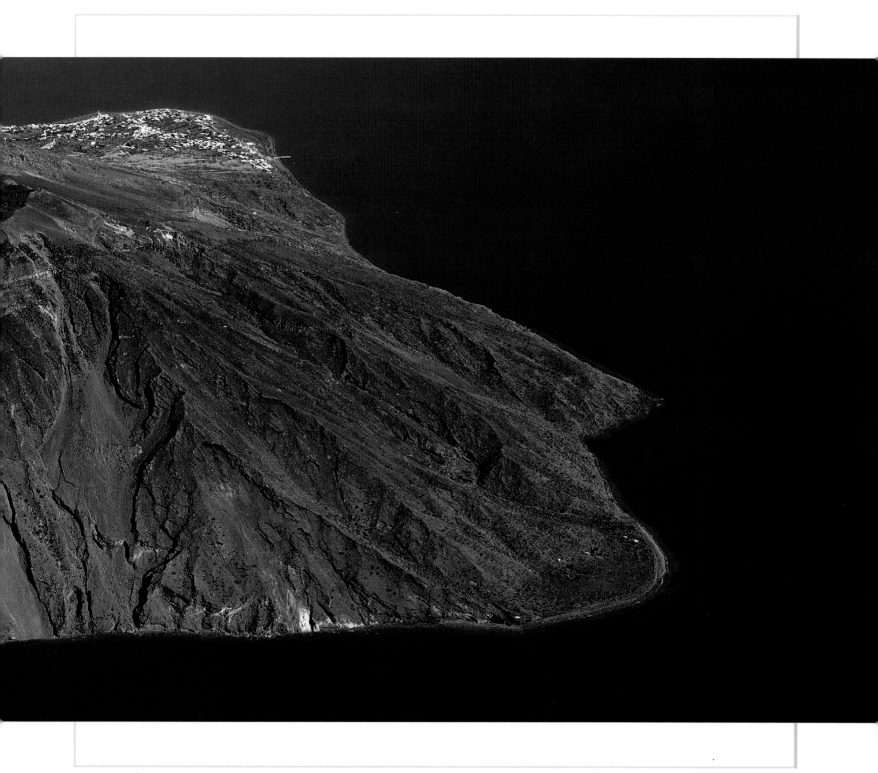

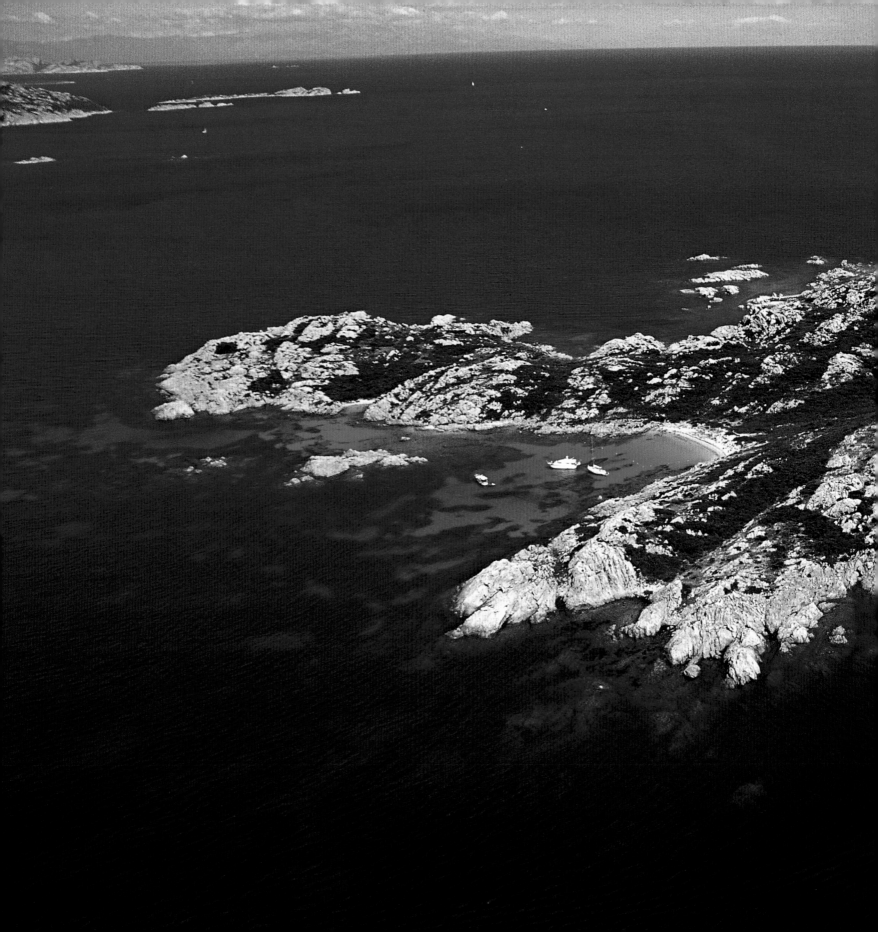

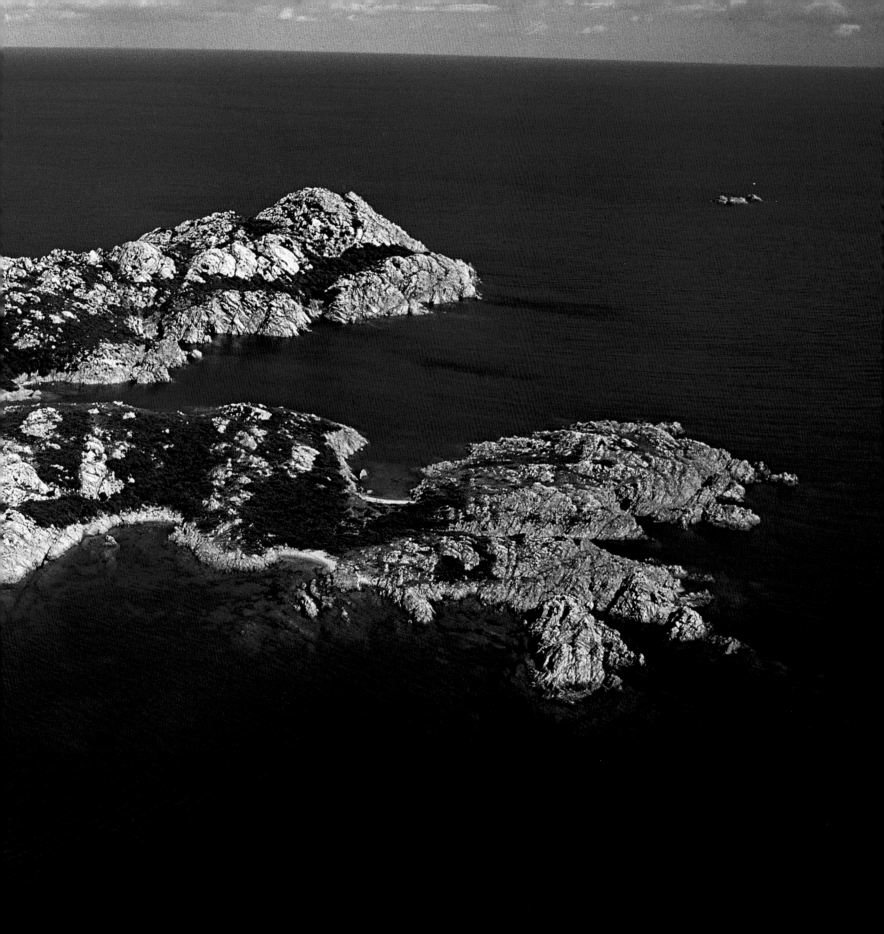

"THE SUN TOUCHED THE CENTER OF THE RENT AND FLOODED THE CLOUDS WITH LIGHT FROM BELOW... THE SEA ALTERED COLOR WITH THE NEW REFLECTION; THE VIOLET DARKENED, THE GREEN AROUND THE ISLAND AND ON THE SAND TURNED A STEADY, PALE EMERALD GREEN..."

Gianni Roghi, 1953

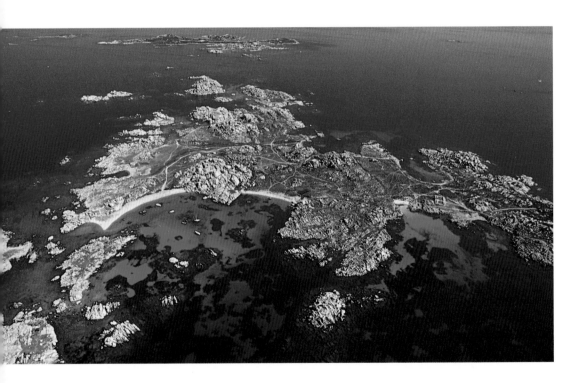

188 ● Mediterranean Sea, Corsica (France) - Lavezzi.

189 ● Mediterranean Sea, islands of Lérins (France) - Ile du Levant.

190-191 ● Atlantic Ocean, Charente-Maritime (France) - Ile de Ré.

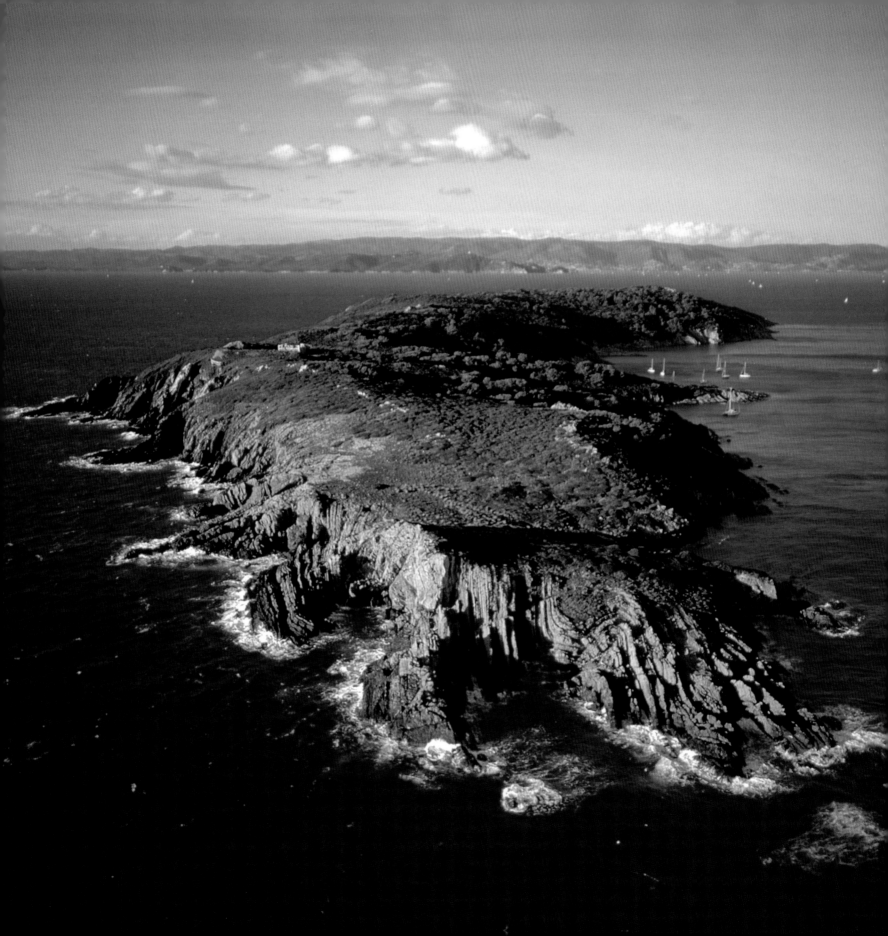

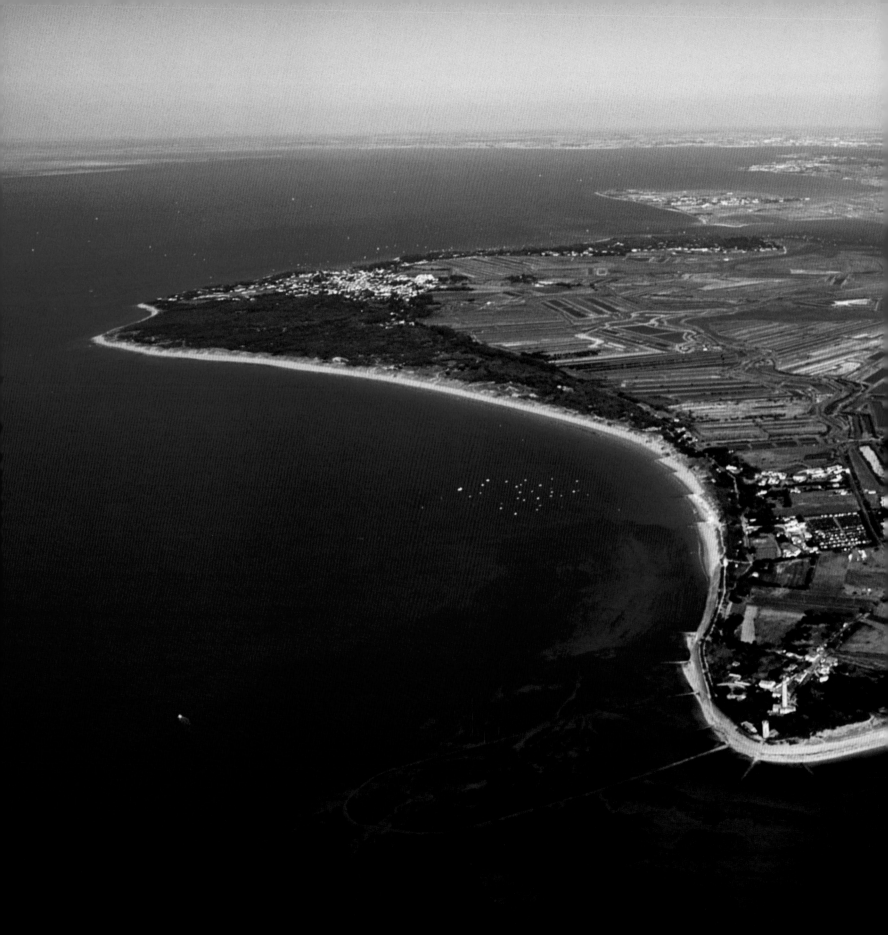

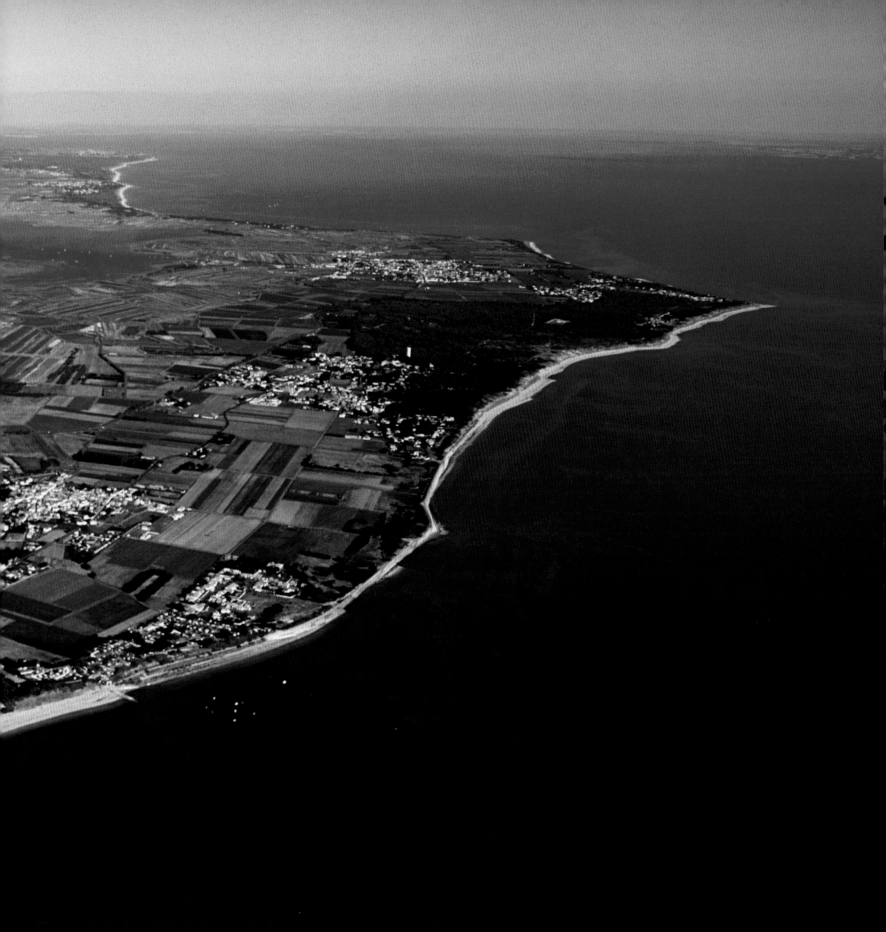

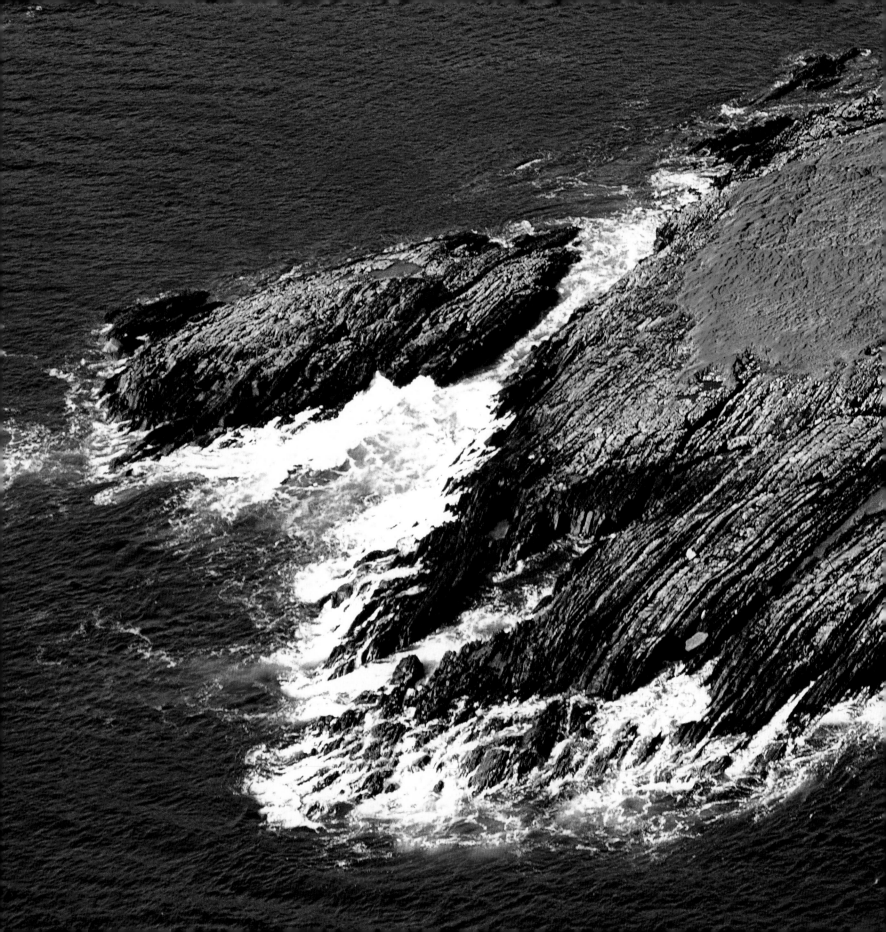

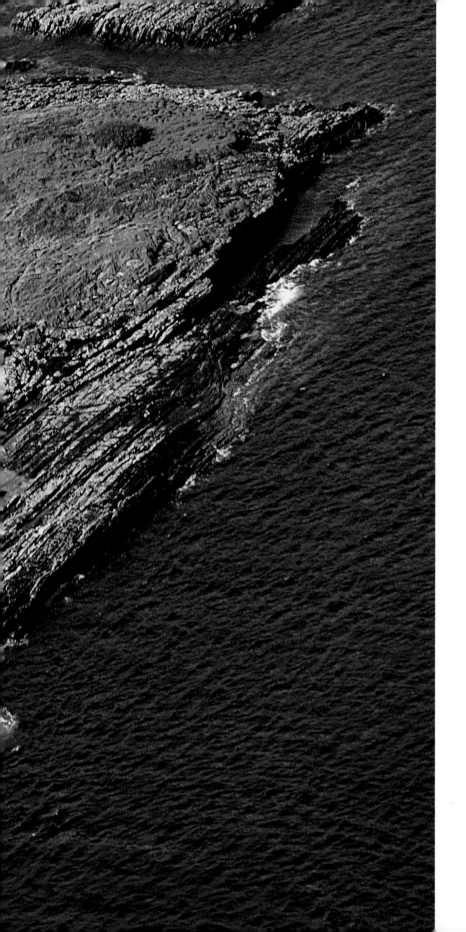

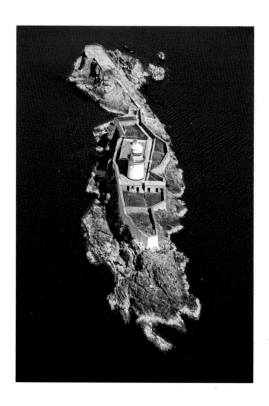

192-193 ● Atlantic Ocean, Cork (Ireland) - Islands in Dumanus Bay.

193 ● Atlantic Ocean, Donegal (Ireland) - Killybergs.

194-195 ● Atlantic Ocean, Quebec (Canada) - Gaspé peninsula.

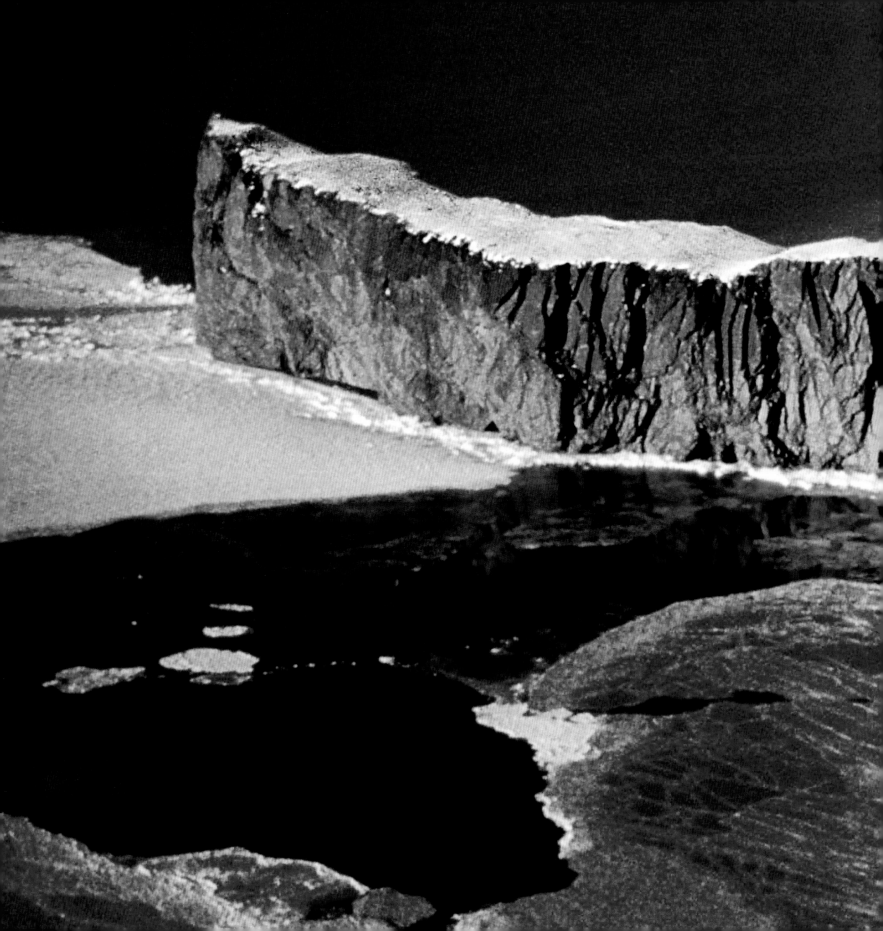

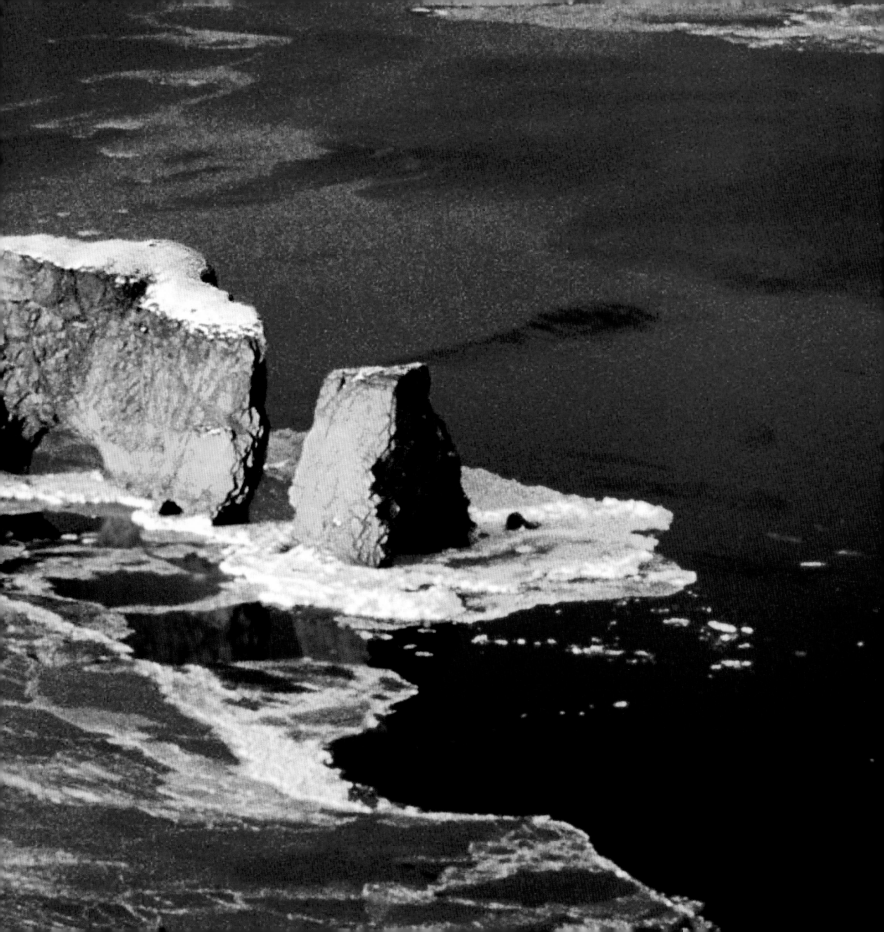

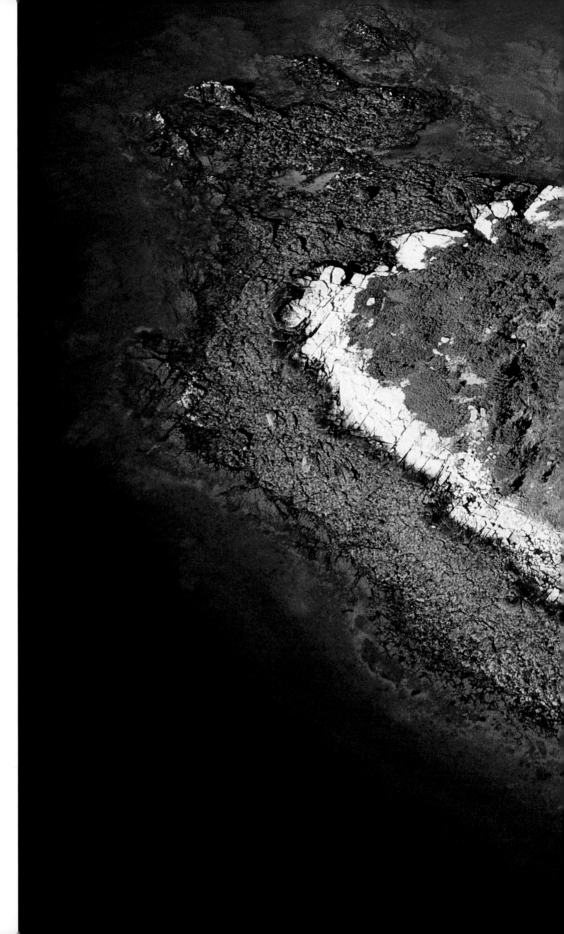

196-197 ● Atlantic Ocean, Penobscot Bay, Maine (USA) - Pumpkin Island.

198-199 ● Caribbean Sea, Guadaloupe - Pointe des Châteaux.

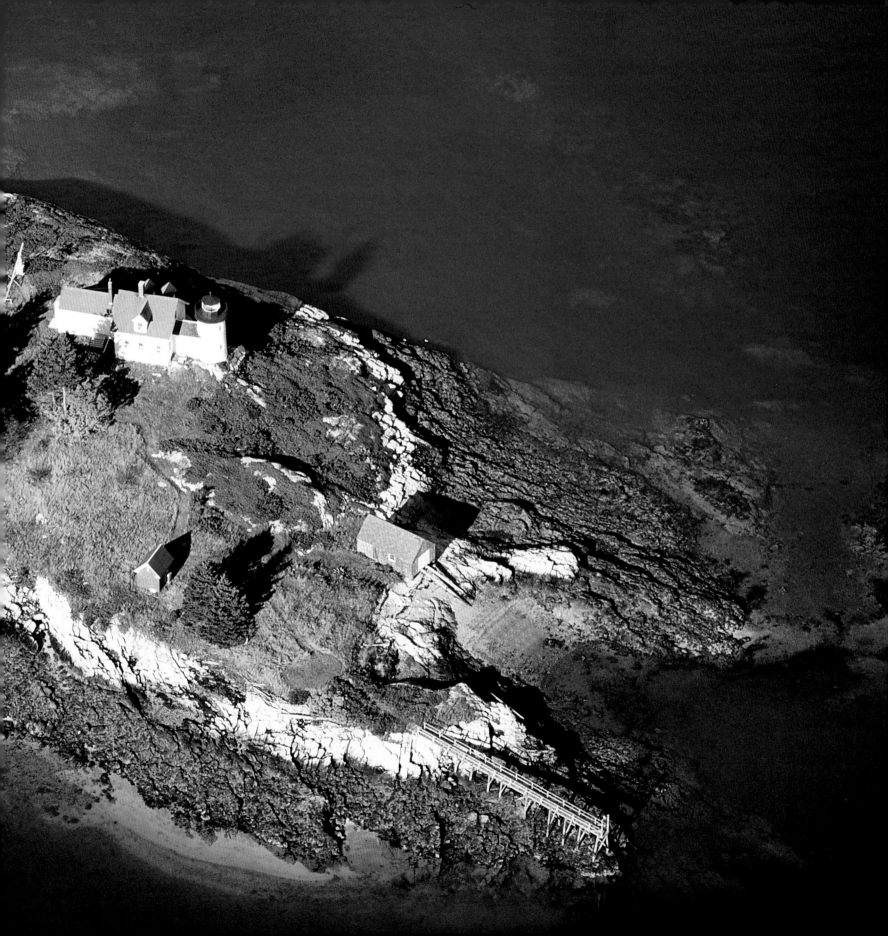

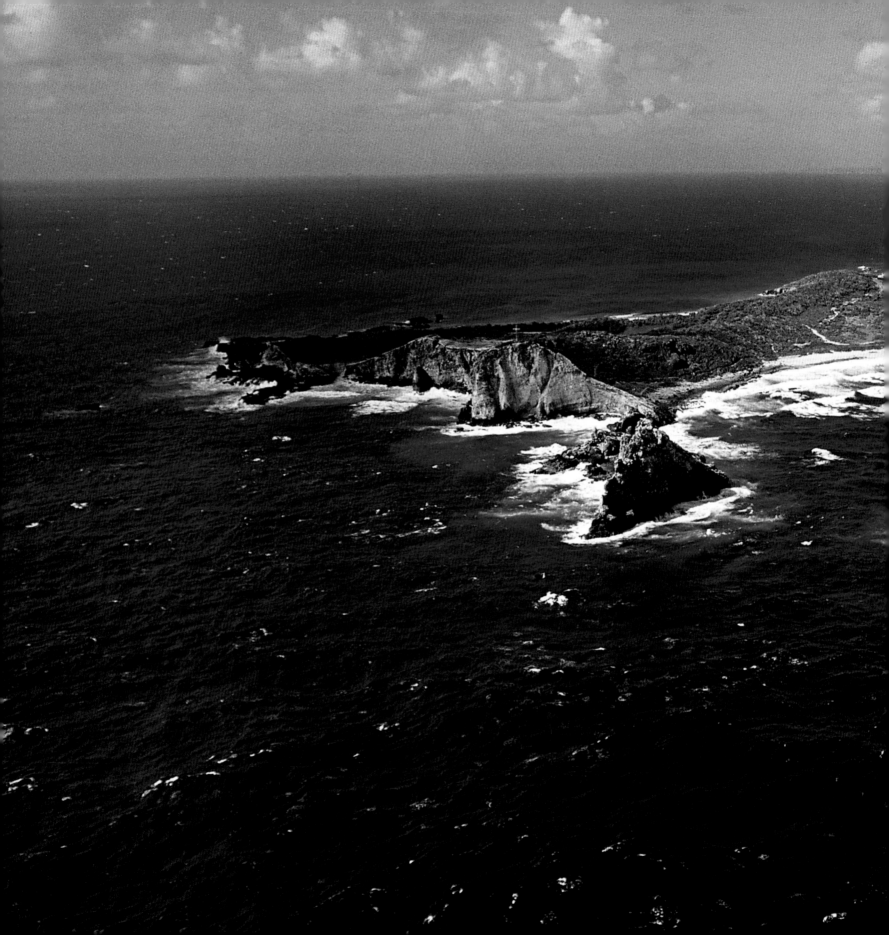

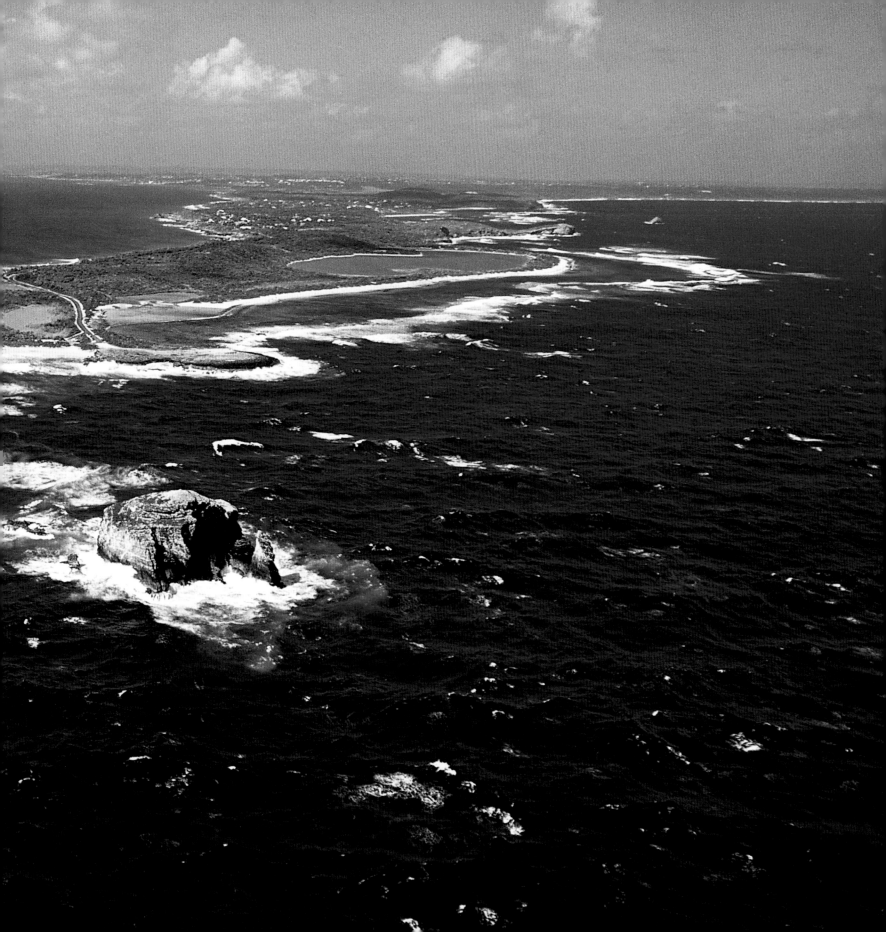

In the Bay of
the Angels

- Pacific Ocean,
California (USA) -
Anacapa Island.

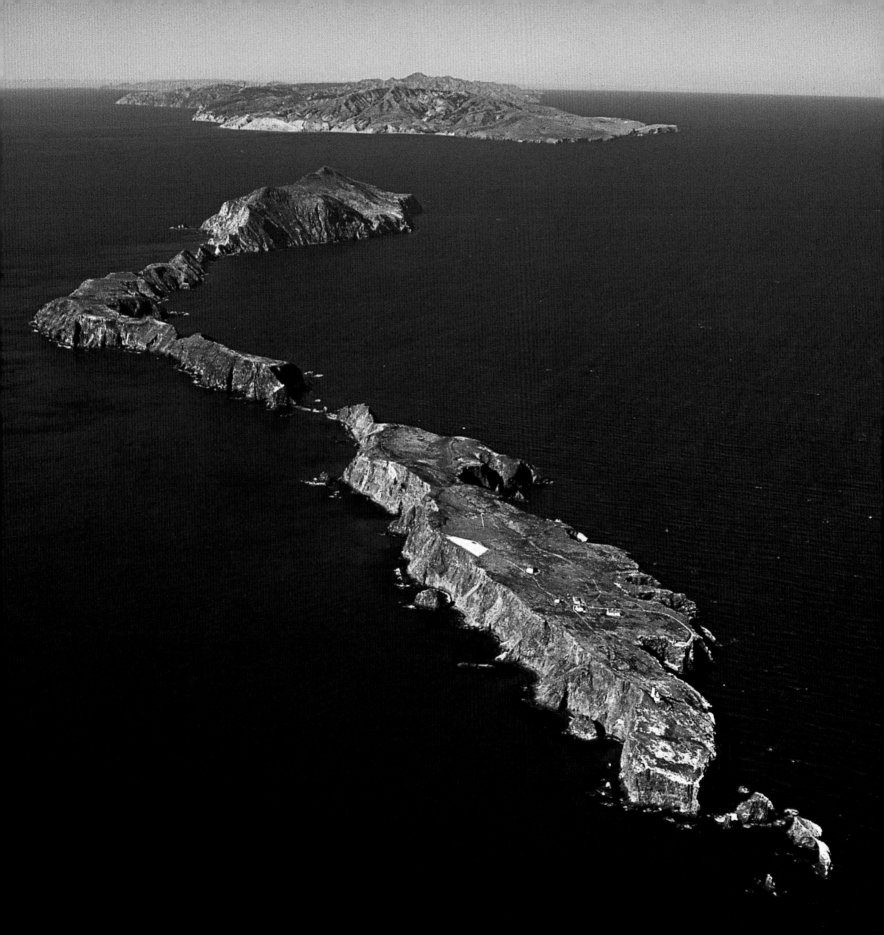

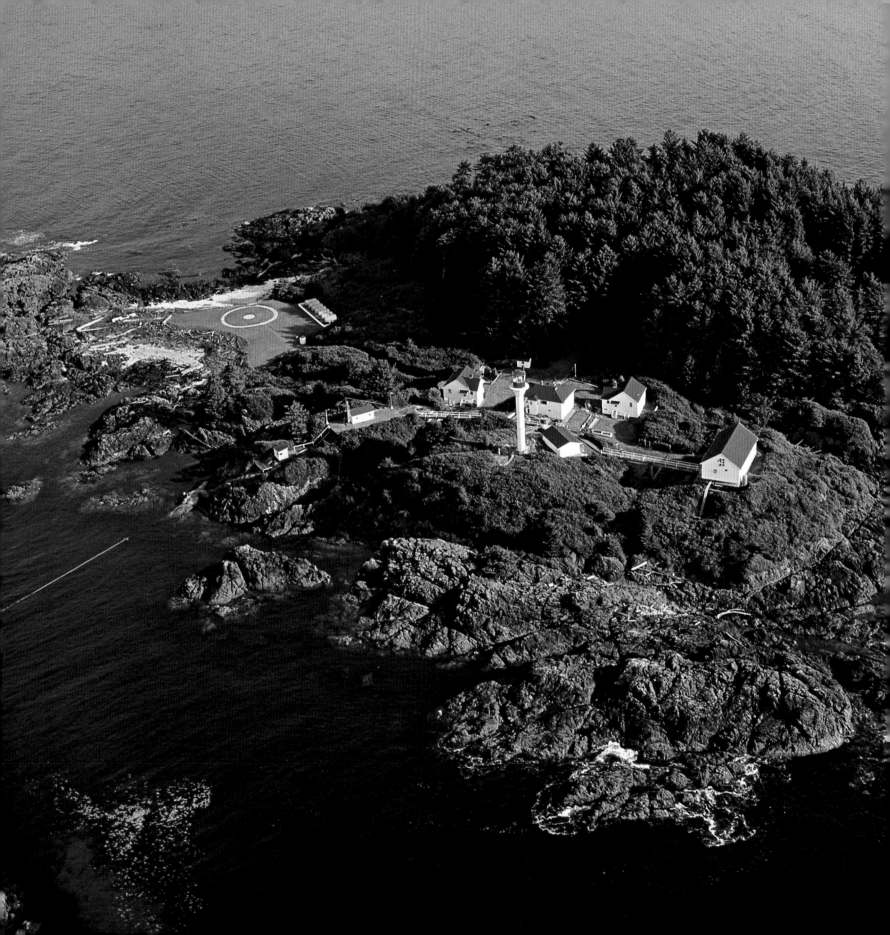

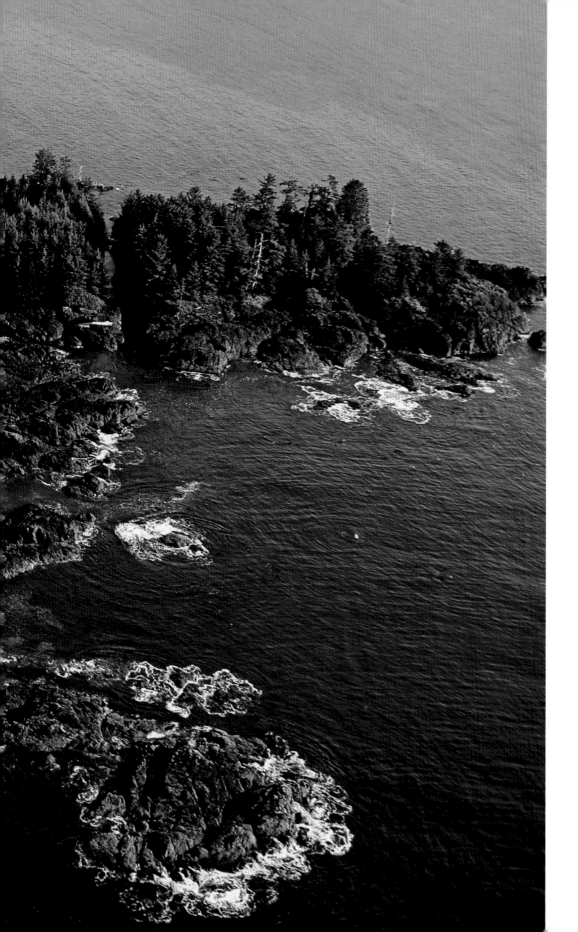

On the limits
of the Arctic

202-203 ● Pacific Ocean,
Vancouver (Canada) -
Islands in front of Tofino.

204-205 ● Atlantic Ocean,
Newfoundland (Canada) -
Great Sacred Island.

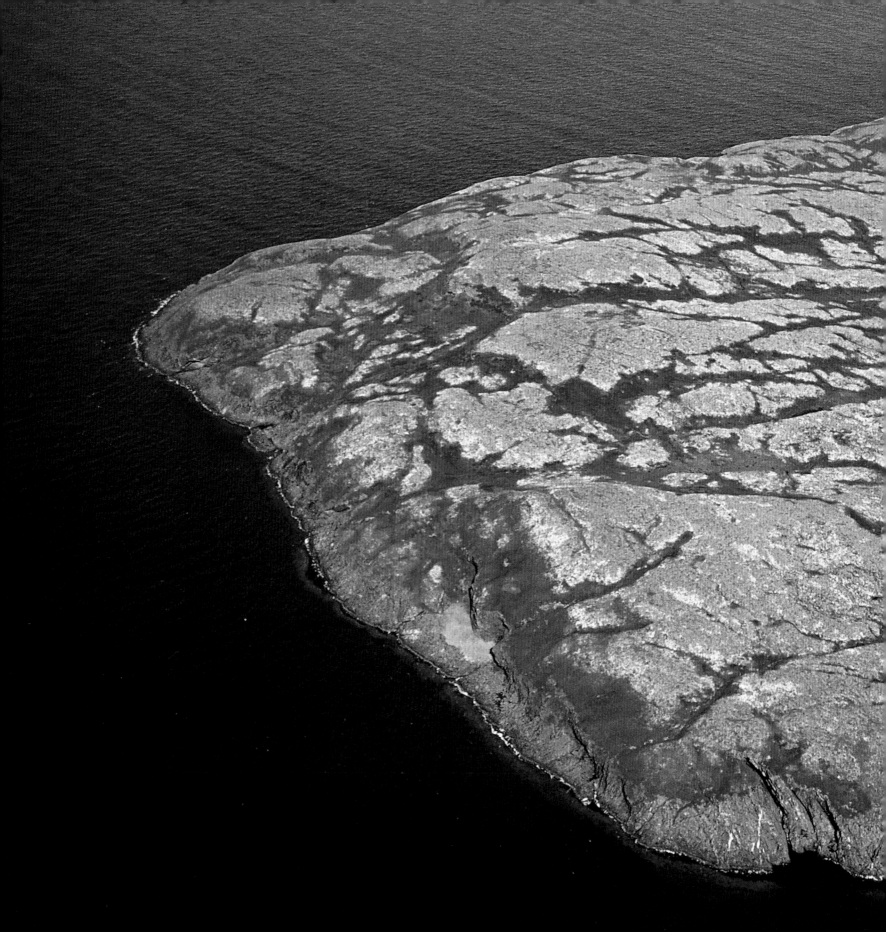

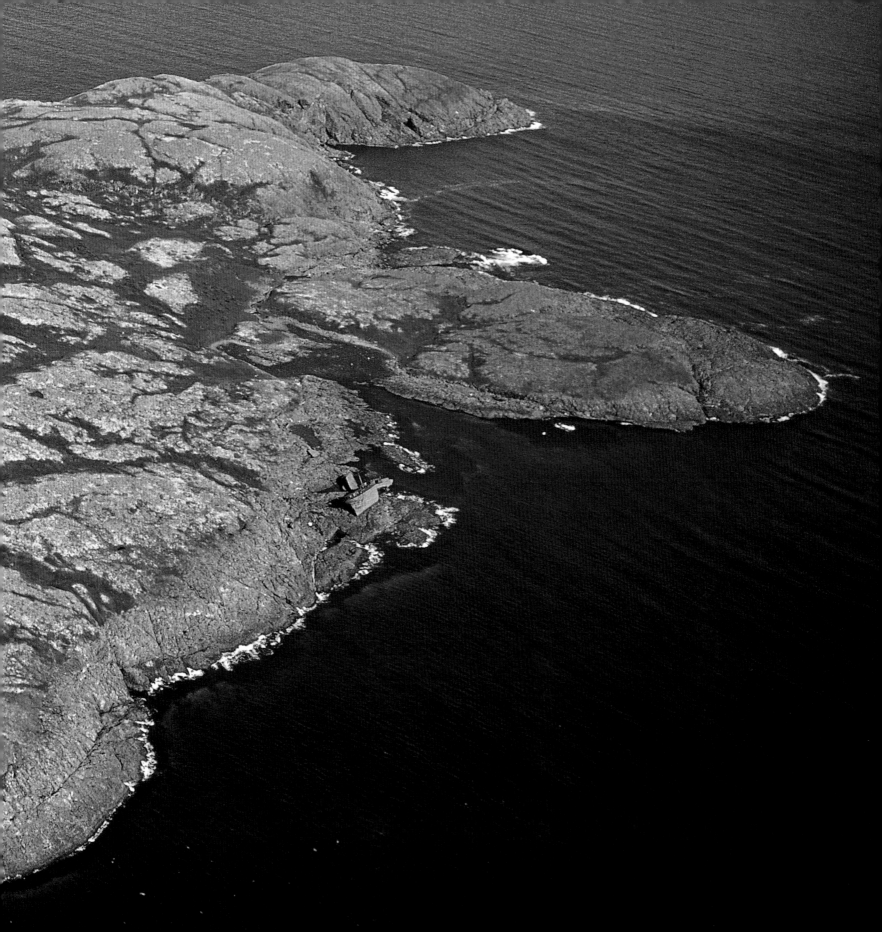

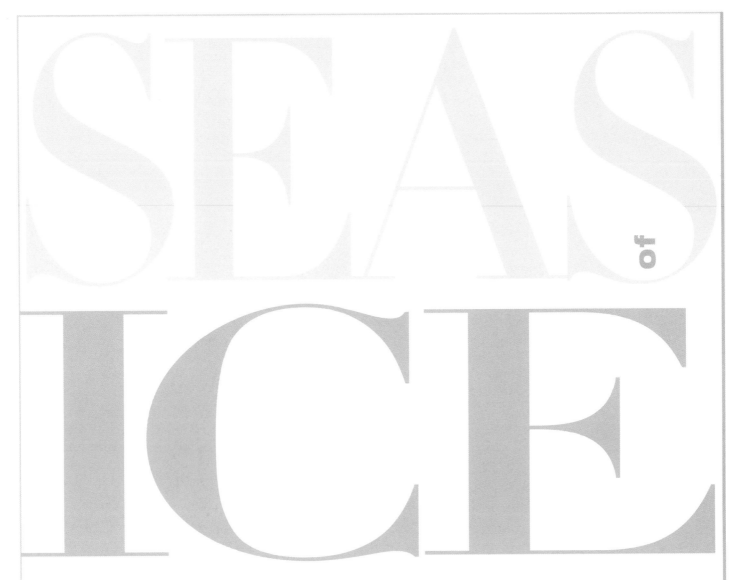

SEAS of ICE

COLIN MONTEATH

● Weddell Sea, Antarctic - On board the icebreaker *Grigorii Mikheev* in the Ronne Ice Shelf.

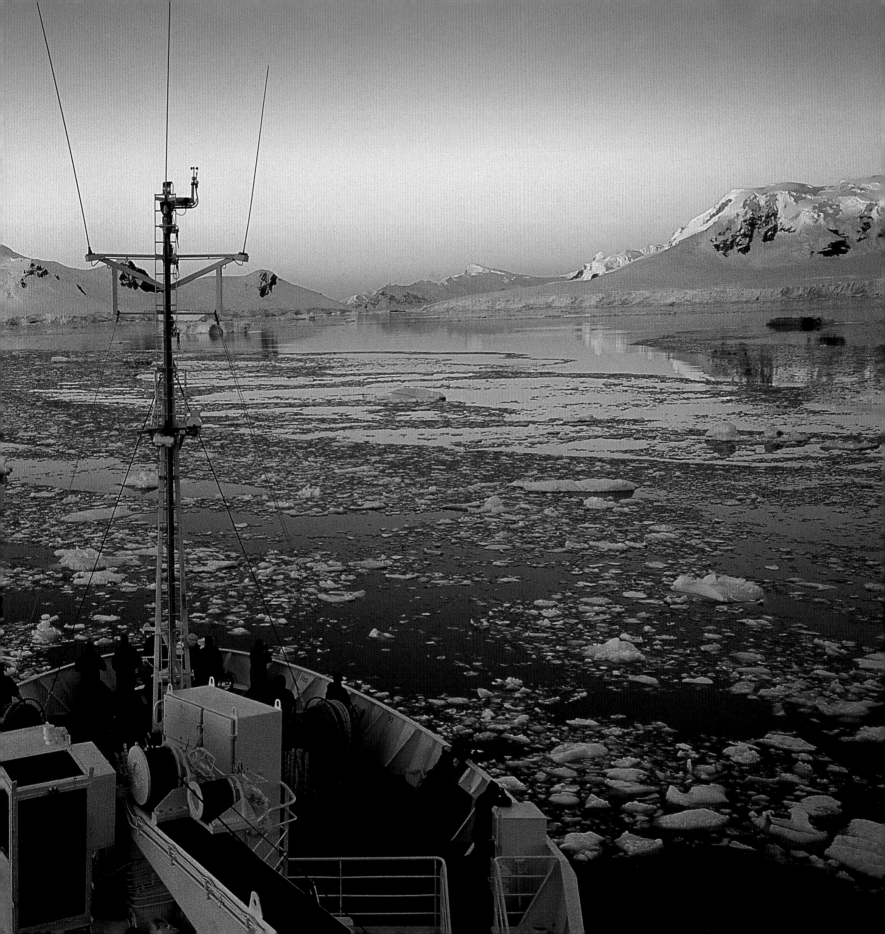

INTRODUCTION Seas of Ice

IN THE WHITE PLANET THE WIND BLOWS AT OVER ONE HUN-

DRED MILES AN HOUR AND THE TEMPERATURE CAN DROP TO MORE

THAN FIFTY BELOW ZERO. AROUND THE ANTARCTIC, THE WAVES IN

THE MOST DANGEROUS SEA IN THE WORLD LASH LIKE POWERFUL

WHIPS. HERE, ON THE SIXTIETH PARALLEL, IS WHERE THE EARTH'S

REAL CONFINES LIE; THESE ARE THE LIMITS THAT NATURE PLACES ON

MAN'S ABILITY TO SURVIVE. THIS IS THE 'END OF THE WORLD' AS THE

CHILEAN WRITER FRANCISCO COLOANE CALLED EVERYTHING

SOUTH OF CAPE HORN. BEYOND THERE IS ONLY A FROZEN DESERT

WHERE THE RAYS OF THE SUN SEEM LIKE BLADES OF ICE THAT CUT

THE SKIN. LIKE A GIANT MONSTER BURIED IN THE SNOW, THE

INTRODUCTION Seas of Ice

ANTARCTIC BREATHES IN KEEPING WITH THE RHYTHM OF THE SEA-

SONS. DURING THE LONG WINTER NIGHT ITS FROZEN BREATH

EXTENDS TO THE OCEAN AND TURNS IT TO ICE TEN FEET THICK.

THESE ARE FOUR LONG MONTHS OF ABSOLUTE DARKNESS,

SCOURGED BY A WIND THAT DOES NOT CEASE FOR A MINUTE. DUR-

ING THE SHORT-LIVED SUMMER, FROM NOVEMBER TO FEBRUARY,

THE LAYER OF ICE THAT COVERS THE SEA MAY BREAK UP AND

RETREAT JUST ENOUGH TO ALLOW ICE-BREAKING SHIPS TO ZIGZAG

BETWEEN ICEBERGS AND REACH LAND. DURING THE FIFTEEN WEEKS

OF SUMMER NIGHT ALMOST CEASES TO EXIST: THE MORNINGS BEGIN

BEFORE THE EVENING COMES TO AN END, MARKED BY A BARELY

Seas of Ice

Introduction

PERCEPTIBLE TWILIGHT DILUTED BY THE MILKY LIGHT OF DAWN. THE BREATH OF THE ANTARCTIC IS A VITAL ONE THAT SPREADS ACROSS THE WHOLE PLANET: THE OXYGEN RELEASED IN ITS COLD WATERS FEEDS A BIOLOGICAL CHAIN THAT EVENTUALLY STRETCHES UP TO THE GIANTS OF THE OCEANS. THIS REGION TEEMS WITH LIFE, AND THE SEA IS SOMETIMES A LEADEN GRAY THAT SEEMS TO PRESAGE A FROZEN HURRICANE, SOMETIMES SILVERY, THAT STRETCHES TO THE HORIZON. ONLY THE FOAM AND THE REFLECTIONS OF THE SUNLIGHT ON CLEAR DAYS BREAK THE MONOTONY OF A PANORAMA THAT GIVES SAILORS THE SAME MALAISE THAT THE NAVIGATORS OF YORE MUST HAVE FELT ON PASSING THROUGH THE PILLARS OF HERCULES.

Arctic Ocean - Greenland, polar bear.

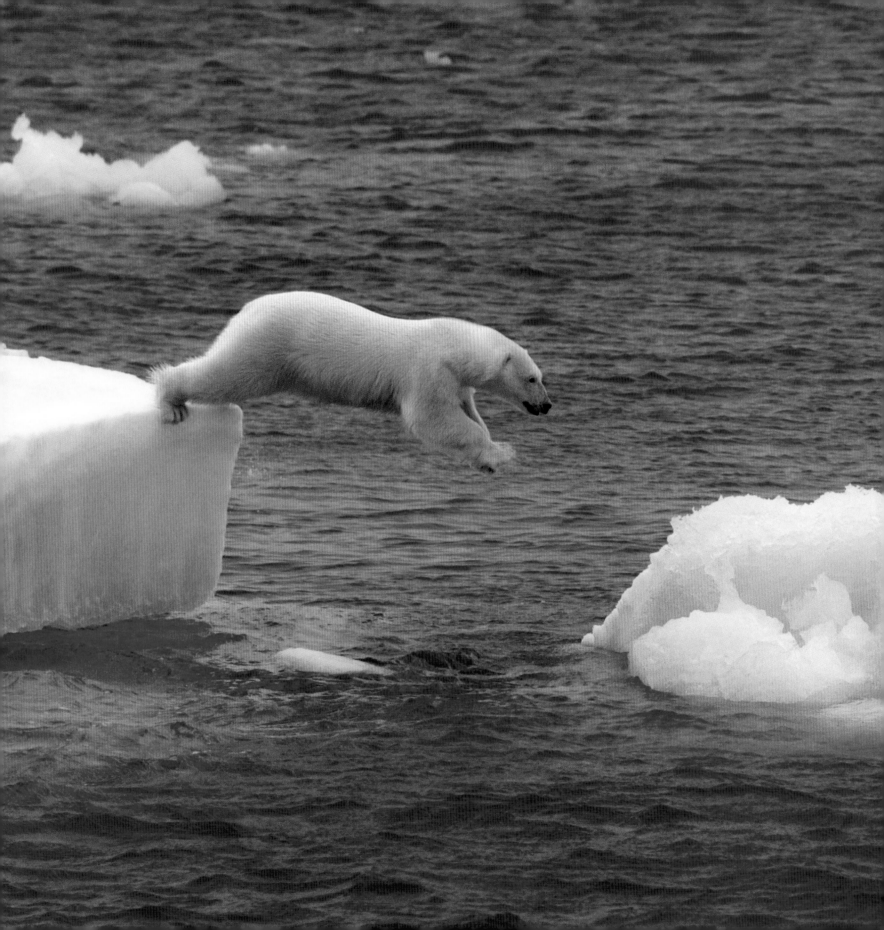

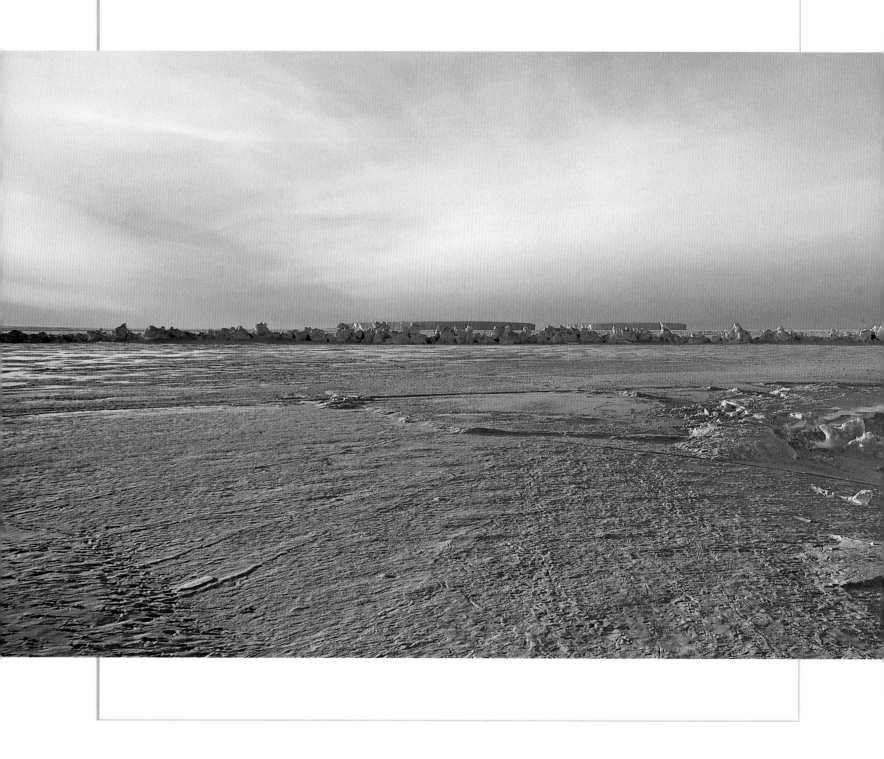

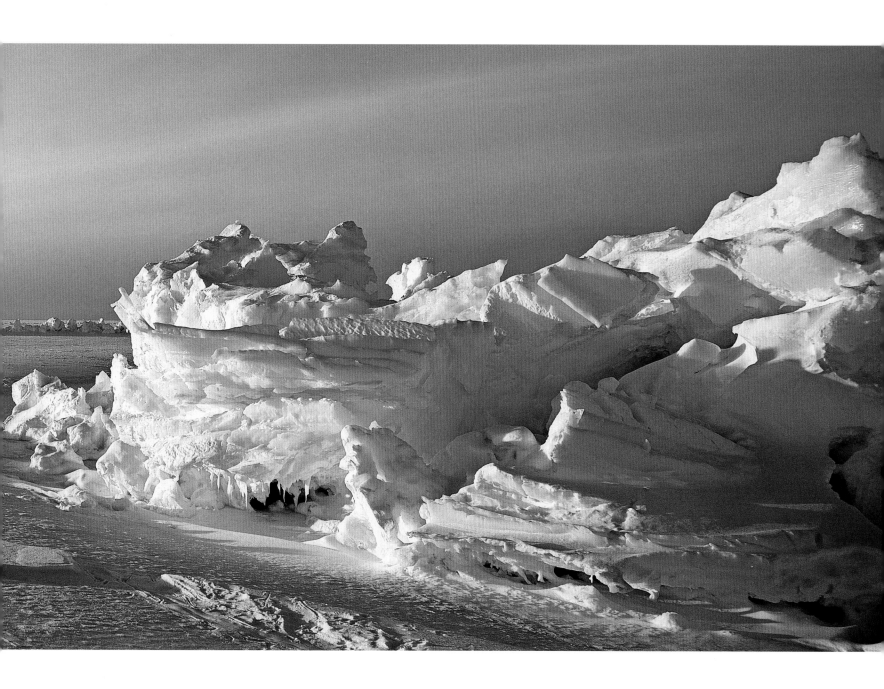

Weddell Sea - Antarctic, ice shelf.

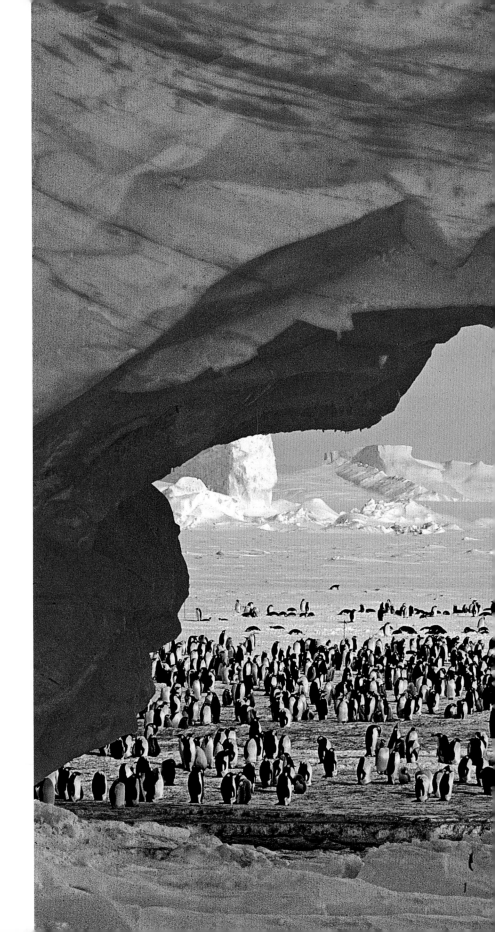

“ **P**ENGUINS FILE SLOWLY AND UNCERTAINLY UP TO THE CREST. SEEING THEM CLIMB AND DESCEND WITH THEIR COMICALLY HUMAN APPEARANCE, THEY SEEM LIKE CHILDREN IN COAT-TAILS AND A DICKEY CONCEN-TRATING IN COMPLETE SERI-OUSNESS ON AN ENJOYABLE GAME. ”

From THE CONQUERORS
OF THE ANTARCTIC
by Francisco Coloane

214-215 ● Atka Bay, Antarctic -
Colony of Emperor penguins.

216-217 ● Arctic Ocean, Canada -
Greenland seals in the St. Lawrence.

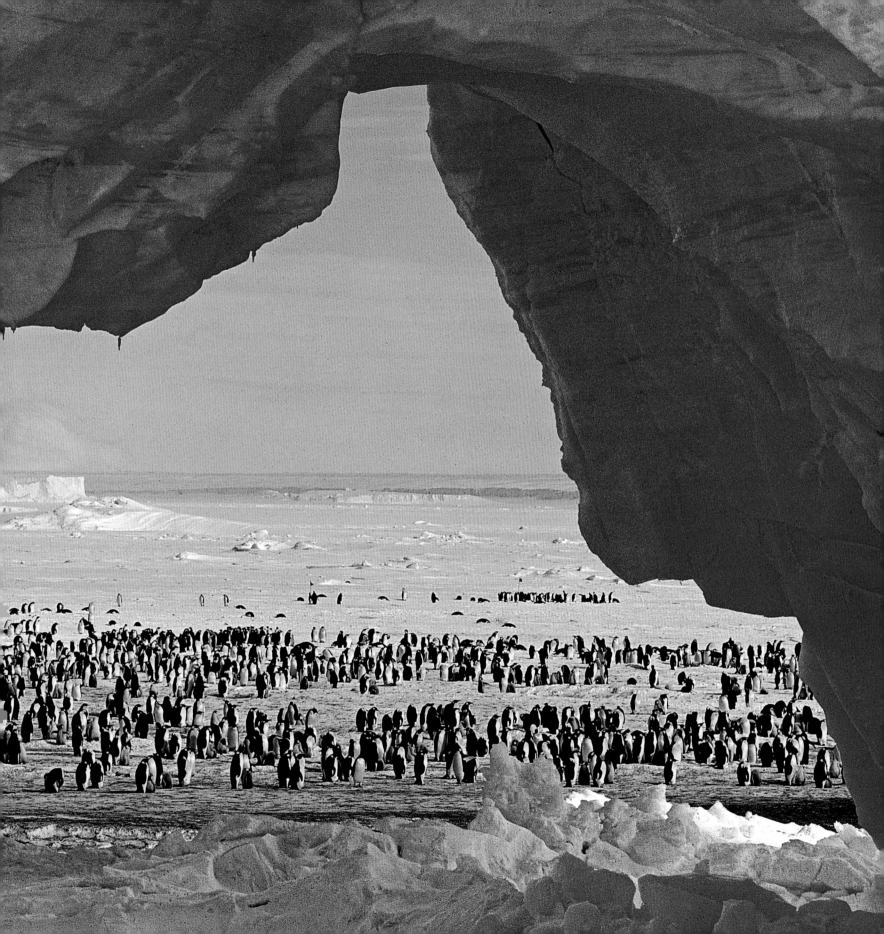

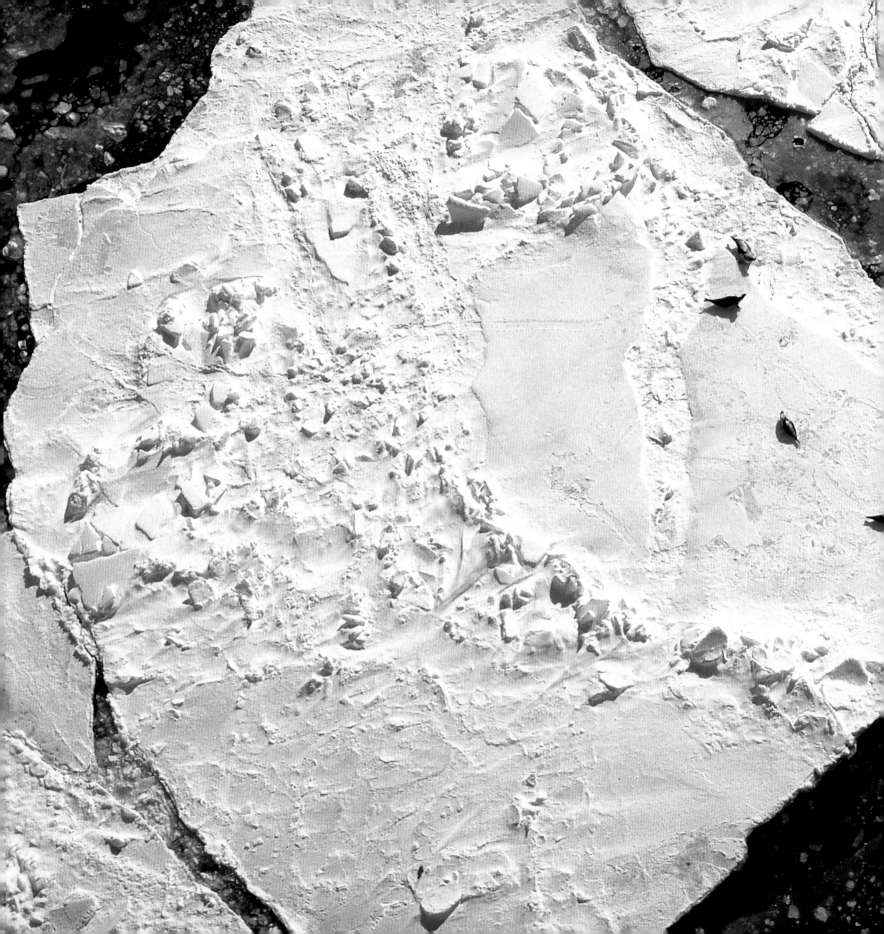

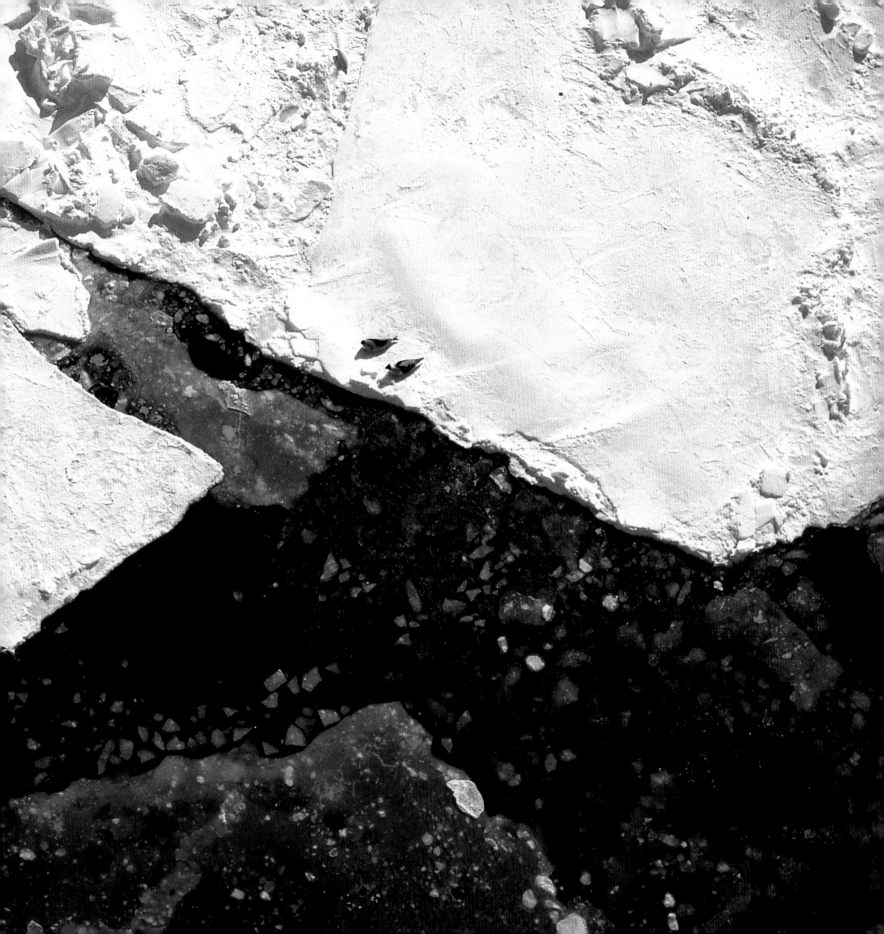

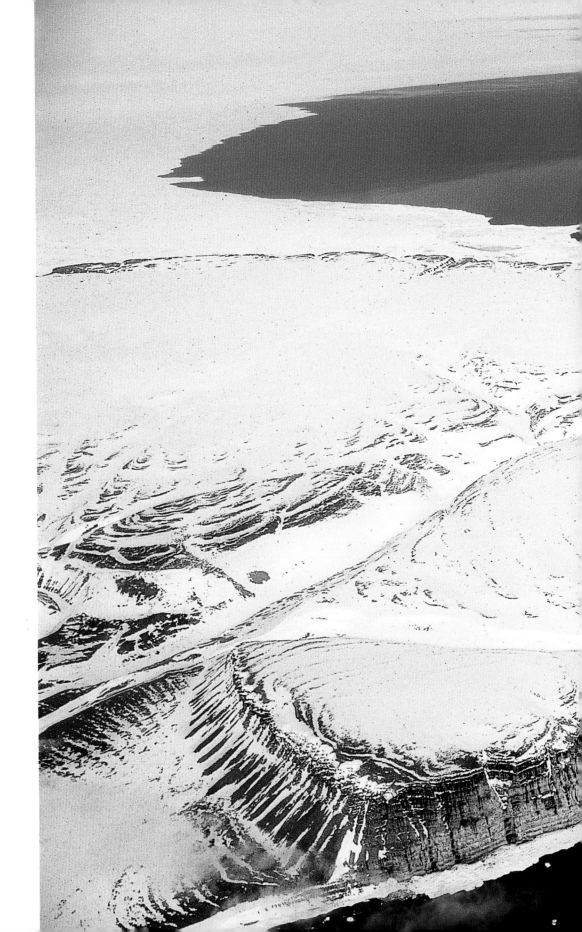

At the ends
of the world

218-219 ● Arctic Ocean, Canada - Baffin Bay.

220-221 ● Indian Ocean, Antarctic - Air bubbles trapped in the ice near Mawson.

222-223 ● Ross Sea, Antarctic - Iceberg.

224-225 ● Atlantic Ocean, Patagonia (Argentina) - The sailing ship *Shenandoah* and the Garibaldi Glacier.

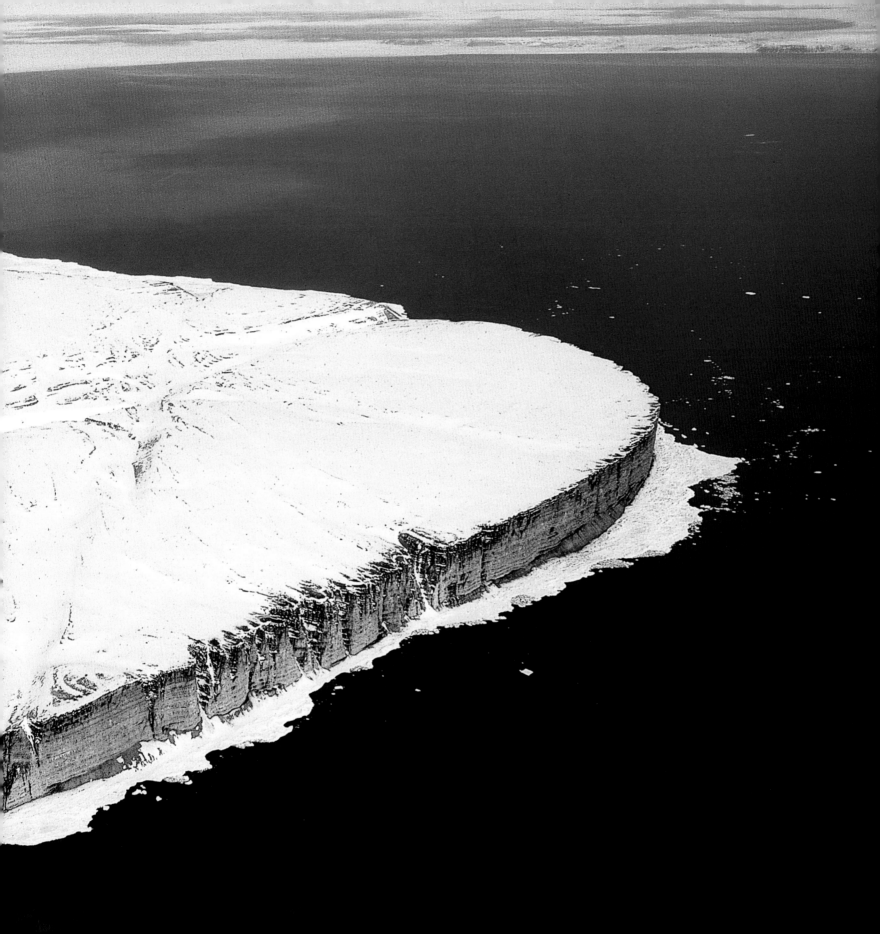

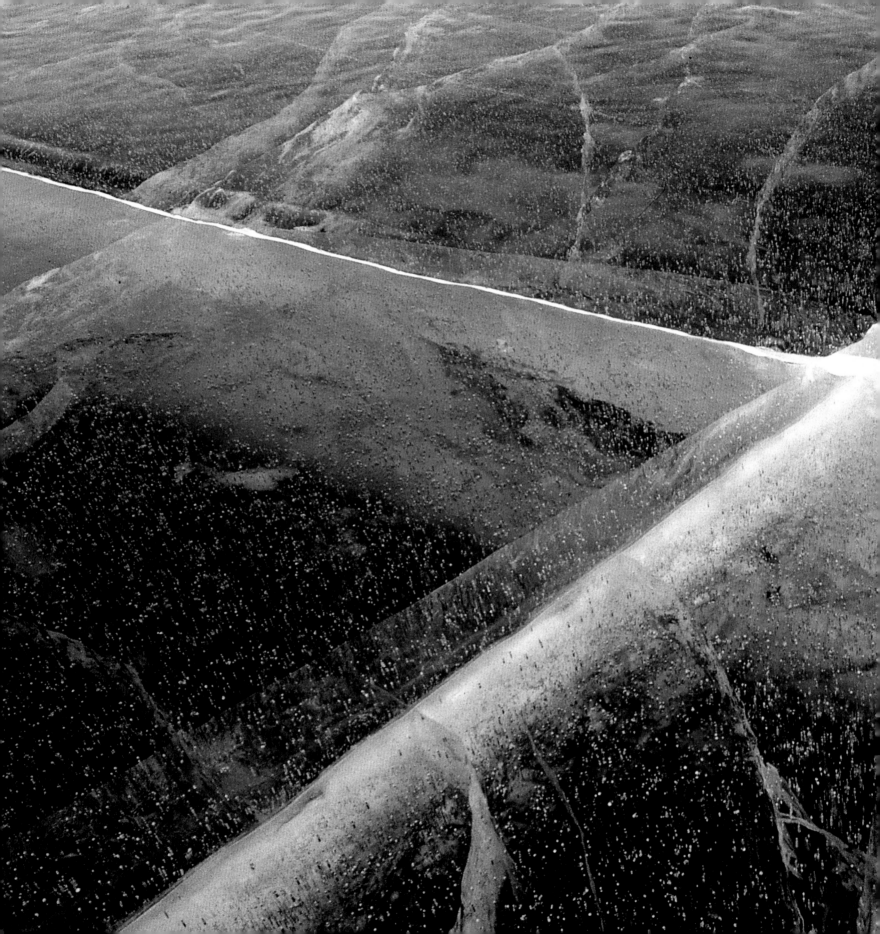

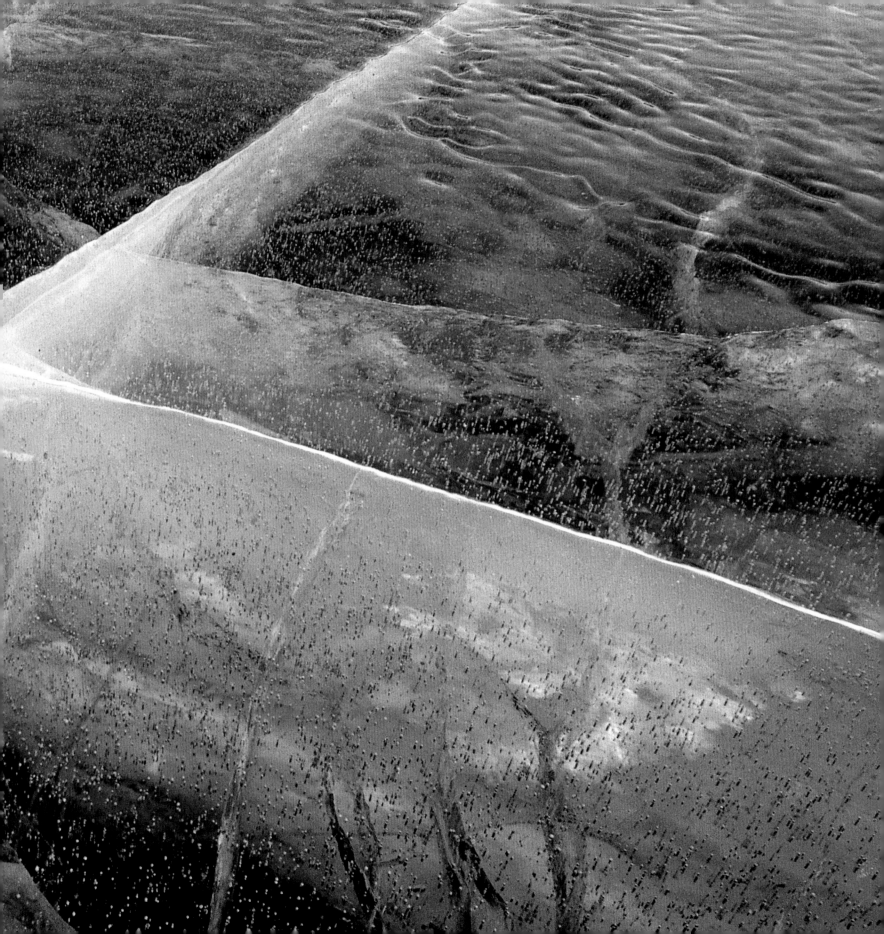

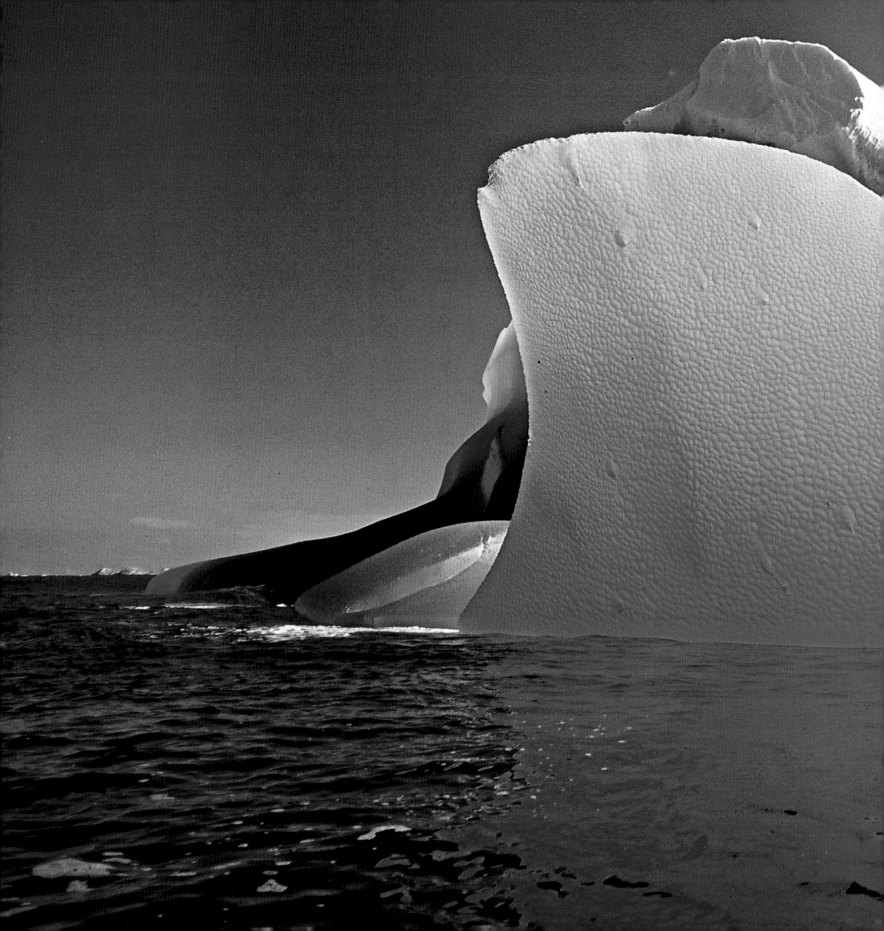

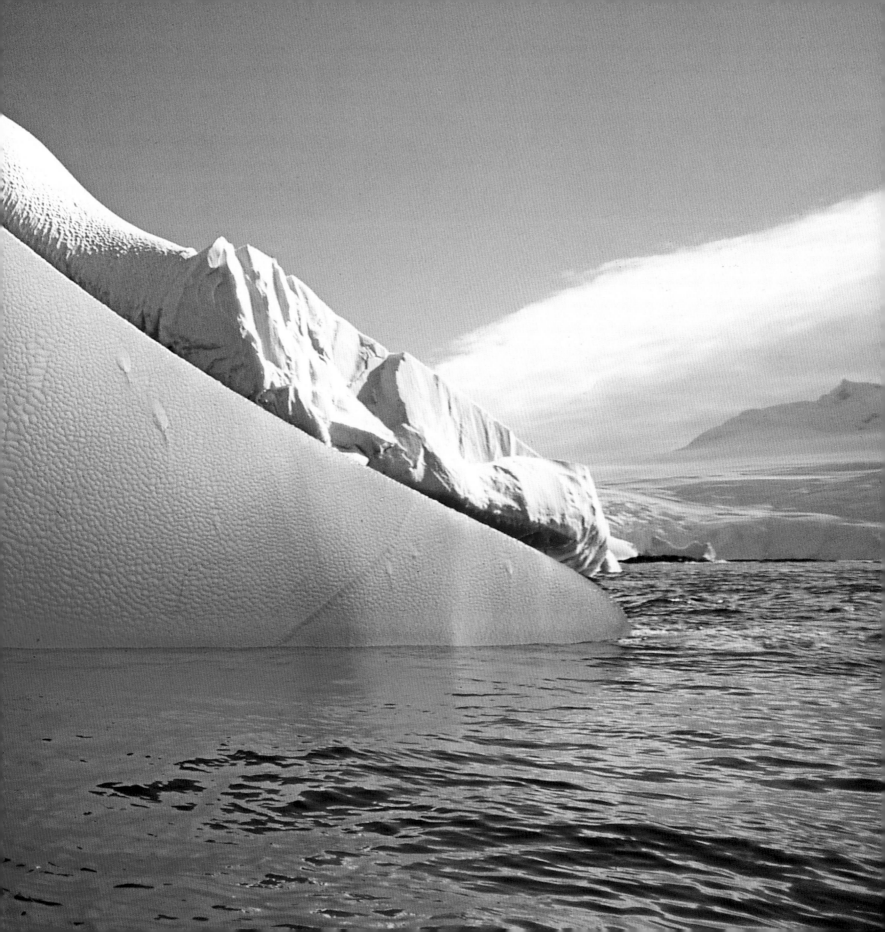

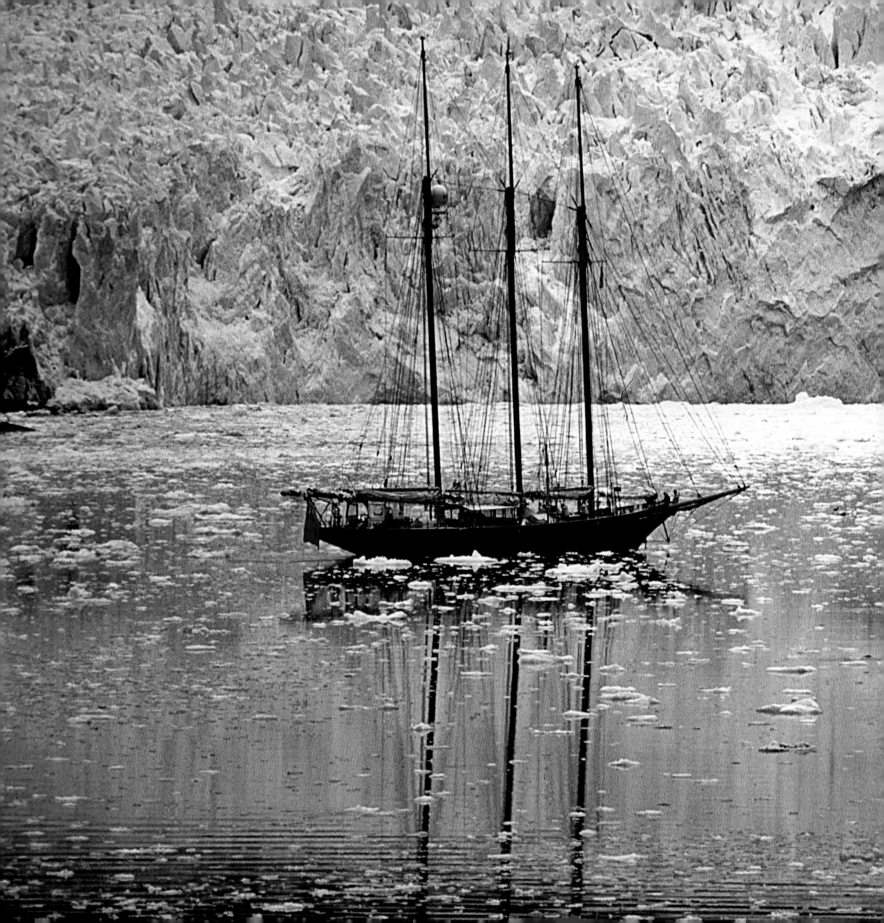

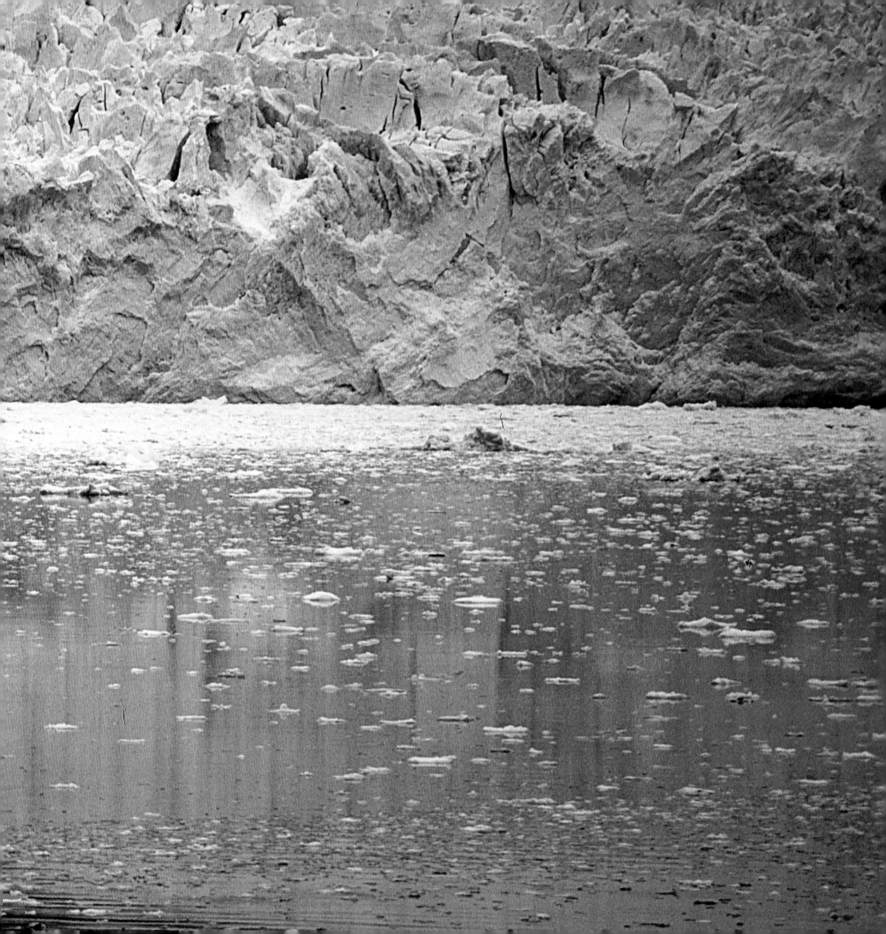

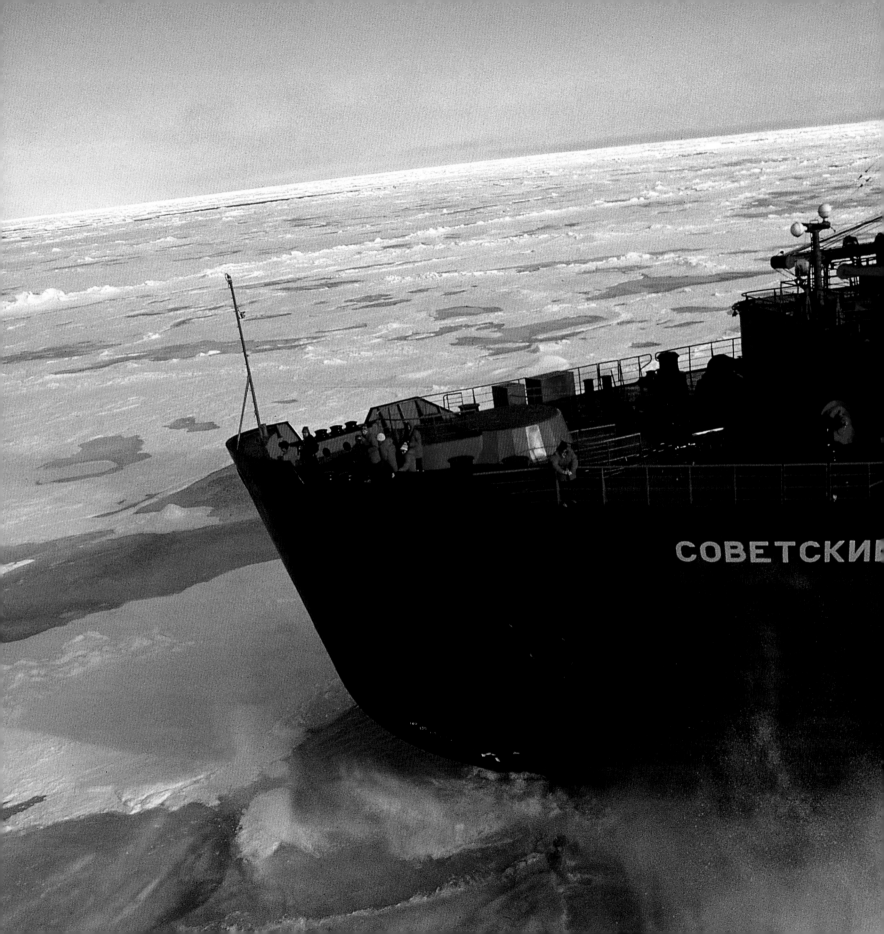

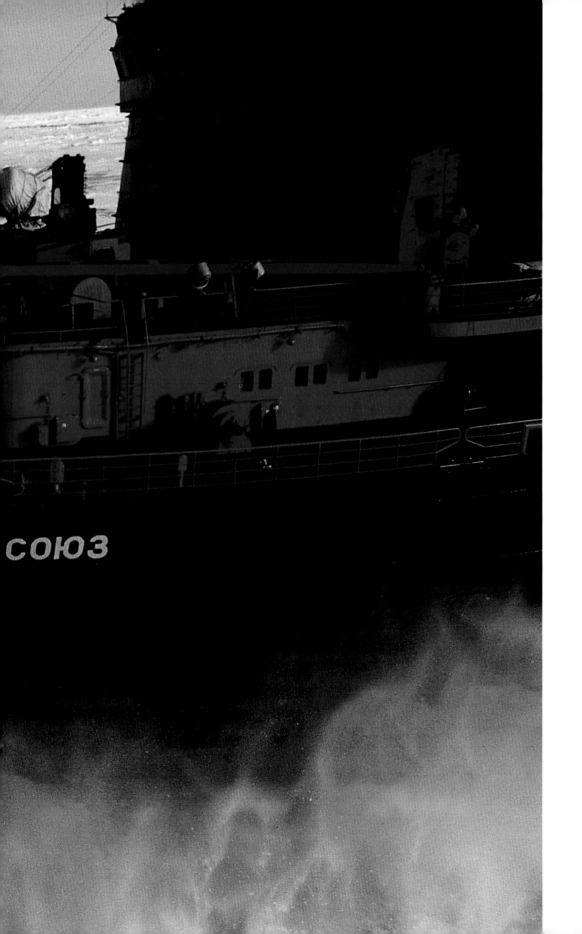

СОЮЗ

226-227 ● Siberian Sea, Russia - The icebreaker *Sovkietsky Soyuz* heading toward the North Pole.

228-229 ● Weddell Sea, Antarctic - Paradise Bay on the Antarctic peninsula.

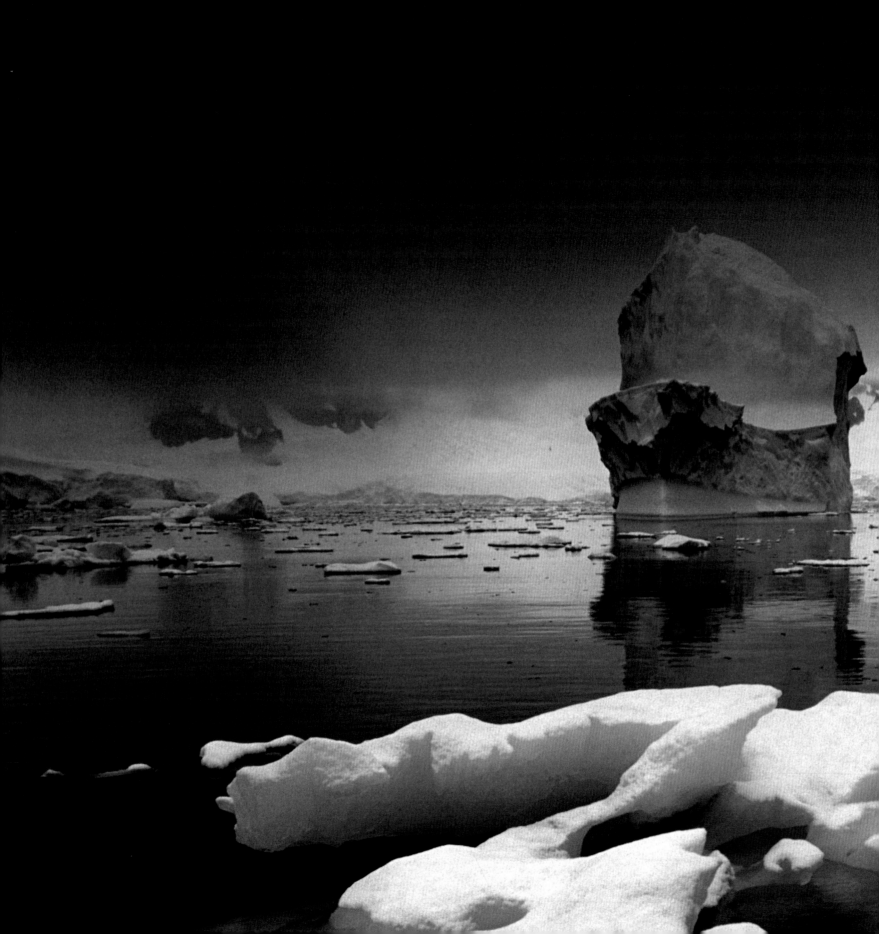

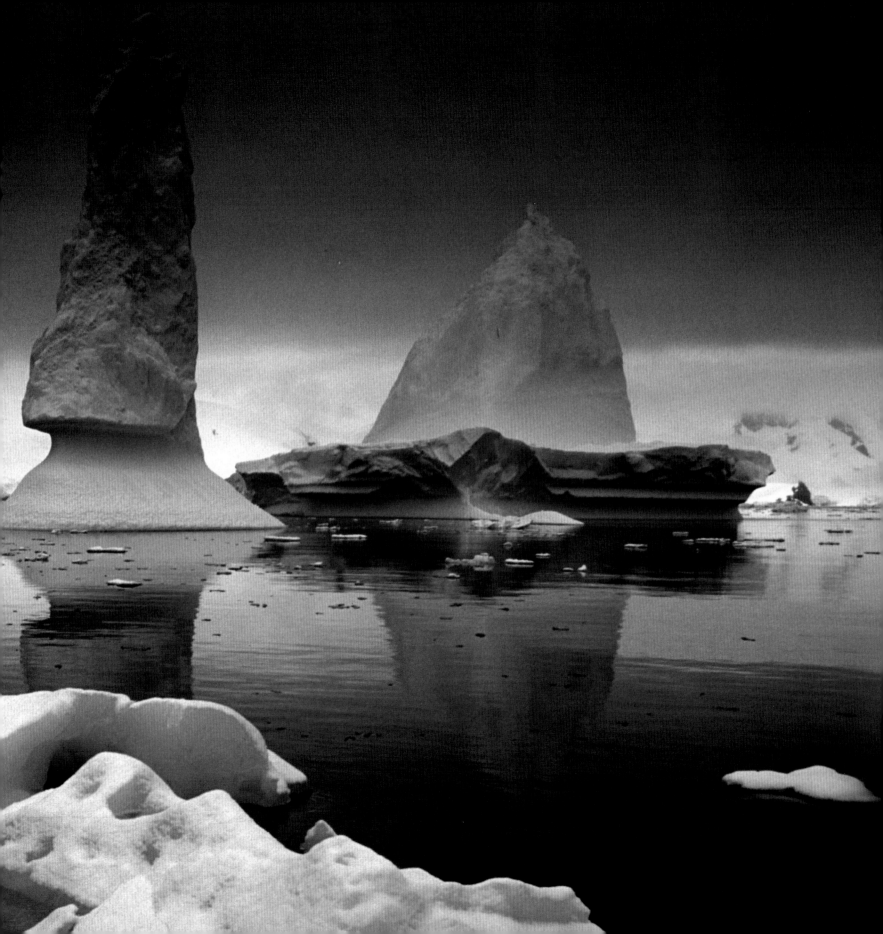

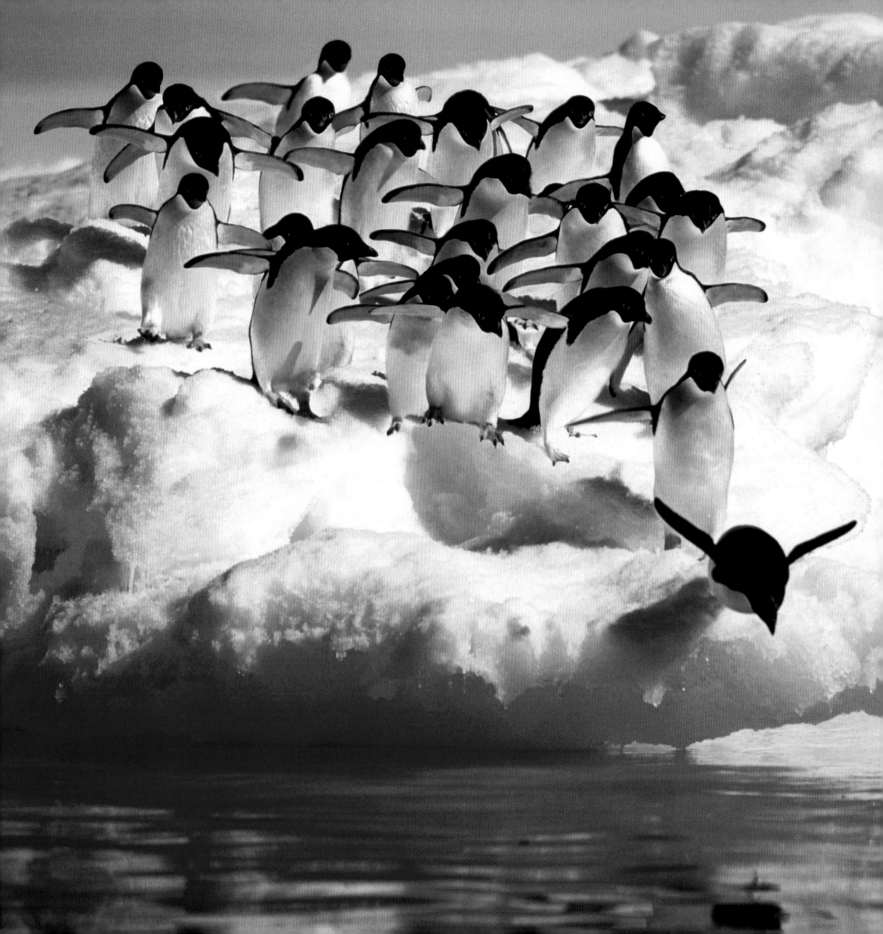

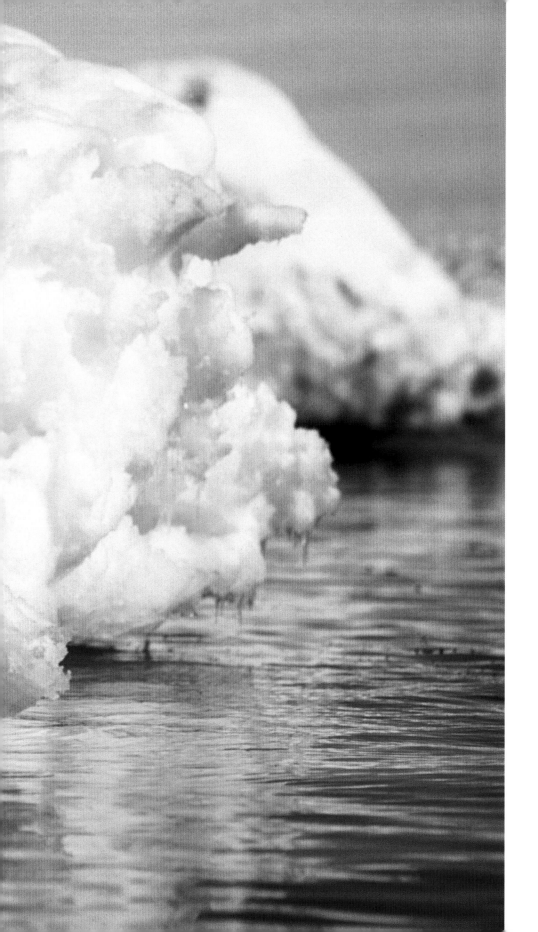

Ross Sea, Antarctic -
Colony of Adélie penguins
at Edmonson Point.

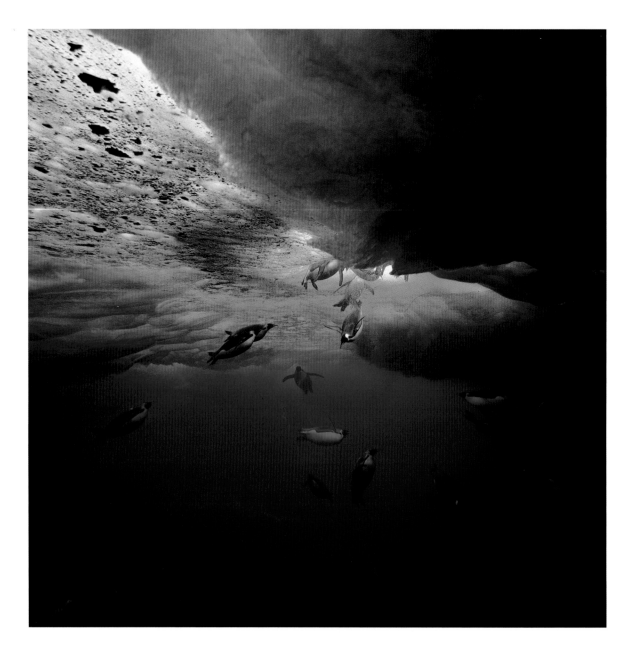

232 ● Ross Sea, Antarctic - Emperor penguins at Cape Washington.

233 ● South Atlantic, Antarctica - Weddell seal.

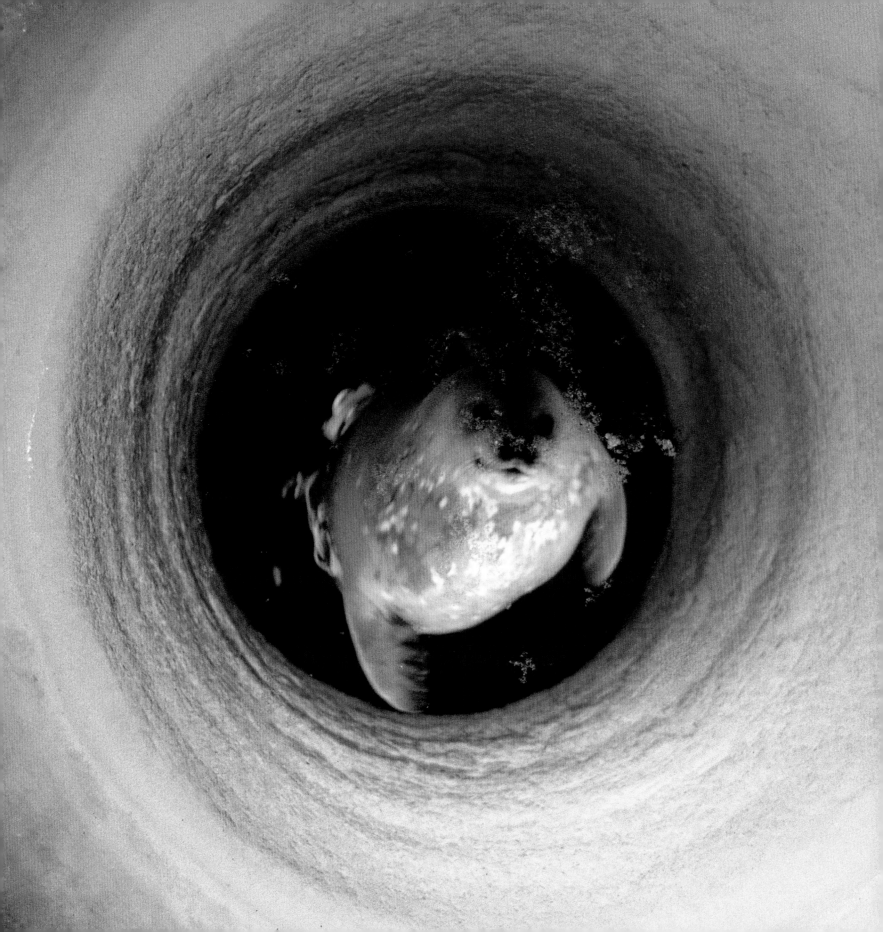

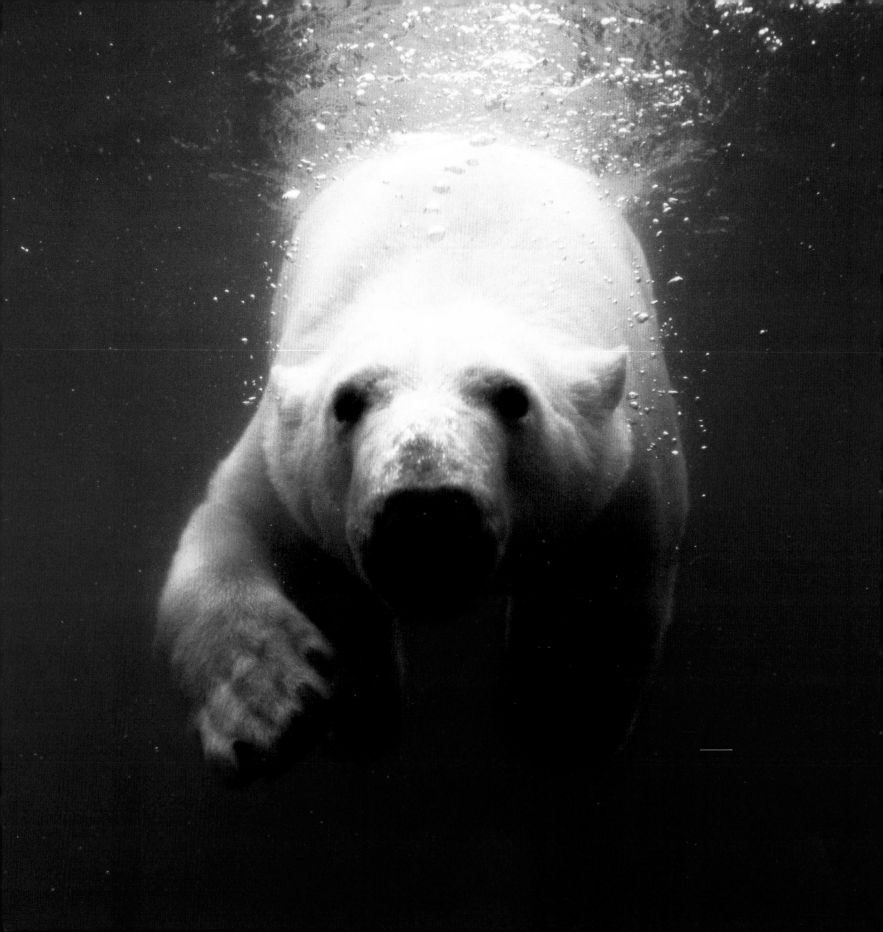

LIFE HAS THE SAME RULES EVERYWHERE - PRED-
ATORS HUNT AND THEIR PREY ATTEMPTS TO ESCAPE ITS
DESTINY. IN THE ANTARCTIC THE MOST VORACIOUS PREDA-
TOR, THE POLAR BEAR, DOES NOT SEEM AT ALL FRIGHTEN-
ING. IT LOOKS LIKE A GIANT BALL OF COTTON WOOL BUT IT
IS ABLE TO TEAR A SEAL TO PIECES IN JUST A FEW MINUTES.

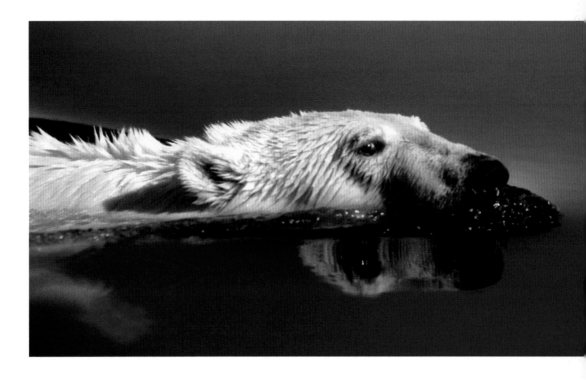

234 and 235 ● Arctic Ocean, Greenland - Polar bears in the water off Thule.

236-237 ● Arctic Ocean, Canada - Narwhal in the fiords of the Northwest Territories.

238-239 ● Weddell Sea, Antarctic - Family of Emperor penguins.

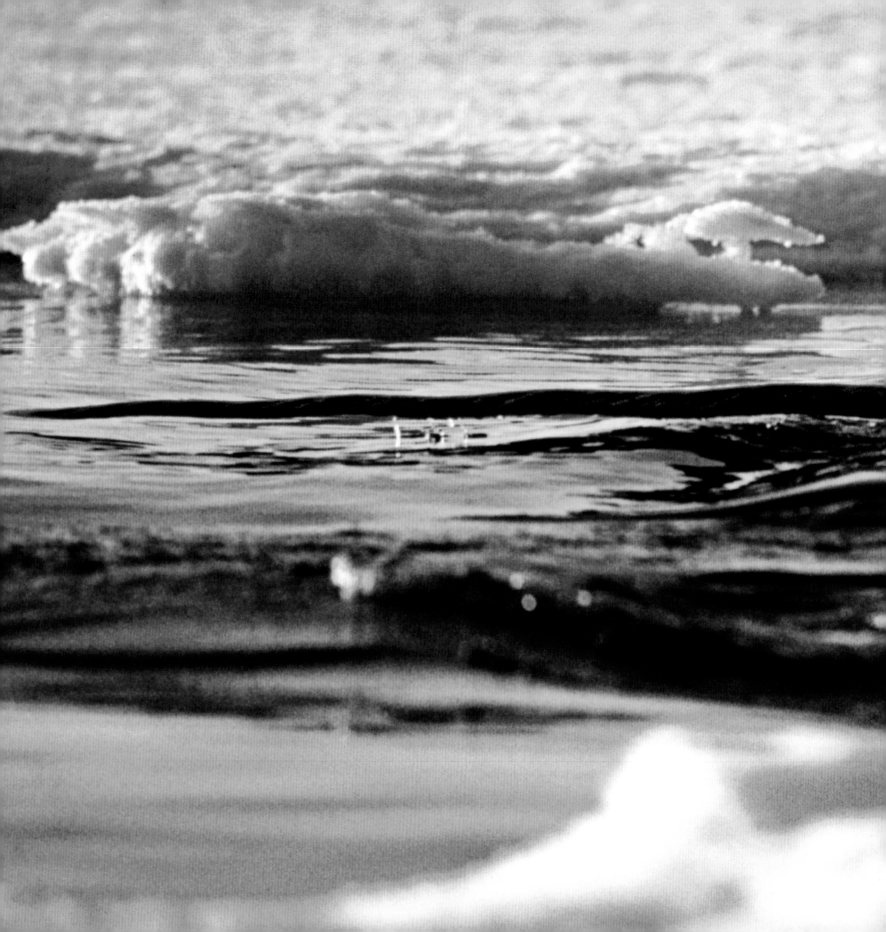

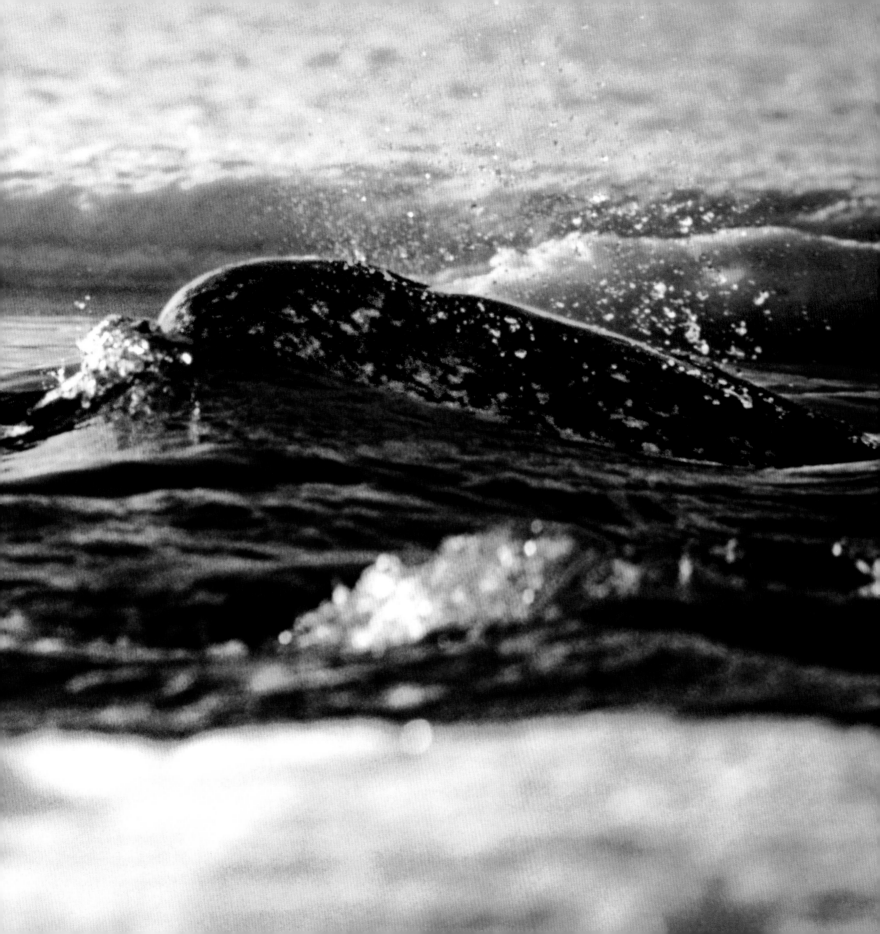

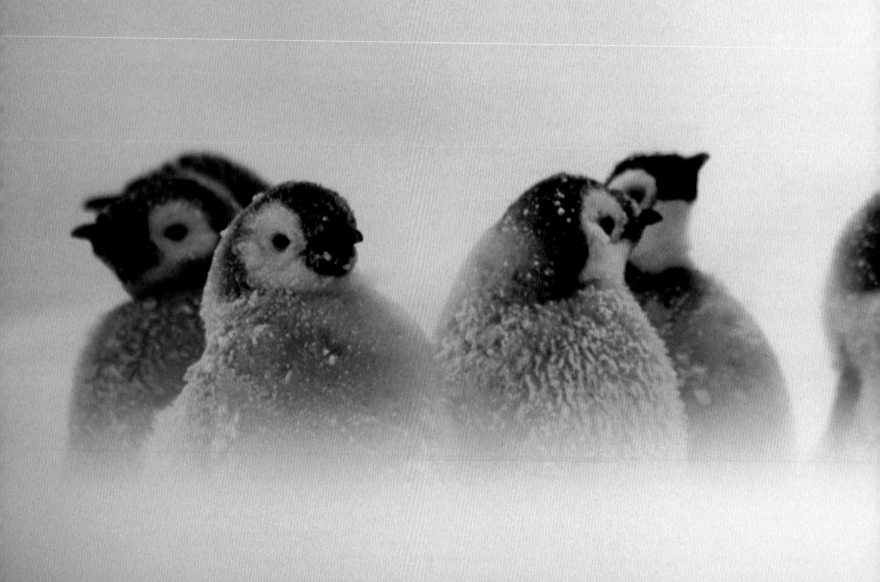

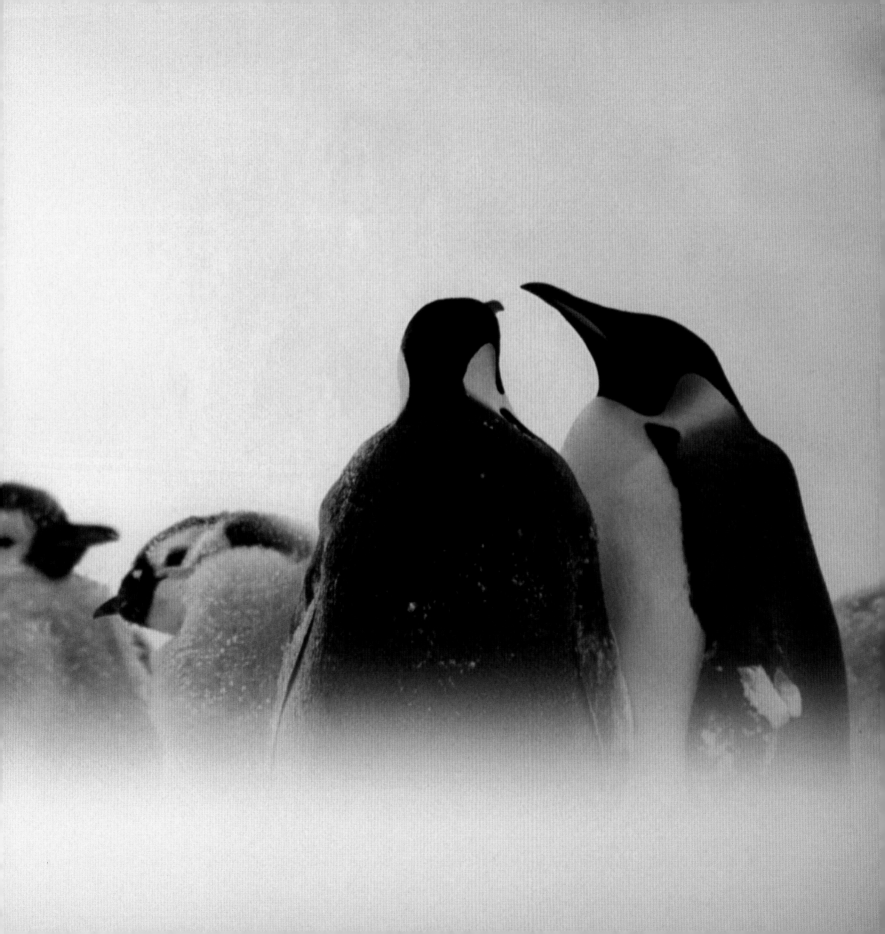

TOWNS and VILLAGES

GAETANO CAFIERO

● Mediterranean Sea, Liguria (Italy) - Camogli.

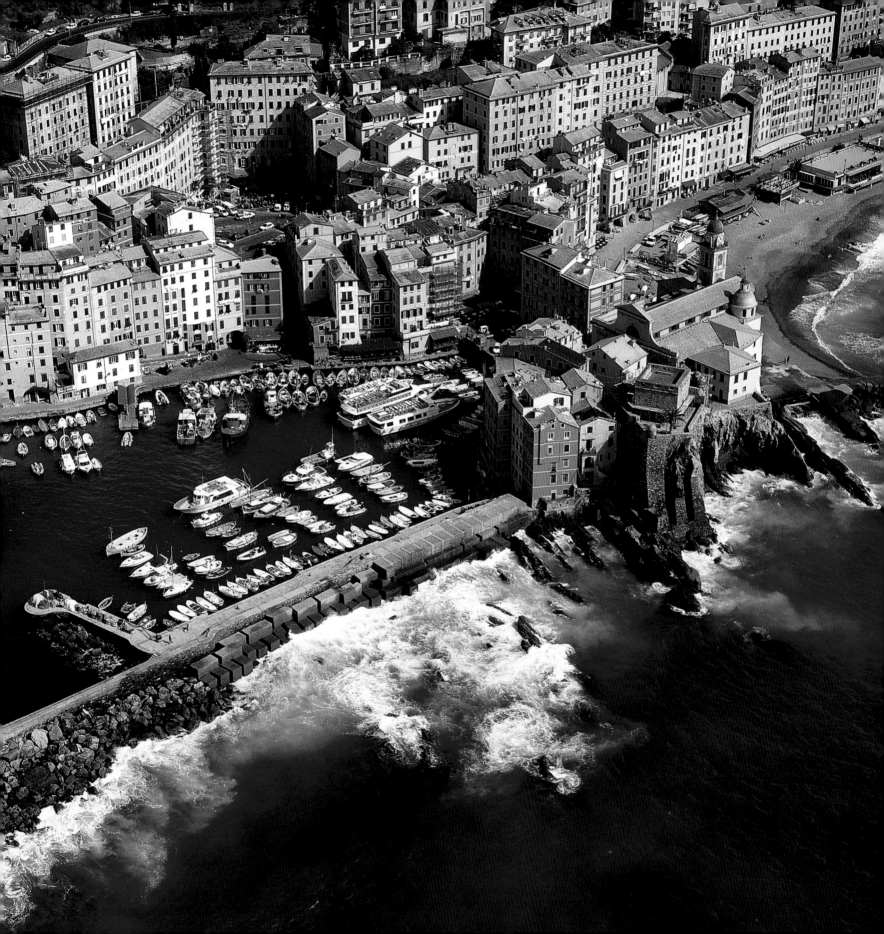

INTRODUCTION Towns and Villages

THE WIND WHISPERS UP THE NARROW, CLIMBING STREETS, BEARING THE TANG OF SEA BRINE AND THE MOISTURE THAT CLINGS TO THE SKIN. THE SHUTTERS SEEM TO BANG TO THE RHYTHM OF THE WAVES WHICH, AT THE BOTTOM OF THE VILLAGE, FOAM AND DIE ON THE WATERLINE. THE FIRST LIGHT OF DAWN GILDS THE SURFACE OF THE SEA AND SWEEPS OVER THE WALLS OF THE HOUSES, BRIGHTENING THEIR PASTEL HUES. A FEW UPTURNED BOATS ON THE BEACH, THAT MAY ONE TIME HAVE BEEN A CHEERFUL RED, BLUE OR WHITE, PATIENTLY AWAIT A NEW COAT OF PAINT NEAR THE TINY PORT. OTHER CRAFT – SMALL, FAT-BELLIED MOTORBOATS – CAN JUST BE MADE OUT IN THE DISTANCE AS THEY TIREDLY DRAG HEAVY NETS PESTERED BY

INTRODUCTION Towns and Villages

FLOCKS OF HUNGRY GULLS. THESE ARE IMAGES OF A SMALL SEASIDE

TOWN OVERLOOKING THE MEDITERRANEAN, BUT THEY COULD JUST

AS EASILY BE THOSE OF A SCANDINAVIAN VILLAGE SET DEEP AMONG

HUNDREDS OF MILES OF FJORDS, OR A PORT IN NORTH AMERICA

FROM WHICH DOZENS OF FISHING BOATS SET OUT EACH DAY OF THE

SEASON IN SEARCH OF SCHOOLS OF SWORDFISH. LIVING BESIDE THE

SEA MEANS SHARED EXPERIENCES BETWEEN THE MILLIONS OF PEO-

PLE WHO HAVE CHOSEN TO LIVE WITH THEIR FEET ON THE LAND BUT

THEIR GAZE AND IMAGINATION DIRECTED OUT OVER THE WAVES. IN

EVERY LATITUDE, WHETHER CARESSED BY THE WARM AND DAMP

BREEZES OF THE TROPICS OR BRUSHED BY RAINY NORTHERN CLIMES,

Towns and Villages
Introduction

THEY HAVE SWORN AN OATH TO THEMSELVES AND THE SEA: NOT TO

GIVE IN, AND TO RETIE EACH DAY THE KNOTS THAT THEIR CHOSEN

LOCATION SLOWLY LOOSENS. THUS, THEY PULL OUT THE WEEDS THAT

GROW BENEATH THEIR ROOFS, REPAINT THEIR HOUSES, SCRAPE THE

SALT OFF OF THE WINDOWS, AND HEAL THE WOUNDS THAT THE SEA

AND ITS CLIMATE CAUSE TO THE SKIN AND PLANKING OF THE BOATS.

THESE ROUTINES SUSTAIN THE UNDERLYING RHYTHM OF LIFE IN EVERY

SEASIDE TOWN: BEHIND THE SMELL OF MEDITERRANEAN HERBS AND

THE PASTEL TINTS OF THE FISHERMEN'S HOUSES, PULSE THE HEARTS

OF THE MEN IN WHOSE VEINS SALT WATER FLOWS.

● Aegean Sea, Cyclades (Greece) - Mykonos.

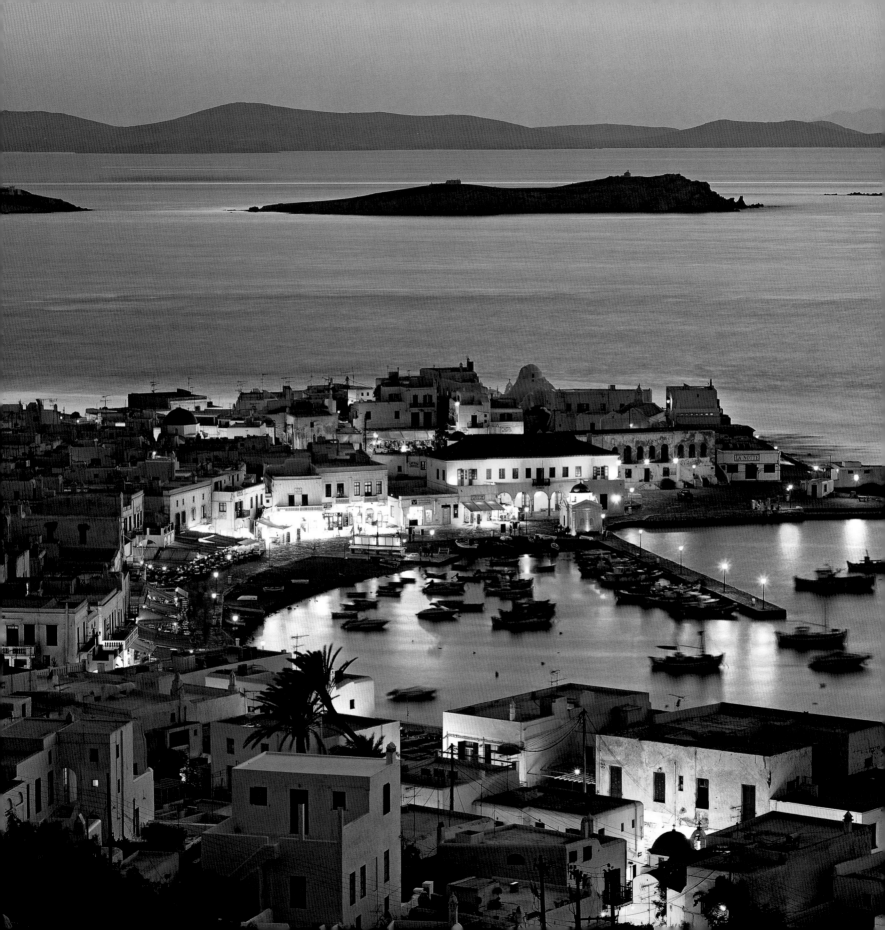

Mediterranean Sea, Liguria (Italy) - San Rocco.

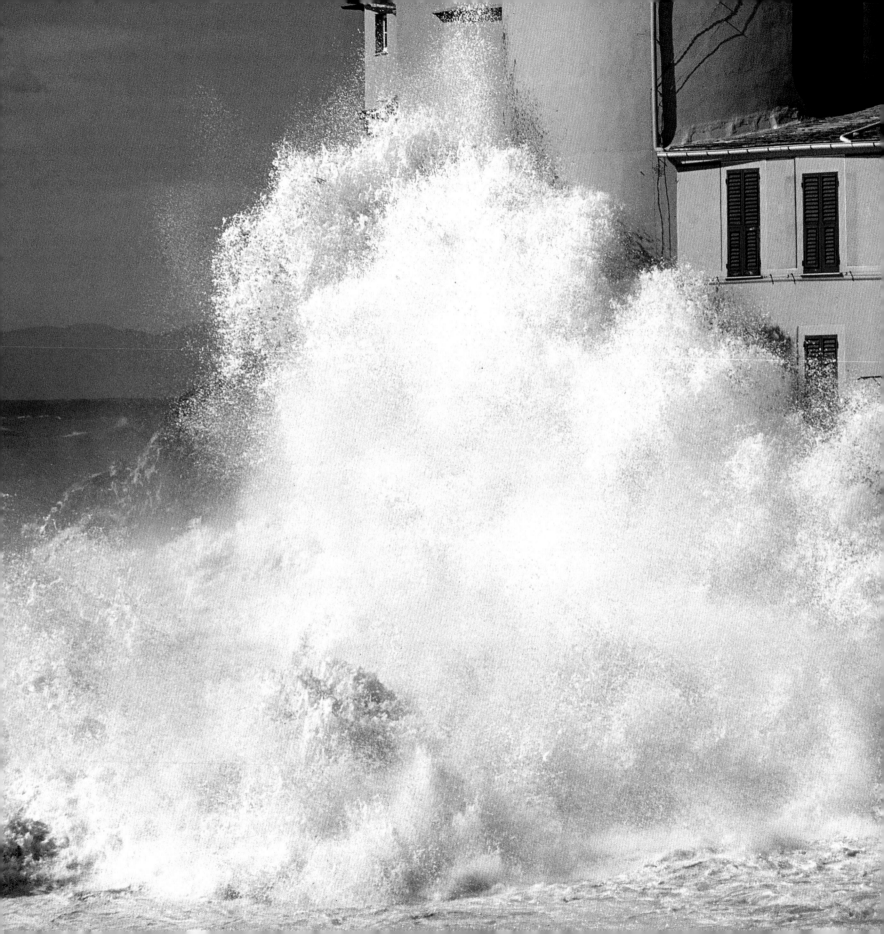

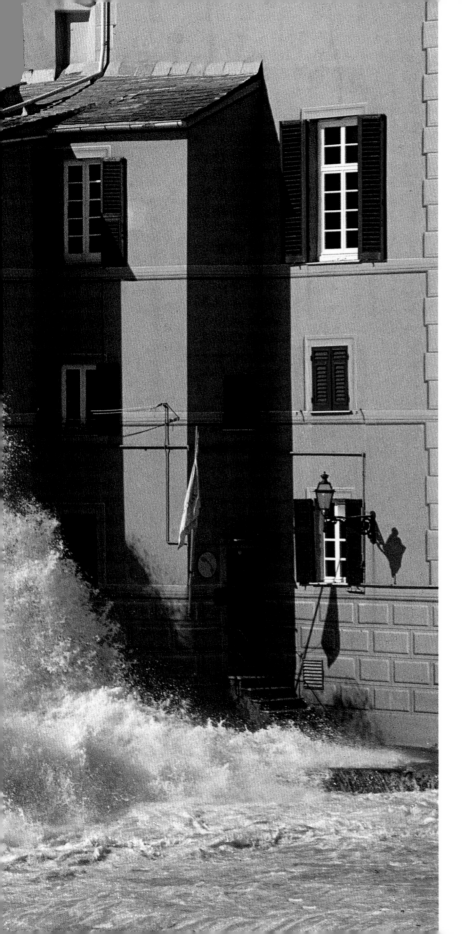

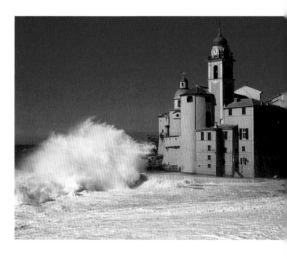

248-249 and 249 ● Mediterranean Sea, Liguria (Italy) - Camogli.

250-251 ● Mediterranean Sea, Liguria (Italy) - Portovenere.

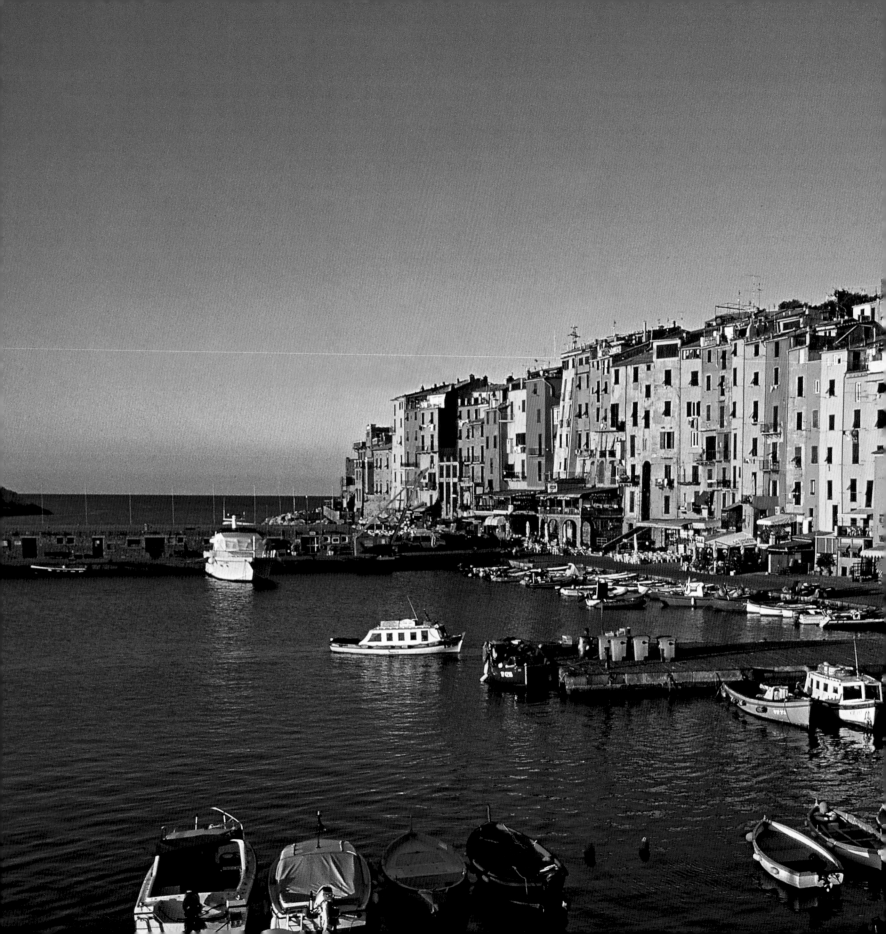

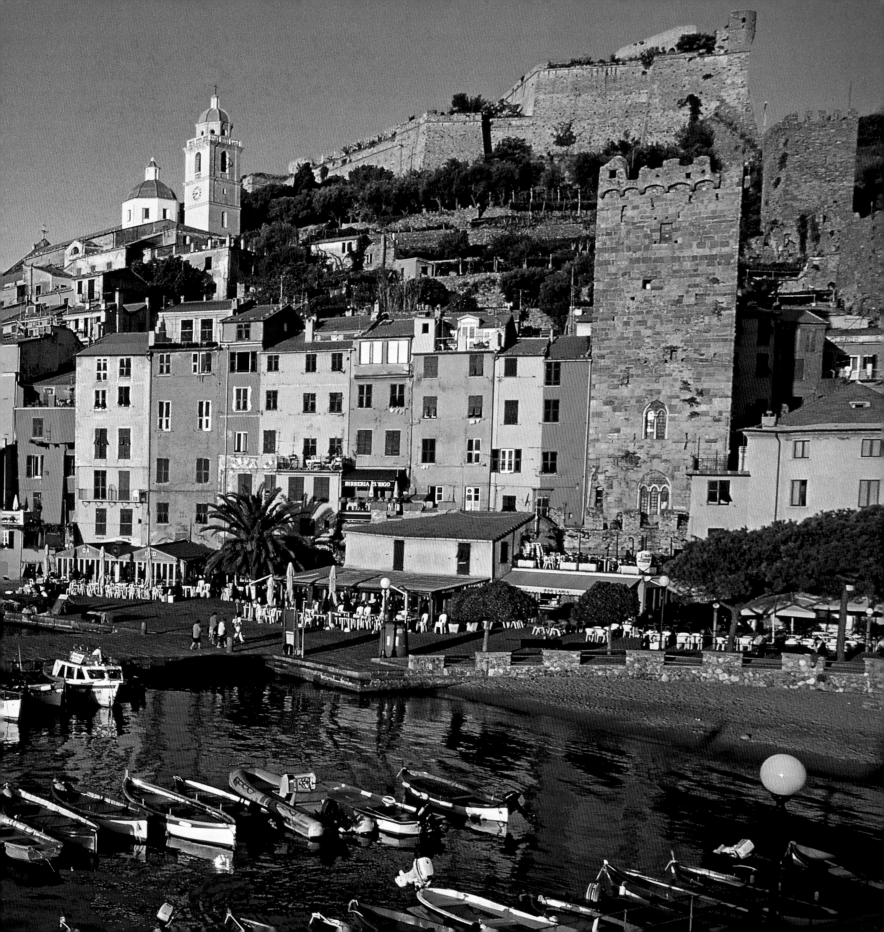

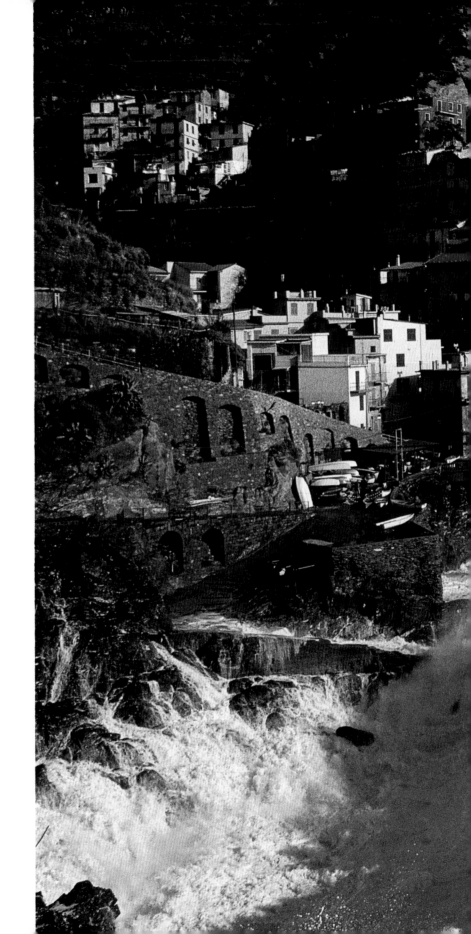

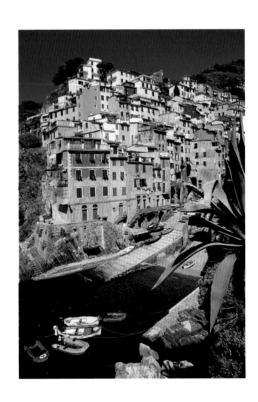

252 ● Mediterranean Sea, Liguria (Italy) -
Riomaggiore.

252-253 ● Mediterranean Sea, Liguria
(Italy) - Manarola.

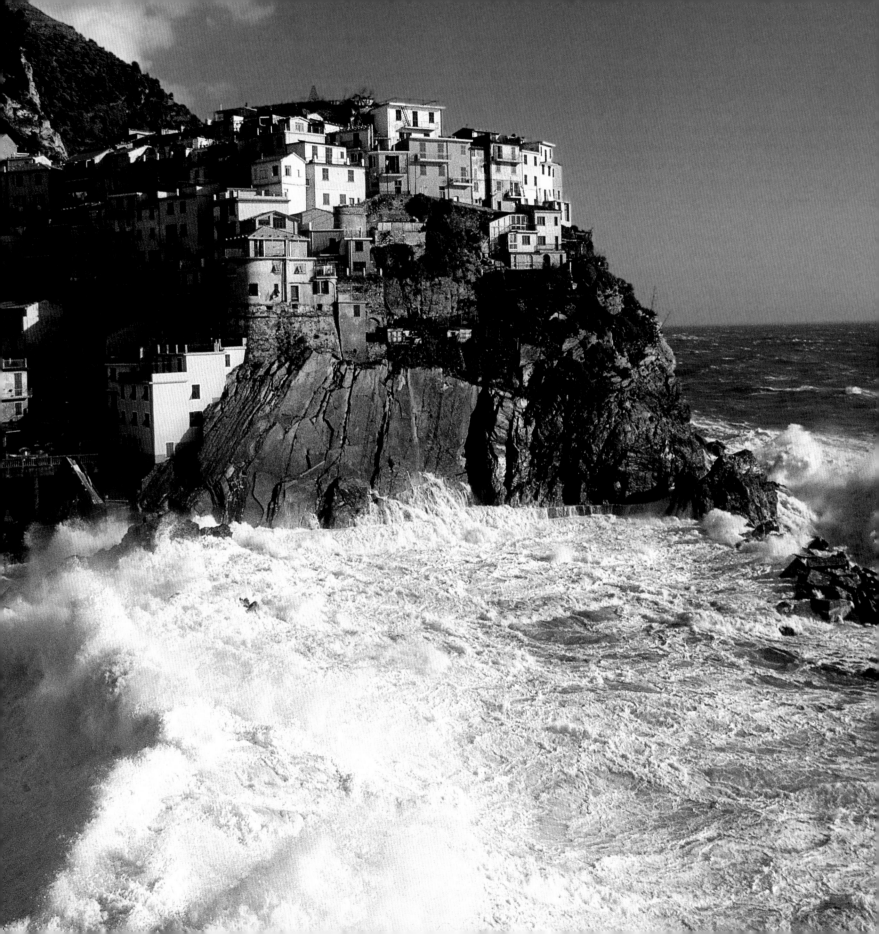

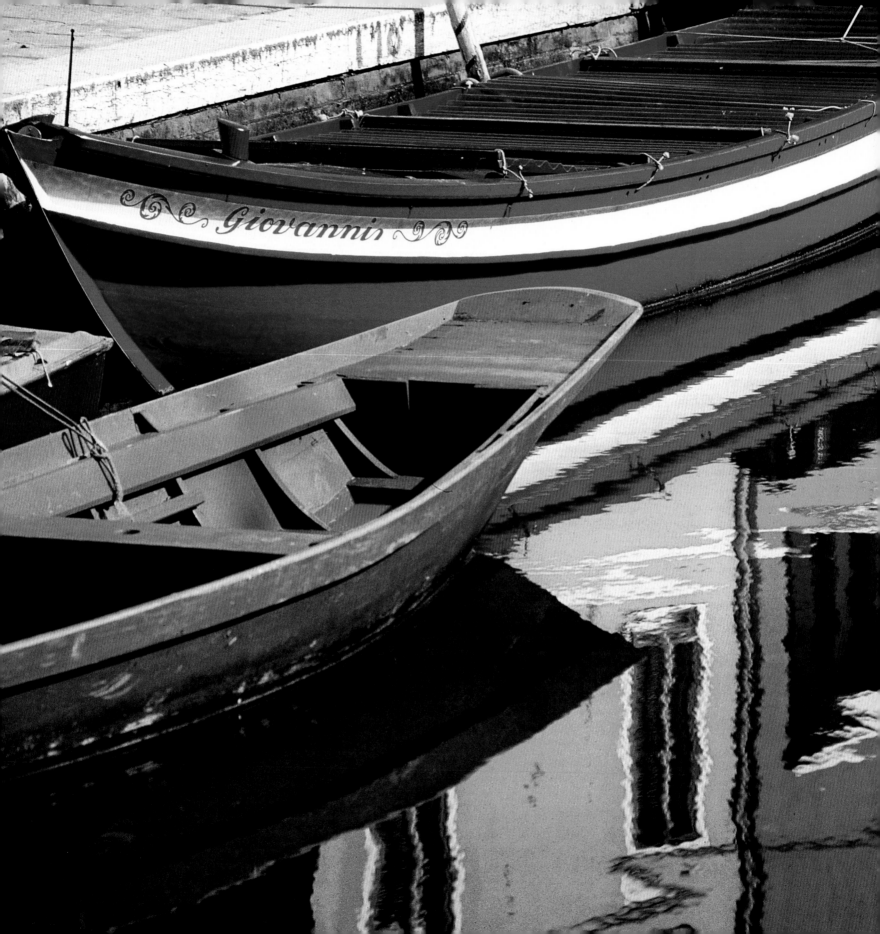

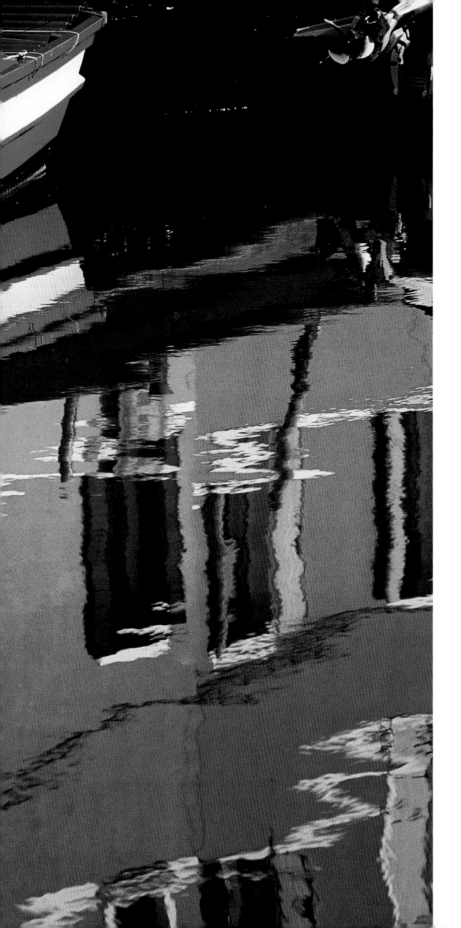

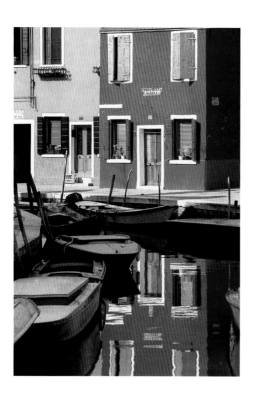

Adriatic Sea, Venetian Lagoon (Italy) - Burano.

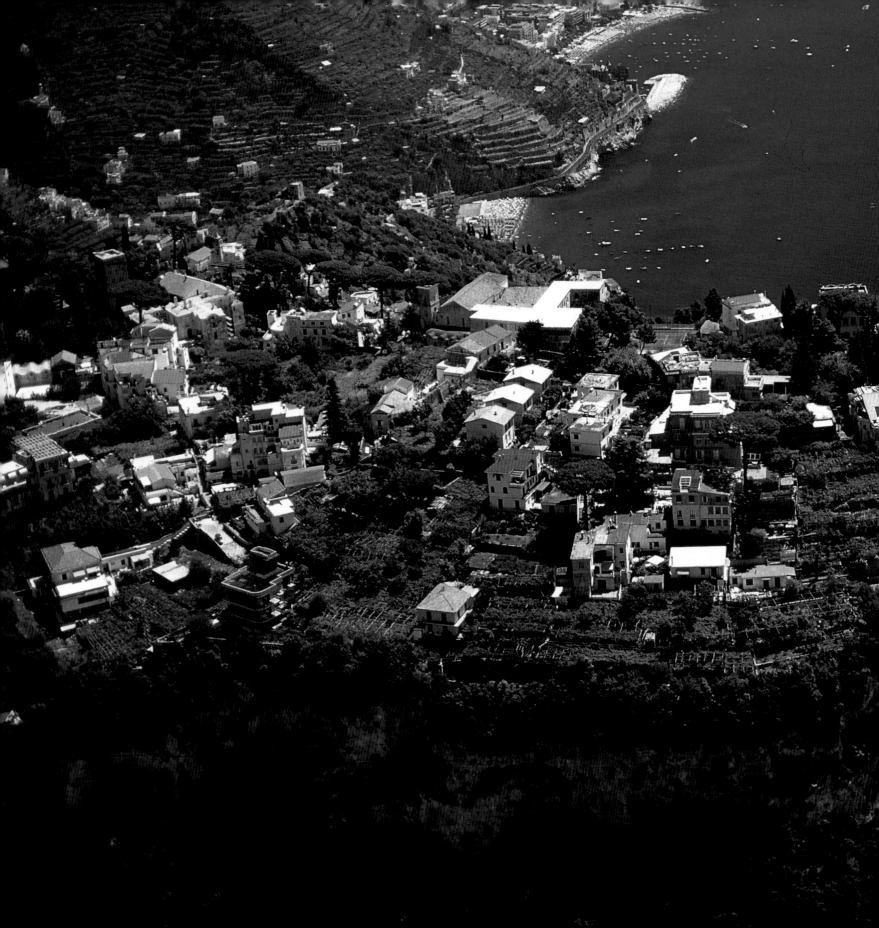

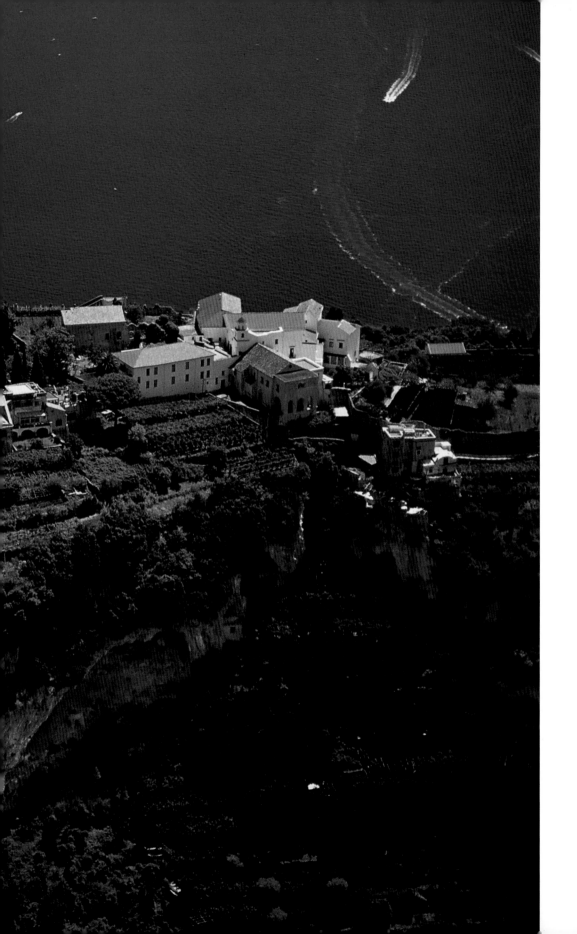

The jewels of the Amalfi coast

● Tyrrhenian Sea, Gulf of Salerno, Campania (Italy) – Ravello.

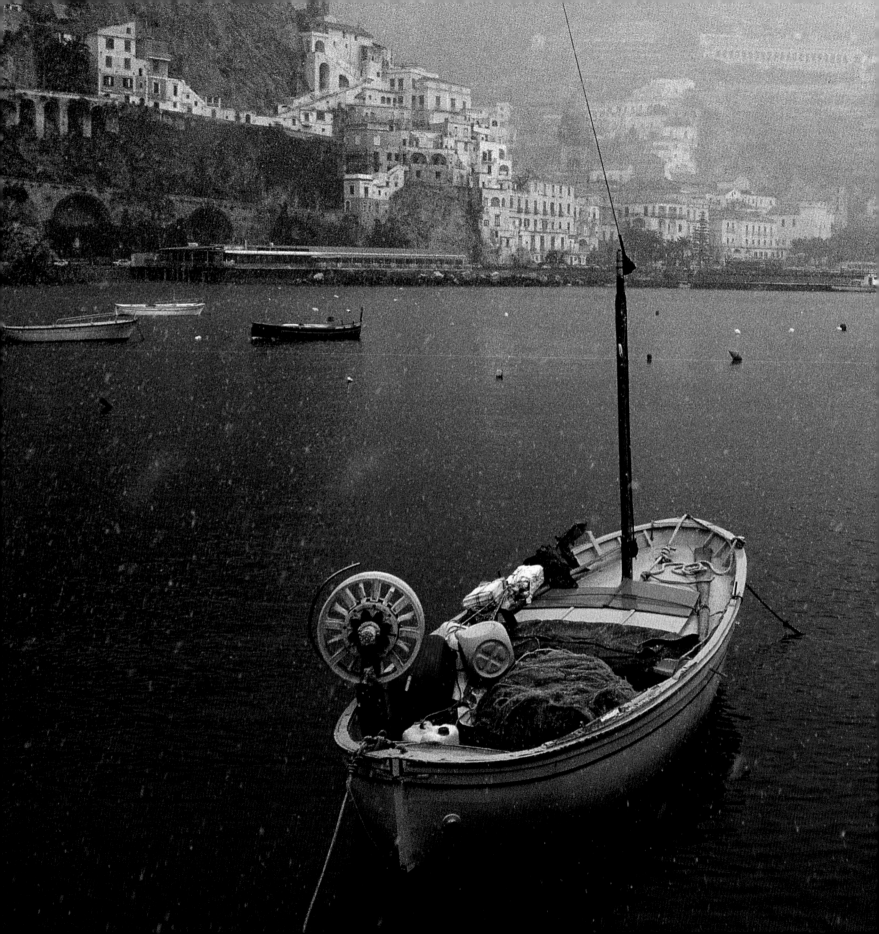

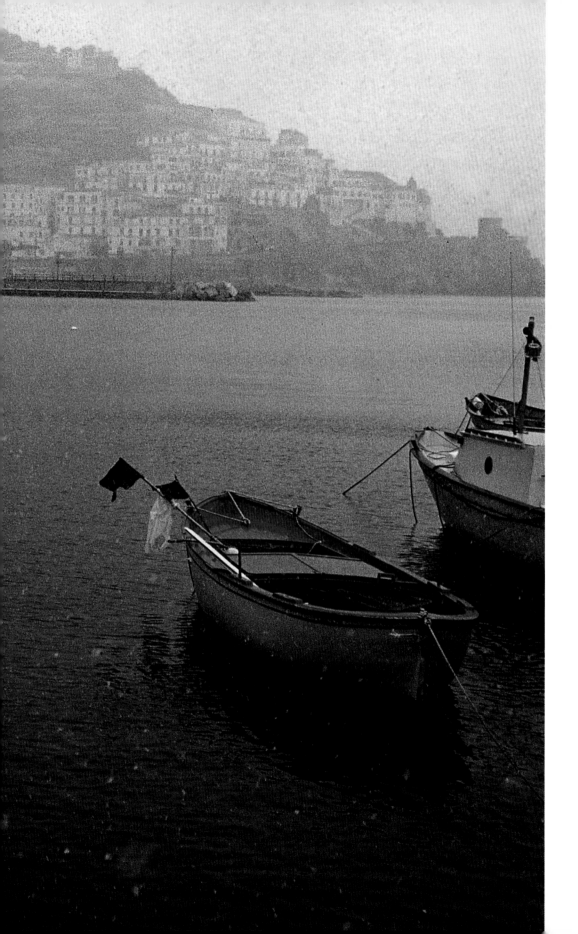

258-259 ● Tyrrhenian Sea, Gulf of Salerno, Campania (Italy) - Amalfi coast.

260-261 ● Tyrrhenian Sea, Gulf of Naples, Campania (Italy) - Ischia.

262-263 ● Tyrrhenian Sea, Gulf of Naples, Campania (Italy) - Procida, La Corricella.

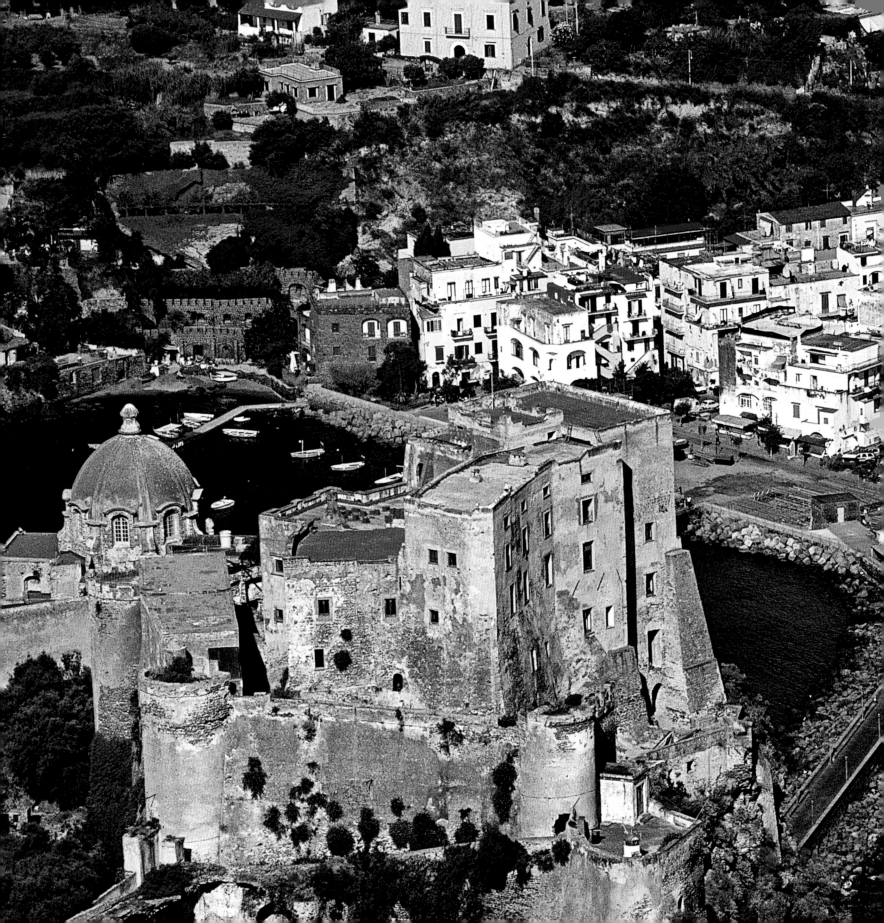

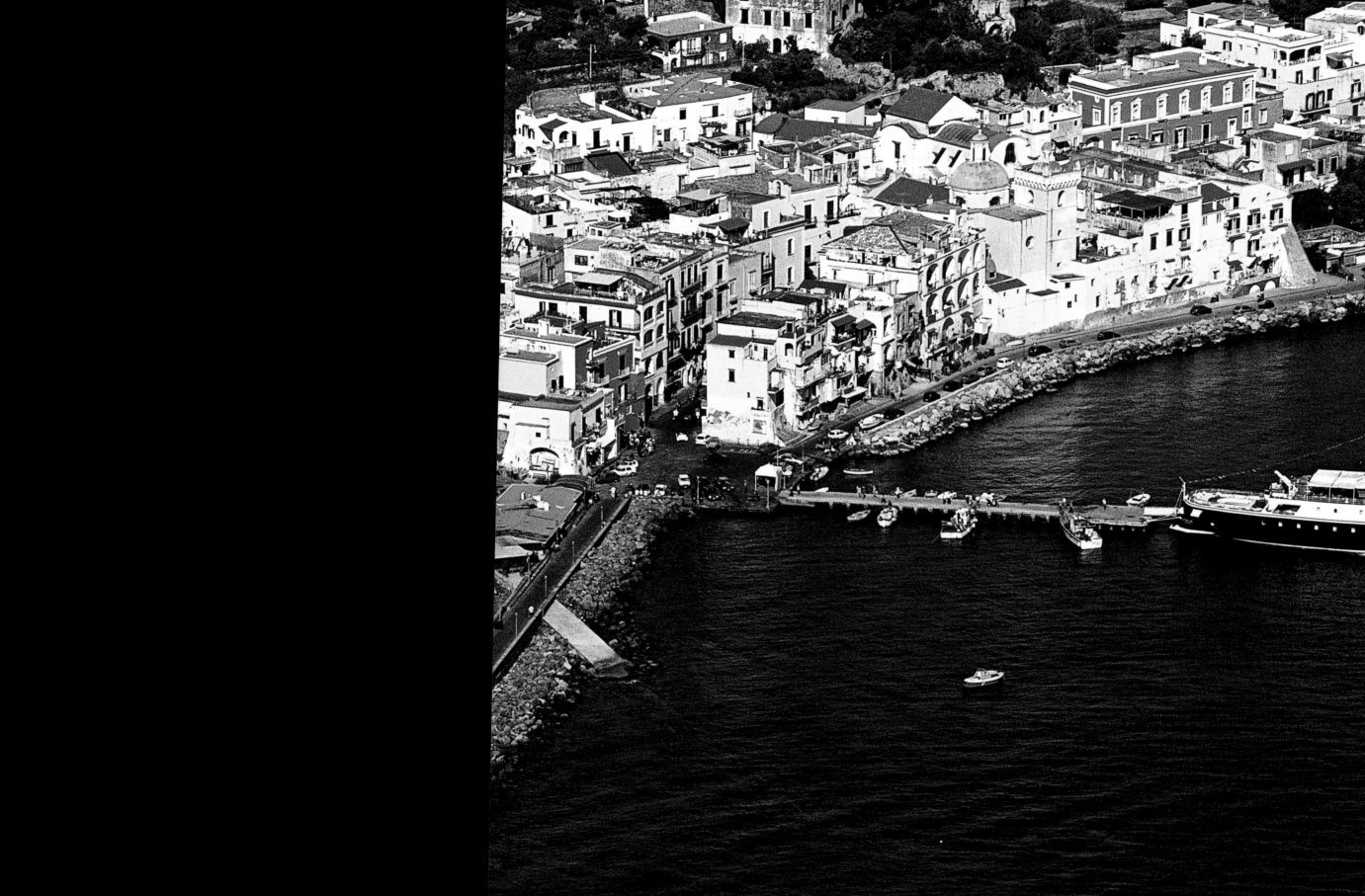

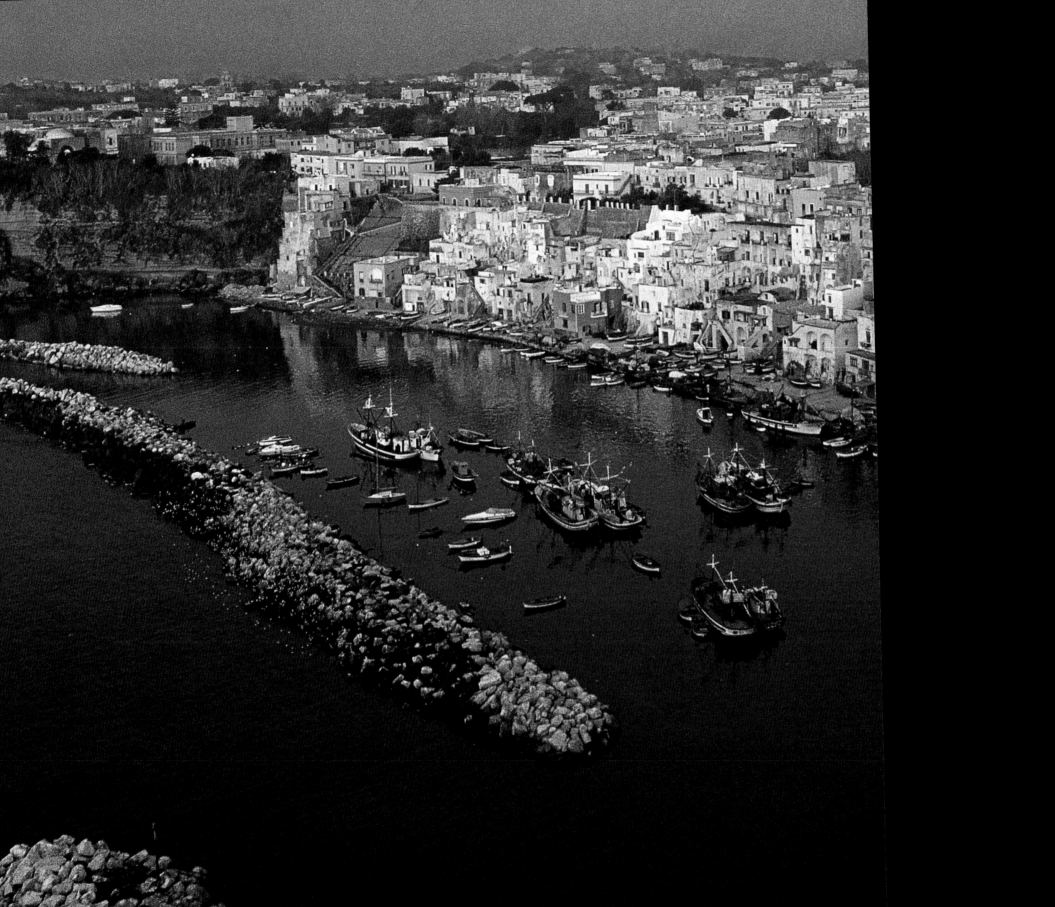

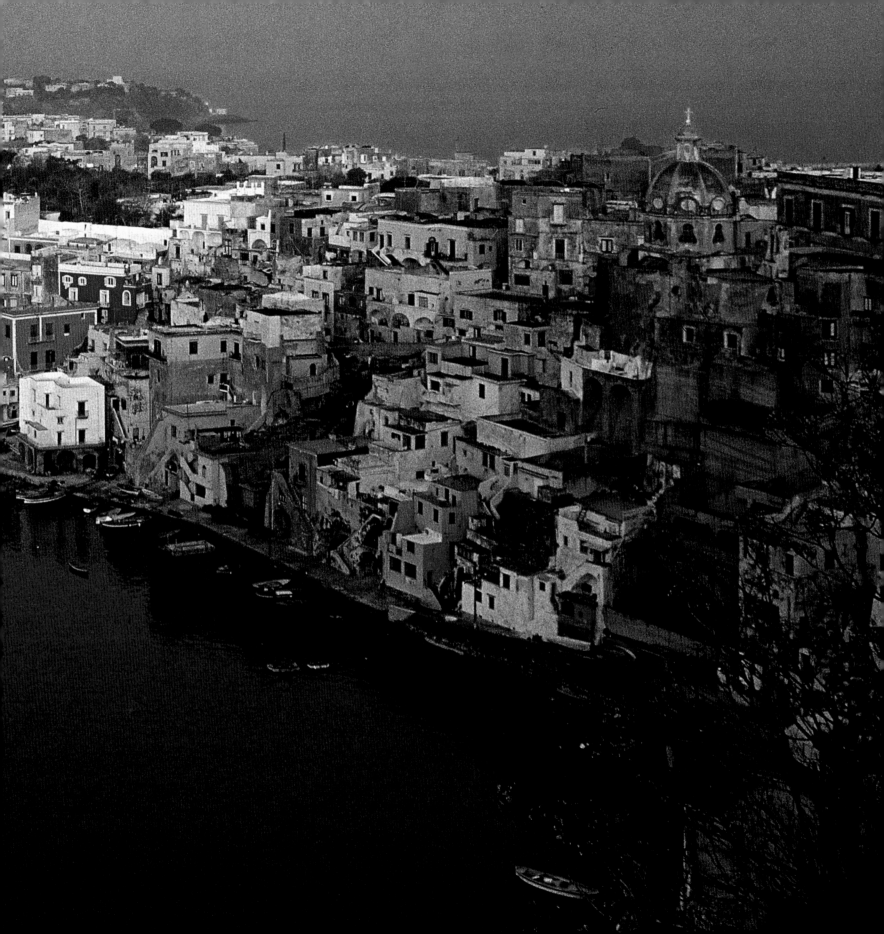

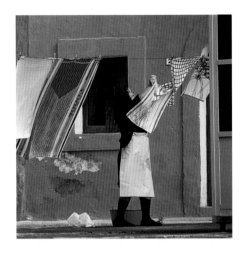 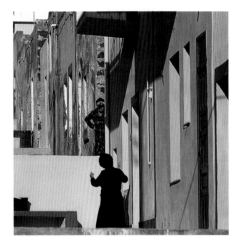 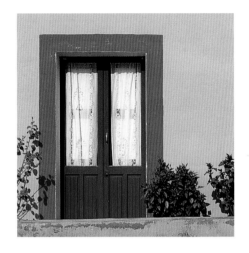

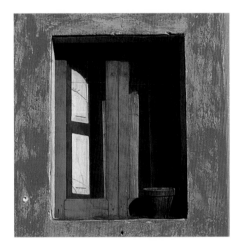 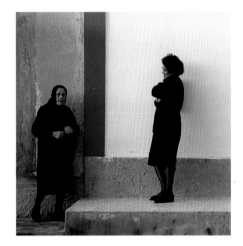

A step away
from Africa

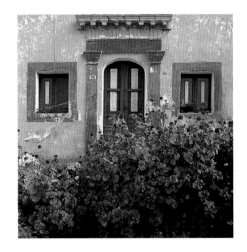

● Mediterranean Sea, Pelagian Islands,
Sicily (Italy) - Linosa.

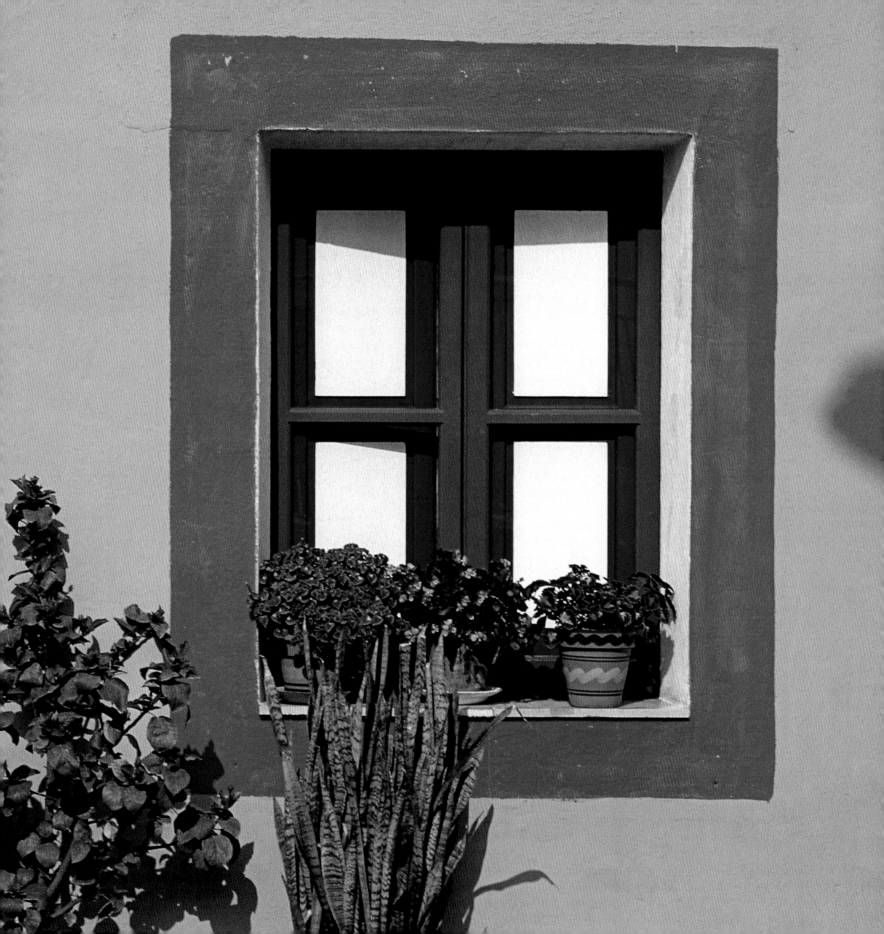

" THE FEW HOUSES THAT STOOD LINED UP AGAINST THE PLATEAU, SO CLOSE TO THE SEA, WERE SHUT OFF FROM THE VIEW OF THE VILLAGE, SET OUT IN A HALF-RING IN THE OTHER BAY OF THE BEACH. AND THERE WAS A GREAT PEACE THERE, A PEACE ALMOST STRUCK DUMB BY THE BOUNDLESS SPECTACLE OF THE SEA. "

from THE OLD GOD *by Luigi Pirandello*

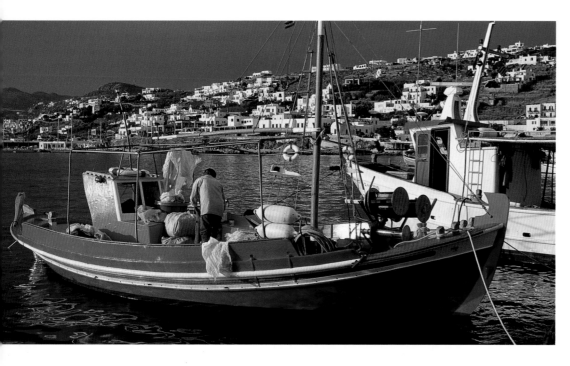

266 ● Aegean Sea, Cyclades (Greece) - Mykonos.

267 ● Aegean Sea, Dodecanese (Greece) - Astipalea, villages of Skala and Chara.

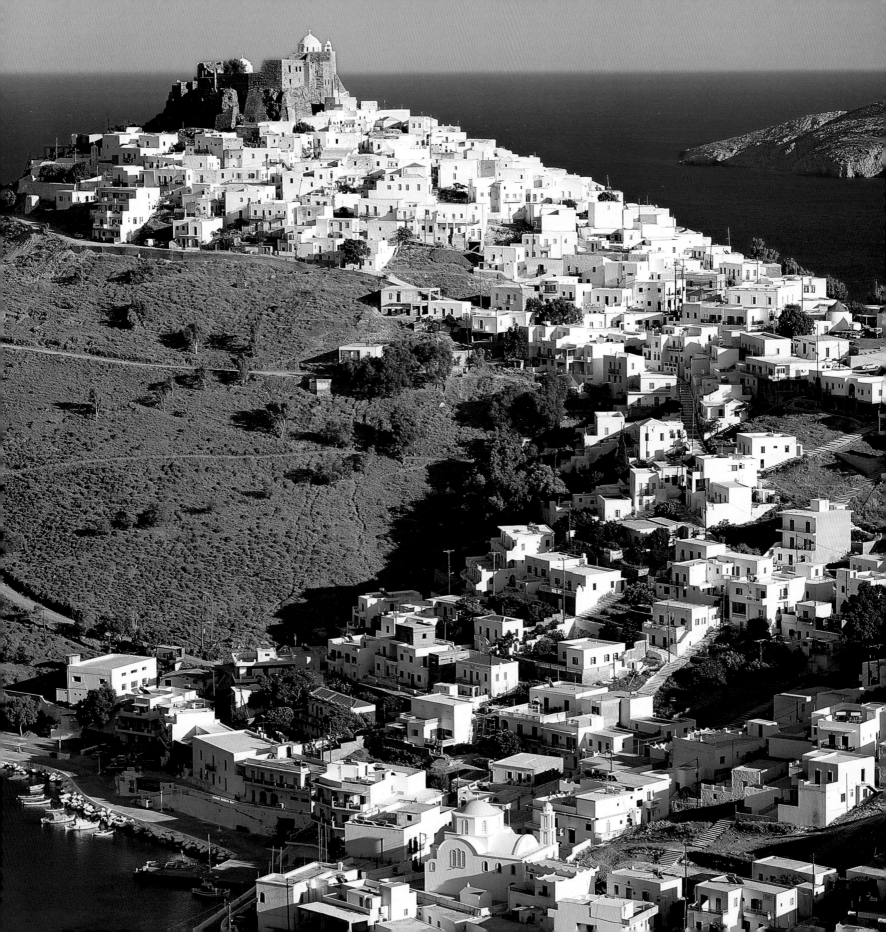

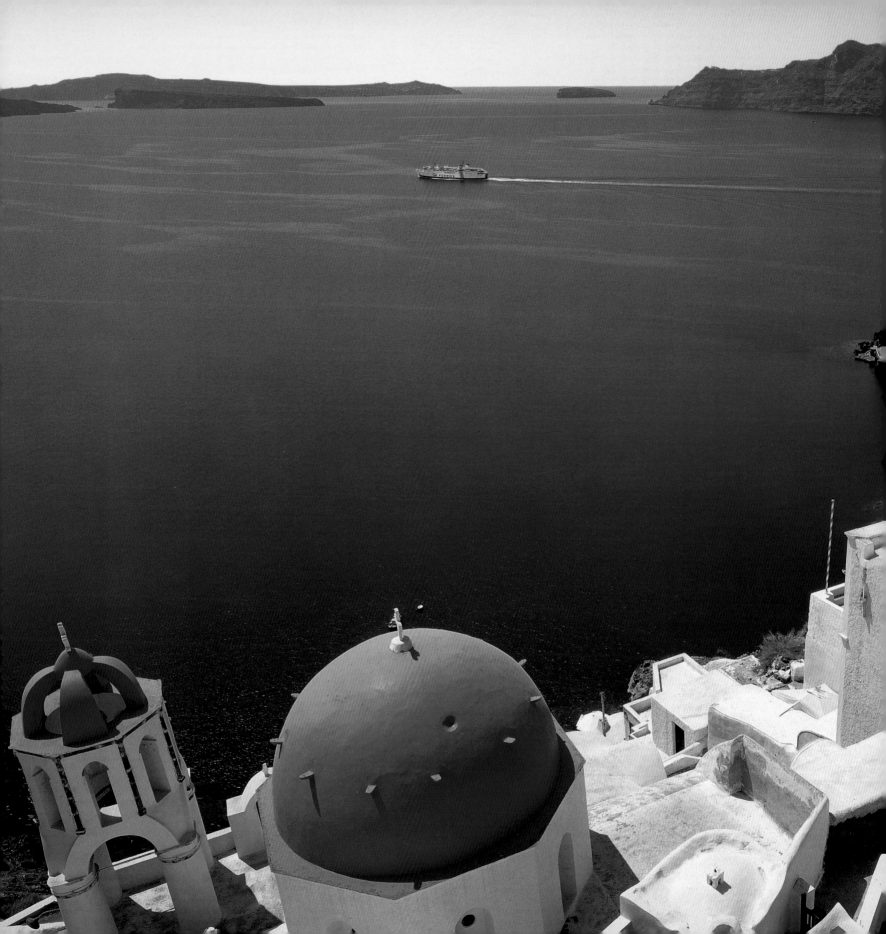

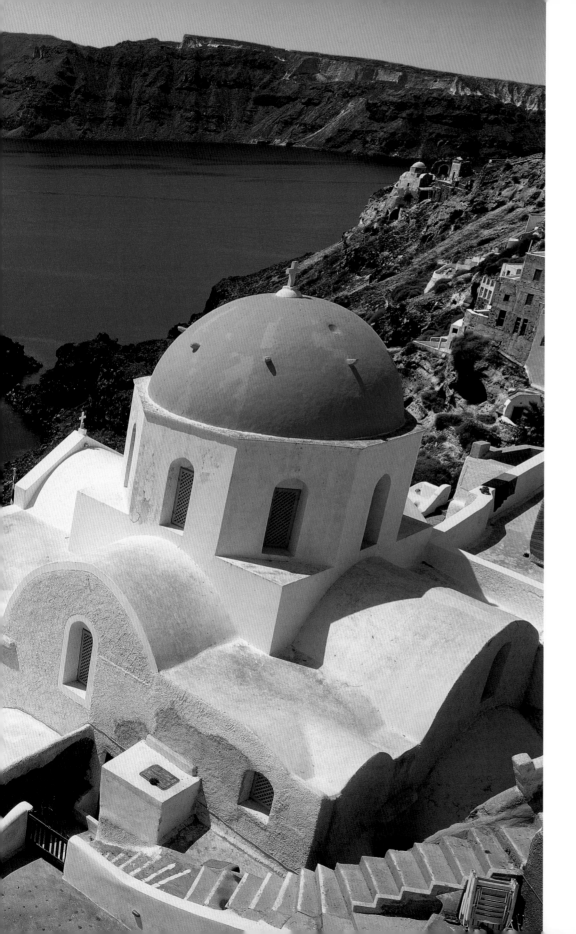

The white
and the blue

- Aegean Sea, Cyclades
  (Greece) - Santorini.

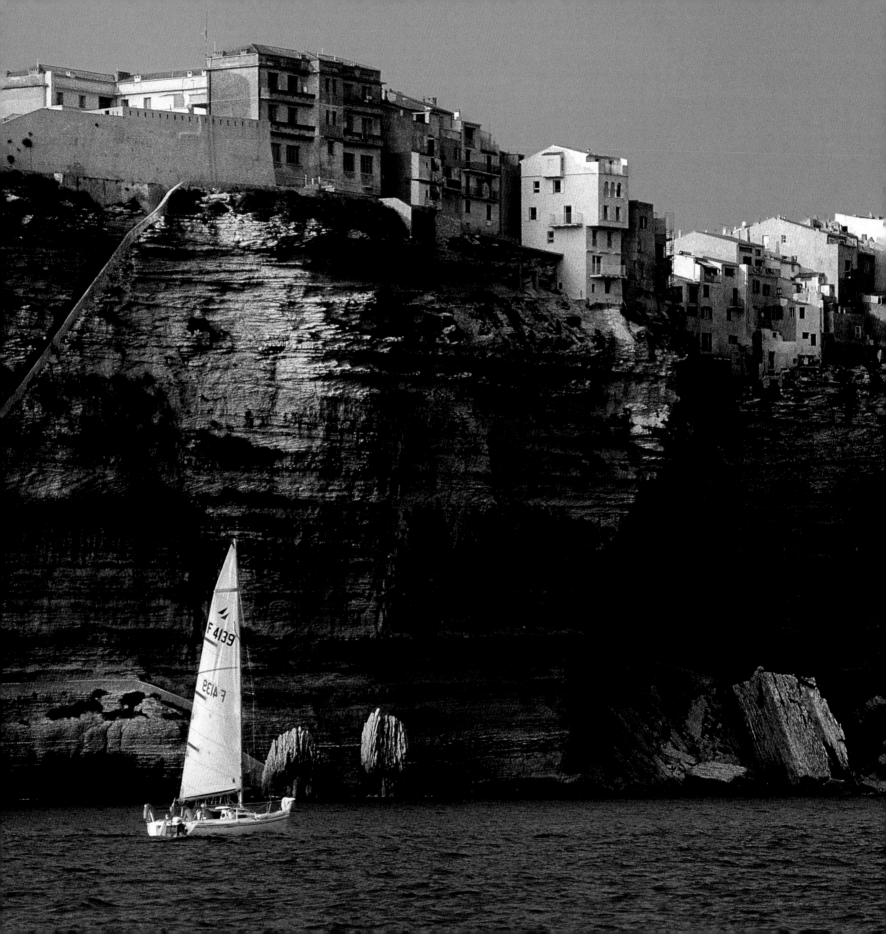

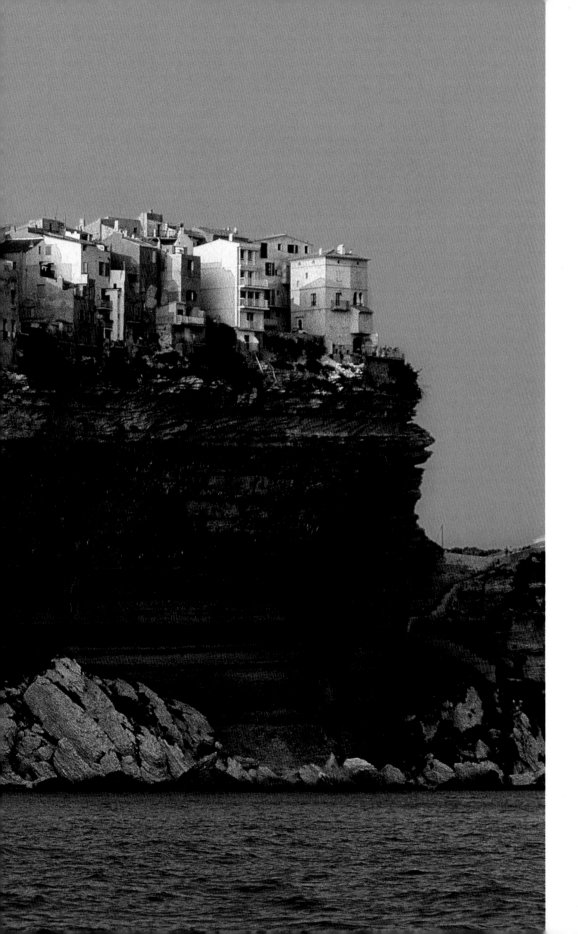

Mediterranean Sea,
Corsica (France) -
Bonifacio.

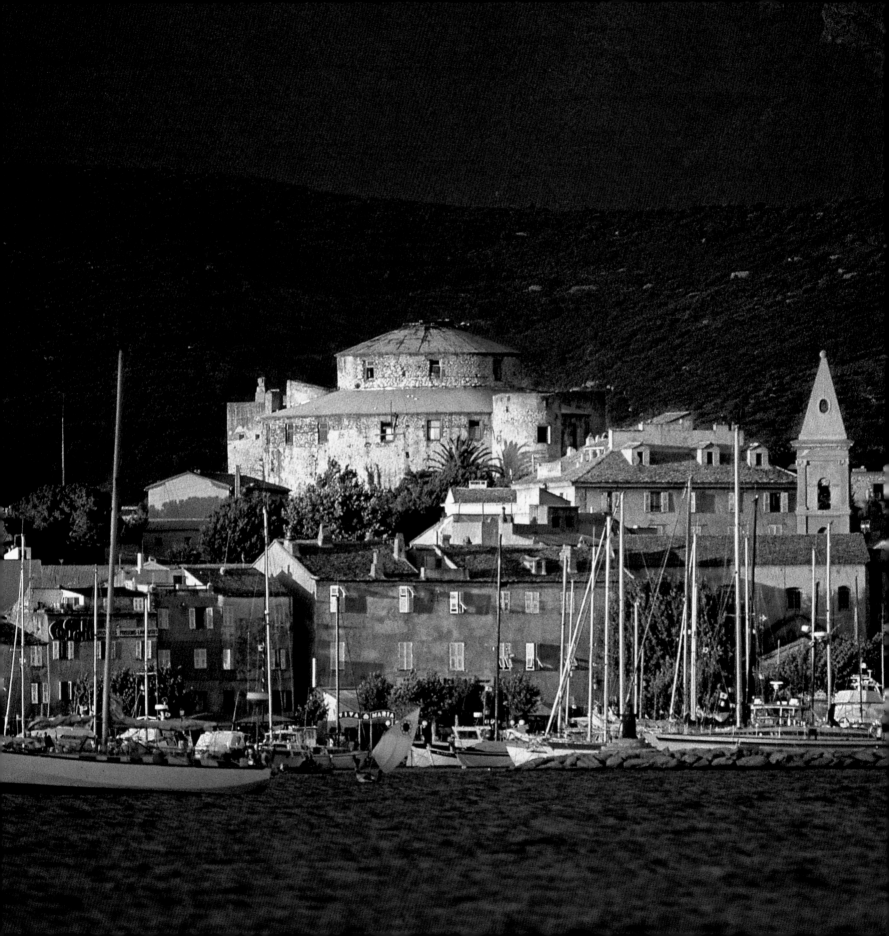

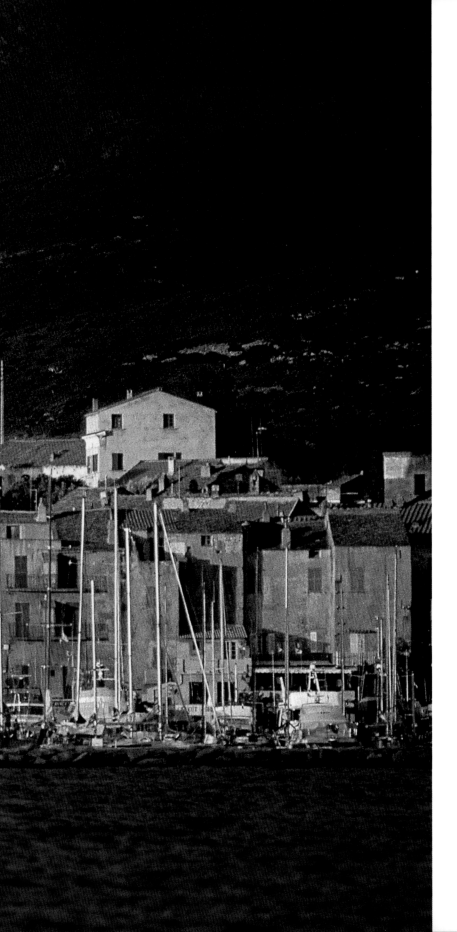

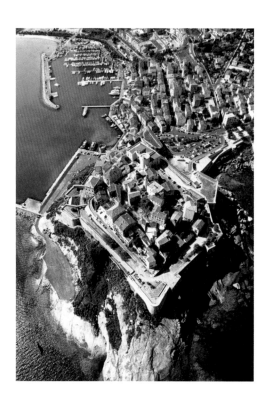

272-273 ● Mediterranean Sea, Corsica
(France) - Saint Florent.

273 ● Mediterranean Sea, Corsica
(France) - Calvi.

274-275 ● Mediterranean Sea, Côte
d'Azur (France) - Saint Tropez.

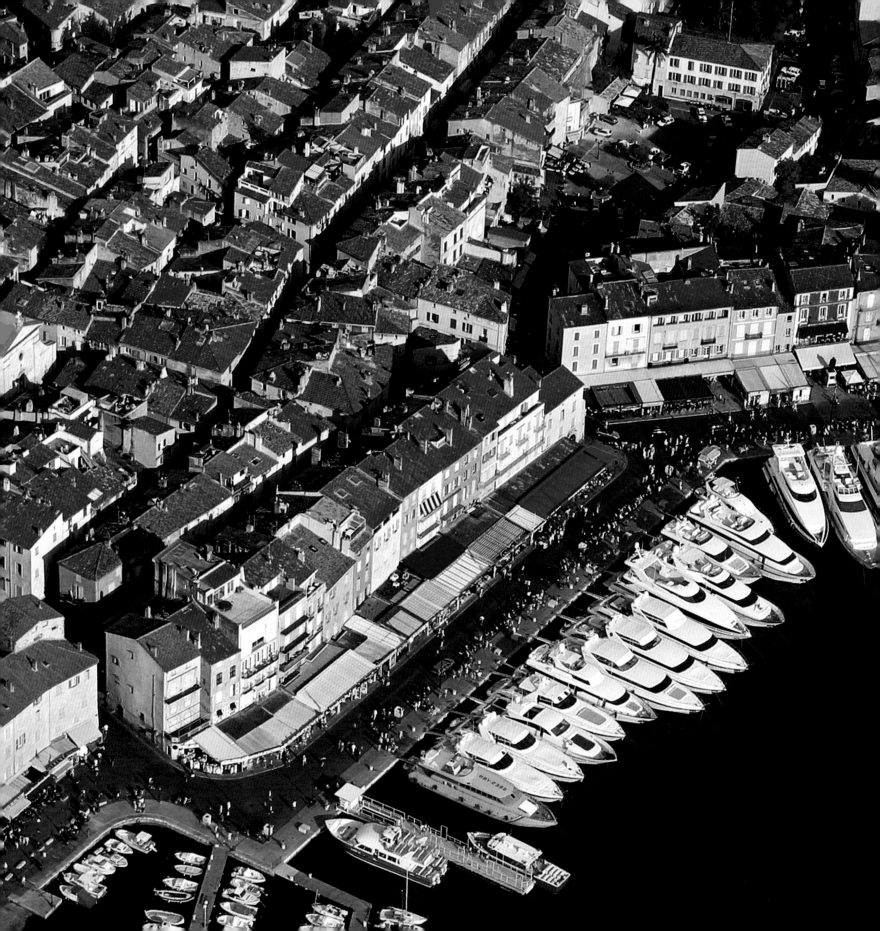

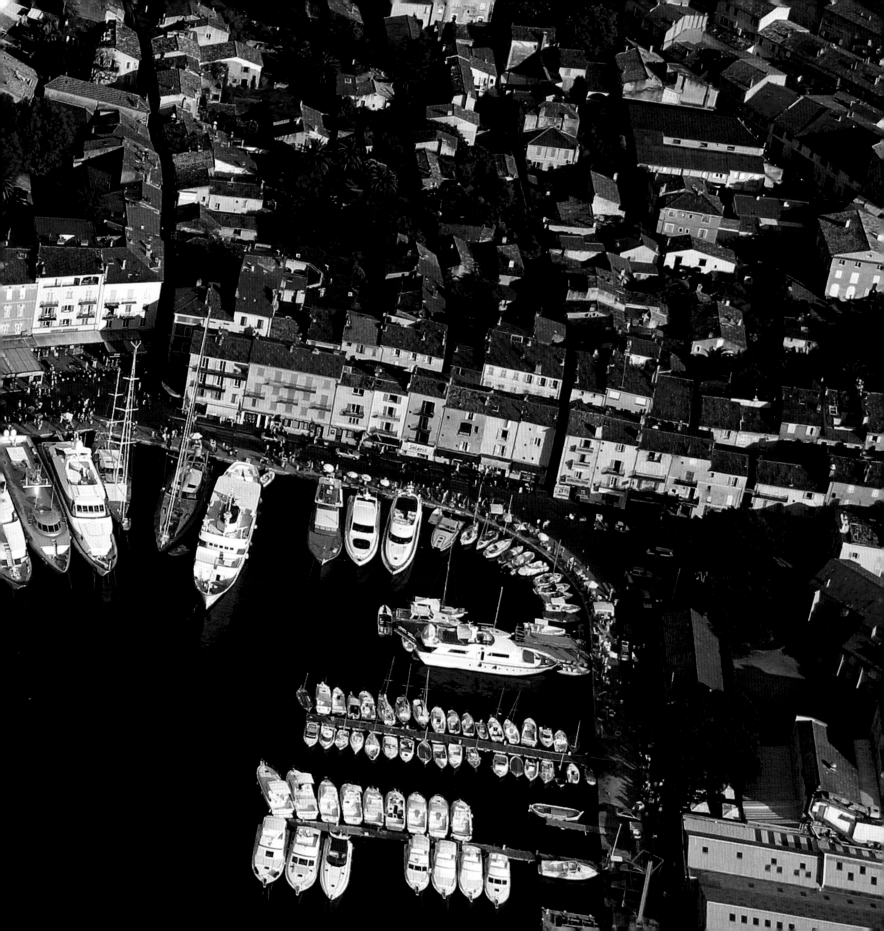

“ALL ROADS END AT THE SEA, I USED TO TELL HIM, WHERE THERE ARE PORTS. FROM THERE ONE WOULD EMBARK AND GO TO THE ISLANDS, WHERE THE ROADS START ONCE MORE...”

from AUGUST HOLIDAY
by Cesare Pavese

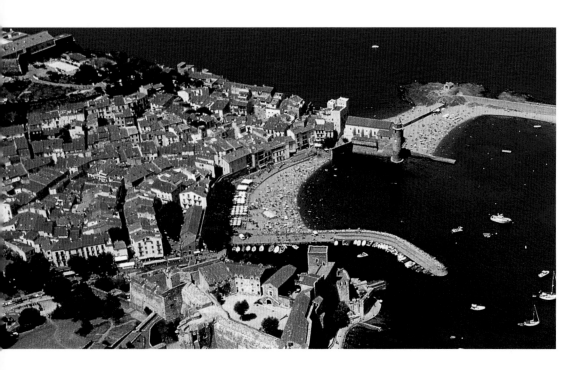

276 ● Mediterranean Sea, Côte Vermeille (France) - Collioure.

277 ● Atlantic Ocean, Ile de Ré (France) - Saint-Martin-de-Ré.

278-279 ● Atlantic Ocean, Côte d'Armor, Brittany (France) - Paimpol.

280-281 ● Mediterranean Sea, Costa Brava (Spain) - Cadaqués.

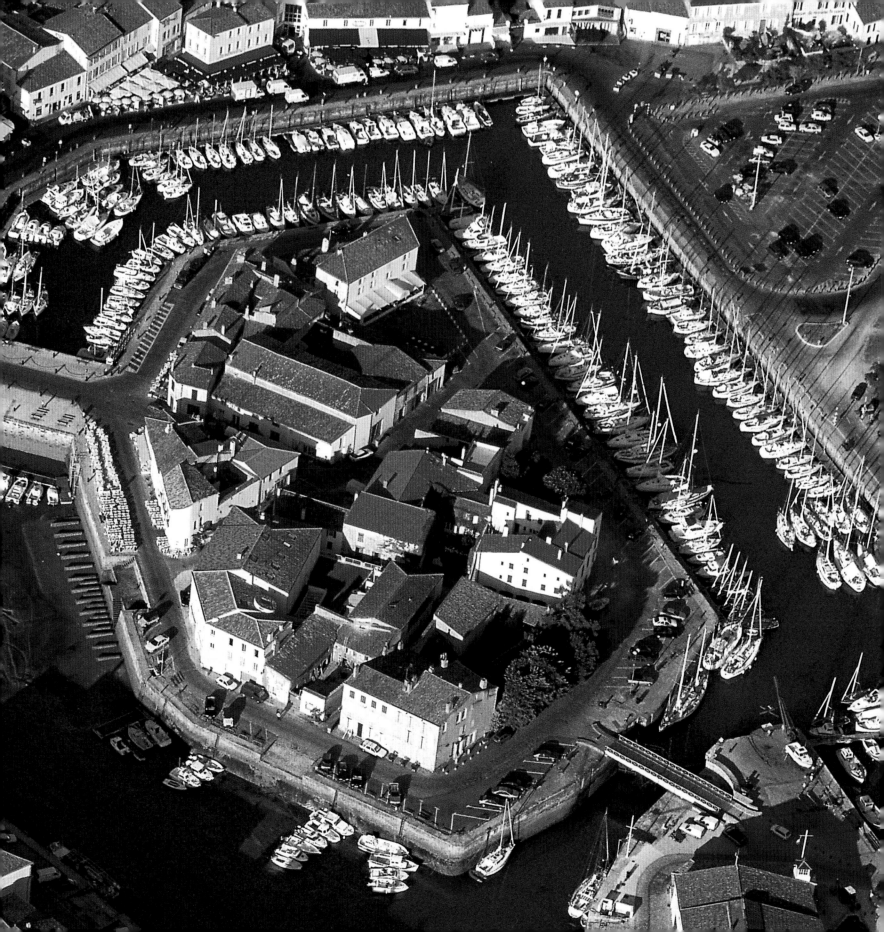

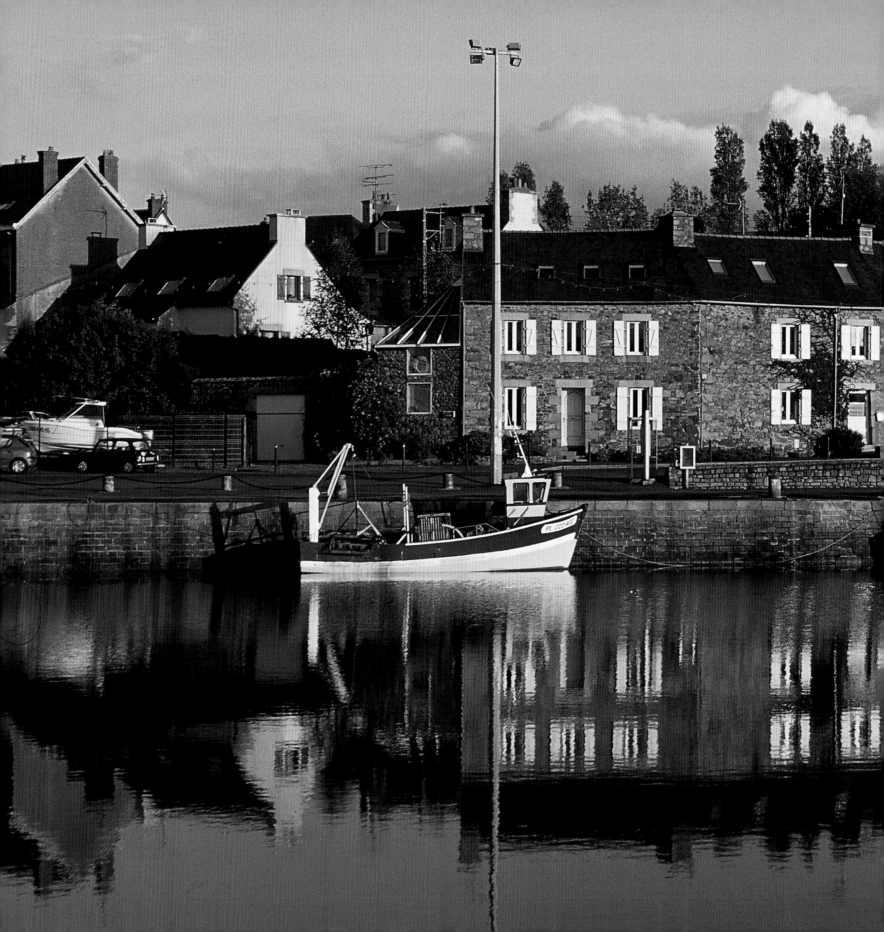

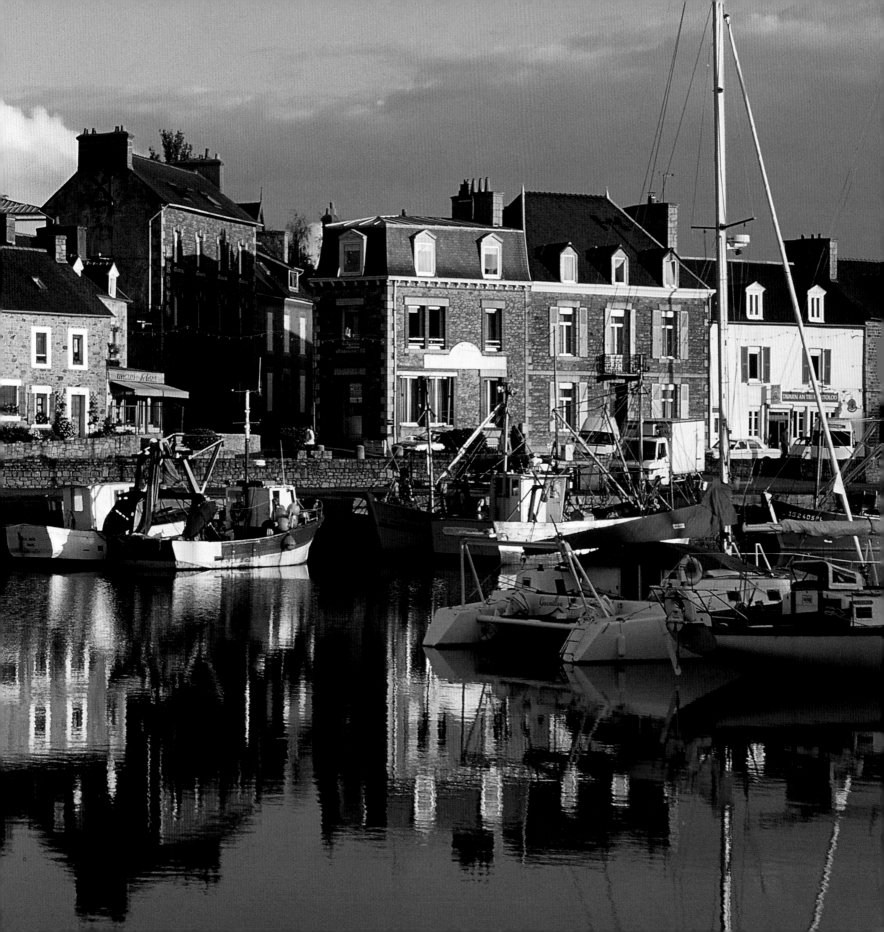

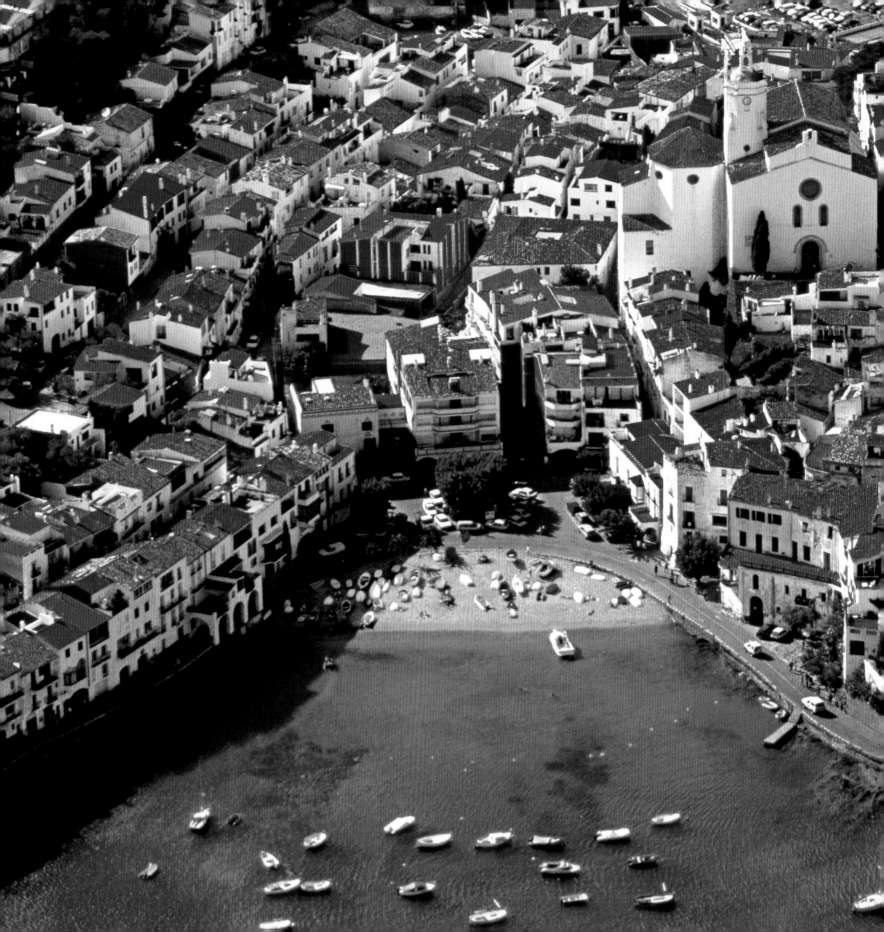

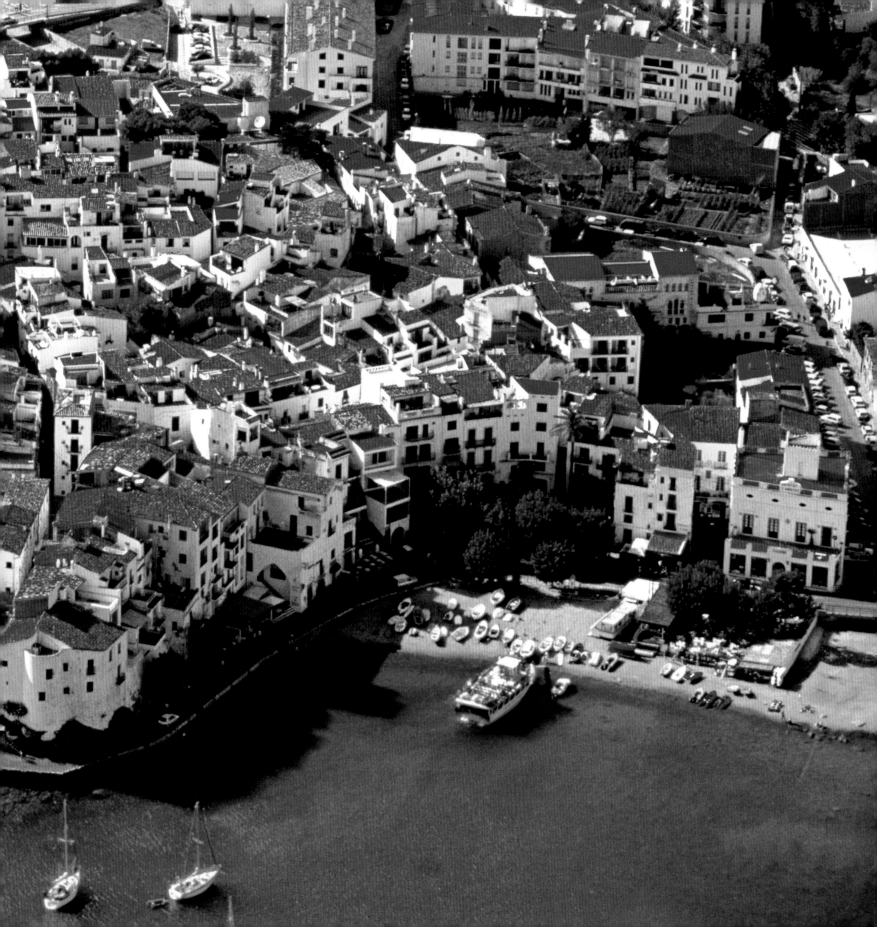

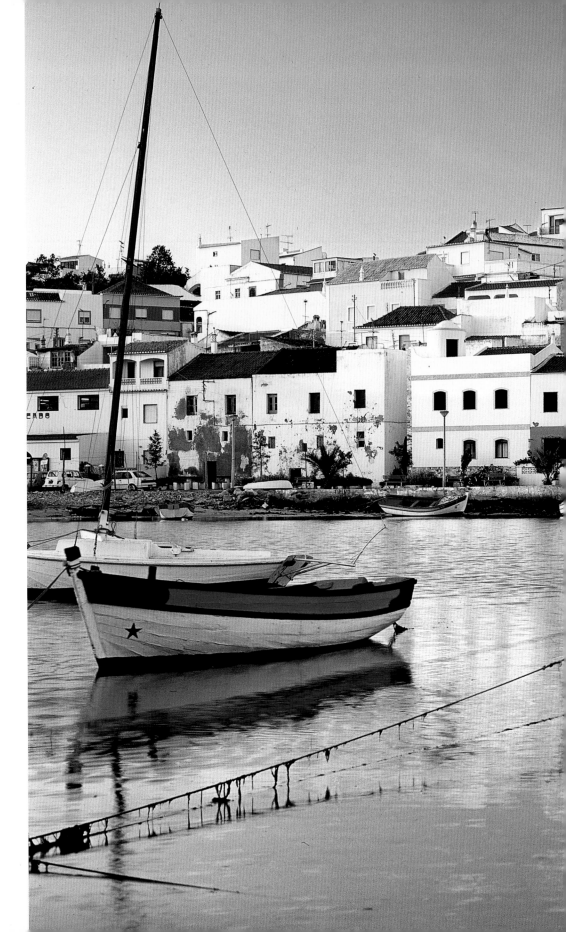

282-283 ● Atlantic Ocean, The Algarve (Portugal) - Ferragudo.

284-285 ● Atlantic Ocean, Cornwall (England) - Polperro.

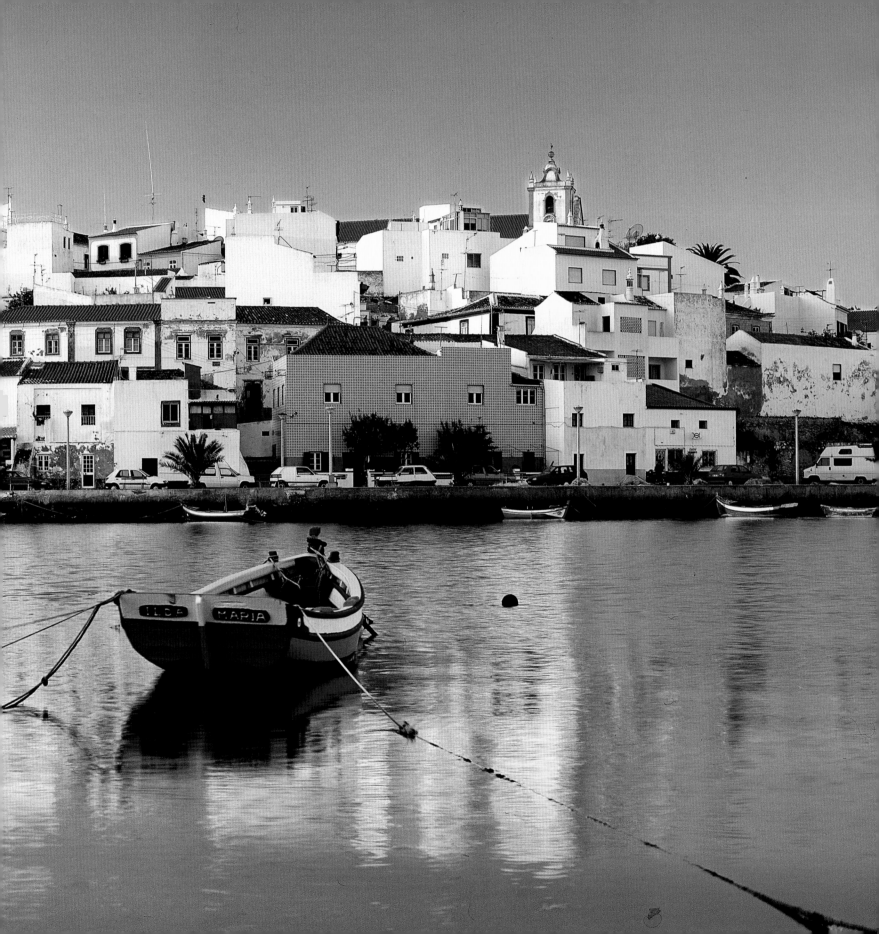

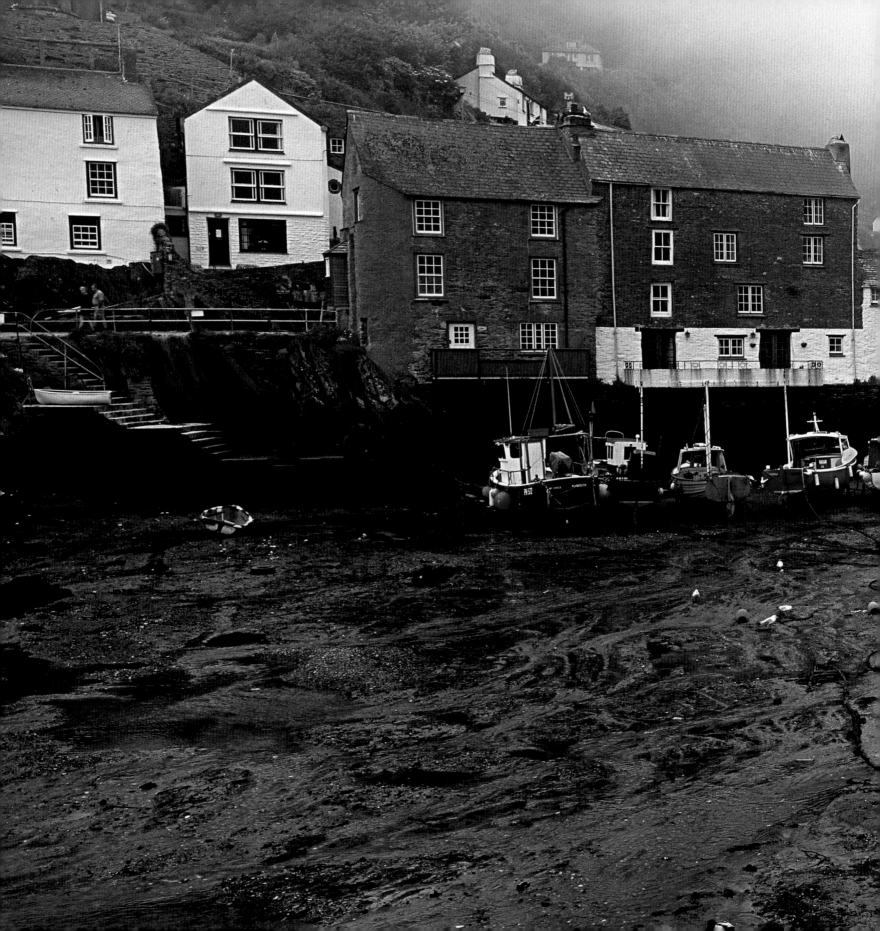

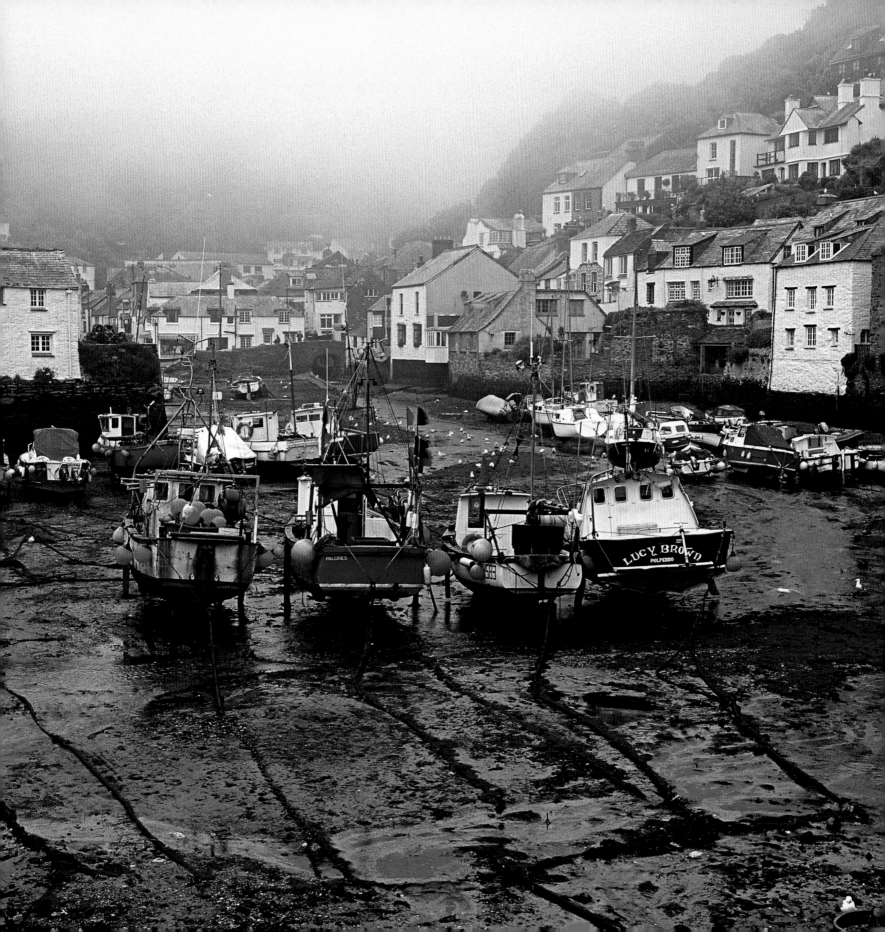

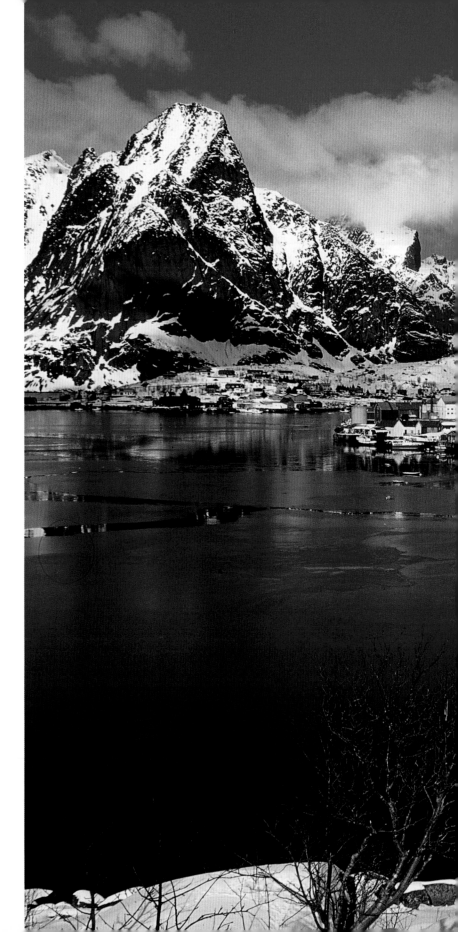

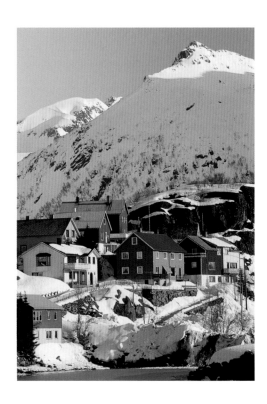

286 ● Atlantic Ocean, Lofoten Islands
(Norway) - Svolvær.

286-287 and 288-289 ● Atlantic Ocean,
Lofoten Islands (Norway) – Meskenes.

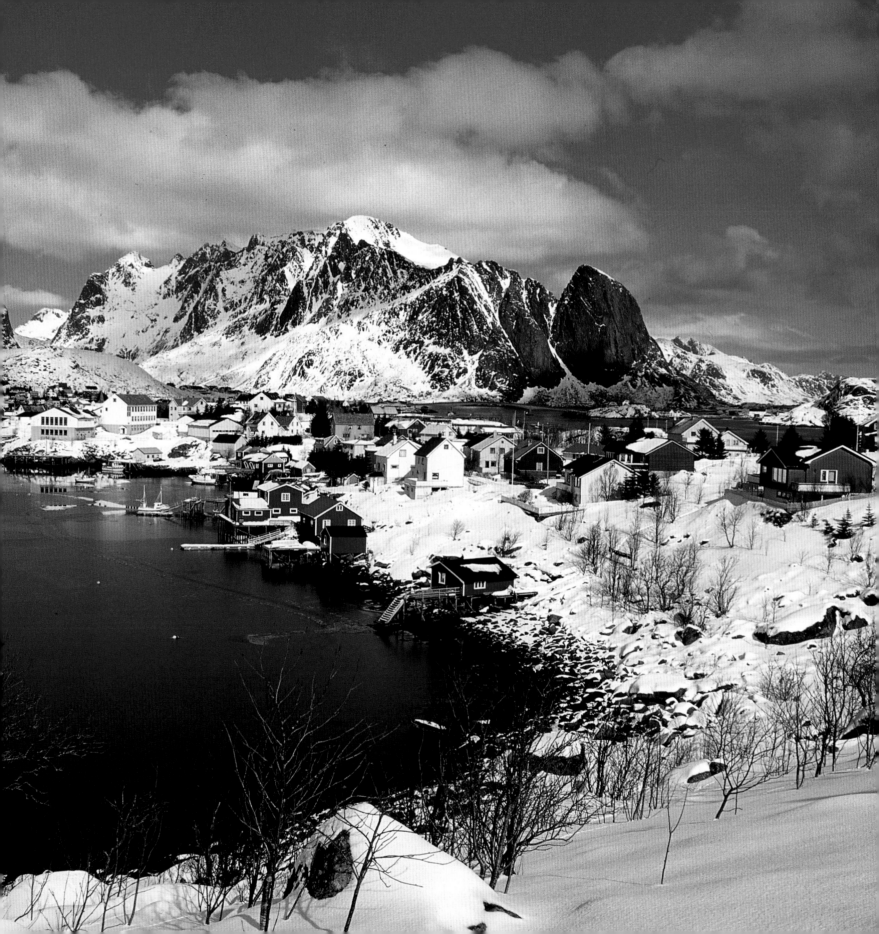

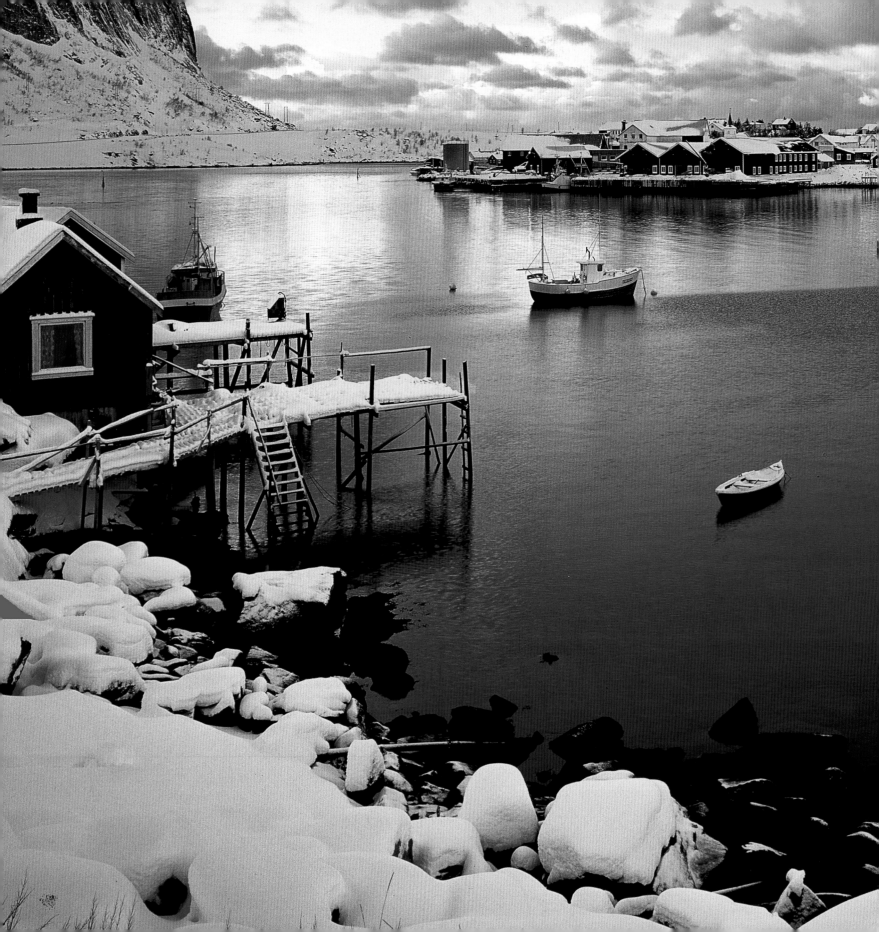

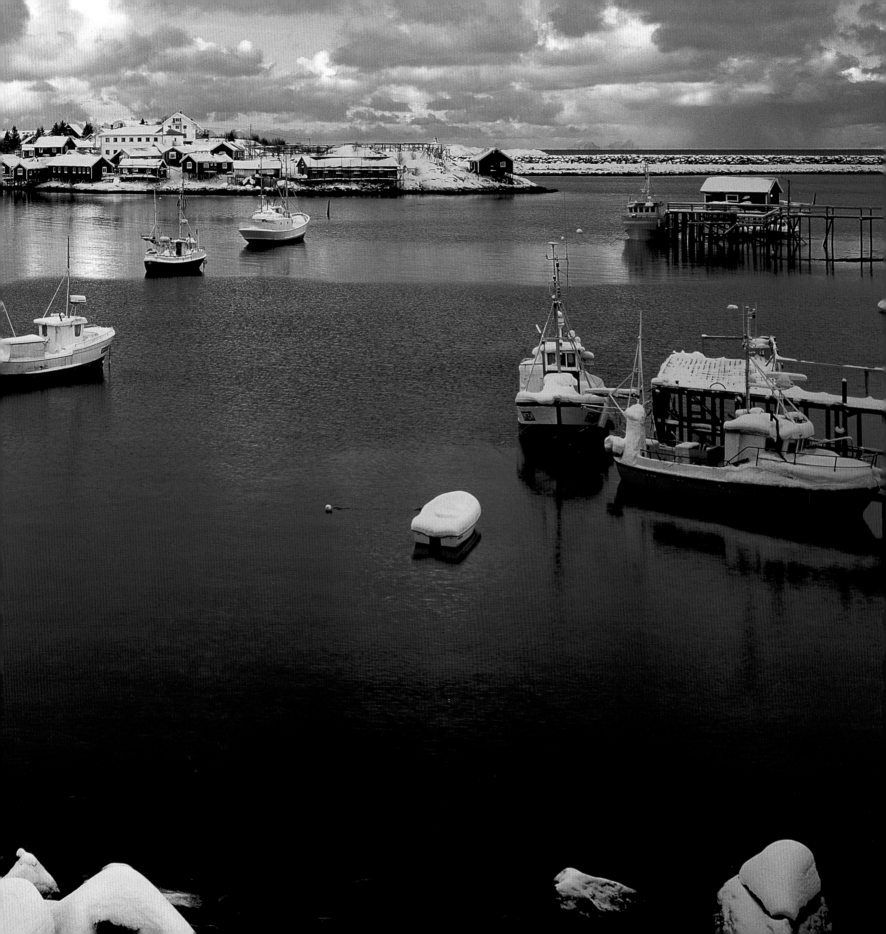

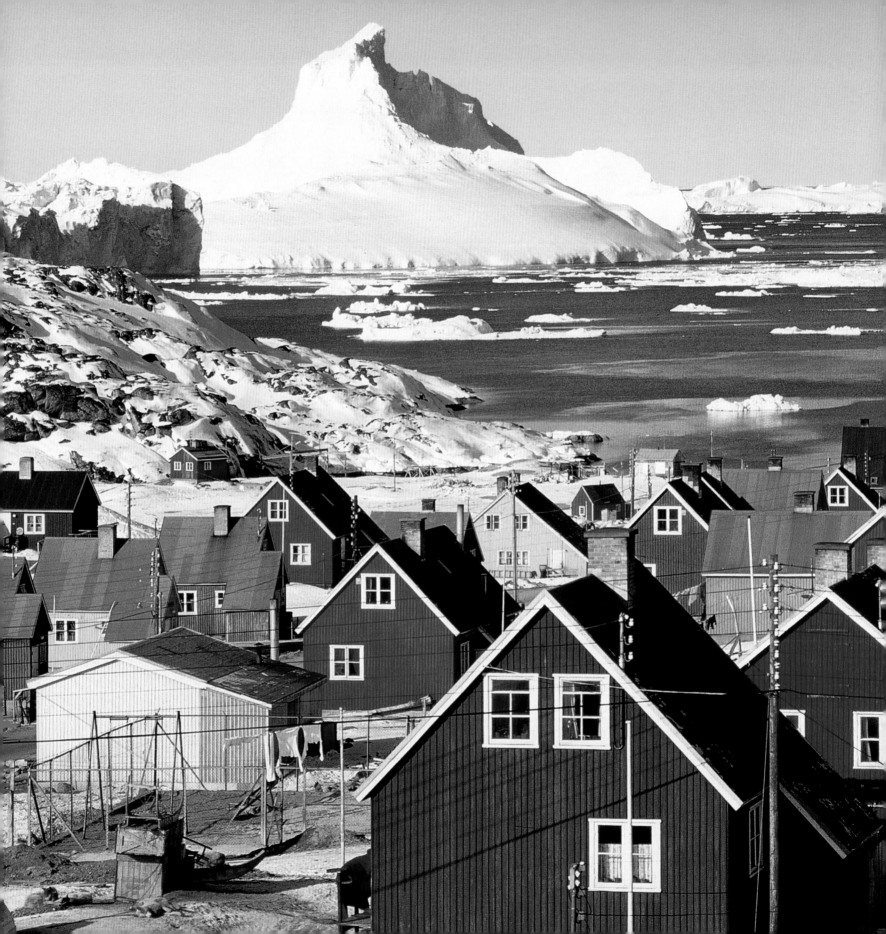

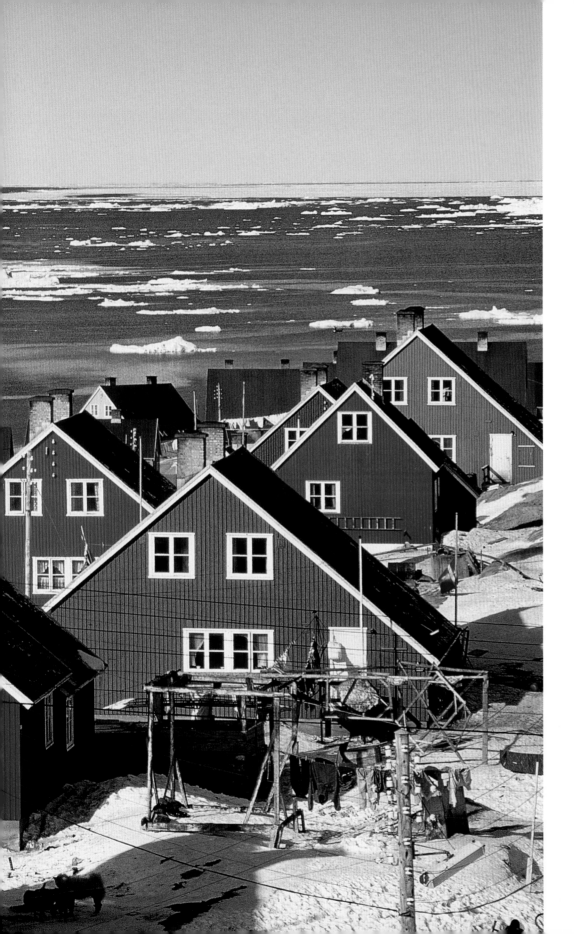

290-291 ● Atlantic Ocean,
Davis Strait (Greenland) -
Ilulissat-Jacobshavn.

292-293 ● Atlantic Ocean,
Maine (USA) - York.

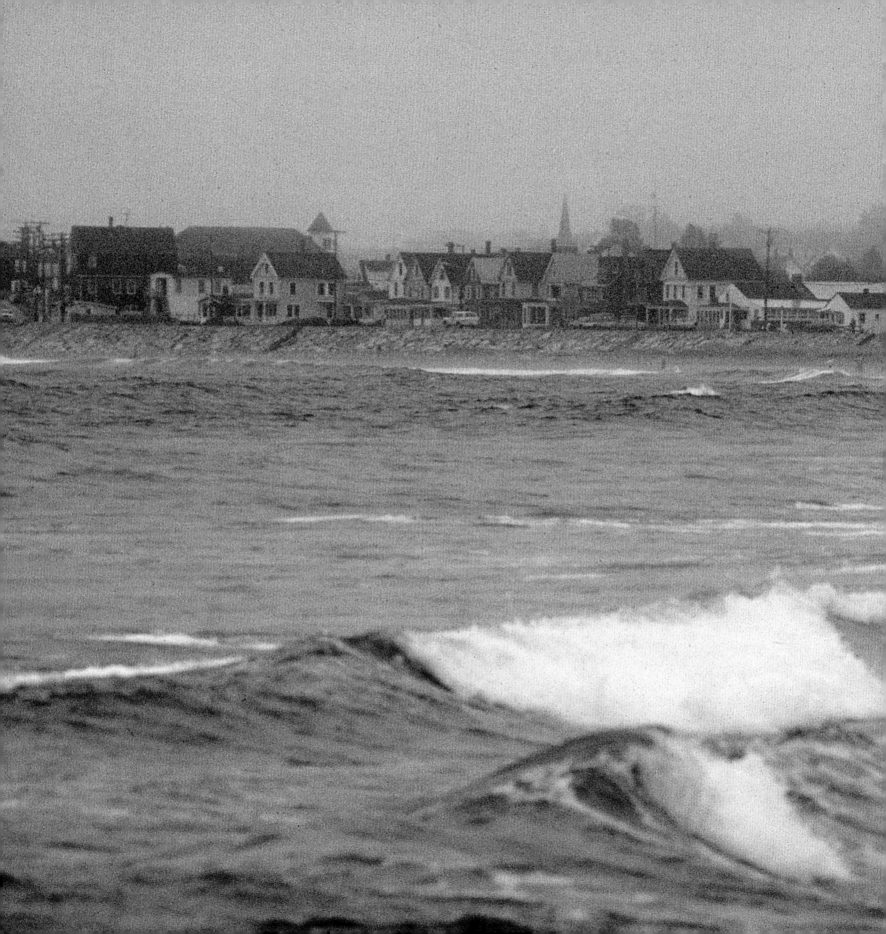

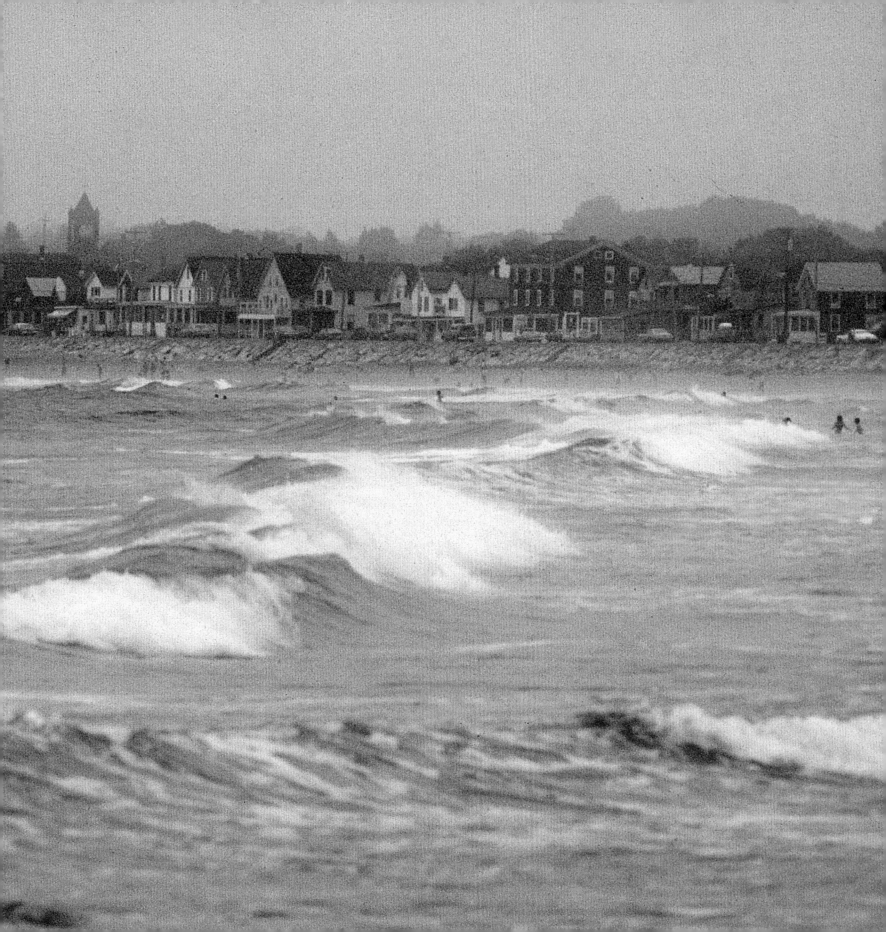

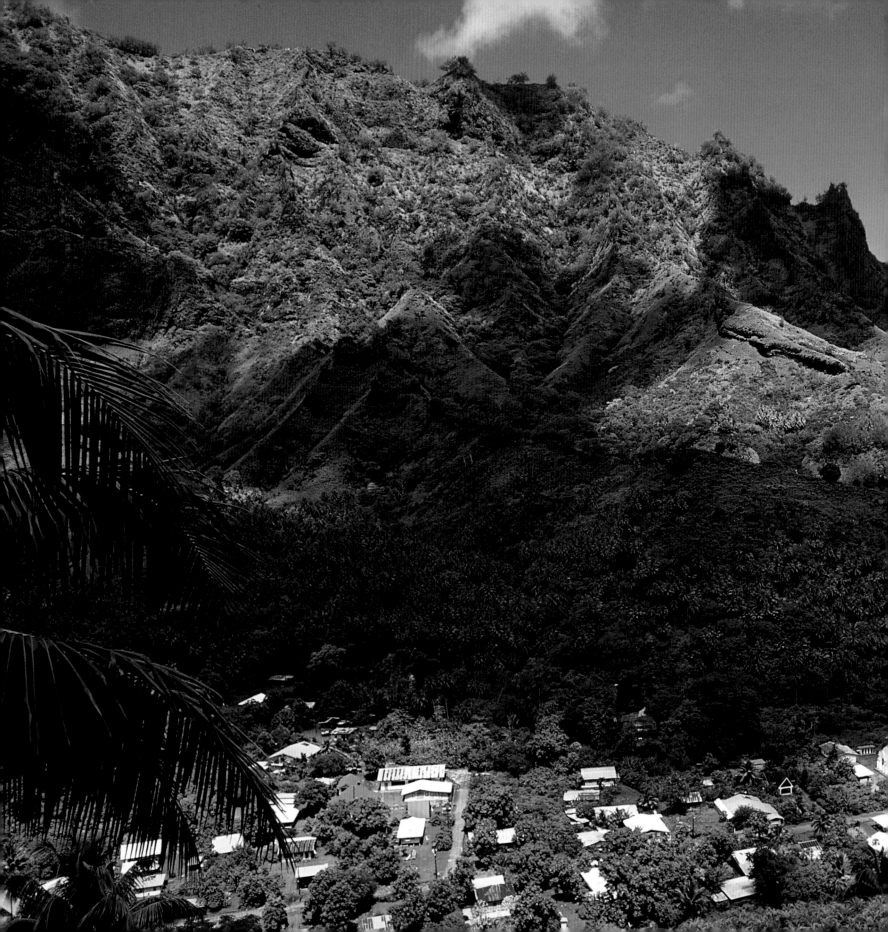

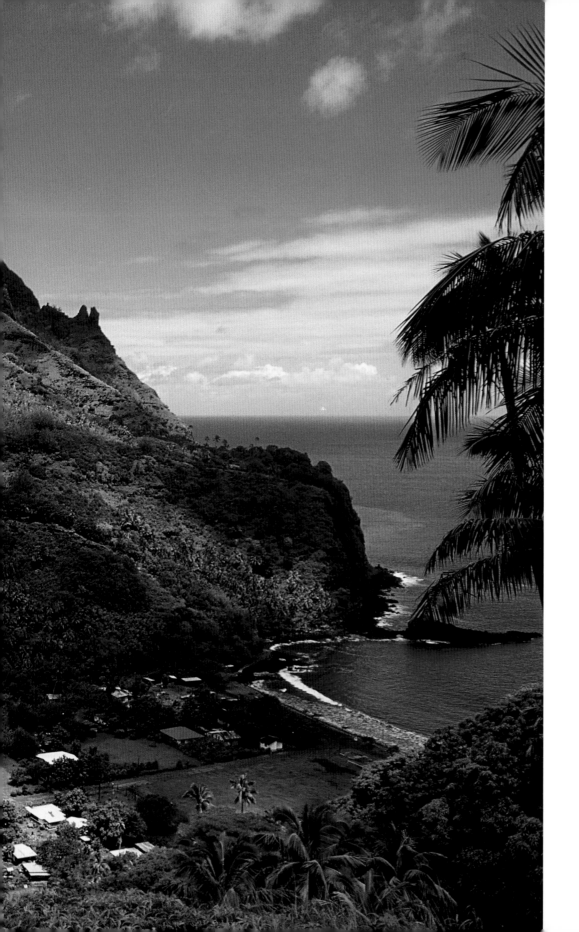

The South Seas

● Pacific Ocean,
Marquesas Islands
(French Polynesia) - Omoa
on Fatu Hiva.

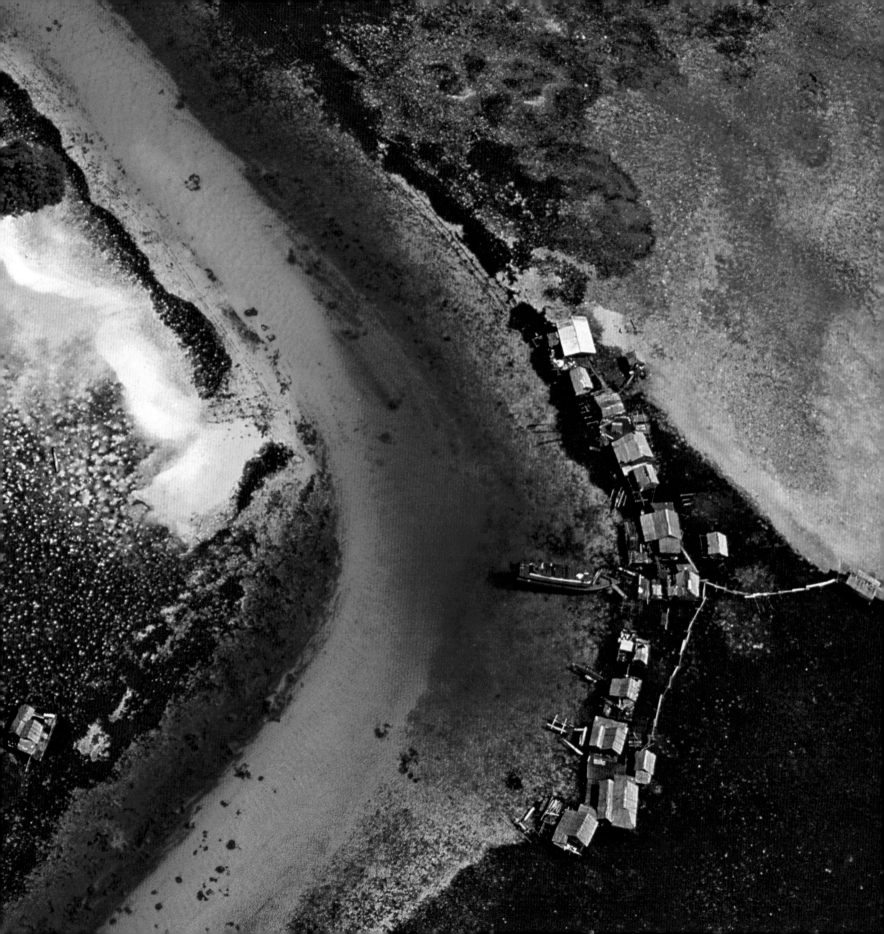

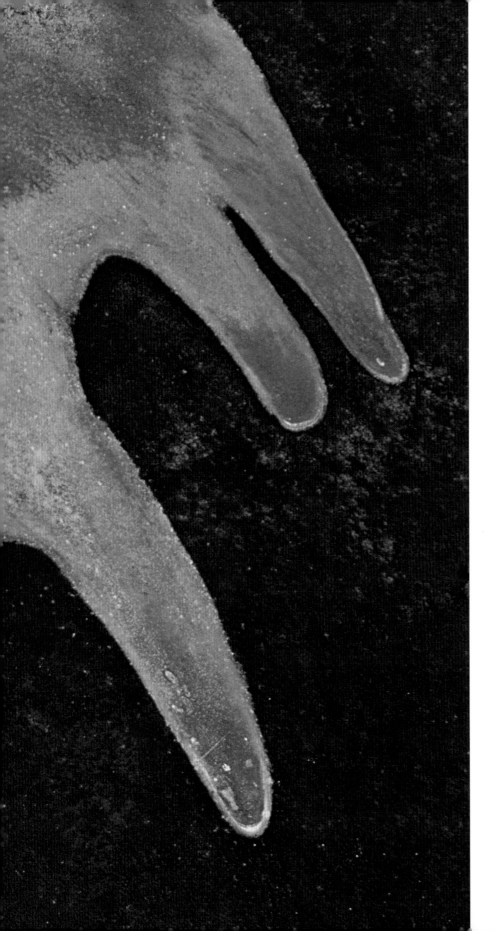

Pacific Ocean, Pantugaran Islands
(Philippines) - Village on Panducan.

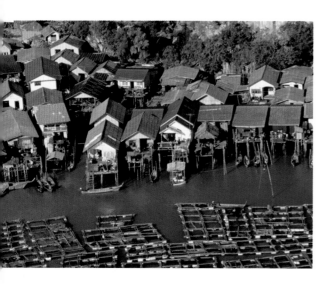

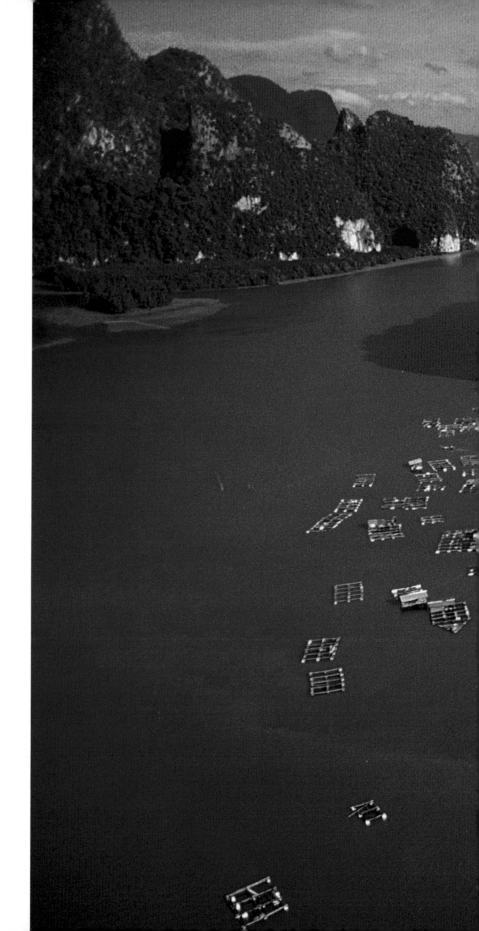

298 and 298-299 ● Indian Ocean, Phuket- Plang Nga Mining District (Thailand) - Fishing village in Ao Bay.

300-301 ● South China Sea, Sabah (Malaysia) - Village at Sipadan.

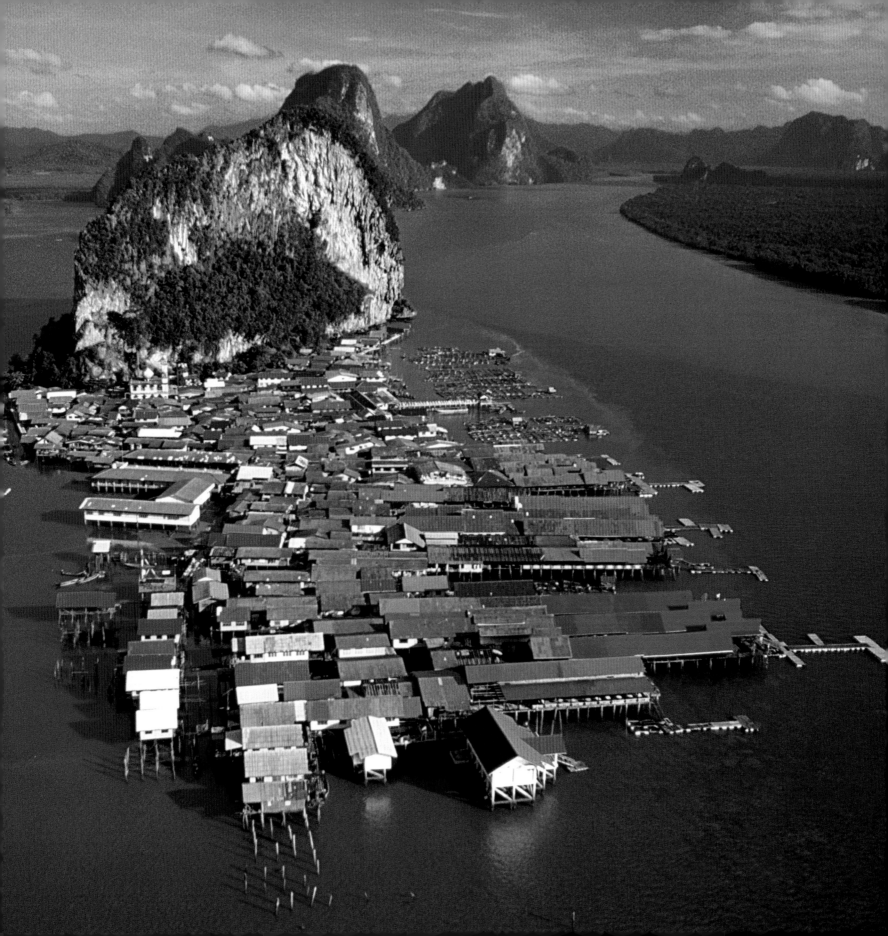

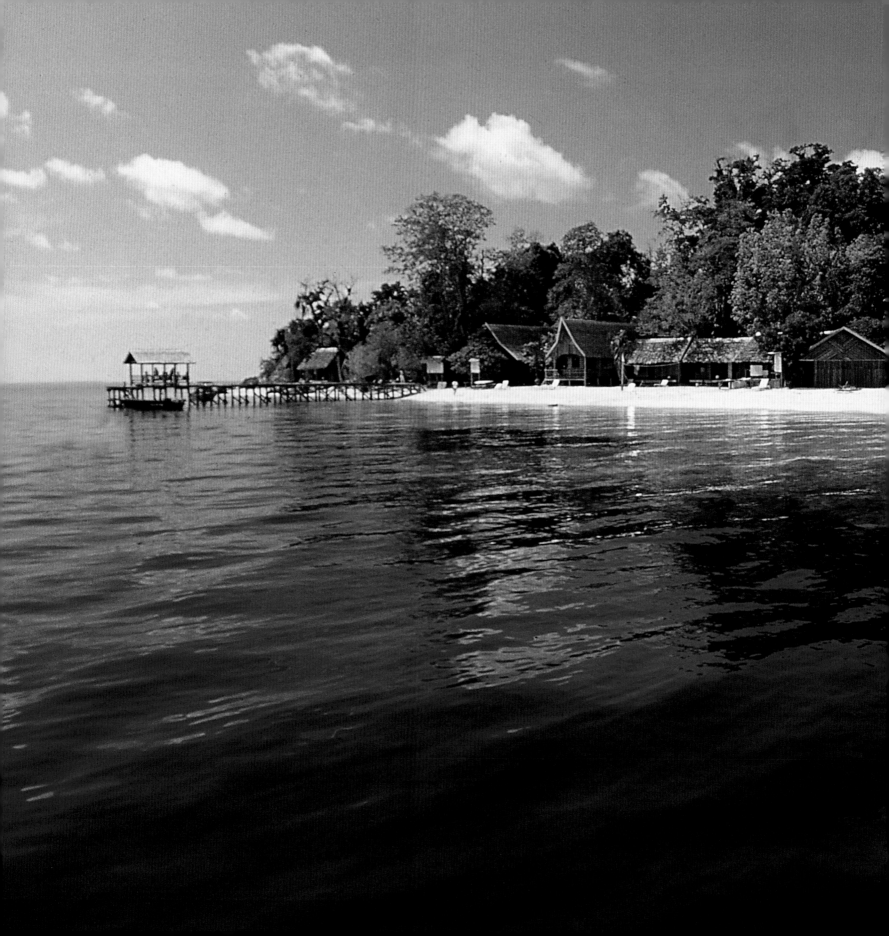

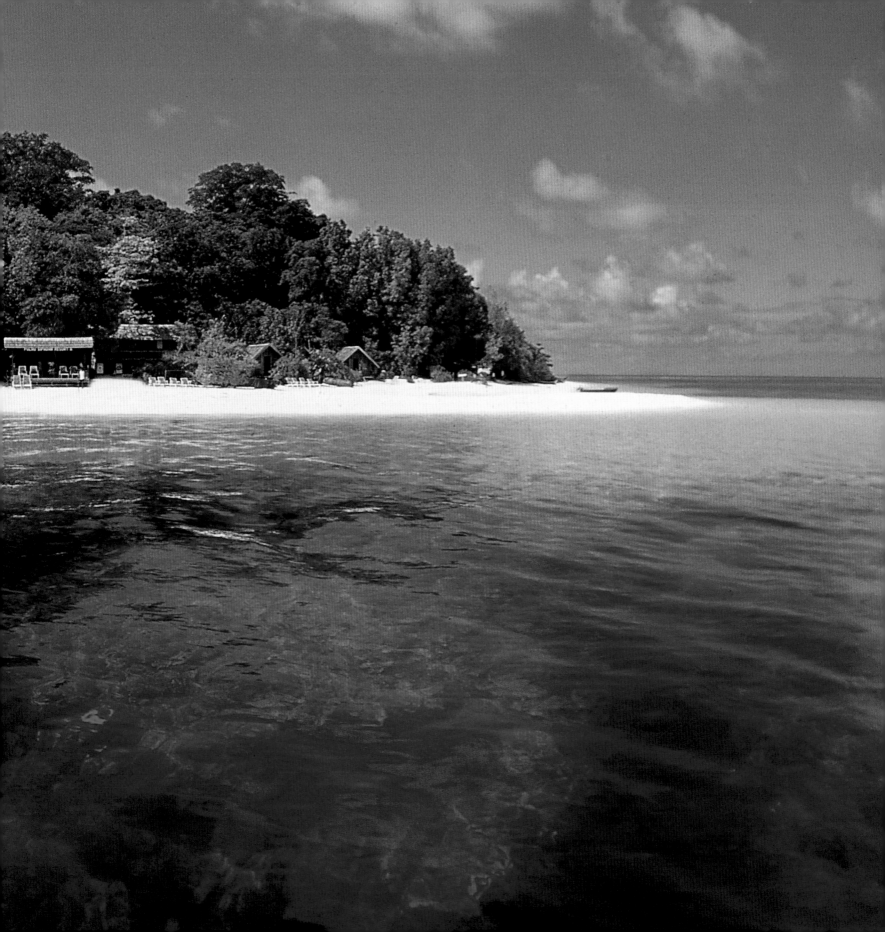

SEA PEOPLE

GAETANO CAFIERO

● Indian Ocean, Kerala (India) - Fishermen at Kovalam.

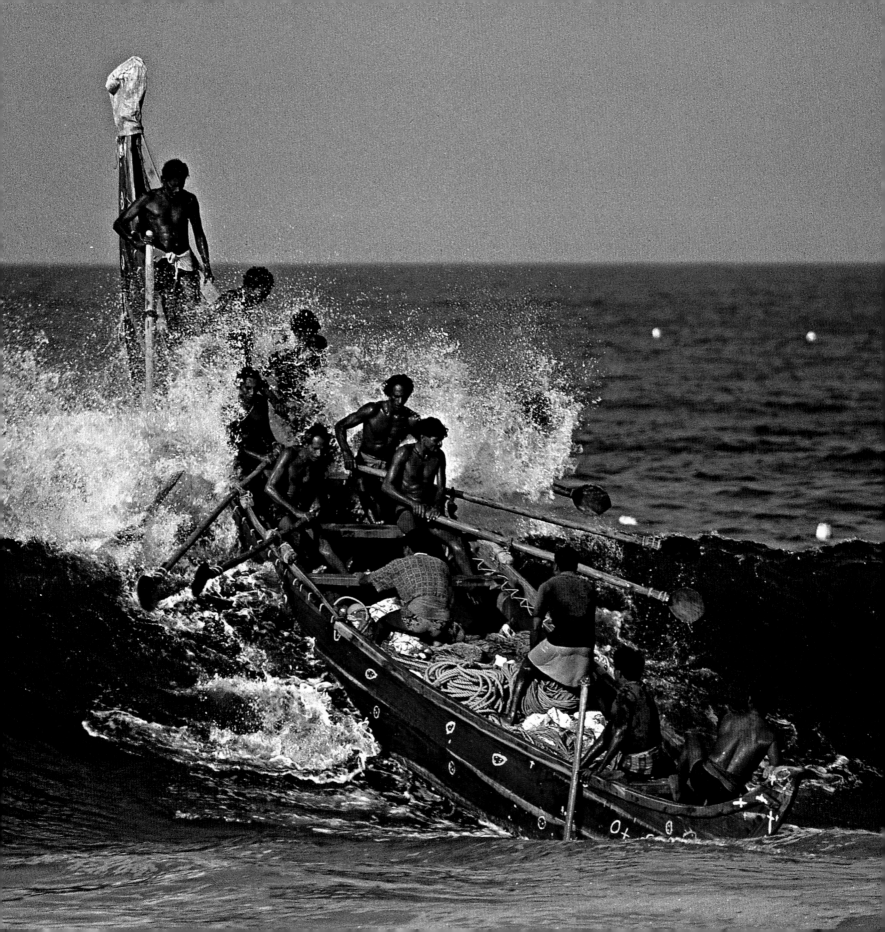

INTRODUCTION Sea People

THEY MAY LIVE ANYWHERE IN THE WORLD – WHETHER A

GREAT CITY OR A VILLAGE – AS LONG AS THEY ARE BESIDE THE OPEN

SEA OR ON THE CLIFF OVERLOOKING A STRAIT. SEA PEOPLE ARE JEAL-

OUS OF THEIR LOCAL TRADITIONS BUT SHARE THEIR DREAMS, SUF-

FERINGS AND CHALLENGES WITH SEA PEOPLE IN OTHER LANDS AND

OTHER SEAS. TO SURVIVE THE HOSTILITY OF THE VAST EXPANSE OF

WATER, EFFORT AND SACRIFICE ARE NECESSARY, PERHAPS HEROISM.

THE SEA OFFERS PRECIOUS GIFTS BUT IT CAN ALSO BE FEARSOME.

WHEN EVENING FALLS, THE FISHERMEN ORGANIZE THE TACKLE ON

THEIR BOATS. LONG SLEEPLESS HOURS ARE SPENT SUPPORTED BY

THE HOPE OF A GOOD CATCH. THEY LEAVE THE PORT DURING THE

INTRODUCTION Sea People

DEPTH OF NIGHT. A PRAYER IS OFFERED TO GOD FOR THE CATCH TO

BE GOOD. IT IS A NIGHT WITHOUT MUCH LIGHT, BUT THE SAILORS ARE

KEPT COMPANY BY THE THOUGHT OF THE RETURN IN THE WARMTH

OF THE MORNING SUN AND THE KNOWLEDGE THEY WILL DO THEIR

WORK AS IT HAS ALWAYS BEEN DONE. THEY ARE HEROES WITHOUT

ARMOR ON TECHNOLOGICAL BOATS, REPEATING UNIVERSAL RITUALS.

THEY USE LUCKY CHARMS, OATHS AND GESTURES TO HELP ENDURE

THE TERROR OF HUGE WAVES THAT ROLL UP OUT OF THE DARK AND

DISAPPEAR INTO IT ONCE MORE. AND THEN THERE IS THE FEAR OF AN

EMPTY NET, OF POVERTY AND HUNGER. EVERY COASTAL COMMUNI-

TY HAS FOUNDED ITS EXISTENCE ON FISHING THOUGH OTHER TRADES

Sea People

Introduction

HAVE COME AND GONE. THE INDUSTRIAL REVOLUTION DID AWAY WITH THE BUILDERS OF WOODEN BOATS, AND WITH THE CAULKERS WHO MADE HULLS WATERTIGHT WITH OAKUM AND PITCH. PHOTOGRAPHY MADE THE PORT PAINTER OBSOLETE AFTER CENTURIES AT THE SERVICE OF CAPTAINS AND THEIR BOATS. NEW MATERIALS MADE SAILMAKERS REDUNDANT, AND THE SCULPTORS OF FIGUREHEADS AND FLAG-MAKERS PROSPERED BEFORE DECLINING AND PASSING INTO CRAFTSMEN OF THE PAST. TODAY, THE ONLY REMINDERS OF THE OLD TRADES ARE THE NAMES ON THE STREETS OF THE SEASIDE TOWNS AND A WEAK TRACE IN THE COLLECTIVE MEMORY.

● Atlantic Ocean - Sailor on the *Amerigo Vespucci*.

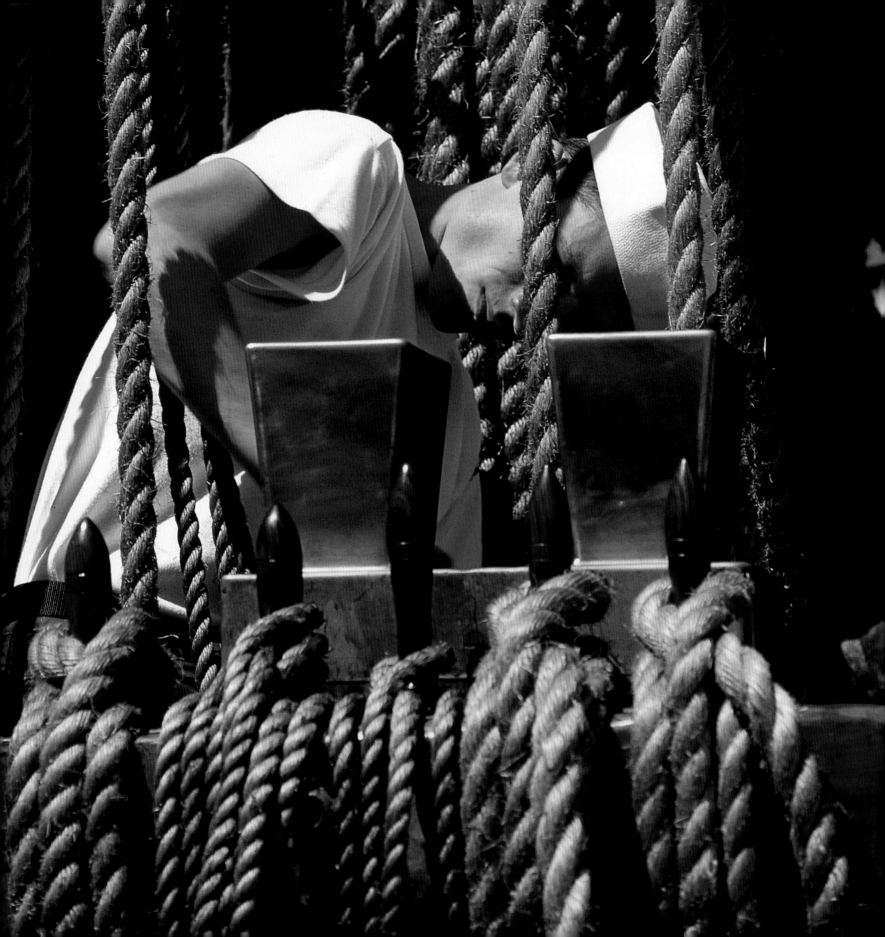

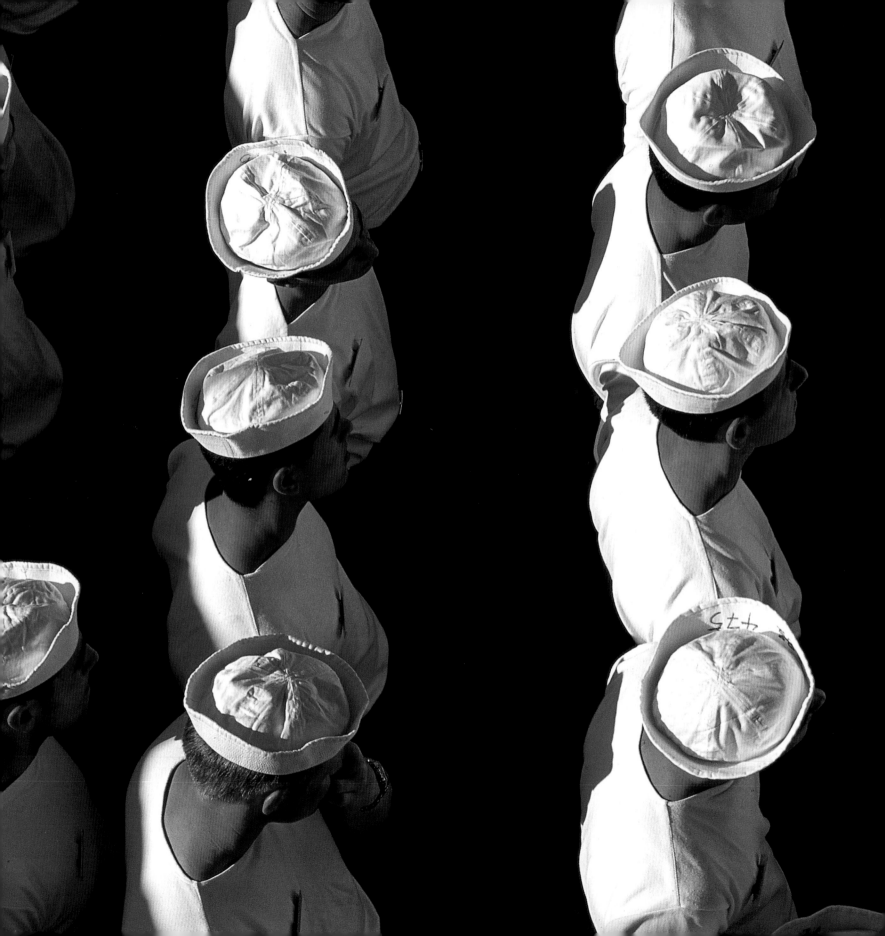

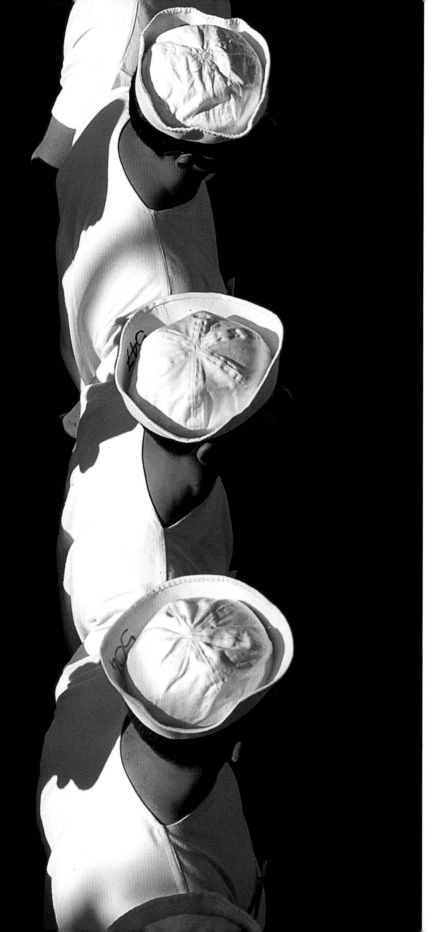

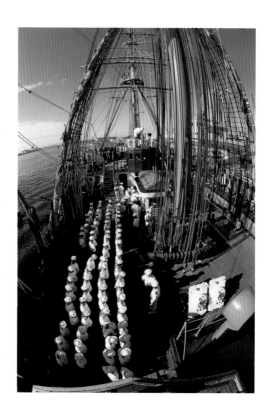

Atlantic Ocean - Sailors on the
Amerigo Vespucci.

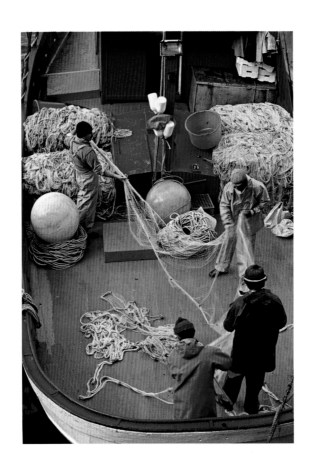

● Tyrrhenian Sea, Campania (Italy) - Fishing boat off Procida.

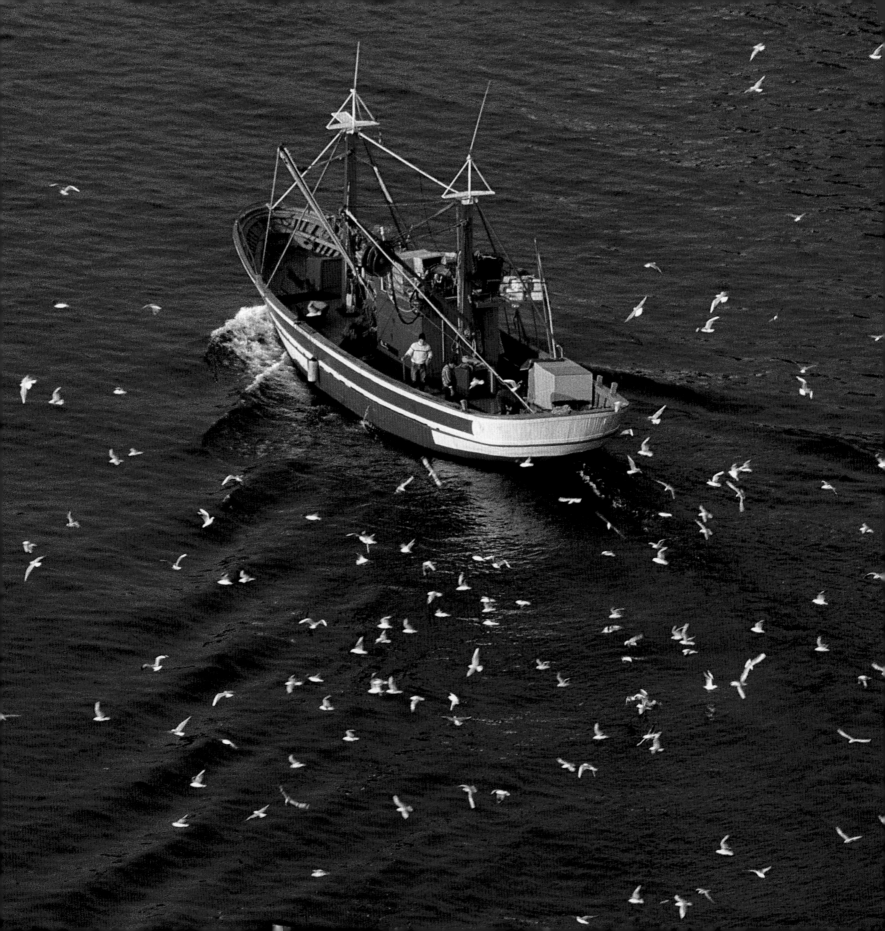

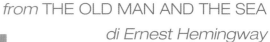

"THE SAIL WAS PATCHED WITH FLOUR SACKS AND, FURLED, IT LOOKED LIKE THE FLAG OF PERMANENT DEFEAT. THE OLD MAN WAS THIN AND GAUNT ... HIS HANDS HAD THE DEEP-CREASED SCARS FROM HANDLING HEAVY FISH ON THE CORDS. BUT NONE OF THESE SCARS WERE FRESH. THEY WERE AS OLD AS EROSIONS IN A FISHLESS DESERT."

from THE OLD MAN AND THE SEA
di Ernest Hemingway

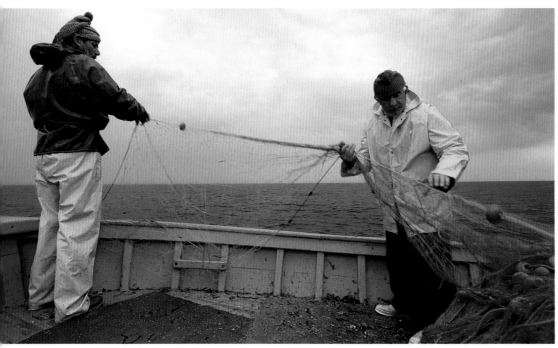

312 and 313 ● Tyrrhenian Sea, Sardinia (Italy) - On board a fishing boat off the island of Maddalena.

314-315 ● Mediterranean Sea, Liguria (Italy) - Tuna fishermen from Camogli.

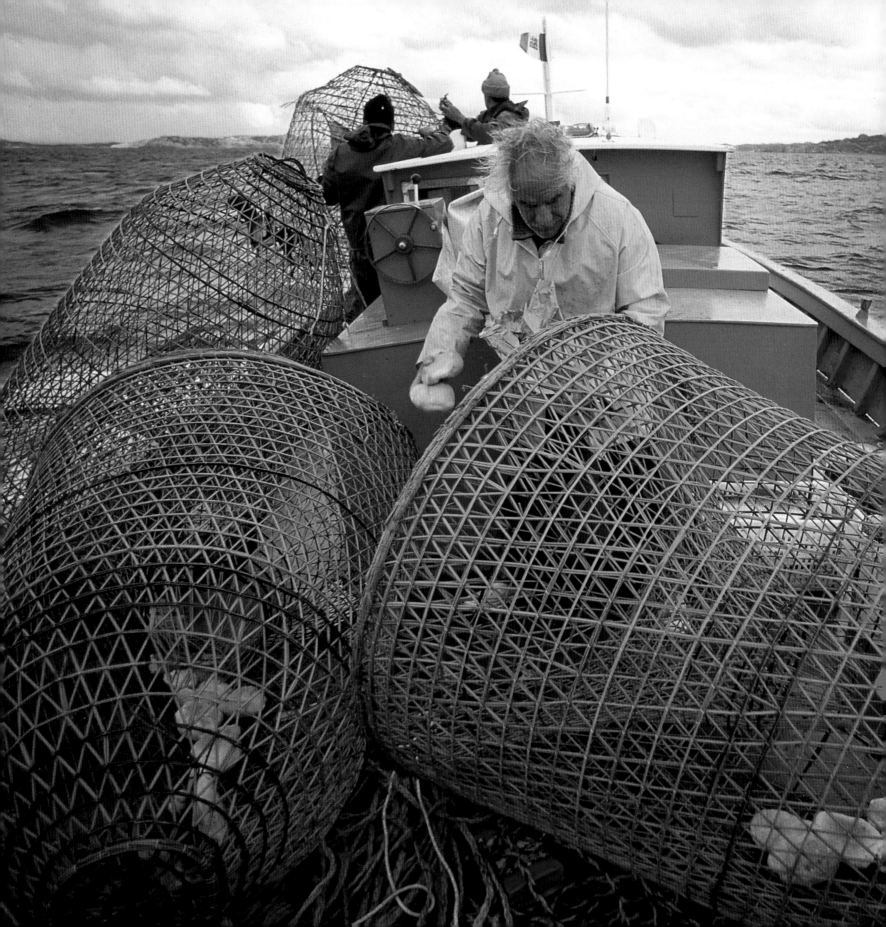

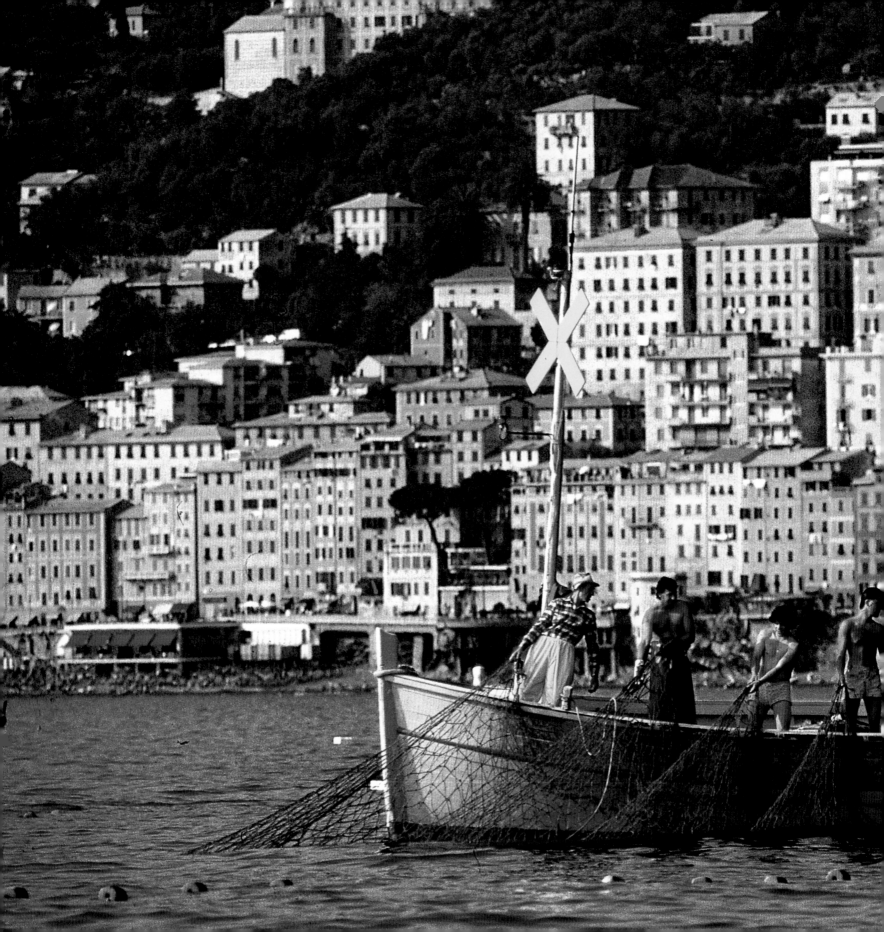

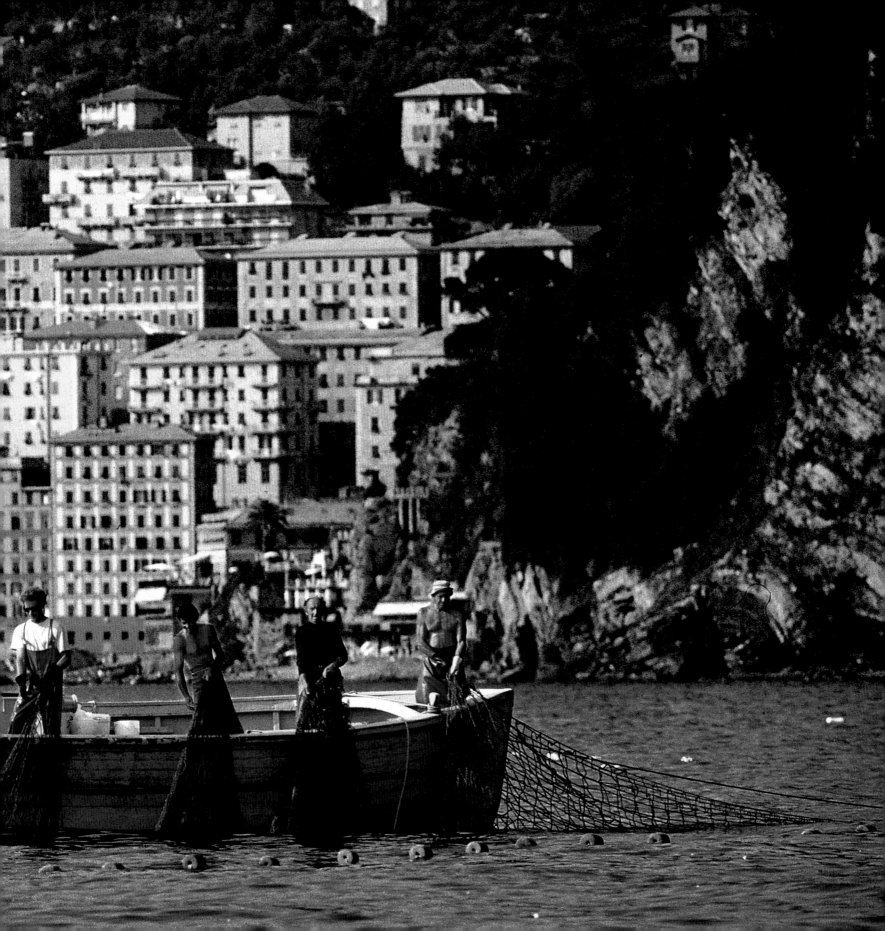

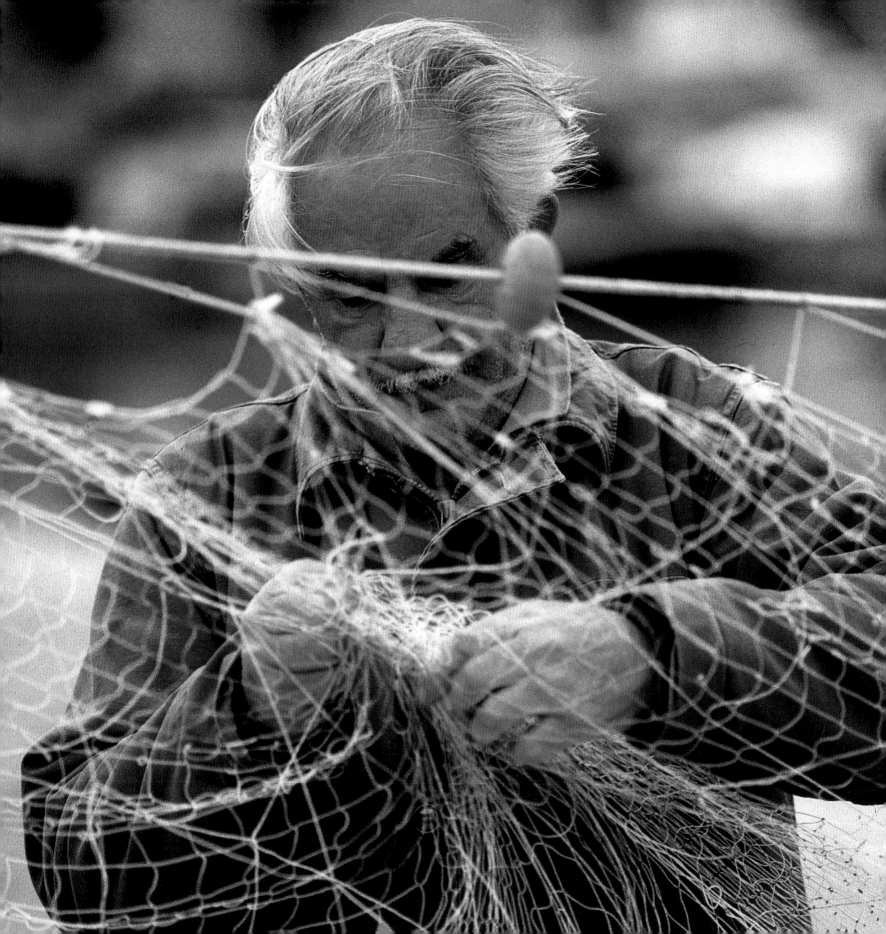

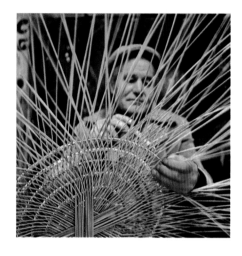
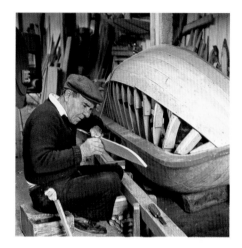
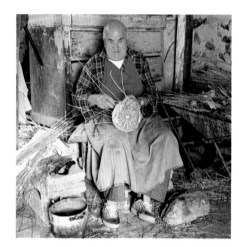

Fishermen
and their pots

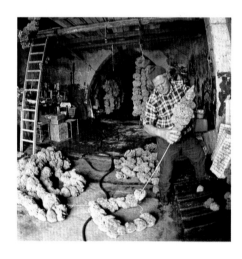
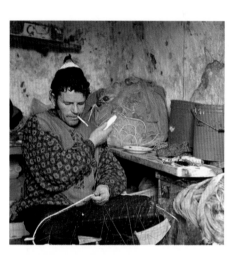
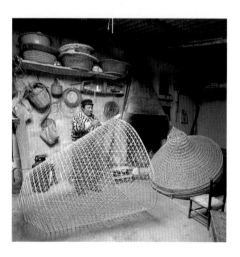

316 ● Mediterranean Sea, Sardinia (Italy) - Mending nets.

317 from left to right, top to bottom:
● Tyrrhenian Sea, Campania (Italy) - Making a fishing pot.
● Tyrrhenian Sea, Calabria (Italy) - Small boatyard in Vibo Marina.
● Tyrrhenian Sea, Procida (Italy) - Making a fishing pot.
● Mediterranean Sea, Sicily (Italy) - Sponge fisherman on Lampedusa.
● Mediterranean Sea, Sicily (Italy) - Mending a net.
● Tyrrhenian Sea, Calabria (Italy) - Repairing a fishing pot.

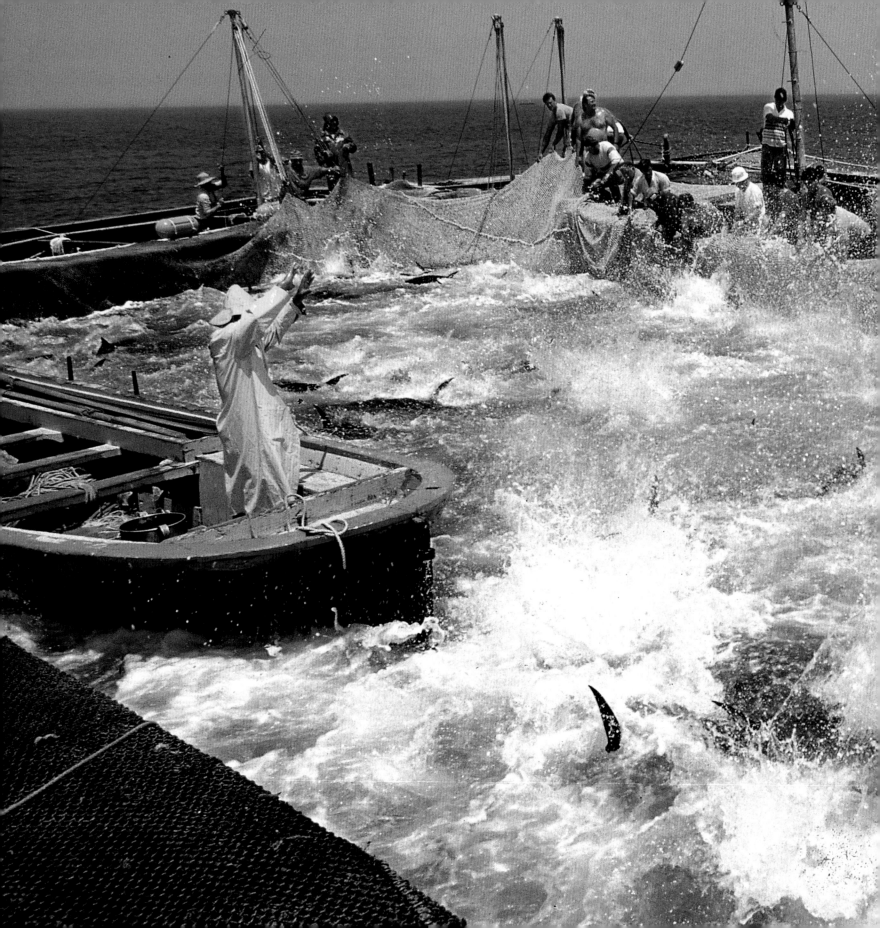

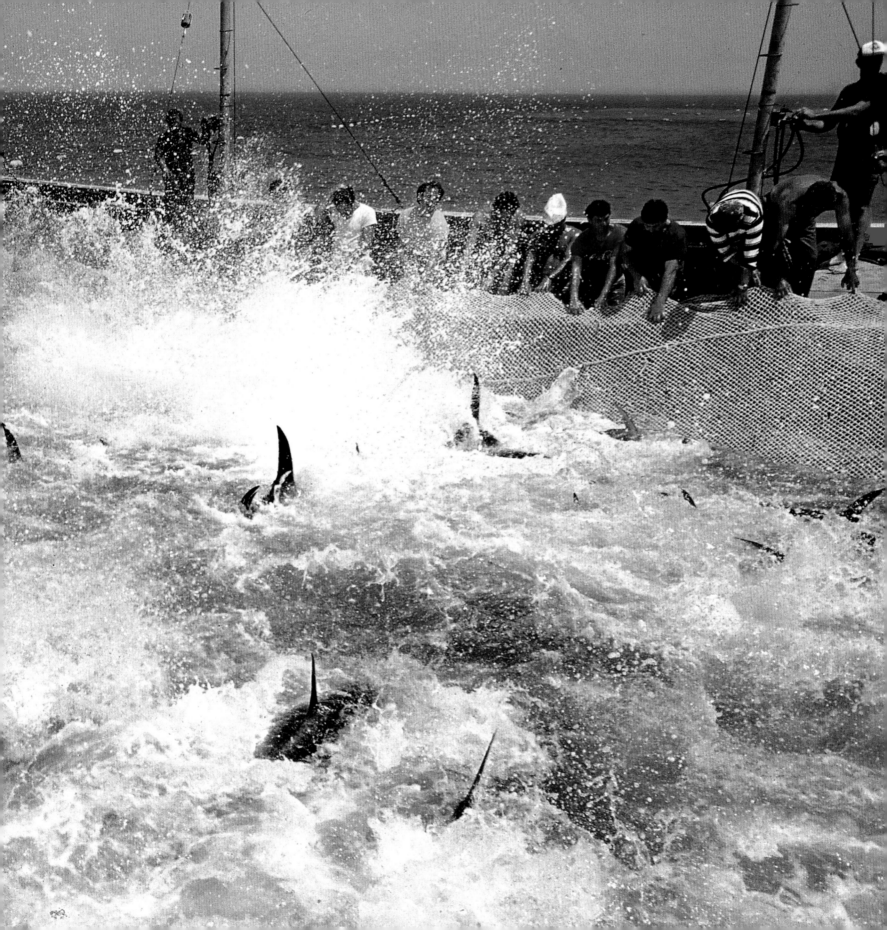

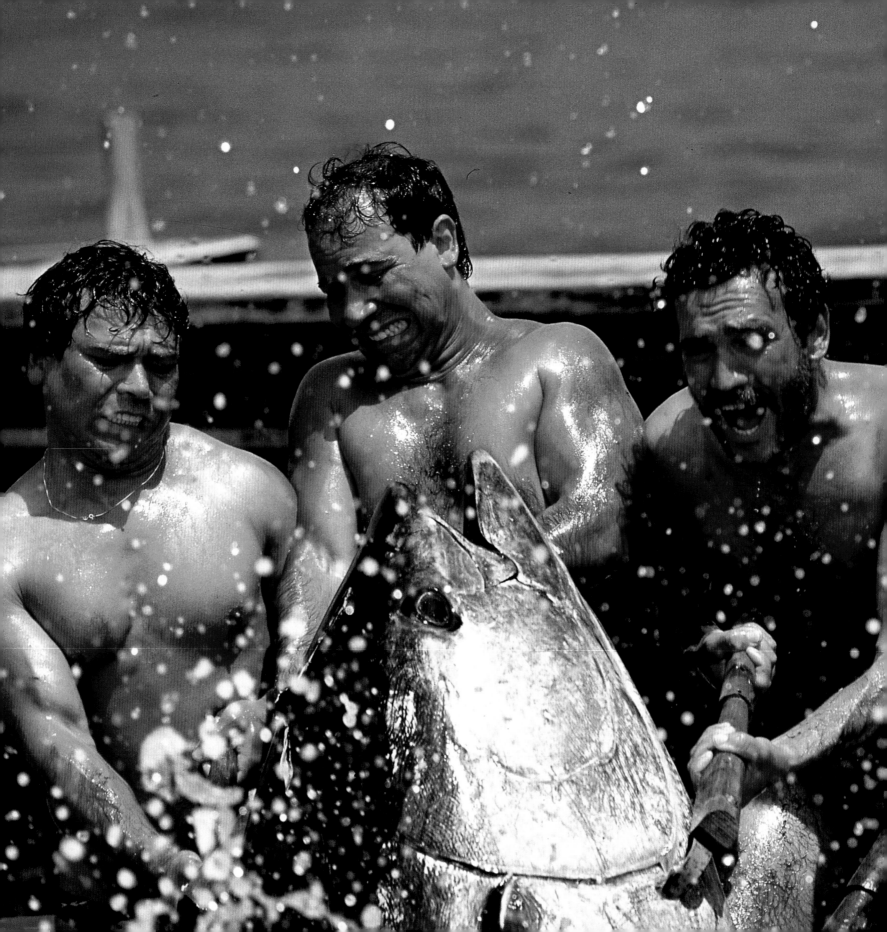

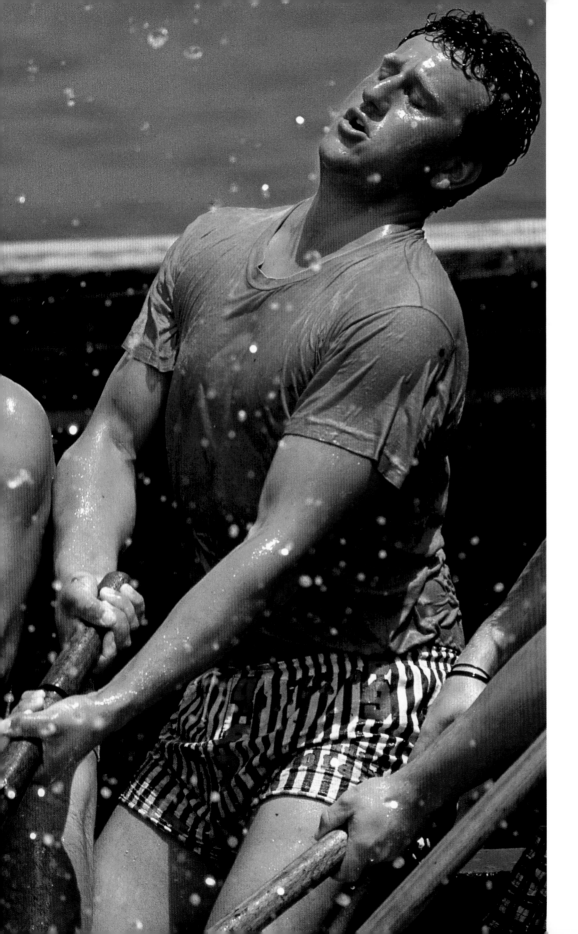

318-319 and 320-321 •
Mediterranean Sea,
Sicily (Italy) - Tuna nets
at San Cusumano.

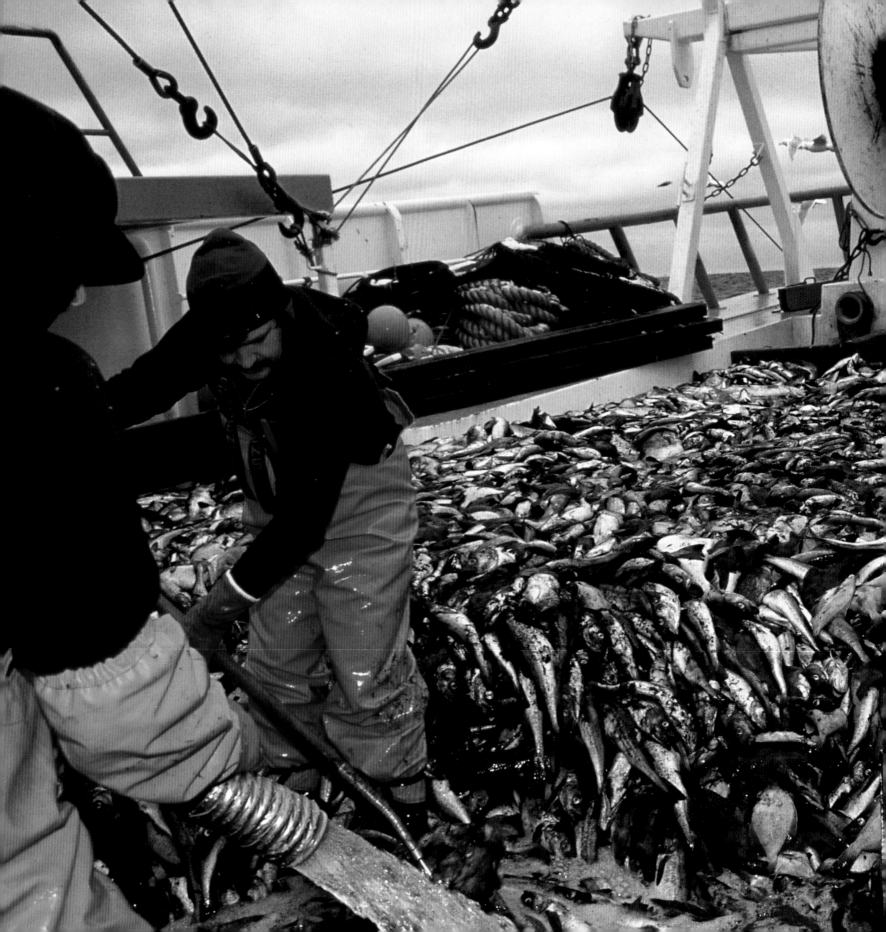

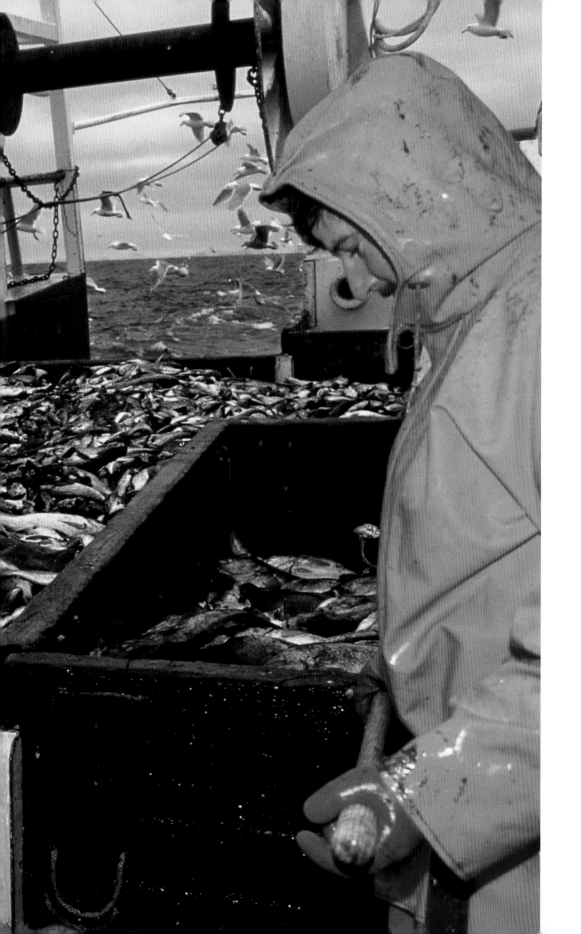

On the
high seas

322-323 ● Pacific Ocean,
Gulf of Alaska (USA) -
On board the fishing boat
Miss Amy.

324-325 ● Atlantic Ocean,
Gulf of Gascony (France) -
On board the fishing boat
Koros off La Rochelle.

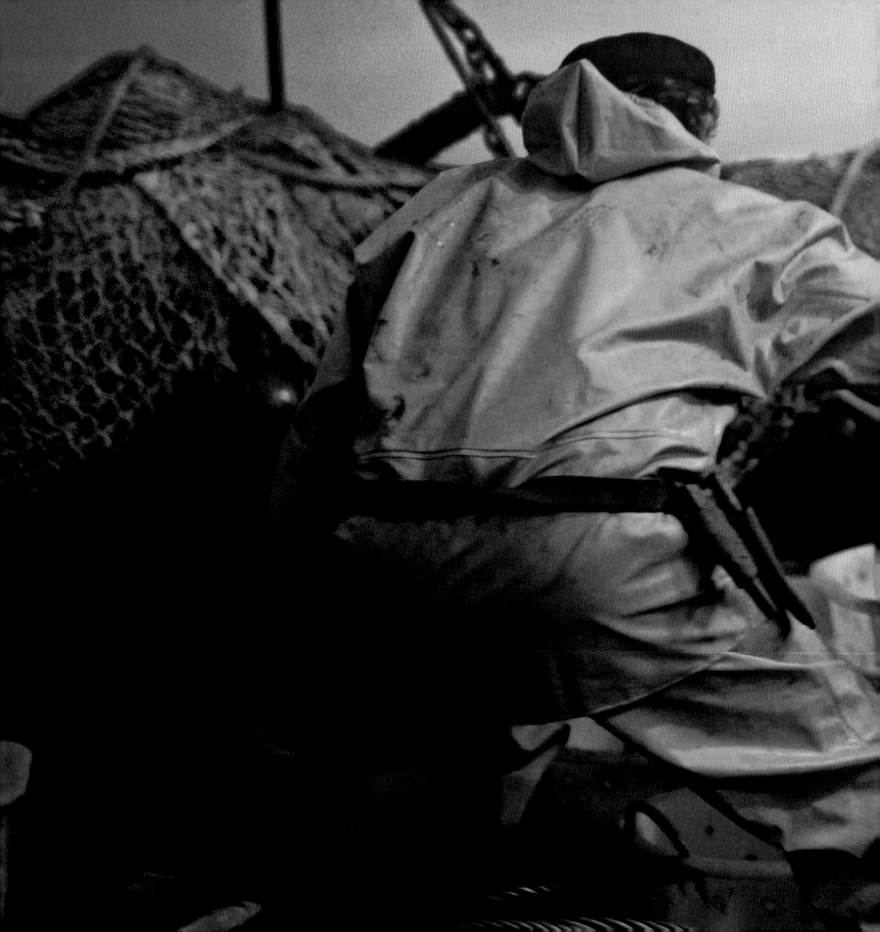

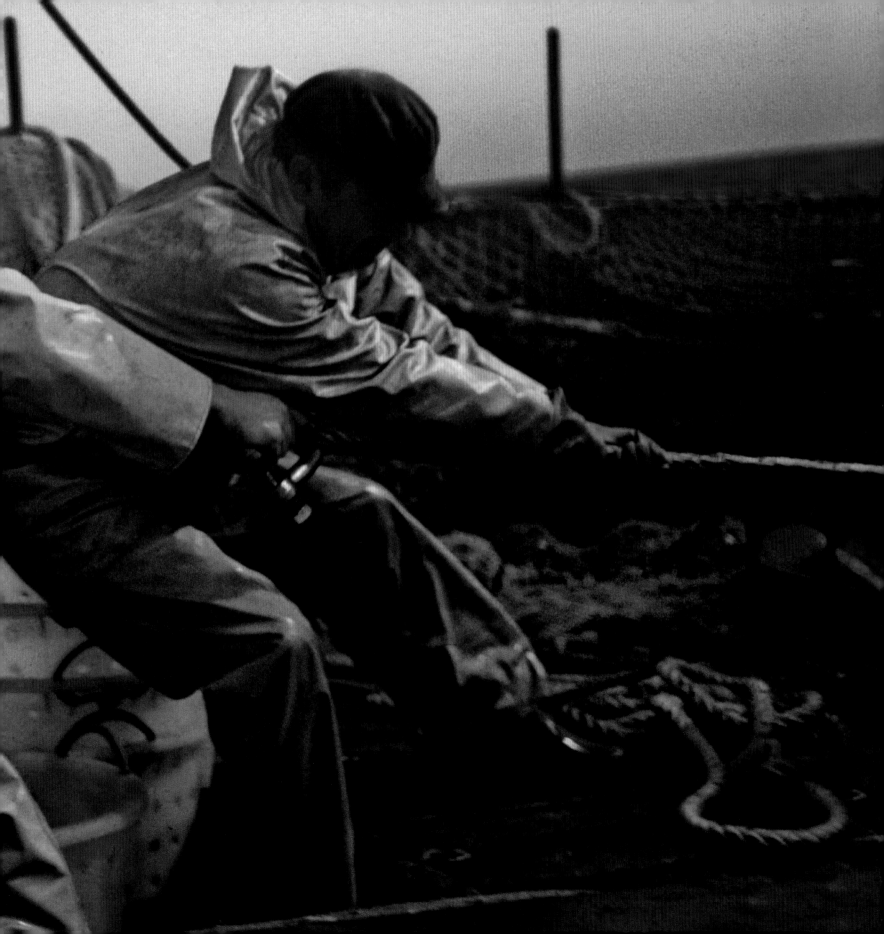

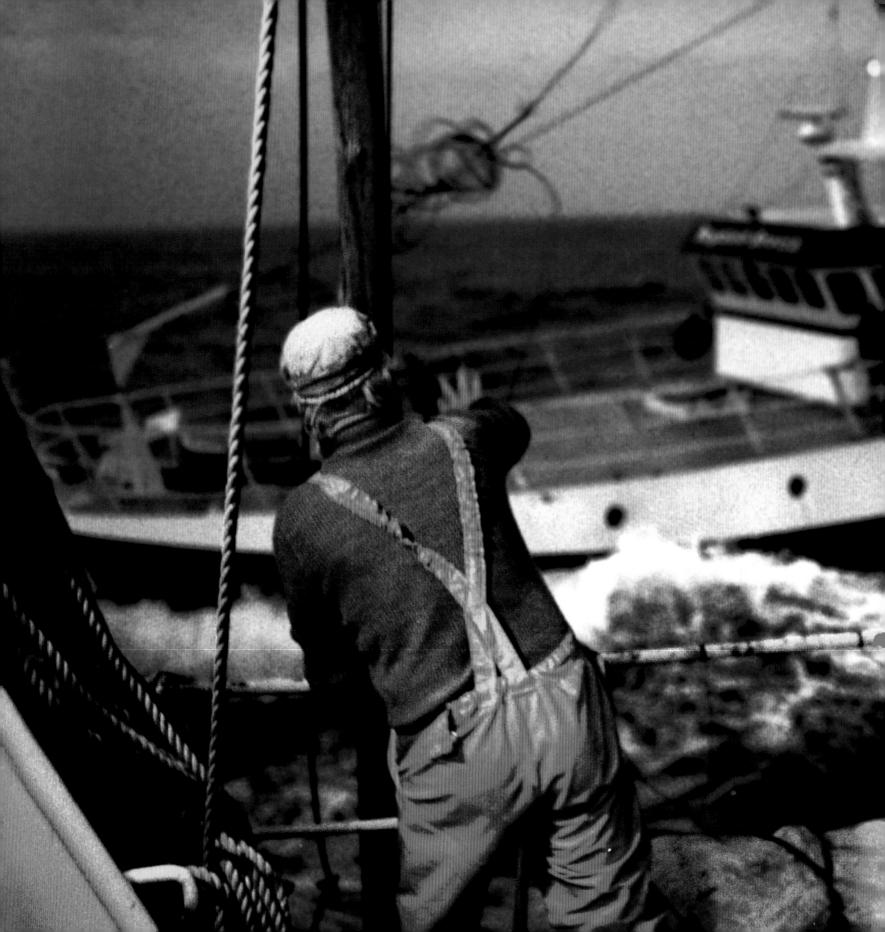

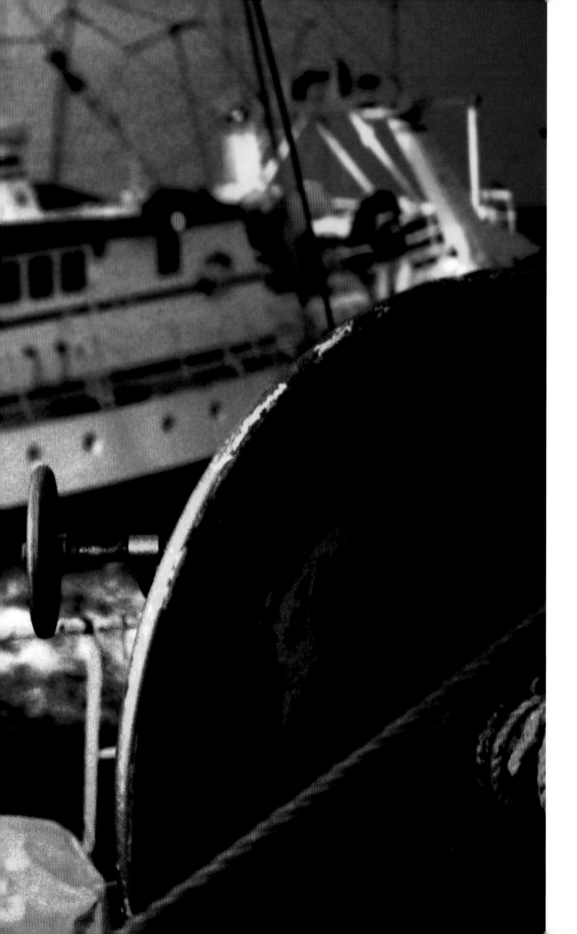

326-327 ● Atlantic Ocean, Gulf of Gascony (France) - Tuna fishing with the *Marie Catherine* and *Bugaled Breizh*.

328-329 ● Atlantic Ocean, Gulf of Gascony (France) - Fishing for swordfish.

330-331 ● Pacific Ocean, Gulf of Alaska (USA) - Pulling up the nets.

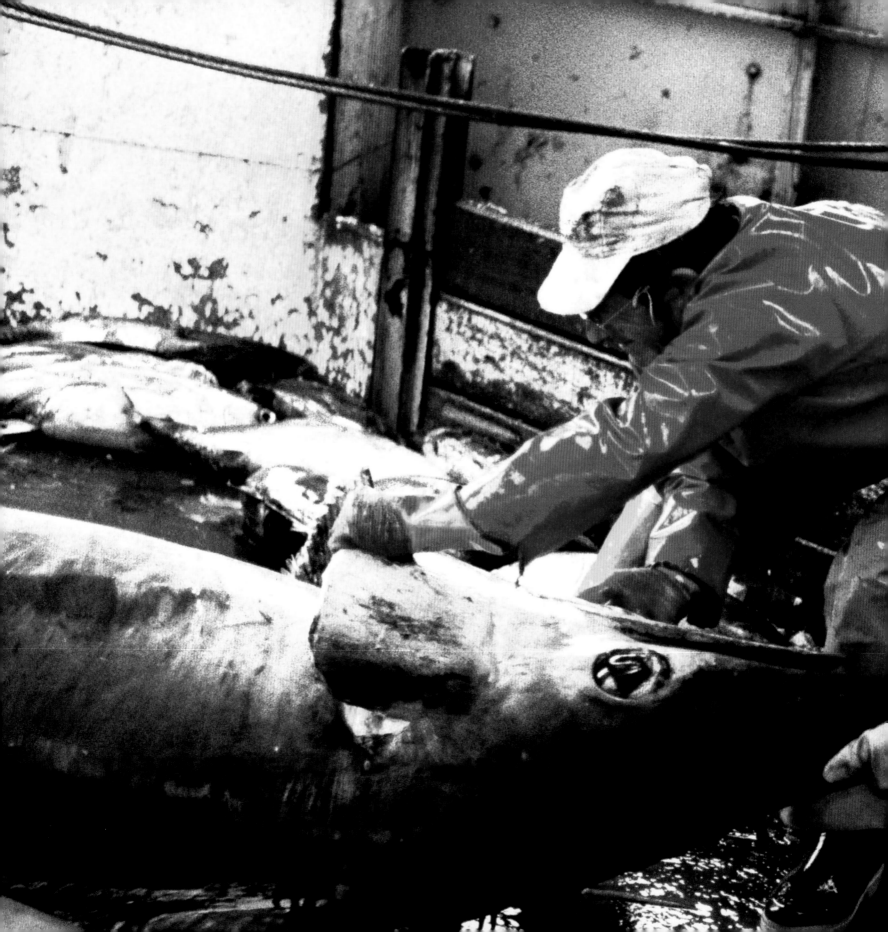

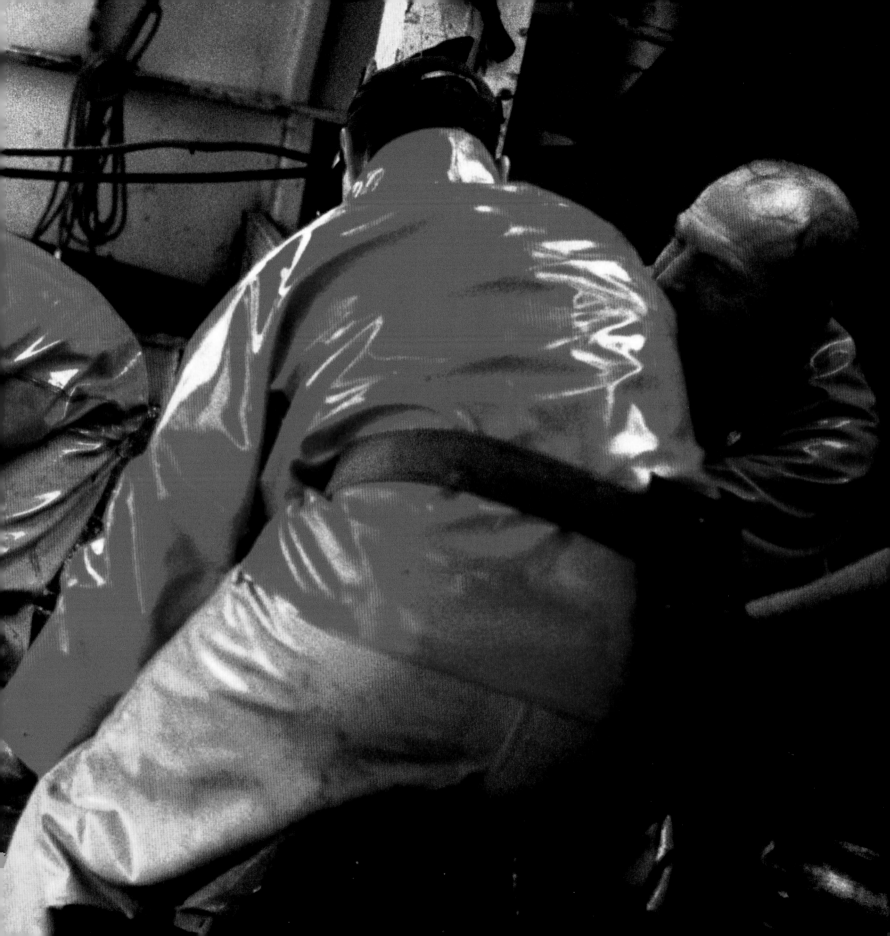

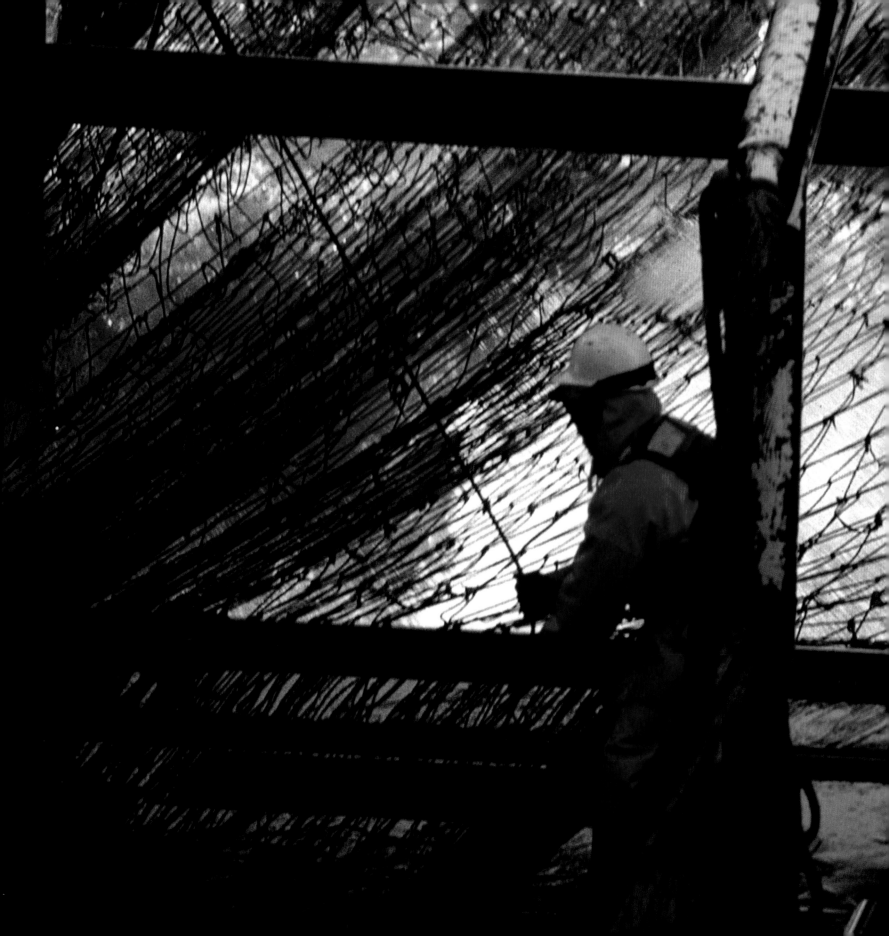

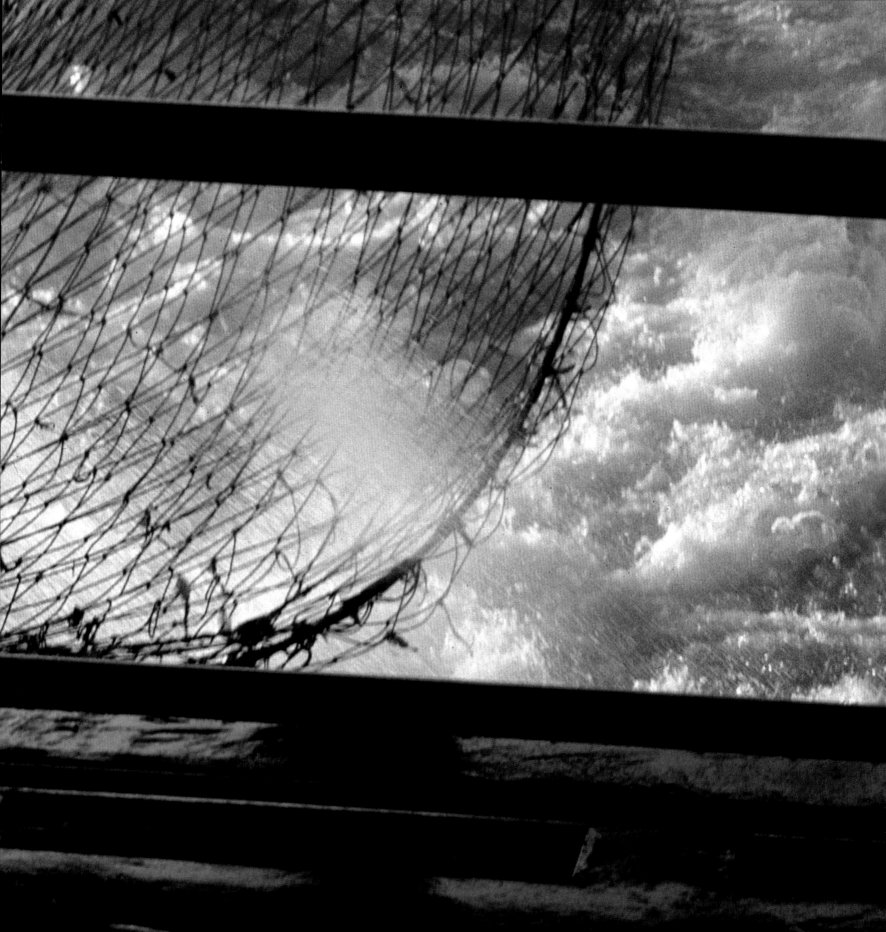

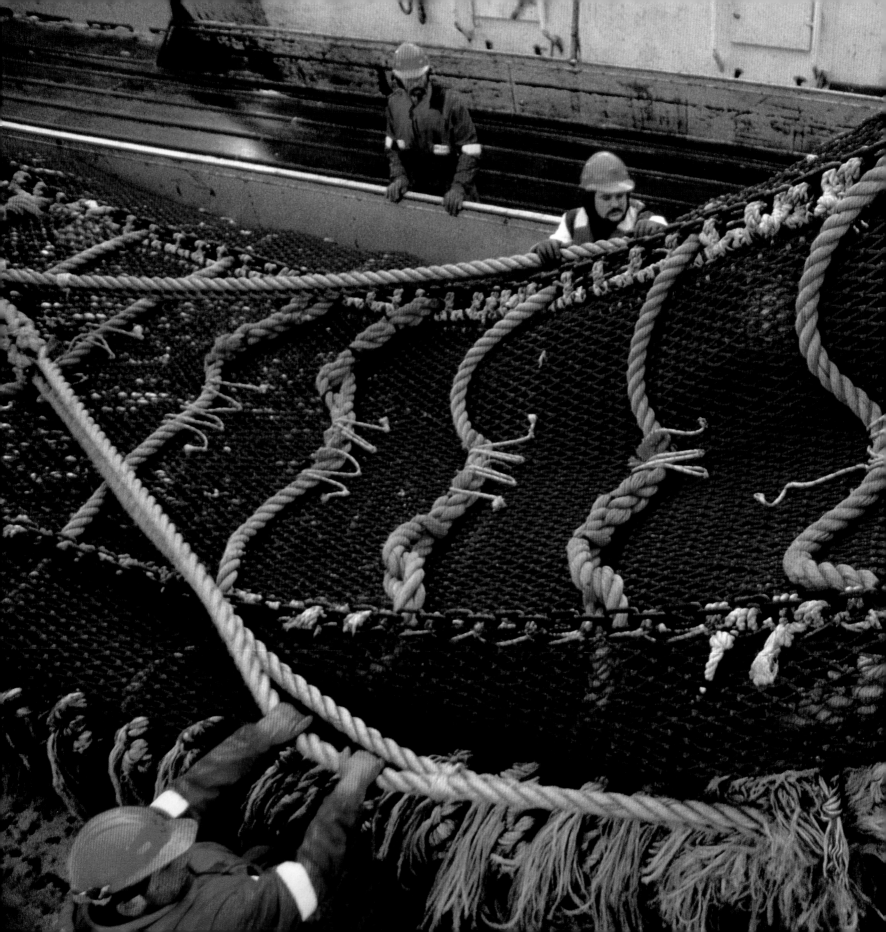

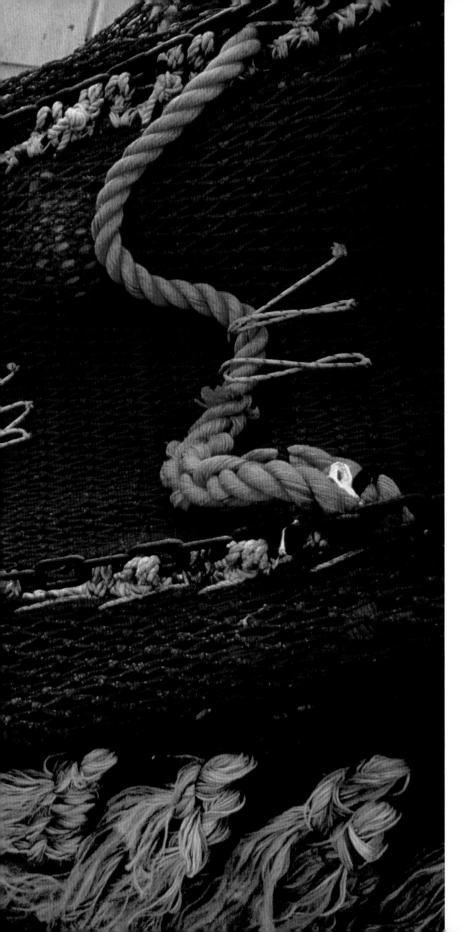

● Pacific Ocean, Gulf of Alaska (USA) - Fishermen letting out the nets.

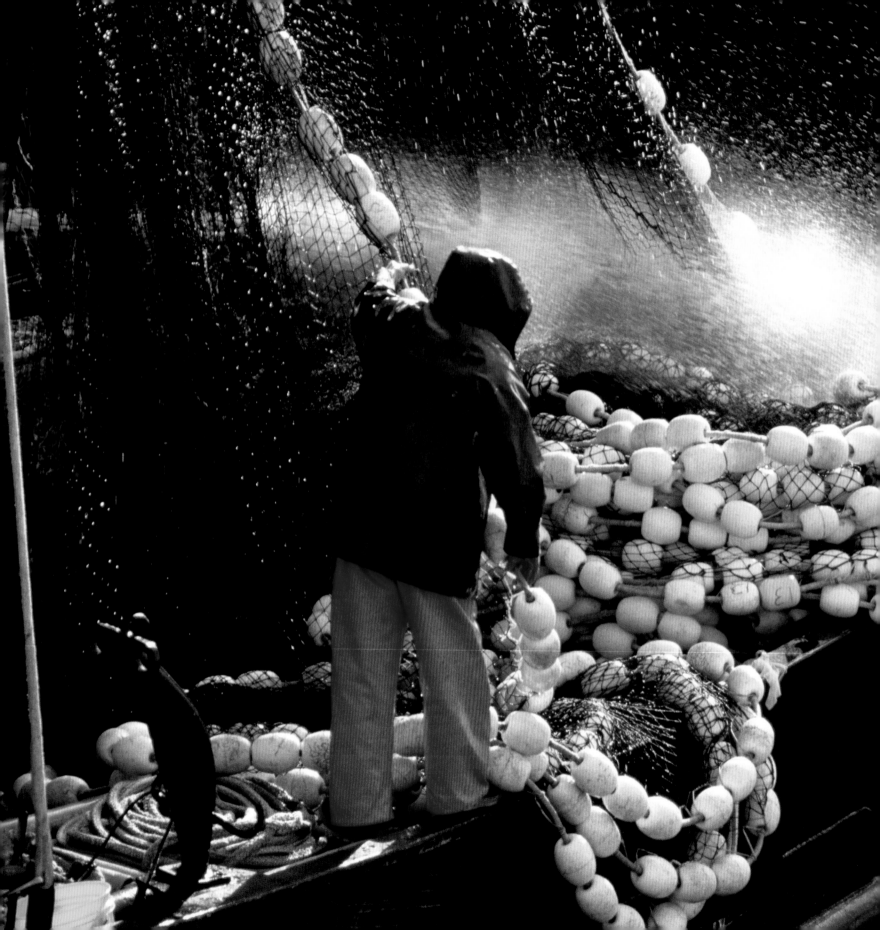

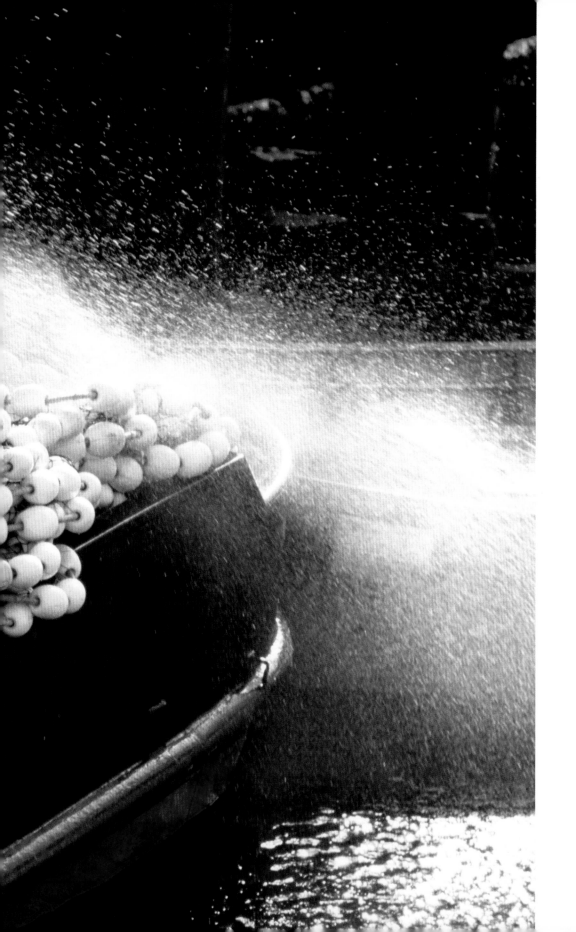

334-335 ● Pacific Ocean, the port of Ketchikan, Alaska (USA) - Washing the nets.

336-337 ● Indian Ocean, Zanzibar (Tanzania) - Collecting seaweed.

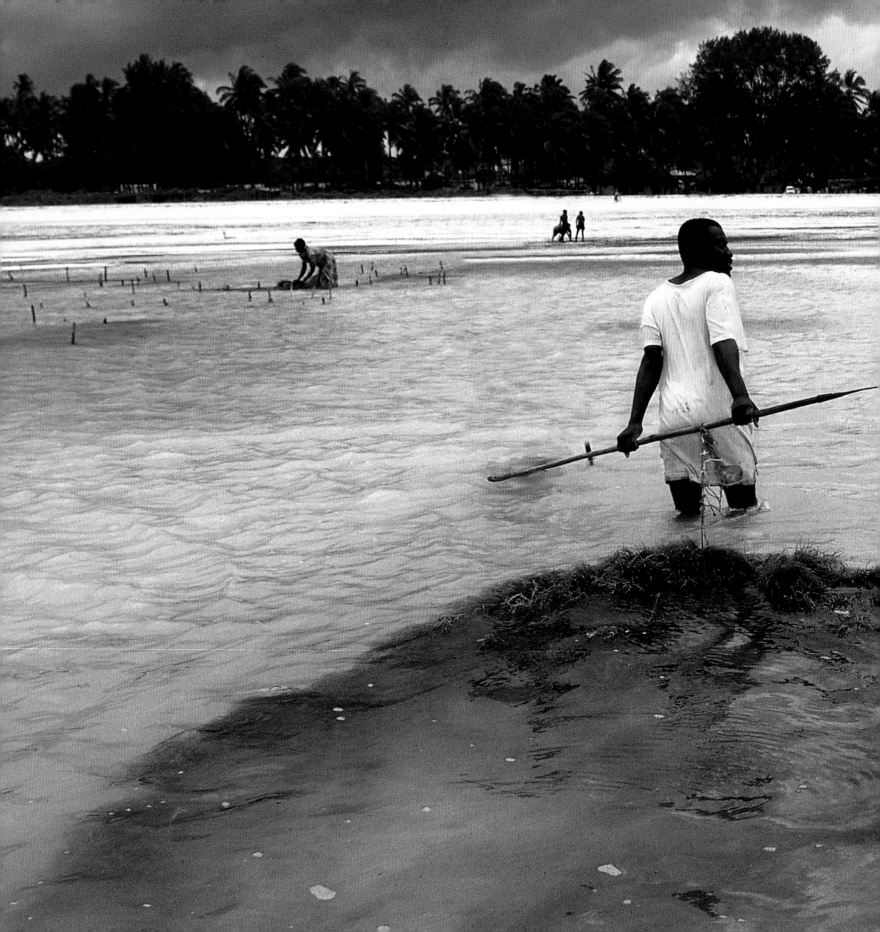

"MEANWHILE, AROUND THE HAMLET, UNDER THE PALMS, WHERE THE BLUE SHADOW LINGERED, THE RED COALS OF COCOA HUSK AND THE LIGHT TRAILS OF SMOKE BETRAYED THE AWAKENING BUSINESS OF THE DAY; ALONG THE BEACH MEN AND WOMEN, LADS AND LASSES, WERE RETURNING FROM THE BATH IN BRIGHT RAIMENT, RED AND BLUE AND GREEN..."

from IN THE SOUTH SEAS
by Robert Louis Stevenson

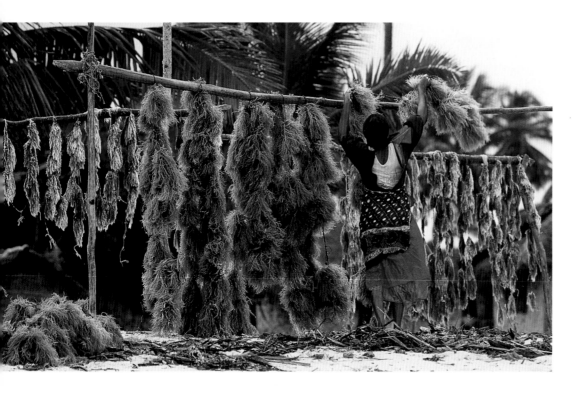

Indian Ocean, Zanzibar (Tanzania) - Collecting and washing seaweed.

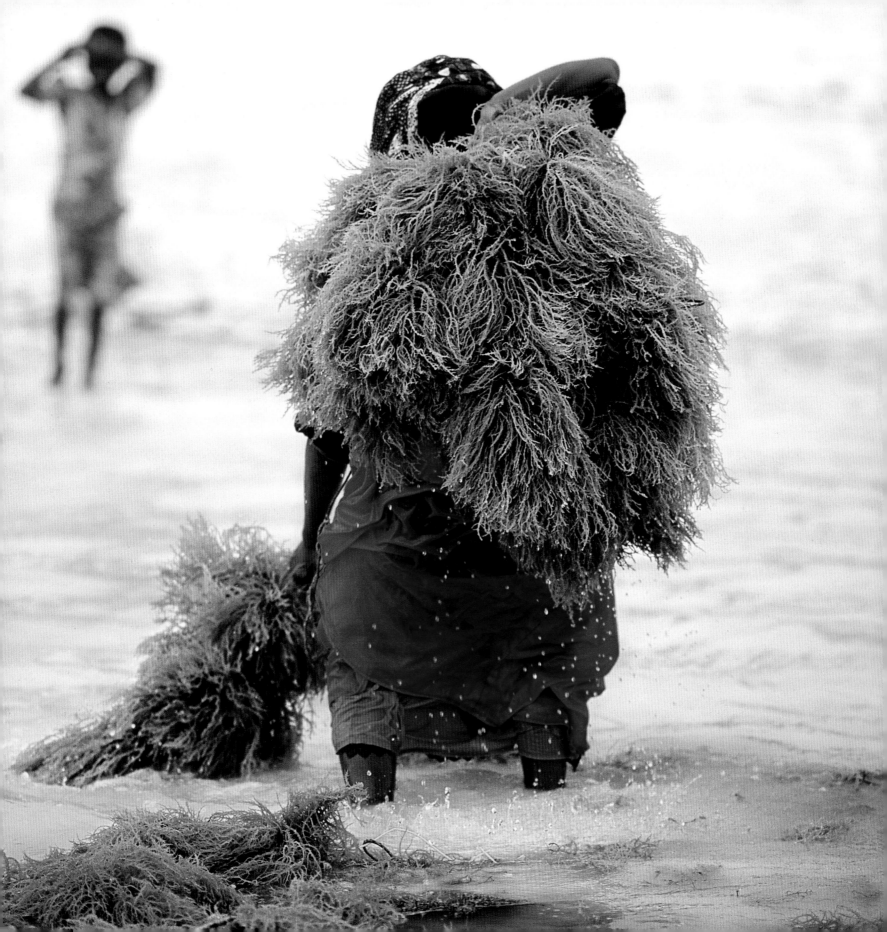

Ancient professions

340-341 and 342-343 ●
Indian Ocean, Bagamoyo
(Tanzania) - Caulking and
repairing a dugout canoe.

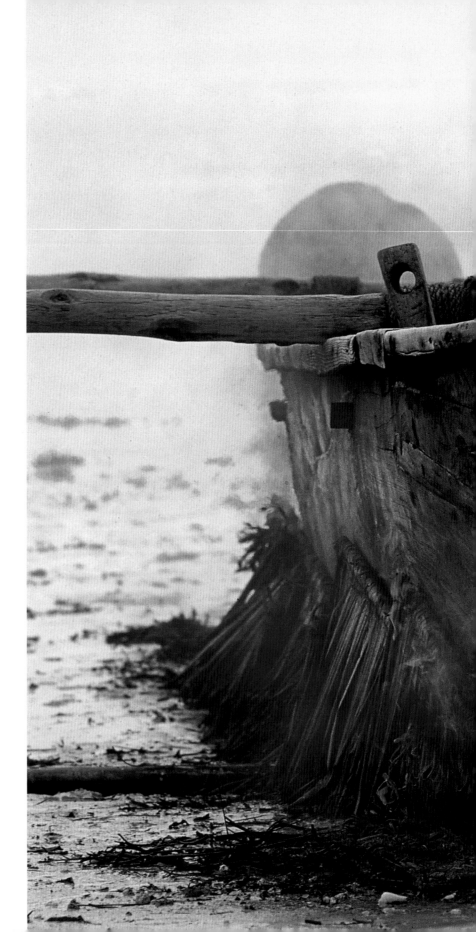

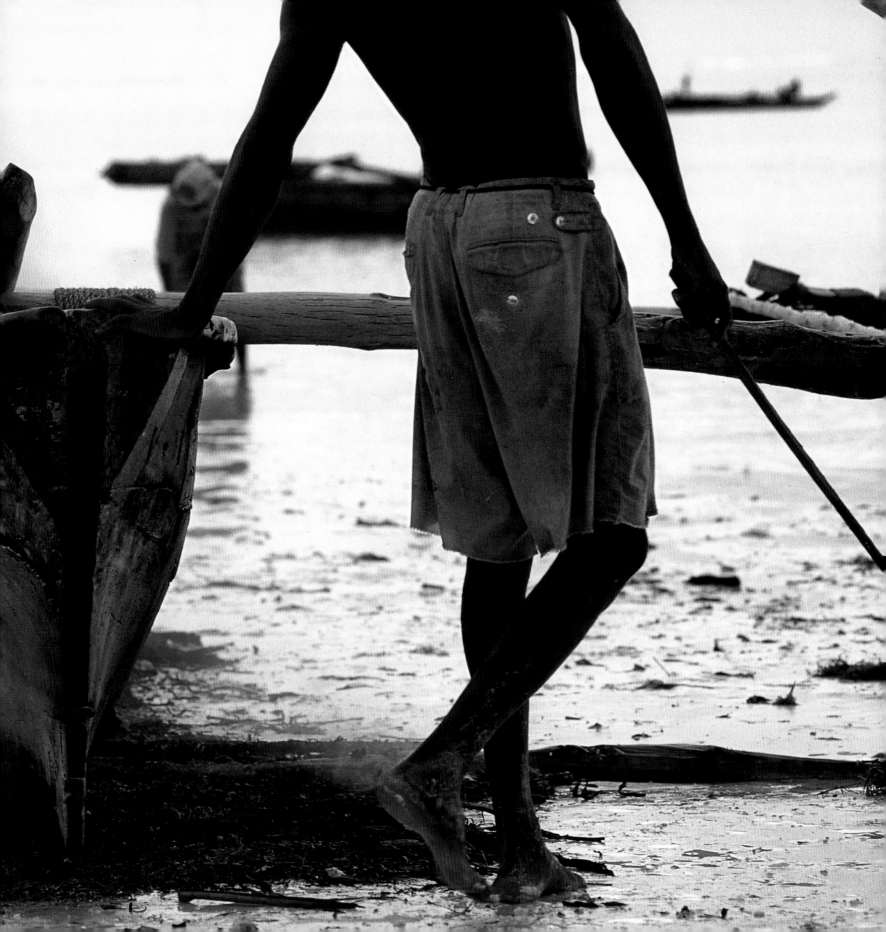

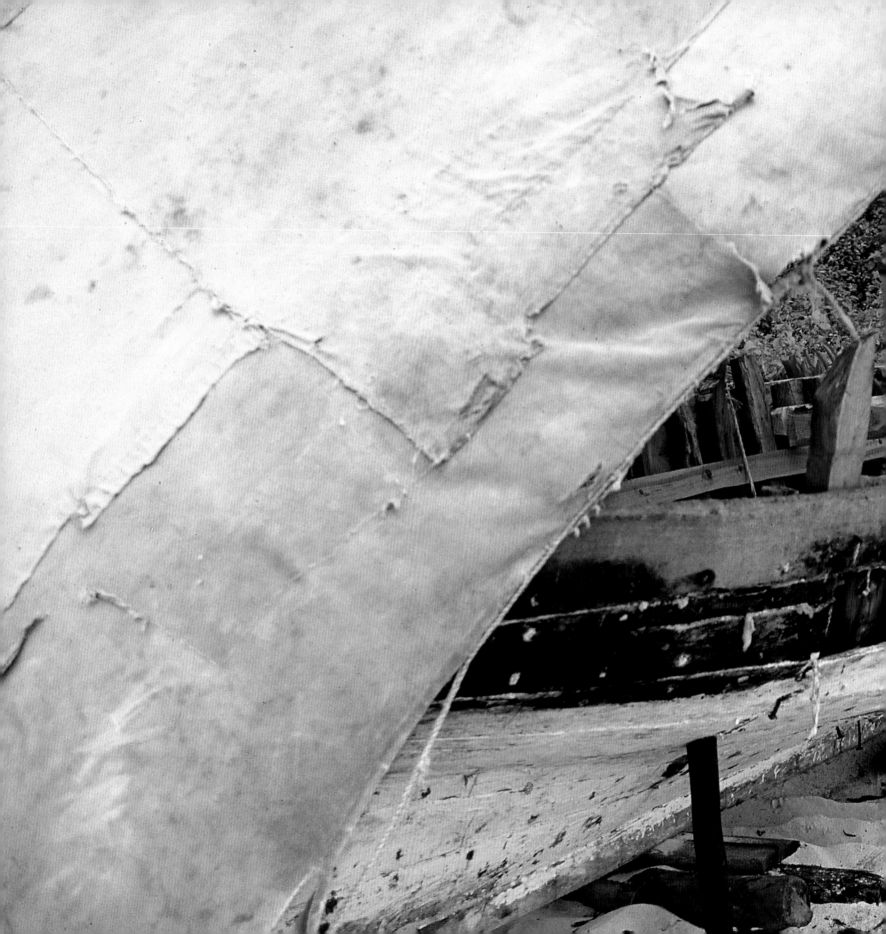

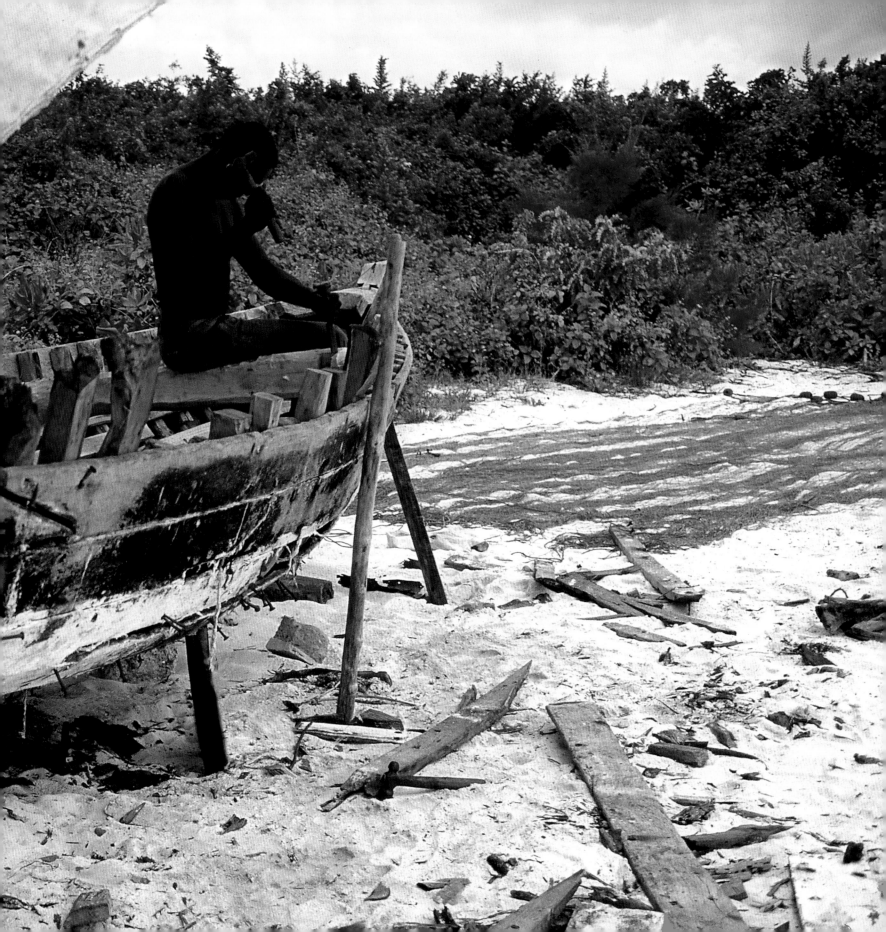

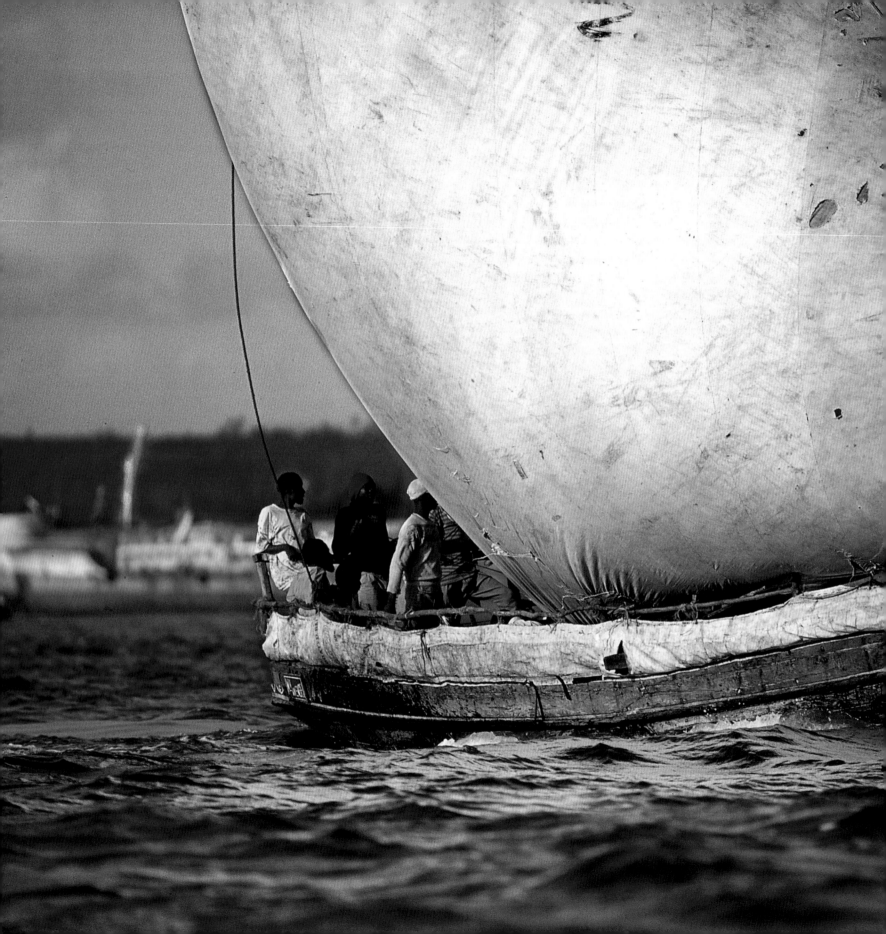

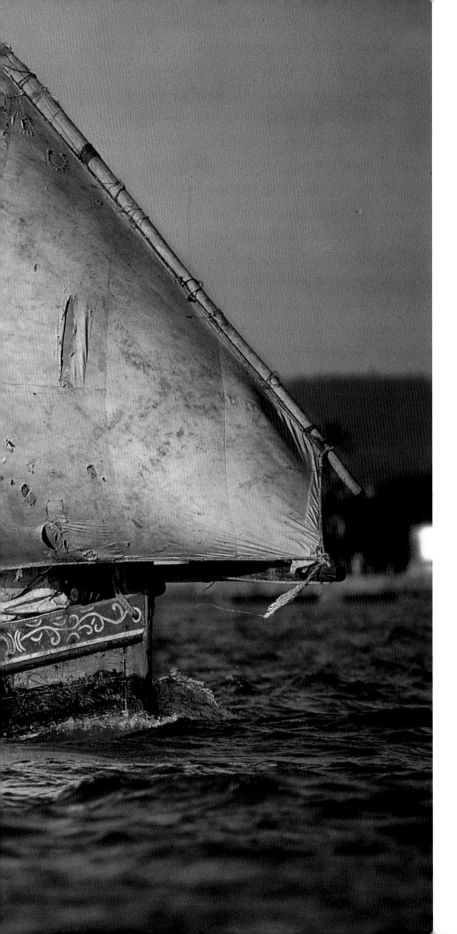

Looking toward
the horizon

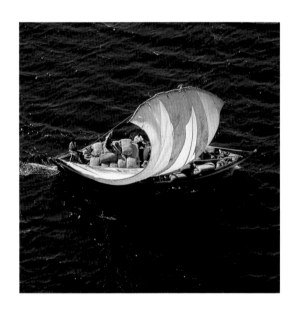

344-345 and 345 ● Olndian Ocean, Zanzibar (Tanzania) - Fishermen on a *dhow*.

346-347 ● Atlantic Ocean, Badagry (Nigeria) - Trawling from the shore.

348-349 ● Pacific Ocean, Bay of Tokyo (Japan) - Trawling.

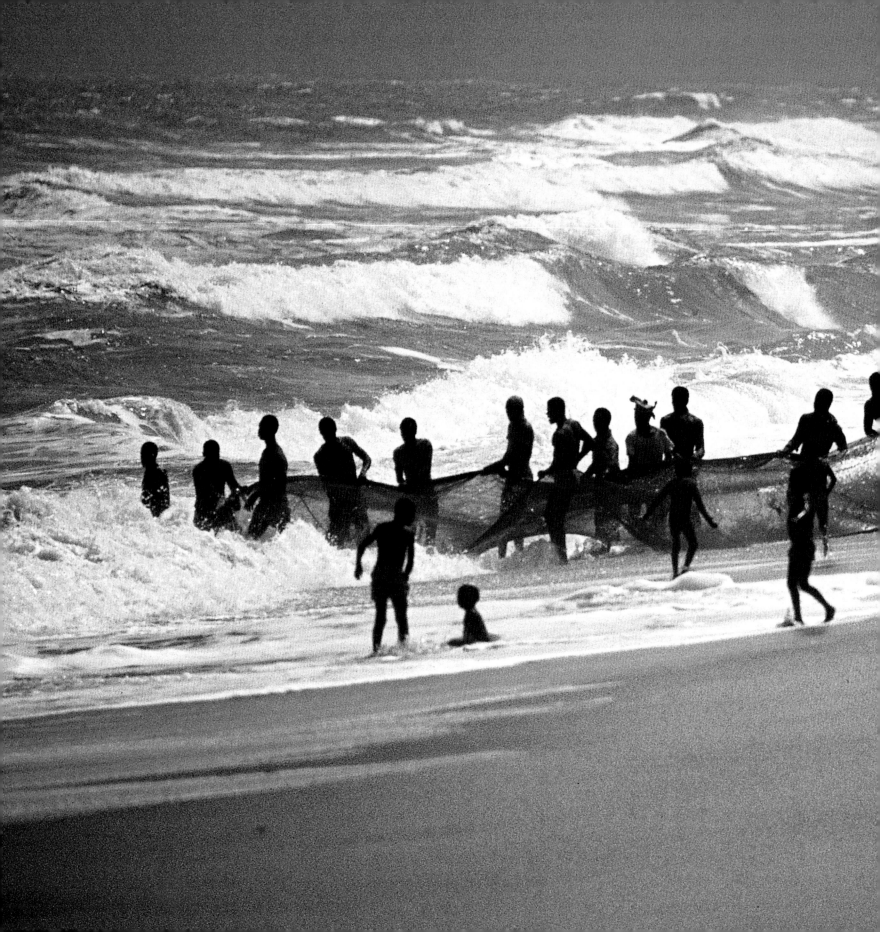

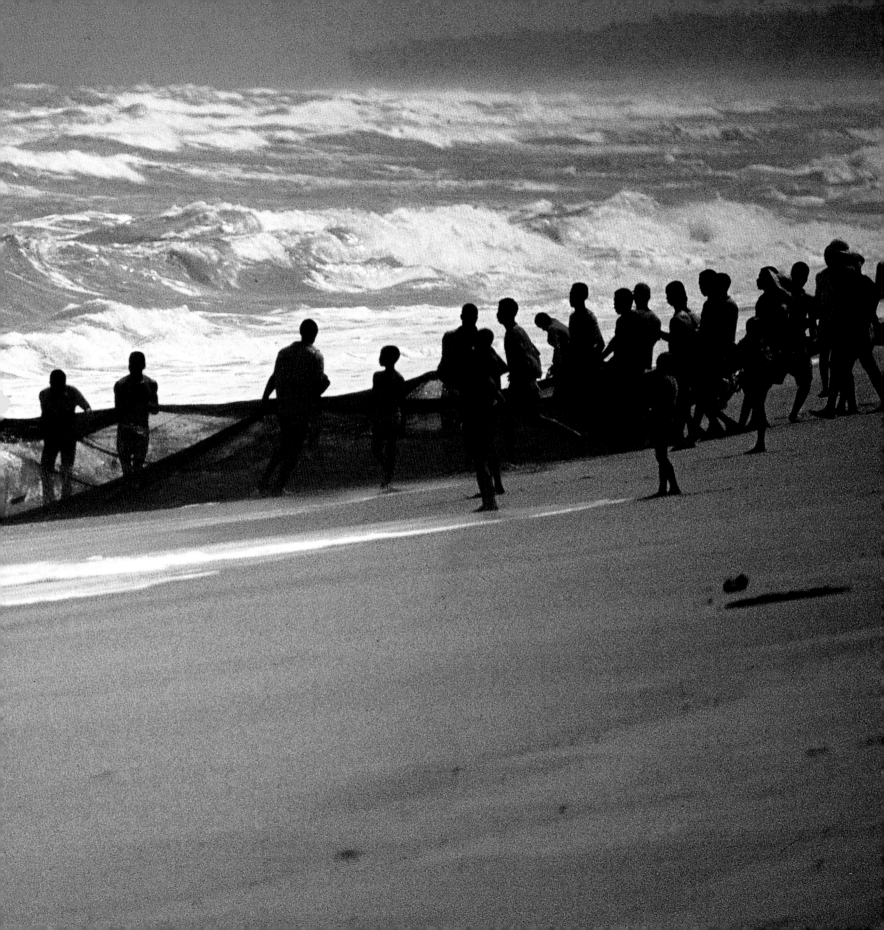

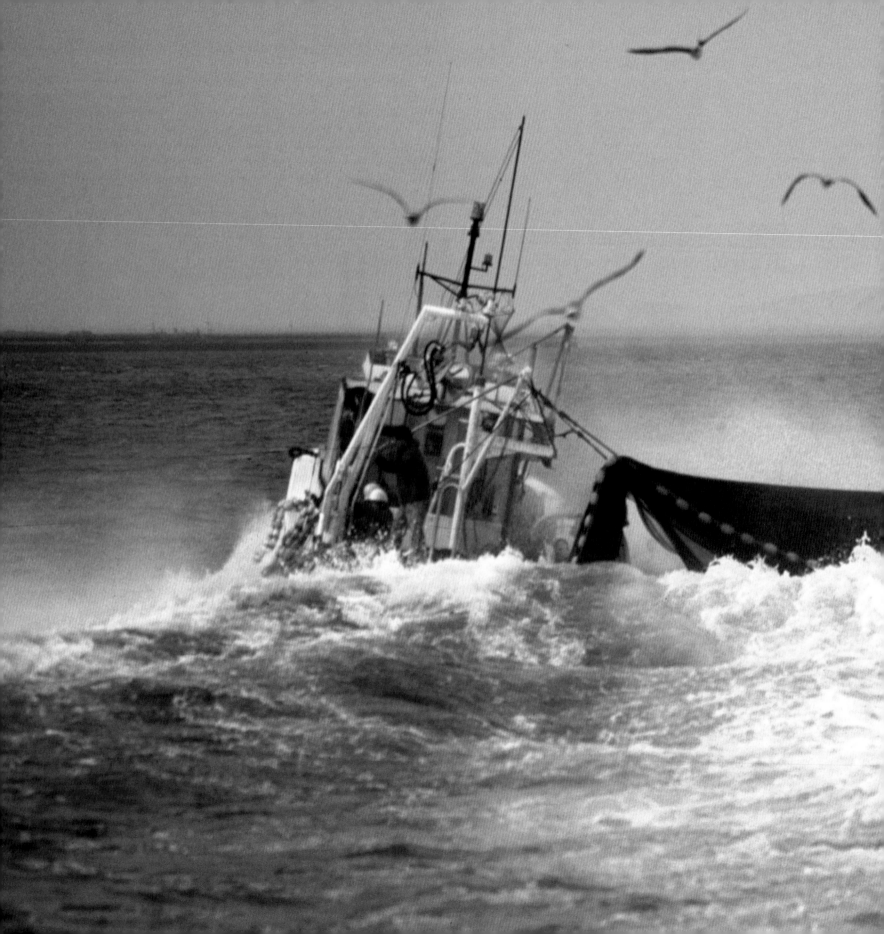

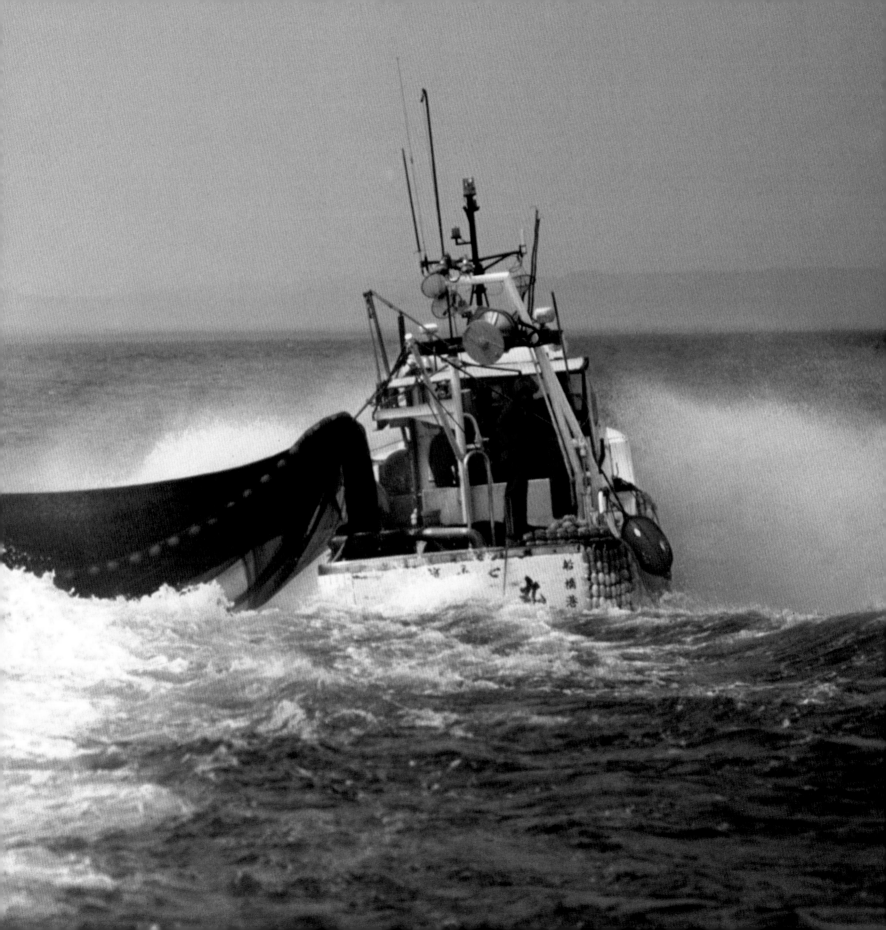

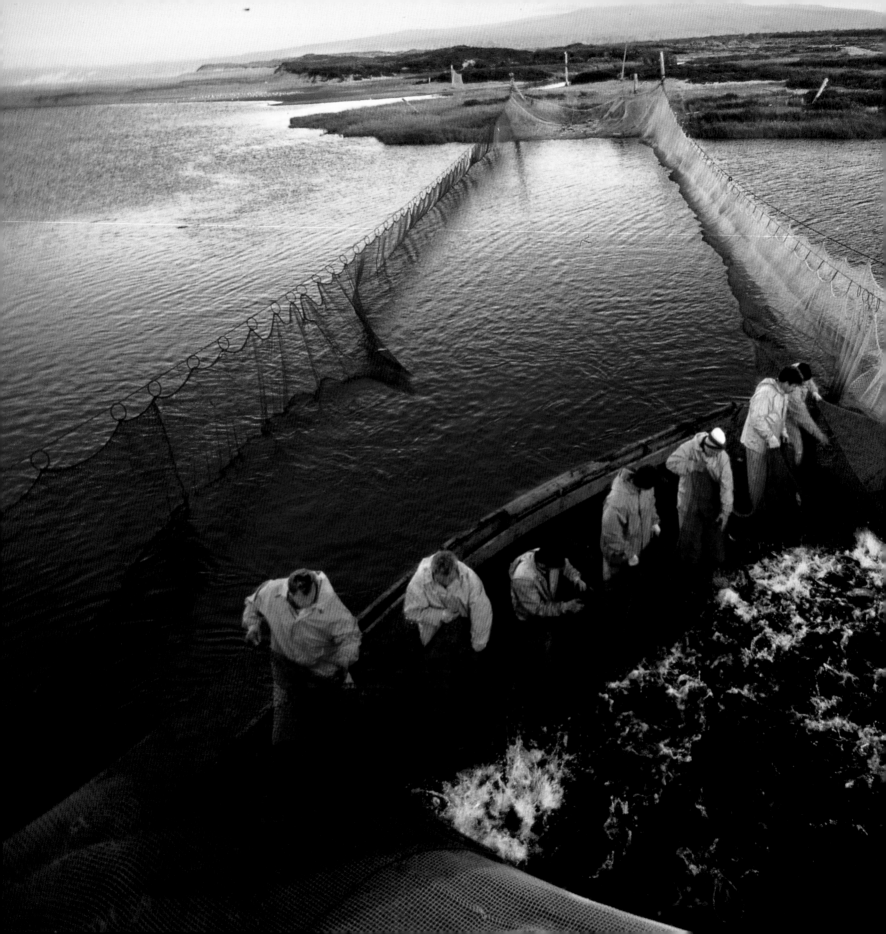

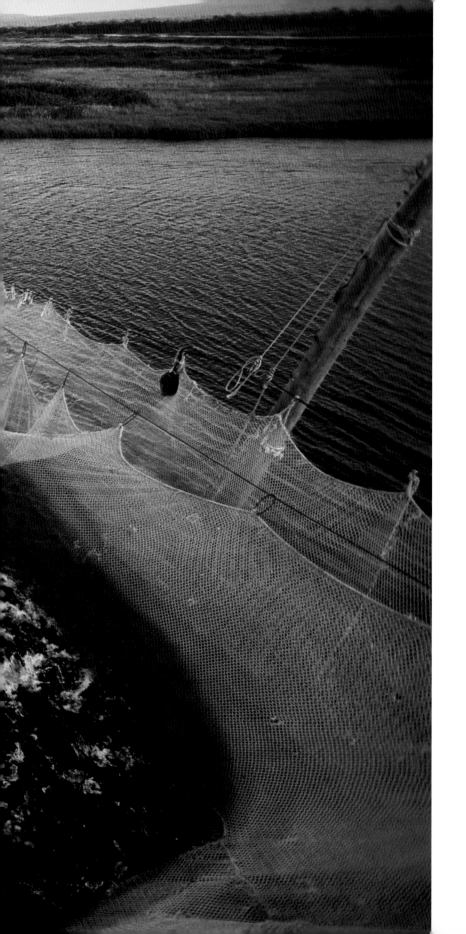
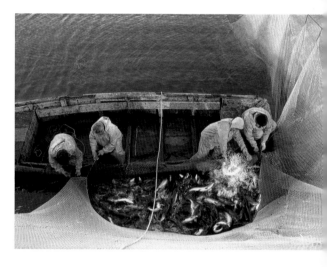

Pacific Ocean, Kuril Islands
(Russia) – Fish gathering.

" SEA PEOPLE ARE NOT NATURALLY JOYFUL. THEIR MELANCHOLY STEMS FROM THE SENSE OF DEATH AND INCOMPREHENSIBLE BOUNDLESSNESS THAT THE SEA HIDES. THEY ARE FISHERMEN, WOOD CUTTERS, FARMERS, LAND- AND SEA-GOING TRADERS, FINANCIERS, THE OWNERS OF SAILBOATS... "

from SEA PEOPLE
by Giovanni Comisso

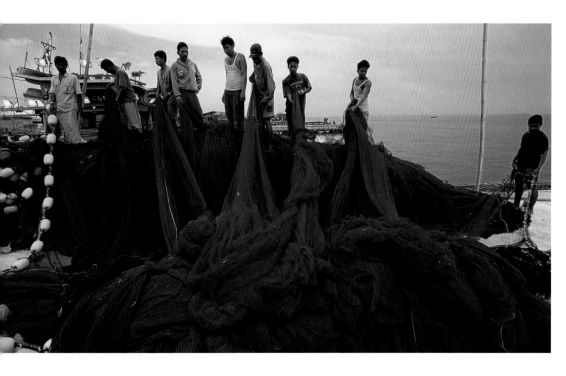

352 ● Pacific Ocean, Indonesia - Fishermen folding up their nets.

353 ● Pacific Ocean, Tohoku (Japan) - Repairing nets.

354-355 ● South China Sea, Kaohsiung (Taiwan) - Unloading the fishing boats.

356-357 ● Pacific Ocean, Indonesia - Shrimp fishermen.

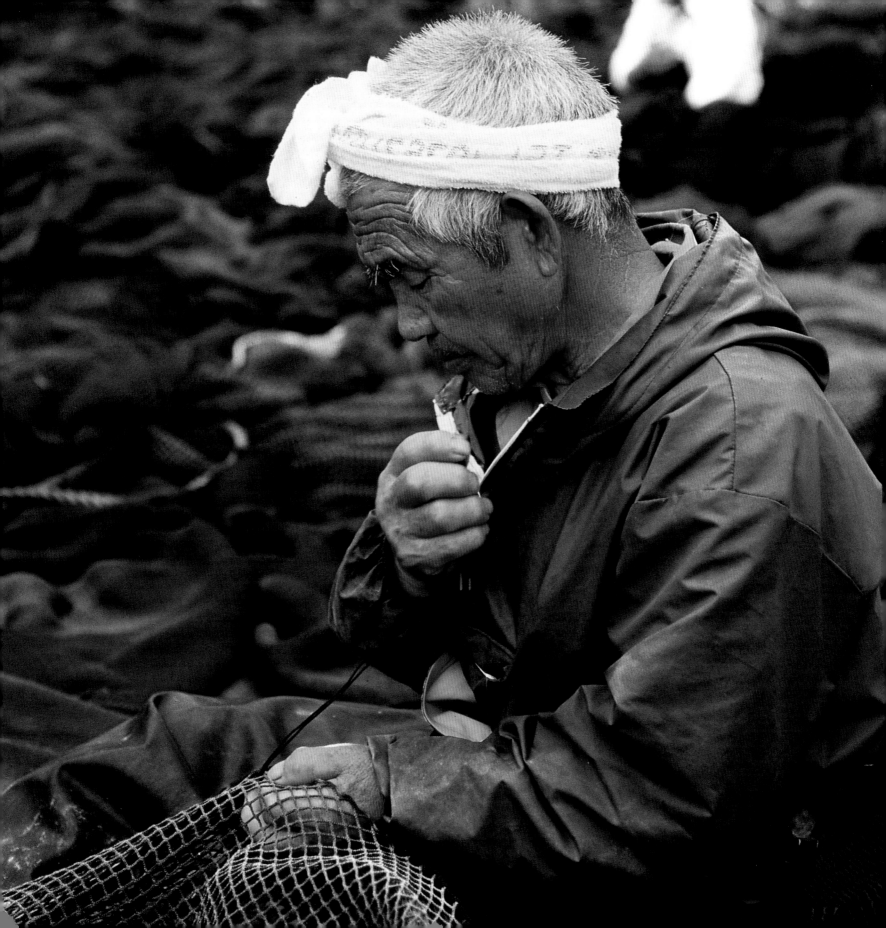

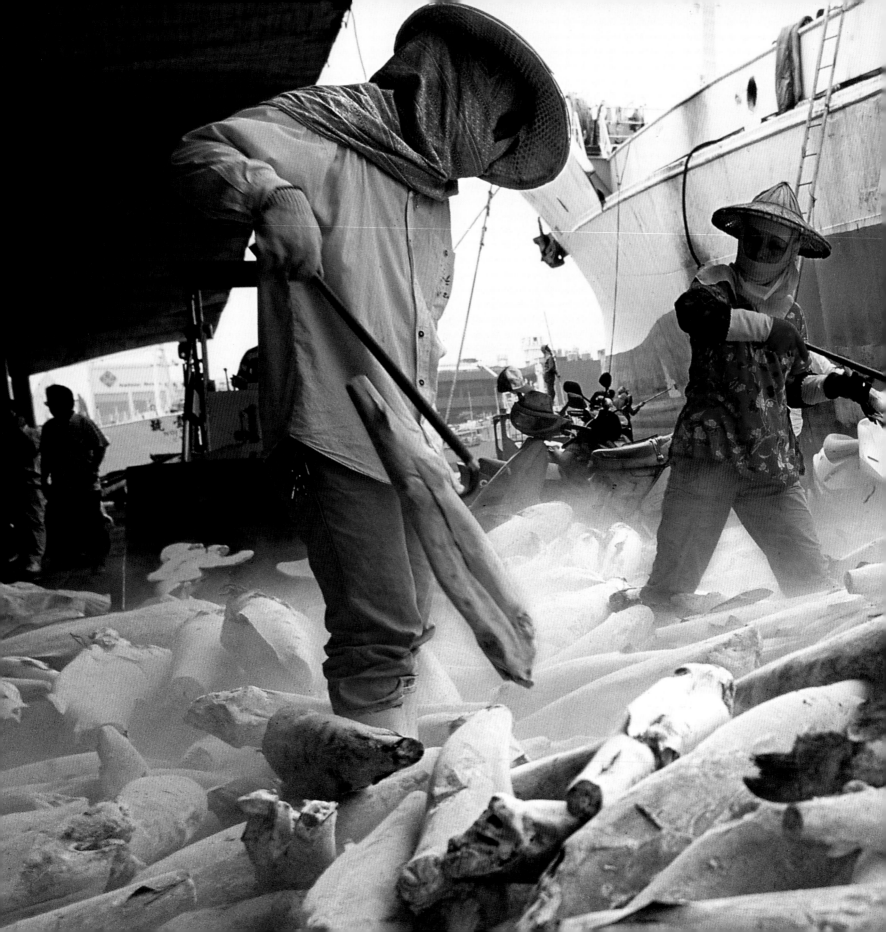

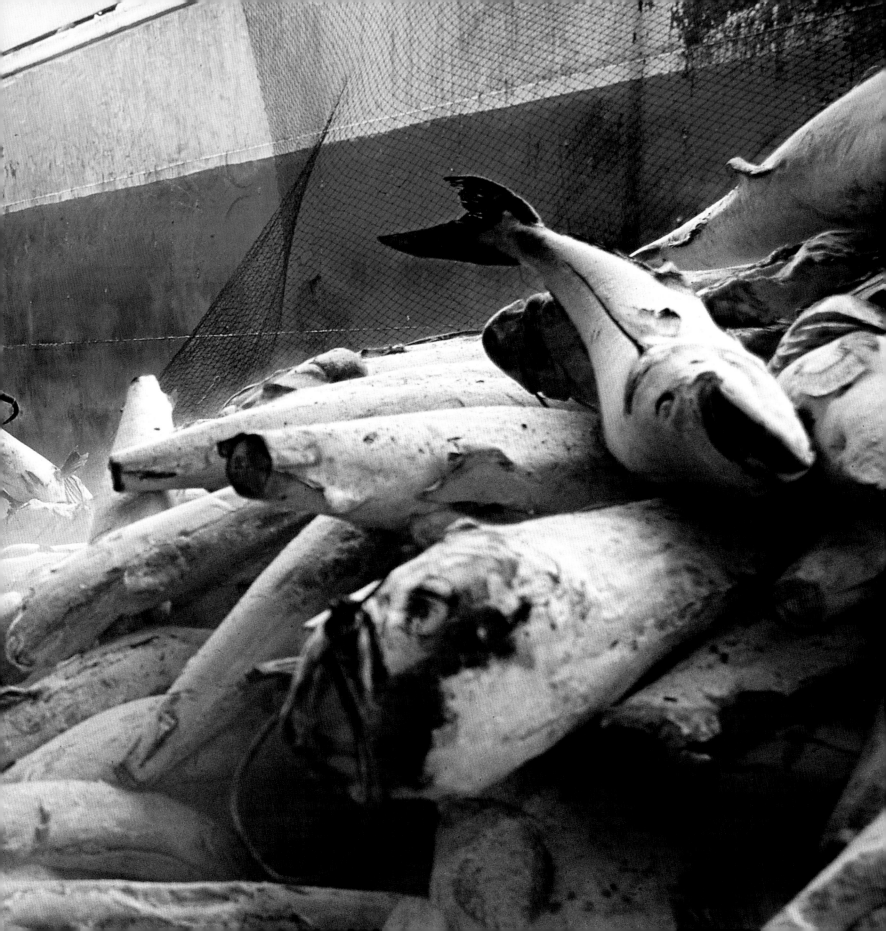

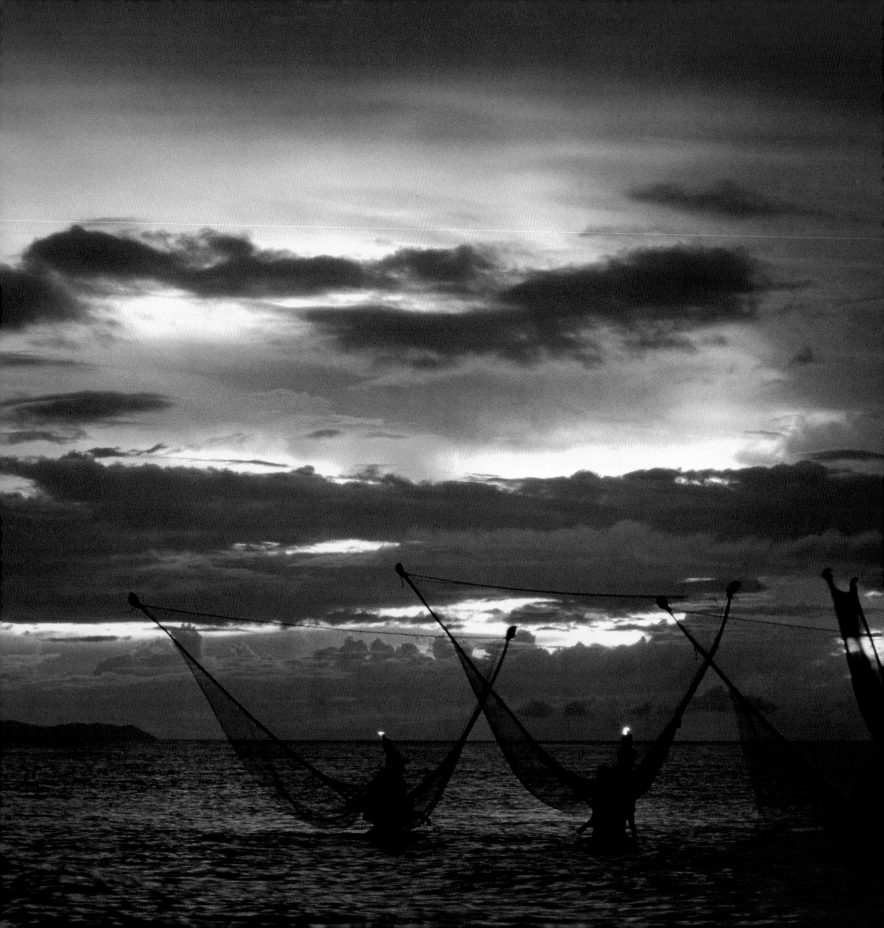

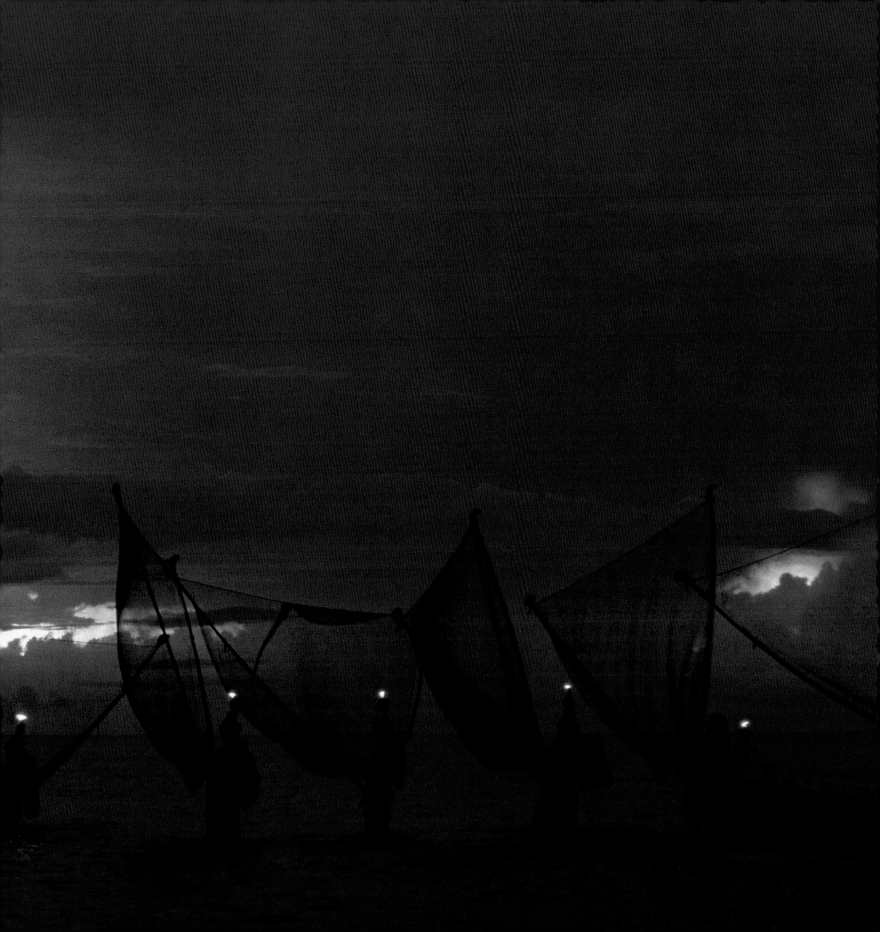

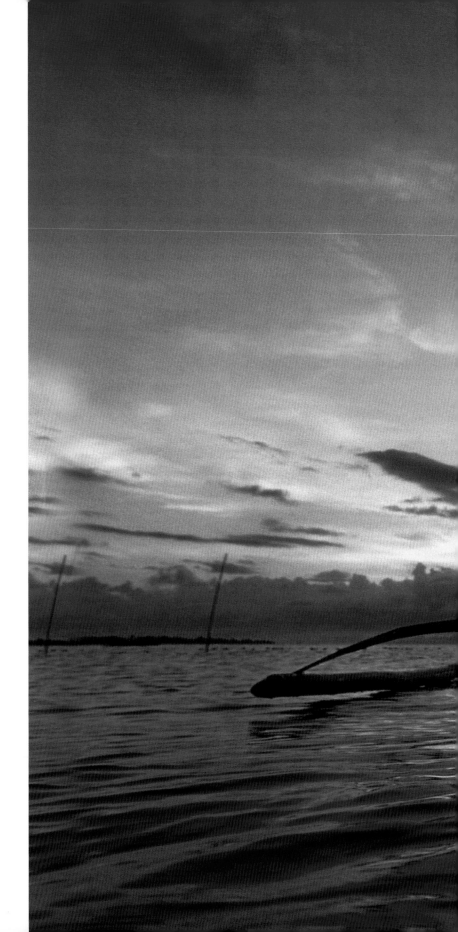

After sundown

358-359 ● Pacific Ocean,
Indonesia - Seahorse fisherman.

360-361 ● Pacific Ocean,
Komodo (Indonesia) - Fishermen.

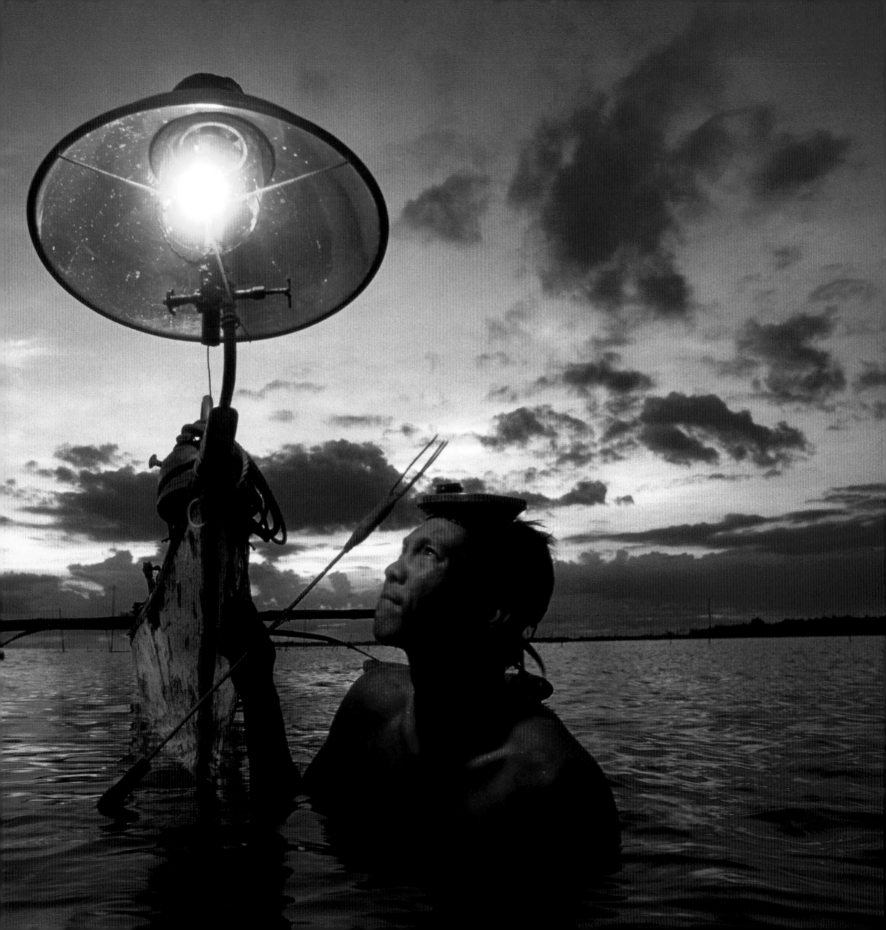

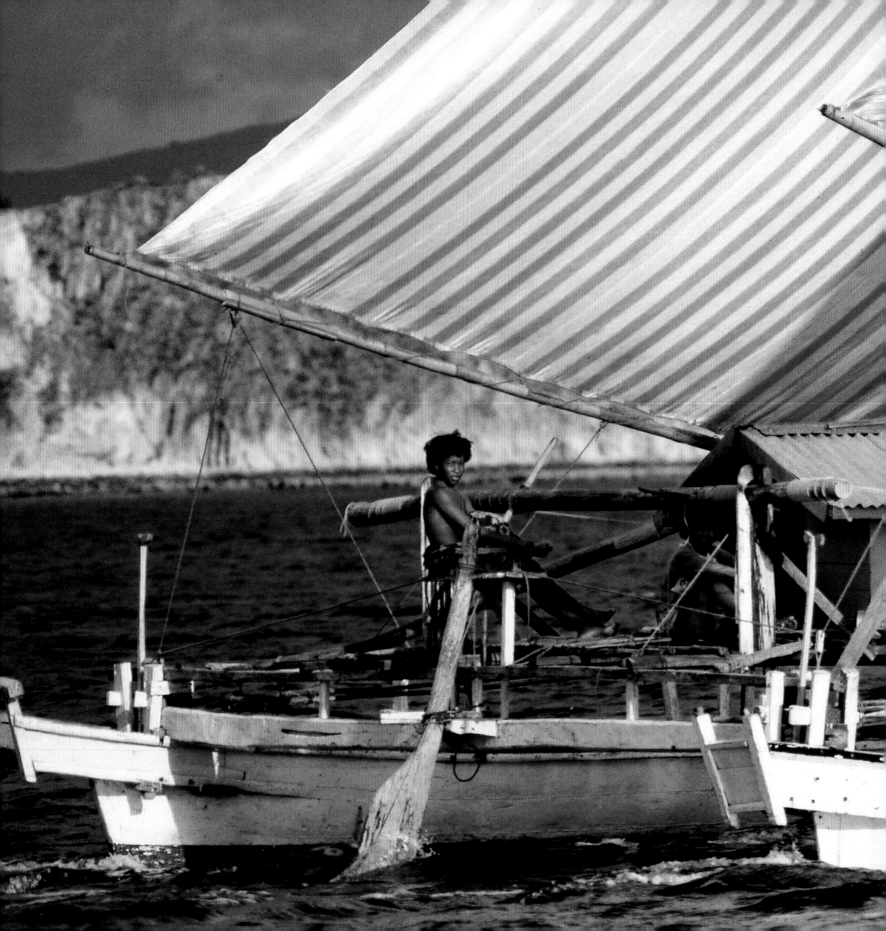

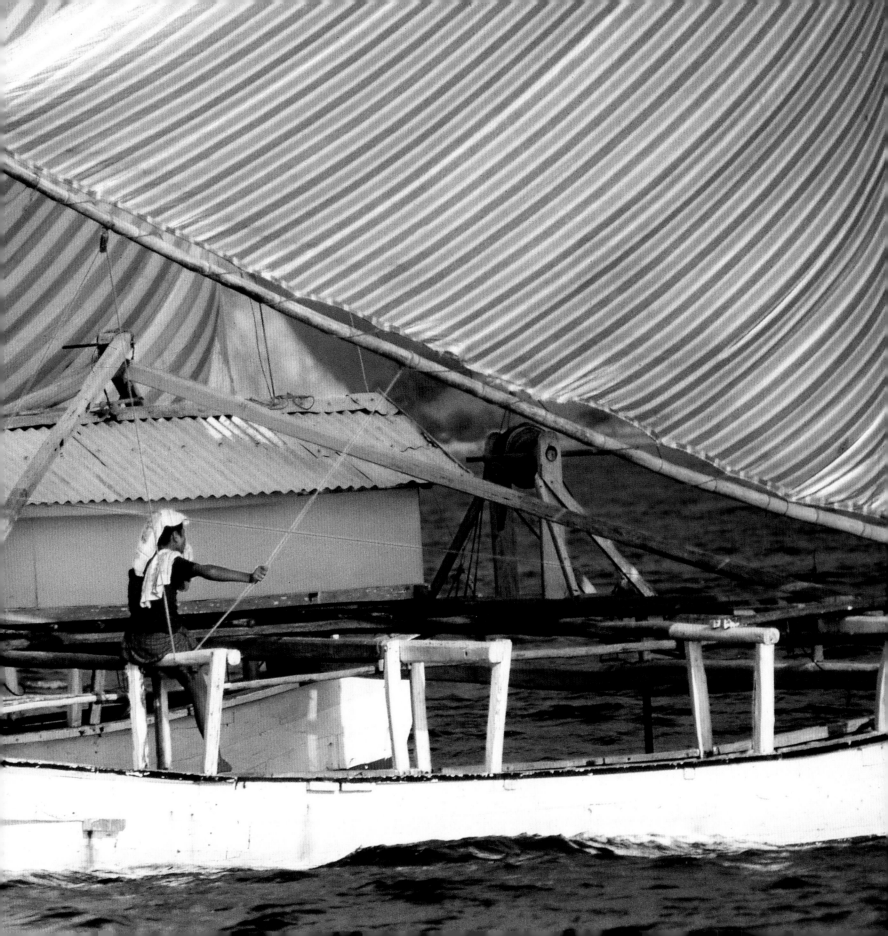

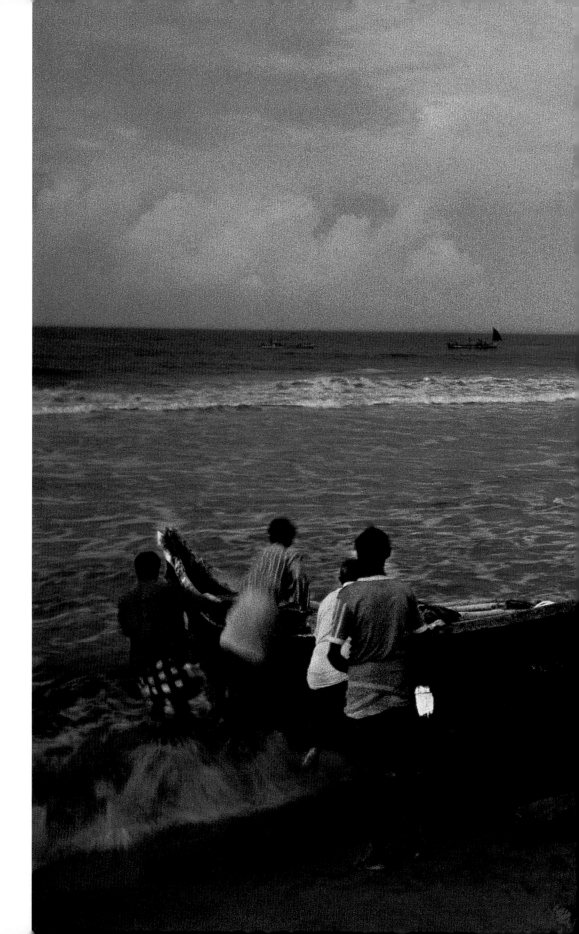

Under the full moon

Indian Ocean, Kerala (India) - Night fishing.

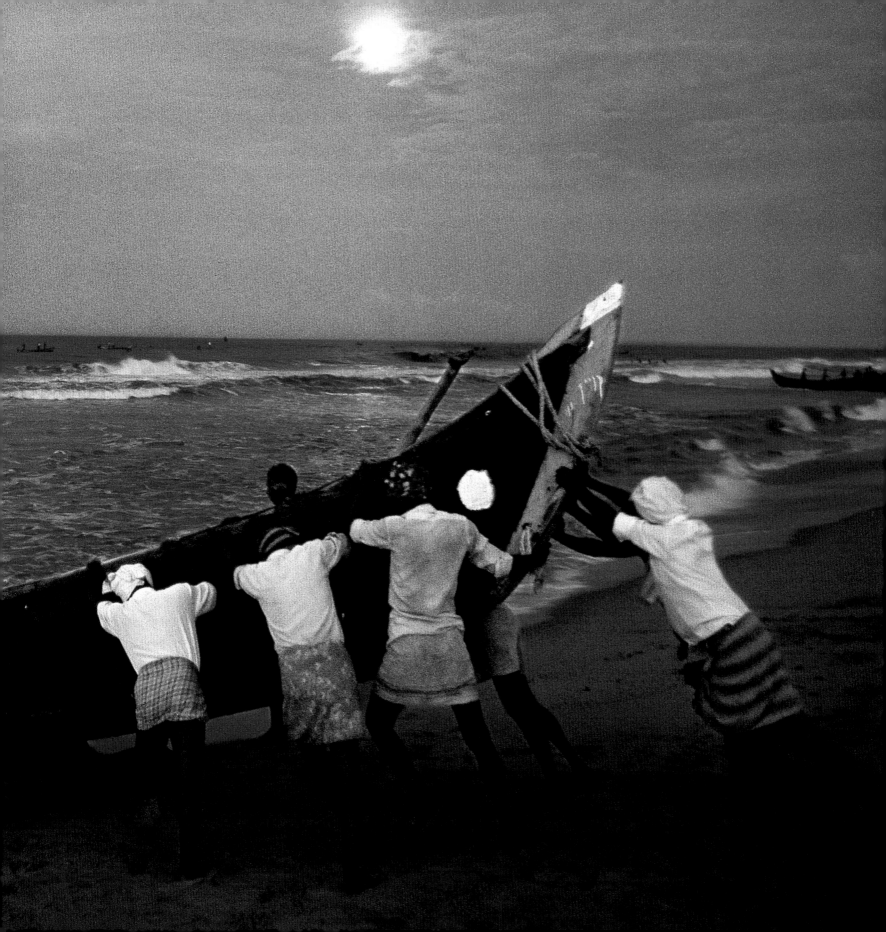

The SENTINELS of the SEA

GIANNI GUADALUPI

• Atlantic Ocean, Rhode Island (USA) - Sakonnet Point Light at Little Compton.

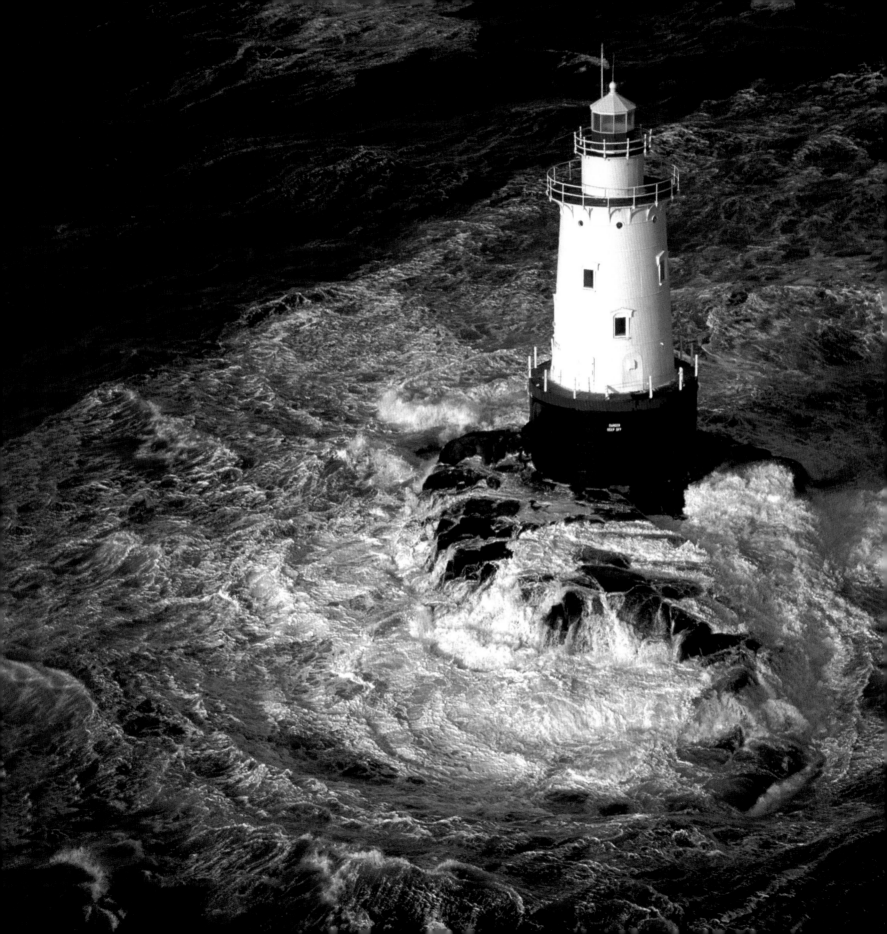

INTRODUCTION The Sentinels of the Sea

PERHAPS THE INVENTION OF THE LIGHTHOUSE WAS PROMPTED BY THE WORRY OF WIVES AND THE ANGUISH THAT, AT THE FALL OF NIGHT, WRACKED THE HEARTS OF THE ELDERLY AND CHILDREN WAITING ON THE BEACH FOR THE RETURN OF SOME SIMPLE CRAFT HELD OFF SHORE BY THE WIND, THE CURRENT, THE TIDE, OR THE HAND OF A HOSTILE GOD. SOMEONE SAID, 'LET'S LIGHT A LARGE FIRE AS HIGH AS POSSIBLE ON THE CLIFF SO THEY CAN SEE THE DIRECTION TO TAKE.' LATER, THE IMPROVISED IDEA WAS TURNED INTO AN INSTITUTION, THE FIRE WAS GIVEN A FIXED LOCATION SO THAT IT WOULD BE AS RADIANT AND EFFECTIVE AS POSSIBLE. IT WAS ASSIGNED A FEEDER, A KEEPER, WHO PERHAPS ENJOYED A SORT OF SACRED,

INTRODUCTION The Sentinels of the Sea

PRIESTLY PRESTIGE WHEN FIRE WAS STILL CONSIDERED A PART OF THE

MYSTERY OF NATURE. AND WHEN CITIES BEGAN TO BE BUILT ON THE

SHORES OF THE SEAS AND OCEANS AND WERE ENDOWED WITH

FRIENDLY STRUCTURES CALLED PORTS, THE FIRE-LIGHTHOUSES GREW

TALLER AND LARGER. THEY BECAME HUGE TOWERS THAT DEMANDED

AN UNENDING SUPPLY OF WOOD, LIKE THE ONE BUILT ON THE ISLAND

OF PHAROS THAT ATTRACTED SHIPS TOWARDS THE EGYPTIAN CITY OF

ALEXANDRIA. THEY ALSO TOOK ON HUMAN FORMS, LIKE THE COLOS-

SUS OF RHODES BETWEEN WHOSE LEGS THE SHIPS HAD TO PASS, OR

THE STATUE OF LIBERTY THAT GREETS THE SHIPS THAT ENTER NEW

YORK HARBOR. HOWEVER THE REAL LIGHTHOUSE, THAT LIGHTHOUSE

The Sentinels of the Sea

Introduction

OF LEGEND, FIRESIDE TALES, FILM AND NOVELS, IS NOT A BURLY PORT BEACON NOR AN EXAGGERATEDLY HIGH URBAN STREET LAMP: IT IS A SMALL, SLENDER TOWER STANDING WAY OUT AMONG THE SURGING ROLLERS OFF A NOISY, JAGGED COASTLINE, SOMEWHERE UP AT THE TOP OF THE WORLD, AND WHICH CAN ONLY BE REACHED BY BOAT. IT IS VISITED ONLY BY SEAGULLS AND LIVED IN BY AN OLD, RETIRED SAILOR WHO HAS A CELLAR AND A LIBRARY FOR COMFORT, AND OCCUPIES HIS TIME BETWEEN A RADIO AND THE WEEKLY MAIL. THIS LIGHTHOUSE IS A COASTAL MINARET IN WHICH ONLY THOSE WHO WORSHIP SOLITUDE CAN ENJOY, CELEBRATING THE CEREMONY OF LIGHTING AND PUTTING OUT THE LIGHT AS PART OF A HERMIT'S EXISTENCE.

● Atlantic Ocean, Wexford (Ireland) - Tuskar Rock.

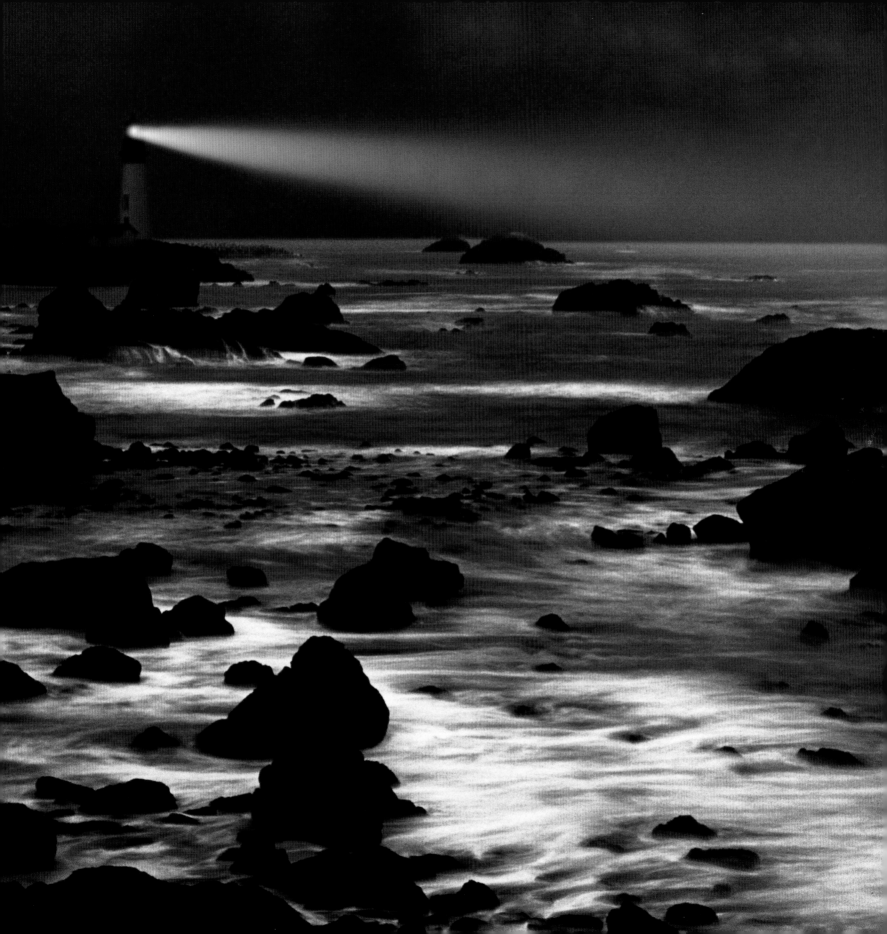

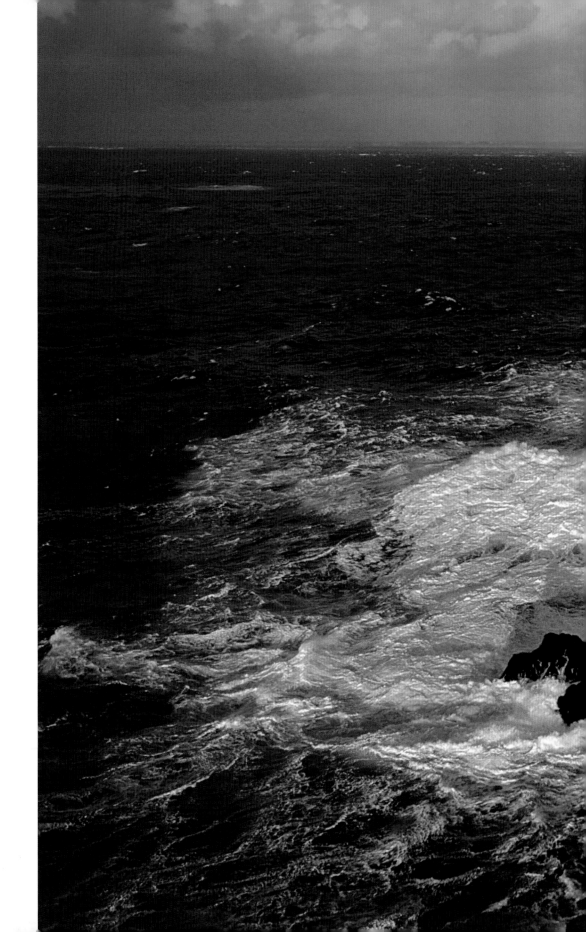

Atlantic Ocean, Brittany
(France) - Phare des
Pierres Noires off Finistère.

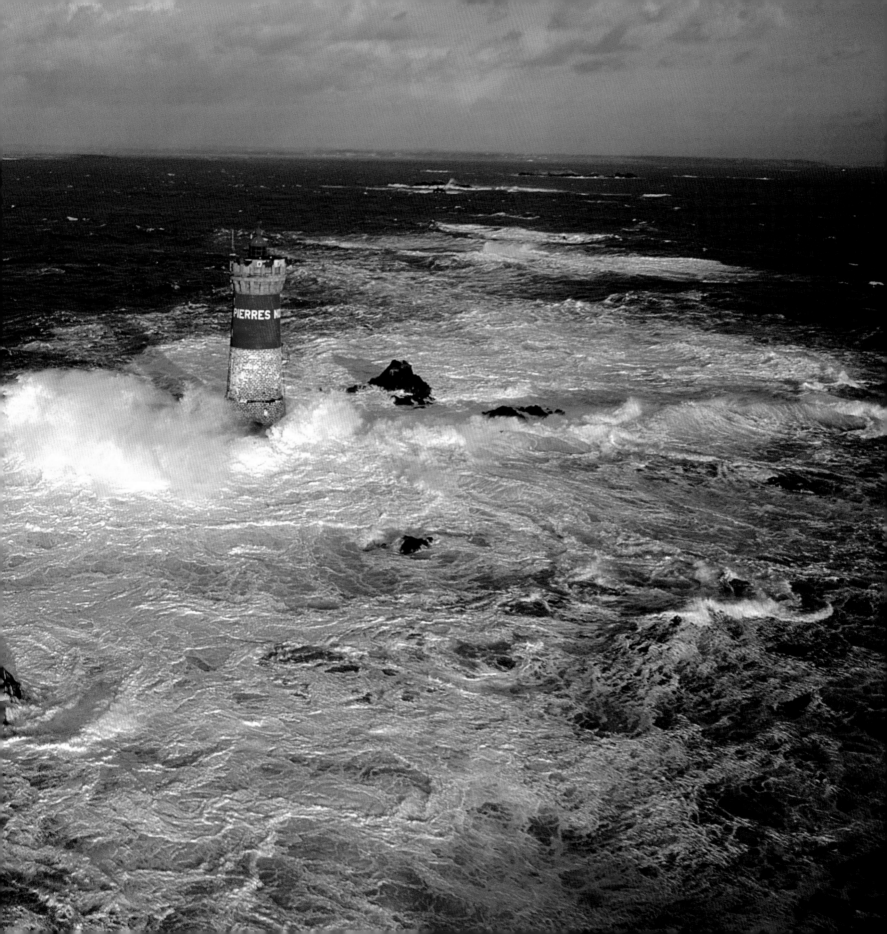

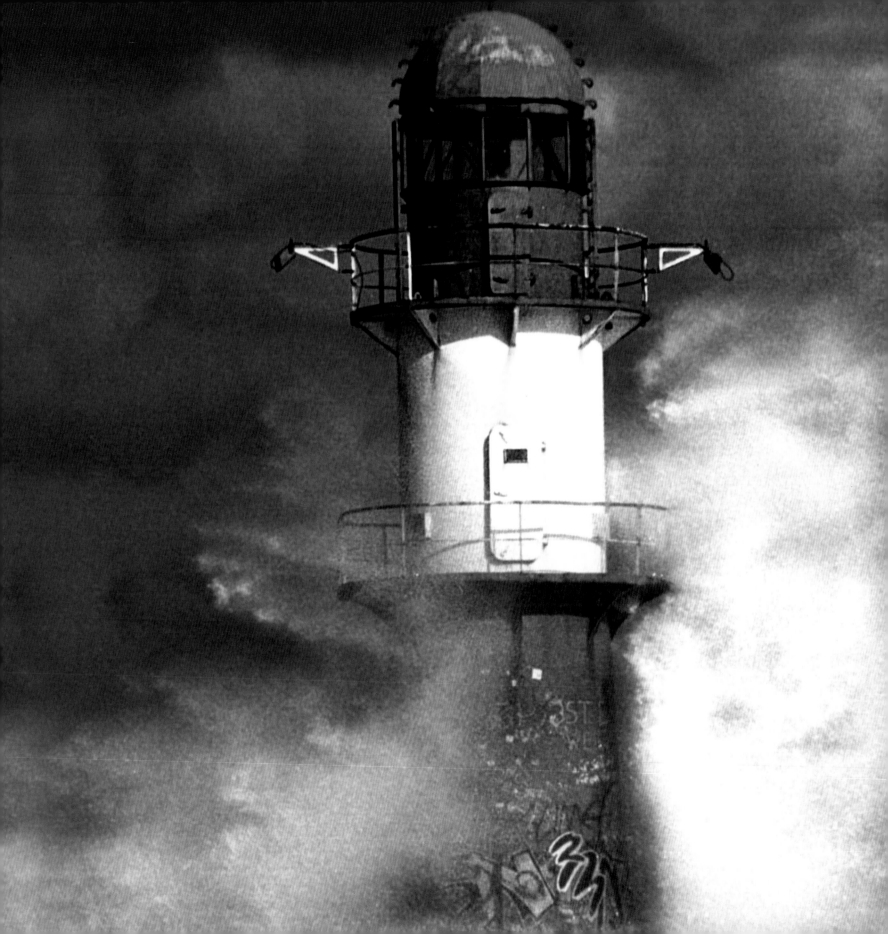

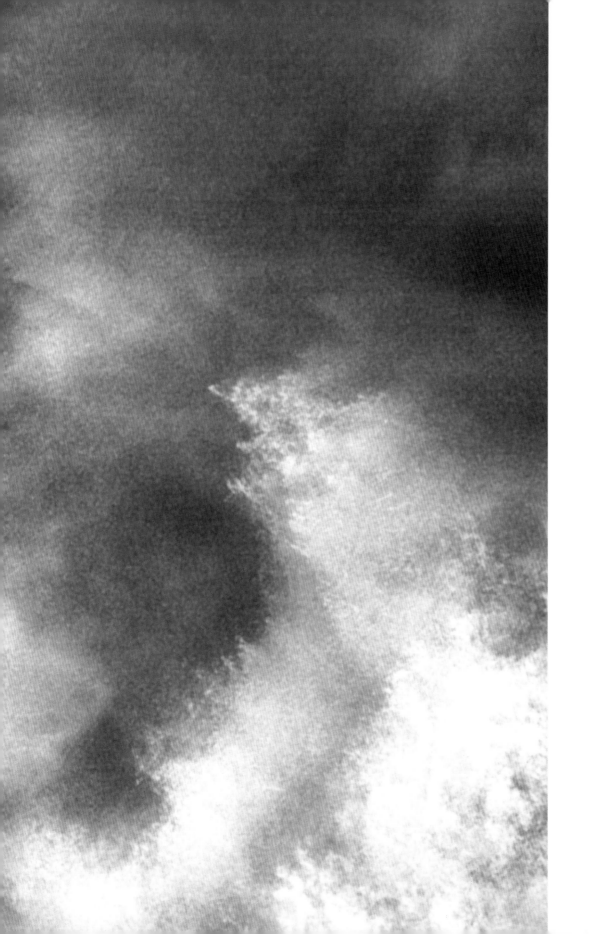

Alone in
the storm

Baltic Sea, Germany -
Warnemünde lighthouse.

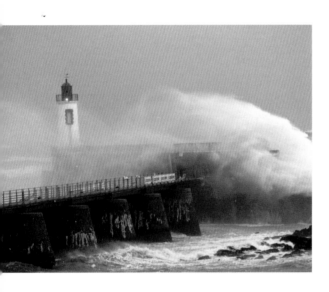

Atlantic Ocean, La Rochelle
(France) - Les Sables d'Olonne.

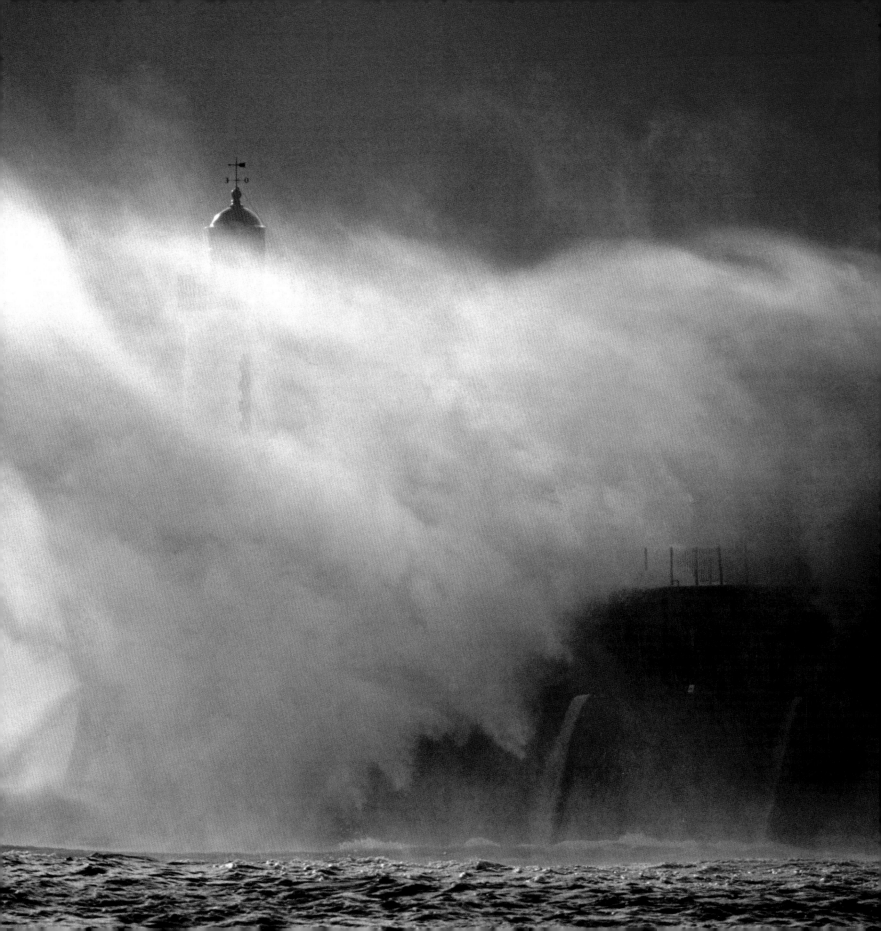

Lights
in the fog

● Atlantic Ocean,
Massachussetts (USA) -
Chatham lighthouse
on Cape Cod.

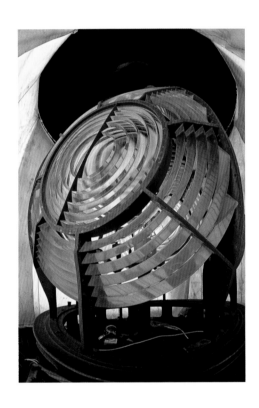

378 and 378-379 • Red Sea, Egypt
- El-Akhawein Island.

380-381 • Pacific Ocean, Oregon
(USA) - Heceta Head near Florence.

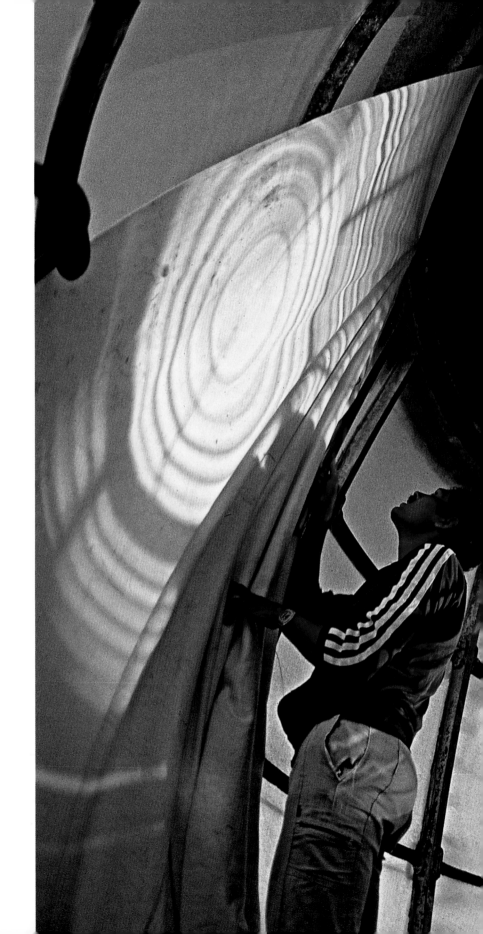

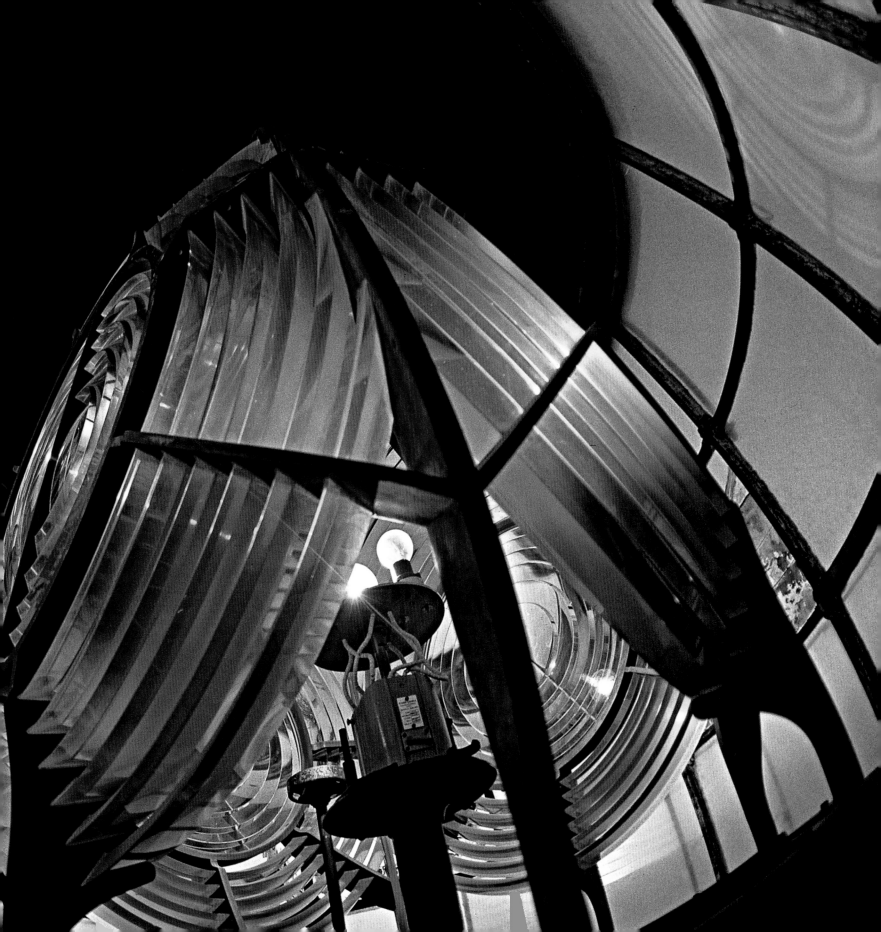

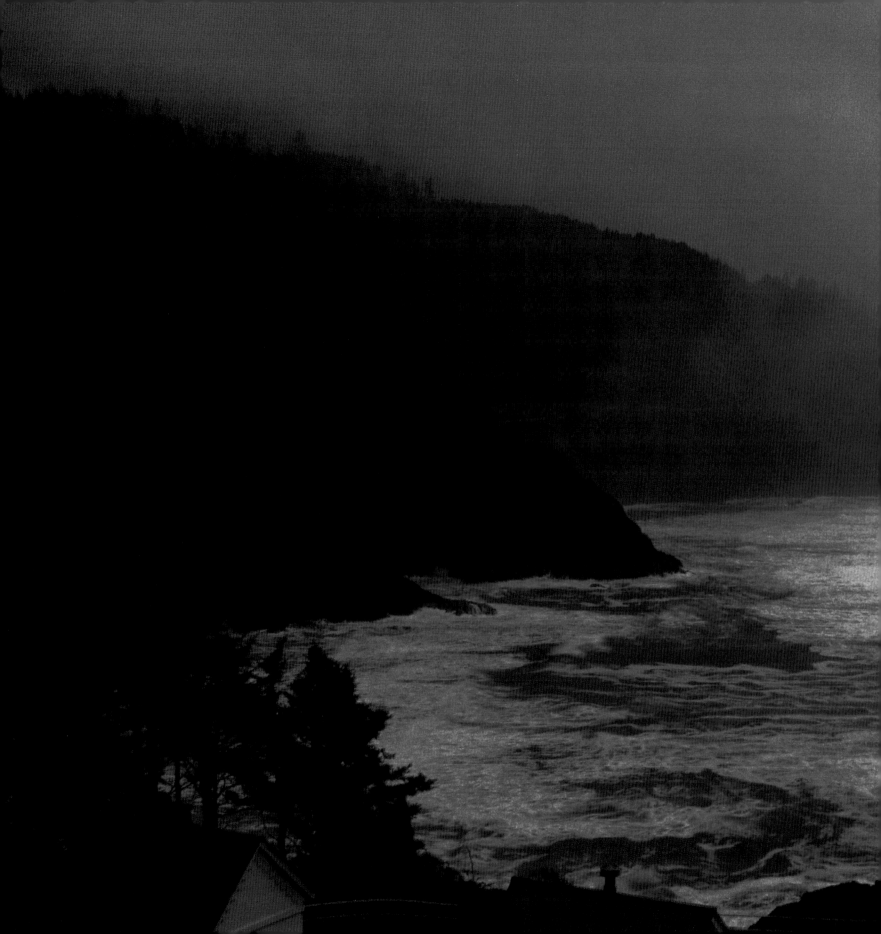

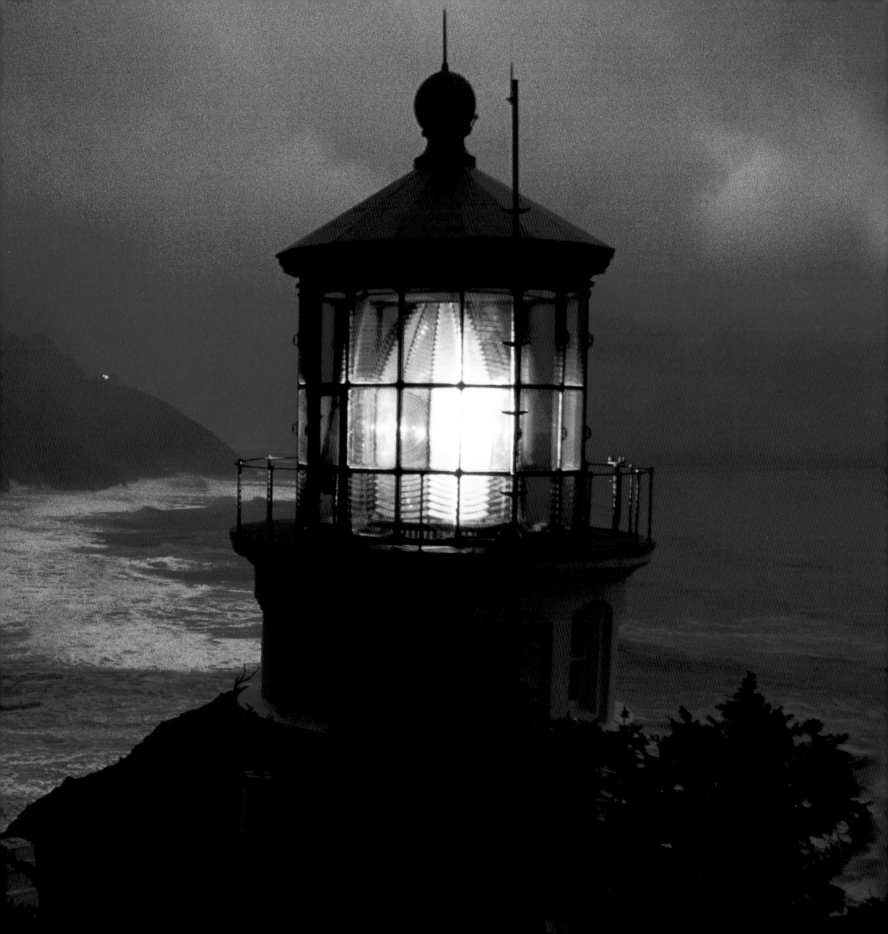

The FURY of NATURE

GIOVANNI SOLDINI

• Pacific Ocean, Hawaii - Coast of Oahu.

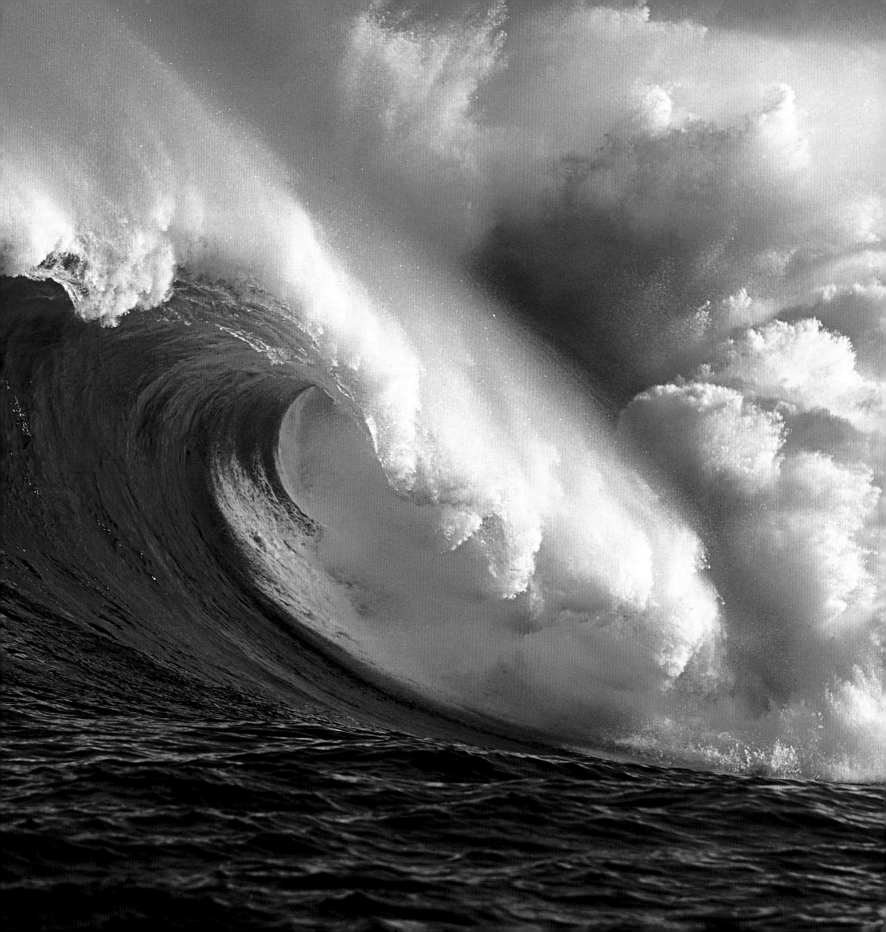

INTRODUCTION The Fury of Nature

I EXPERIENCED 'MY' STORM OFF NEW ZEALAND DURING THE

SINGLE-HANDED ROUND-THE-WORLD RACE. I HAD SEEN IT ON THE

WEATHER MAPS BUT DID NOT KNOW WHEN IT WOULD ARRIVE NOR

HOW STRONG IT WOULD BE, AND THERE IS A HELL OF A DIFFERENCE

BETWEEN WINDS OF 50 AND 80 KNOTS. I PREPARED FOR THE WORST

BY REEFING THE SAILS AND SHELTERING IN THE CABIN. THE BOAT WAS

SAILING CLOSE-HAULED AND WAS BUFFETED BY LARGE WAVES.

THEN, THE WIND STRENGTHENED AND I WAS FORCED TO GO UP ON

DECK AND TAKE DOWN ALL THE SAILS. IN CONDITIONS LIKE THOSE

YOU HAVE TO SECURE YOURSELF SOLIDLY OR YOU MAY WELL END UP

IN THE SEA. HARNESSED AS BEST AS I COULD, I HAULED MYSELF ON

INTRODUCTION The Fury of Nature

DECK, HOLDING ON WHEREVER POSSIBLE, AND BEGAN TO LOWER

THE SAILS THOUGH THE SEA WAS BREAKING OVER THE BOAT, CREAT-

ING AN INFERNAL ROAR. THEN I RETURNED TO THE CABIN WHERE IT

WAS VERY COLD (THOUGH WARMER THAN OUTSIDE OF COURSE). IT

TOOK 36 FRIGHTENING HOURS, EITHER SPENT IN THE DARKNESS OF

THE CABIN OR TIED TO THE WHEEL OF THAT FLOATING SHELL, TOSSED

AND TURNED BY AN INFINITELY STRONG FORCE. I SUFFERED VIOLENT

AND CONFLICTING EMOTIONS: ON ONE HAND, THE TENSION AND PER-

HAPS FEAR CAUSED BY THE WALLS OF WATER, THE ROAR OF THE

WIND, AND THE HUGE CLOUDS AS BLACK AS PITCH. ON THE OTHER,

THE CALM THAT CAME FROM REPEATING THE SAME GESTURES AND

The Fury of Nature
Introduction

FROM ASSERTING MY SELF-CONTROL. THIS COMPOSURE WAS DIC-

TATED BY EXPERIENCE AND THE CERTAINTY OF HAVING ONLY MY

OWN RESOURCES TO COUNT ON FOR SURVIVAL. FOR EXAMPLE, AS I

PULLED MYSELF UP ON THE DECK TO HAUL DOWN THE SAILS, MY

ONLY CONCERN WAS TO DO ONE THING AT A TIME. AND WHILE DOING

ONE THING, I WAS STUDYING WHAT I WOULD NEED TO DO NEXT. ONE

SMALL ERROR OR SOME UNEXPECTED EVENT COULD HAVE PUT AN

END TO THE BOAT AND MYSELF. AT SEA, AS IN LIFE, YOU NEVER CEASE

LEARNING. WHAT COUNTS IS YOUR ACCUMULATED EXPERIENCE AND

THE EVENTS THAT BRING YOU NEW KNOWLEDGE. A STORM IS THE

TOUGHEST AND MOST UNFORGIVING OF TESTS.

● Mediterranean Sea, Liguria (Italy) - Storm at Camogli.

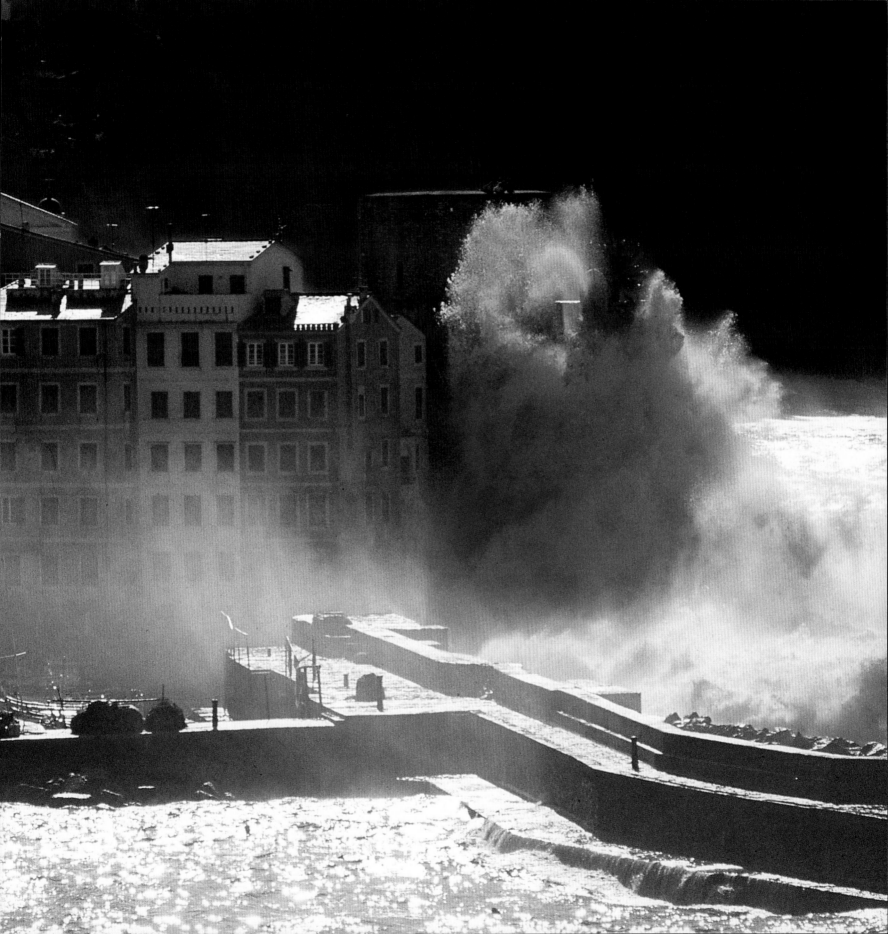

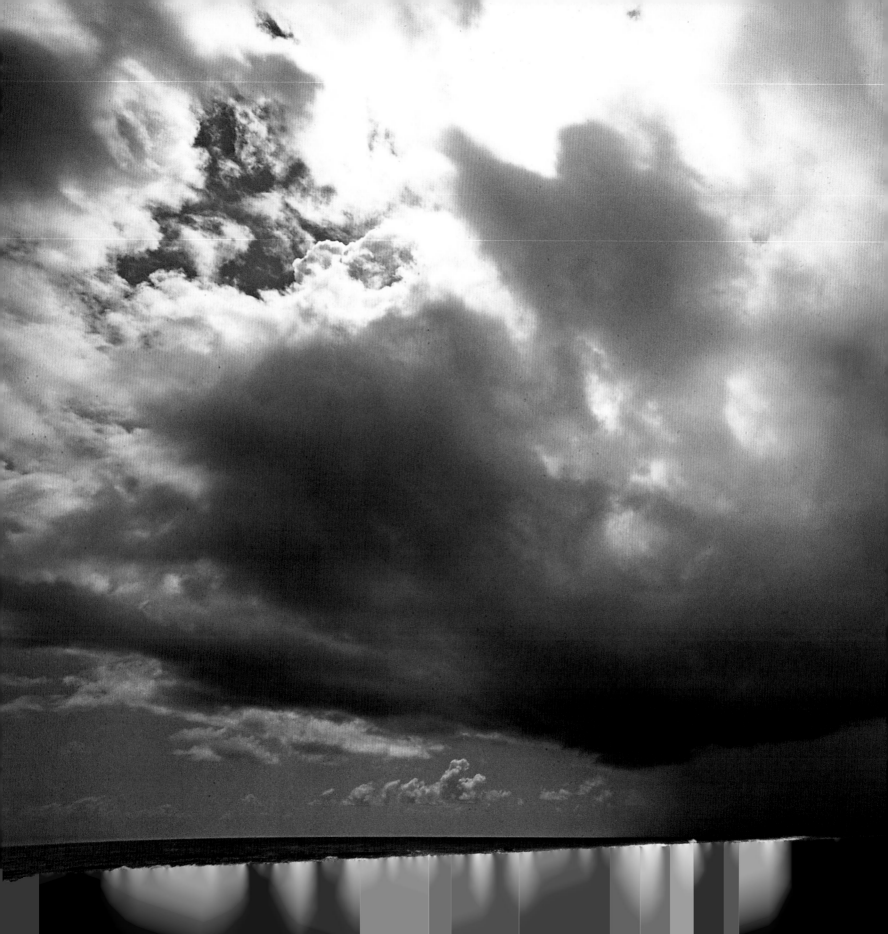

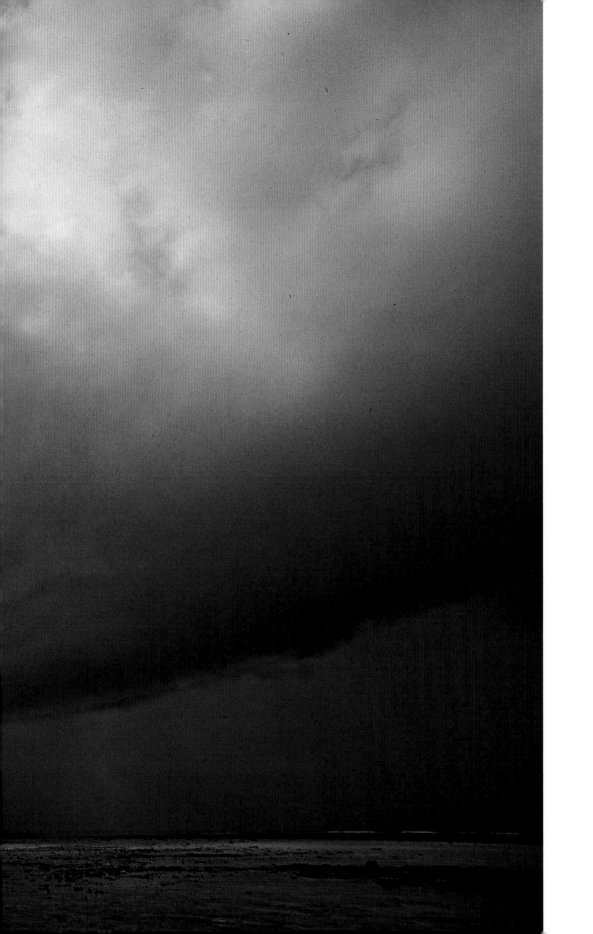

Pacific Ocean,
French Polynesia -
Storm on the coast
of Rangiroa.

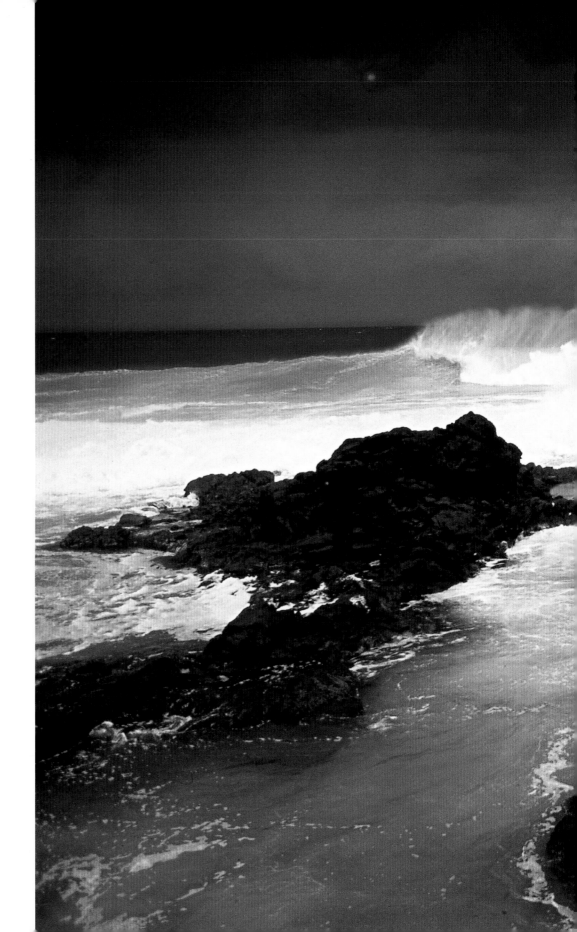

The anger of the sea over the rocks

390-391 ● Pacific Ocean, Hawaii (USA) - North coast of Mauii.

392-393 ● Mediterranean Sea, Liguria (Italy) - Storm over the cliffs.

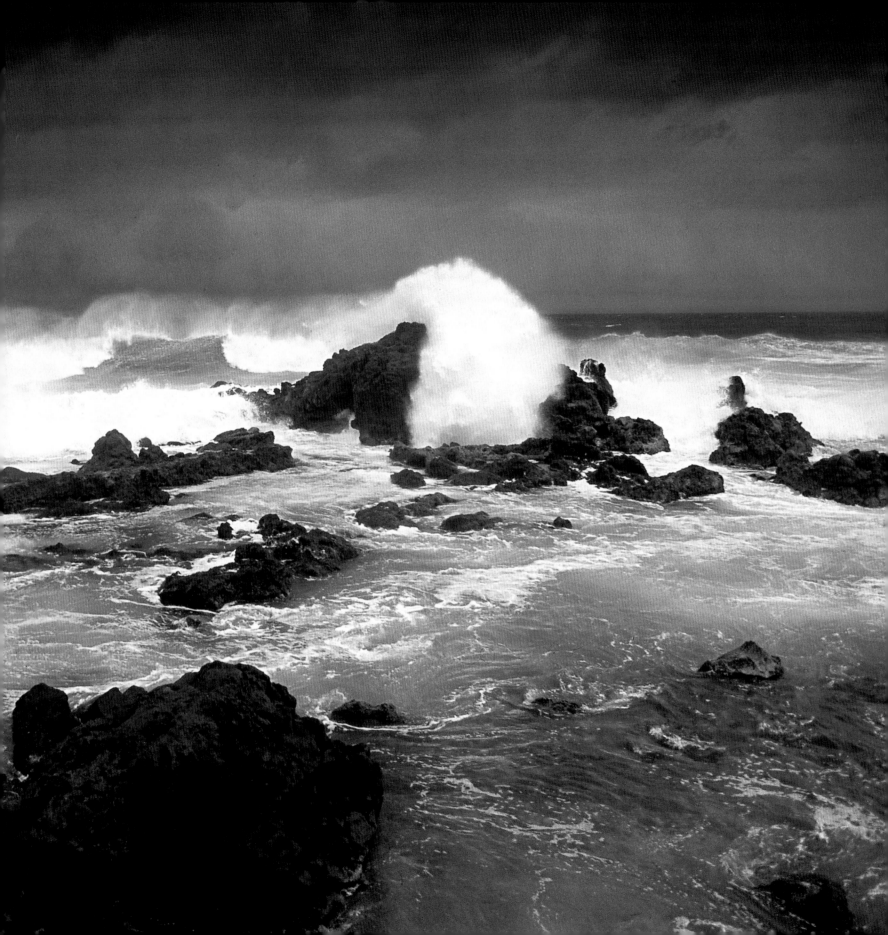

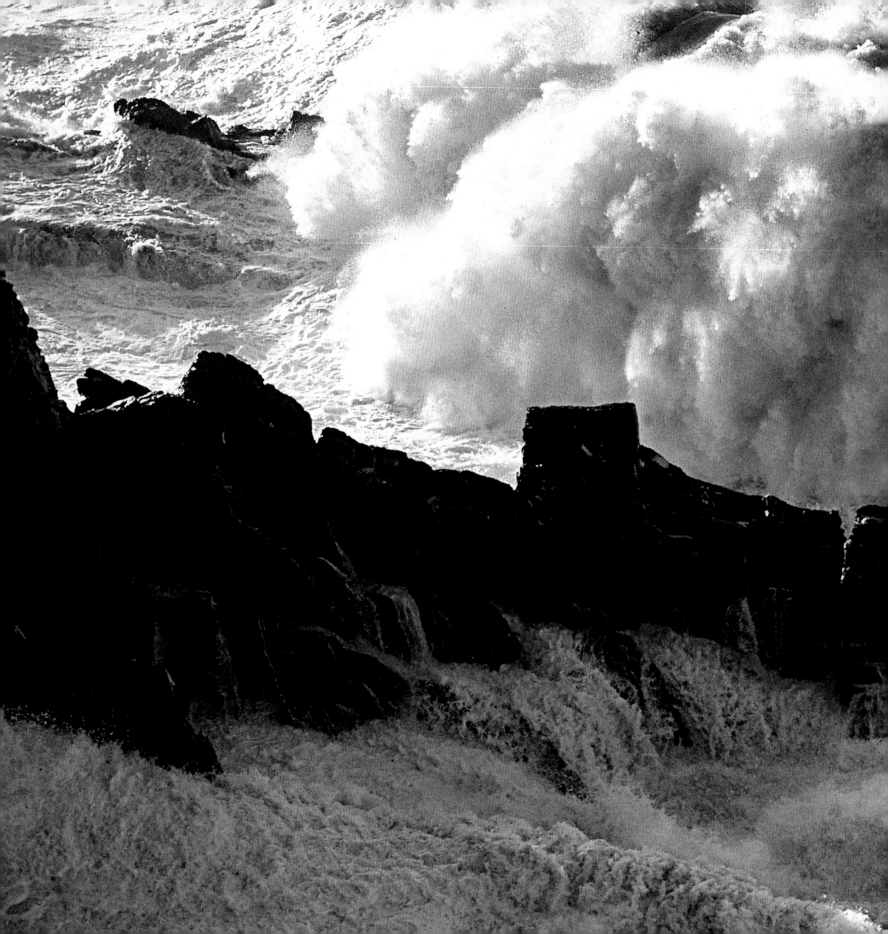

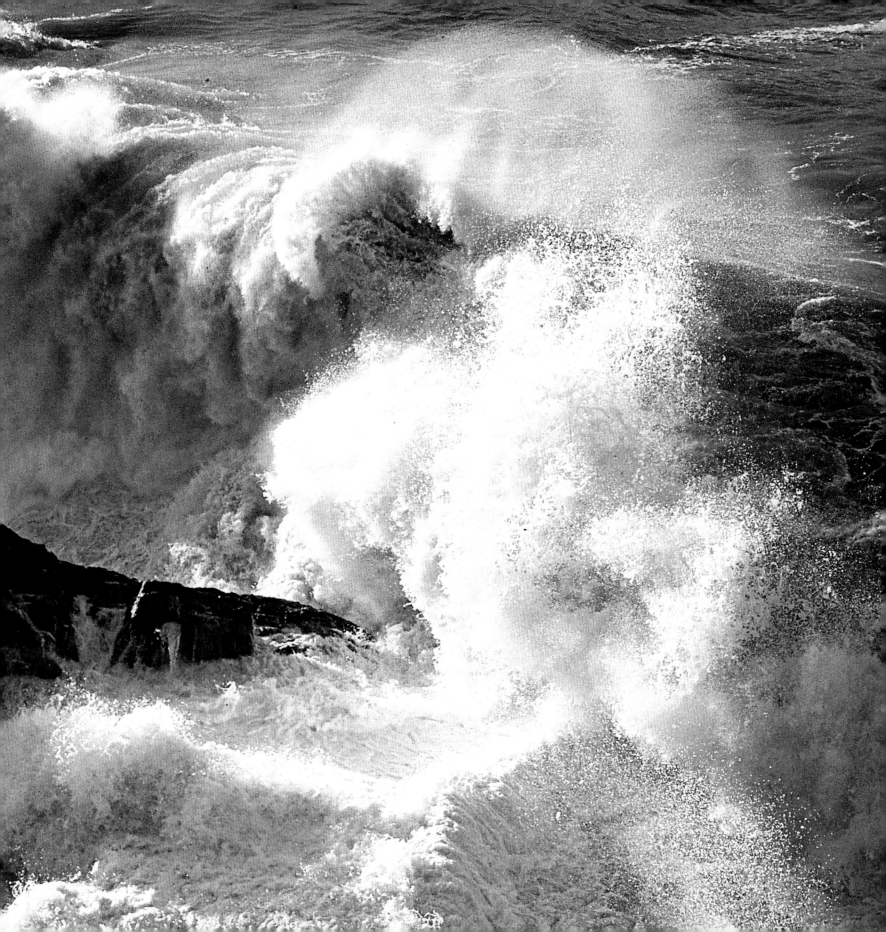

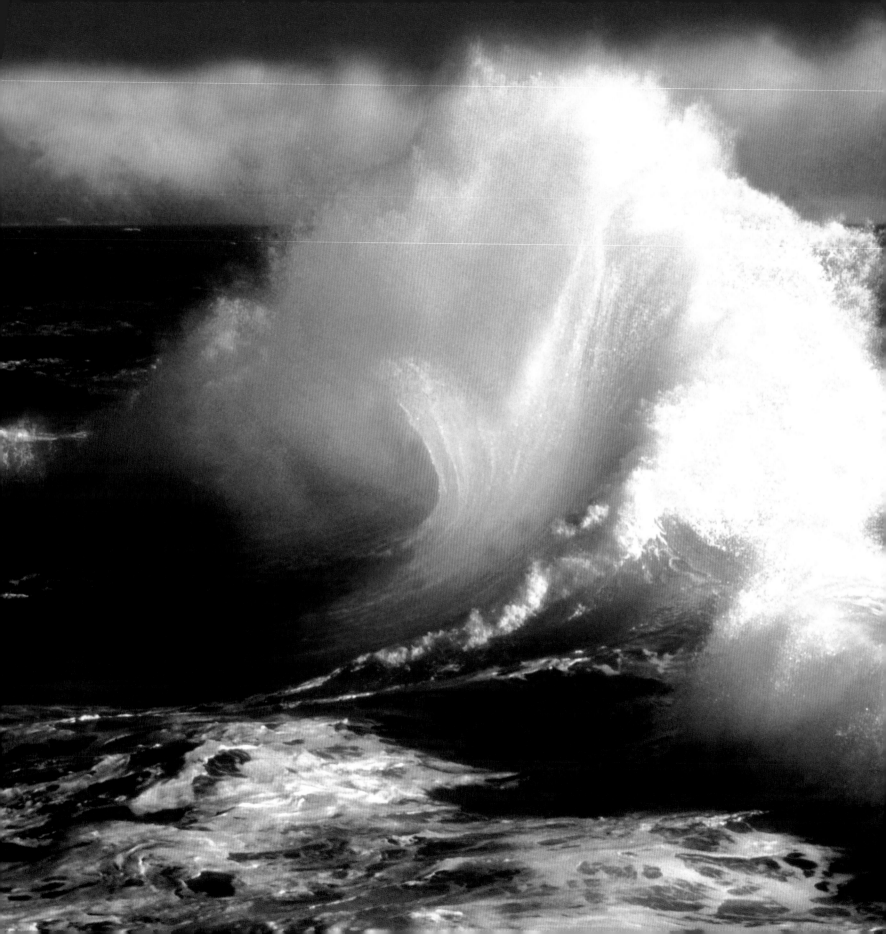

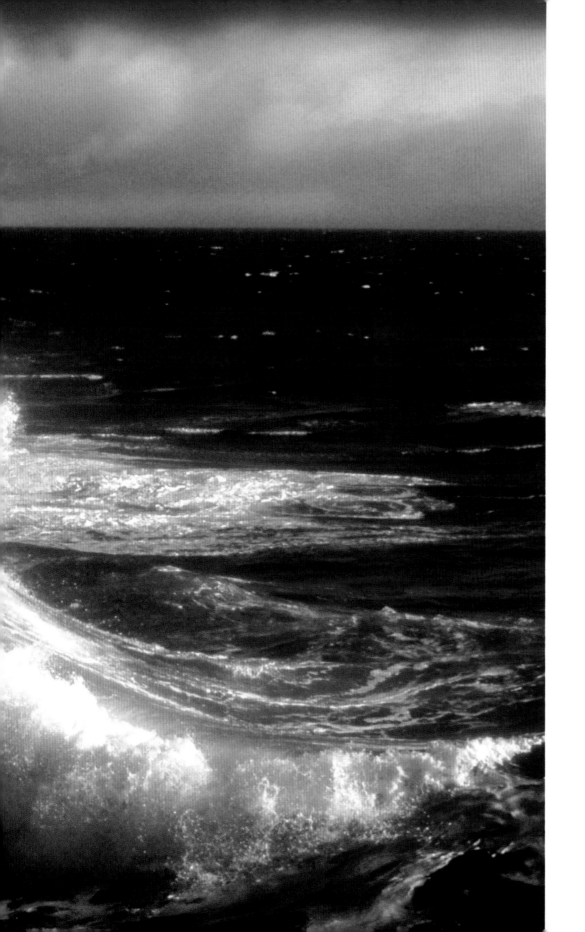

Atlantic Ocean,
France - Storm at
Le Havre.

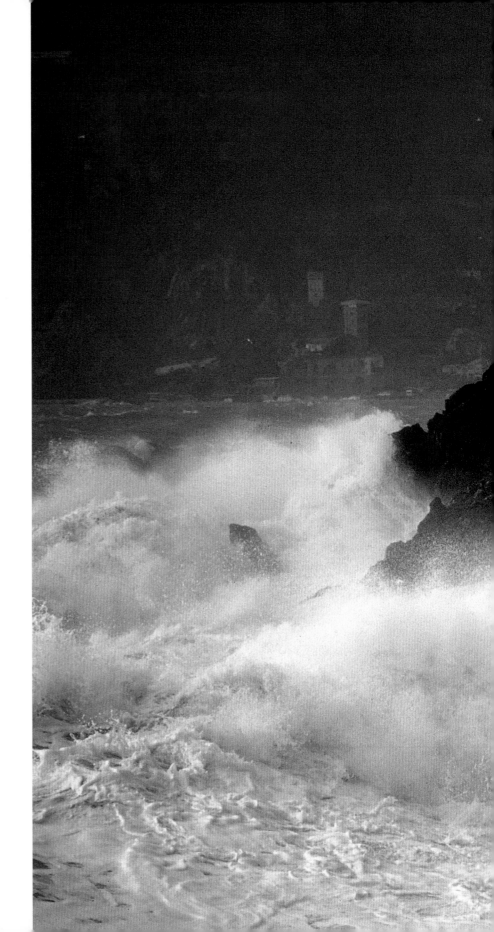

"J OVE'S LIGHTNING ...
THE FIRE AND CRACKS OF
SULPHUROUS ROARING THE
MOST MIGHTY NEPTUNE
SEEM TO BESIEGE, AND MAKE
HIS BOLD WAVES TREMBLE,
YEA, HIS DREAD TRIDENT
SHAKE."

from THE TEMPEST
by William Shakespeare

396-397 ● Mediterranean Sea,
Liguria (Italy) - Gale at Vernazza.

398-399 ● Atlantic Ocean, Tierra
del Fuego (Argentina) - Storm over
Cape Horn.

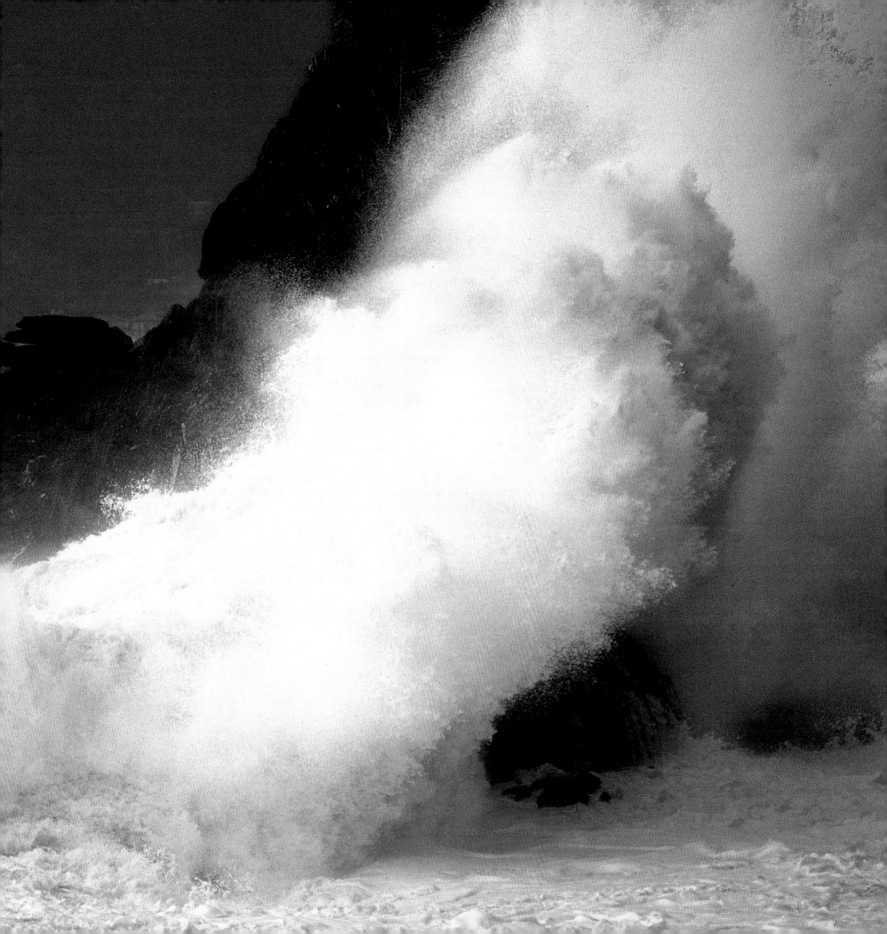

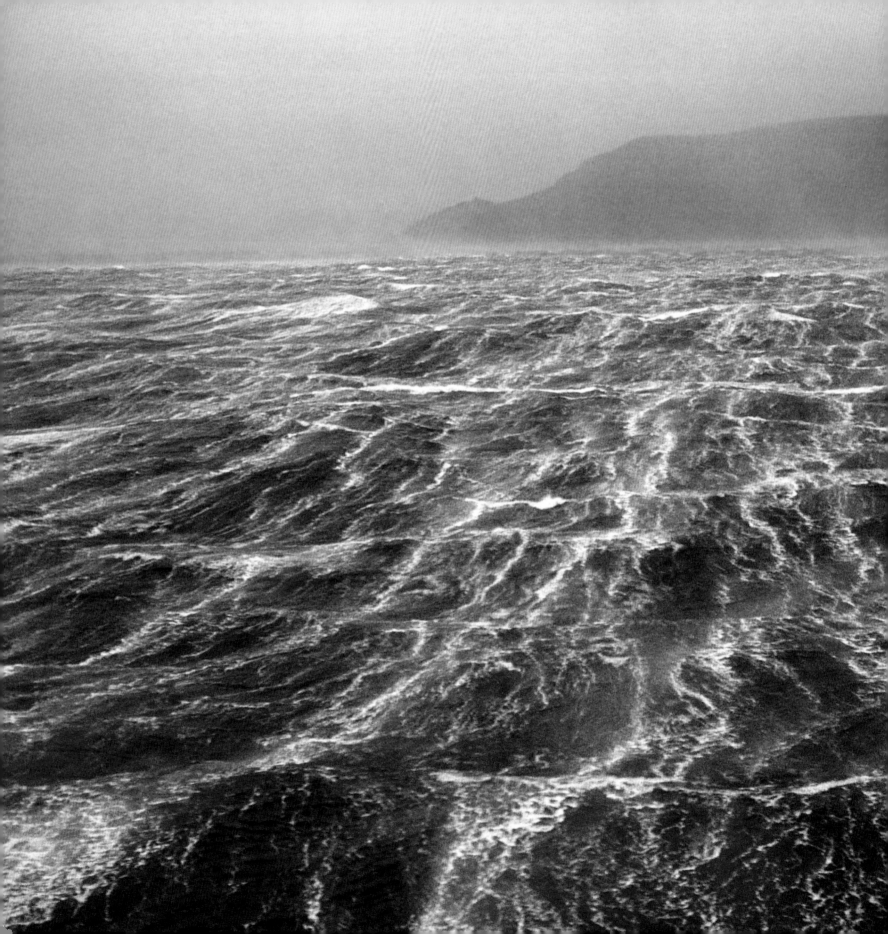

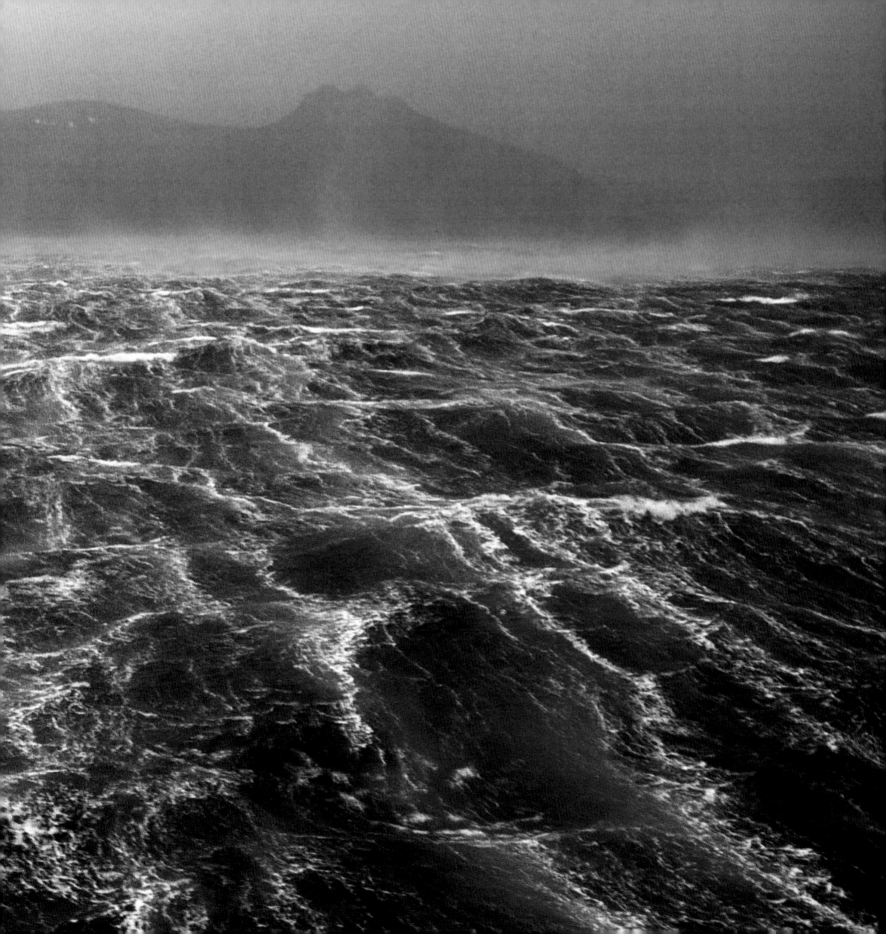

North Sea, Norway -
Oil platform.

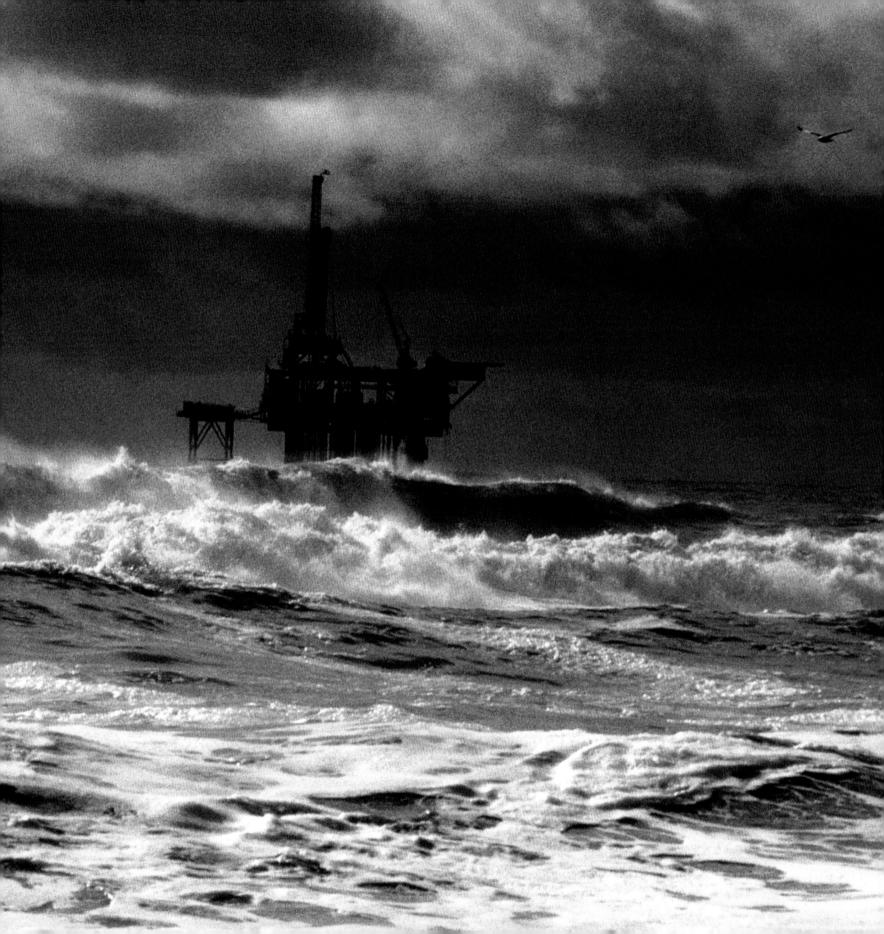

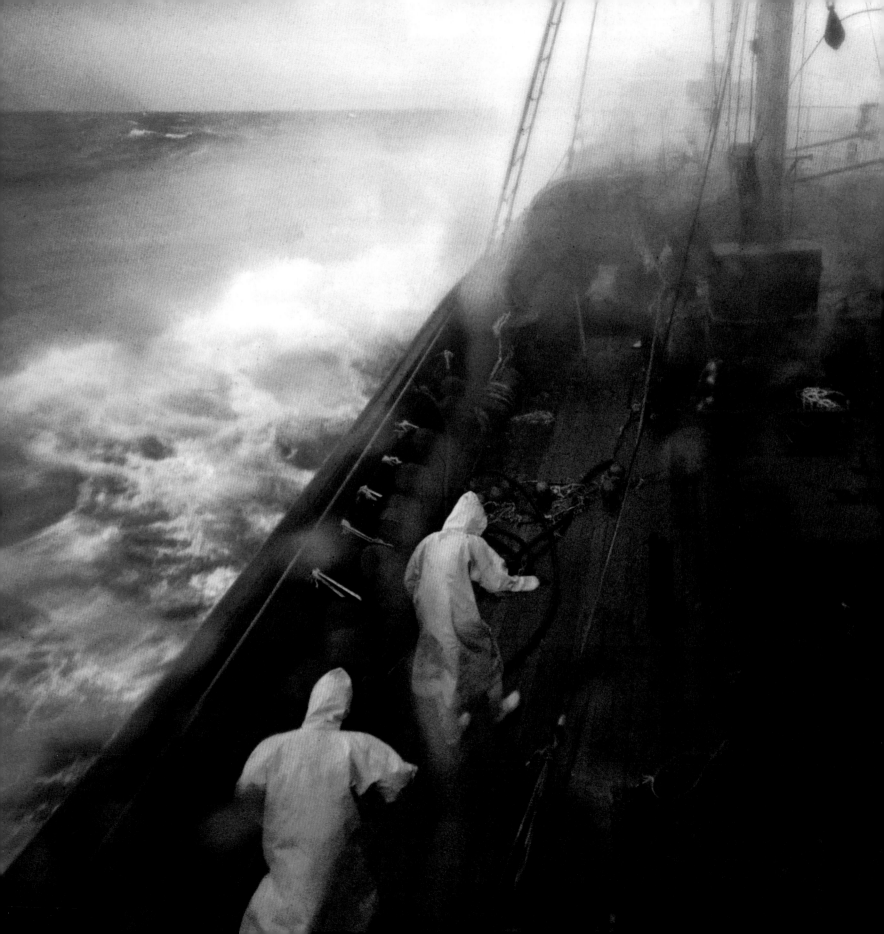

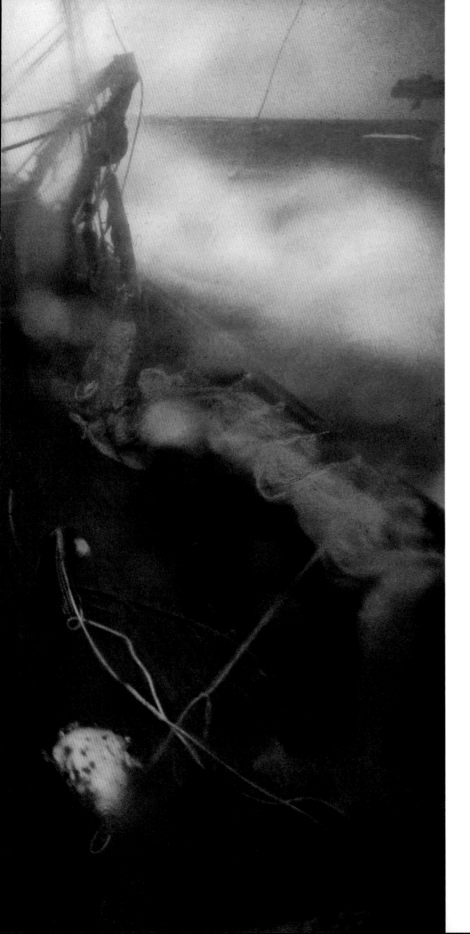

At the mercy
of the waves

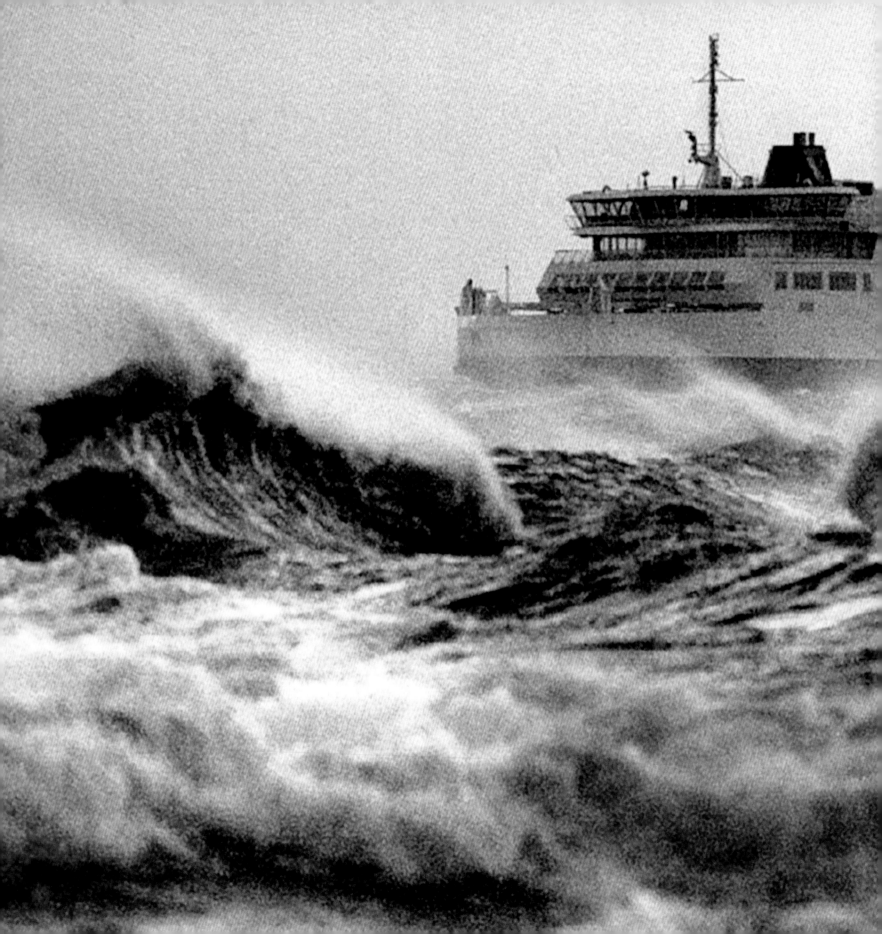

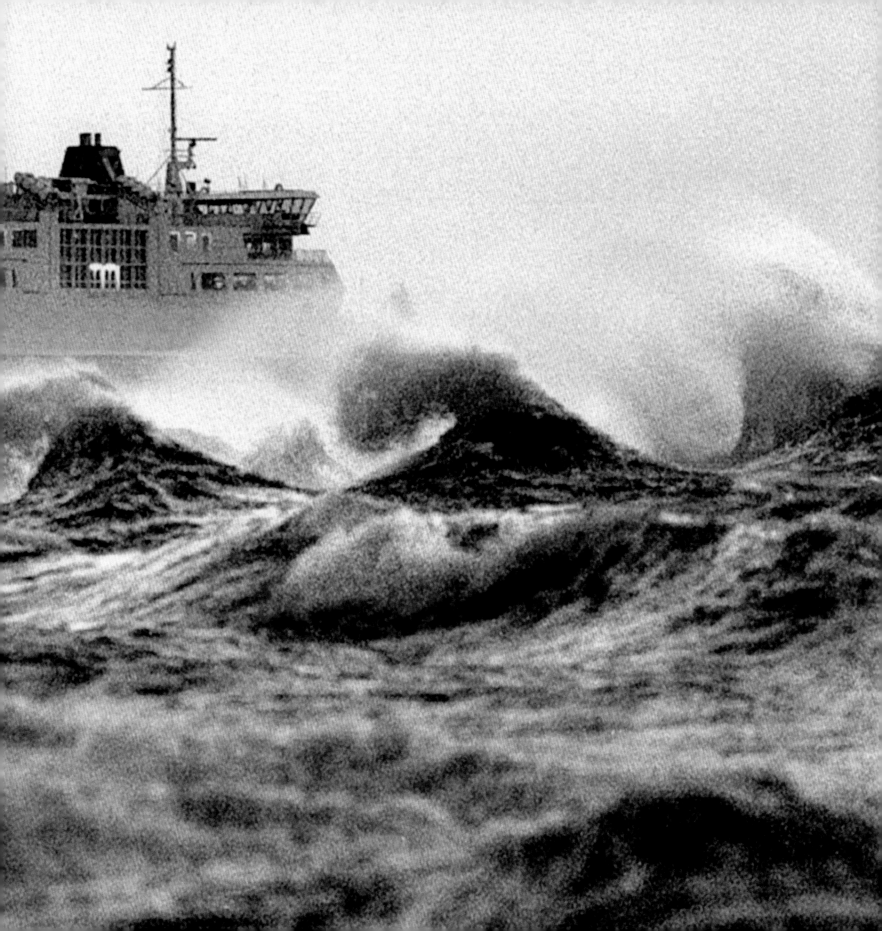

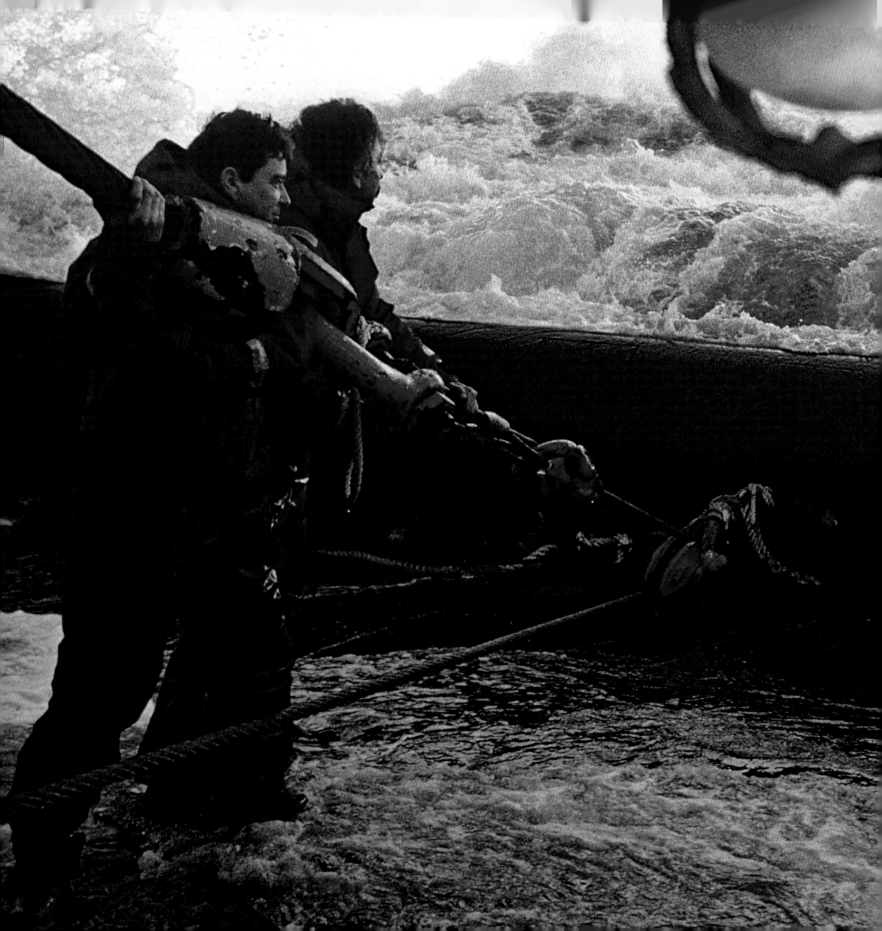

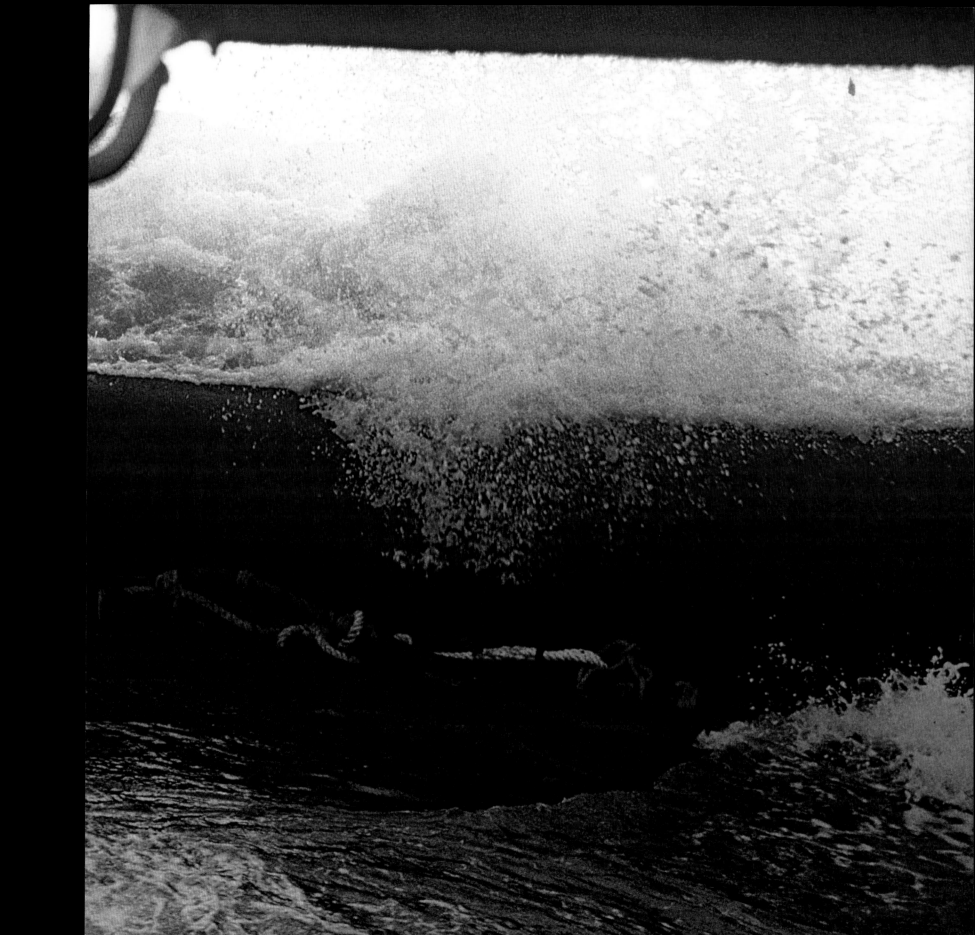

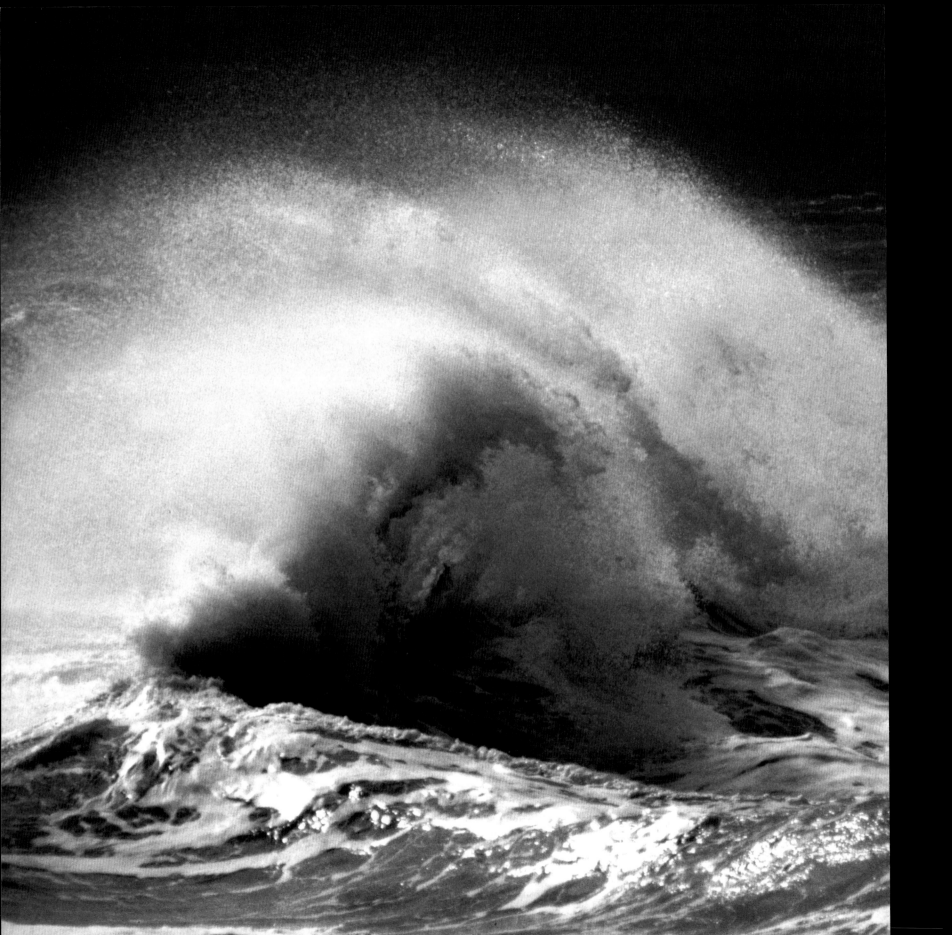

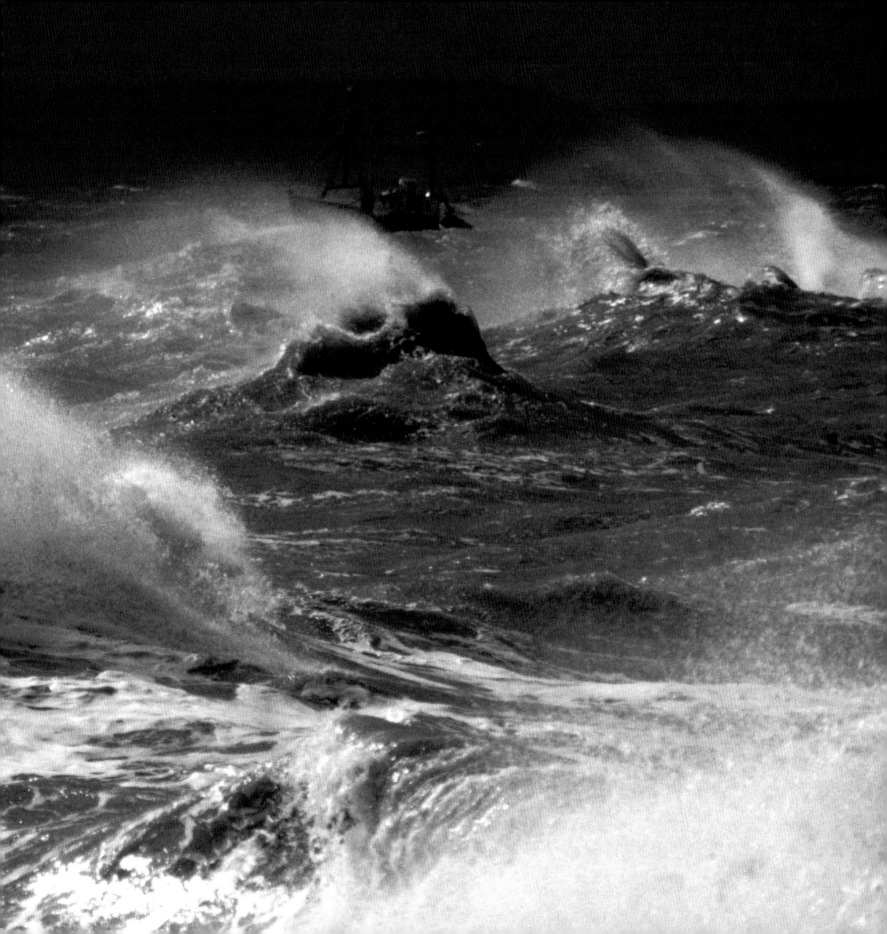

On the WINGS of the WIND

CARLO MARINCOVICH

Caribbean Sea - Antigua Classic Week, *Velsheda*.

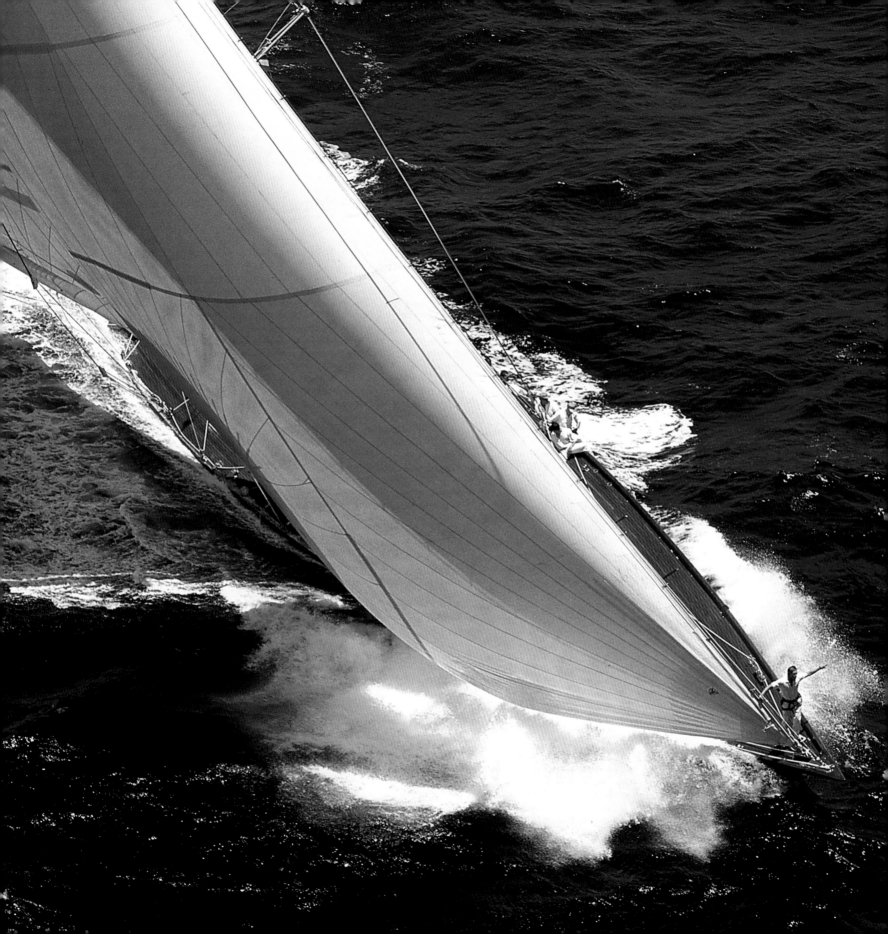

INTRODUCTION On the Wings of the Wind

I FIRST FLEW ON THE WINGS OF THE WIND WHEN I WAS A

CHILD. I HAD BEEN TAKEN ON A SAILING BOAT WITH A MAJESTIC

WHITE SPANKER, WHICH TO ME WAS IMMENSE, AND IT WAS ONLY AS

AN ADULT THAT I FOUND OUT THE BOAT WAS JUST A SIXTEEN-FOOT-

ER! HOWEVER, BEING ALONE FOR THE FIRST TIME ON A BOAT WHOSE

CLOSEST FRIENDS ARE THE WIND AND WAVES IS ENOUGH TO MAKE

YOUR HAIR STAND ON END. MY VESSEL WAS HAULED UP ON THE

BEACH; THE SAILOR FITTED THE SAIL AND SAID, 'RIGHT, I'LL SHOW

YOU HOW IT'S DONE.' I WAS LIFTED INTO THE AIR AND PLACED BY THE

TILLER. THEN HE SAID, 'NOW I'LL PUSH THE BOAT OUT. YOU HOLD THE

TILLER STEADY.' I FELT LIKE CAPTAIN HORNBLOWER AND HAPPILY DID

INTRODUCTION On the Wings of the Wind

AS I WAS TOLD. BUT THE SAILOR DID NOT CLIMB ON BOARD AND ALL

I HEARD FROM BEHIND WAS A SHOUT, 'HAUL ON THE SHEET.' FORTU-

NATELY, I HAD LEARNED ENOUGH FROM OTHERS TO KNOW THAT THIS

MEANT PULL ON THE SAIL TO LET IT CATCH THE WIND. I DID SO AND

THE BOAT SHOT OUT TOWARD THE OPEN SEA. THE SIROCCO WAS

BLOWING UP NASTY WAVES, THE SEA WAS GREEN AND THE WATER

CHURNED UP THE SAND. I LOOKED BEHIND FEARFULLY AND SAW THE

SHORE ALREADY DISTANT AND THE SAILOR SHOUTING SOMETHING.

ALL OF A SUDDEN, AND FOR THE FIRST TIME, I FELT ALONE AND

SCARED. BUT I MANAGED. I HAULED, LUFFED, TURNED AND DID

EVERYTHING NECESSARY TO GET BACK TO THE SHORE, AND, FROM

On the Wings of the Wind

Introduction

THAT MOMENT, MY LOVE FOR THE SEA BEGAN. ON OCCASIONS EVEN

SMALL WAVES SEEMED MONSTERS, ON OTHERS I HAD THE DREAD-

FUL SENSATION OF BEING UTTERLY ALONE AND THE PREY OF AN

UNSTOPPABLE FORCE. HOWEVER, WHEN I MANAGED TO DOMINATE

MY FEAR AND GET BACK MY SELF-CONTROL, I EXPERIENCED A

HEADY ELATION AND THE CONVICTION I COULD TAME THE BIZARRE

HORSE I HAD SO RASHLY MOUNTED. THIS WAS THE START OF A

LONGING TO GO TO SEA. WHAT I HAVE RETAINED FROM THOSE

YEARS IS THE PLAYFUL SPIRIT THAT COMES OVER ME EVERY TIME I

PUT OUT FROM THE SHORE.

● Atlantic Ocean, South Africa, Around Alone - *the Fila* and, at the bow, Giovanni Soldini.

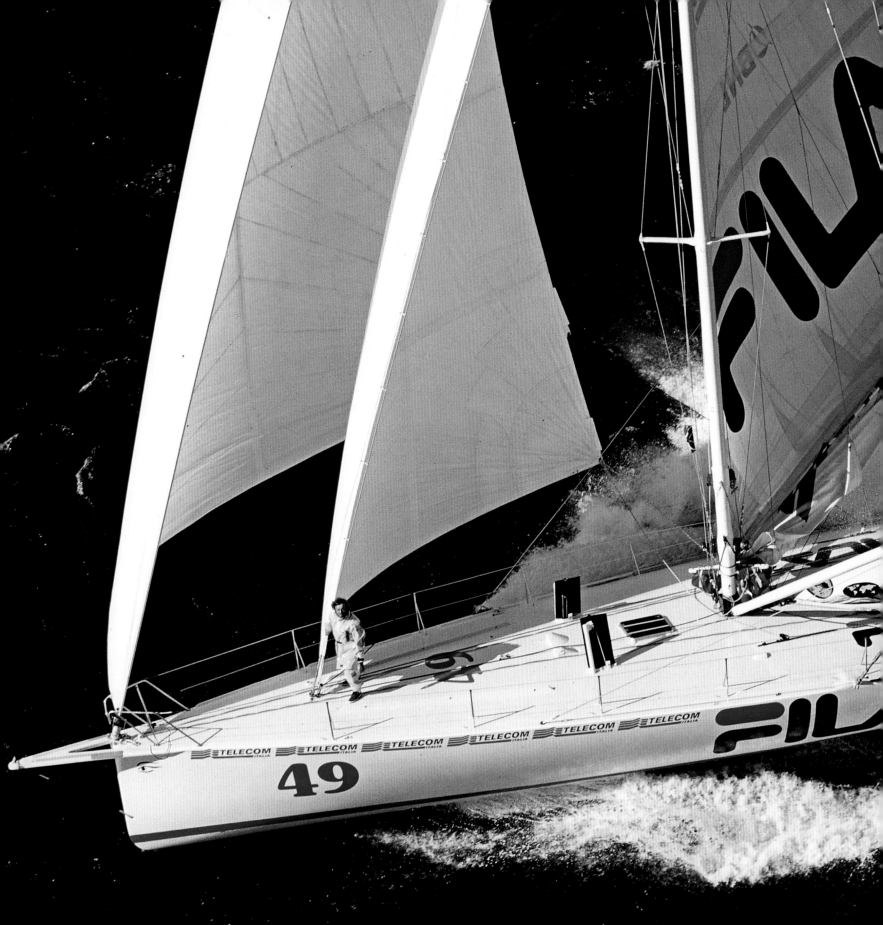

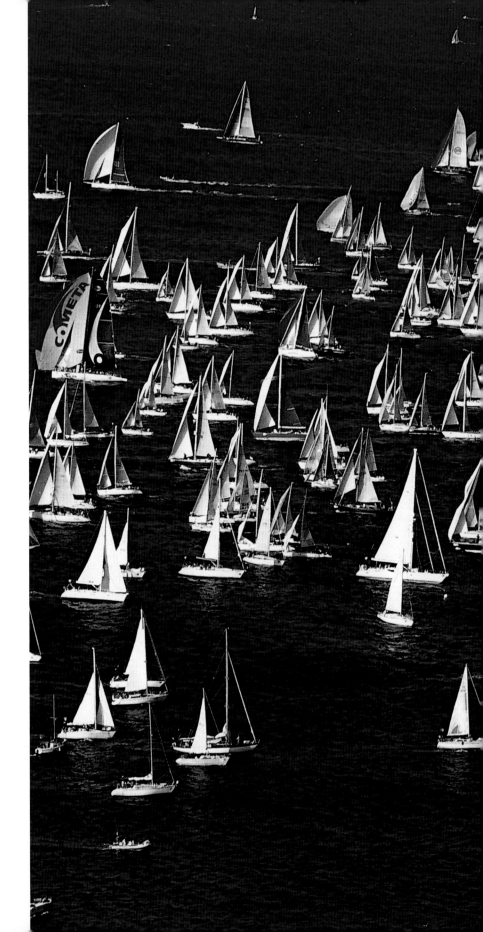

A SWARM OF WHITE SAILS LIKE A FLOCK OF GULLS IN THE SKY, SNOWFLAKES OR SEEDS SCATTERED IN THE WIND.

416-417 ● Adriatic Sea, Trieste (Italy) - Start line of the Trieste race.

418-419 ● Caribbean Sea - Antigua Classic Week, the *Velsheda*.

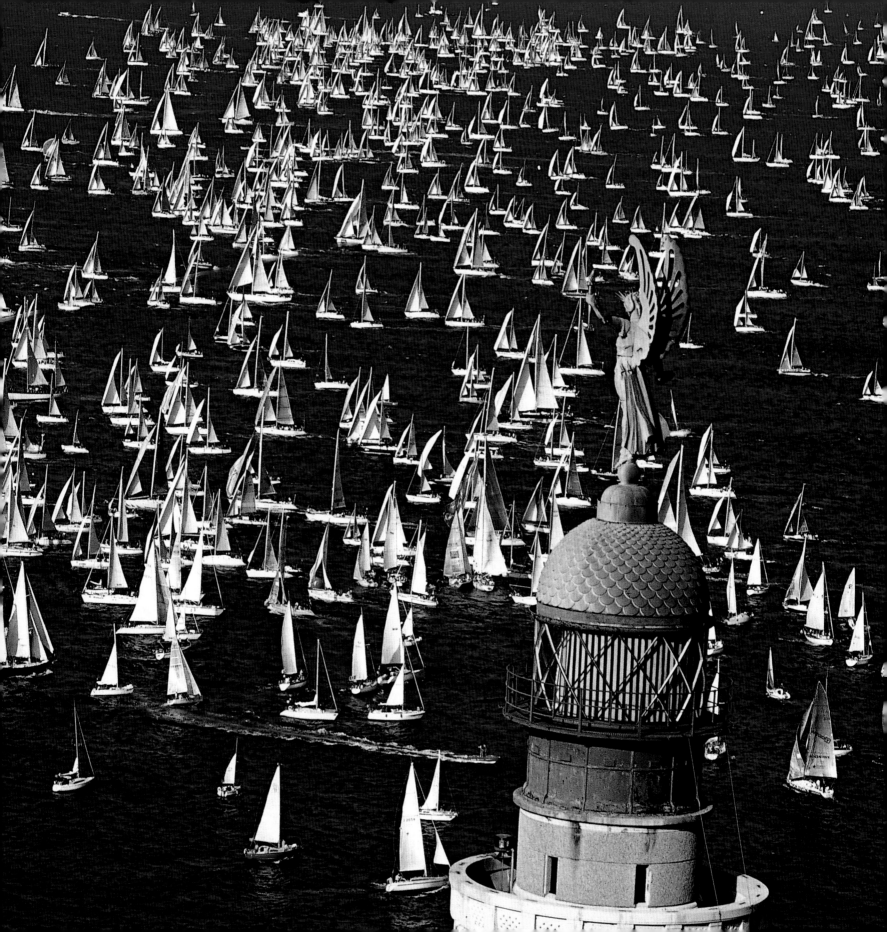

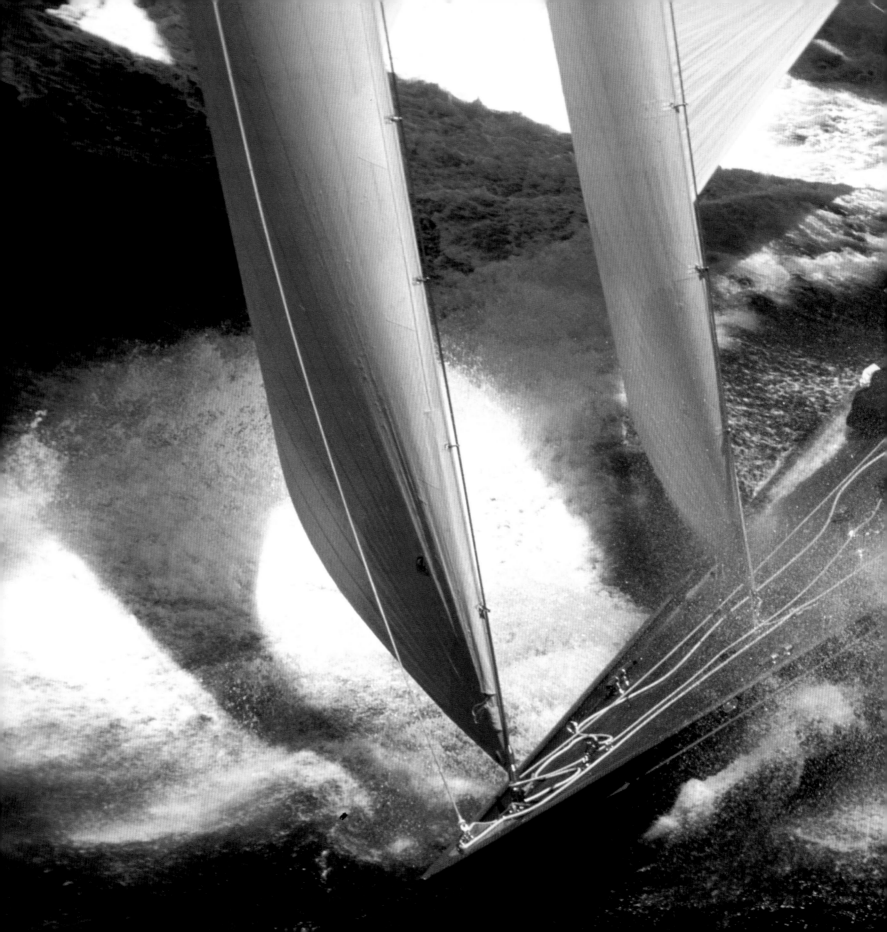

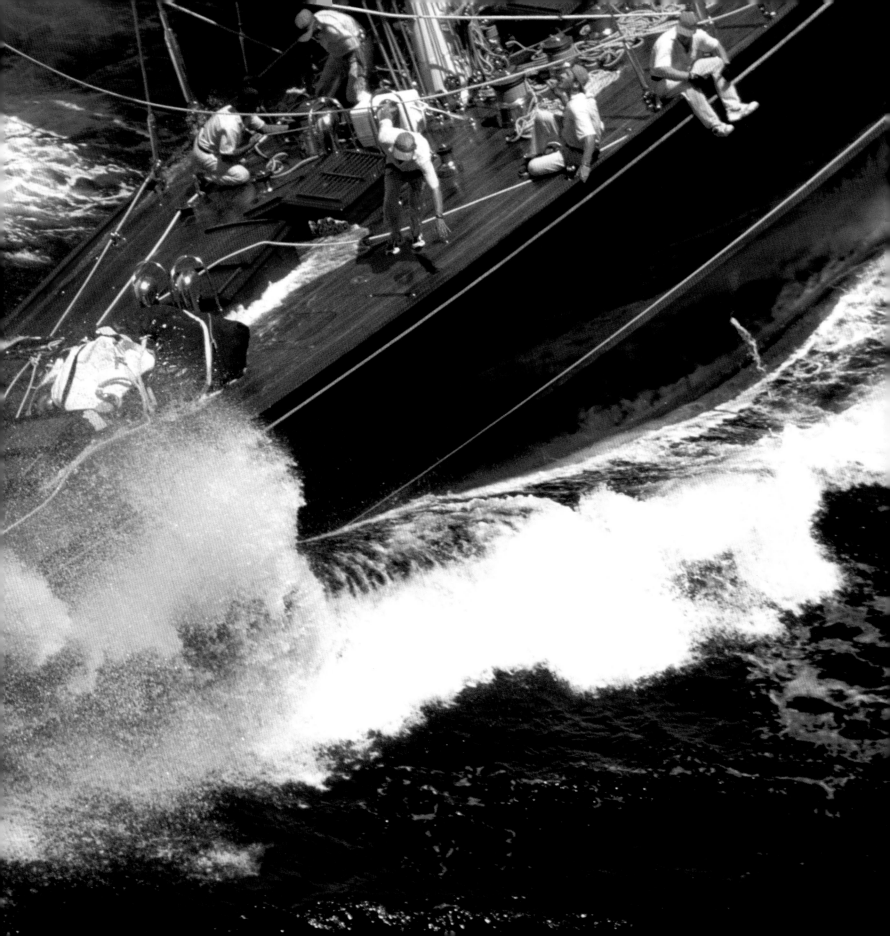

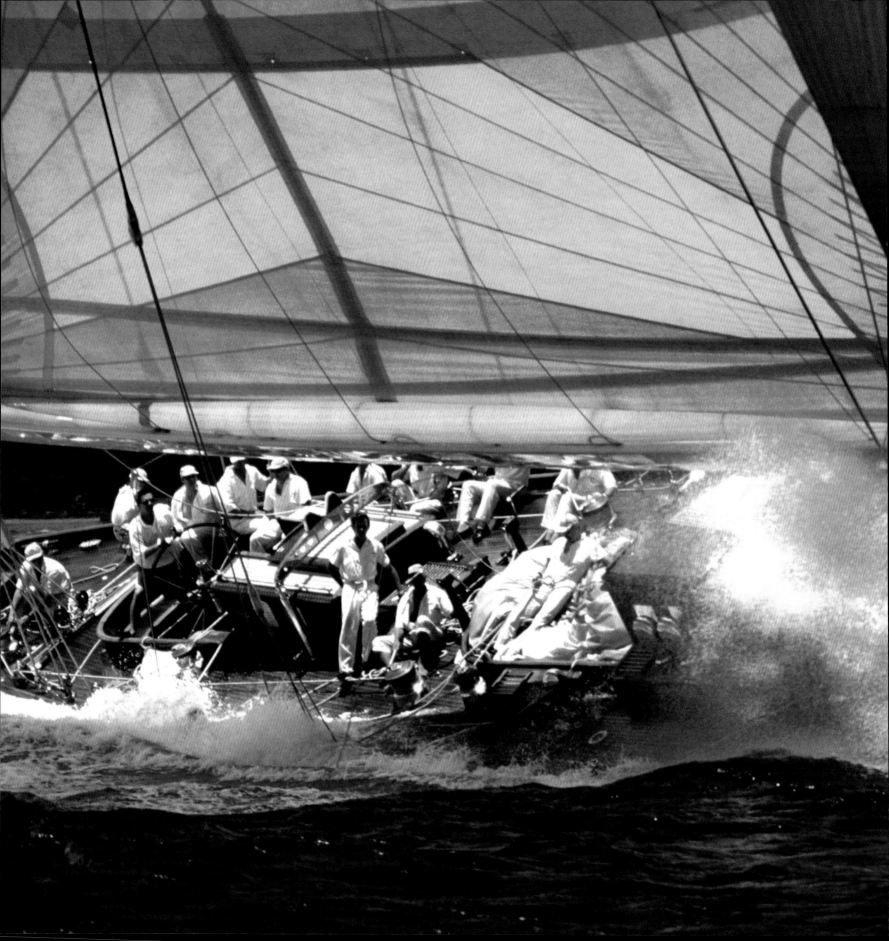

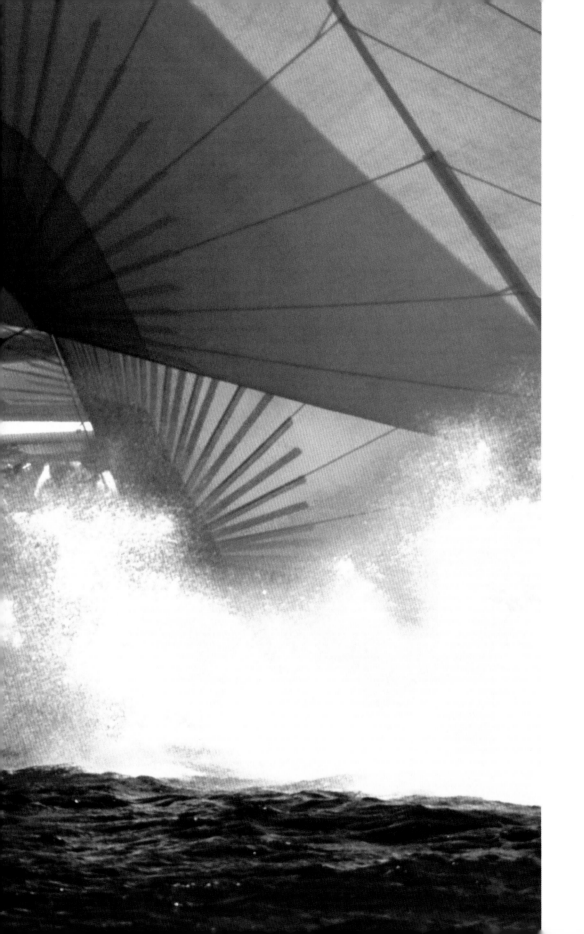

Caribbean Sea -
Antigua Classic Week,
the *Velsheda*.

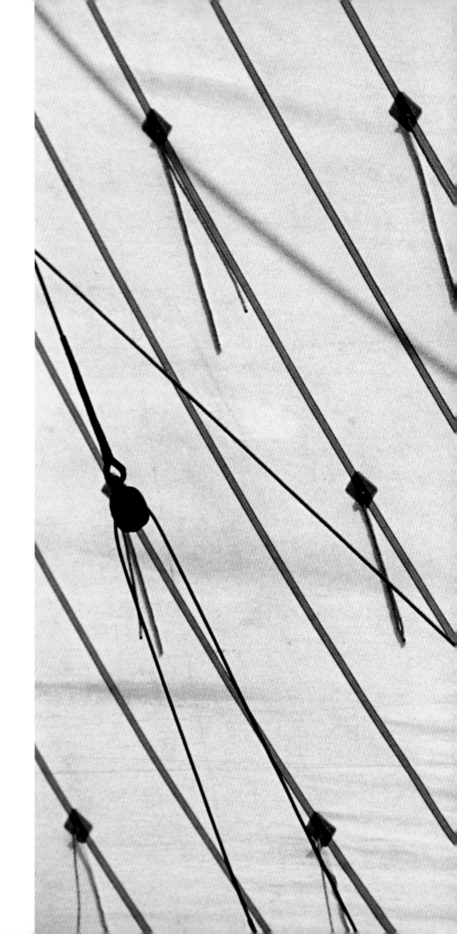

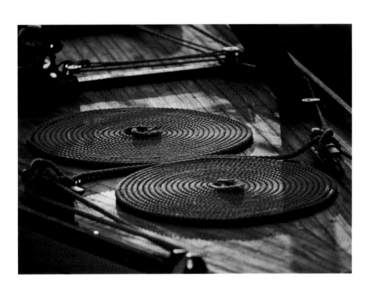

422 ● Atlantic Ocean, Cowes (England) - On board the *Cambria*, lines ready for a maneuver during the America's Cup Jubilee.

422-423 ● Atlantic Ocean, Brest (France) - The sails of the *Pesa*.

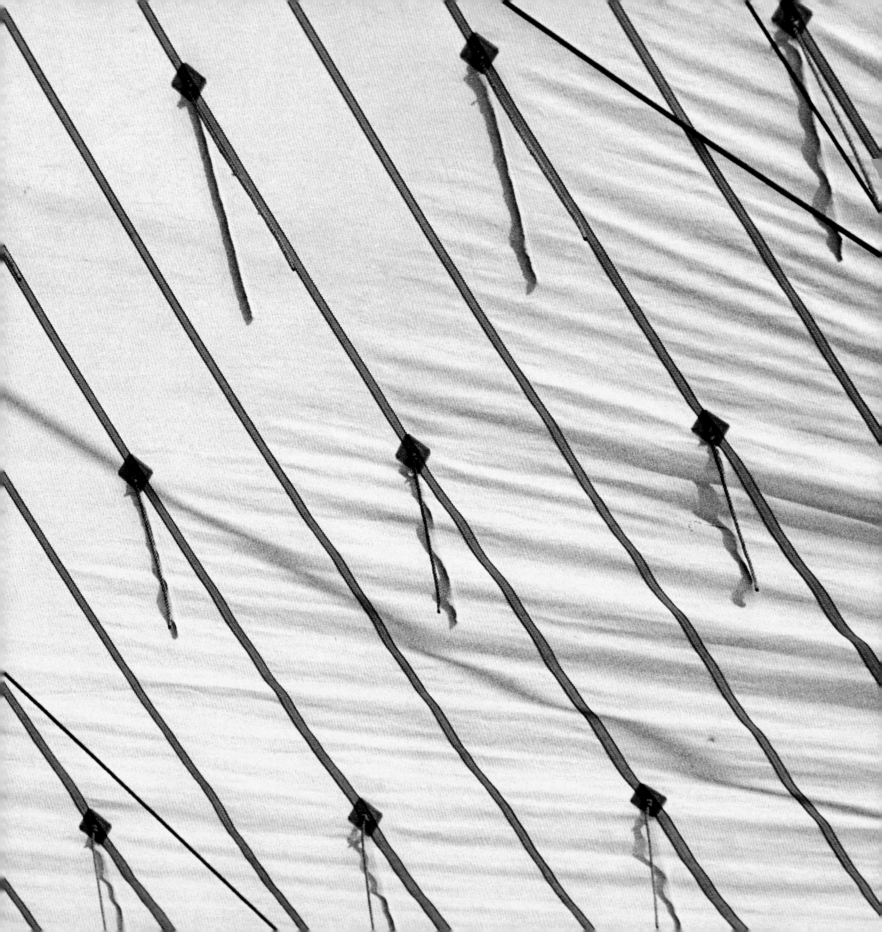

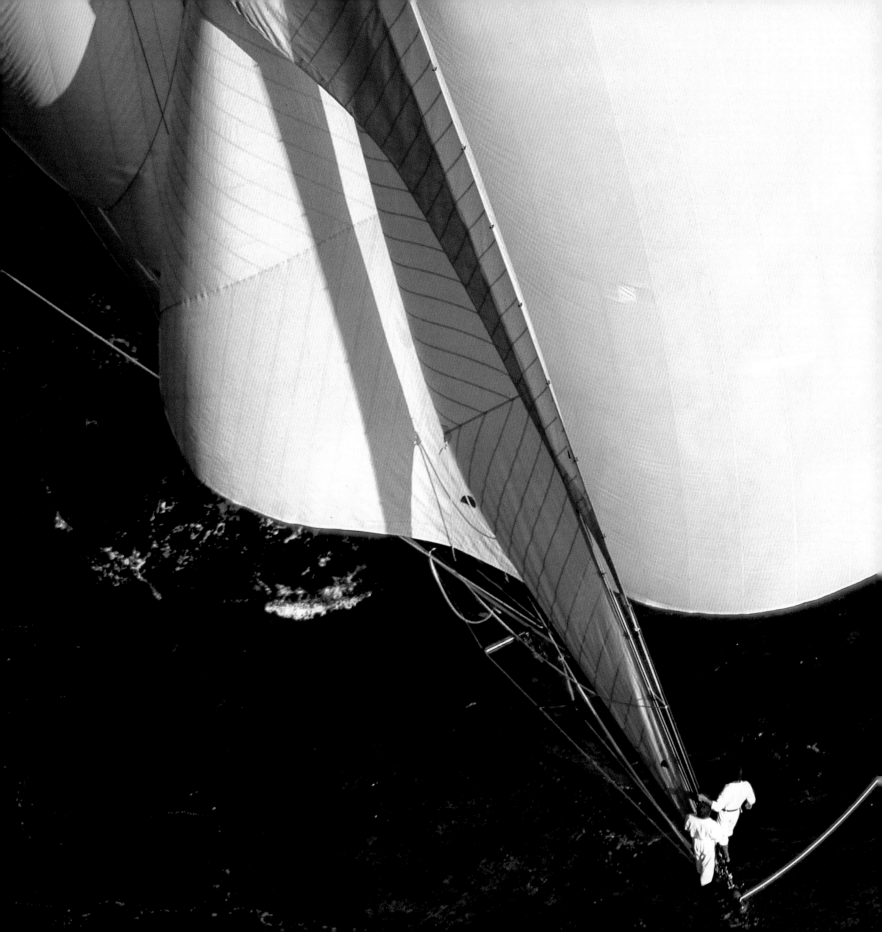

424-425 ● Mediterranean Sea, St. Tropez (France) - Les Voiles de Saint-Tropez event (Nioulargue), the *Altair*.

426-427 ● Atlantic Ocean, Brest (France) - the *Pesa*.

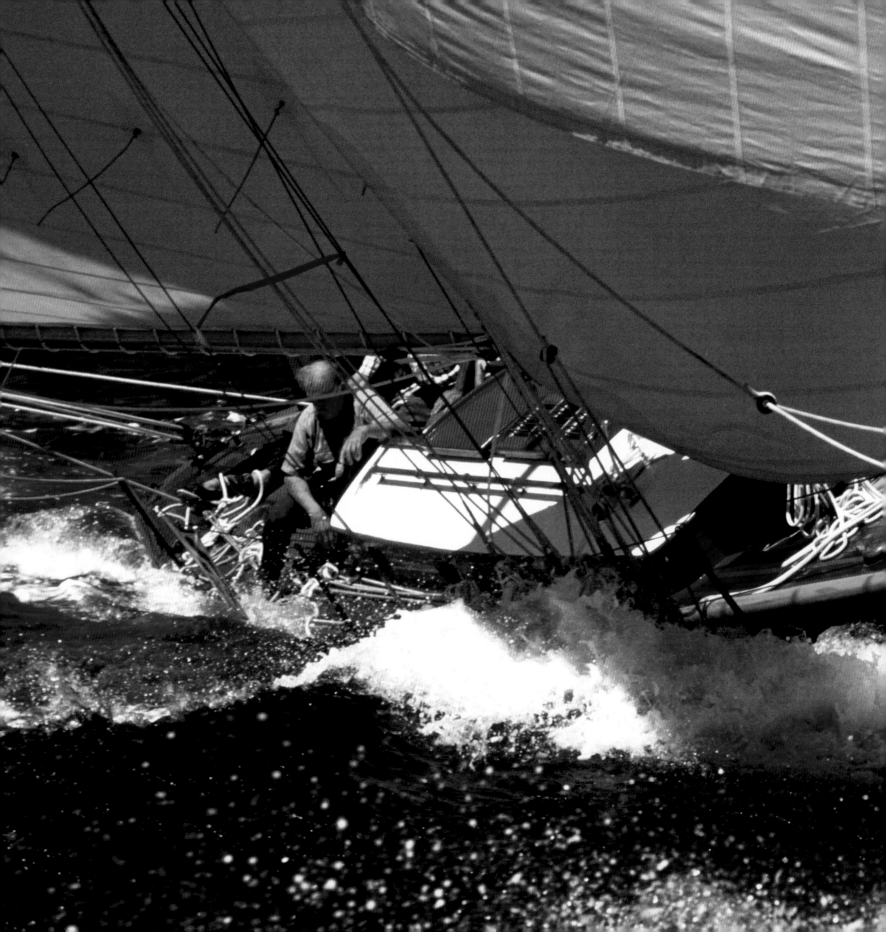

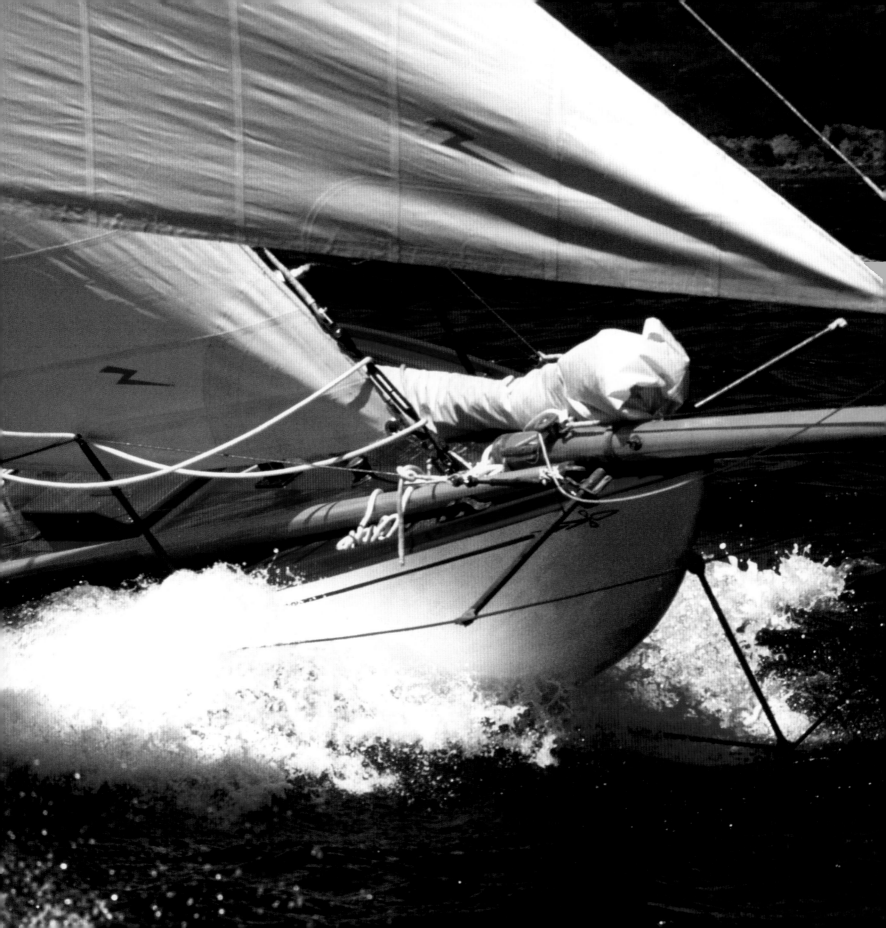

" T HE SOUTHWESTERLY WHISTLED THROUGH THE RIGGING AND SHOOK THE LOWERED SAILS. GUSTS OF RAIN BEAT MILITARY DRUMROLLS ON THE PLANKING... "

from TO THE ENDS OF THE EARTH
by William Golding

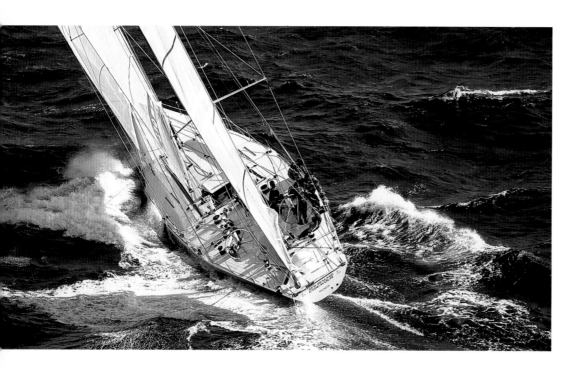

428 ● Pacific Ocean, New Zealand - Whitbread Cup.

429 ● Pacific Ocean, San Diego (USA) - Vuitton Cup in 1992, *Moro*.

430-431 ● Indian Ocean, Fremantle (Australia) - America's Cup, 1987.

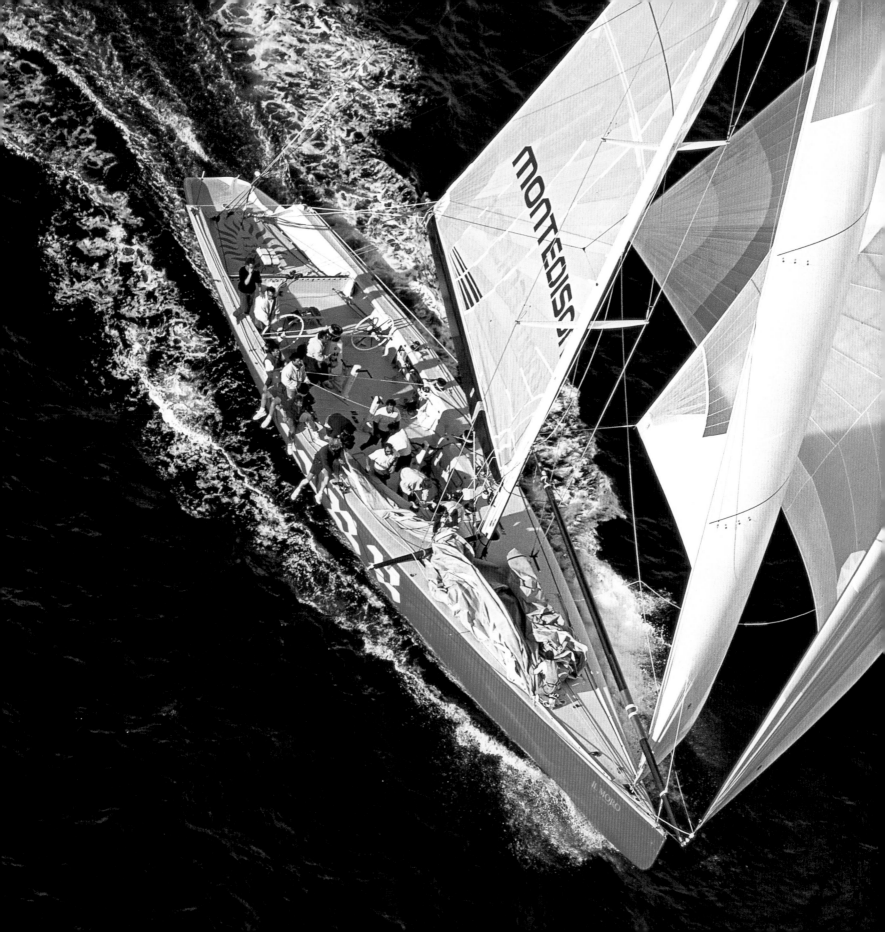

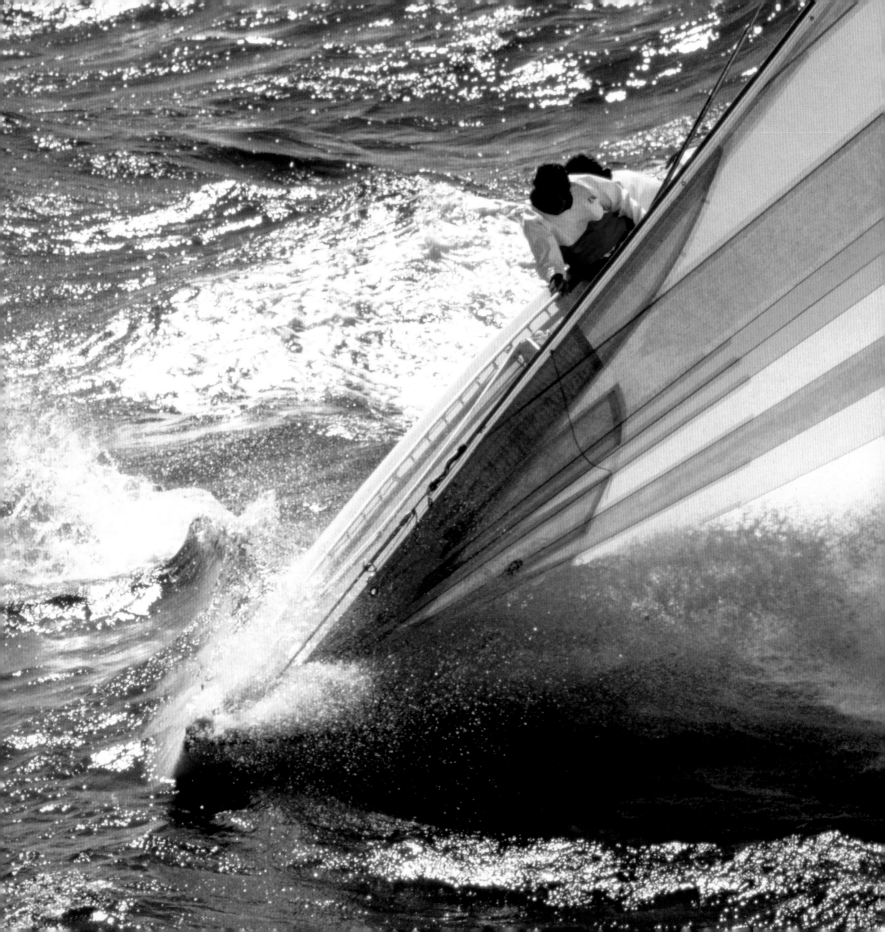

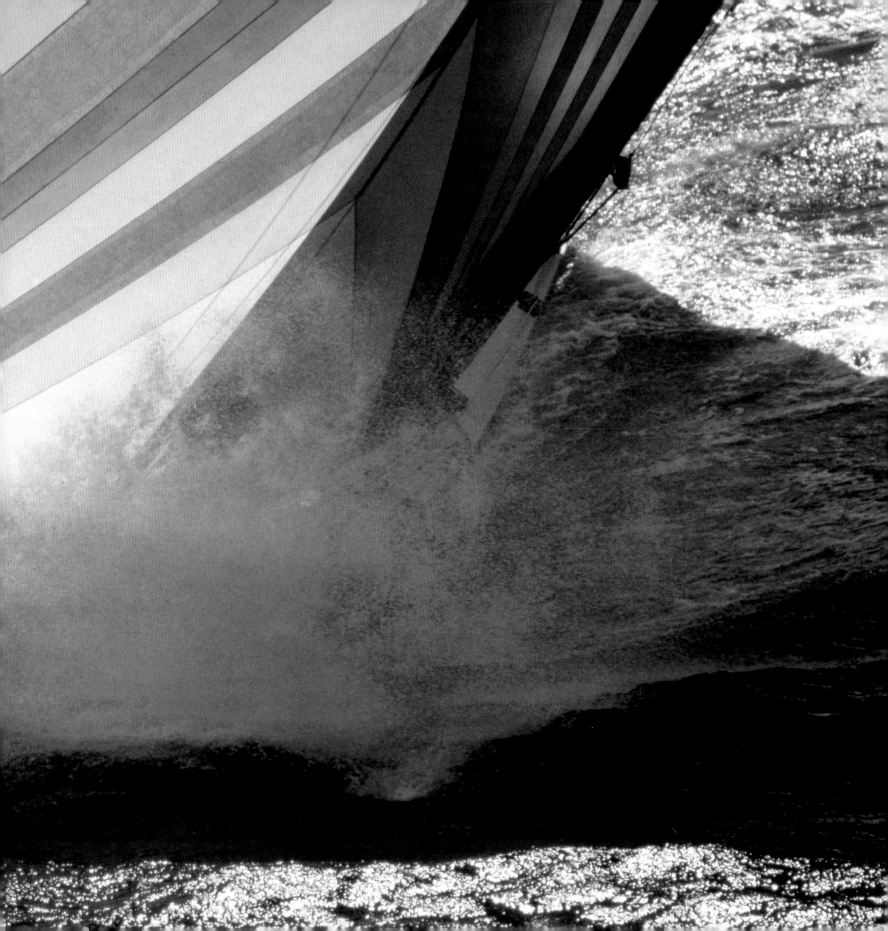

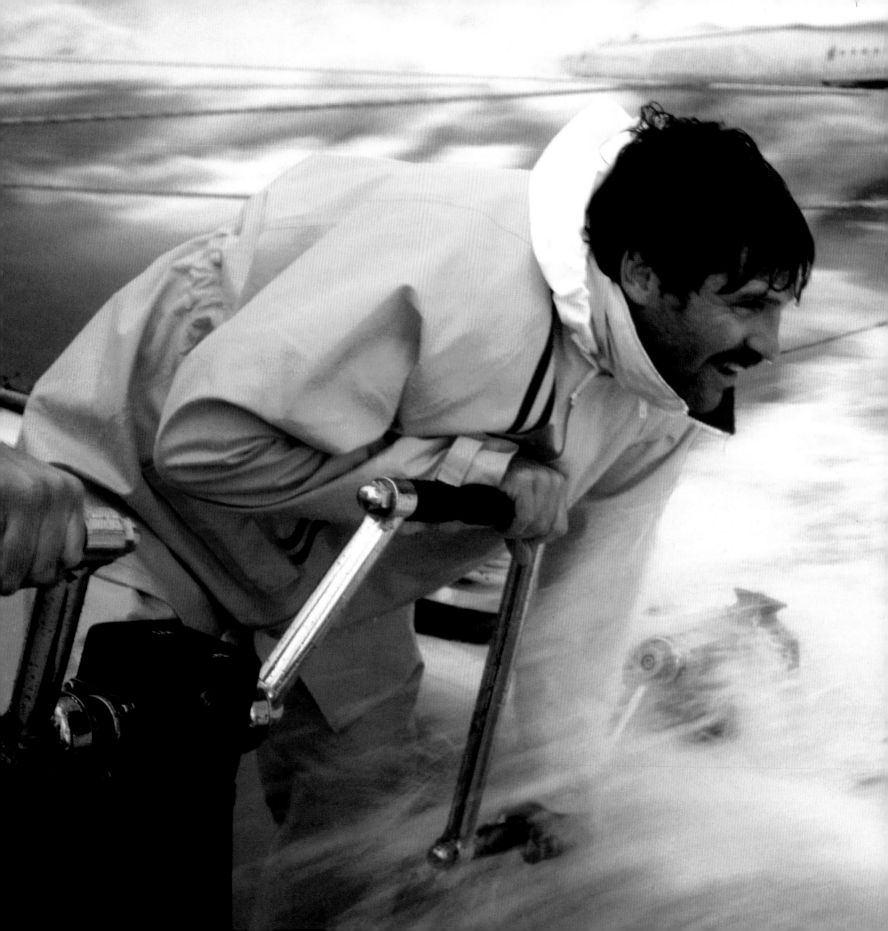

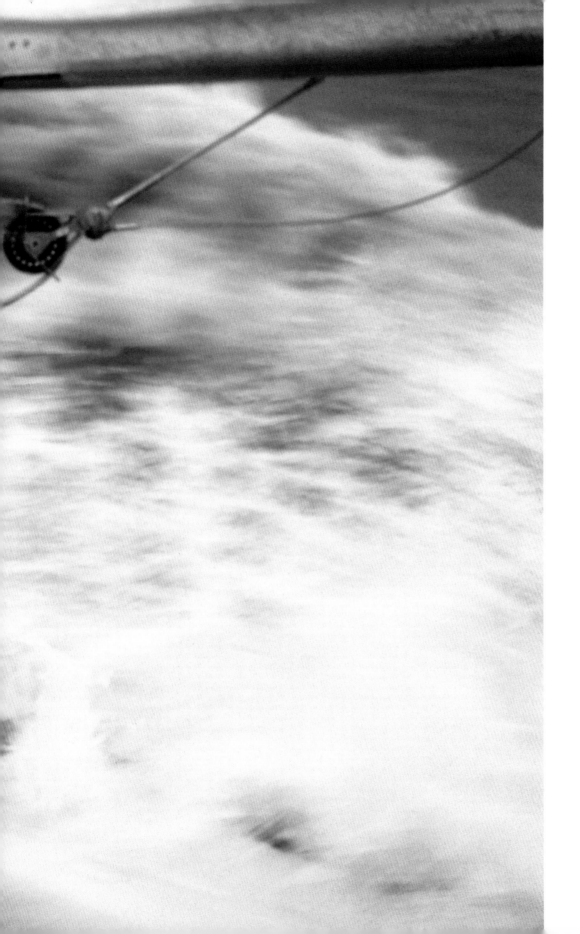

● Pacific Ocean,
San Francisco (USA) -
A member of the crew on
the 12-meter *USA*

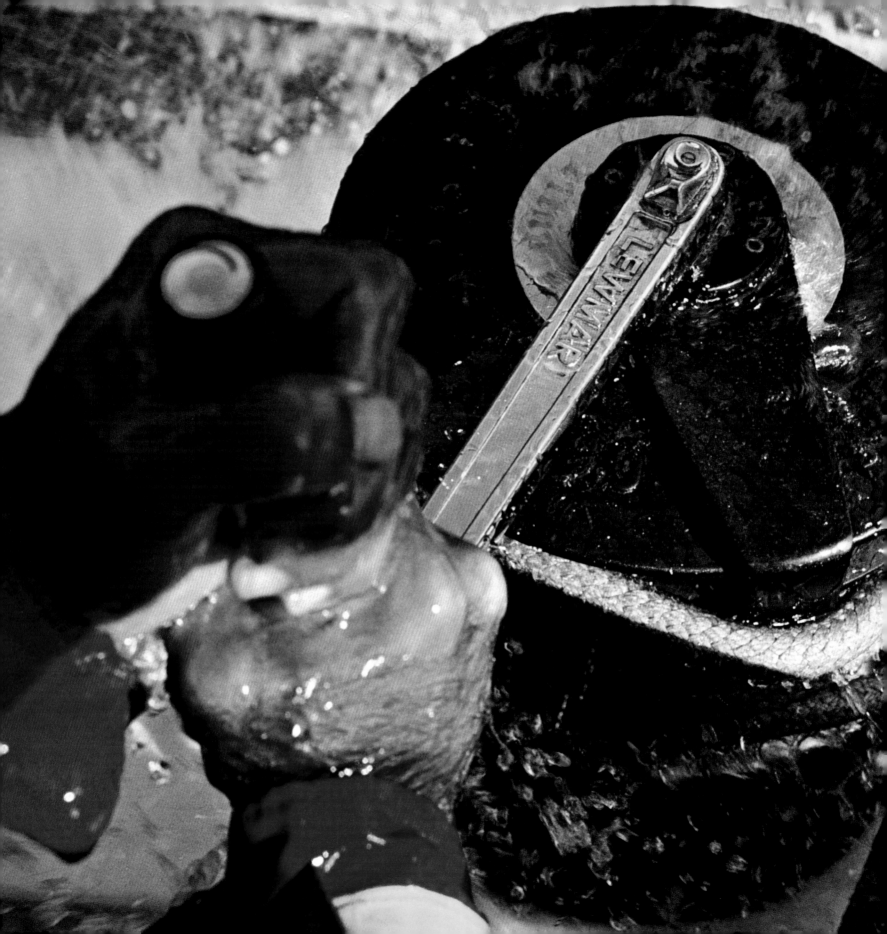

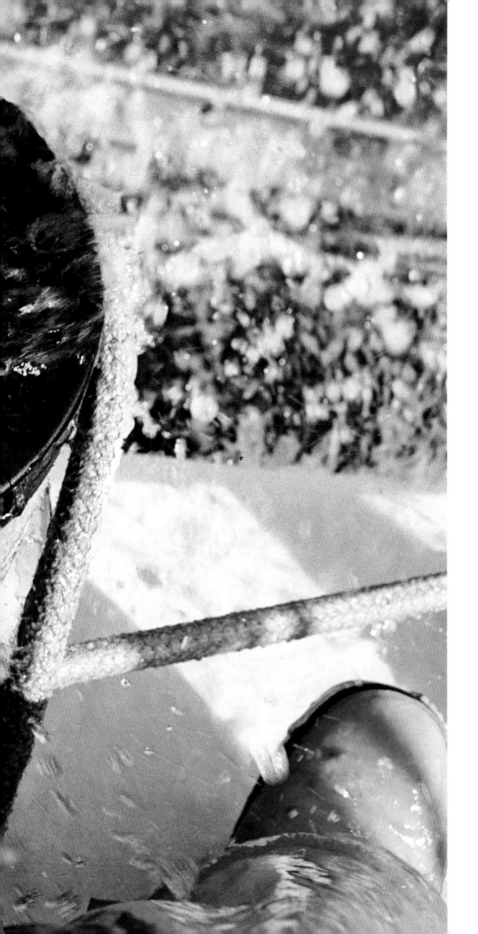

Indian Ocean, Fremantle
(Australia) - Vuitton Cup 1992,
on board one of the
challengers.

435

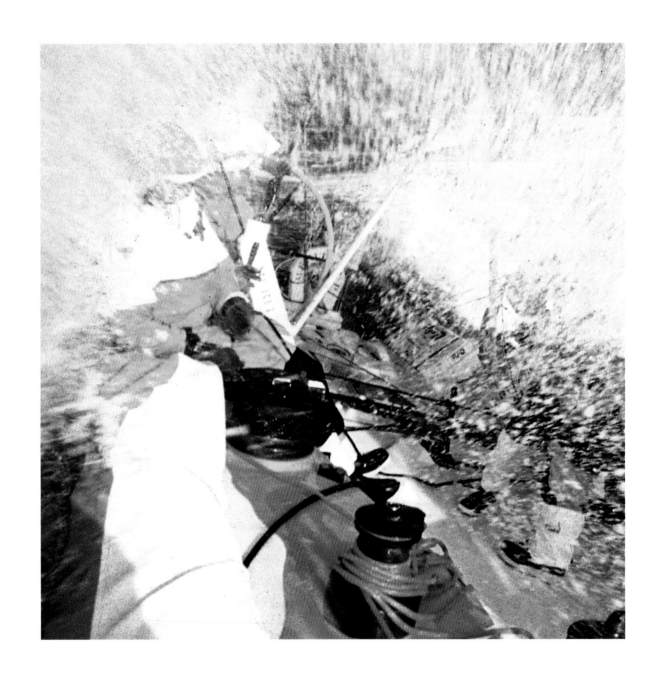

● Atlantic Ocean, Whitbread Cup - On board the *Merit*.

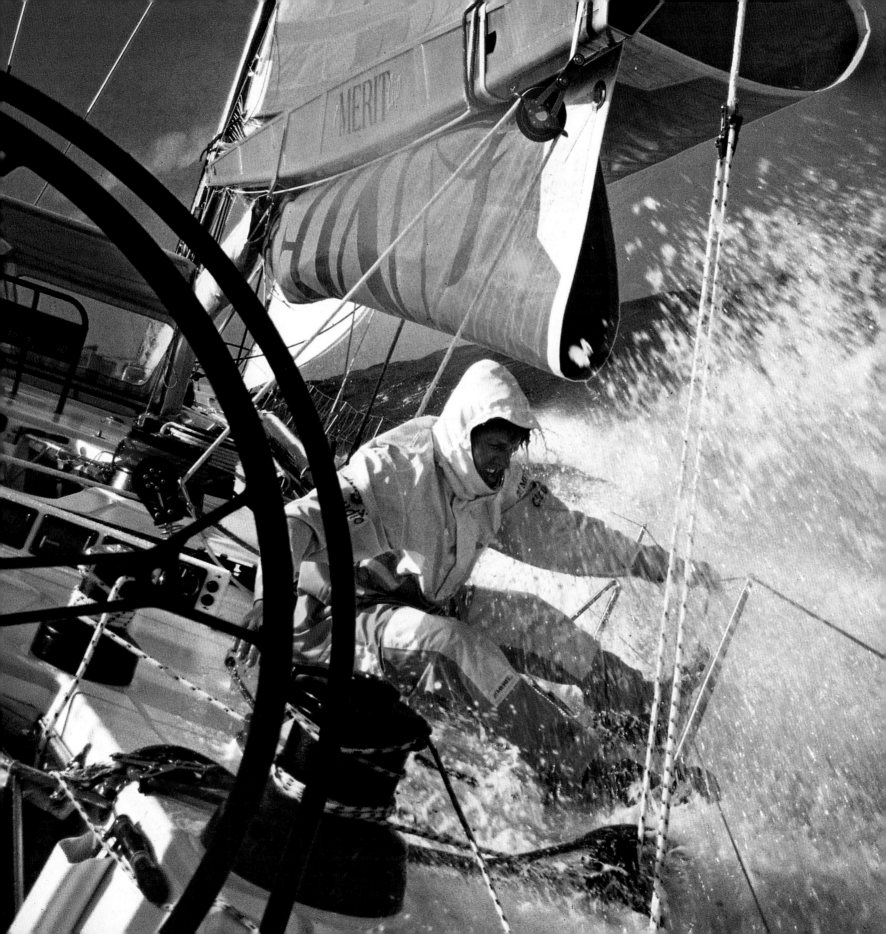

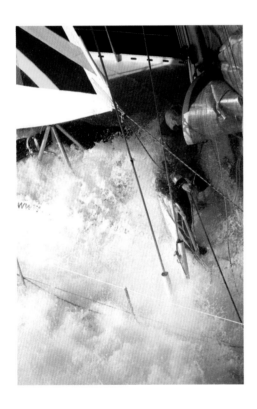

438 and 438-439 ● Pacific Ocean, Volvo Ocean Race 2002 - On board *Amer Sports One*.

440-441 ● Atlantic Ocean, Brest (France) - Global Challenge 2002-2003, *Adrien* di Jean-Luc van den Heede.

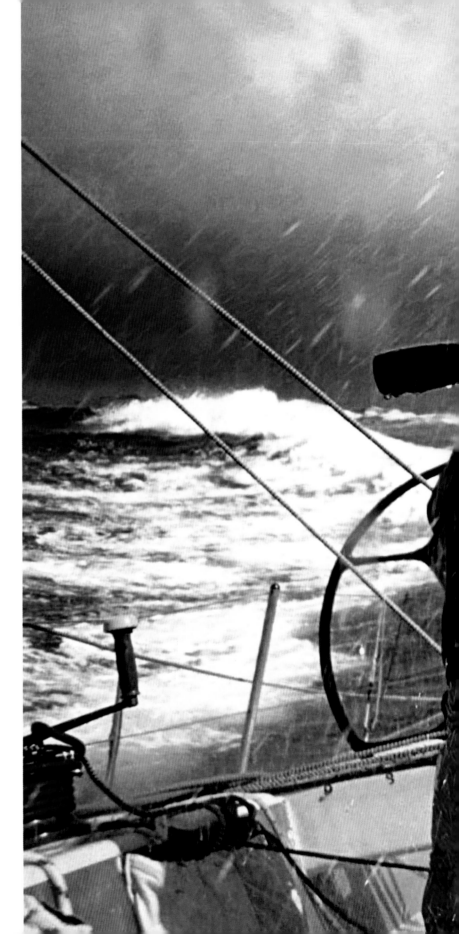

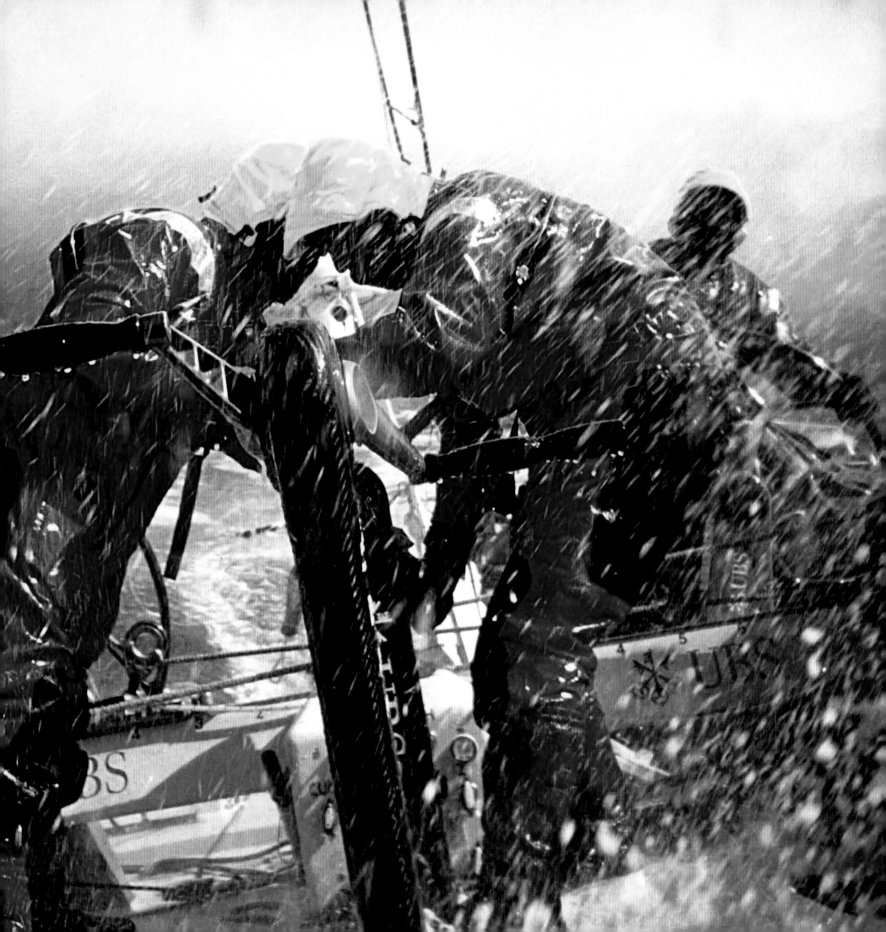

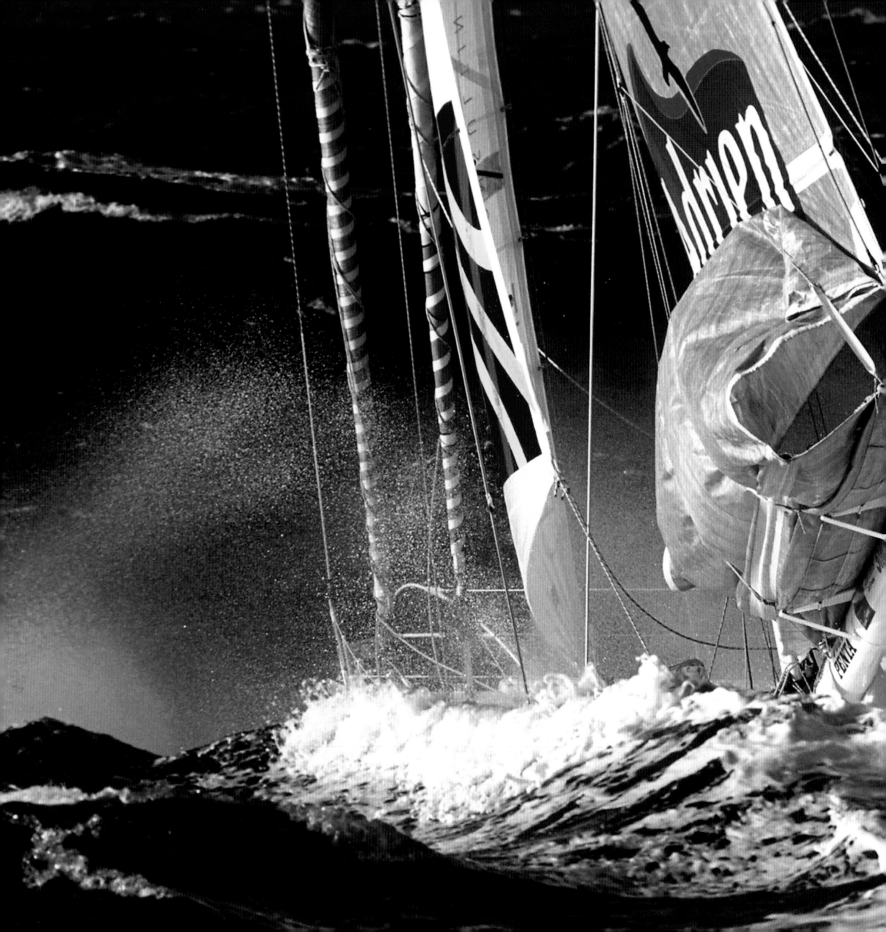

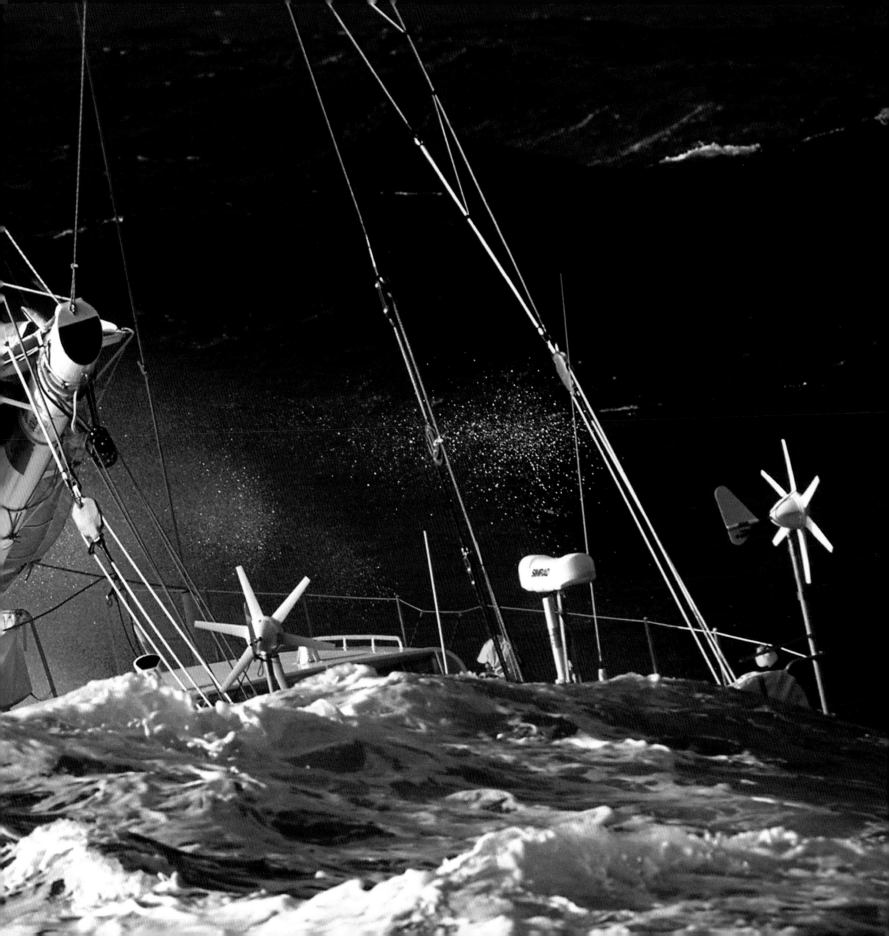

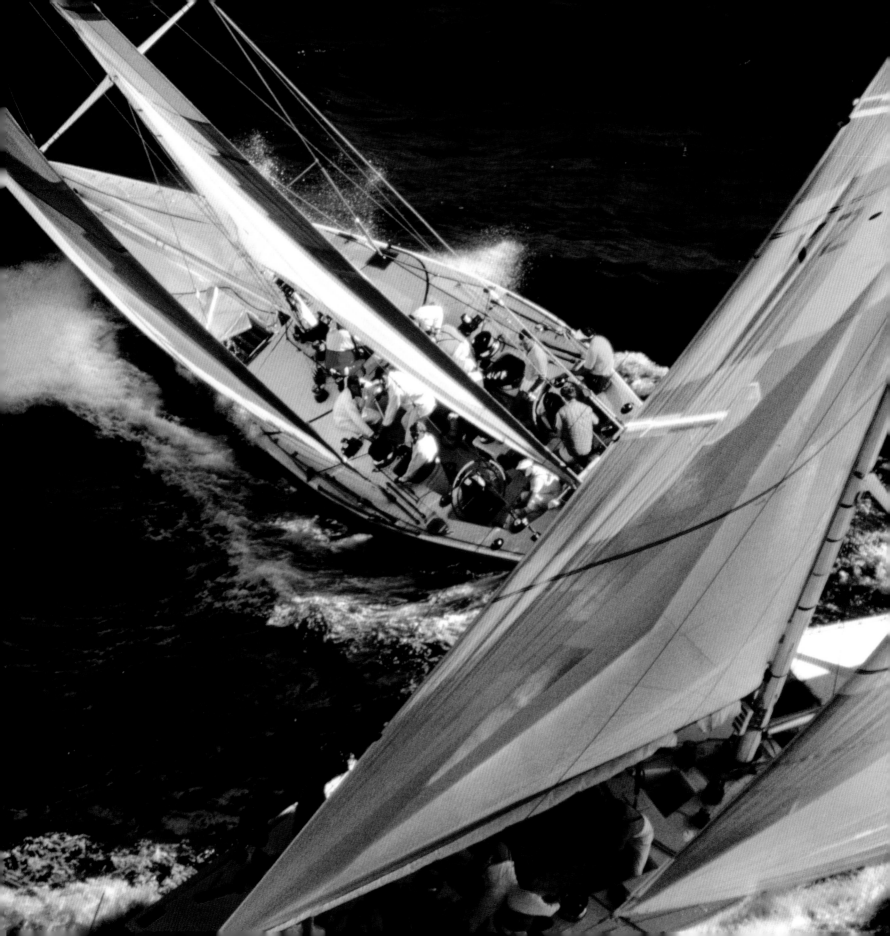

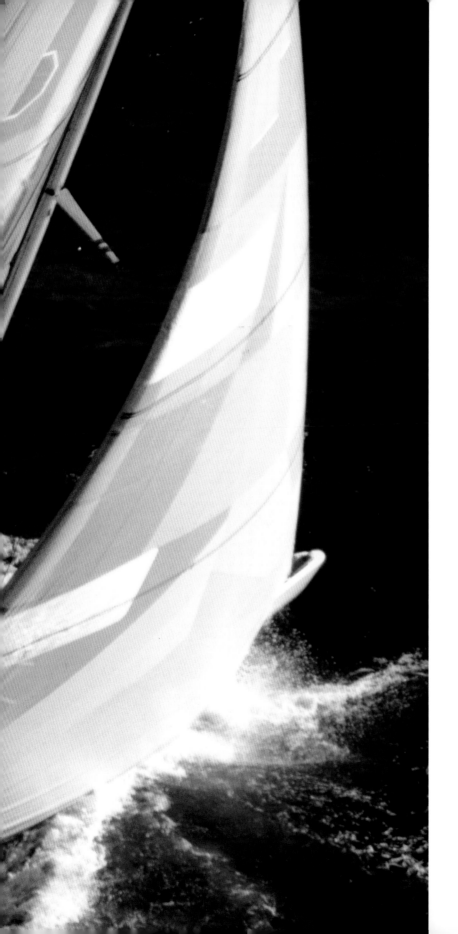

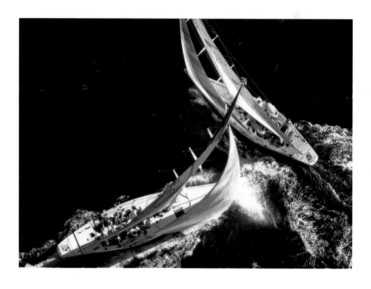

442, 443 ● Indian Ocean, Fremantle (Australia) - America's Cup 1987.

444-445 ● Pacific Ocean, sailing race in a rough sea.

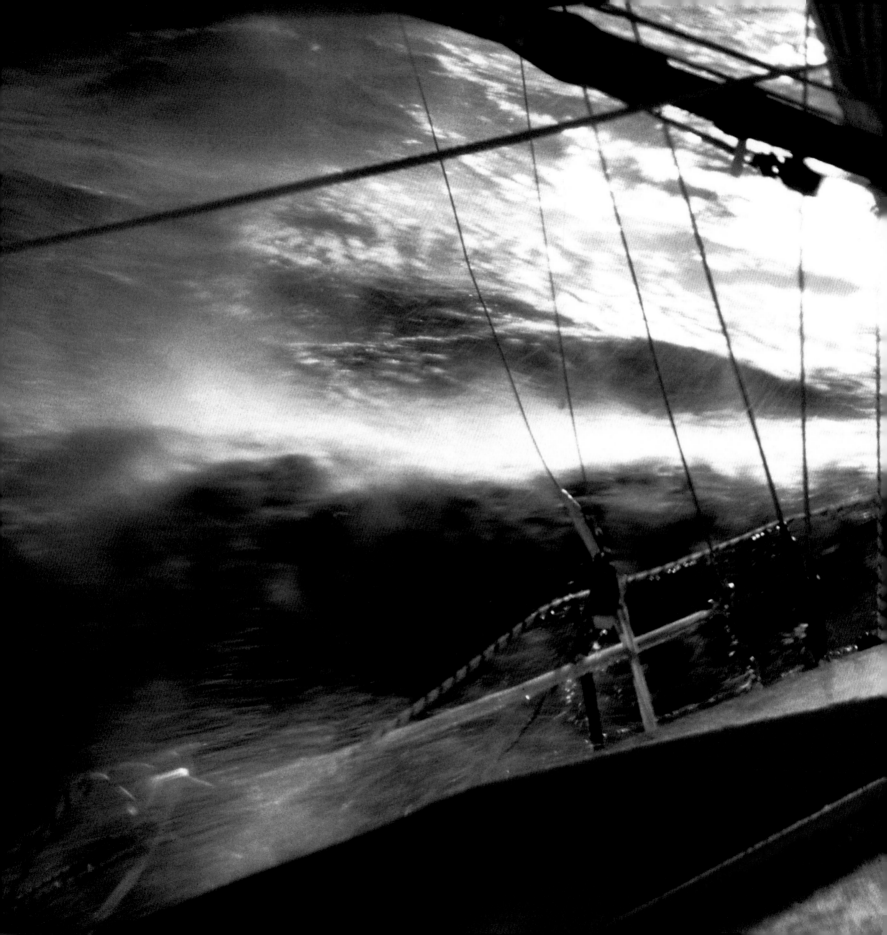

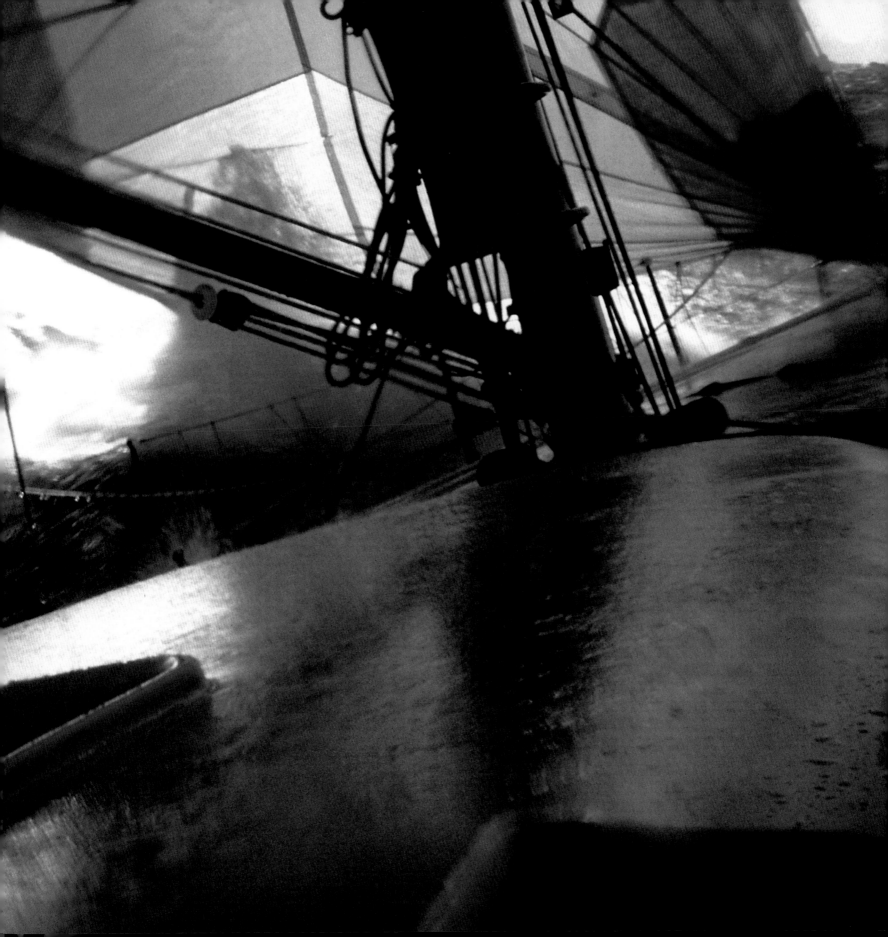

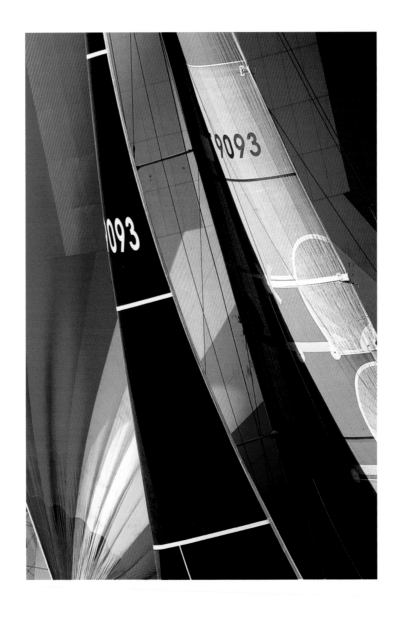

446 and 447 ● Mediterranean Sea, St. Tropez (France) - Colored jibs and spankers during Les Voiles de Saint-Tropez event (Nioulargue).

448-449 ● Pacific Ocean, New Zealand - America's Cup 2003, the *Luna Rossa*.

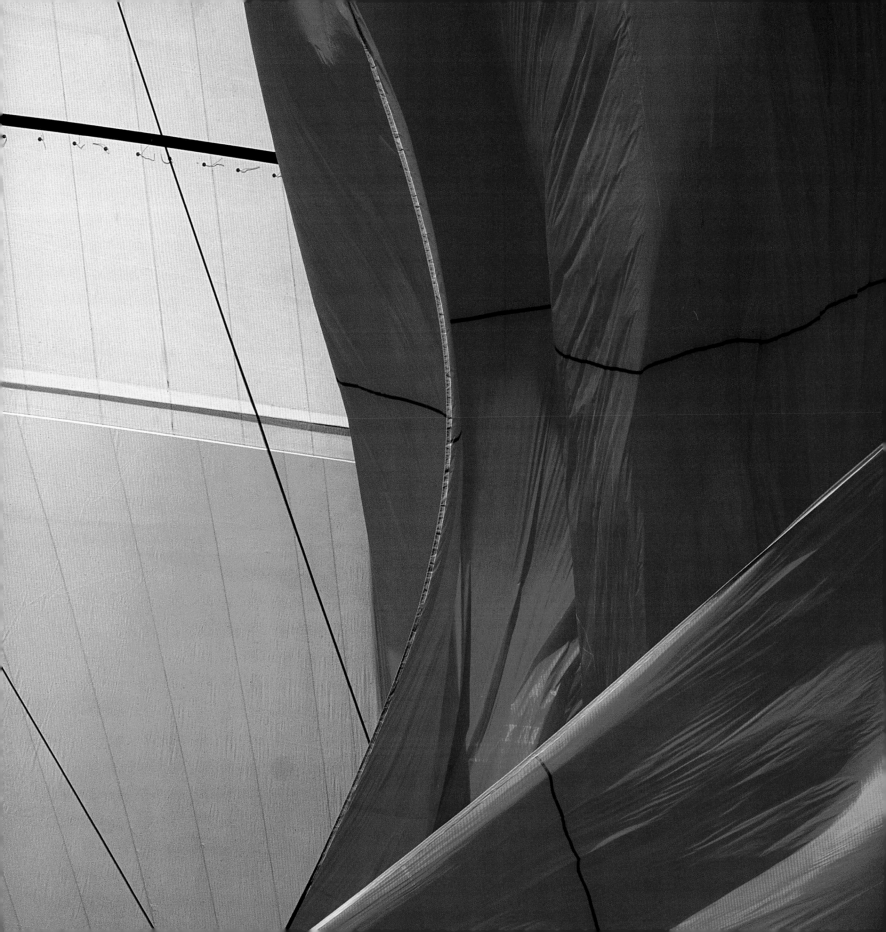

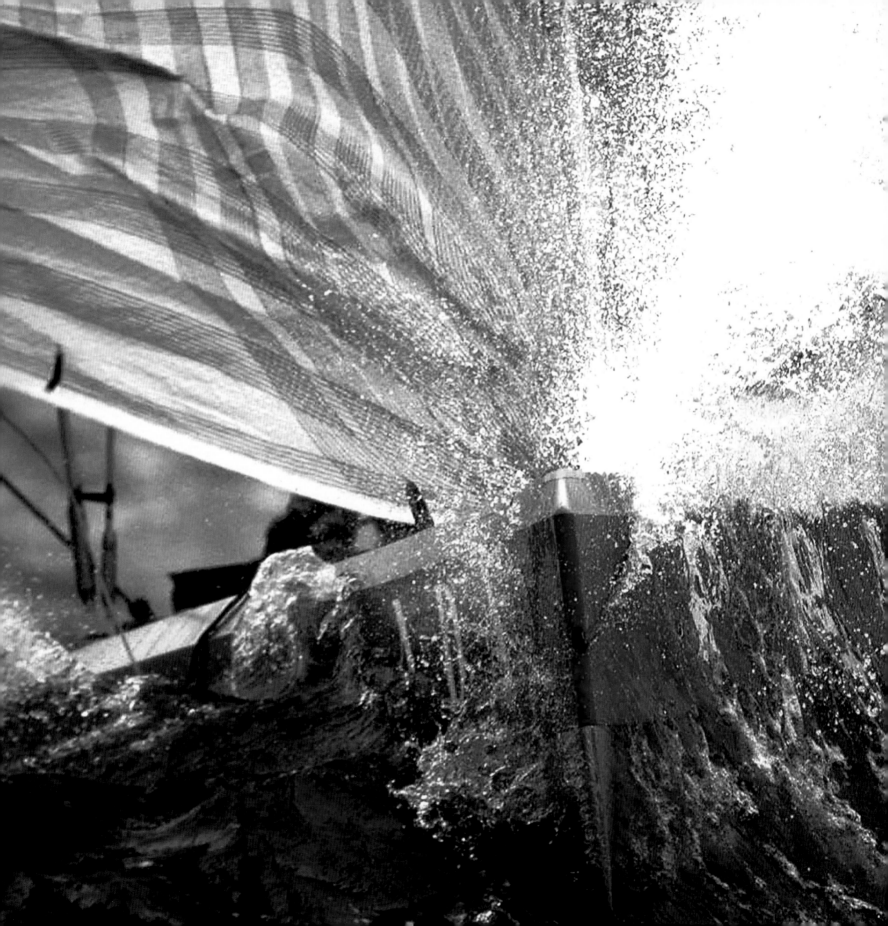

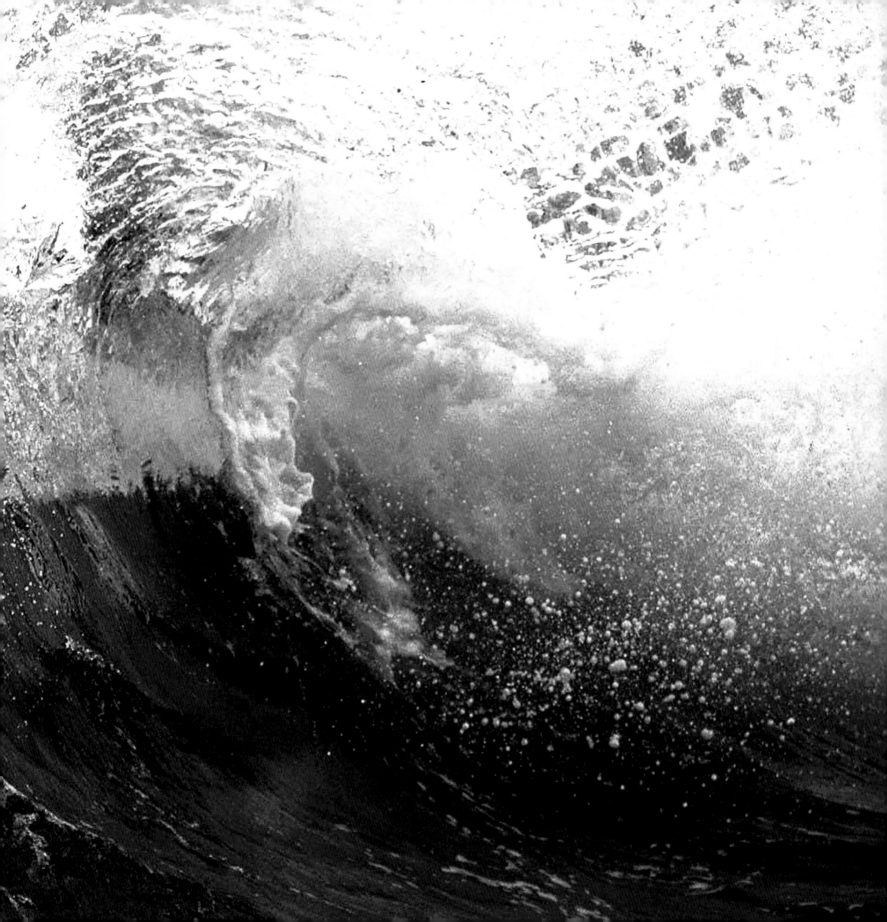

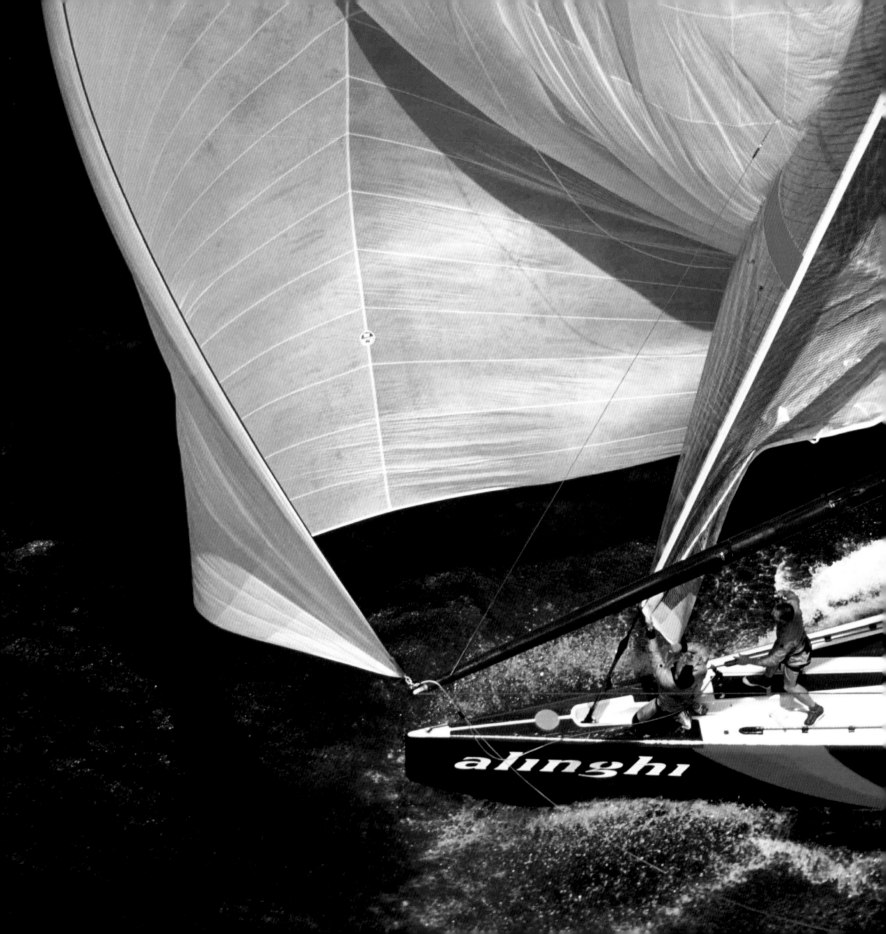

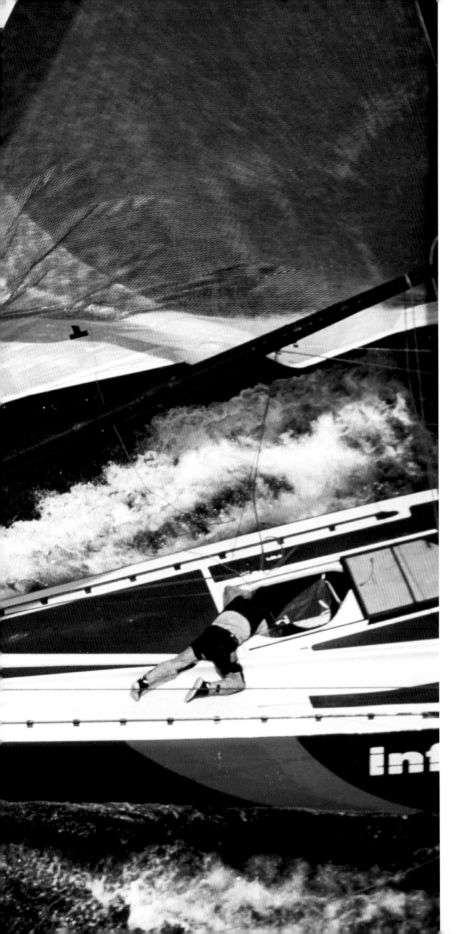

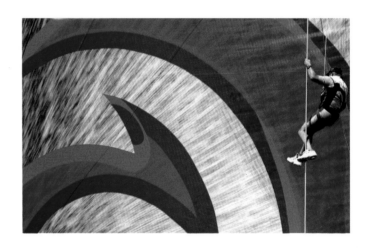

● Pacific Ocean, New Zealand -
America's Cup 2003, the *Alinghi*.

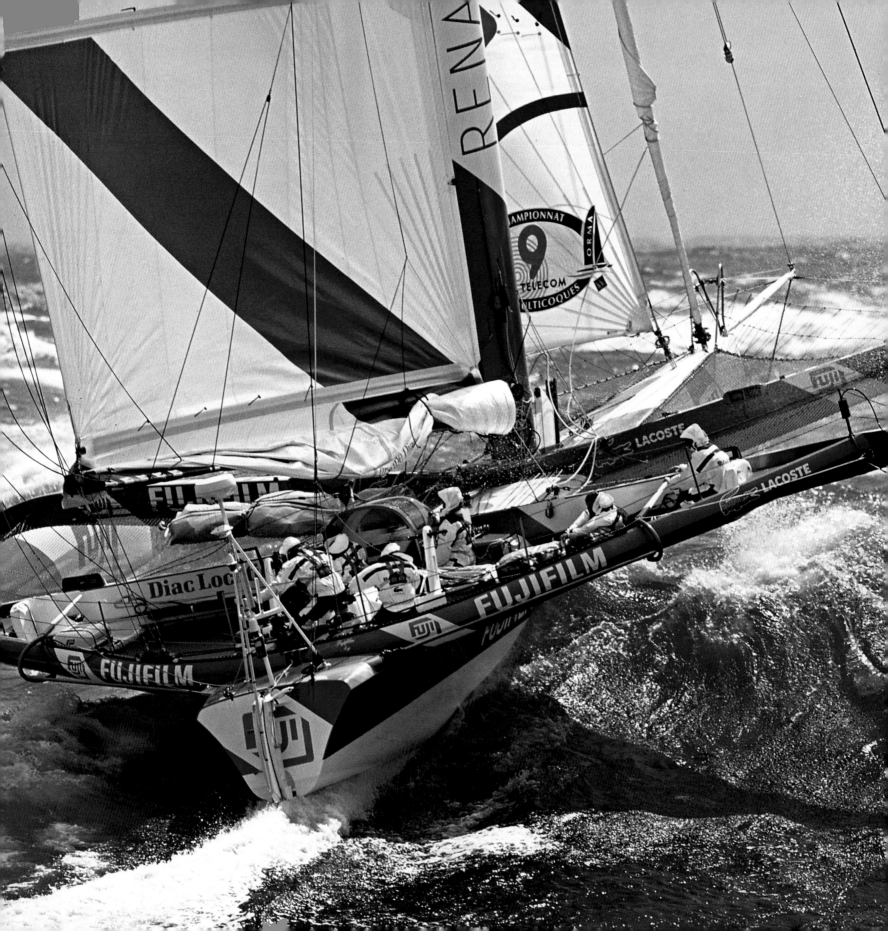

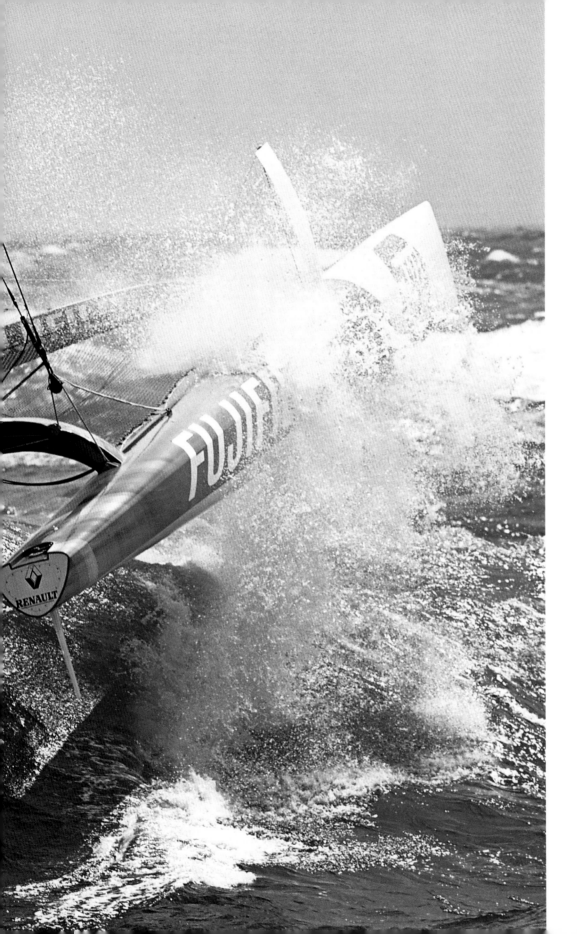

Atlantic Ocean,
Transatlantic Rum Race
2002 - The trimaran *Fujifilm*.

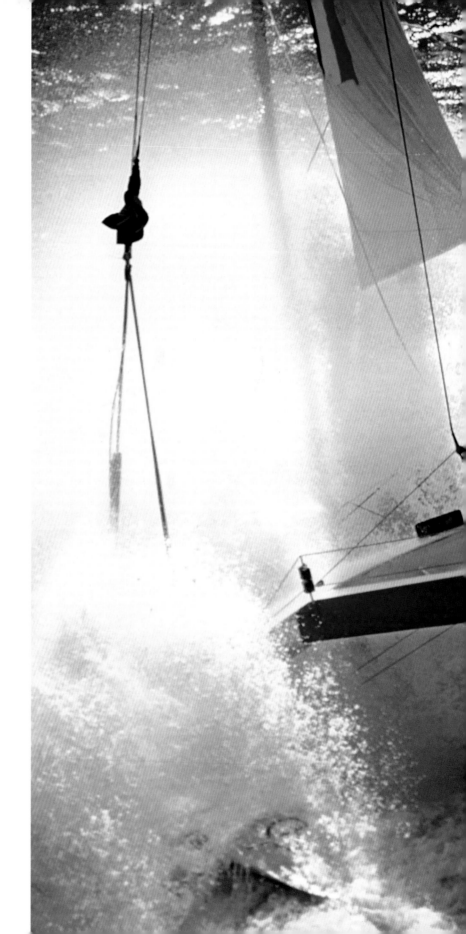

C HILDREN OF THE WIND AND ADVANCED TECH-NOLOGY, THAT SAME TECH-NOLOGY THAT SENT MAN TO THE MOON, CATAMARANS ARE THE OFF-ROADERS OF HIGH SEA COASTAL NAVIGA-TION, WATER-BORNE MISSILES CAPABLE OF HIGH SPEEDS.

Atlantic Ocean - Transatlantic Rum Race 2002, the trimaran *Belgacom*.

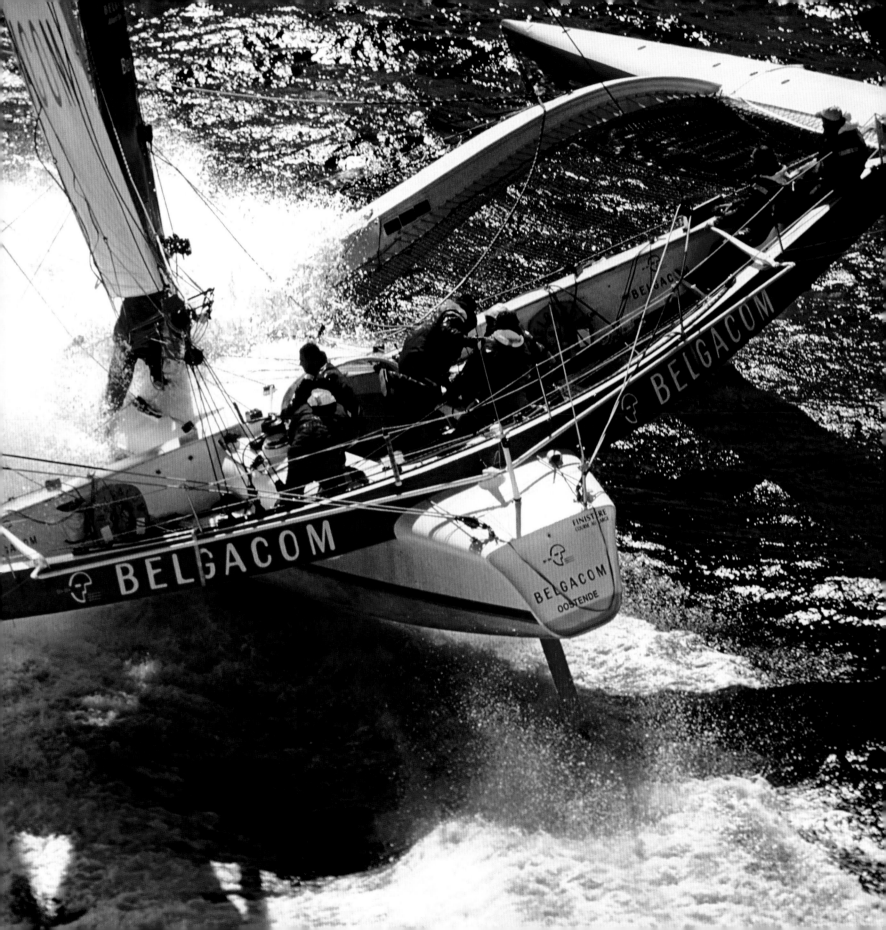

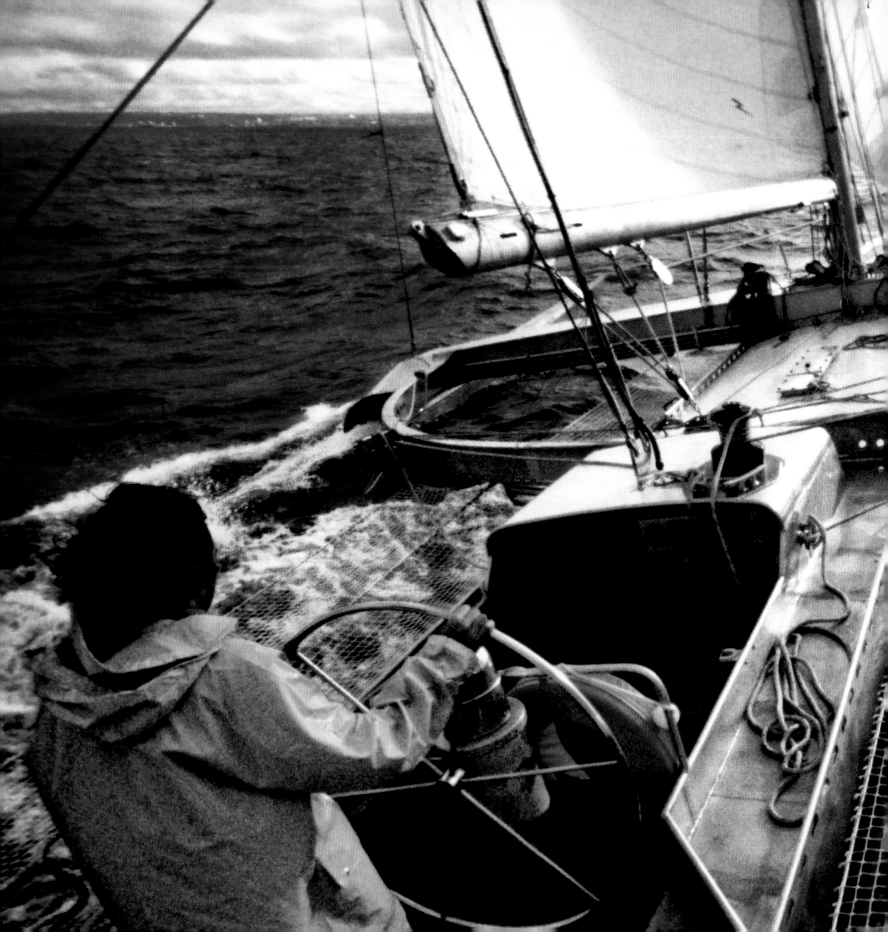

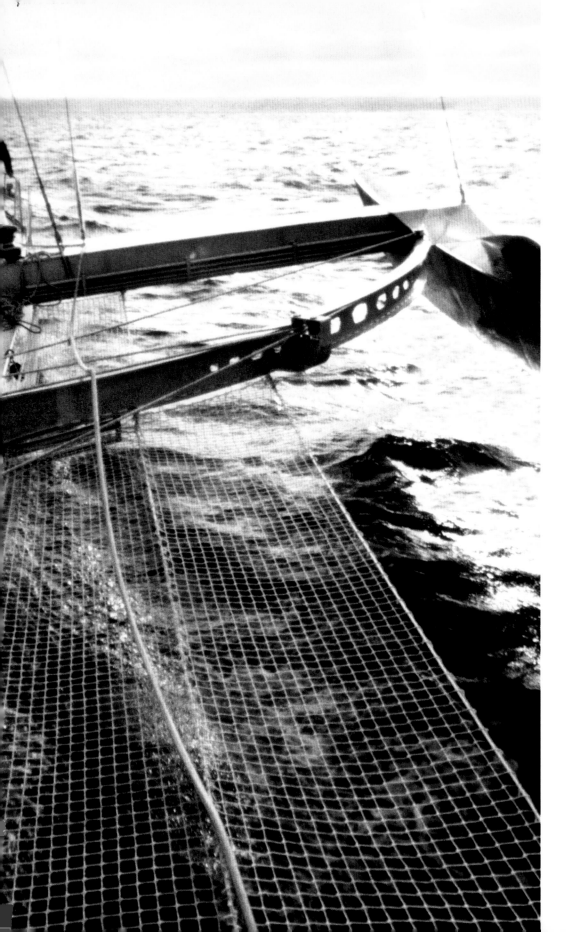

Atlantic Ocean -
Transatlantic Rum Race
1978, the trimaran *Krite IV*.

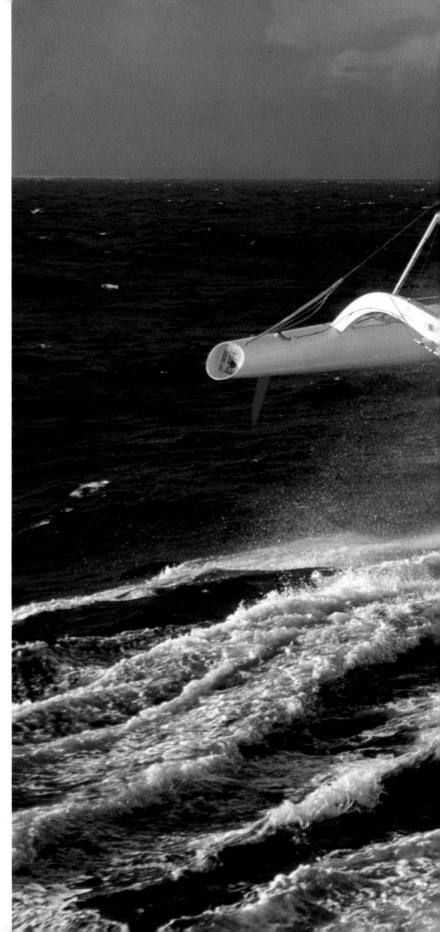

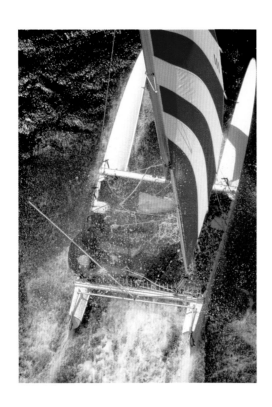

458 ● Caribbean Sea - Mini-catamaran.

458-459 ● Atlantic Ocean - Challenge Mondial Assistance 2003, the trimaran *Foncia*.

460-461 ● Atlantic Ocean - Transatlantic Rum Race 1978, the trimaran *Dupon*.

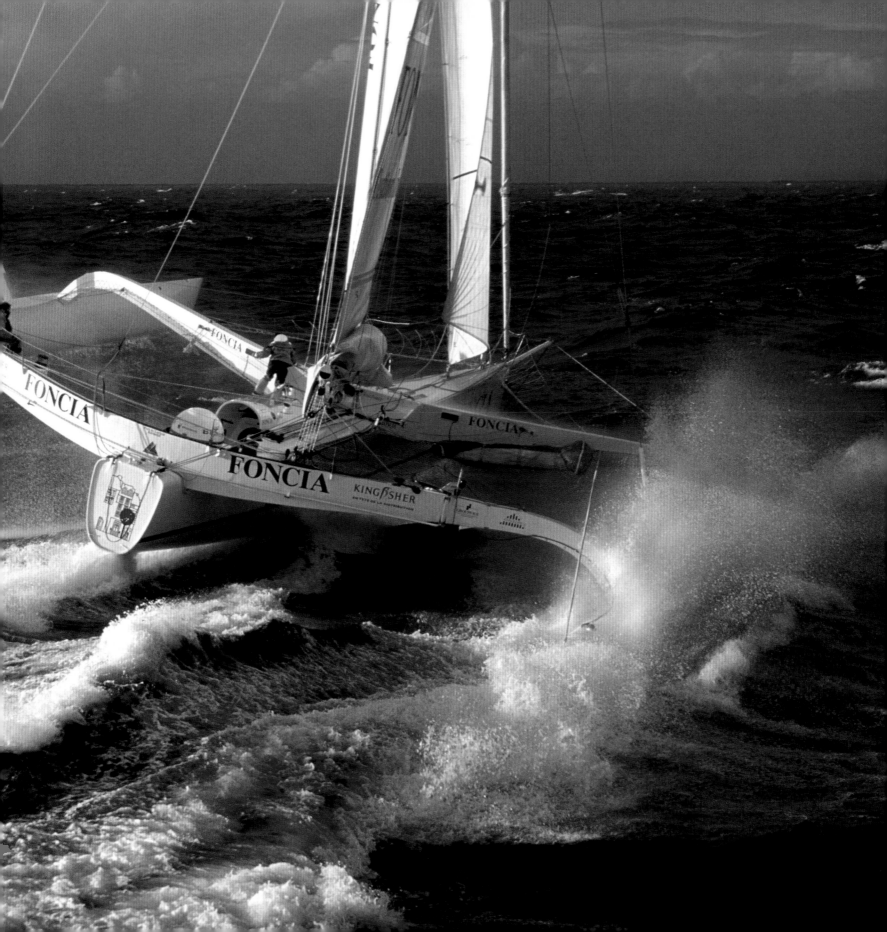

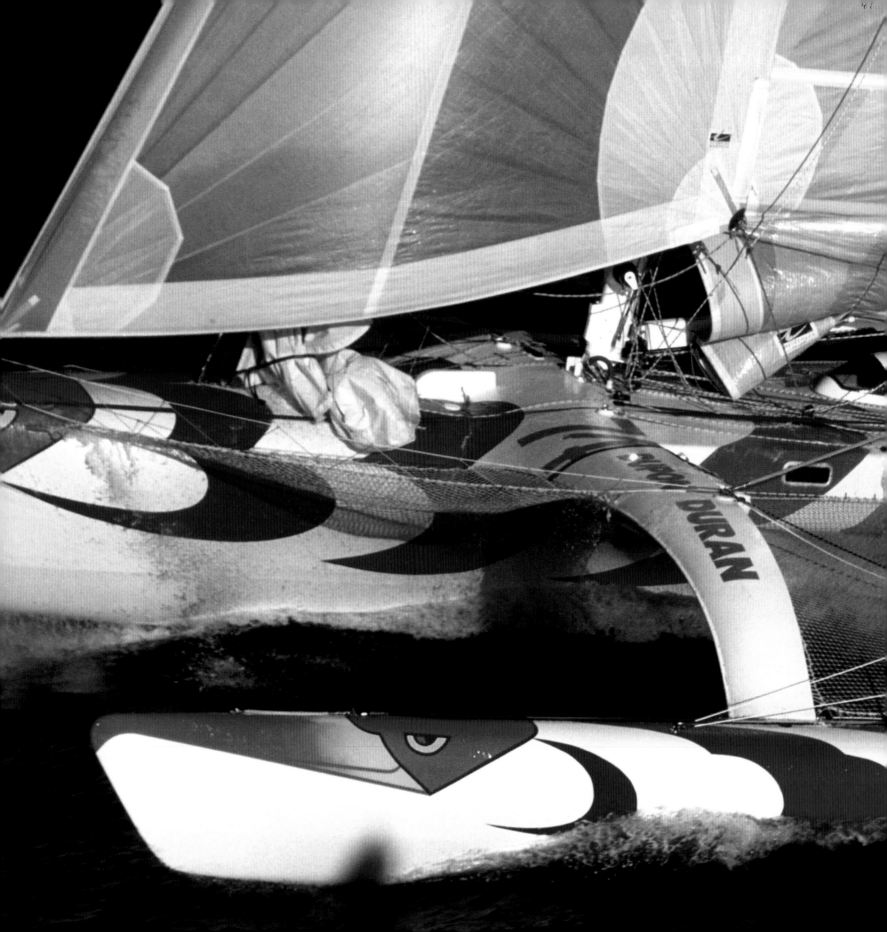

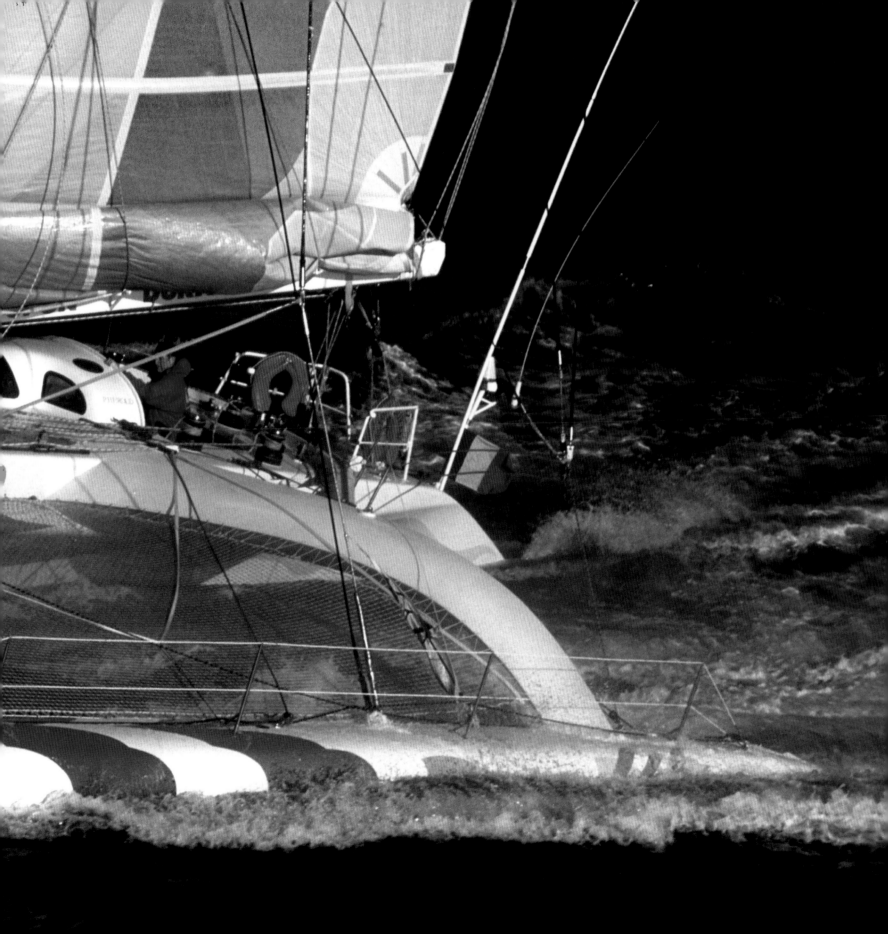

On the CREST of a WAVE

ALESSANDRA SENSINI

California (USA) - "Floating" on a breaking wave.

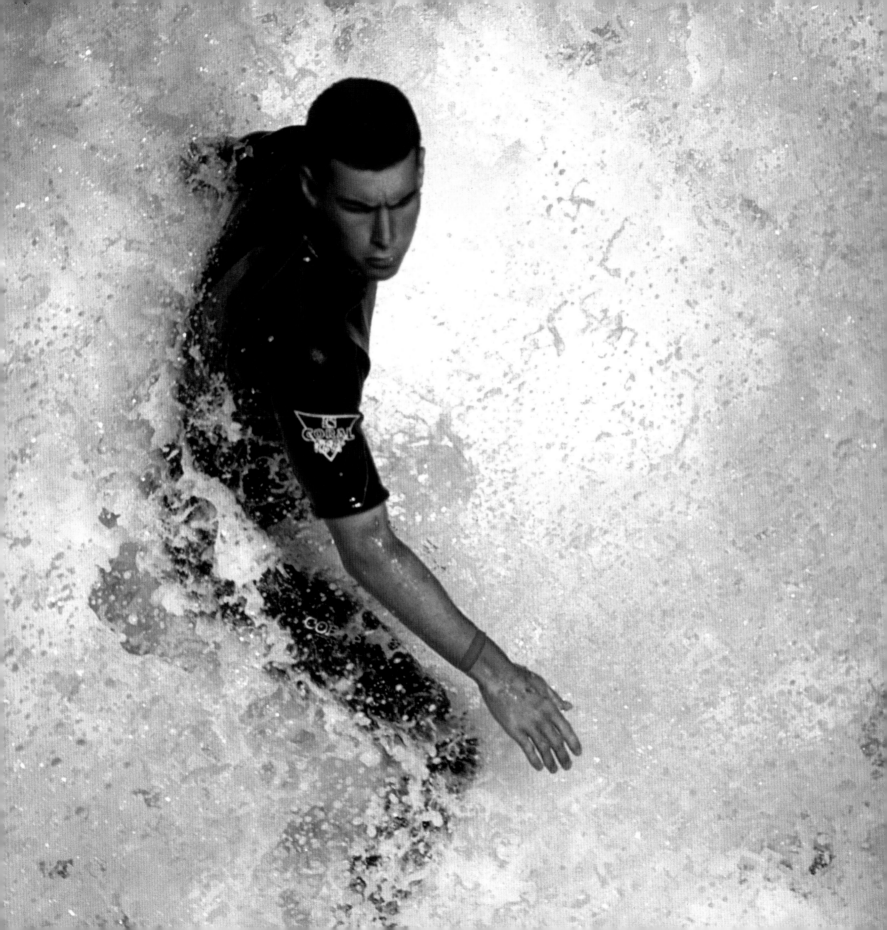

INTRODUCTION On the Crest of a Wave

THE FIRST TIME OCCURRED IN THE HAWAIIAN ISLANDS. A GROUP OF DAREDEVILS CLUNG TO THE TOP OF A WAVE WITH THE FOAM CURLING OVER THEIR HEADS. THESE WERE WAVES FIFTEEN FEET HIGH, MAYBE EIGHTEEN. TO GET UP THERE IT WAS NECESSARY TO CIRCUMVENT THEM IN SOME WAY, TO STUDY THE SEA, UNDERSTAND HOW IT WORKED AND TRICK IT. GOOD WAVES COME IN CYCLES, ONE EVERY THREE, FOUR OR FIVE DEPENDING ON THE PLACE AND THE CIRCUMSTANCES. IT IS EASY TO KNOW WHEN A GOOD WAVE HAS ARRIVED: IT GROWS IN SIZE, CLIMBS TILL IT IS VERTICAL AND THEN CRASHES DOWN ONTO THE SHORELINE. DEPENDING ON THE TIDE, THE CURRENT PUSHES IN OR PULLS OUT, AND OTHER FACTORS ARE THE WIND AND THE

INTRODUCTION On the Crest of a Wave

DEPTH OF THE WATER. THE RHYTHM OF THE WAVES IS CREATED BY A

NATURAL CLOCK. FINALLY THE PERFECT WAVE ARRIVES. TO BEGIN

WITH IT IS A SMALL SWELLING OF THE WATER THAT HARDLY SEEMS TO

MOVE, THEN IT BEGINS TO GROW. YOU HAVE TO CATCH IT AT THE RIGHT

MOMENT, NOT A SECOND BEFORE, NOT A SECOND LATER. WHEN YOU

ARE AT THE TOP YOU KNOW YOU HAVE NO MORE STRENGTH THAN A

TWIG. THE POWER OF A WAVE IS FRIGHTENING. THE SENSATIONS YOU

FEEL ARE EXHILARATING, SOMETIMES OVERWHELMING, BUT ONCE

YOU HAVE LEARNED THE SECRET OF DOMINATING IT, THE WAVE

BECOMES EVERYTHING: NATURE AS FRIEND, AND A VITAL ENERGY. IT

GIVES YOU THE SENSE THAT YOU ARE ALIVE. TO EXPERIENCE THE

On the Crest of a Wave

Introduction

CREST OF A WAVE MEANS KNOWING HOW TO GOVERN YOUR BALANCE: BEHIND THAT WHITE FOAM AND INSIDE THOSE BLUE DEPTHS LIES THE VIBRATING POWER OF THE SEA. TO LET YOURSELF BE CARRIED OR OVERTURNED? THIS IS A DILEMMA THAT EXISTS BOTH IN SPORT AND IN LIFE. MANAGING SUCCESS IS MORE DEMANDING. HOW MANY TIMES IN LIFE HAS A WAVE TAKEN ME AND THROWN ME OVER, JUST WHEN I THOUGHT I WAS IN CONTROL? ONLY ONE TIME THAT I AM SURE OF: IT WAS AFTER I HAD WON THE GOLD MEDAL AT THE OLYMPICS IN SYDNEY WHEN I SAW THE SQUARE IN GROSSETO, BACK HOME IN ITALY, FILLED WITH PEOPLE, WITH MUSIC AND CONFETTI, PEOPLE CRYING AND THANKING ME. RIGHT THEN I FAINTED AND BEGAN CRYING TOO.

467 ● Australia - The surfboard slashes the face of the wave like a knife.

468-469 ● Hawaii (USA) - Wind and breakers at Pavillions on Hookipa Beach Park.

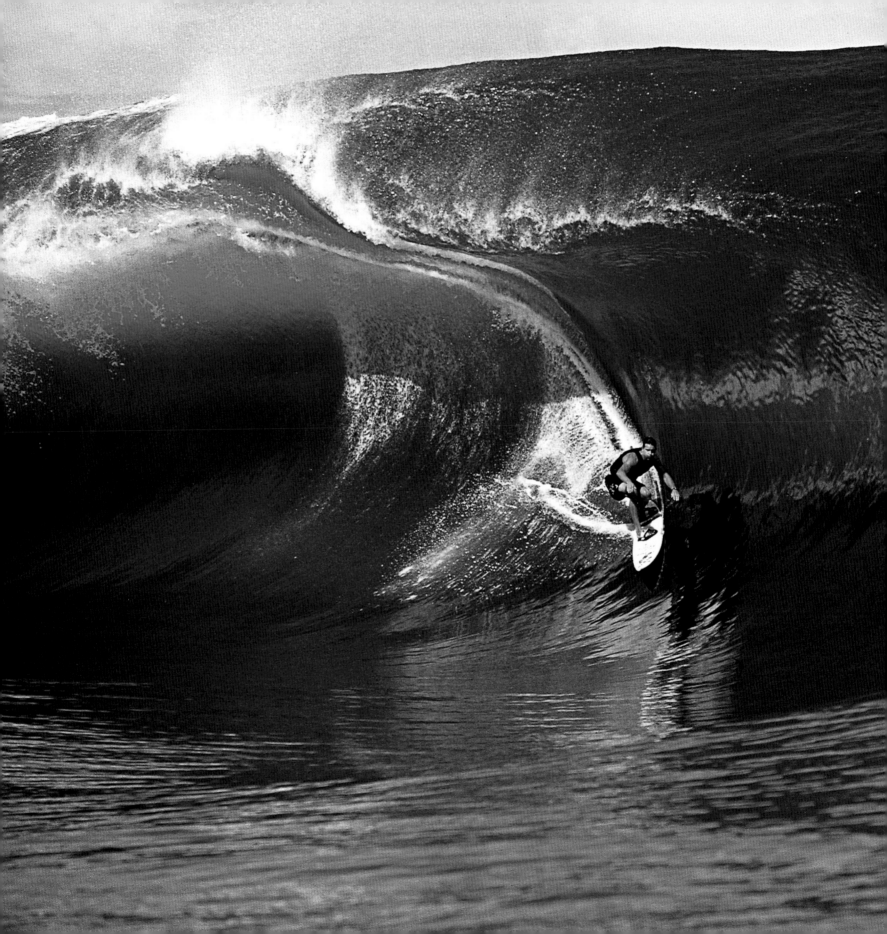

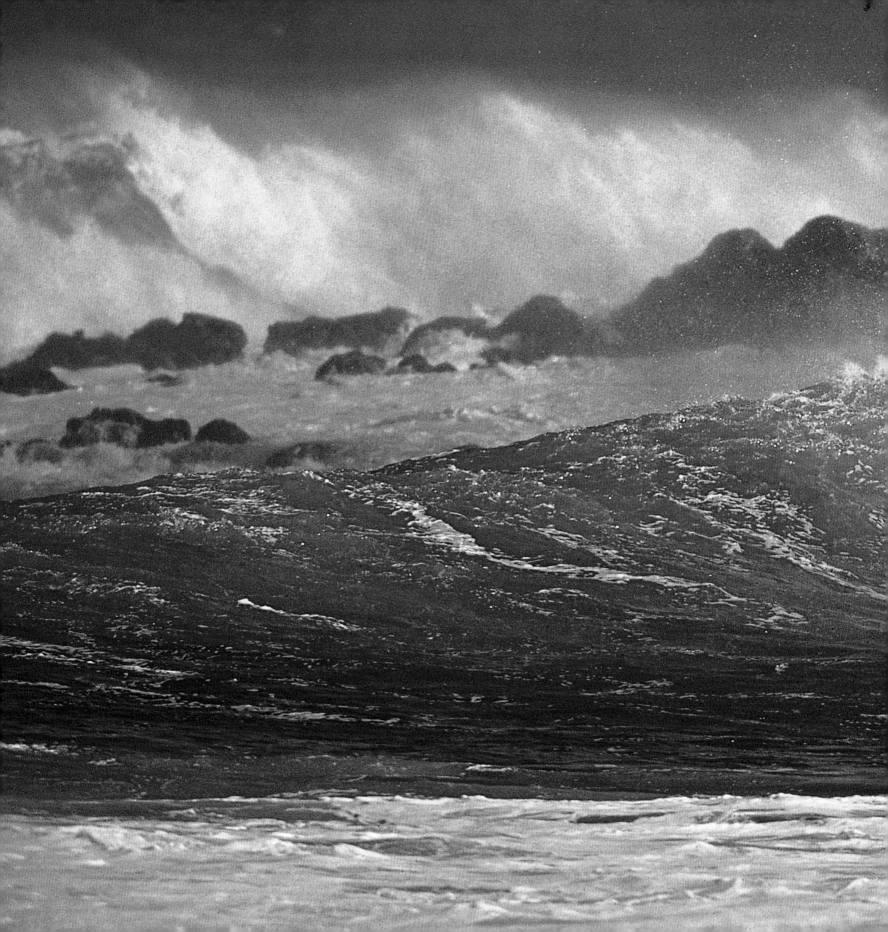

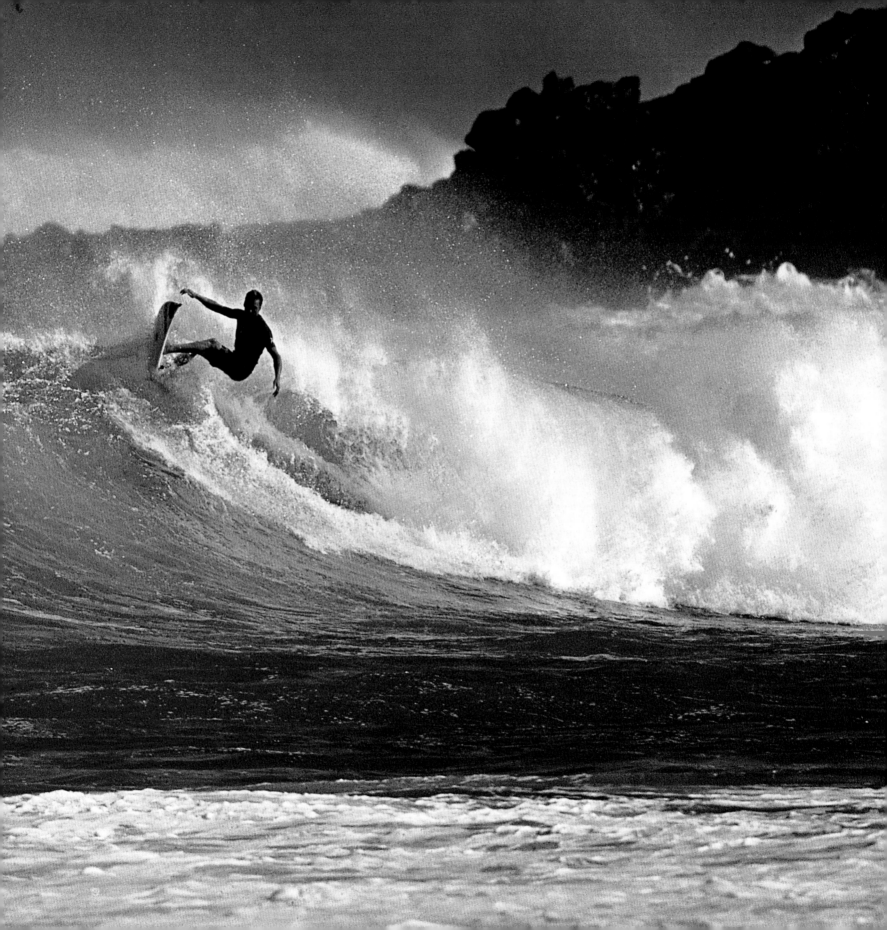

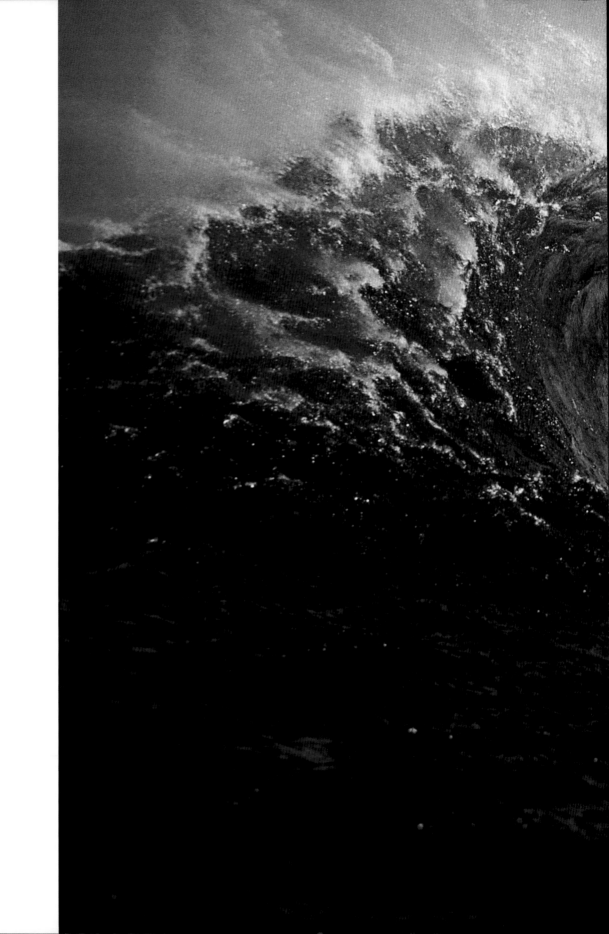

● Hawaii (USA) - In the hollow of a wave.

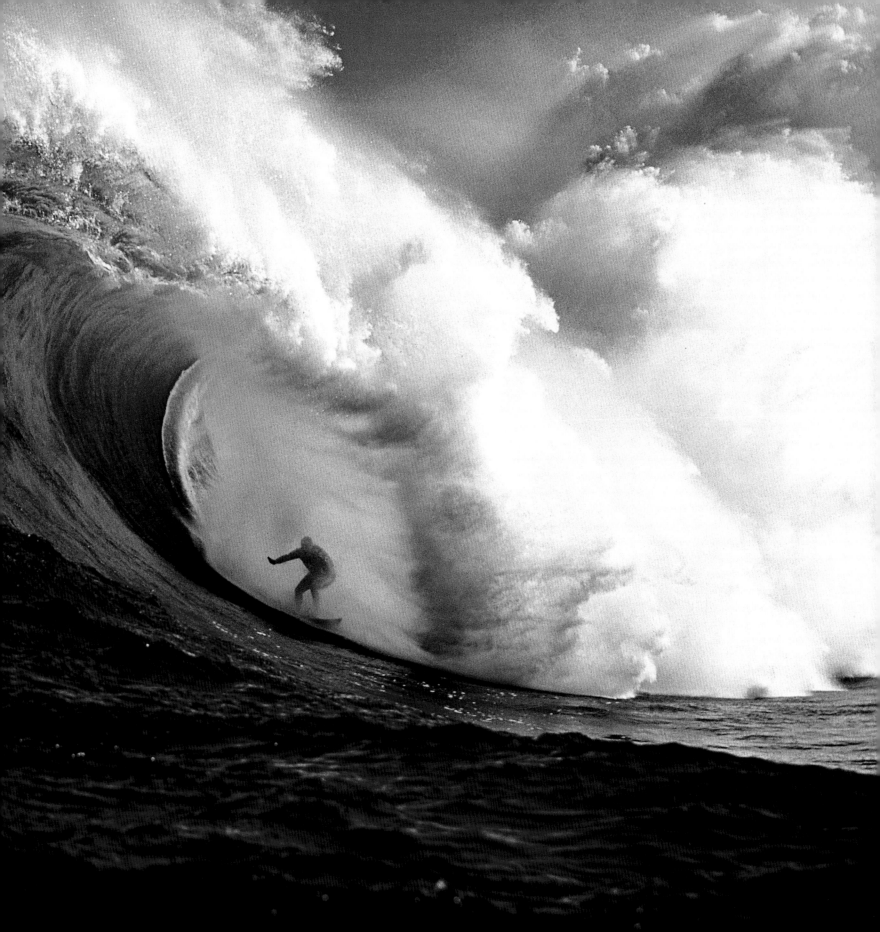

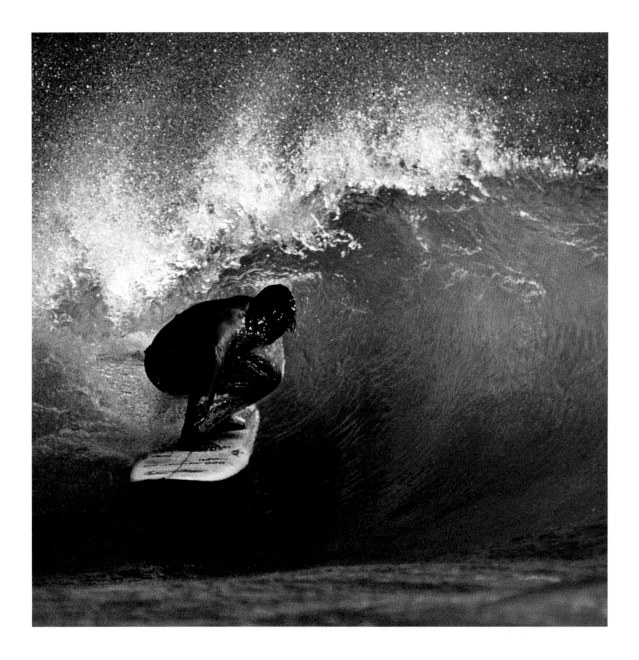

472 ● California (USA) - Rolled up in a liquid film, man and board break out of the tunnel.

473 ● Maui (USA) - Slipping and sliding, the surfer flees from an angry wall of water.

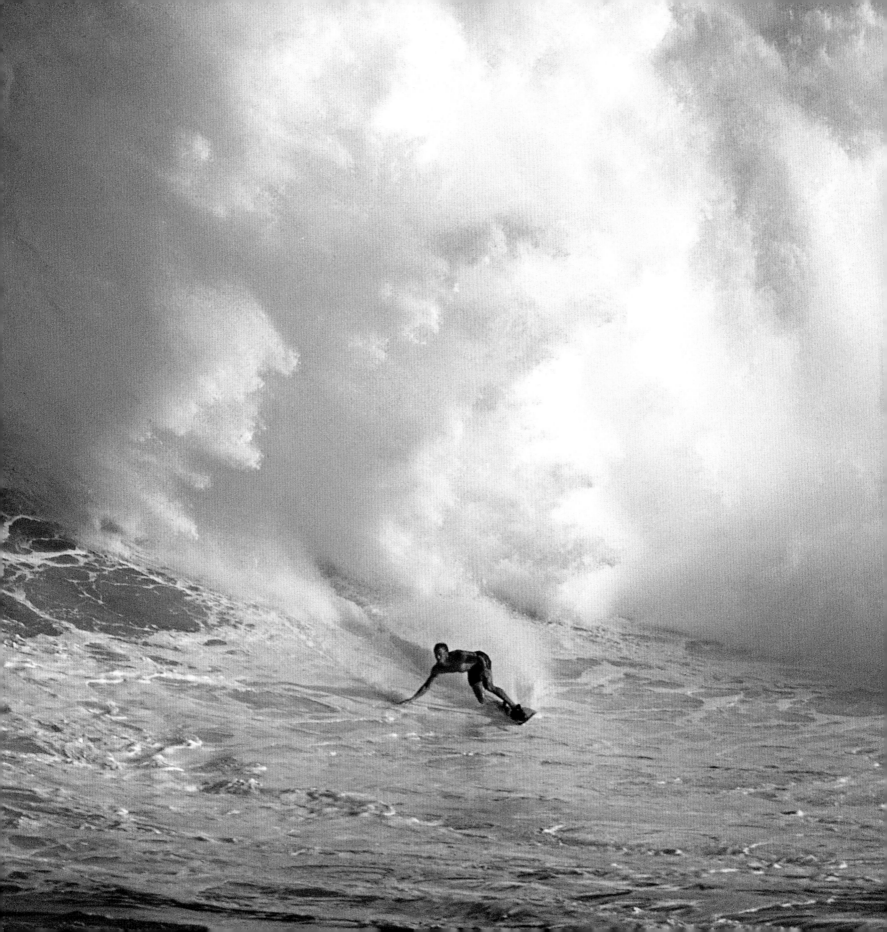

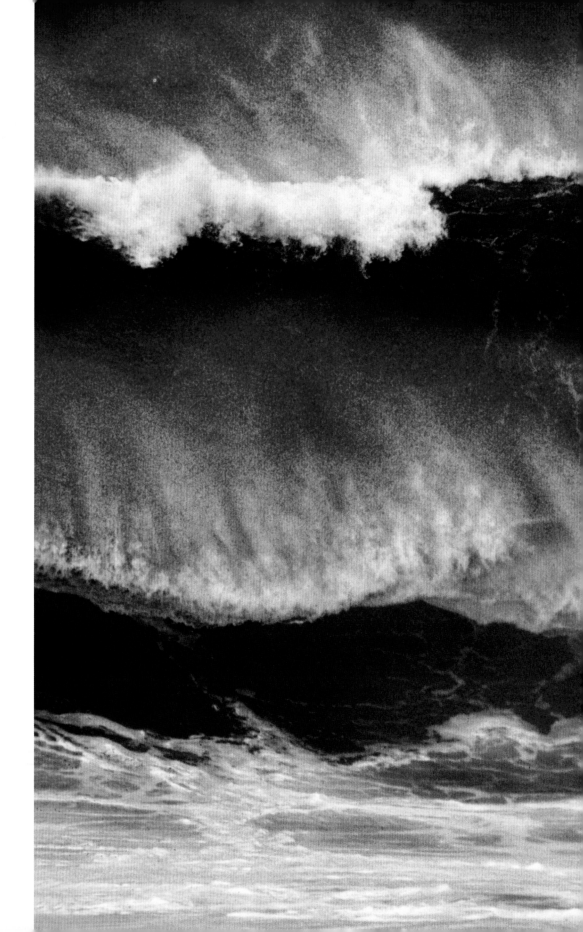

The perfect wave

474-475 ● Gigantic waves gather and smash down on the coasts of Hawaii.

476-477 ● Australia - Riding the breakers.

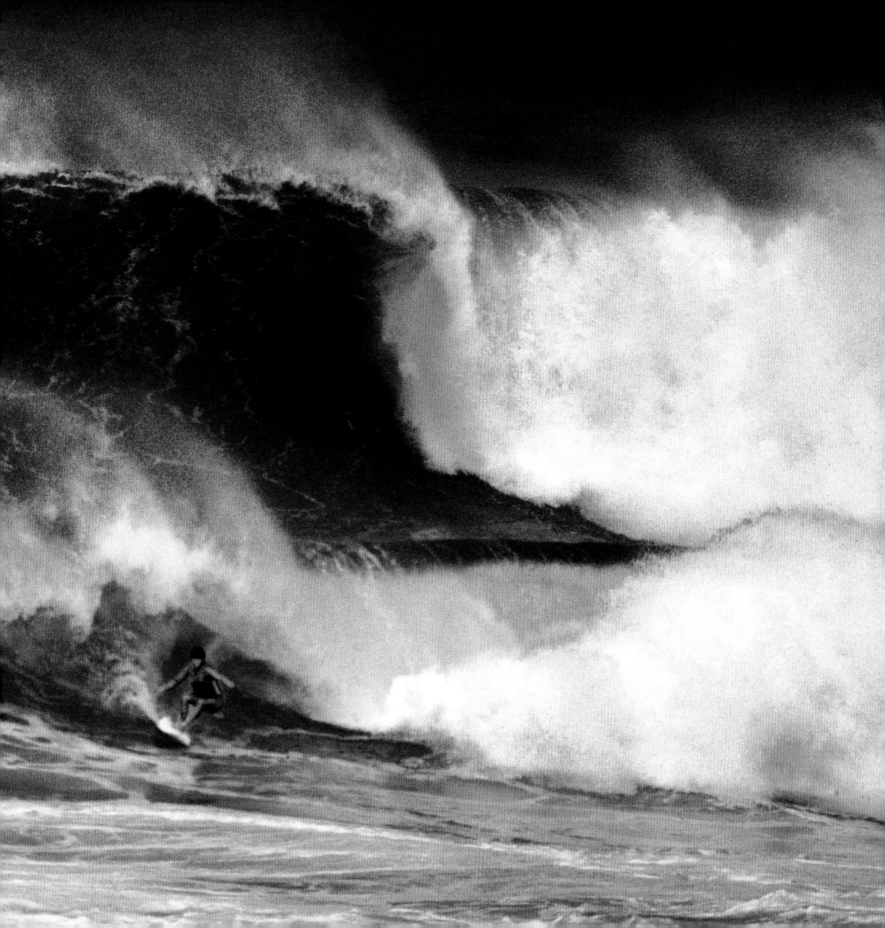

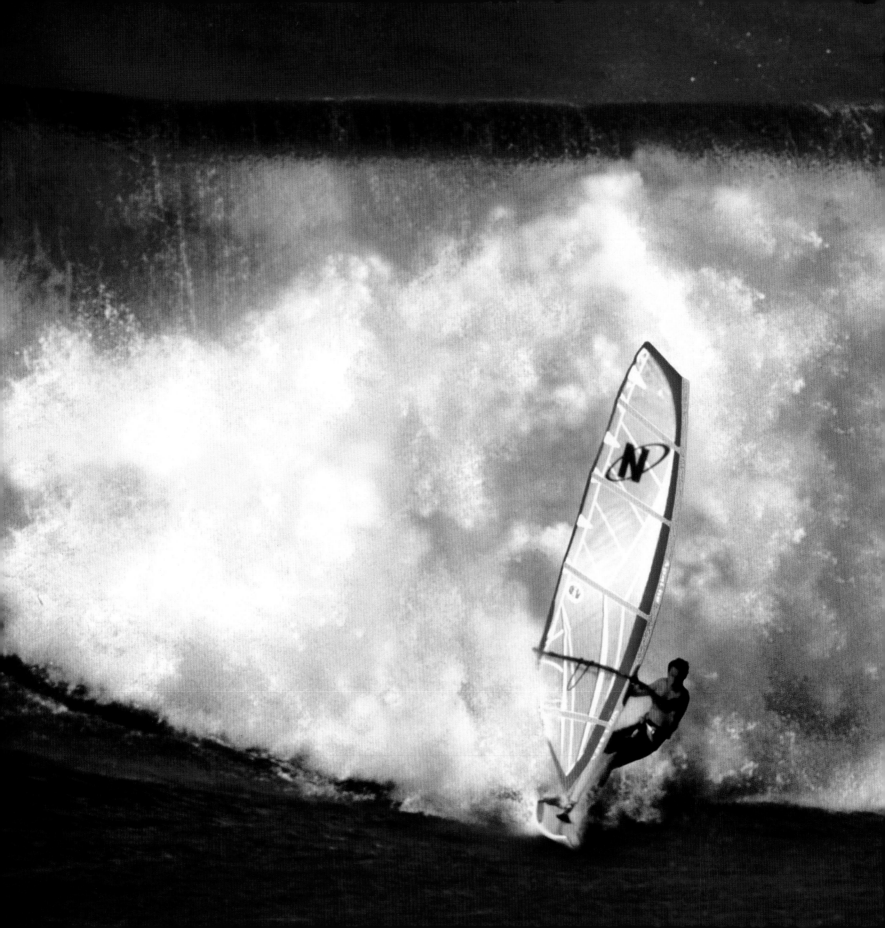

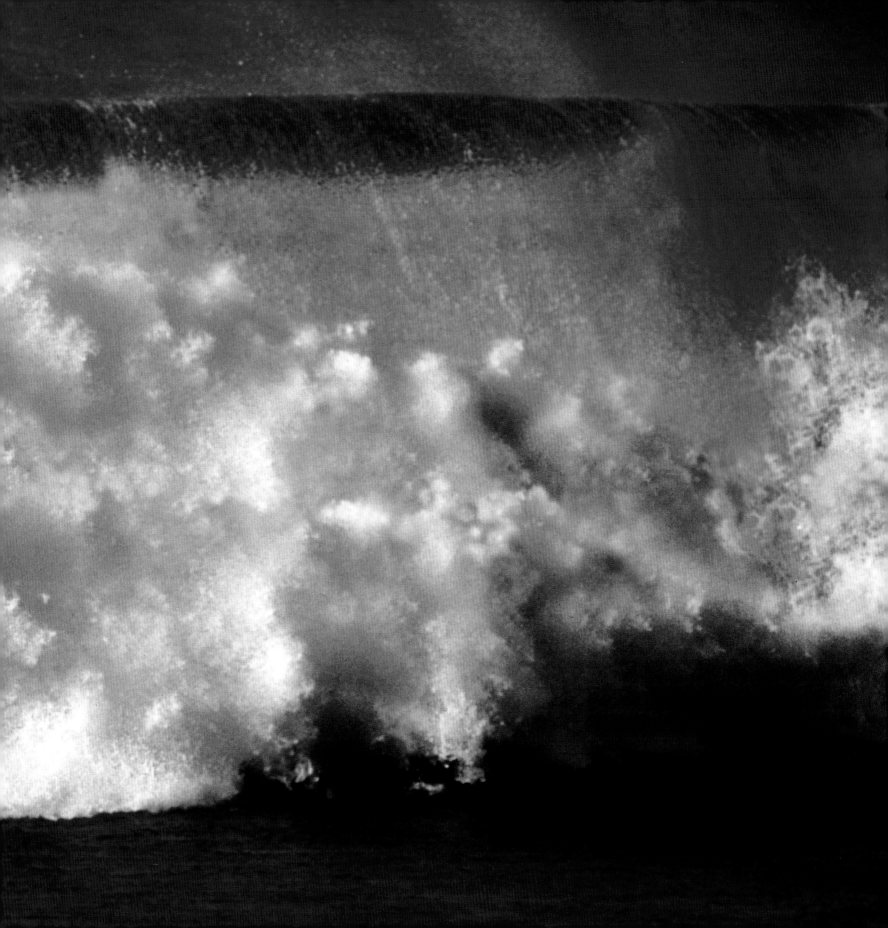

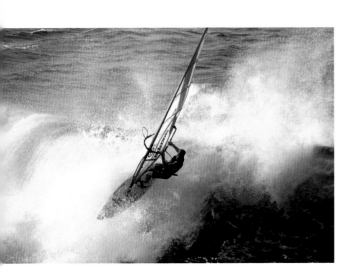

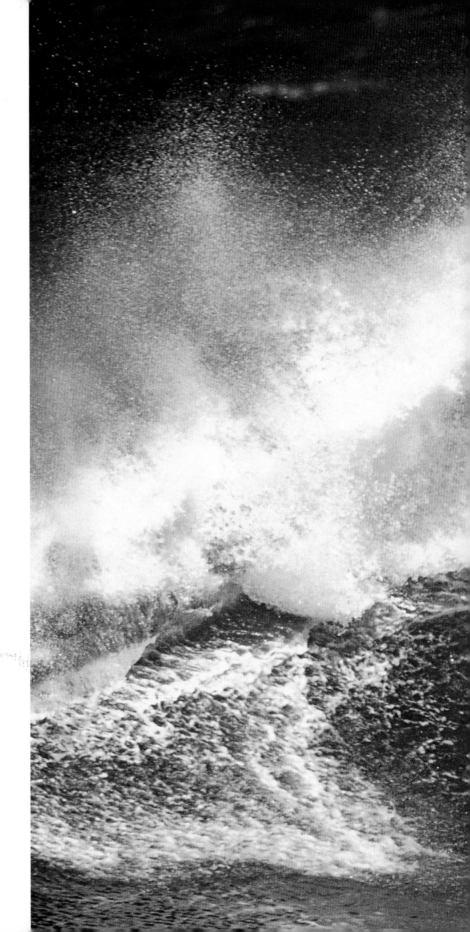

478 ● California (USA) - Safely on
the crest, a windsurfer controls the
forces of the wave and wind.

478-479 ● Australia - Acrobatics
above the waves.

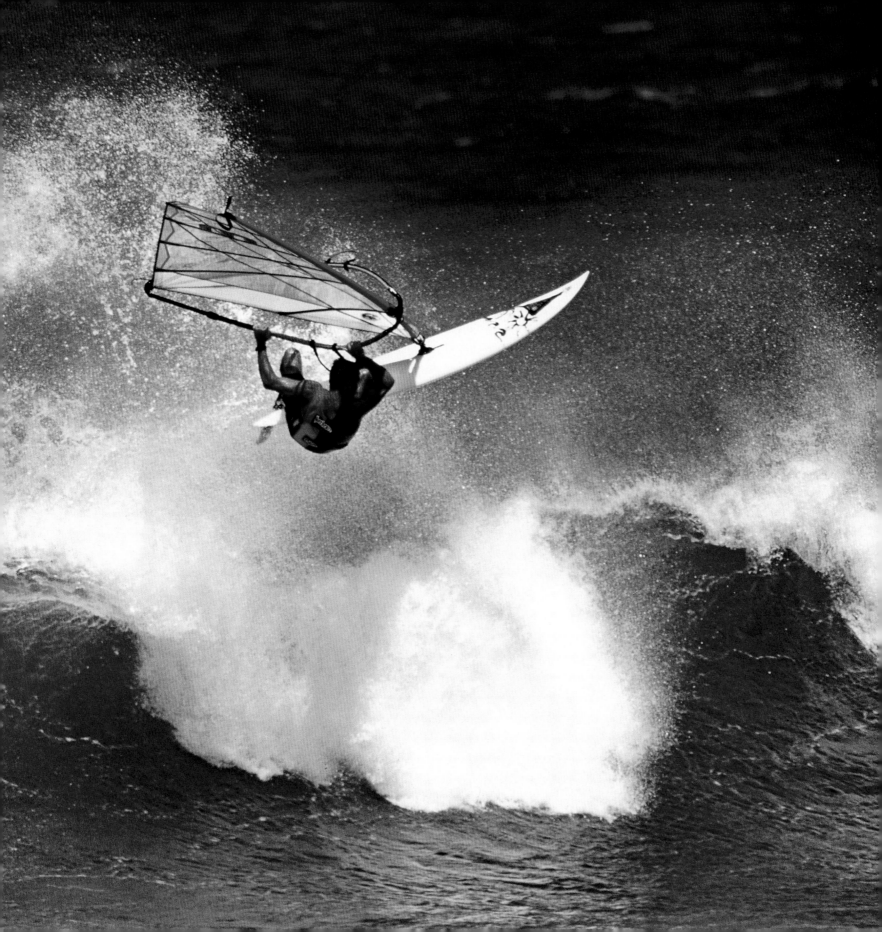

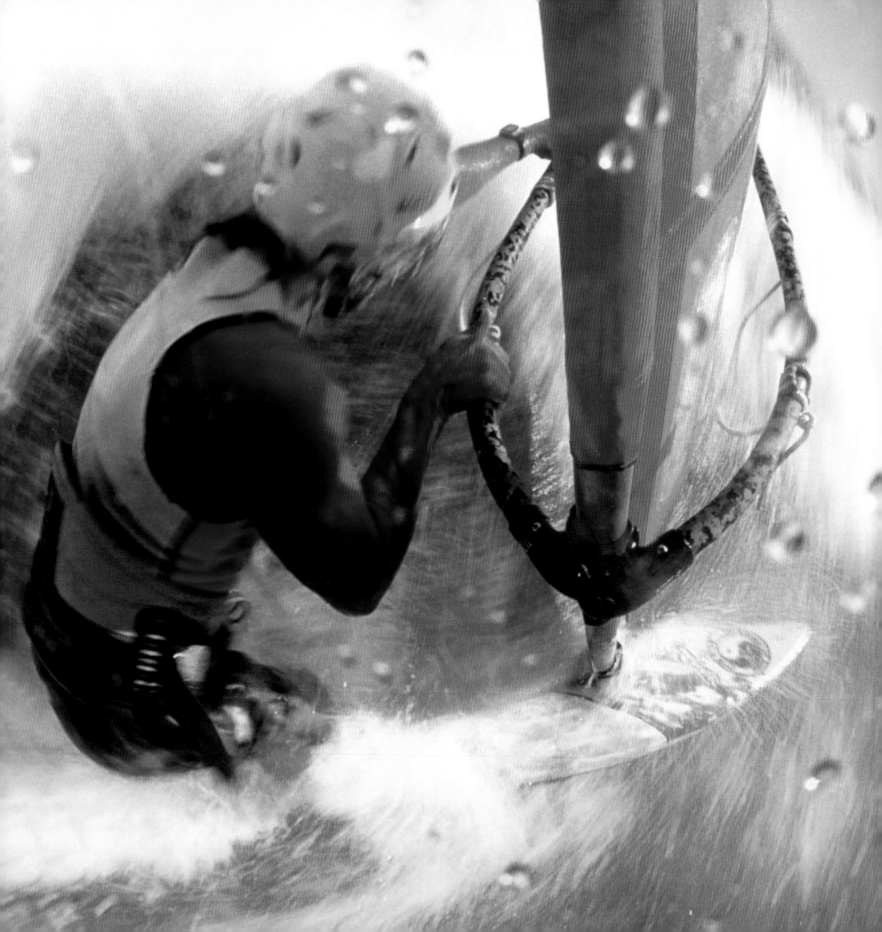

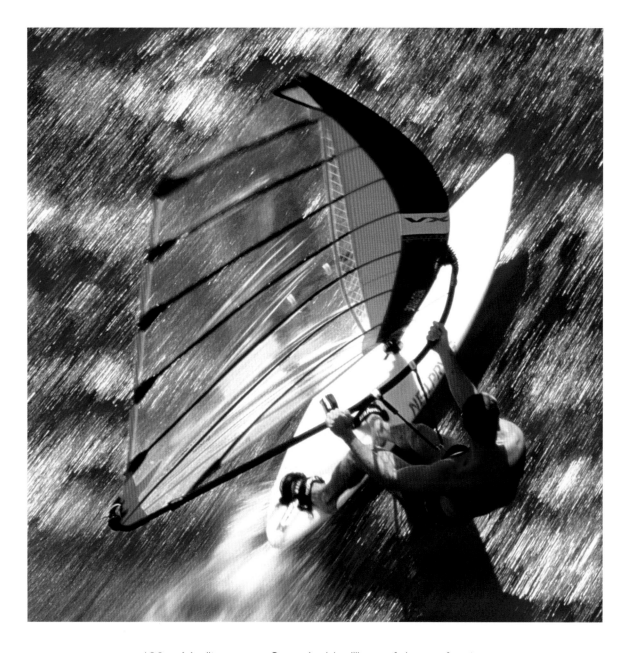

480 ● Mediterranean Sea - Amid millions of drops of water.

481 ● California (USA) - Powered by the wind, the windsurfer skims lightly and rapidly.

482-483 ● Hawaii (USA) - At the foot of a blue mountain, the crest lashed by the wind.

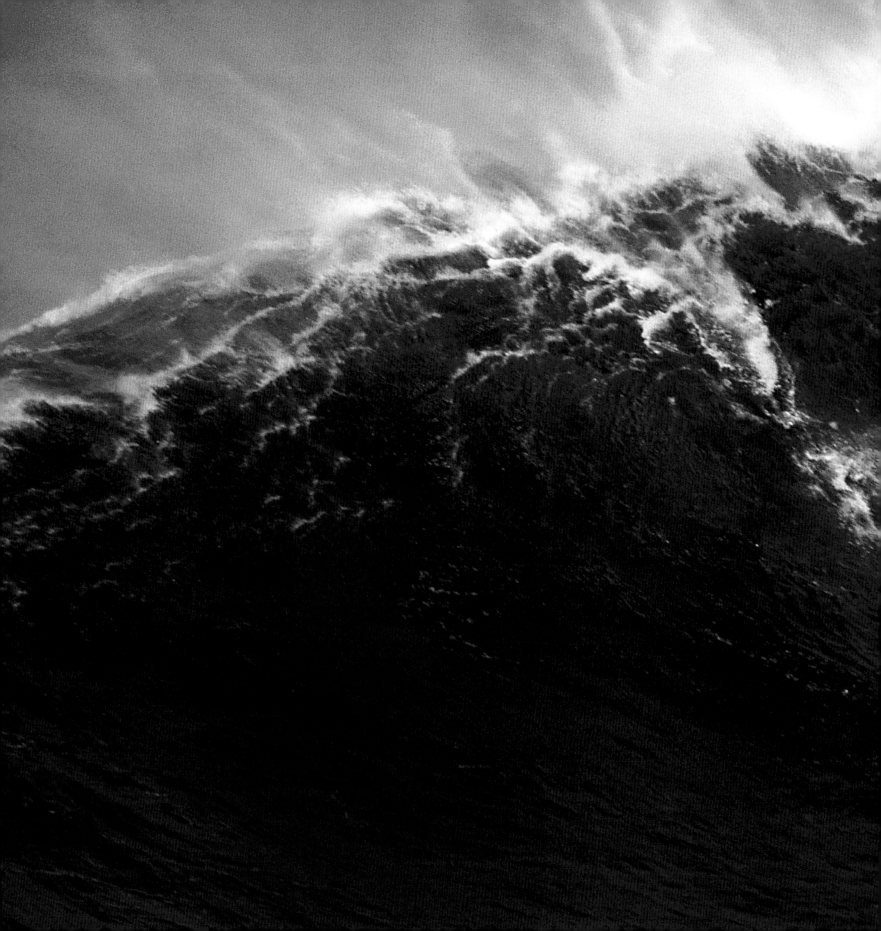

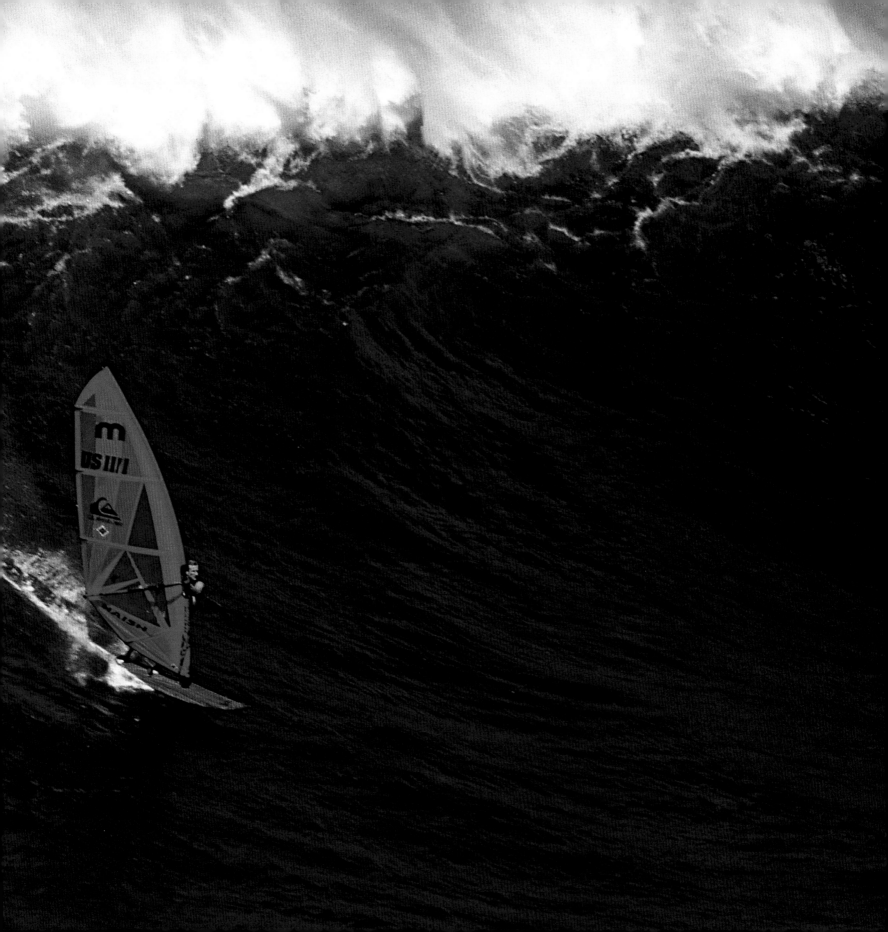

CREATURES between AIR and WATER

ANGELO MOJETTA

● Pacific Ocean, Gálapagos Islands (Ecuador) - Iguana.

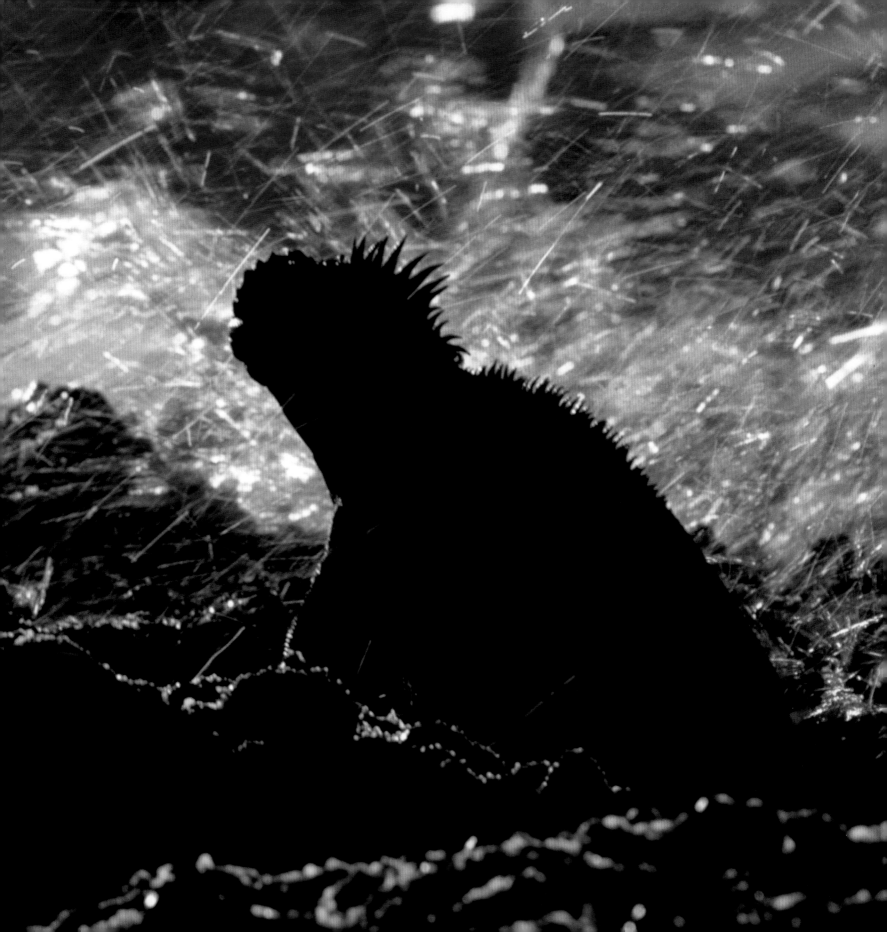

INTRODUCTION Creatures between Air and Water

On the night of a full moon, a female turtle heaves her bulk slowly out of the sea and crawls up the beach. With enormous effort she digs a hole with her hind flippers, lays her eggs and covers them over. In the morning only traces in the sand – destined to be washed away by the rising tide – record her ephemeral link with dry land. Turtles, like sea snakes, crocodiles and iguanas, belong to two contrasting but neighboring worlds. On the borderline between land and sea, these species have risked their probability of survival: it is a bet they have won thanks to the cruel but crucial laws that underlie evolu-

INTRODUCTION Creatures between Air and Water

TION, WHICH FAVOR CREATURES THAT ARE CAPABLE OF ADAPTA-

TION. THESE SAME LAWS HAVE ALSO PROVIDED PENGUINS WITH THE

ABILITY TO MOVE BETWEEN THE TWO HABITATS. THESE STRANGE,

WINGLESS BIRDS, APPARENTLY GARBED IN EVENING DRESS, ABAN-

DONED THE SKY FOR THE SEA EONS AGO AND ARE NOW ABLE TO

DART THROUGH THE WATER IN THE SEARCH FOR FOOD FASTER

THAN MANY FISH. A SIMILAR TALE CAN BE TOLD BY CERTAIN TER-

RESTRIAL MAMMALS, SUCH AS SEALS, SEA LIONS AND WALRUSES,

WHICH ALL EAT, PLAY, HUNT AND MATE IN THE WATER AND ONLY

RARELY RETURN TO LAND, AND FOR SHORT PERIODS AT THAT.

ALMOST ALL SEA BIRDS INHABIT THE THREE ENVIRONMENTS OF THE

Creatures between Air and Water
Introduction

SEA, THE LAND AND THE AIR. ALBATROSSES CAN GLIDE FOR THOU-

SANDS OF MILES ON THE AIR CURRENTS JUST ABOVE THE SURFACE

OF THE SEA, DIPPING DOWN TO PICK OUT FISH ONLY WHEN THEY

NEED TO FEED. GANNETS AND FRIGATES WHEEL ON HIGH TO SPY

THE FOAM CREATED BY LARGE SCHOOLS OF FISH FORCED TO THE

SURFACE BY ATTACKING SCHOOLS OF TUNA, DOLPHINS OR SHARKS;

FROM THIS VANTAGE POINT THEY ATTACK FROM ABOVE, DIVING

STEEPLY AND PLUMMETING INTO THE WATER TO CAPTURE THEIR

PREY. A SHORT DIP AND THEY RISE TO THE SURFACE, WINGS FLAP-

PING WILDLY, A FISH IN THEIR BEAK, TO RETURN TO LAND TO FEED

THEIR YOUNG OR REST FOR THE NIGHT.

• Pacific Ocean, Gálapagos Islands (Ecuador) - Red crabs.

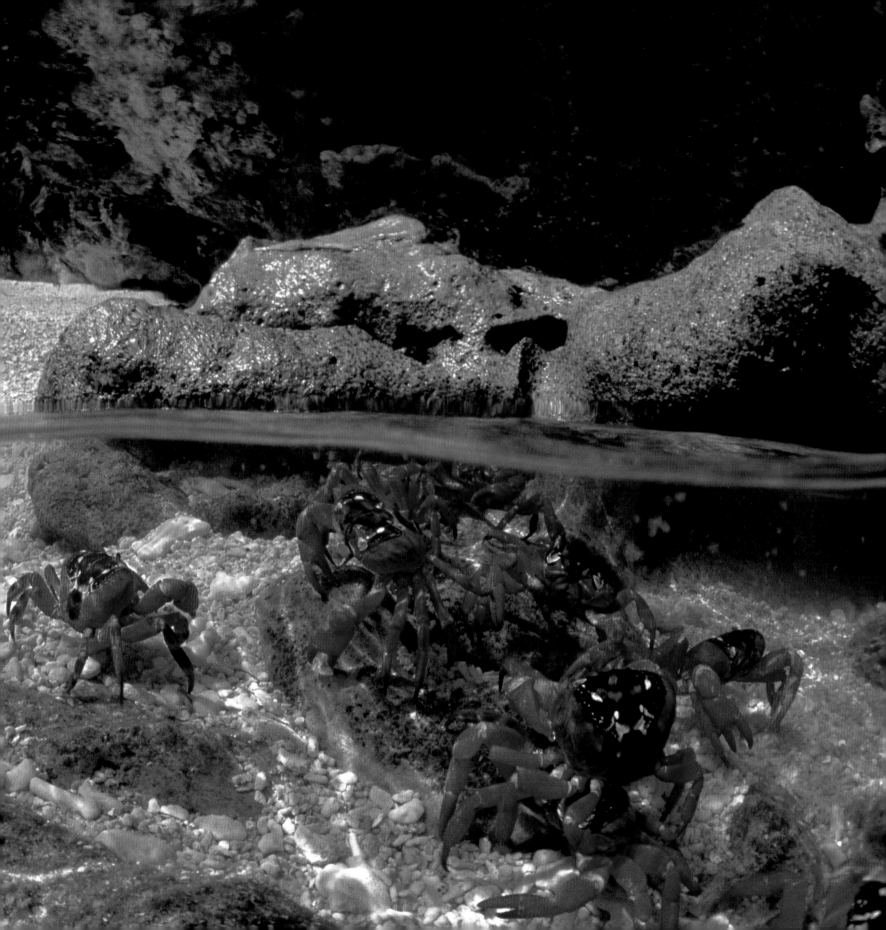

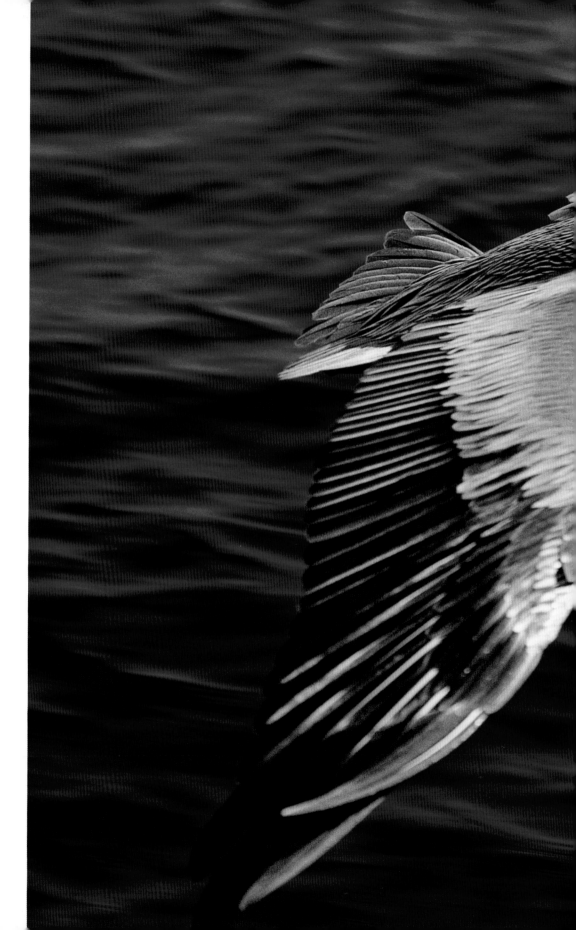

490-491 ● Pacific Ocean, Newport Beach, California (USA) - Brown pelican.

492-493 ● Atlantic Ocean, South Georgia Island (UK) - Royal penguins.

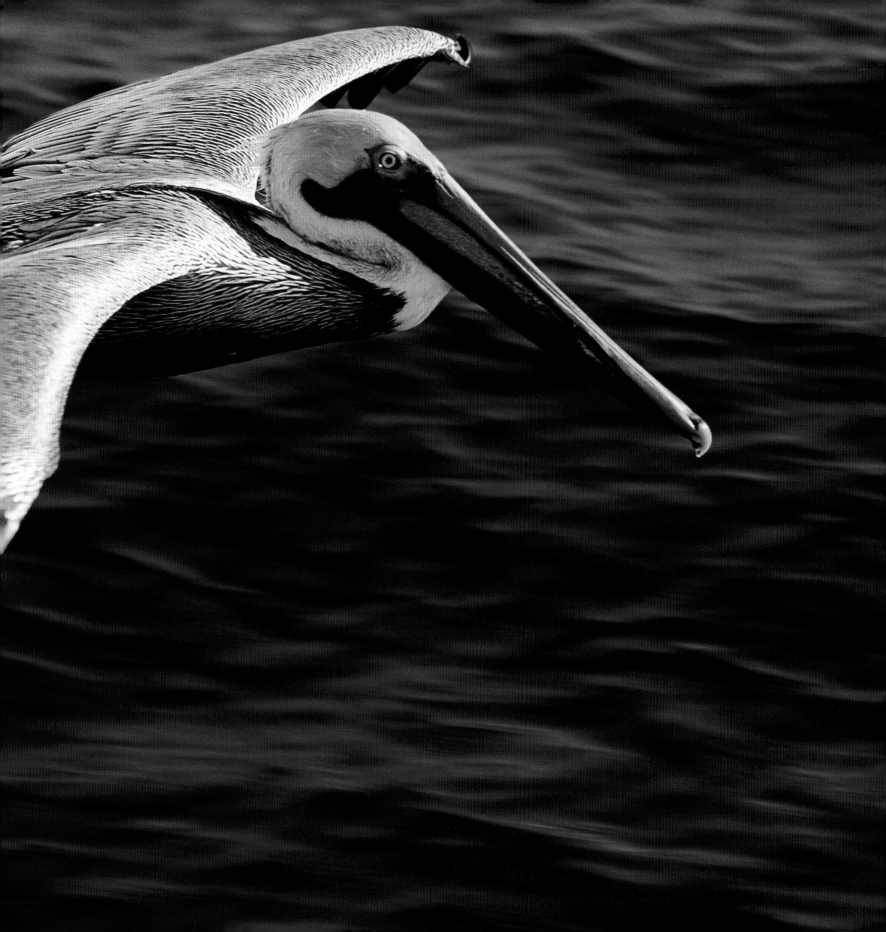

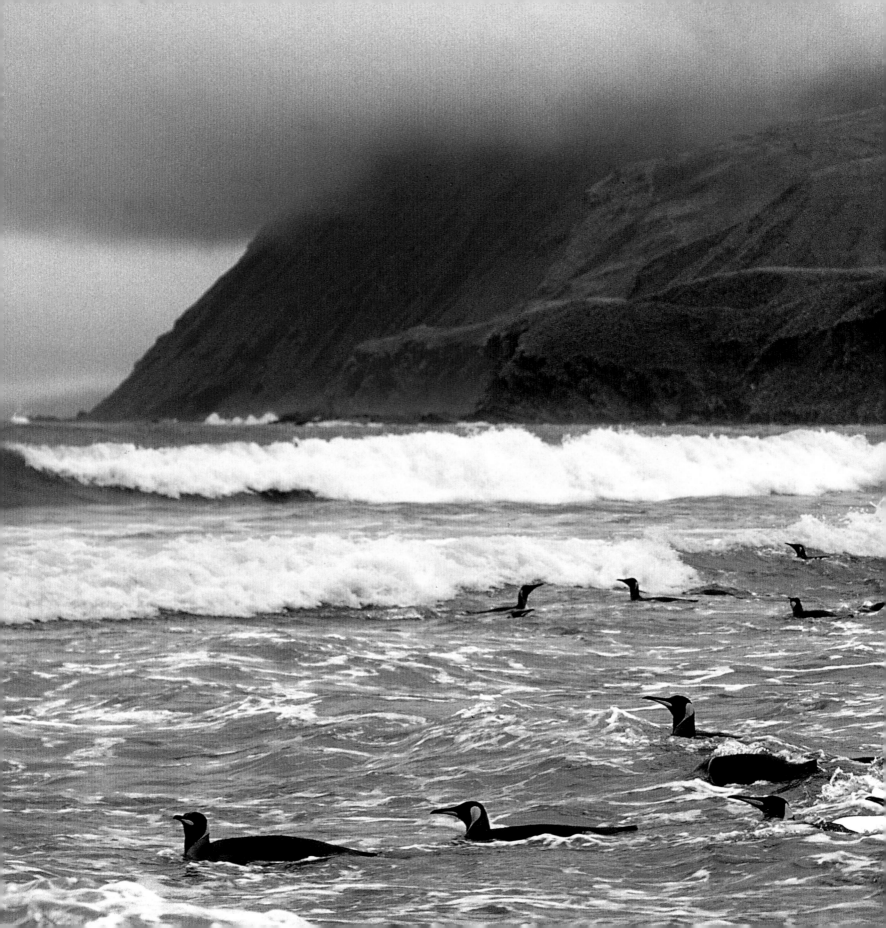

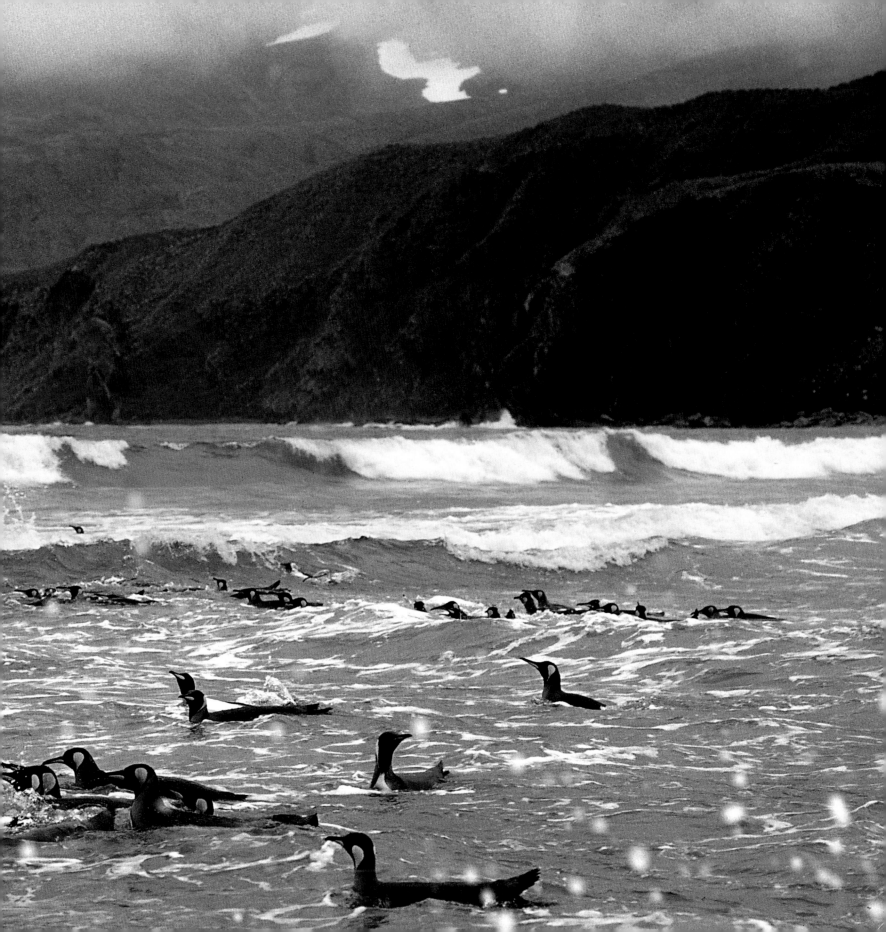

" **S**LUGGISH EXISTENCES GRAZING THERE SUS-PENDED, OR SLOWLY CRAWLING CLOSE TO THE BOTTOM, THE SPERM-WHALE AT THE SURFACE BLOWING AIR AND SPRAY, OR DISPORTING WITH HIS FLUKES, THE LEADEN-EYED SHARK, THE WALRUS, THE TURTLE, THE HAIRY SEA-LEOPARD, AND THE STING-RAY... "

from WORLD BELOW
THE BRINE
by Walt Whitman

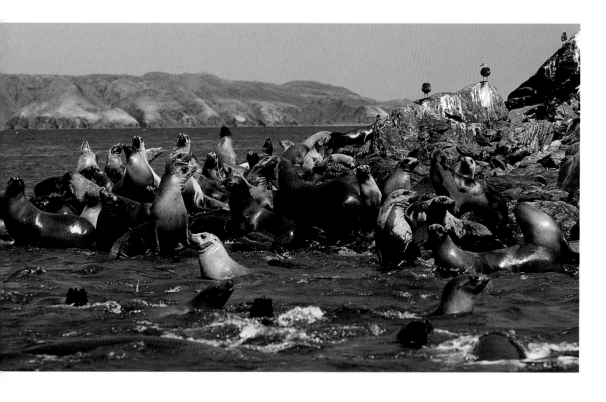

494 ● Pacific Ocean, Baja California (Mexico) - Sea lions.

495 ● Pacific Ocean, Macquarie Island (Antarctic) - Sea elephant and royal penguin.

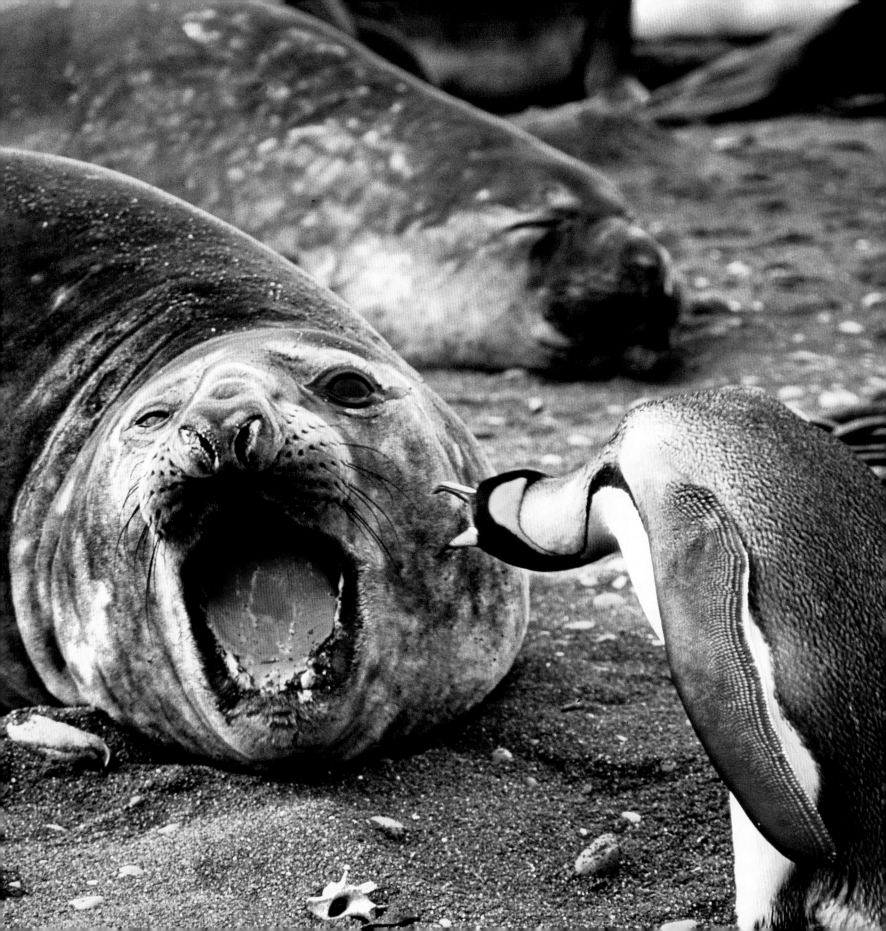

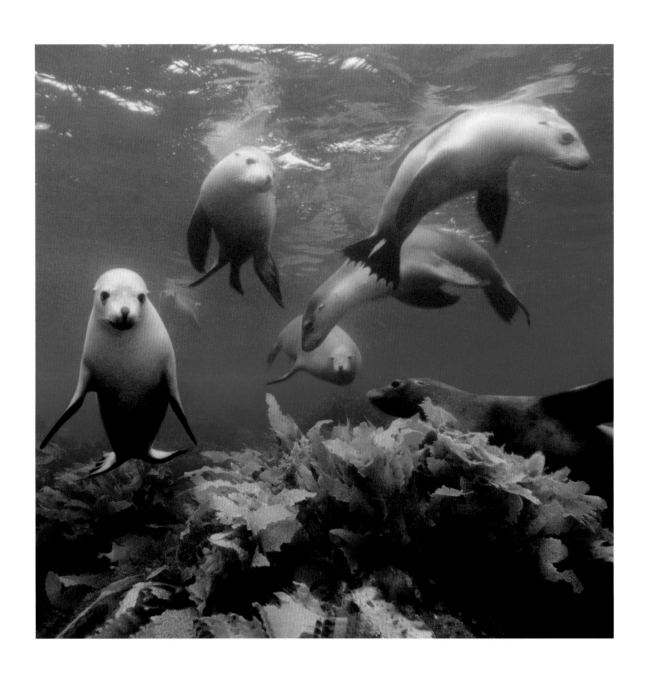

● Atlantic Ocean, Florida (USA) - Sea lion.

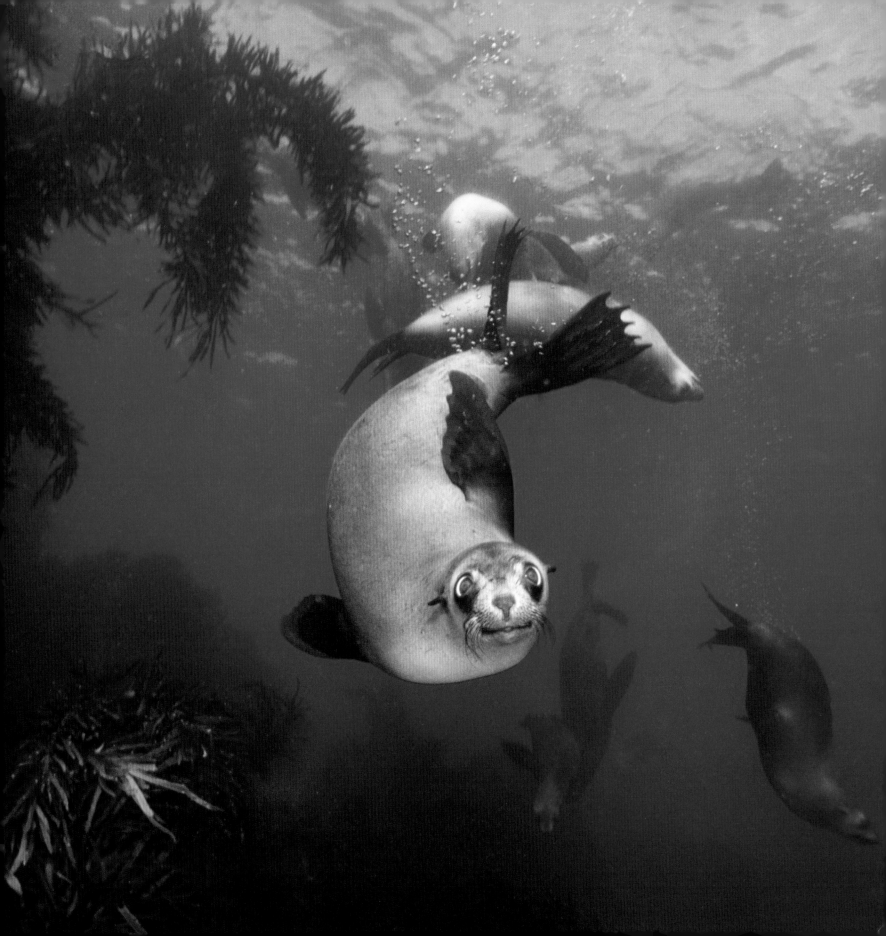

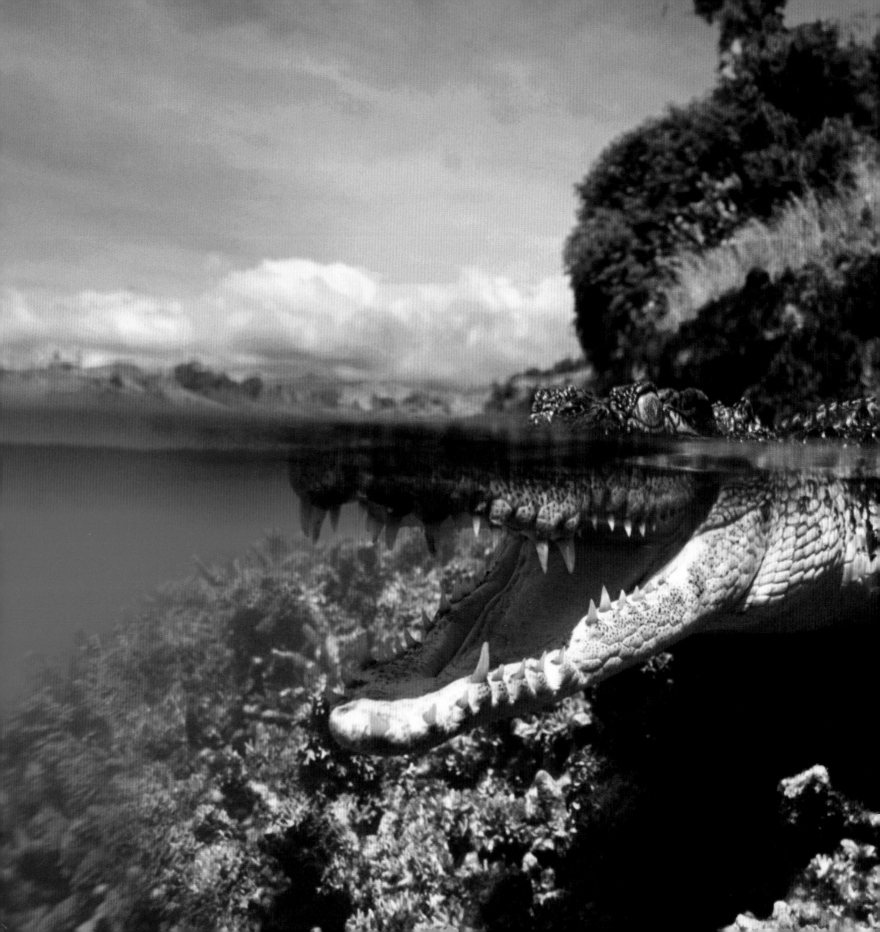

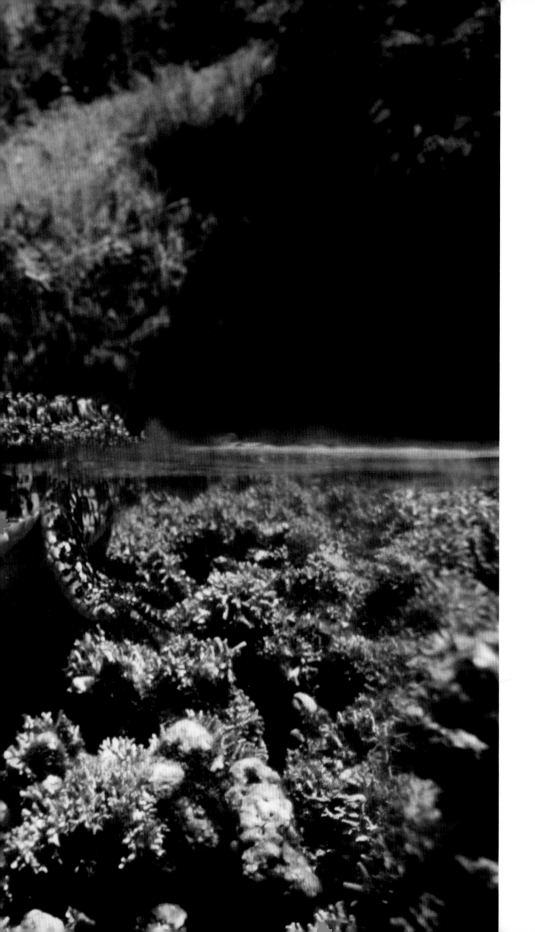

Atlantic Ocean, Florida
(USA) - Alligator.

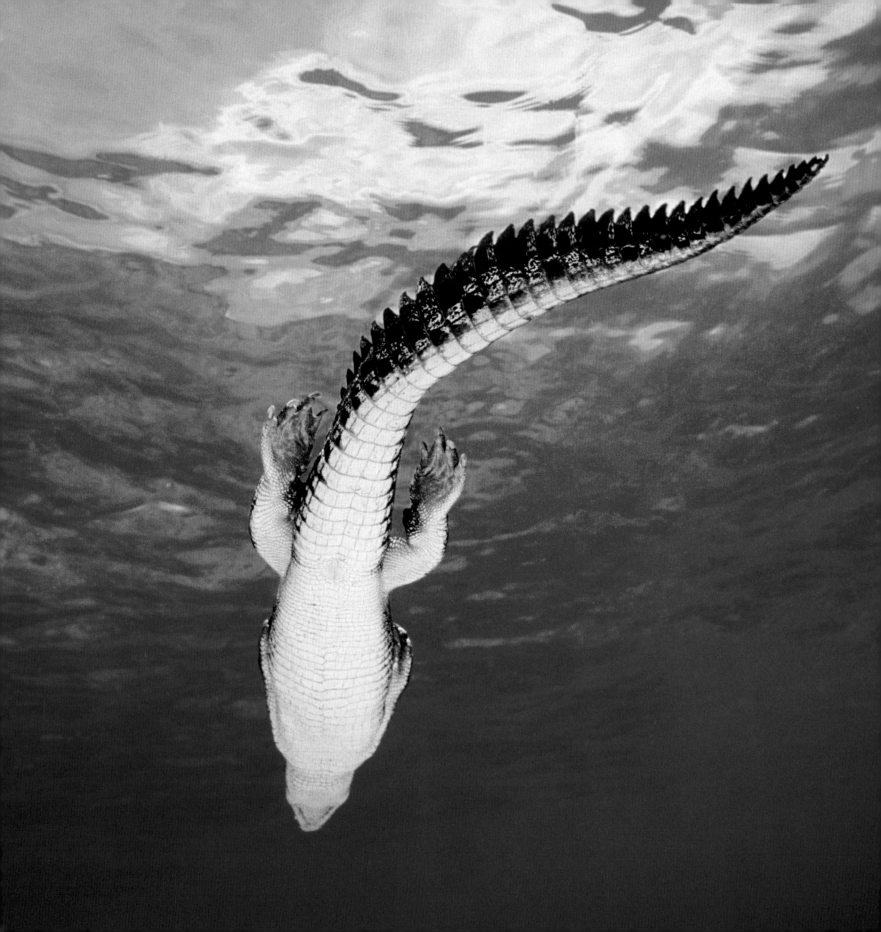

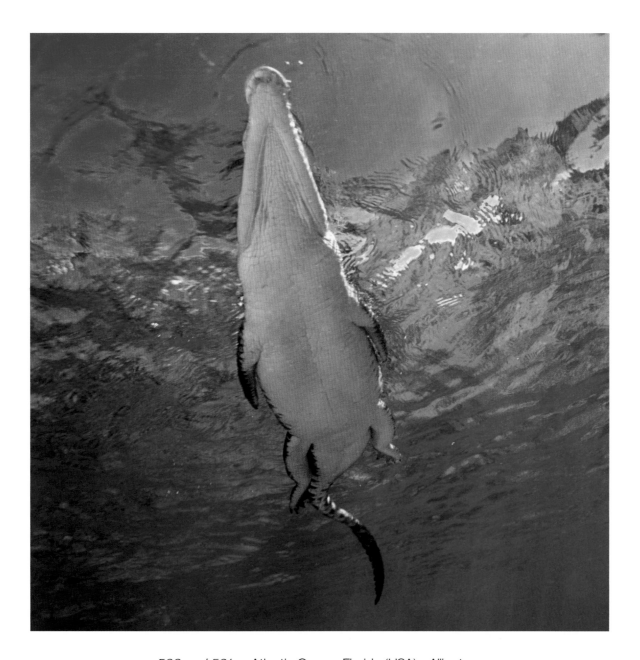

500 and 501 ● Atlantic Ocean, Florida (USA) - Alligators.

502-503 ● Pacific Ocean (Australia) - White-breasted sea eagle.

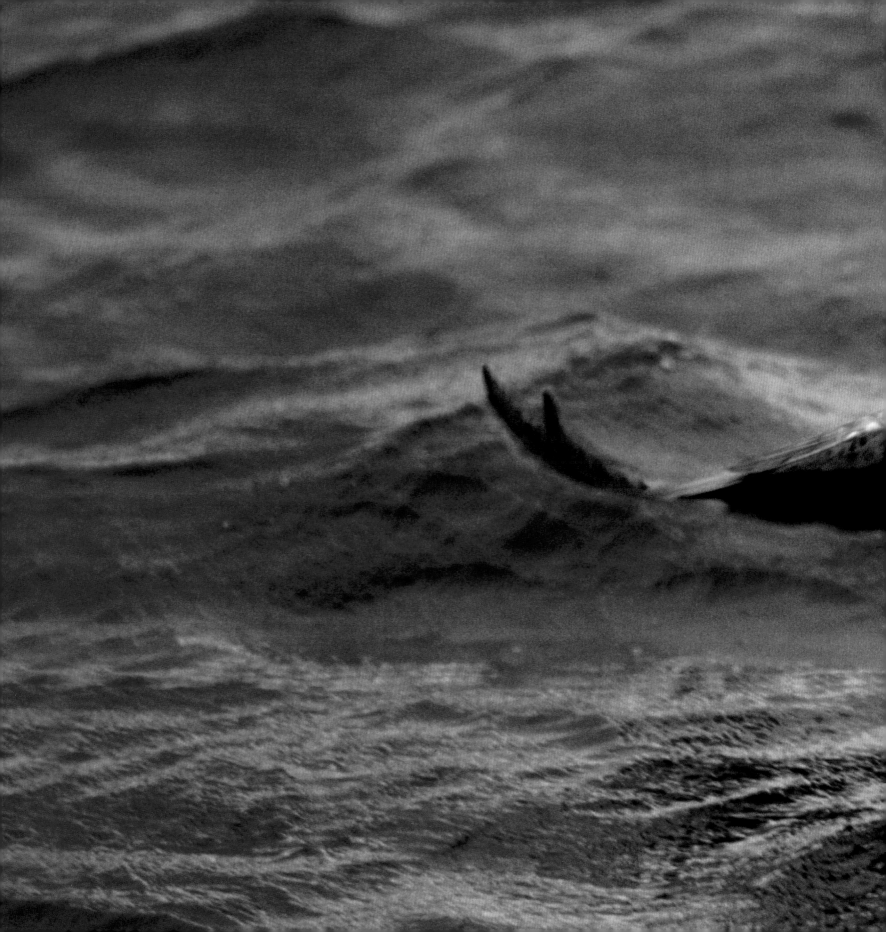

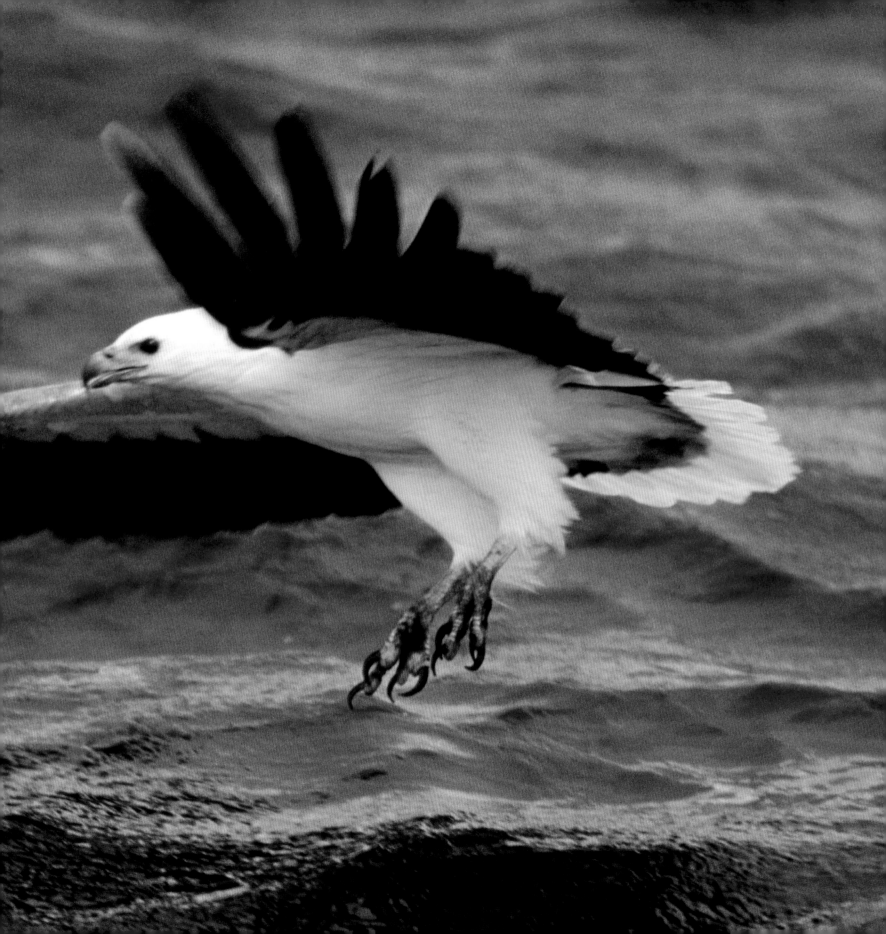

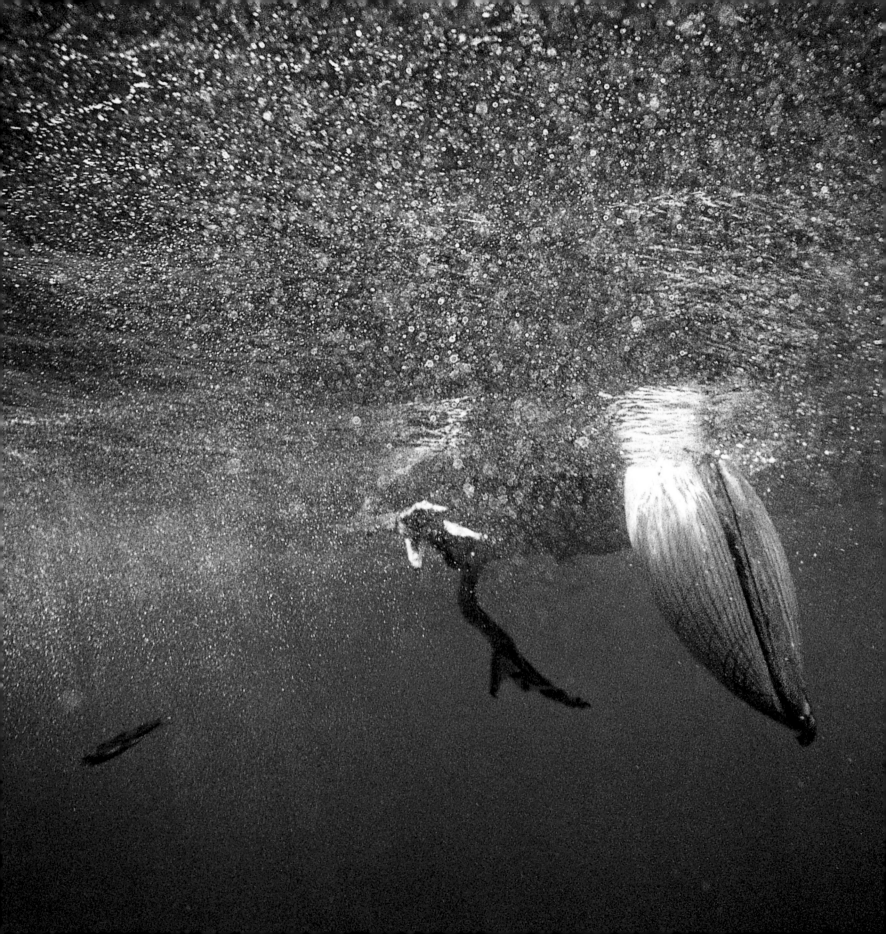

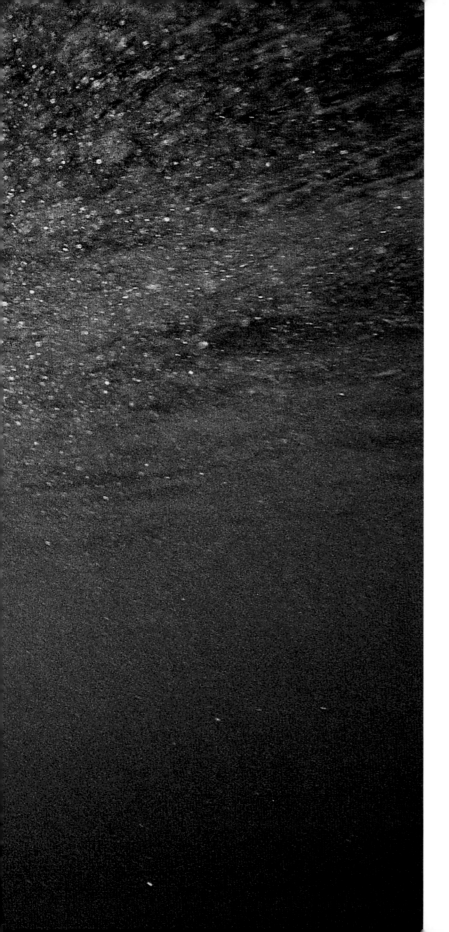

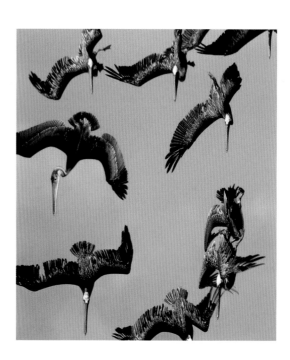

● Pacific Ocean, Gálapagos Islands
(Ecuador) - Brown pelicans.

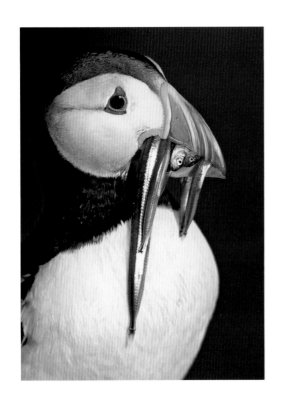

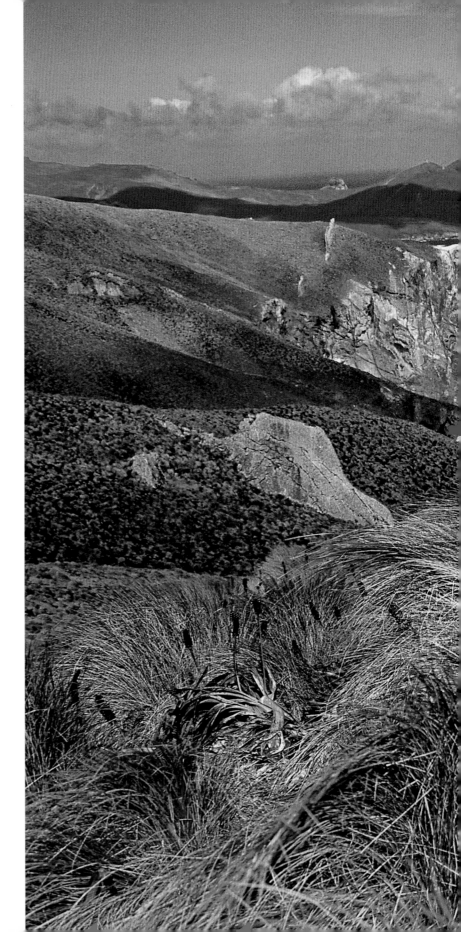

506 ● North Sea, Scotland (Great Britain) - Puffin.

506-507 ● Pacific Ocean, Campbell Island
(New Zealand) - Royal albatrosses.

508-509 ● Red Sea, Dahlak Islands
(Eritrea) - Terns.

510-511 ● Indian Ocean, Maldives -
Striped heron.

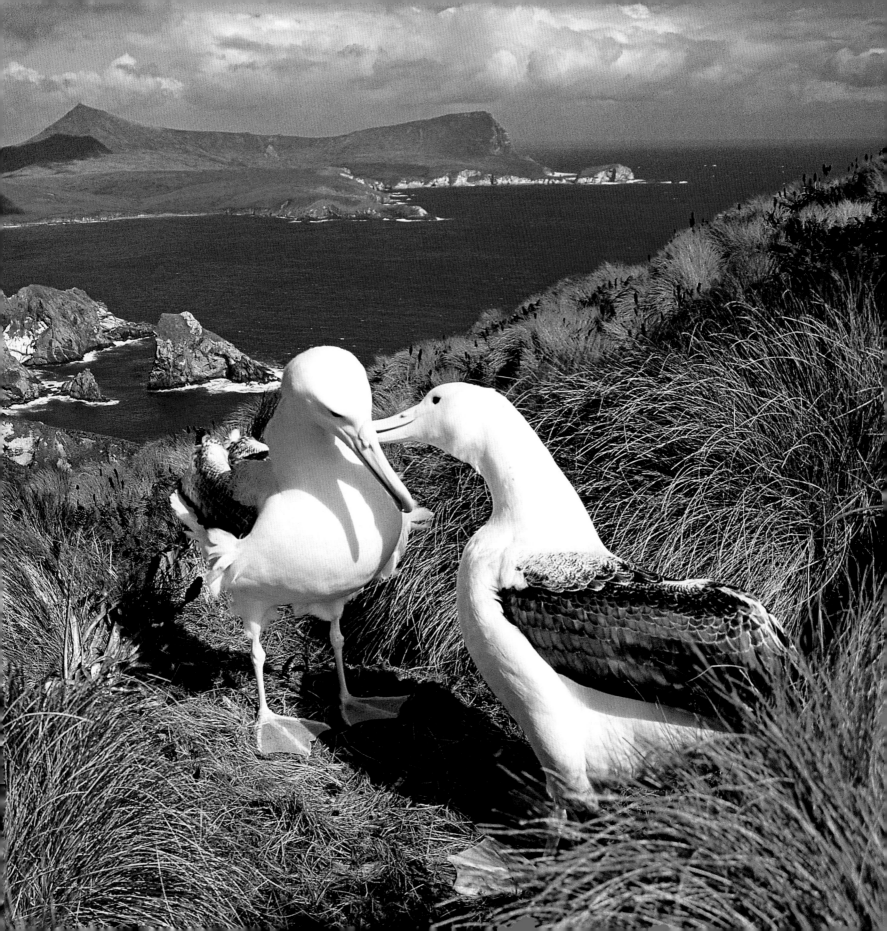

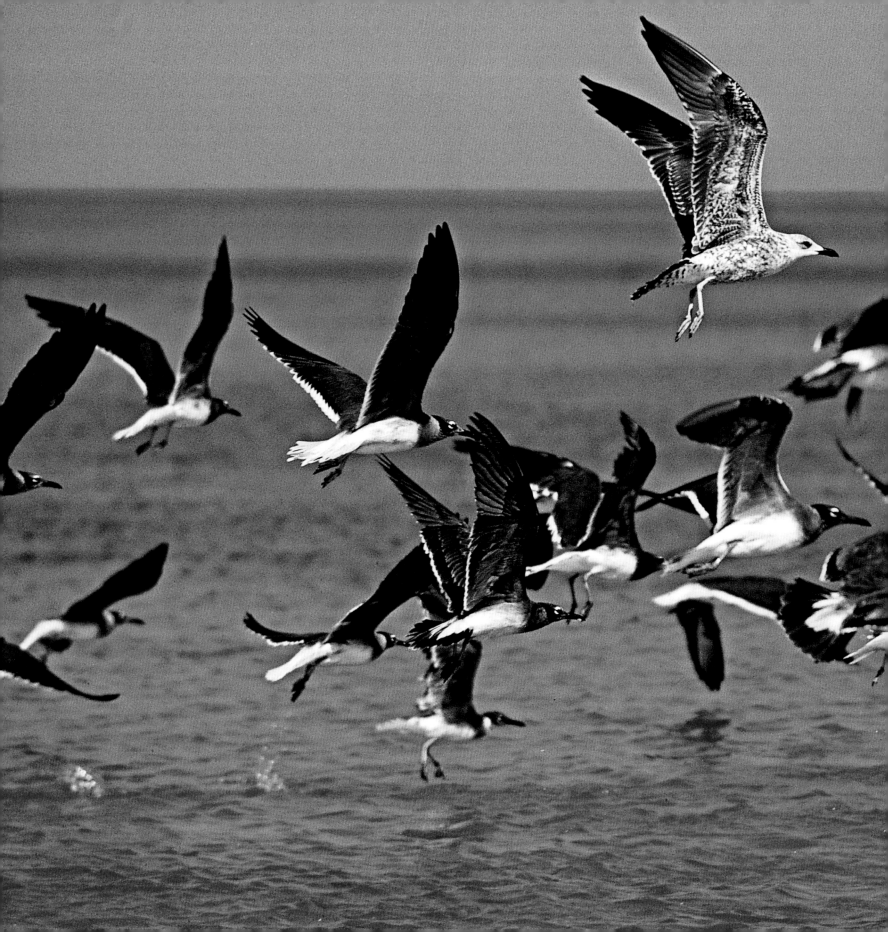

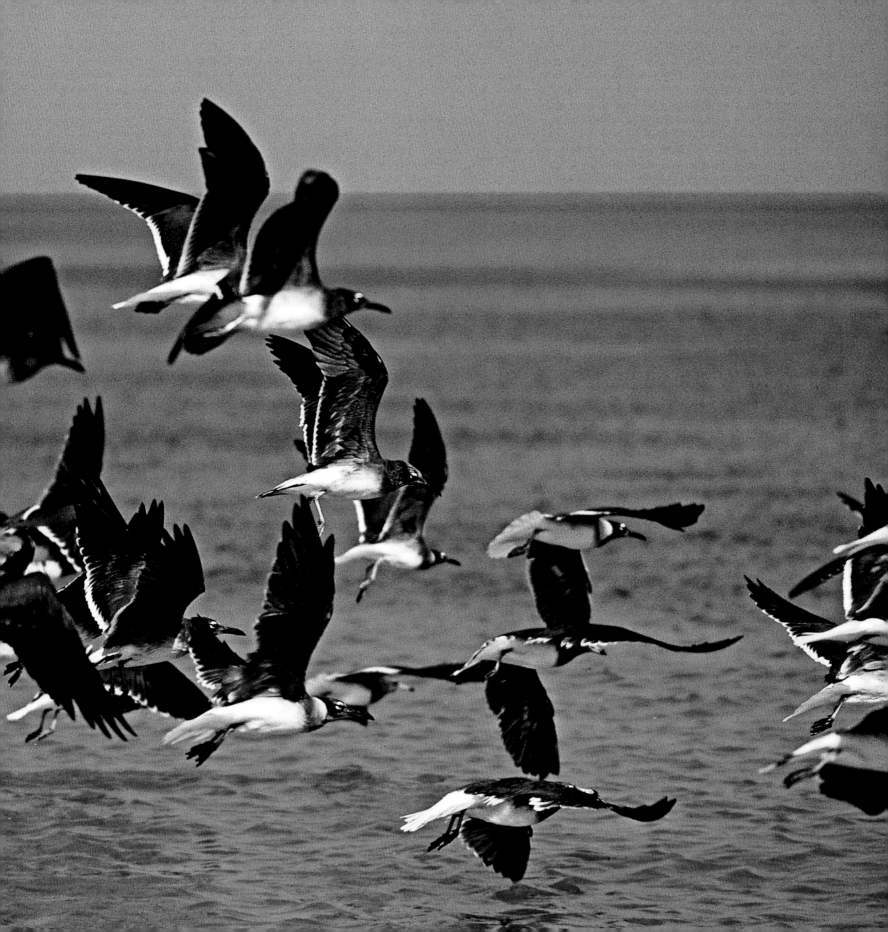

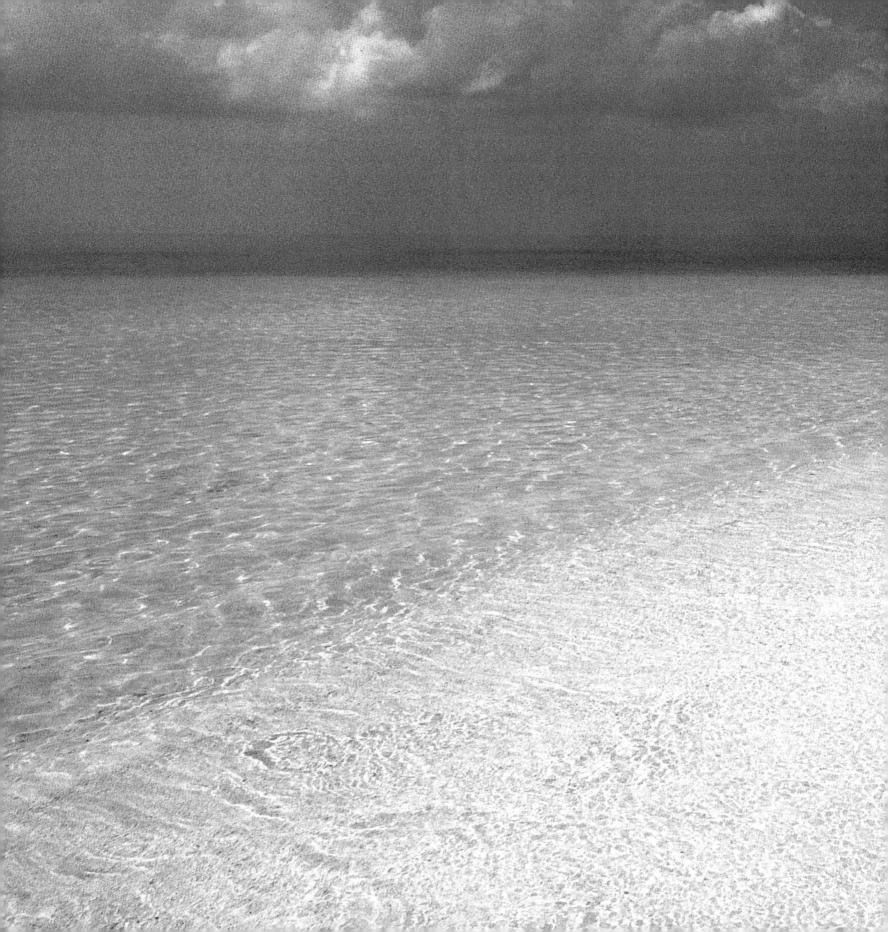

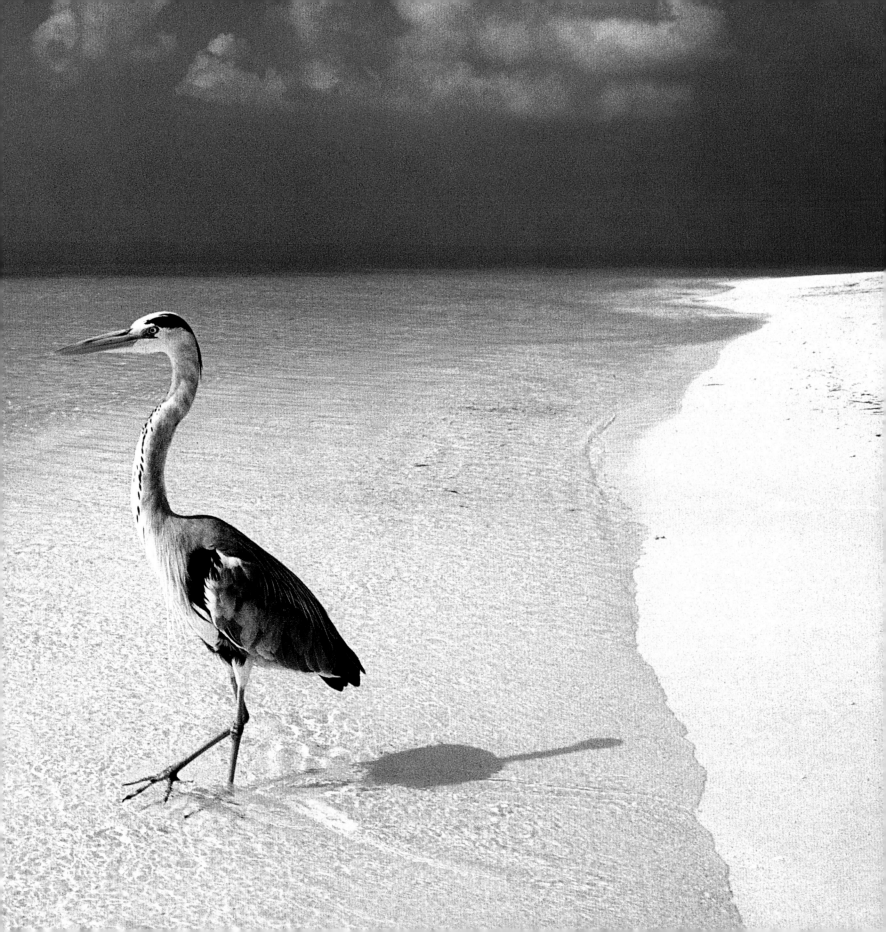

CORAL GARDENS

ANGELO MOJETTA

Red Sea, Egypt - Clown fish and sea anemone.

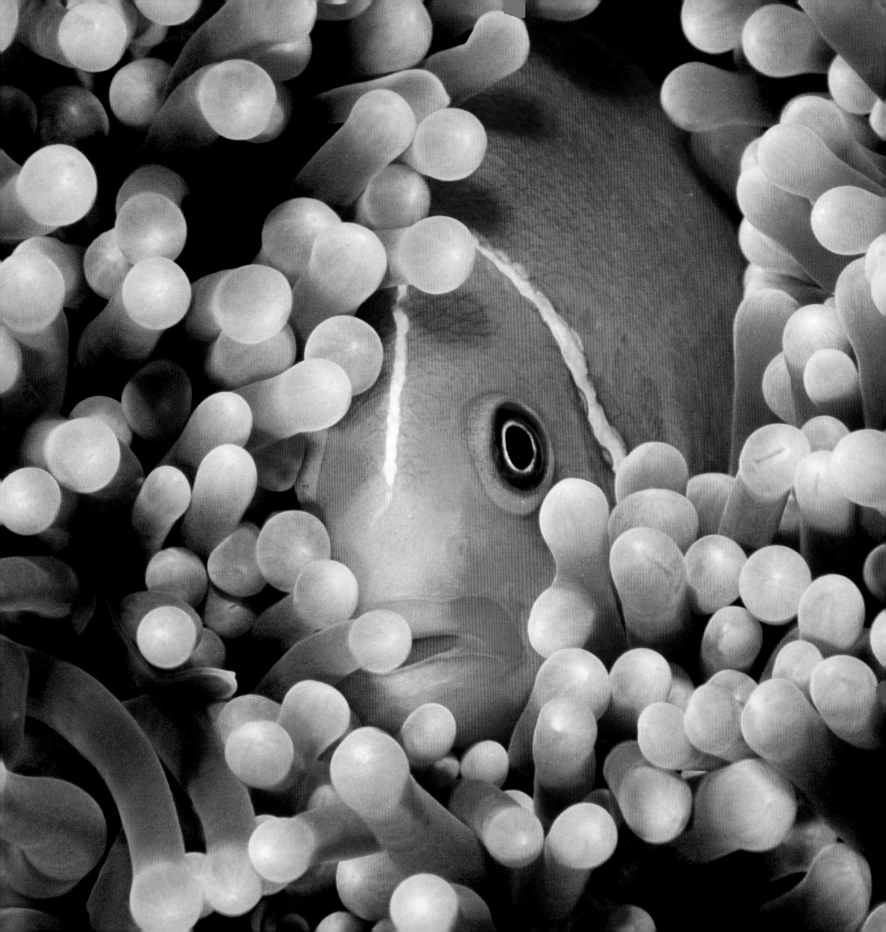

INTRODUCTION Coral Gardens

It is because of their colors that they are called coral gardens. In fact they are meadows, mountains, plains, walls, canyons, galleries, grottoes and many other features. Enveloped and supported by water, and using breathing equipment (or even without), man can float freely through this dreamlike space where sounds are dampened. Each dive is a new adventure, an encounter with extraordinary animals like mantas or whale sharks, or with tiny organisms of surprising beauty, such as nudibranchia, also known as 'sea butterflies.' As though in a dream, you swirl lightly and may encounter large preda-

INTRODUCTION Coral Gardens

TORS THAT EITHER IGNORE YOU OR APPROACH YOU CURIOUSLY,

PROBABLY FEELING A LITTLE SCARED. SLIPPING WEIGHTLESSLY PAST

A TROPICAL REEF – IT DOES NOT MATTER WHETHER YOU ARE IN THE

RED SEA, THE MALDIVES, THE CARIBBEAN OR THE GREAT BARRIER

REEF – YOU RECOGNIZE THE TRUE SENSE AND RICHNESS OF LIFE,

WHICH HERE TAKES ON THE MOST FANCIFUL ASPECTS. A GLANCE

OUT TO THE OPEN SEA REVEALS A LARGE RING OF BARRACUDA OR

JACK CIRCLING, AND A QUICK KICK OF THE FINS LAUNCHES YOU

TOWARD A WALL OF FISH THAT MAGICALLY OPENS AS YOU PASS

THROUGH AND THEN CLOSES BEHIND YOU. ALONG THE CORAL WALL

LARGE GORGONIAS DIVIDE THE SPACE INTO THOUSANDS OF SMALL

Coral Gardens
Introduction

WINDOWS THROUGH WHICH MULTICOLORED FISH SLIP; ALL IT TAKES TO SCARE THEM AWAY IS A CLUSTER OF BUBBLES BLOWN OUT NOISILY. BUT YOU ARE ONLY ALONE FOR A FEW SECONDS BECAUSE THE TEEMING LIFE ON THE REEF IS IRREPRESSIBLE. YOU ARE ENRAPTURED BY THE COMPLICATED STRUCTURES CREATED BY THE POLYPS ON THE MADREPORE, THE BUILDERS OF THIS UNDERWATER EMPIRE. TOGETHER THE CORAL PLUMES AND TENTACLES, MADREPORE AND SEA ANEMONES CREATE A MOSAIC IN WHICH EACH ONE IS A PERFECT TESSERA, A SURPRISINGLY COLORFUL FRAGMENT THAT FITS PERFECTLY AGAINST ITS NEIGHBORS TO FORM A WONDERFUL AND INDESCRIBABLE PATTERN.

● Red Sea, Egypt - Red coral grouper.

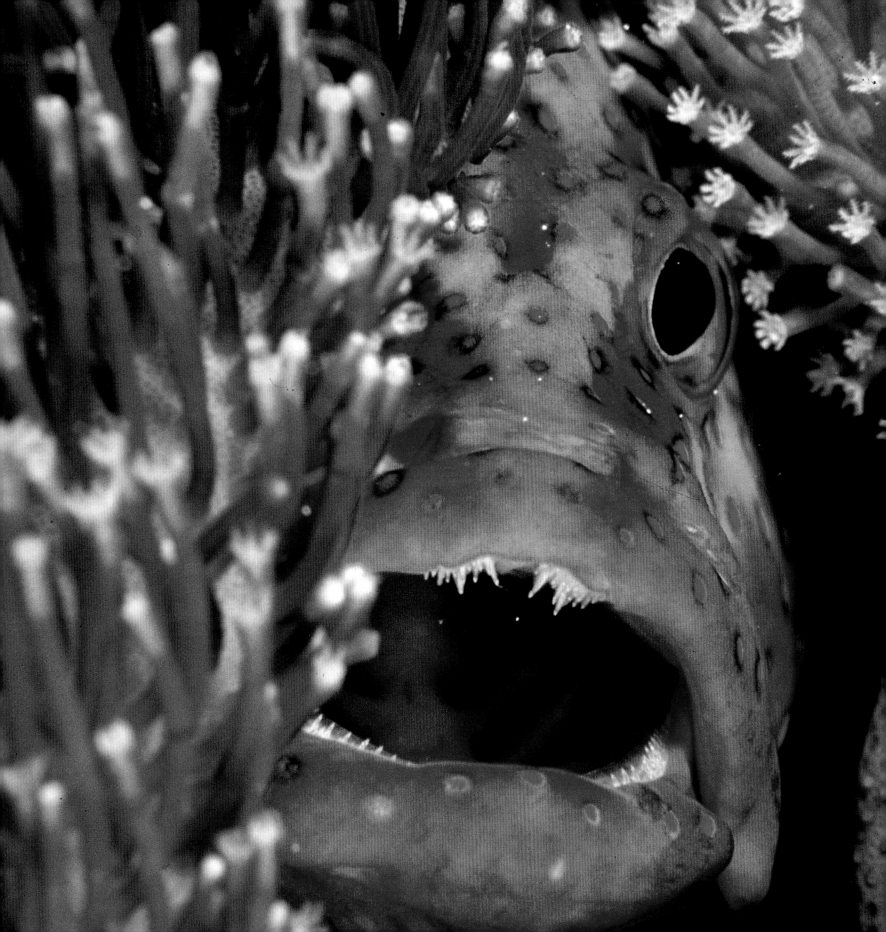

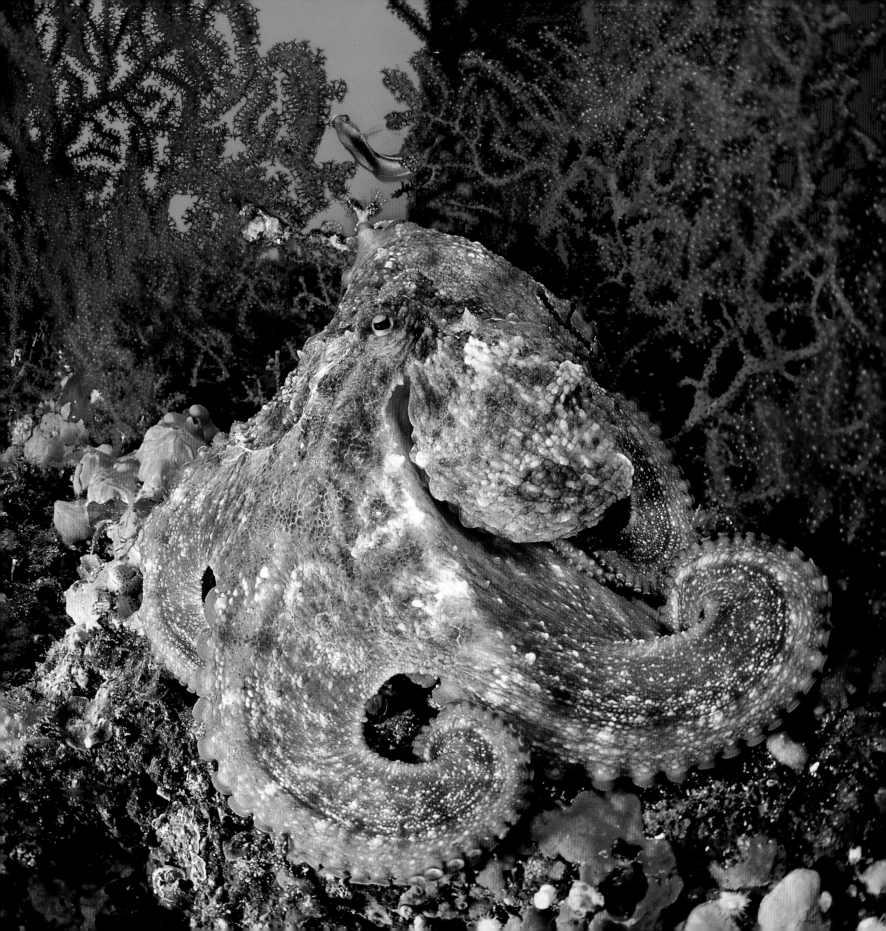

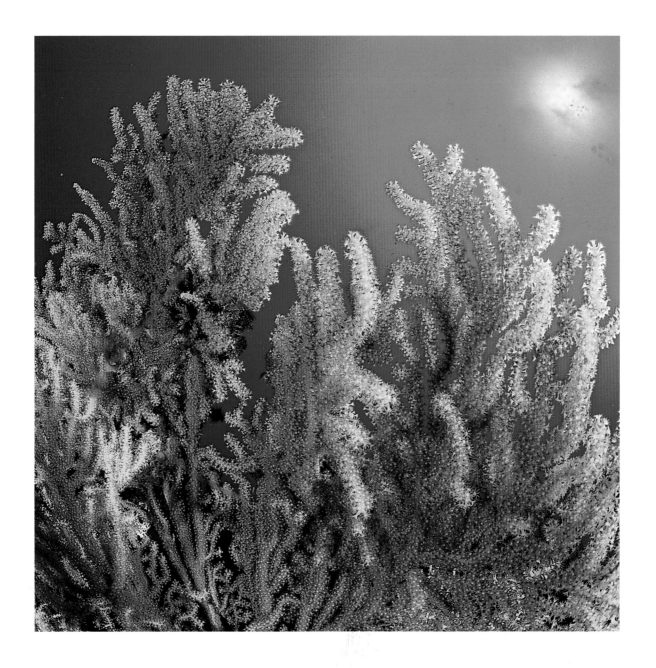

518 ● Mediterranean Sea, Sardinia (Italy) - Common octopus.

519 ● Mediterranean Sea, Gozo (Malta) - Alcyonaria.

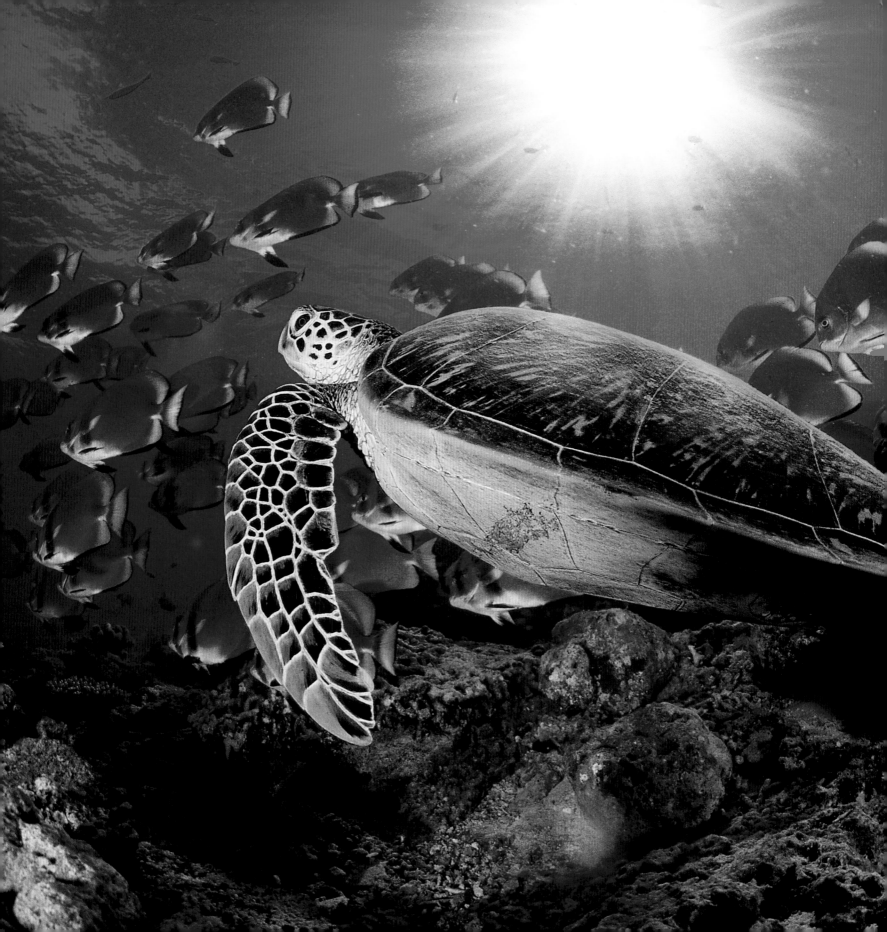

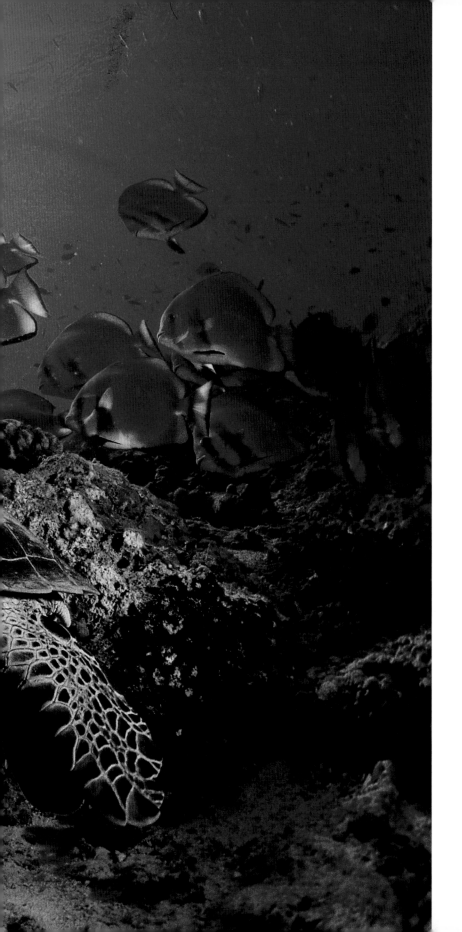

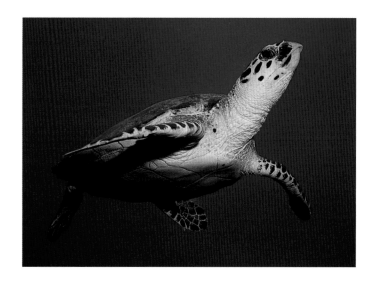

520-521 ● Indian Ocean, Sipadan
(Malaysia) - Sea turtle.

521 ● Red Sea, Sharm el-Sheikh (Egypt) -
Sea turtle.

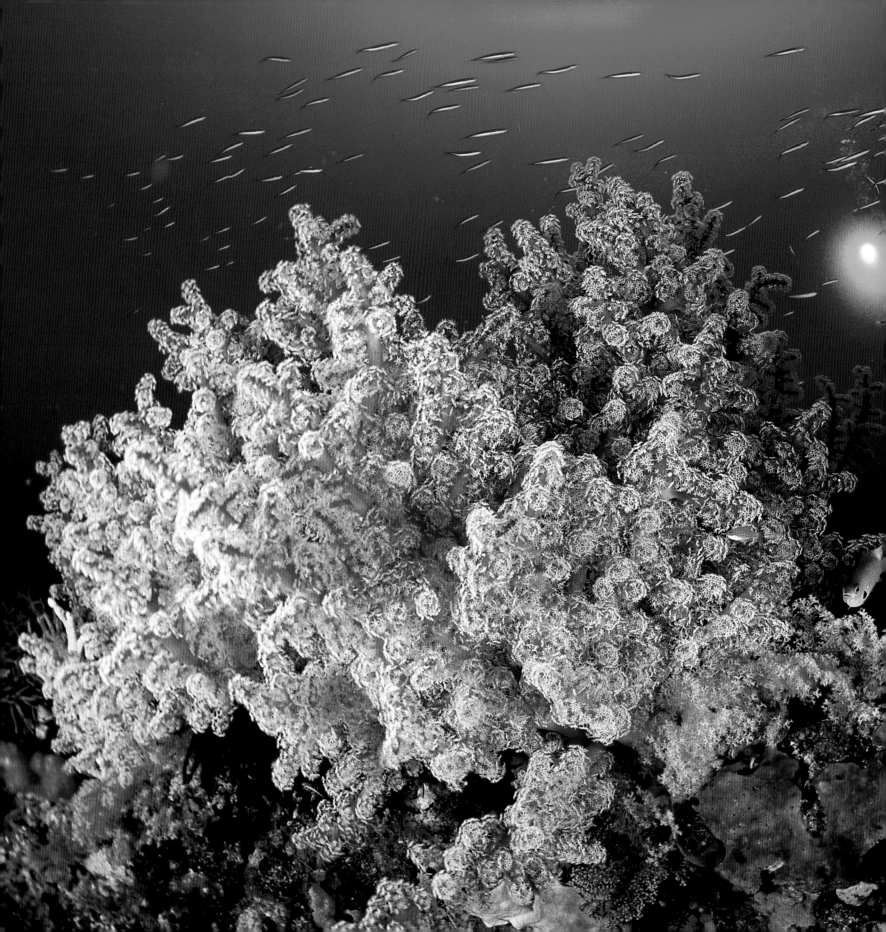

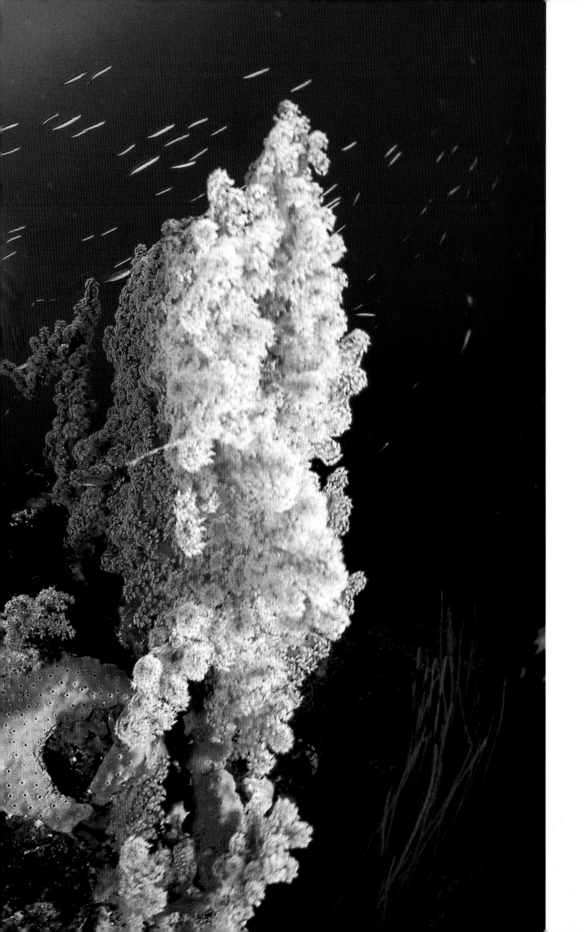

Pacific Ocean, Papua New Guinea - Forest of alcyonaria.

523

" | WAS AMAZED BY THE SIGHT THAT WAS PRESENT-
ED BEFORE ME IN THE WATERS OF LE MOURILLON - ROCKS
COVERED WITH GREEN, BROWN AND SILVER FORESTS OF
SEAWEED AND FISH, SOME I HAD NEVER SEEN, THAT
DANCED IN THE CRYSTALLINE WATER. I FOUND MYSELF IN
A JUNGLE THAT HAD NEVER BEEN SEEN BY THOSE THAT
SAIL OVER ITS OPAQUE ROOF. "

Jacques-Yves Cousteau, 1936

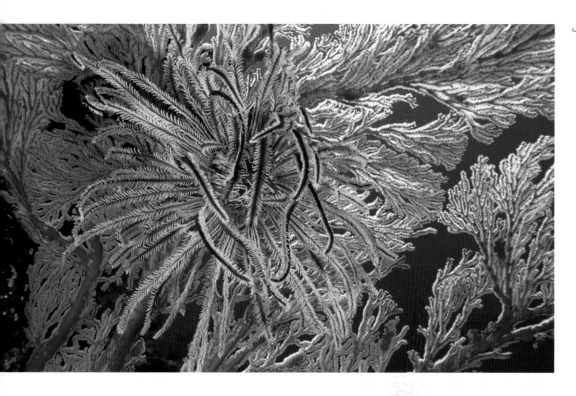

524 ● Caribbean Sea, Cayo Largo (Cuba) - Crinoids and sea fans.

525 ● Red Sea, Sharm el-Sheikh (Egypt) - Sea fans.

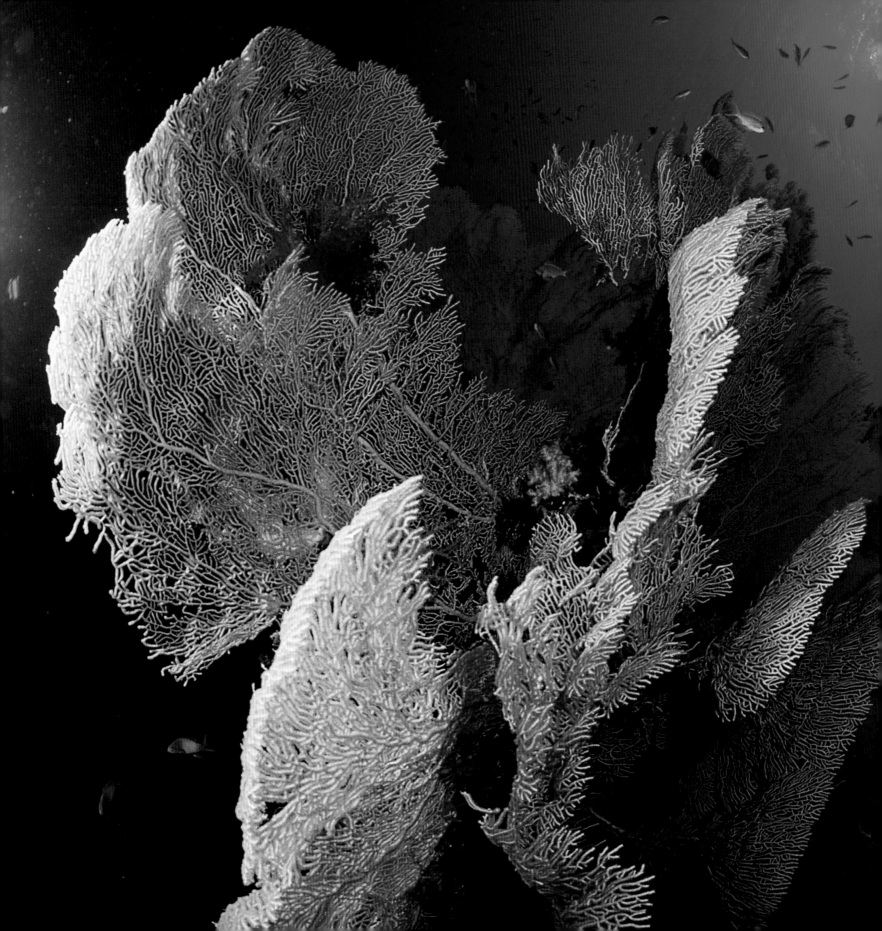

Red Sea, Egypt -
Gorgonias and glass fish.

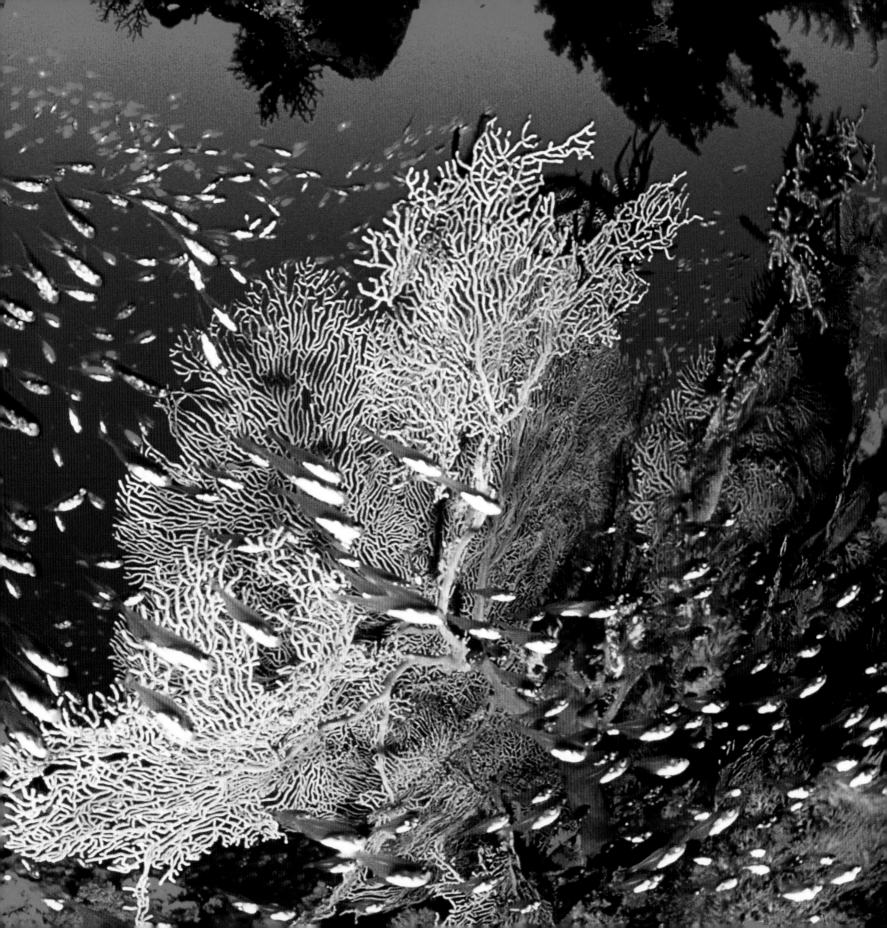

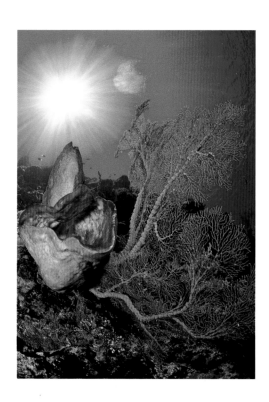

528 ● Pacific Ocean, Manado,
Sulawesi (Indonesia) - Barrel
sponge and giant sea fan.

528-529 ● Pacific Ocean, Papua New
Guinea - Elephant ear sponge.

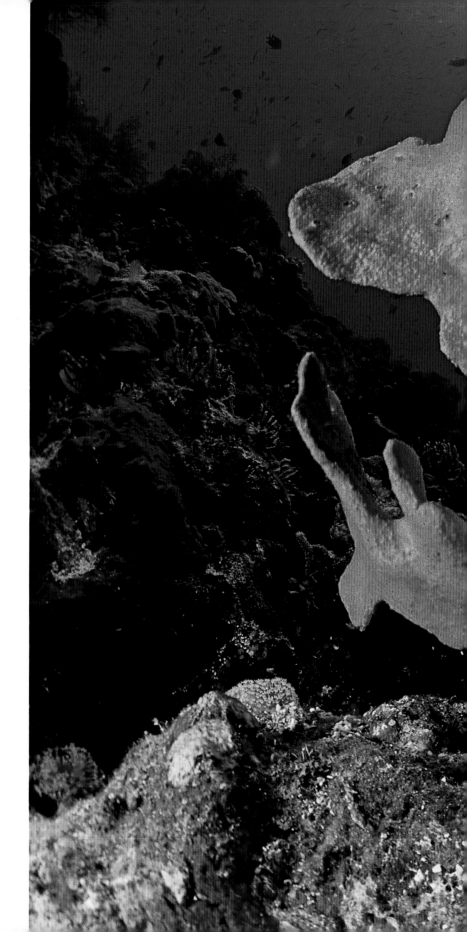

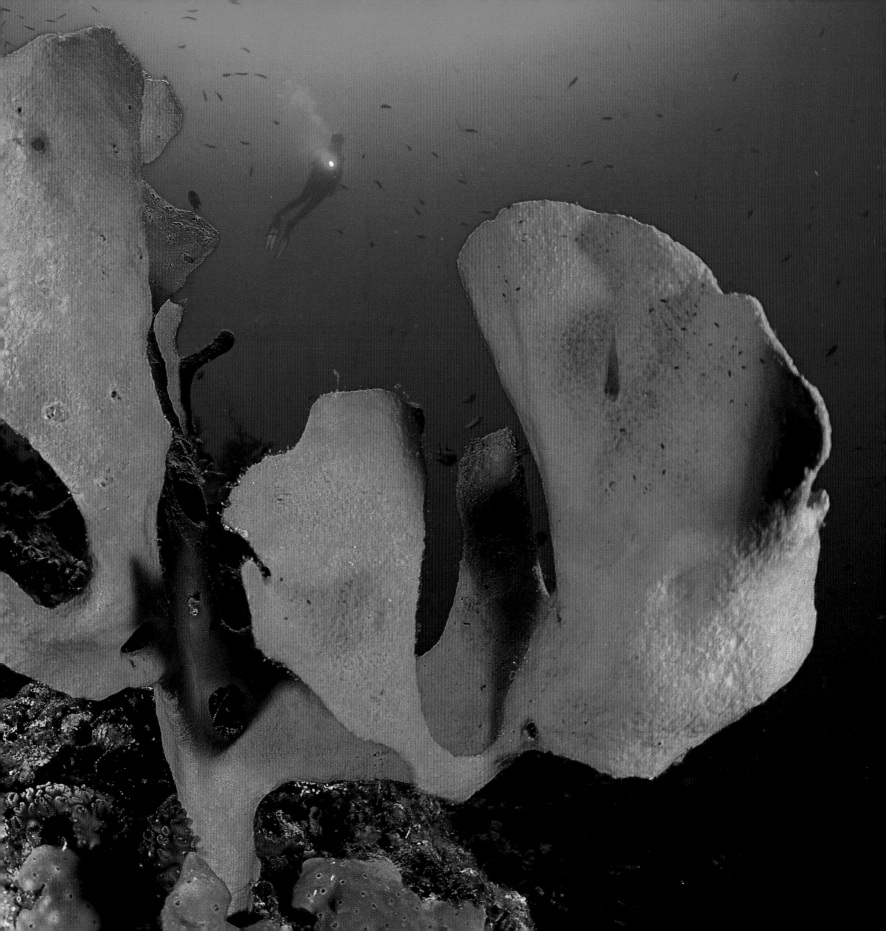

The clowns of the sea

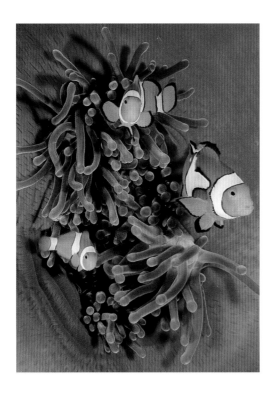

530 ● Pacific Ocean, Malaysia
- False clown fish.

530-531 ● Pacific Ocean, Philippines -
Clown fish.

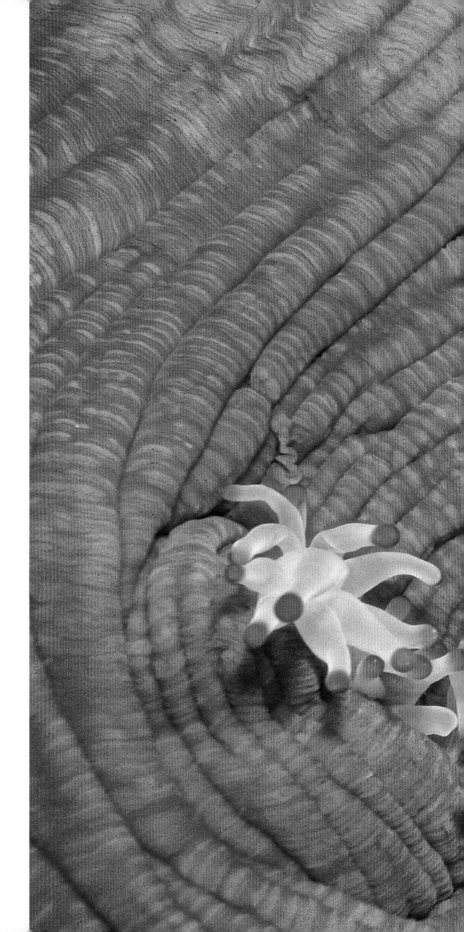

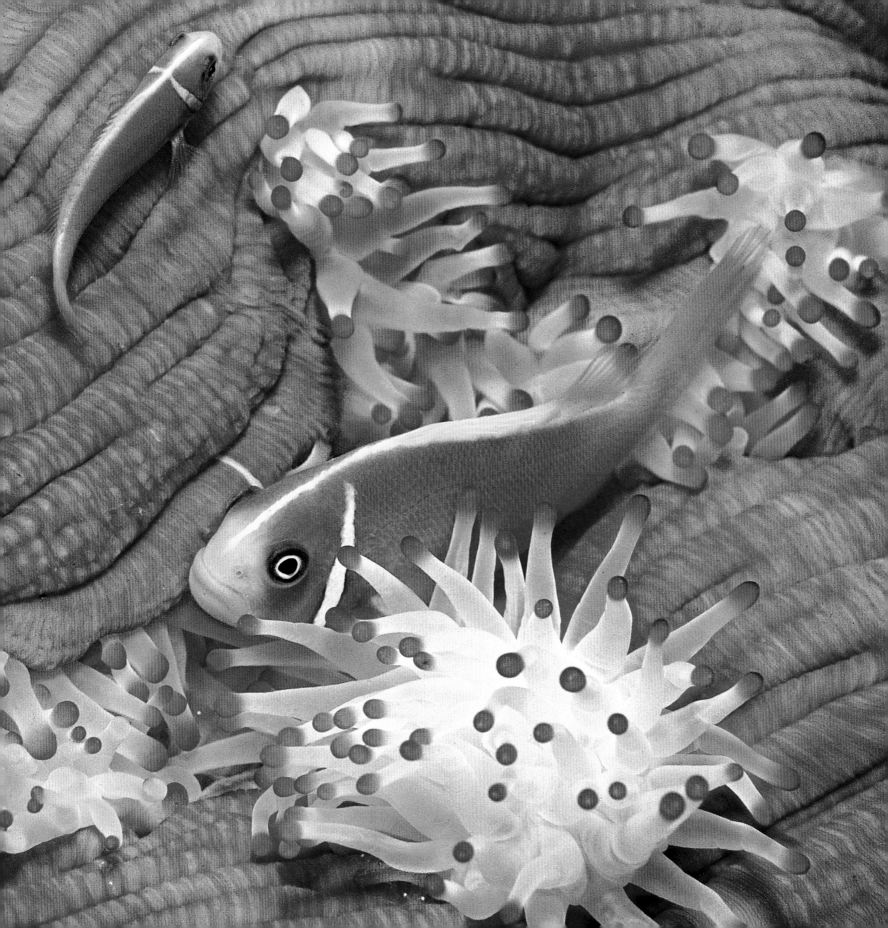

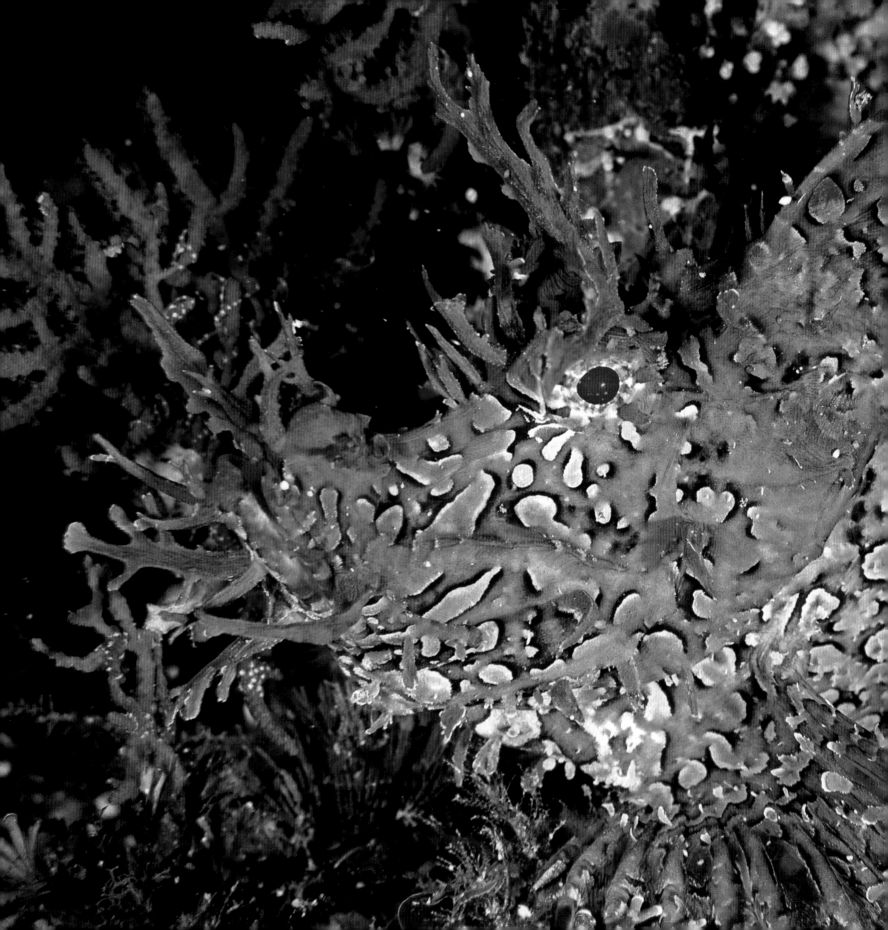

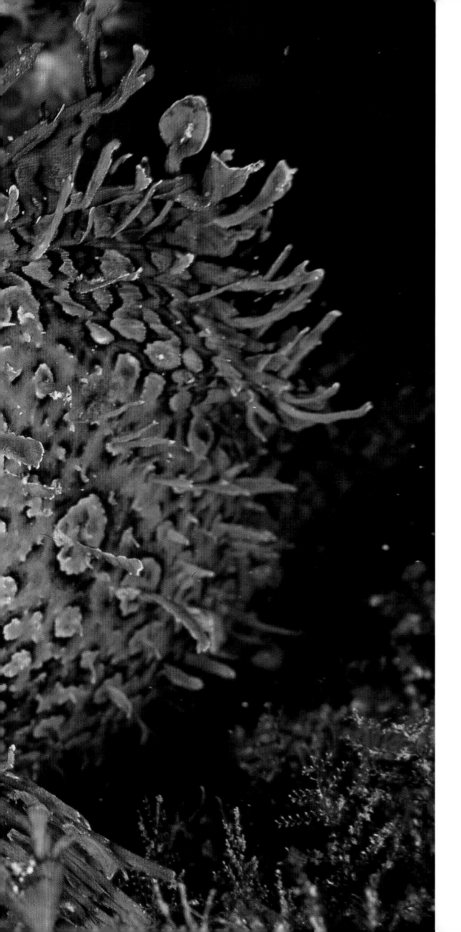

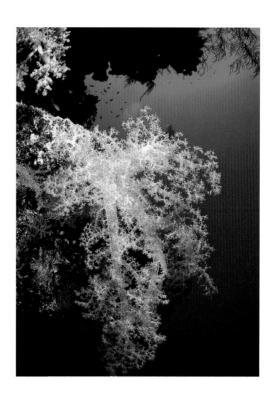

532-533 ● Indian Ocean, Papua New Guinea - Leafy scorpion fish.

533 ● Red Sea, Egypt - Alcyonaria.

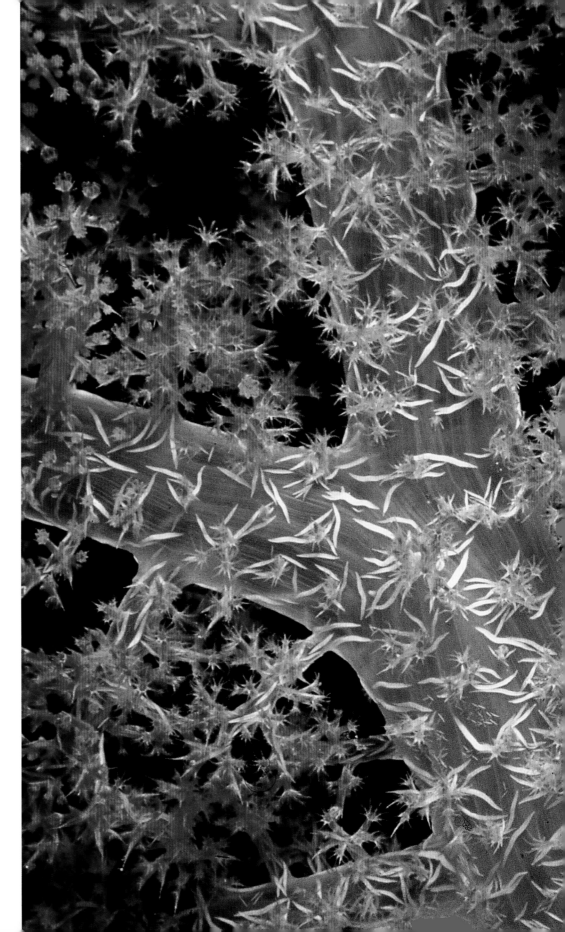

Red Sea, Egypt -
Alcyonaria.

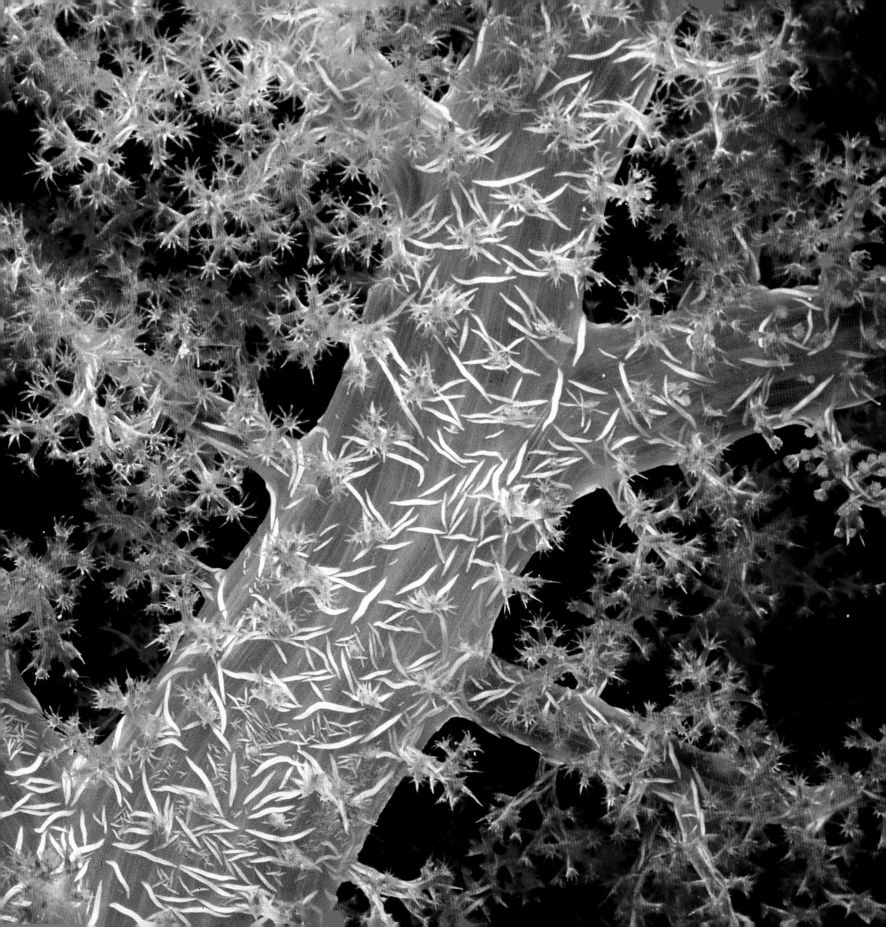

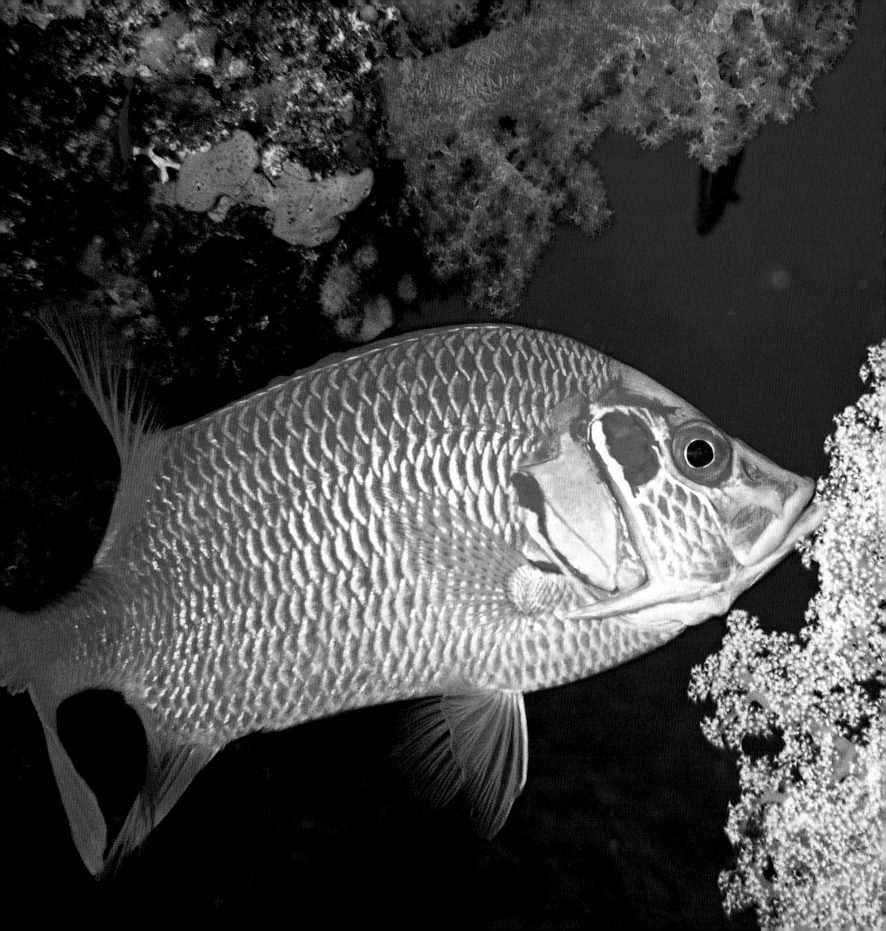

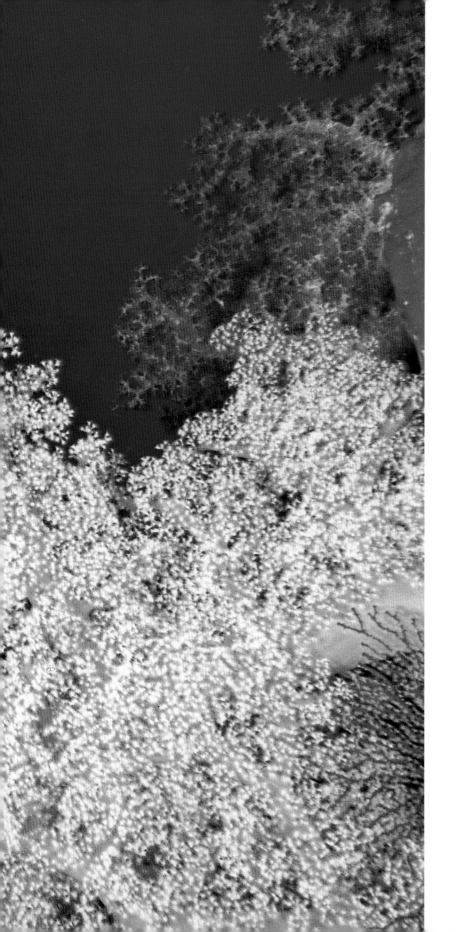

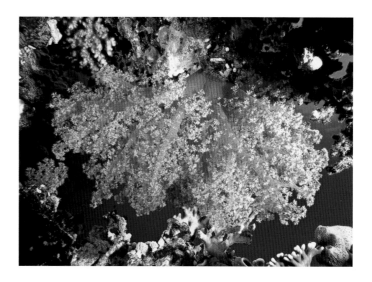

536-537 ● Red Sea, Egypt - Squirrel fish.

537 ● Red Sea, Egypt - Alcyonaria.

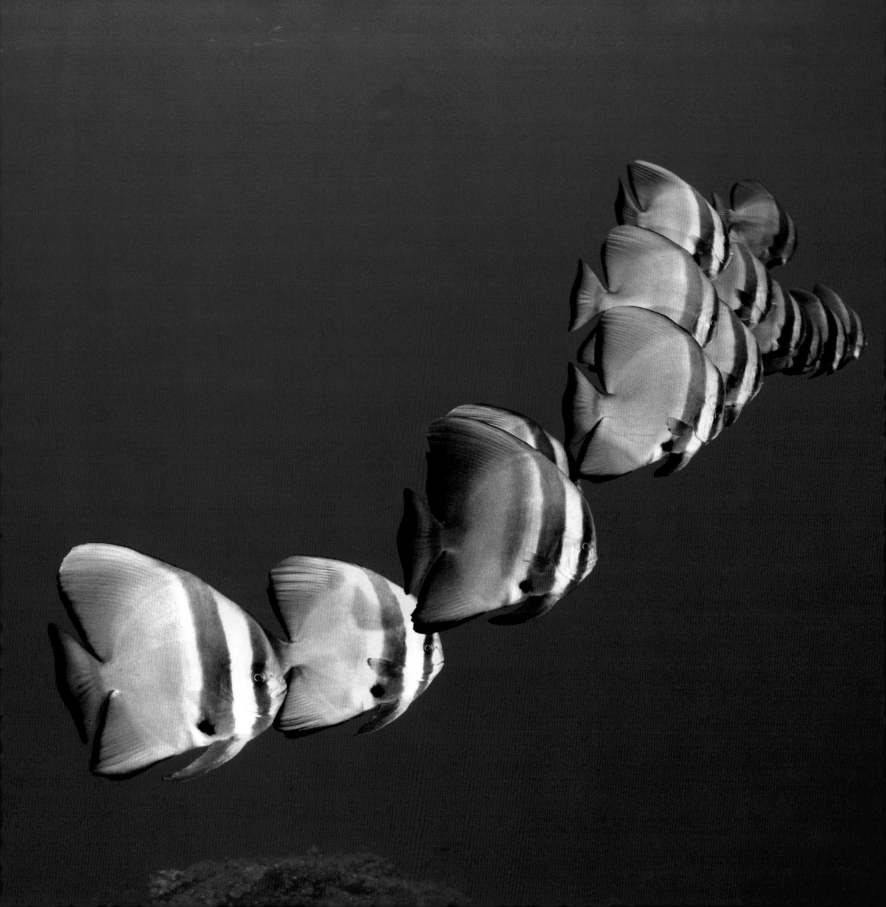

Underwater patterns

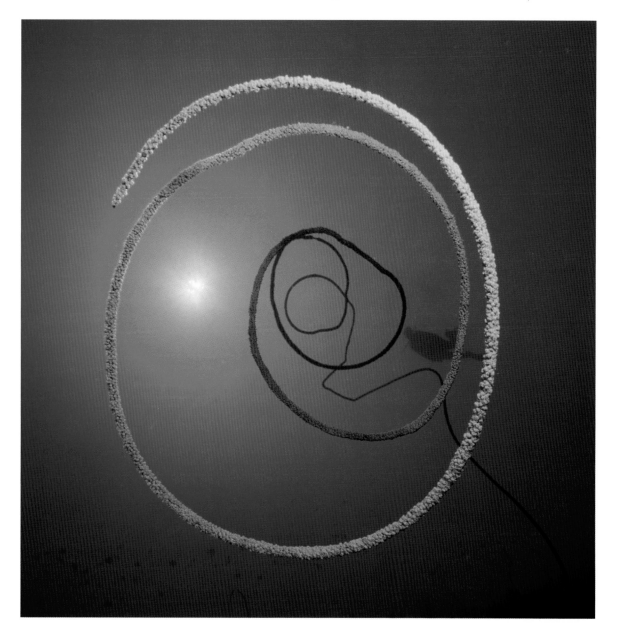

538 ● Indian Ocean, Malaysia - Bat fish.

539 ● Pacific Ocean, Australia - Sea whip.

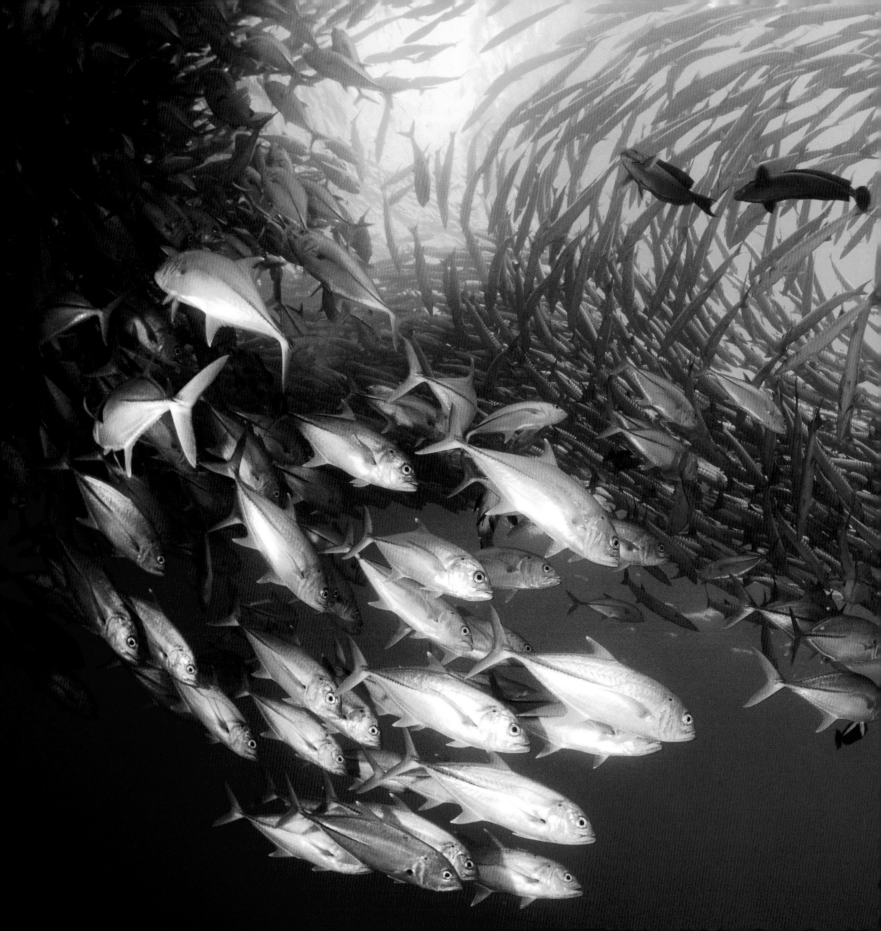

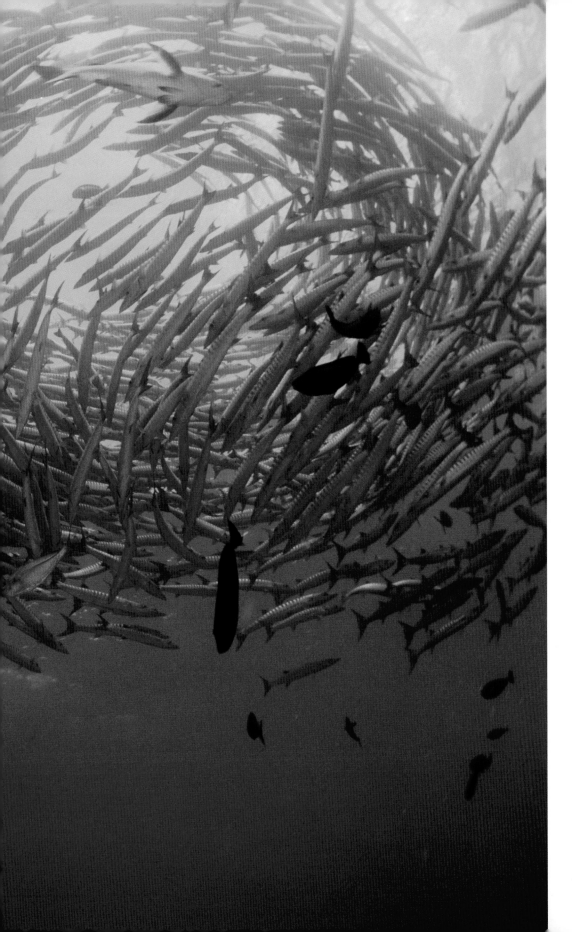

540-541 ● Indian Ocean,
Maldives - Barracuda
and jacks.

542-543 ● Indian Ocean,
Maldives - A school
of fusiliers.

544-545 ● Indian Ocean,
Maldives - Stingrays.

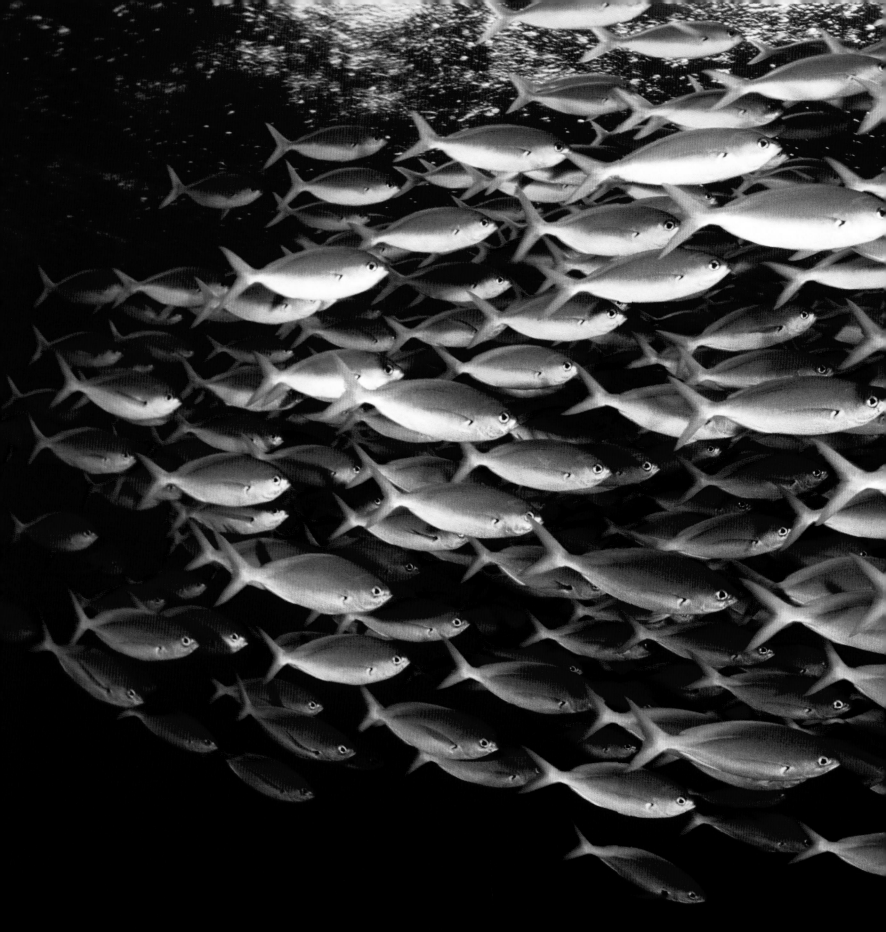

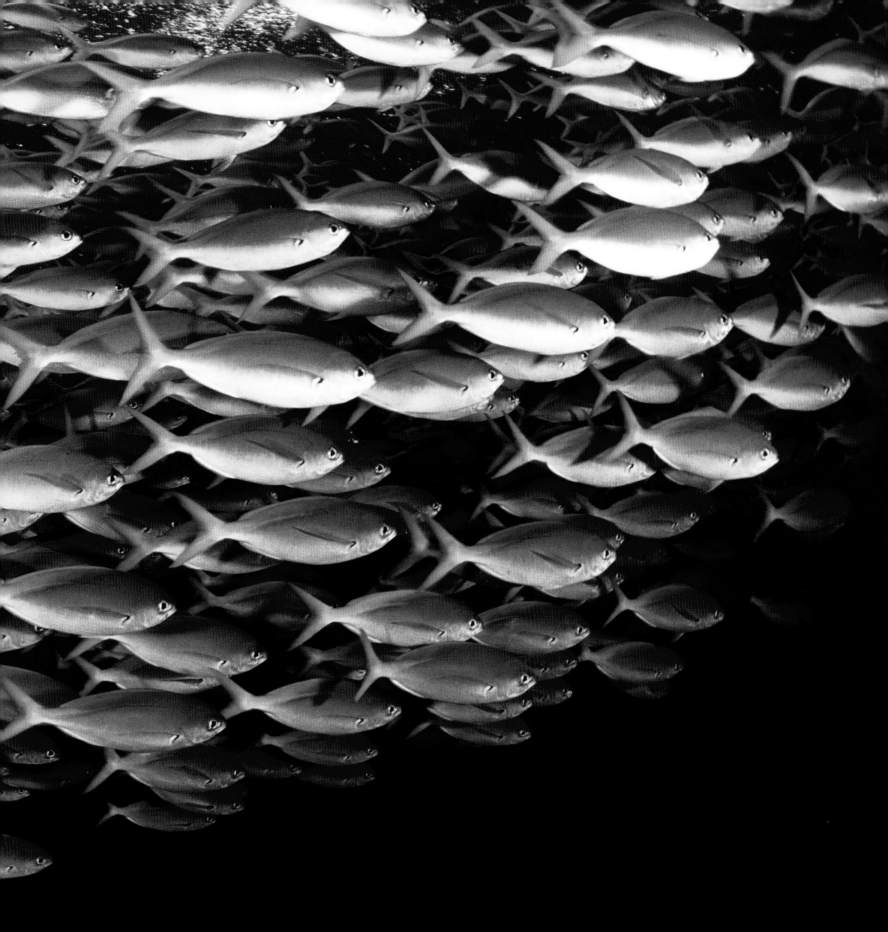

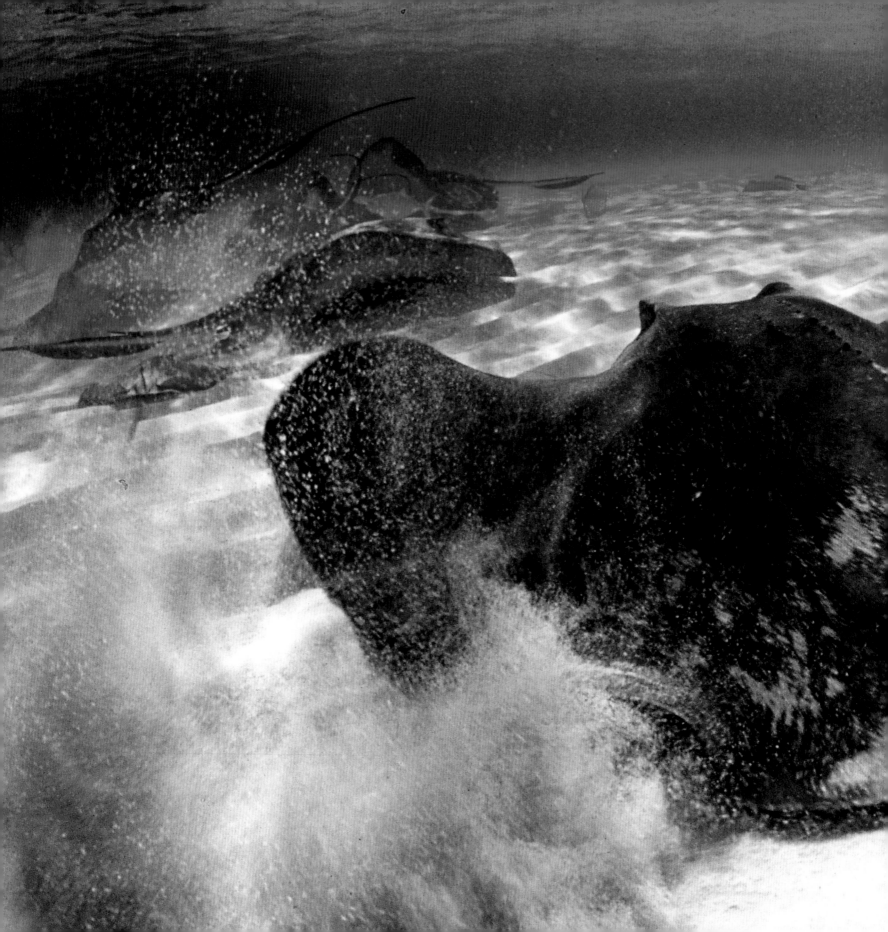

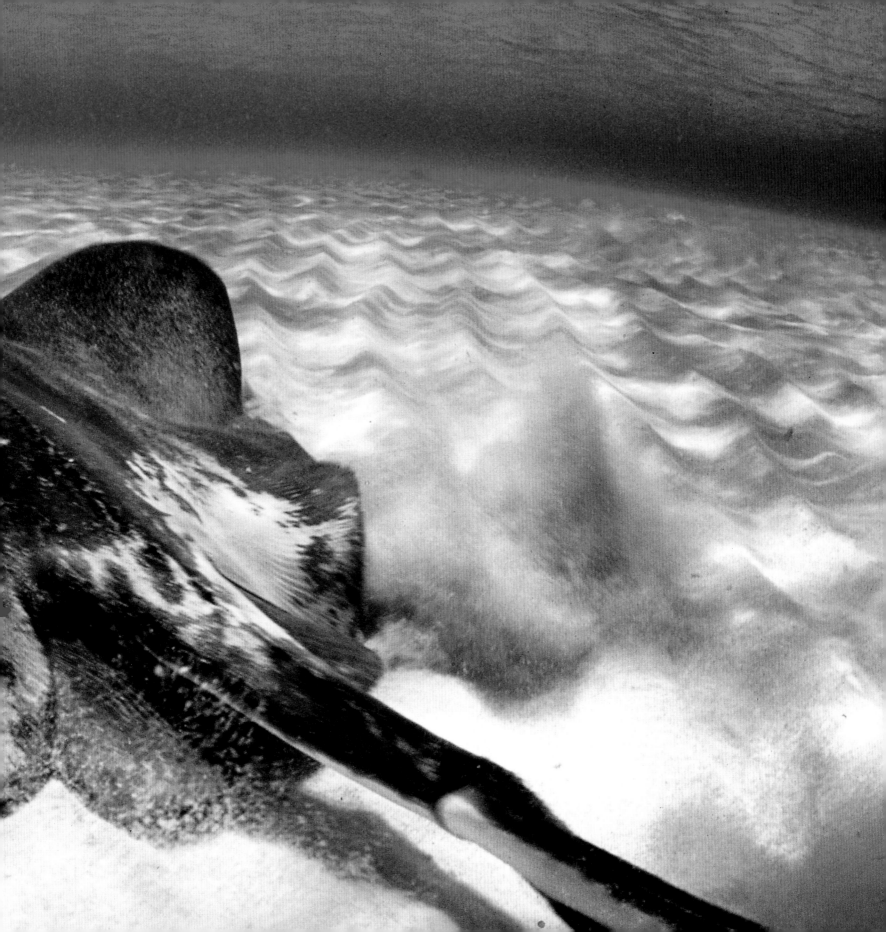

LIKE ENCHANTED FORESTS, THE SEA BEDS ARE PLACES OF LIGHT AND SUFFUSED COLORS WHERE SEA FANS CEASELESSLY TREMBLE, WAVE AND TURN. ONCE YOU LEAVE THE SURFACE, THERE IS ONLY THE NOISE OF THE BUBBLES TO BREAK THE SPELL UNDER WHICH YOU FALL.

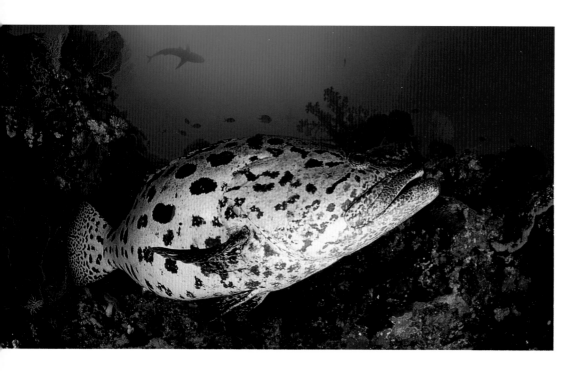

546 ● Pacific Ocean, Australia - Giant grouper.

547 ● Caribbean Sea, Florida (USA) - Black grouper.

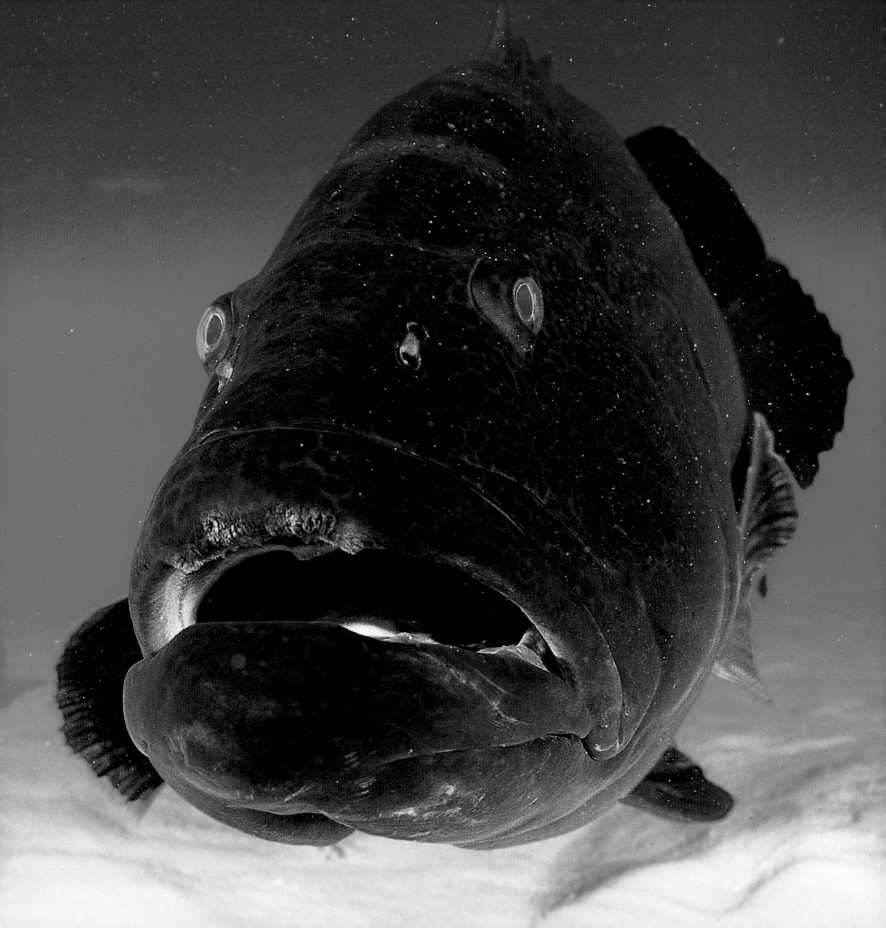

Red Sea, Egypt -
Parrot fish.

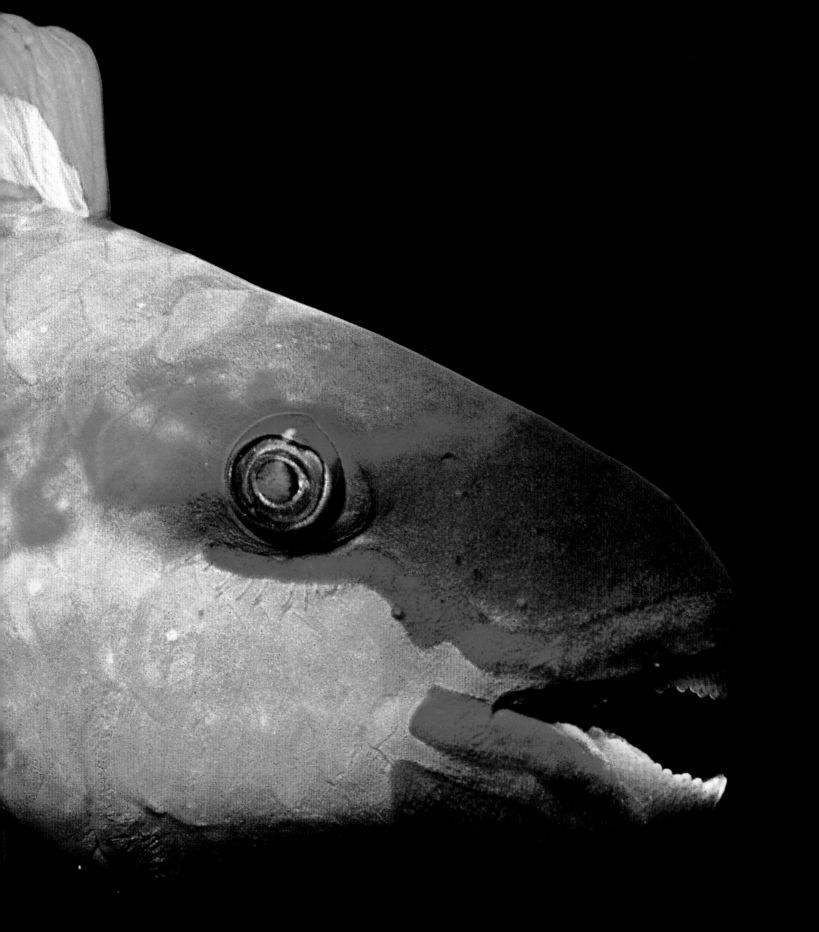

550-551 ● Caribbean Sea, Florida (USA) - Queen angel fish.

552-553 ● Red Sea, Egypt - Red Sea bannerfish.

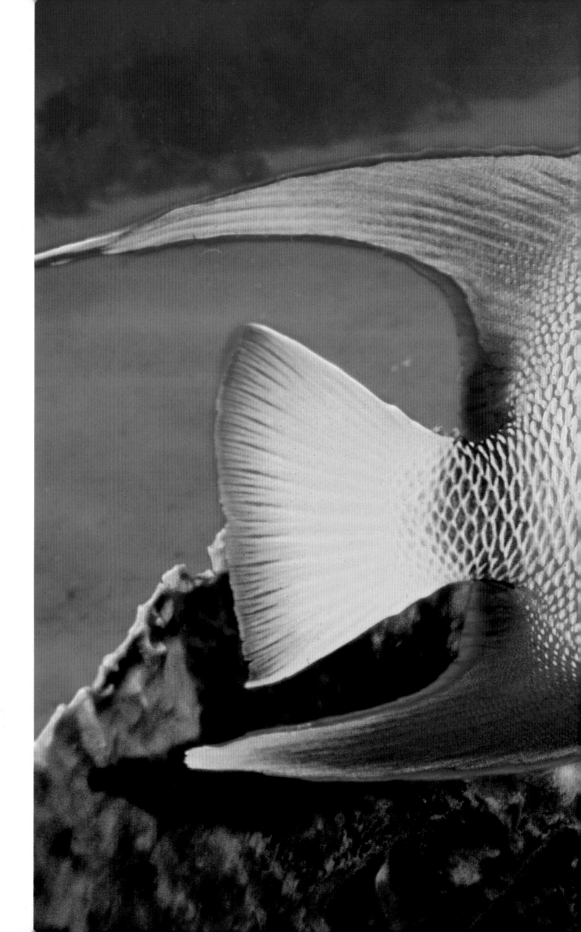

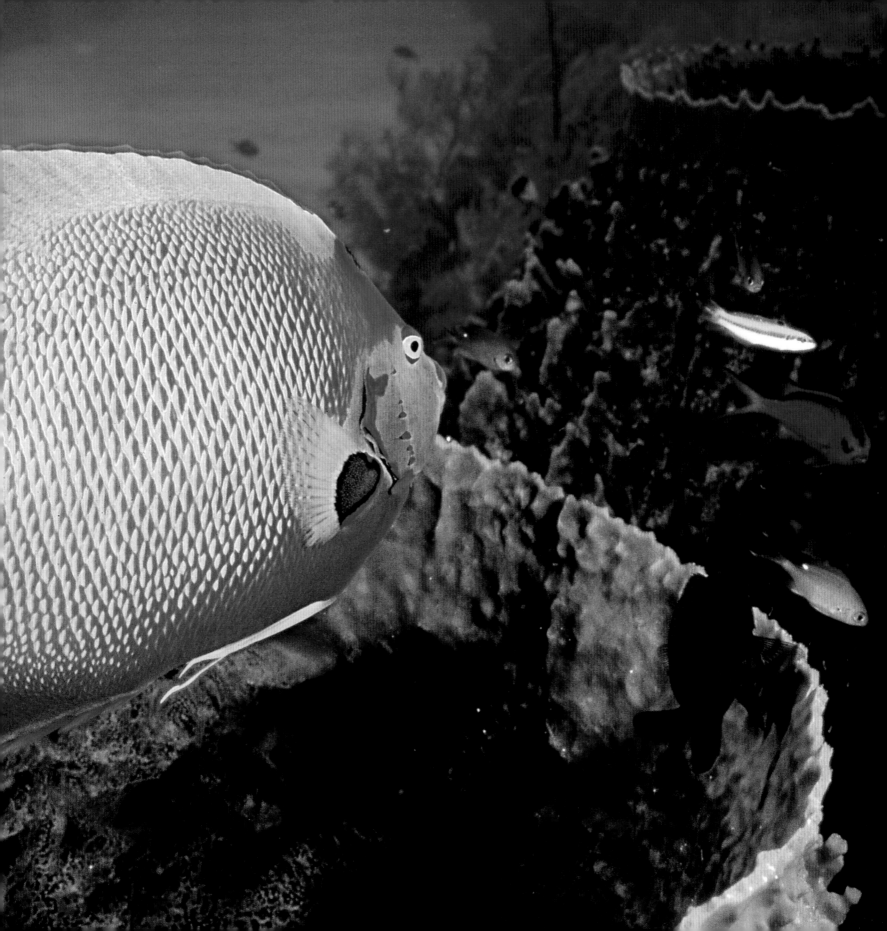

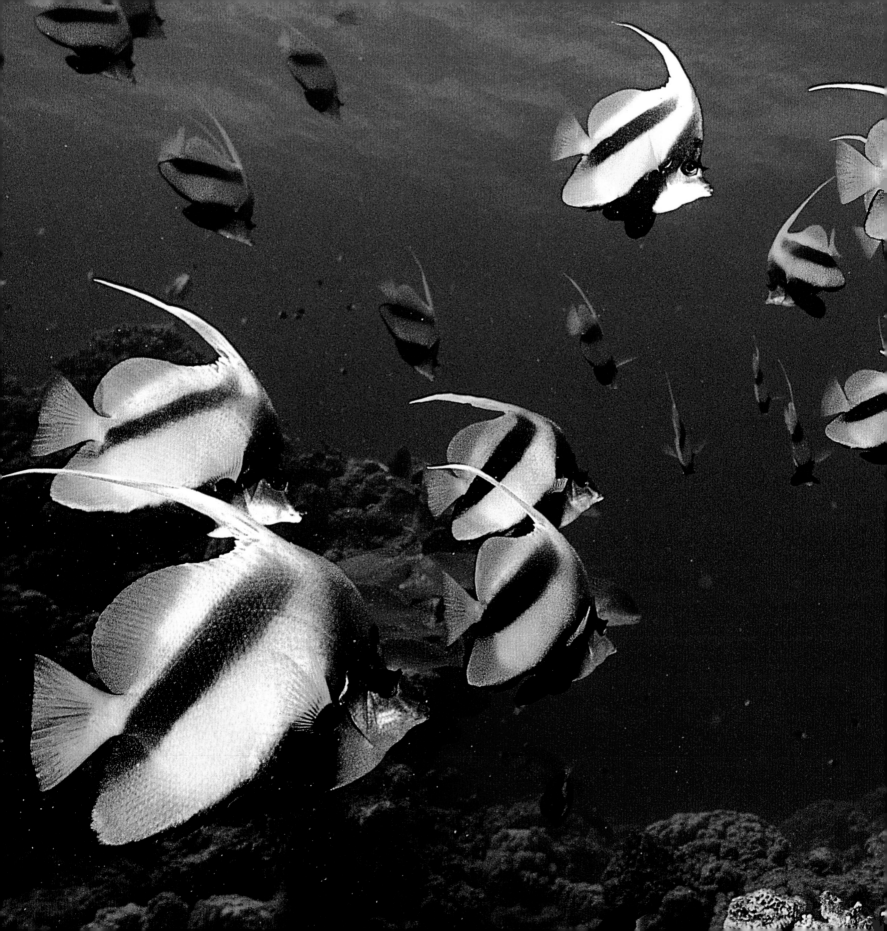

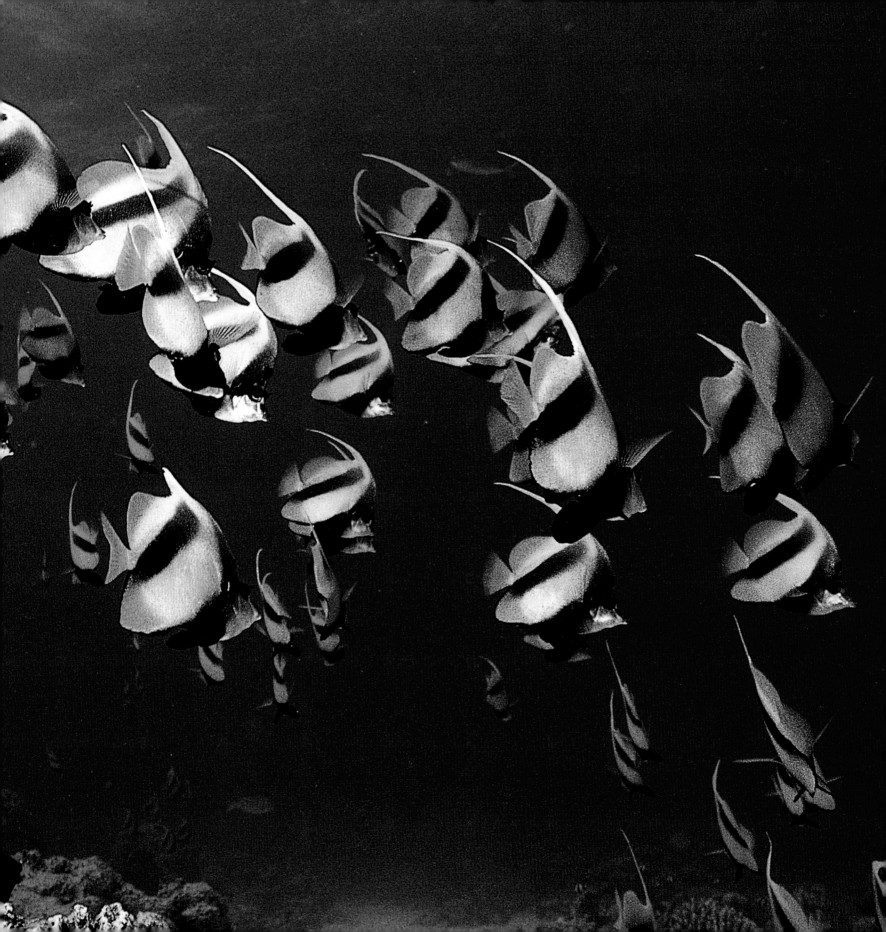

The GIANTS of the SEA

NORA L. DEANS

● Pacific Ocean, Queensland (Australia) - Humpback whale in Platypus Bay.

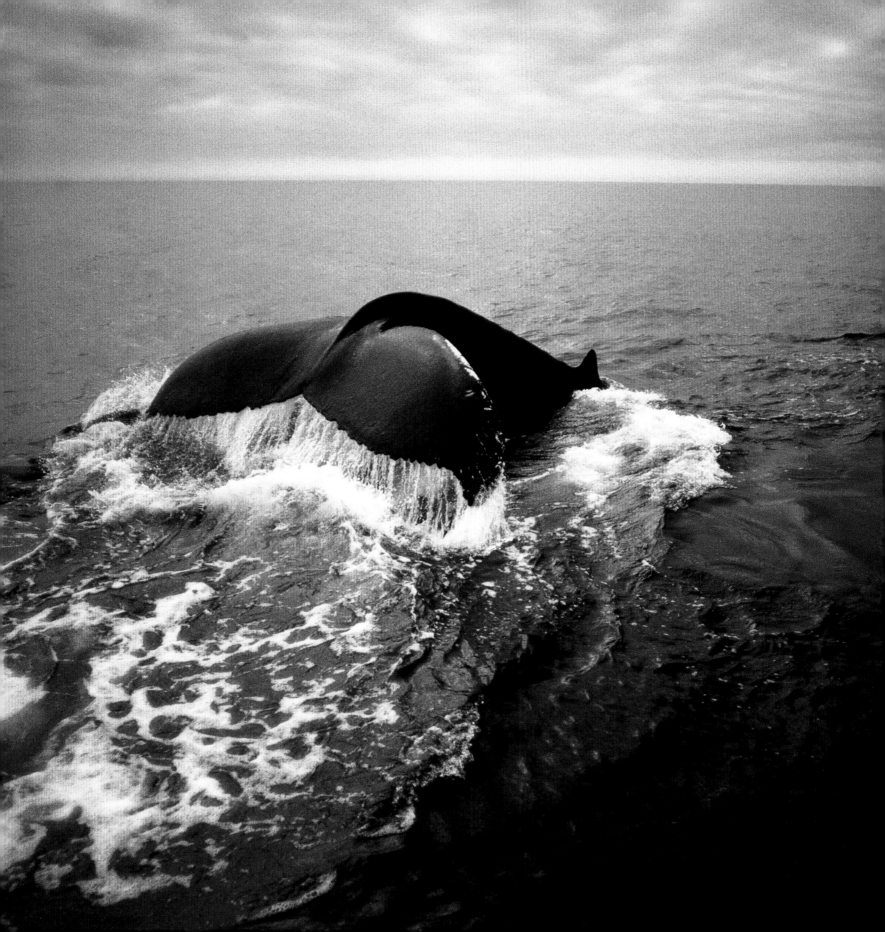

INTRODUCTION The Giants of the Sea

LIKE A SPECTER IN THE MIST, A HUGE SHAPE DARKENED THE WATER. I GLANCED BEYOND THE BOWS THAT ROLLED OVER THE SWELLS OF THE SEA, MY EYES TIRED WITH SEARCHING. THEN, I FELT THE BREATH OF THE CREATURE, ALMOST THE DAMPNESS OF THE COLUMN OF WATER IT SPOUTED 30 FEET HIGH. AND FINALLY, I CAUGHT SIGHT OF ITS SHINY, GRAY-BLUE BACK AS IT ARCED OVER THE SURFACE AND DIVED DOWN TOWARD THE DEPTHS. THE IMMENSE TAIL ROSE HIGH INTO THE AIR BEFORE SLIPPING BENEATH THE SURFACE AND, IN JUST A FEW SECONDS, THE LARGEST CREATURE ON EARTH WAS FAR AWAY. THERE! I HAD SEEN MY FIRST BLUE WHALE. THE SEA IS HOME TO MANY GIANTS BUT

INTRODUCTION The Giants of the Sea

THE BLUE WHALE IS THEIR QUEEN. ONLY AN OCEAN IS CAPABLE OF

PROVIDING THIS GARGANTUAN WITH A HABITAT, AS, ON LAND, IT

WOULD BE UNABLE TO MOVE EVEN A YARD. ALTHOUGH WHALES

WERE ONCE TERRESTRIAL CREATURES FAMILIAR WITH GRAVITY,

THEY LONG AGO MIGRATED TO THE SEA WHERE THEY BECAME

THE LARGEST MAMMALS ON THE PLANET. BUT NOT ALL THE SEA'S

GIANTS ARE WHALES: WHALE SHARKS ARE DAPPLED MASTODONS

AS LARGE AS A FISHING BOAT, ELEPHANT SHARKS JUST SLIGHTLY

SMALLER, AND MANTAS, THE 'BLACK DEVILS' WITH A HUGE

WINGSPAN, ARE ACTUALLY FISH THAT HAVE EVOLVED IN THE SEAS

LIKE THE HUGE PREDATOR, THE GREAT WHITE SHARK. FAR

The Giants of the Sea

Introduction

BENEATH THE SURFACE, ANOTHER COLOSSUS HUNTS IN THE ICE-COLD DARKNESS: A LEGENDARY CREATURE, THE GIANT SQUID INHABITS THE DEPTHS OF THE OCEAN AND OUR SUBCONSCIOUS. IT IS ONLY SEEN WHEN, DEAD OR DYING, IT HAS BECOME STRANDED ON THE SHORE OR TRAPPED IN A TRAWL NET. BELIEVED IN THE PAST TO BE THE MOST FEARSOME INHABITANT OF THE SEAS, THE MASSIVE SIZE OF THE GIANT SQUID HAS RECENTLY BEEN OUTDONE BY A NEWLY DISCOVERED SPECIES CAPTURED IN THE WATERS OF THE ANTARCTIC: THE COLOSSAL SQUID. DOES THIS SPECIES BATTLE THE SPERM WHALES IN THE ABYSS FOR ITS SURVIVAL, IN FEROCIOUS CLASHES BETWEEN THE GIANTS OF THE DEEP?

● Pacific Ocean, Australia - White shark in Spencer Gulf.

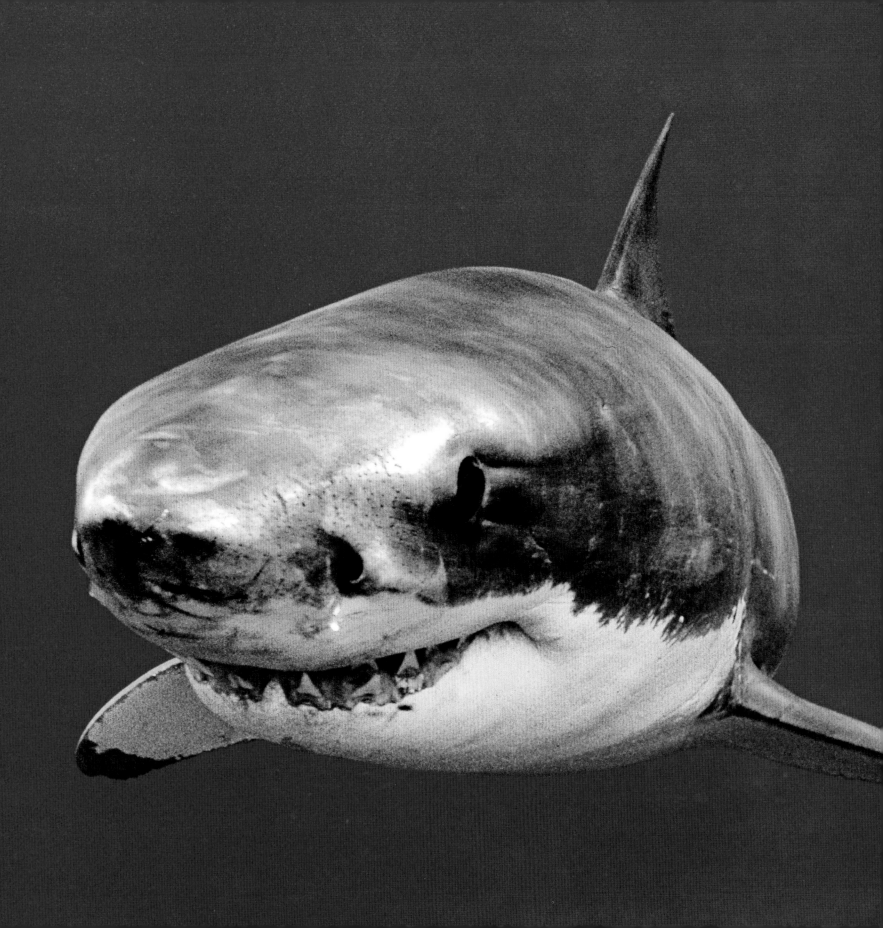

560-561 ● Atlantic Ocean, Patagonia (Argentina) - Southern right whale.

562-563 ● Pacific Ocean, California (USA) - Gray whale near the Channel Islands.

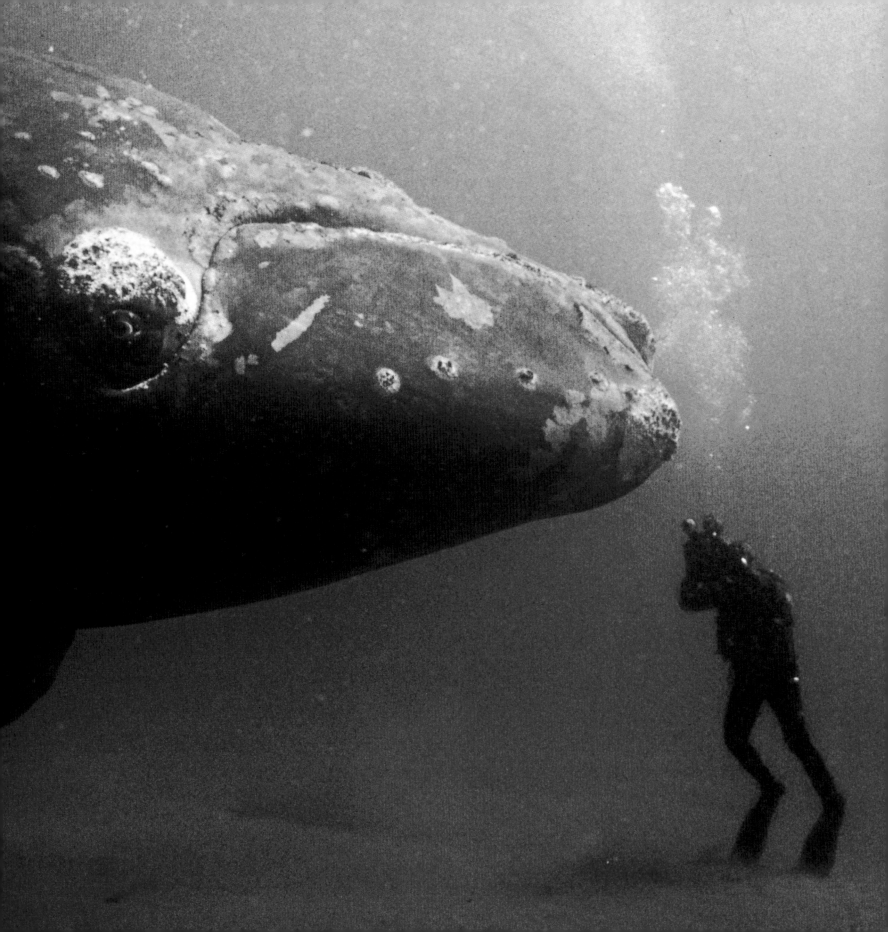

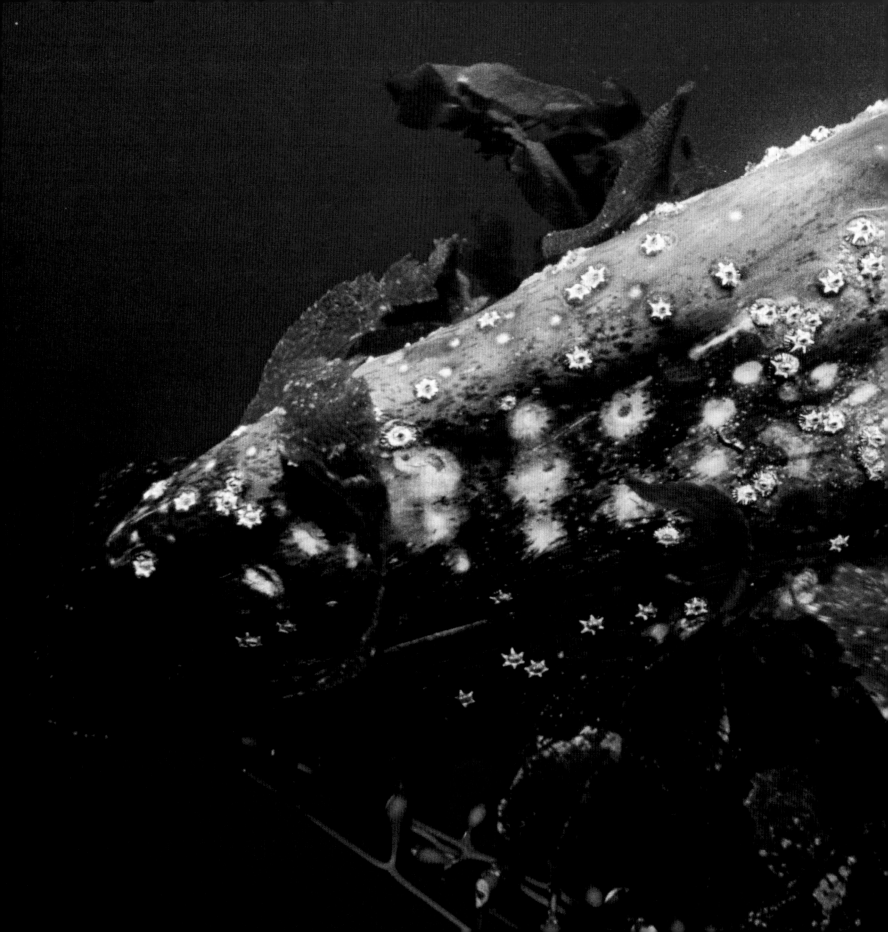

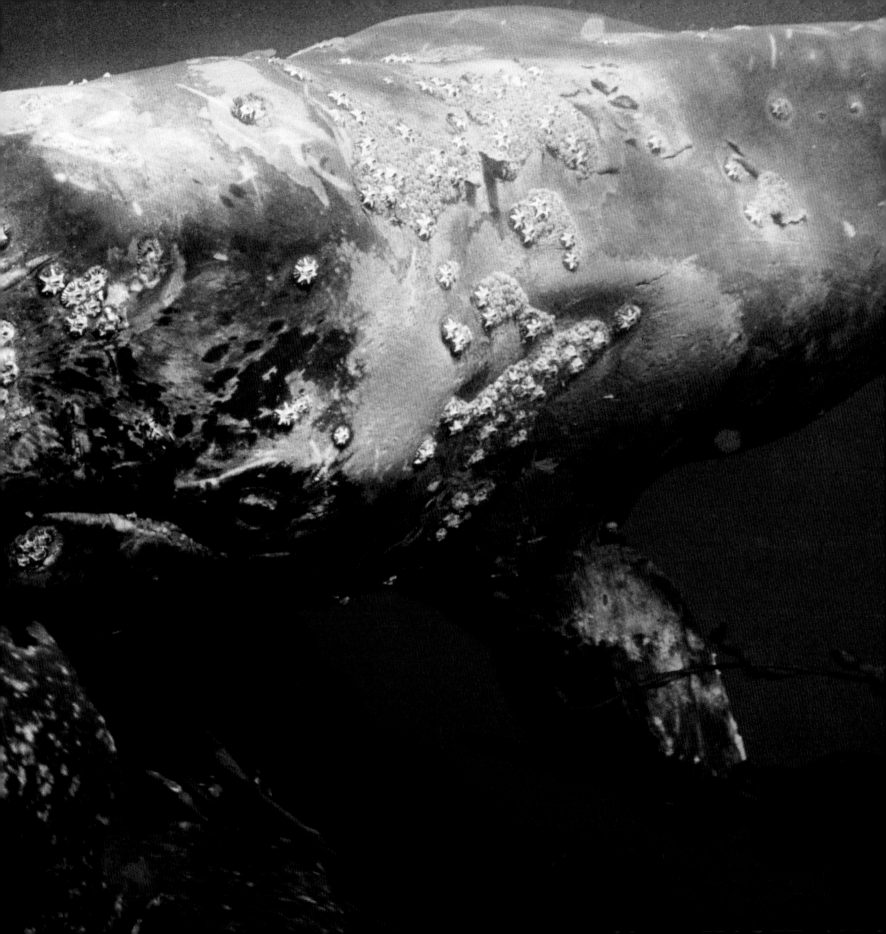

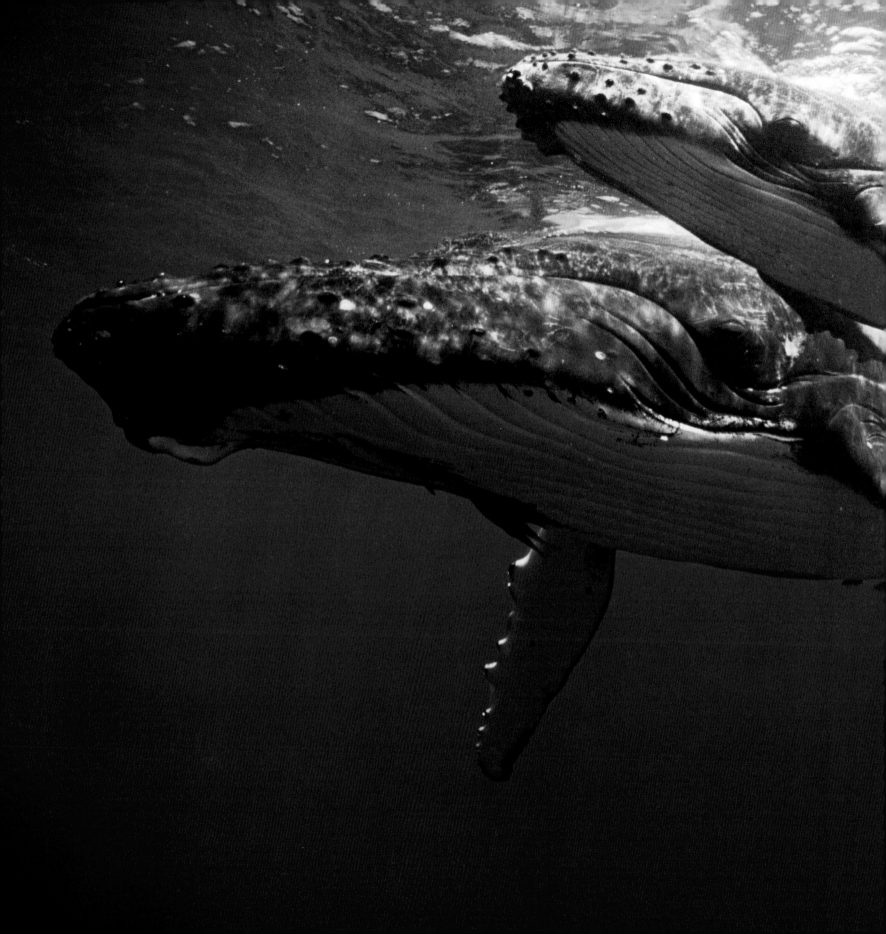

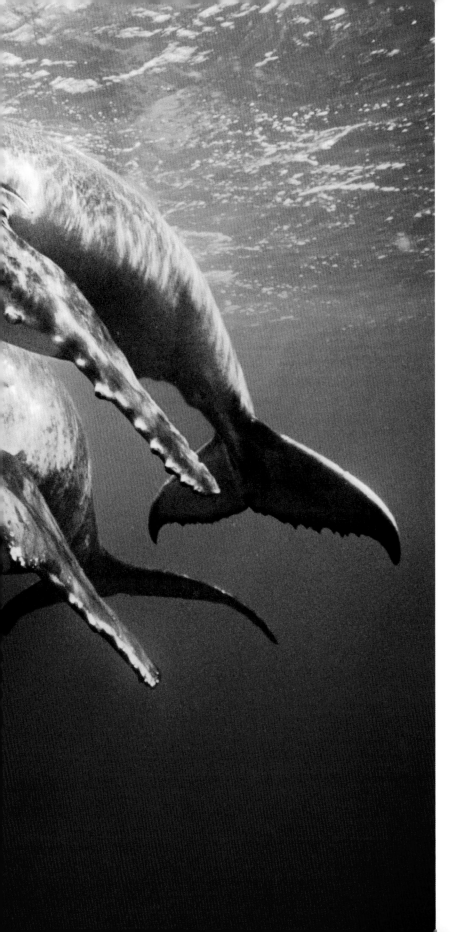

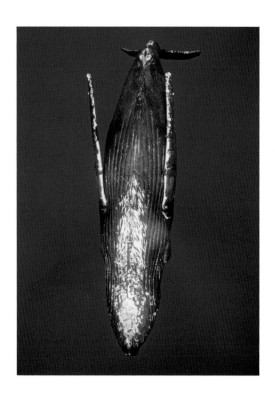

Pacific Ocean, Hawaii (USA) -
Humpback whales.

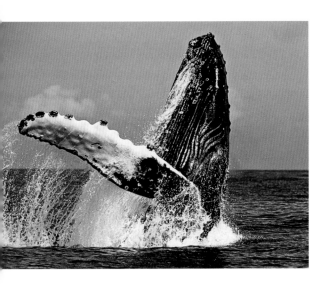

Bering Sea, Alaska (USA) -
Humpback whales.

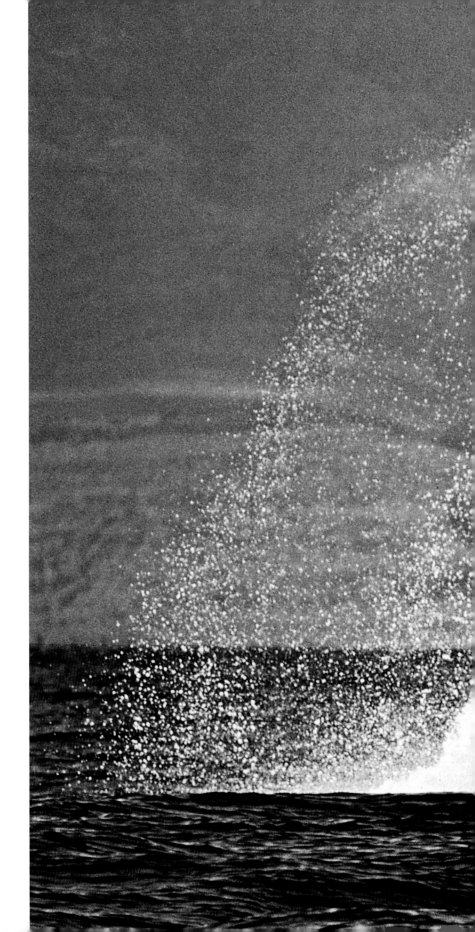

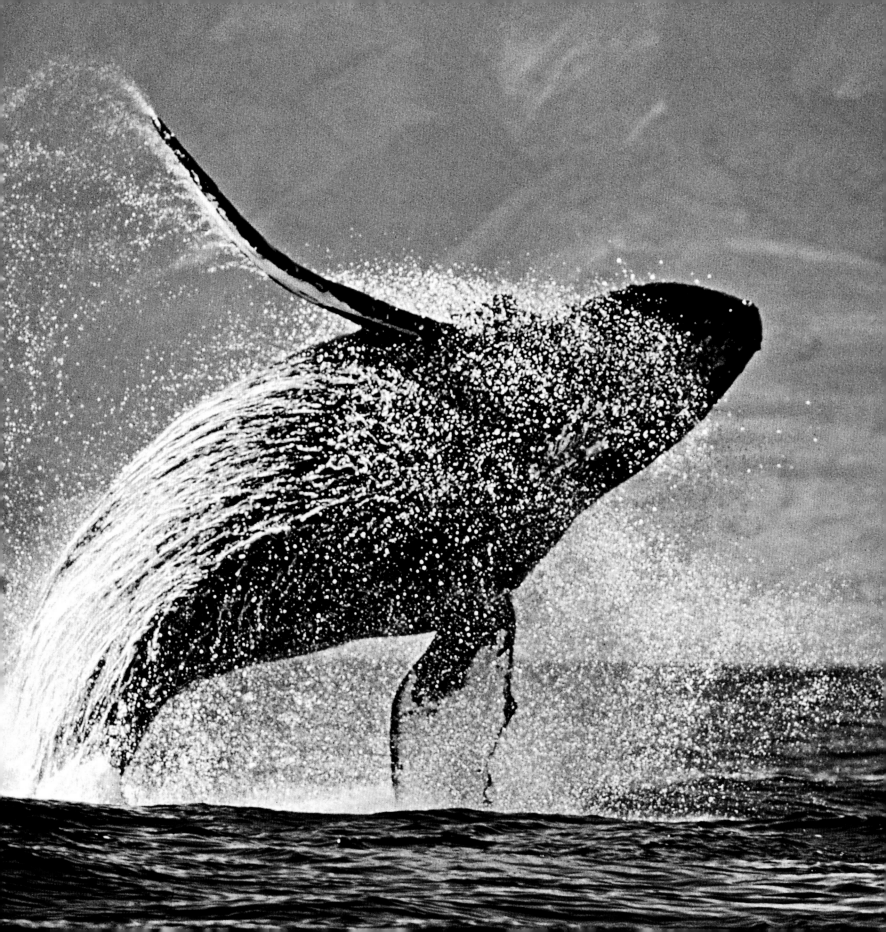

568 and 569 ● Atlantic Ocean - Killer whales off the coasts of Norway.

570-571 ● Pacific Ocean, Australia - Whale shark at Ningaloo Reef.

572-573 ● Pacific Ocean, Great Barrier Reef (Australia) - Whale shark.

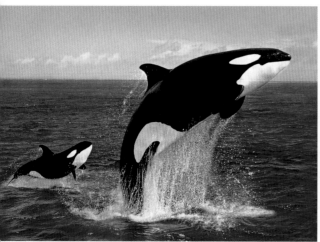 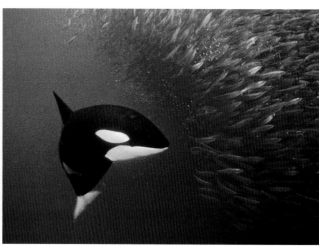

" HITHER, AND THITHER, ON HIGH, GLIDED THE SNOW-WHITE WINGS OF SMALL, UNSPECKLED BIRDS; THESE WERE THE GENTLE THOUGHTS OF THE FEMININE AIR; BUT TO AND FRO IN THE DEEPS, FAR DOWN IN THE BOTTOMLESS BLUE, RUSHED MIGHTY LEVIATHANS, SWORD-FISH, AND SHARKS; AND THESE WERE THE STRONG, TROUBLED, MURDEROUS THINKINGS OF THE MASCULINE SEA. "

from MOBY DICK *by Herman Melville*

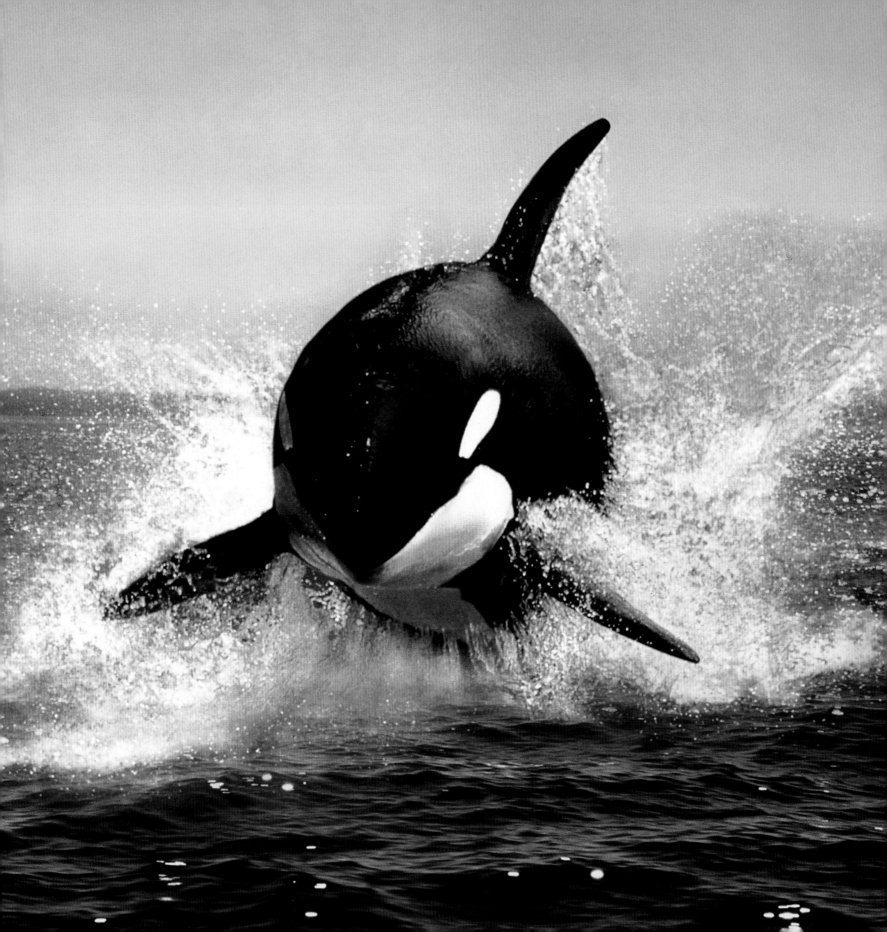

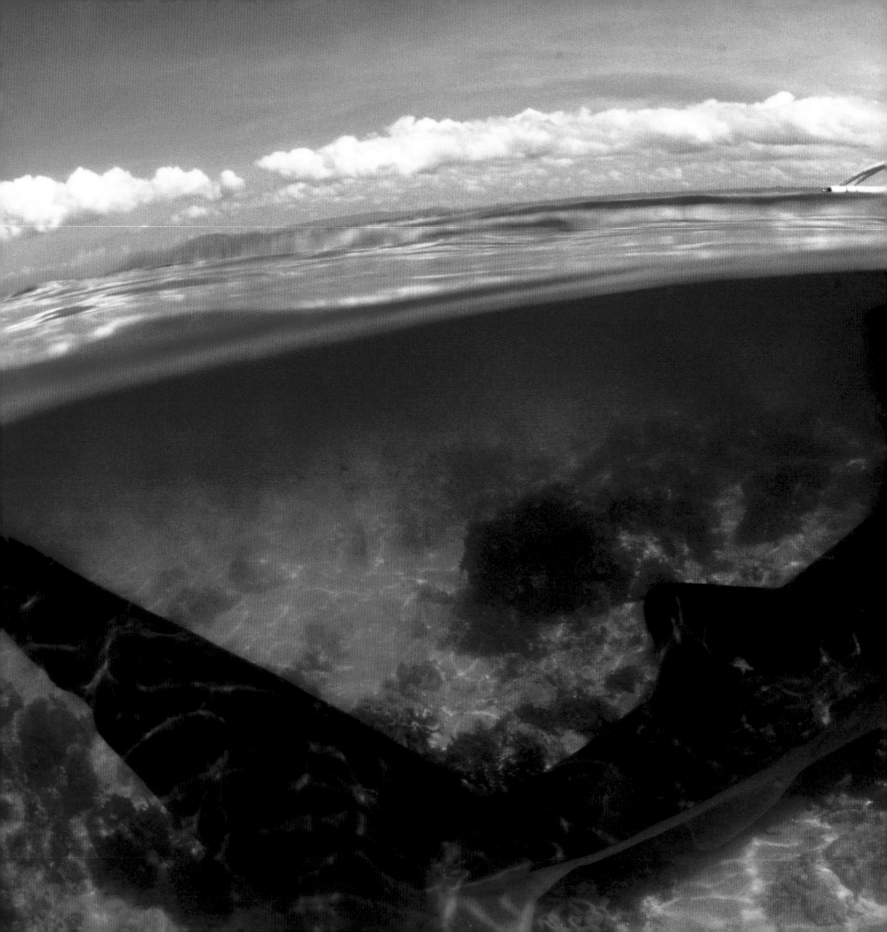

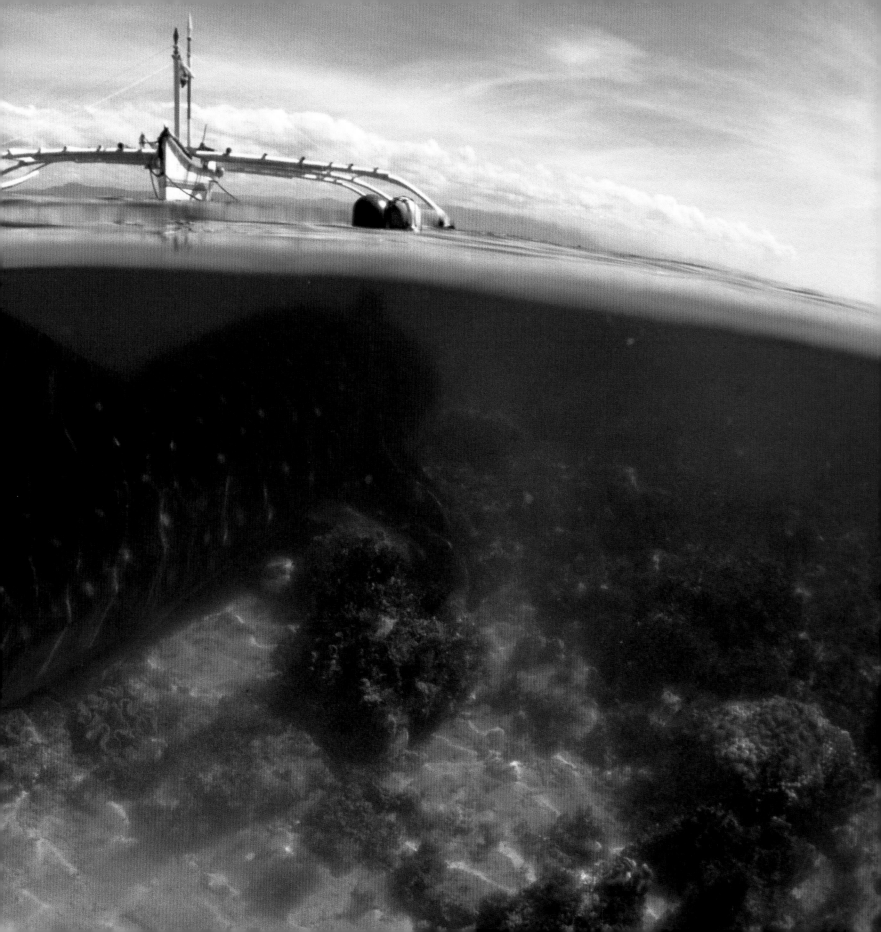

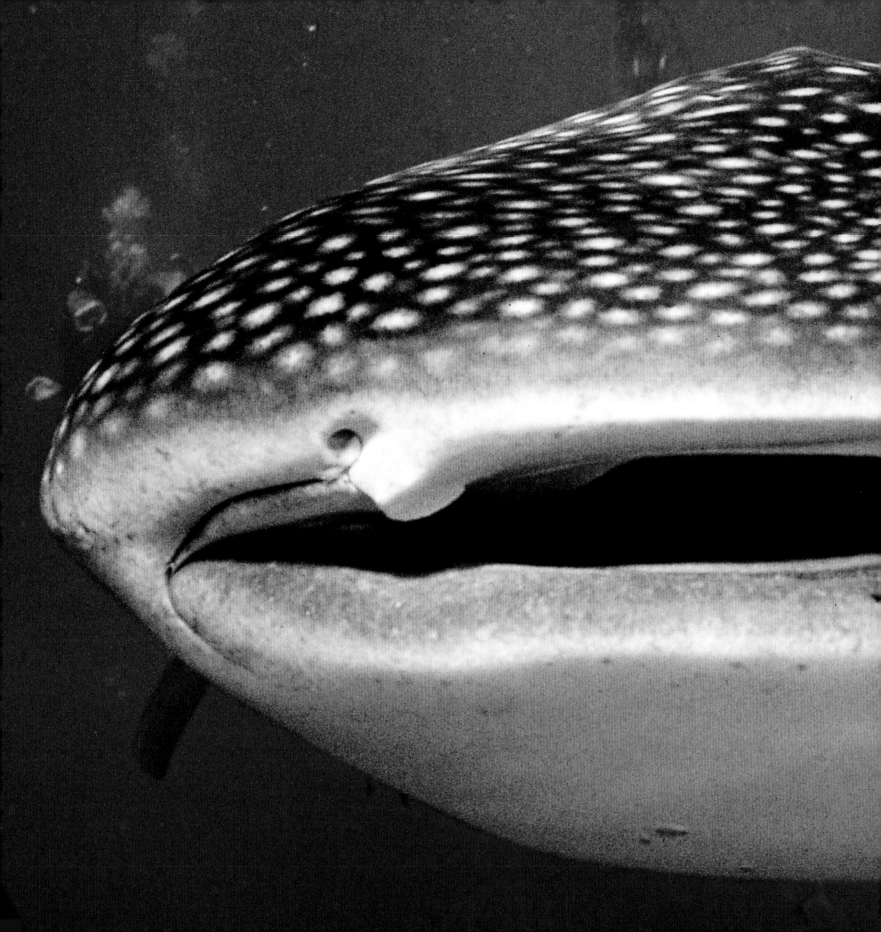

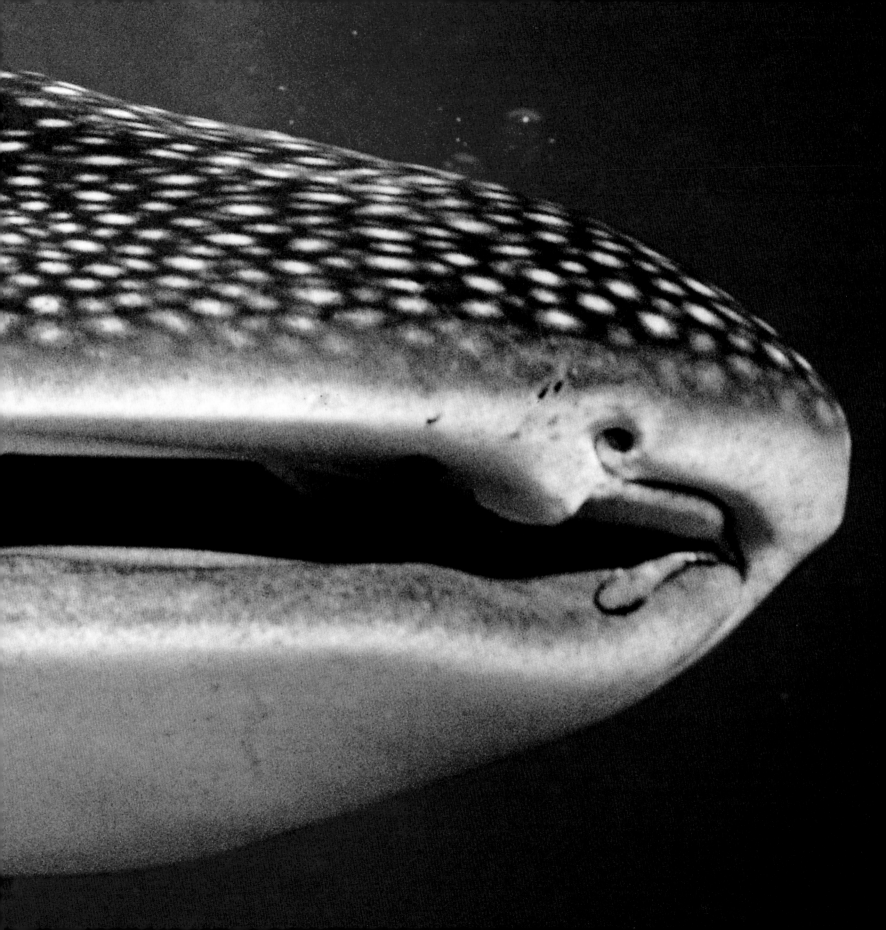

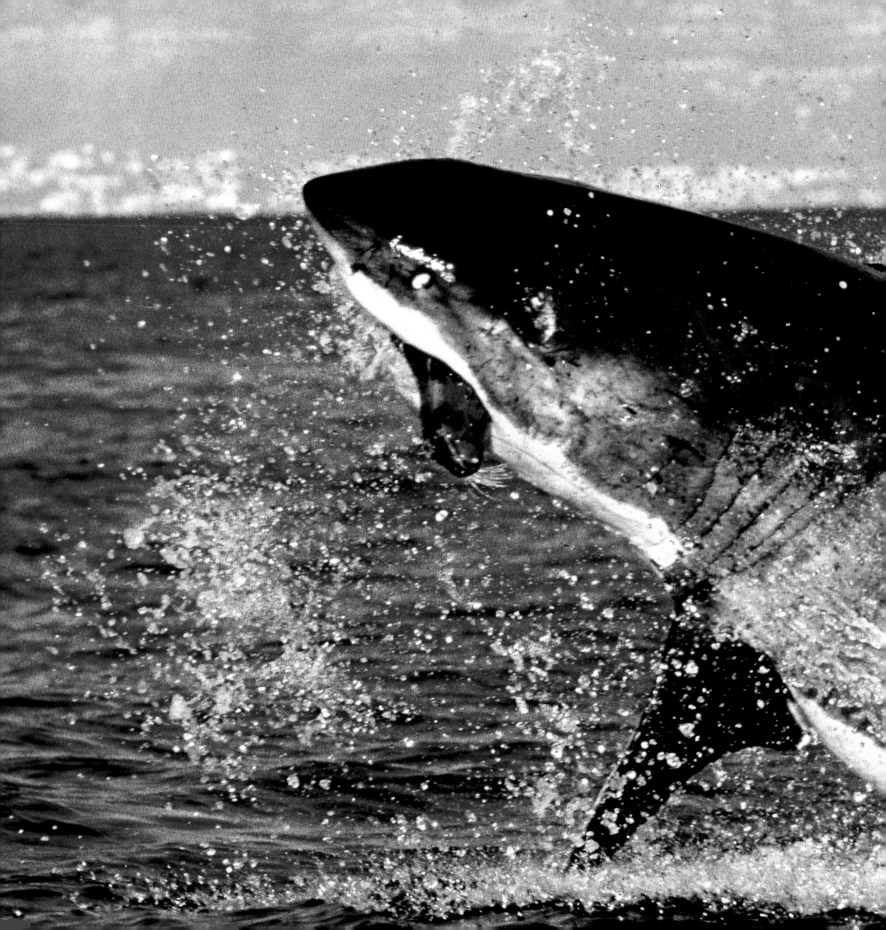

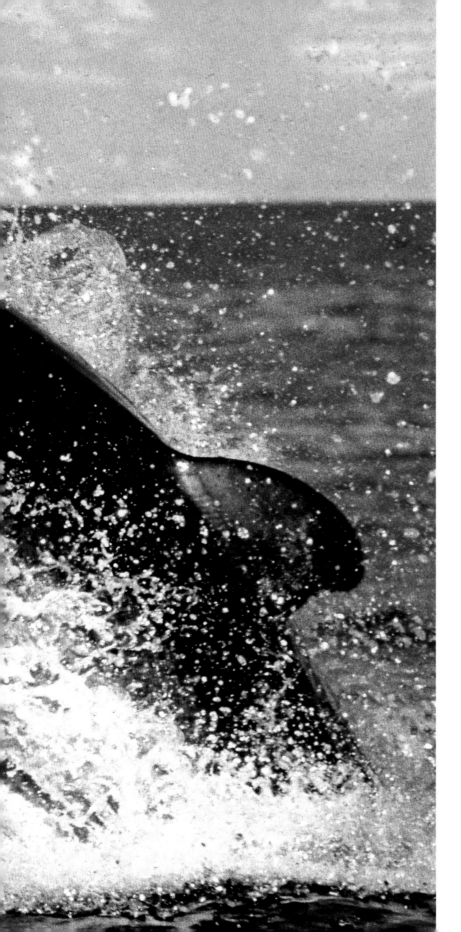

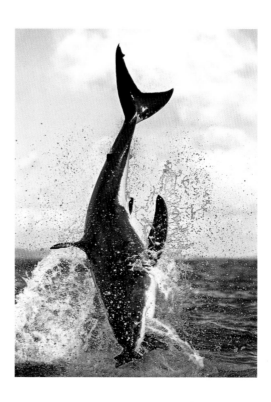

● Indian Ocean, South Africa
- White shark.

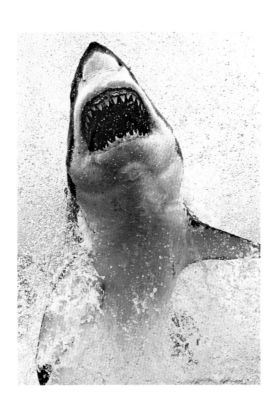

● Southern Atlantic Ocean,
South Africa - White shark in False Bay,
near Cape Town.

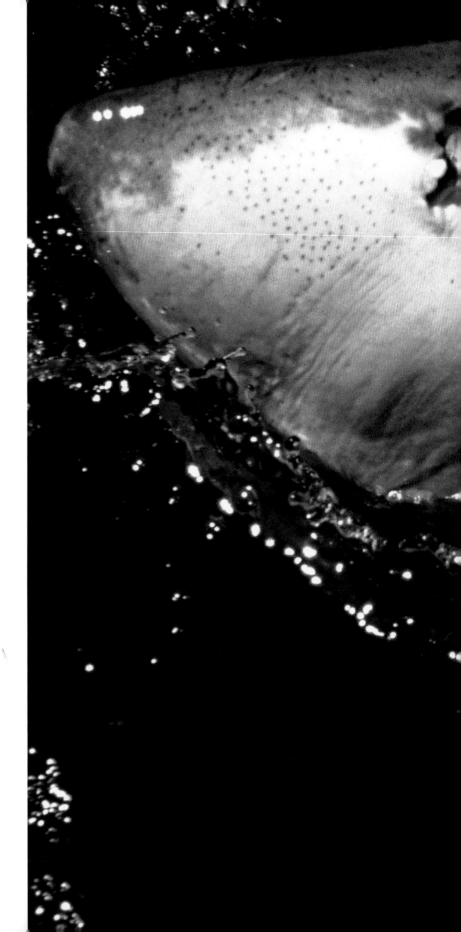

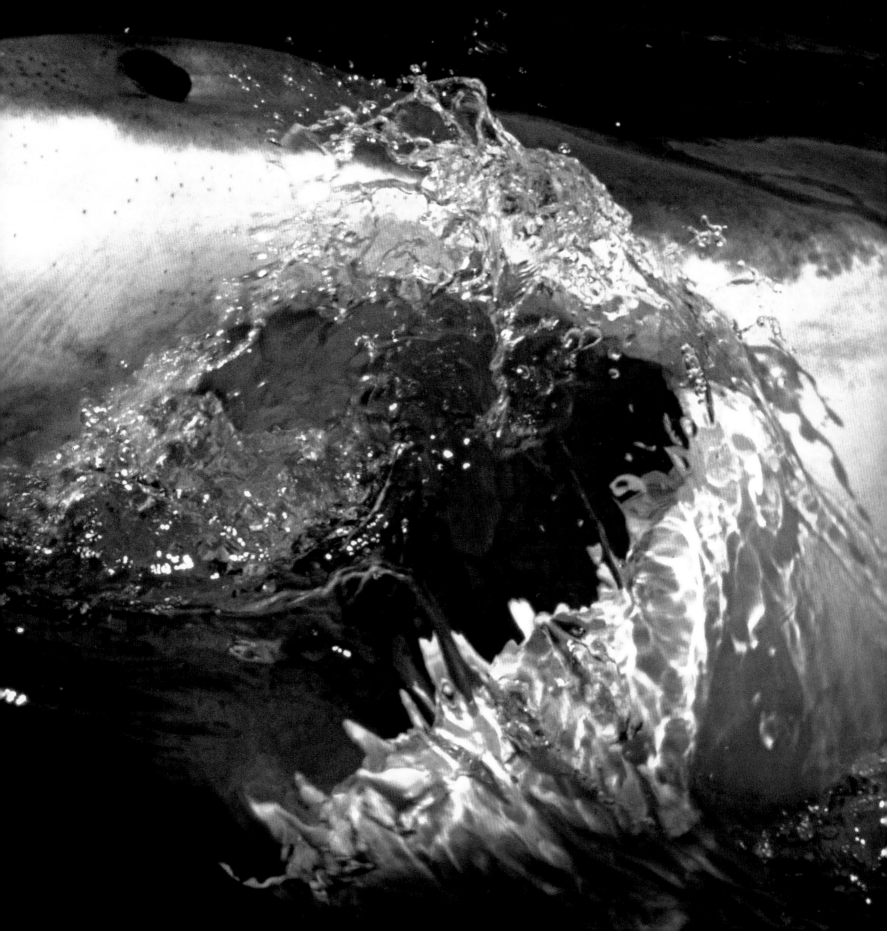

"HE REDOUBLED HIS EFFORTS AND SWAM AS HARD AS HE COULD TOWARD THE WHITE ROCK. HE WAS ALMOST HALFWAY OVER, WHEN SUDDENLY A HORRIBLE SEA MONSTER STUCK ITS HEAD OUT OF THE WATER, AN ENORMOUS HEAD WITH A HUGE MOUTH, WIDE OPEN, SHOWING THREE ROWS OF GLEAMING TEETH, THE MERE SIGHT OF WHICH WOULD HAVE FILLED YOU WITH FEAR."

from PINOCCHIO
by Carlo Collodi

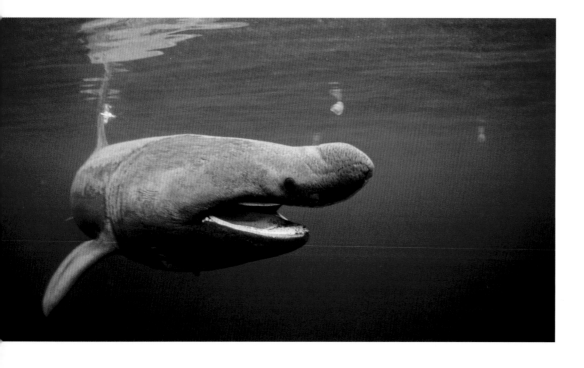

578 ● Atlantic Ocean, Isle of Man (Great Britain) - Elephant shark.

579 ● Pacific Ocean, California (USA) - Elephant shark.

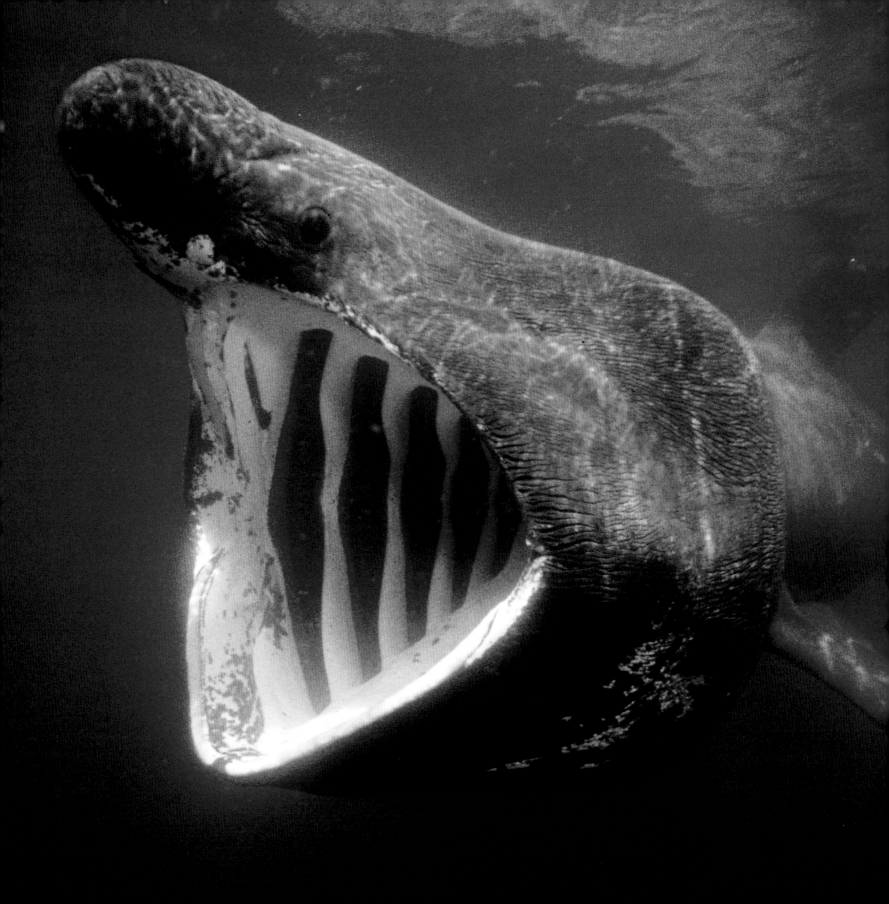

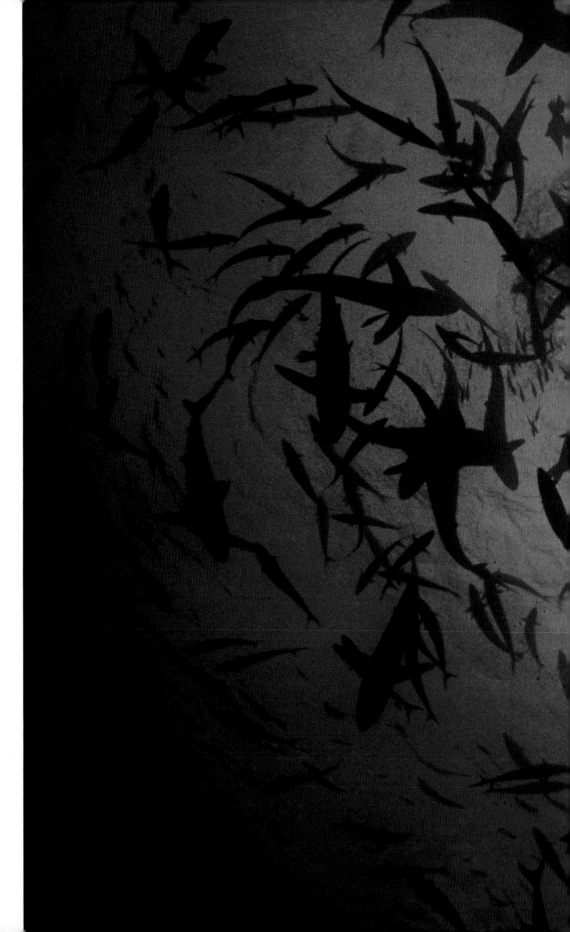

Feeding
frenzy

● Pacific Ocean, Costa Rica
- Silky sharks off Cocos
Island.

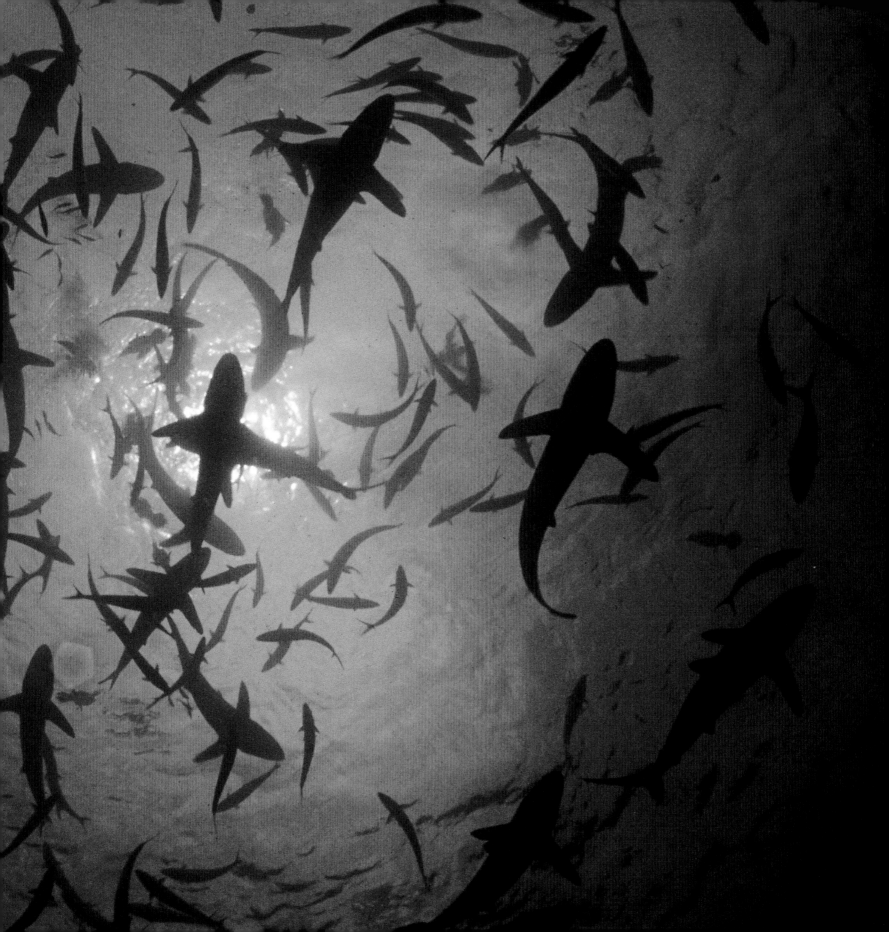

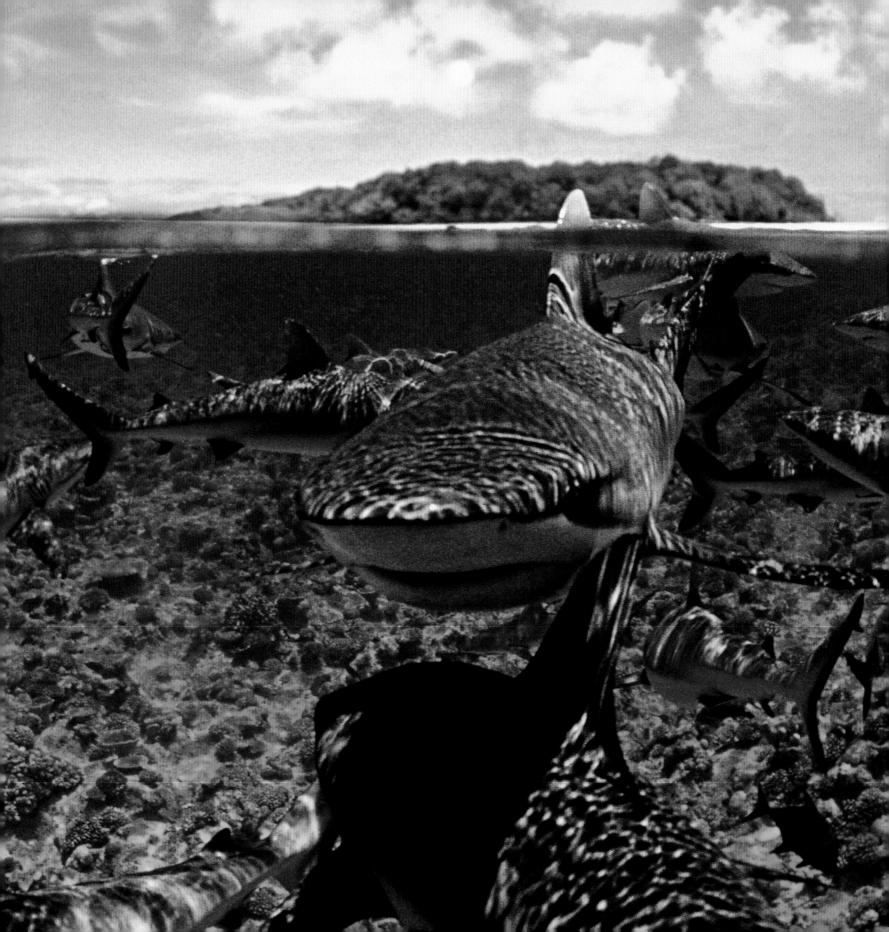

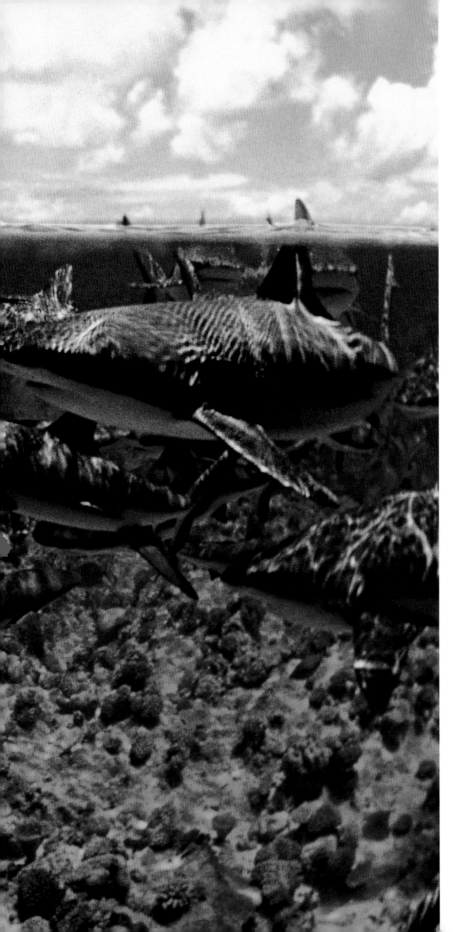

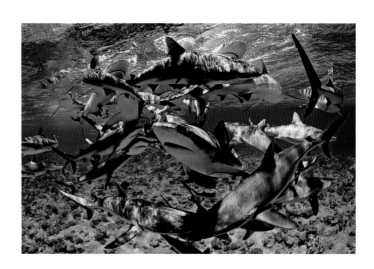

● Pacific Ocean, Marshall Islands (USA) -
Gray reef sharks near Bikini Atoll.

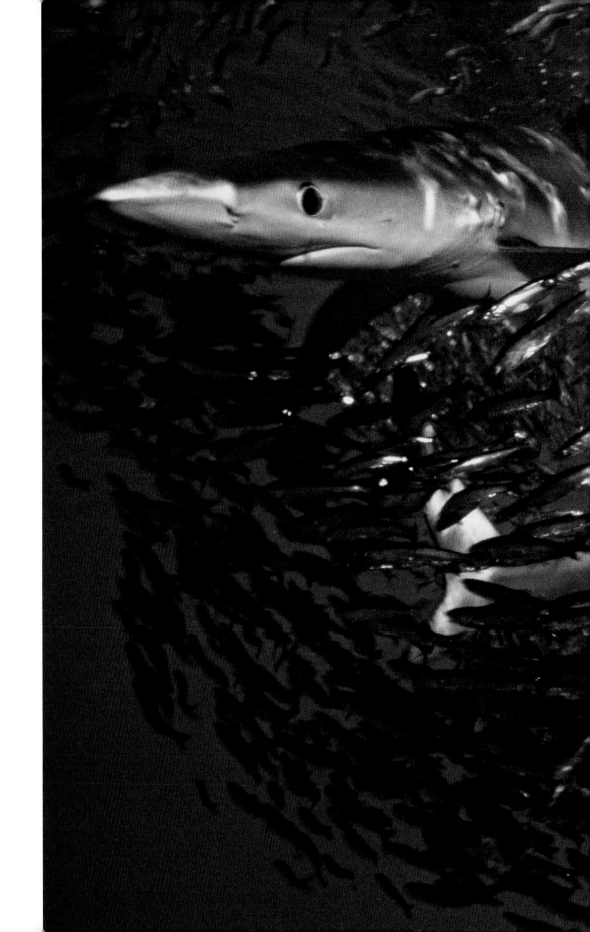

● Pacific Ocean, California (USA) - Blue sharks near San Diego.

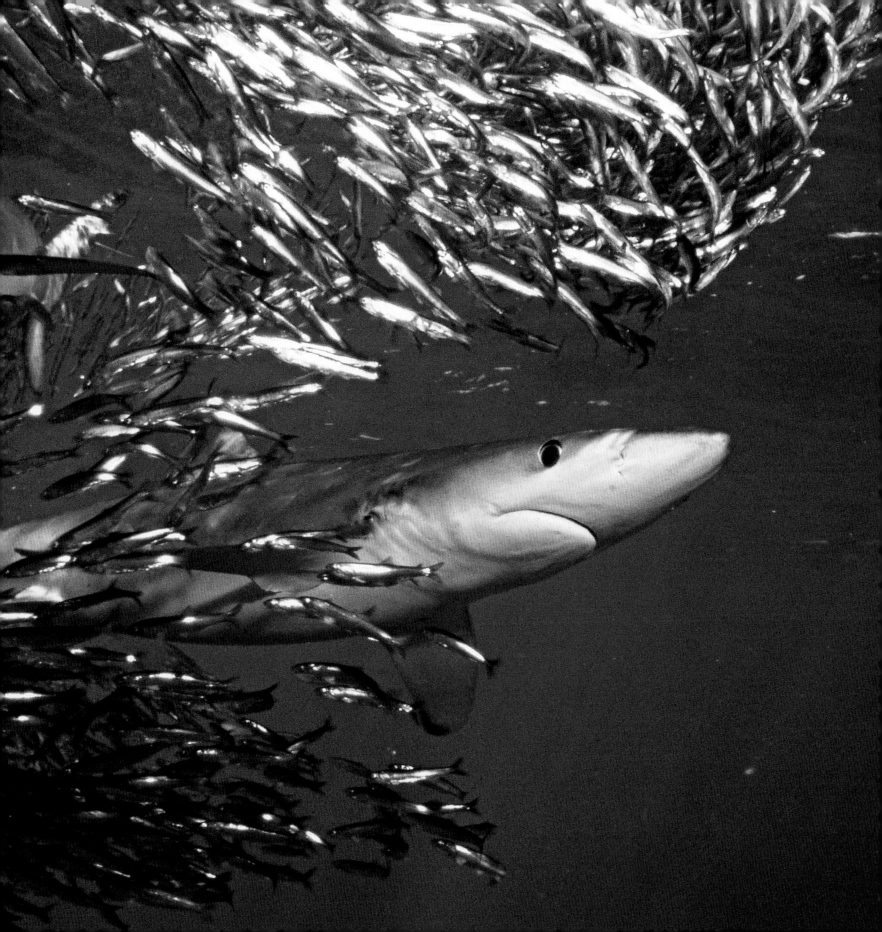

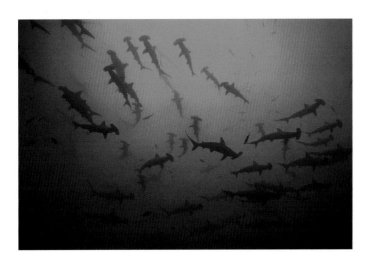

586 ● Pacific Ocean, Costa Rica -
Hammerhead sharks off Cocos Island.

586-587 ● Sargasso Sea, Bahamas -
Hammerhead shark.

588-589 ● Atlantic Ocean, North Carolina
(USA) - Sand tiger shark.

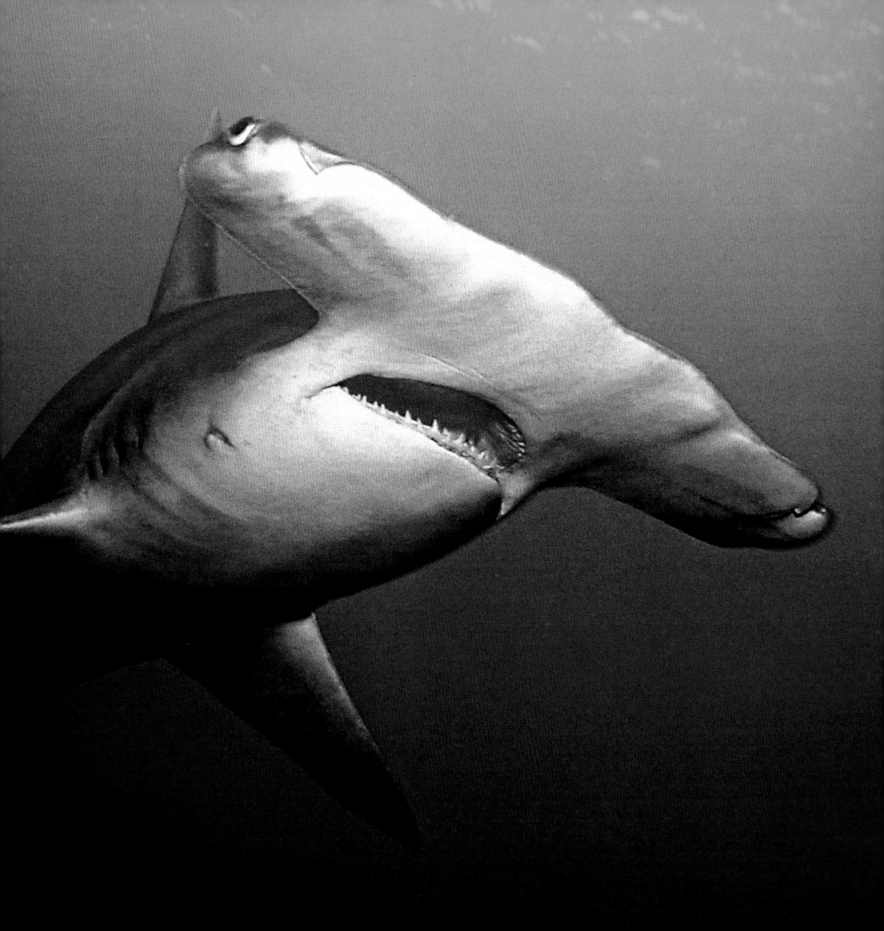

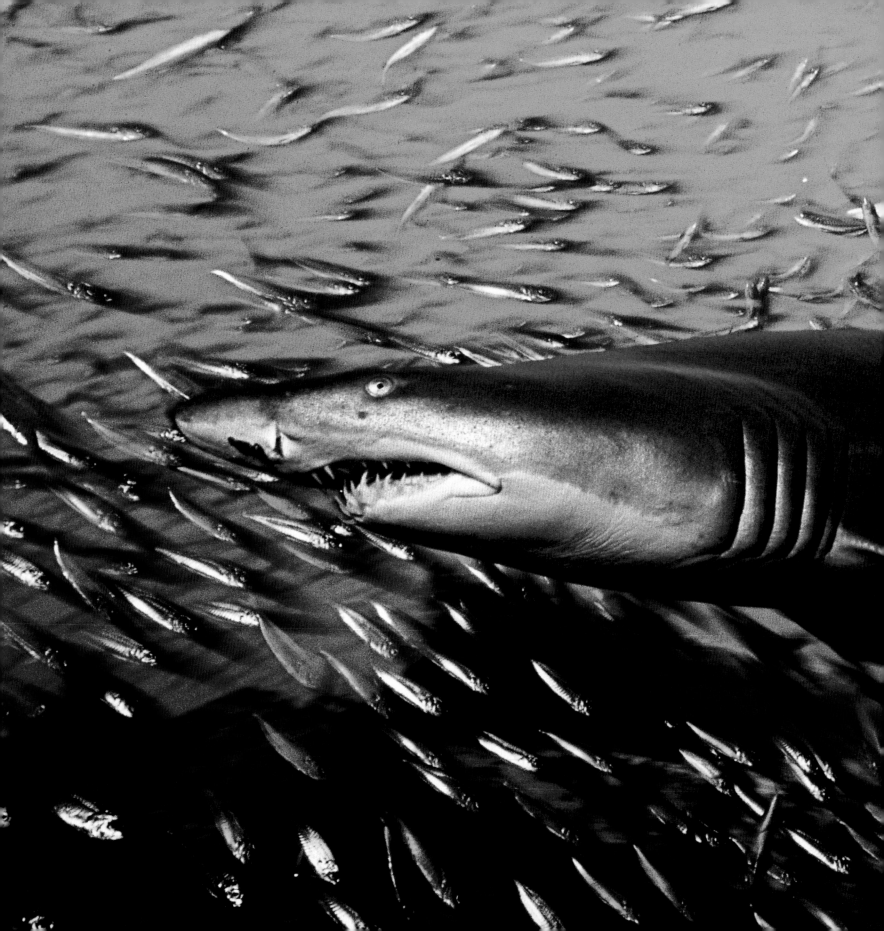

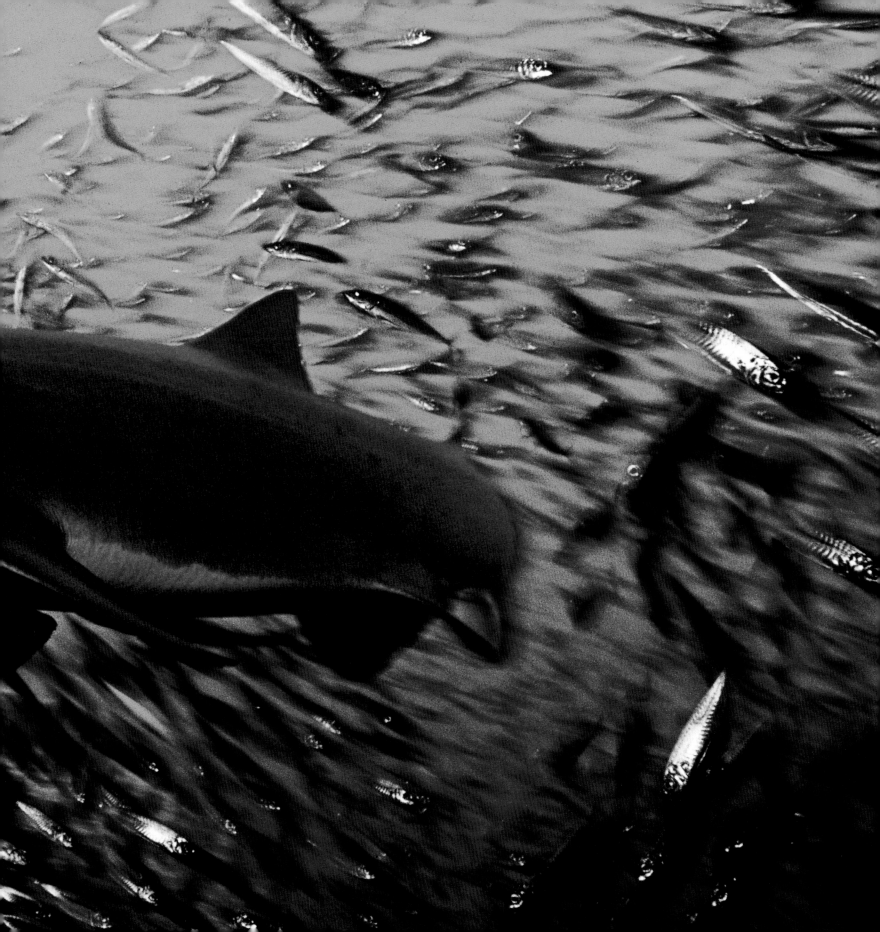

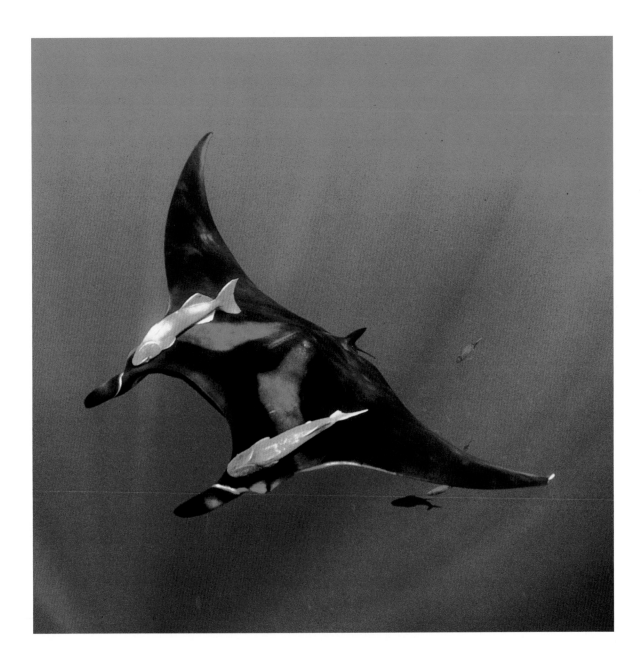

590 and 591 ● Gulf of Mexico, Mexico - Giant mantas off Socorro Island.

592-593 ● Pacific Ocean, Big Island (Hawaii) - Giant manta near Kona.

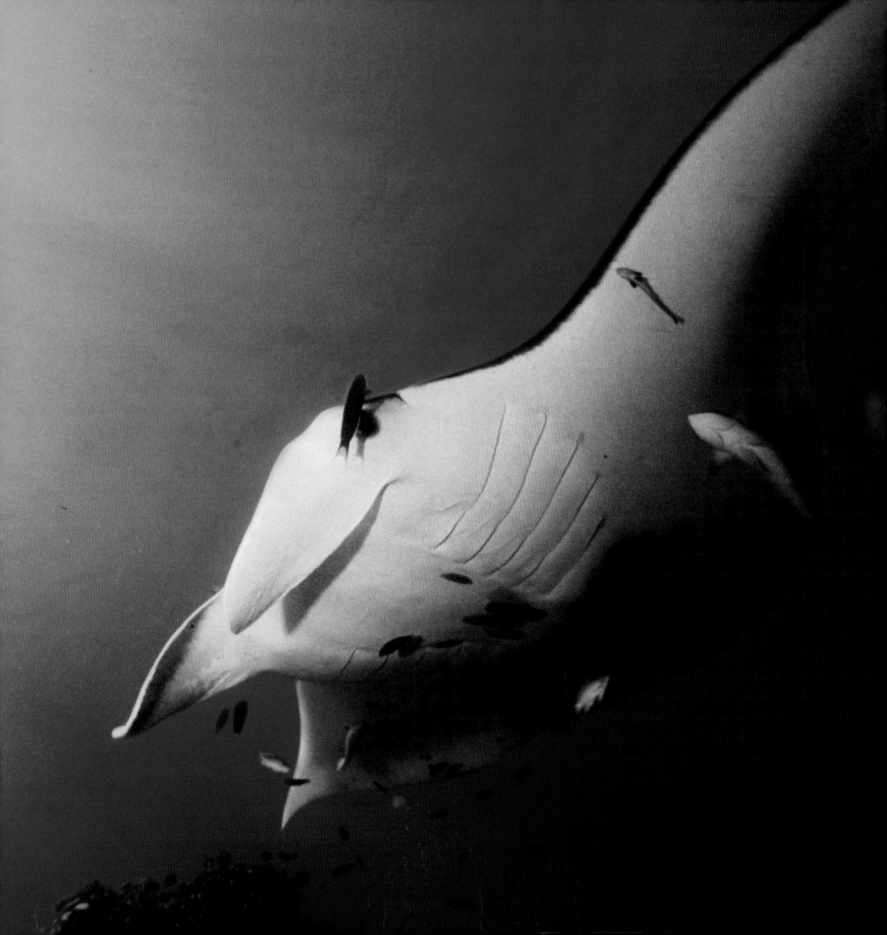

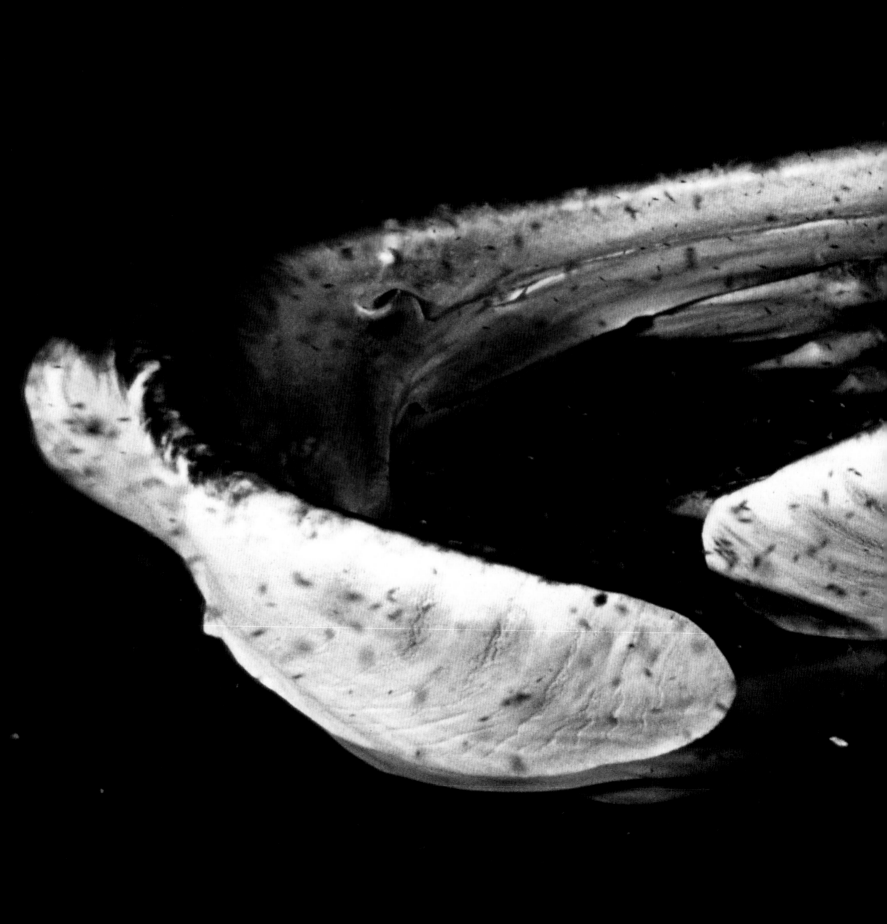

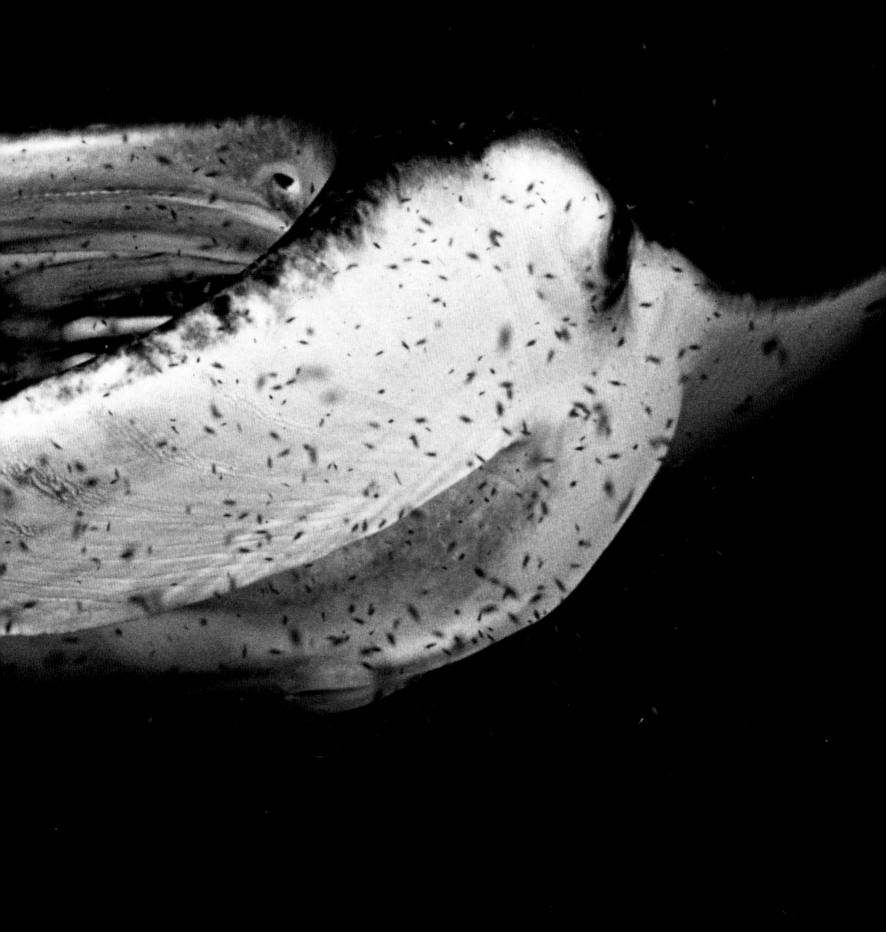

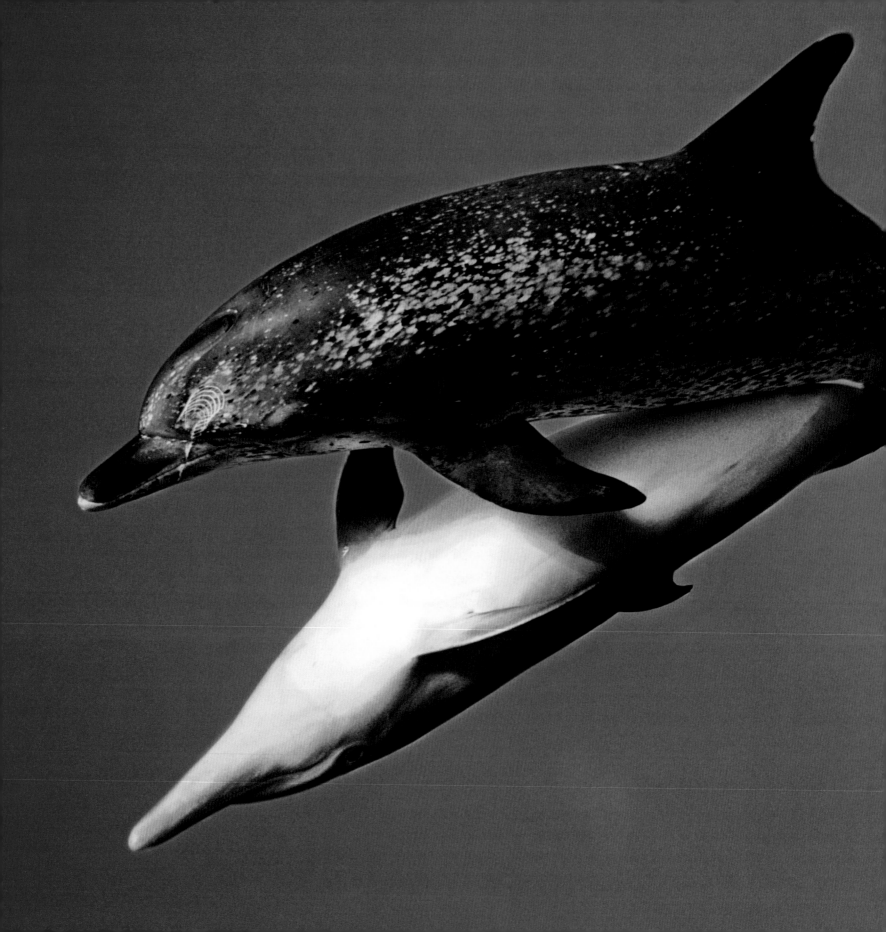

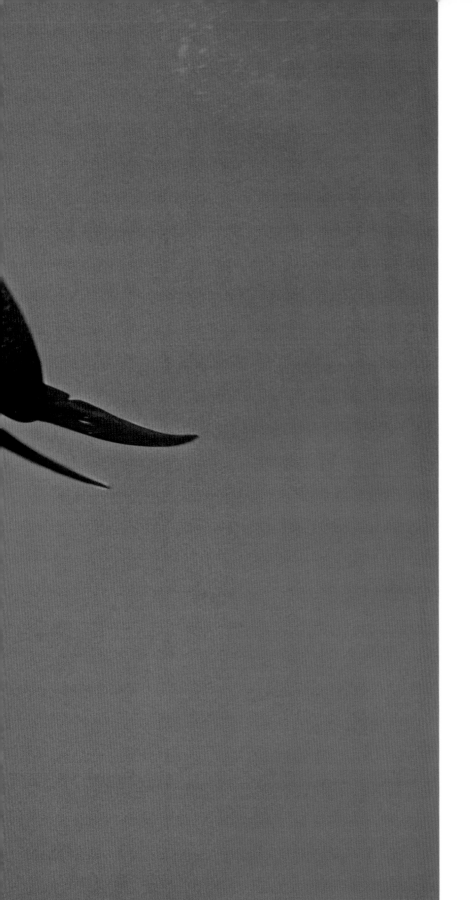

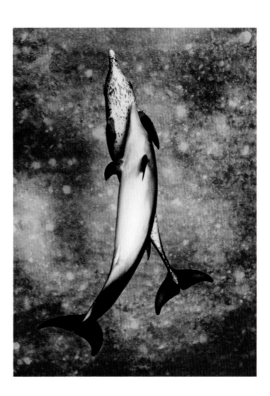

Sargasso Sea, Little Bahama Bank -
Spotted dolphins.

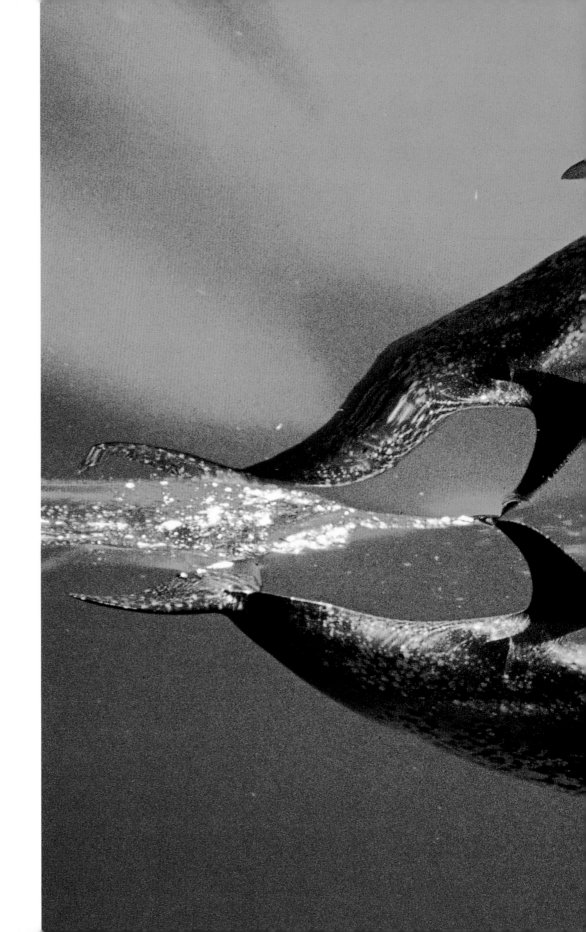

Sargasso Sea, Bahamas
- Spotted dolphins.

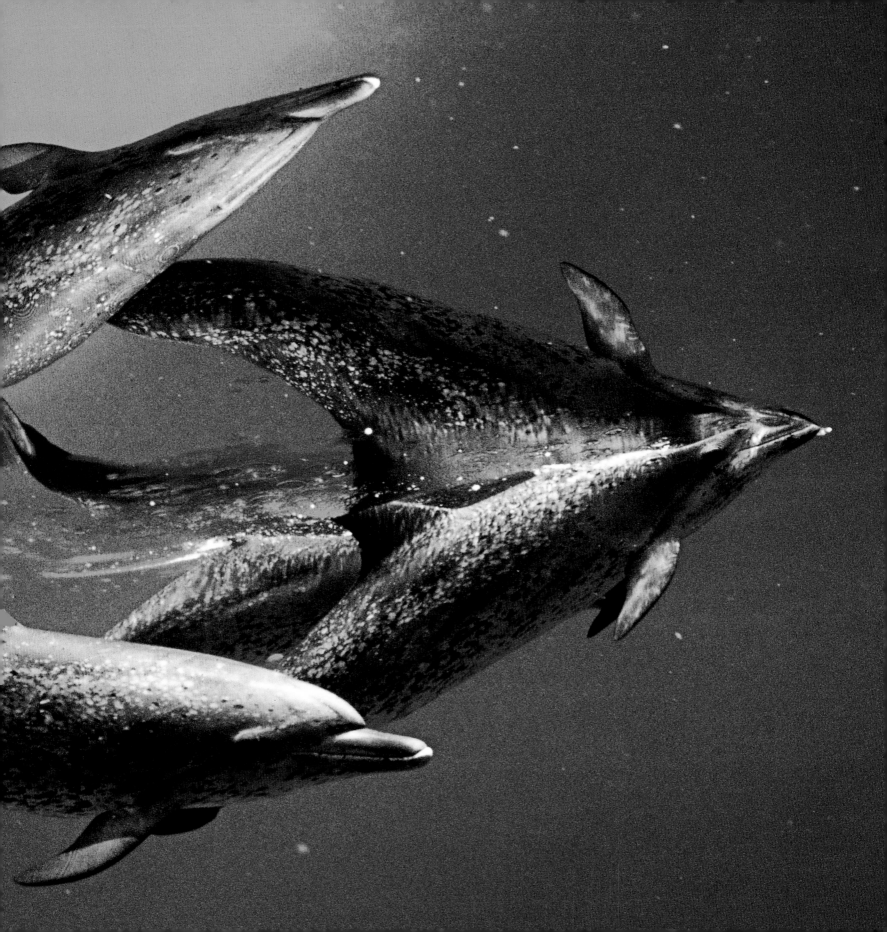

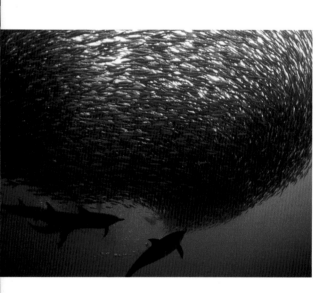

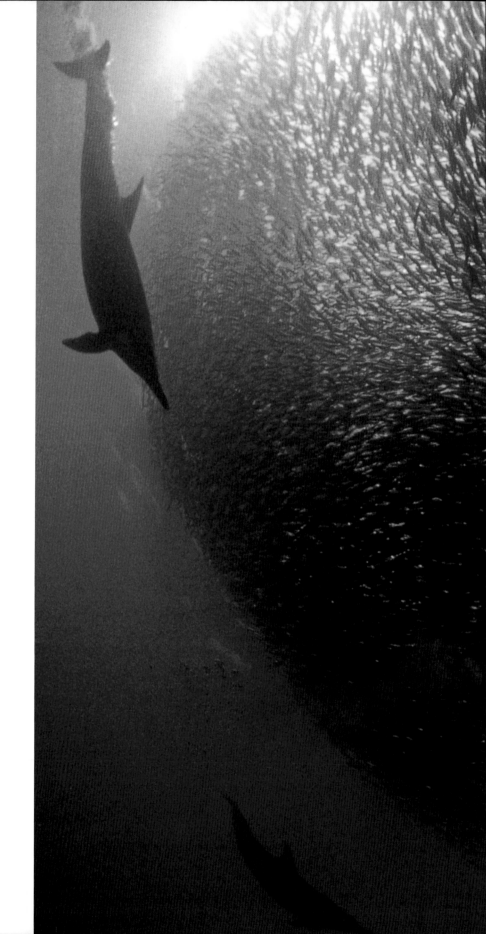

598 and 598-599 ● Indian Ocean,
South Africa - Common dolphins.

600-601 ● Red Sea, Egypt -
Bottle-nosed dolphins.

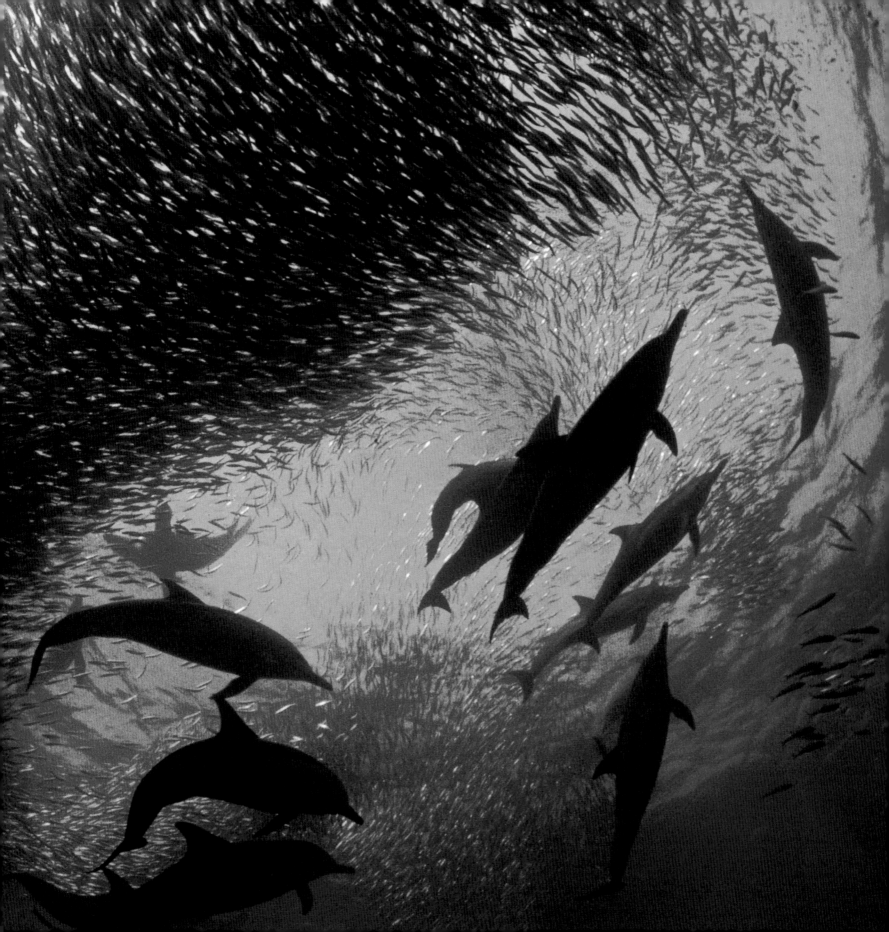

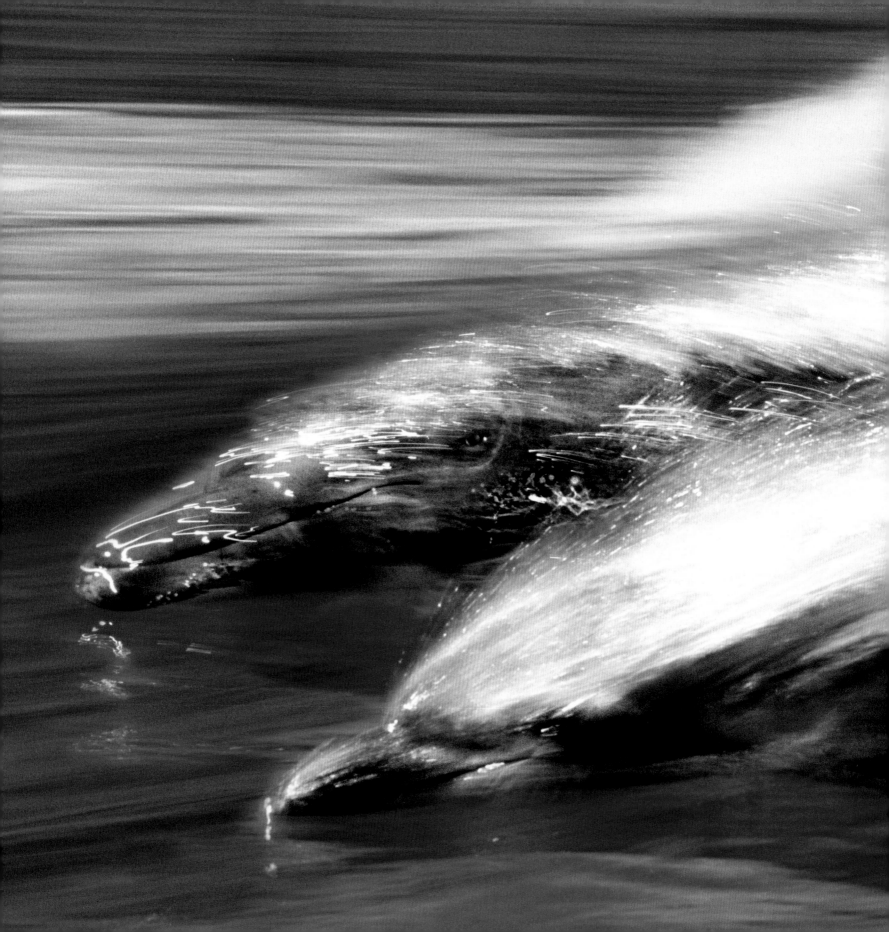

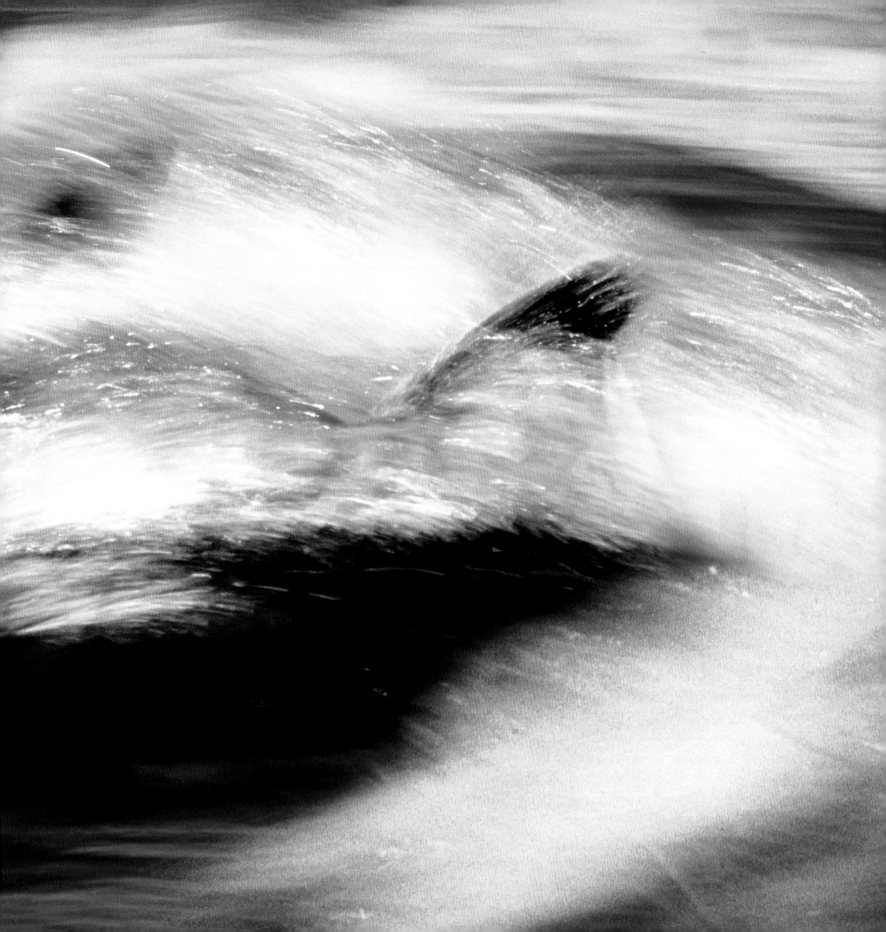

UNDERWATER HISTORY

GAETANO CAFIERO

• Atlantic Ocean, Newfoundland (Canada) - The *Titanic*.

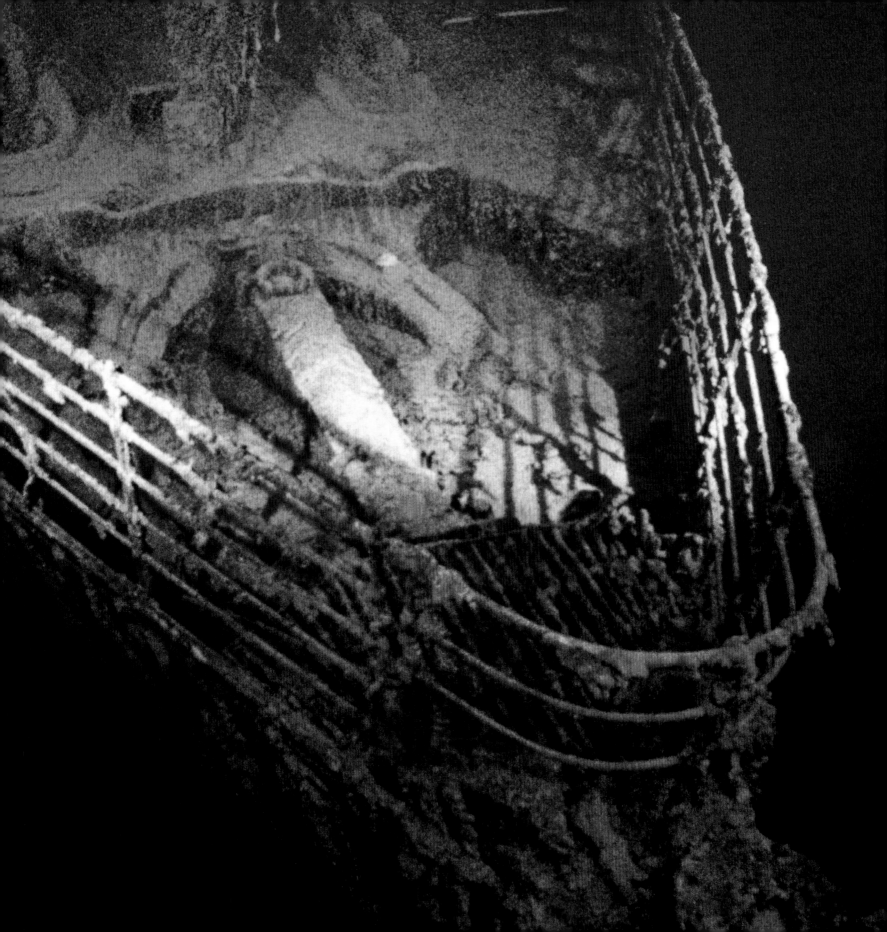

INTRODUCTION Underwater History

"Roll on, thou deep and dark blue ocean – roll!

Ten thousand fleets sweep over thee in vain; man marks

the earth with ruin – his control stops with the shore."

So wrote Lord Byron almost two hundred years ago.

And it's true, man does not leave indelible marks on the

immense body of the ocean: the most powerful ships are

no more than pinheads on the immeasurable mass of

water. When they sink, they may disappear into abysses

miles deep. Thus the ocean has become a witness – mute

but incapable of falsehood – to terrestrial history, a

chest of tangible proofs – produced by art and knowl-

EDGE – OF THE TUMULTUOUS PROGRESS OF CIVILIZATION. THE

REMAINS OF WRECKS, ANCIENT PORTS AND OTHER RUINS ARE

NOW ACCESSIBLE TO MAN, IF NOT DIRECTLY THEN THROUGH HIS

MACHINES, WHICH CAN SHOW US THEIR STATE OF PRESERVATION,

PHOTOGRAPH AND FILM THEM. SINCE PROGRESS HAS FREED US

FROM THE DIVER'S AIR PIPE AND WE HAVE BEEN ABLE TO

BREATHE UNDERWATER UNCONNECTED WITH THE SURFACE, WE

HAVE BEEN ABLE TO OBSERVE NATURE BENEATH THE WAVES AS

FAR AS THE SUNLIGHT REACHES. EXPLORING THE WRECK OF A

SUNKEN SHIP OR A FALLEN PLANE CAN BRING FORTH EMOTIONS

THAT ARE DIFFICULT TO PUT INTO WORDS: THE ANXIETY FELT

Underwater History

Introduction

BEFORE THE DIVE, THE REVERENCE TOWARD THE HISTORY, POS-SIBLY DRAMATIC, OF THE WRECK TO BE EXPLORED. THEN, EACH TIME YOU DESCEND TOWARD THE REMAINS, HOWEVER WELL IT IS KNOWN, THERE IS A MOMENT OF PURE MAGIC: AS YOU GO DOWN, WITH THE ONLY SOUND BEING THE RELEASE OF THE BUBBLES, THE DARK OUTLINE OF THE WRECK SLOWLY BECOMES APPARENT IN THE DARKNESS. ITS FORMS BEGIN TO TAKE SHAPE AND YOU RECOGNIZE VARIOUS PARTS: STRUCTURES AND PILES OF TWISTED WRECKAGE ON THE BRIDGE OR THE SEABED. YOU FIN DOWN TOWARD THE MASS IN THE CERTAIN KNOWLEDGE YOU ARE ABOUT TO MAKE IMPORTANT DISCOVERIES. BROKEN SHEETS OF

Underwater History

METAL HAVE BECOME PART OF THE SEABED ITSELF AND PROVIDE A HABITAT TO THOUSANDS OF LIVING CREATURES, FROM LARGE FISH TO TINY INVERTEBRATES. THEY ABSORB THE WRECK AND TURN IT INTO A REFUGE. THE INVASION OF LIVING ORGANISMS THAT ENCRUST THE SURFACES HAS TRANSFORMED WHAT WAS A HUMAN ENVIRONMENT INTO THEIR OWN. SOME OF THE SPANISH SHIPS THAT SANK IN THE CARIBBEAN ARE NO LONGER VISIBLE, THEIR WOOD HAS BEEN DEVOURED, THE IRON, SILVER AND GOLD THAT THEY CARRIED HAVE BEEN LOCKED IN INACCESSIBLE MAR-BLE FORTS BY THE INCESSANT CONSTRUCTION WORK OF MIL-LIONS OF CORAL POLYPS.

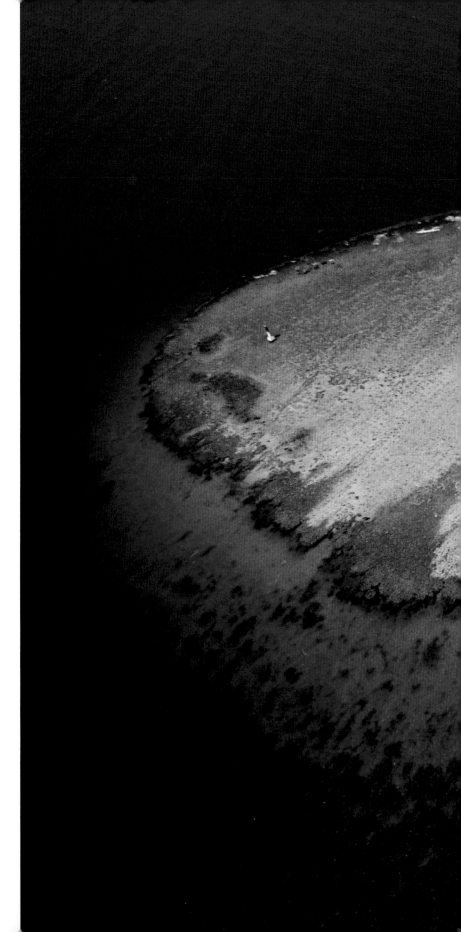

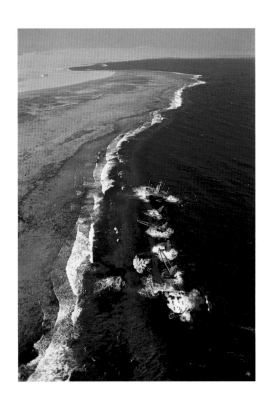

608 ● Red Sea, Nabq oasis (Egypt) - The merchant ship *Hedoromo Million Hope*.

608-609 ● Red Sea, Gordon Reef (Egypt) - The merchant ship *Louilla*.

610-611 ● Atlantic Ocean, Skeleton Coast (Namibia) - The *Dunedin Star*.

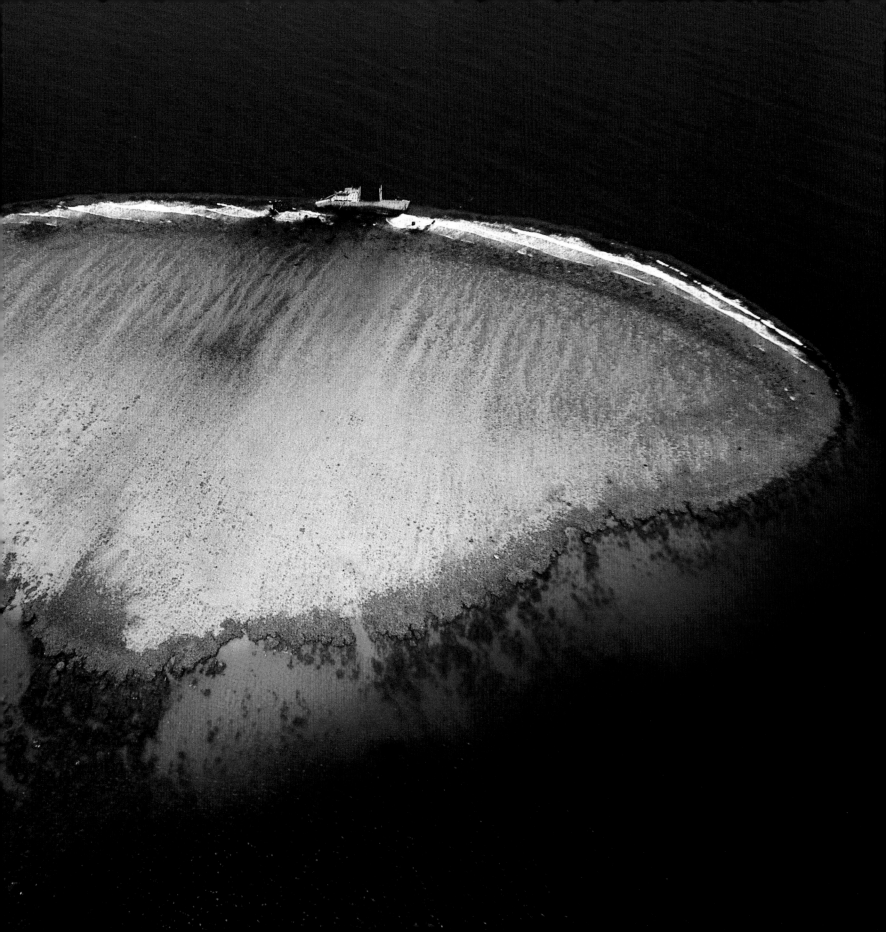

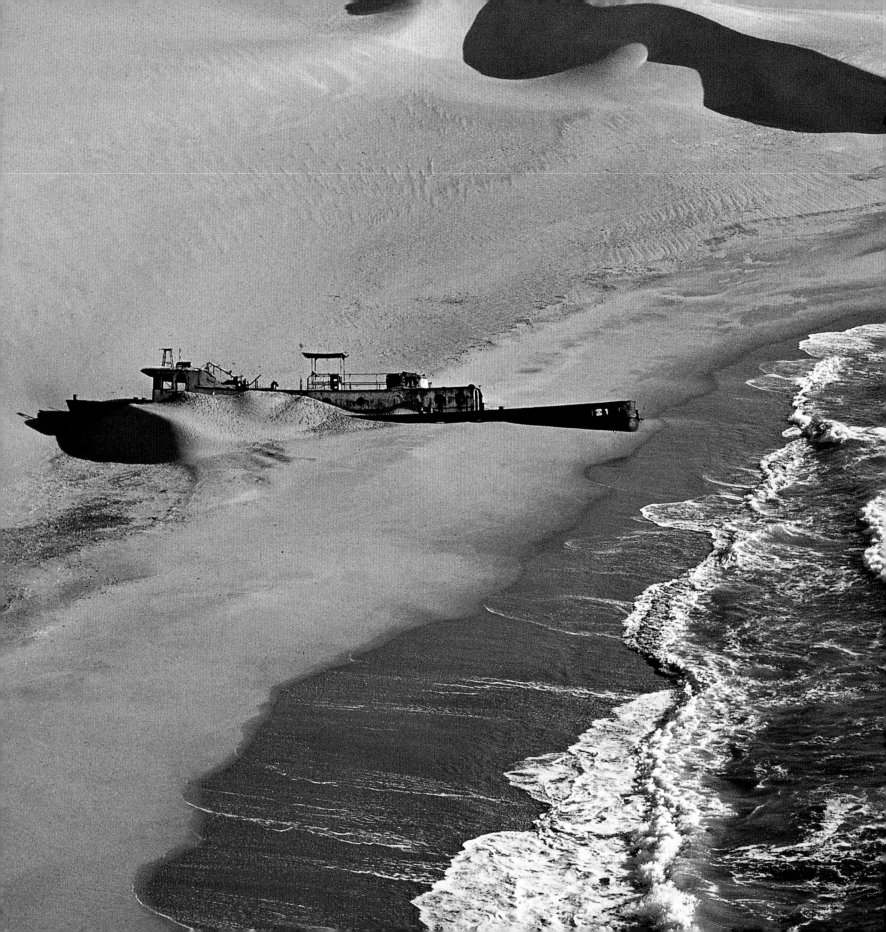

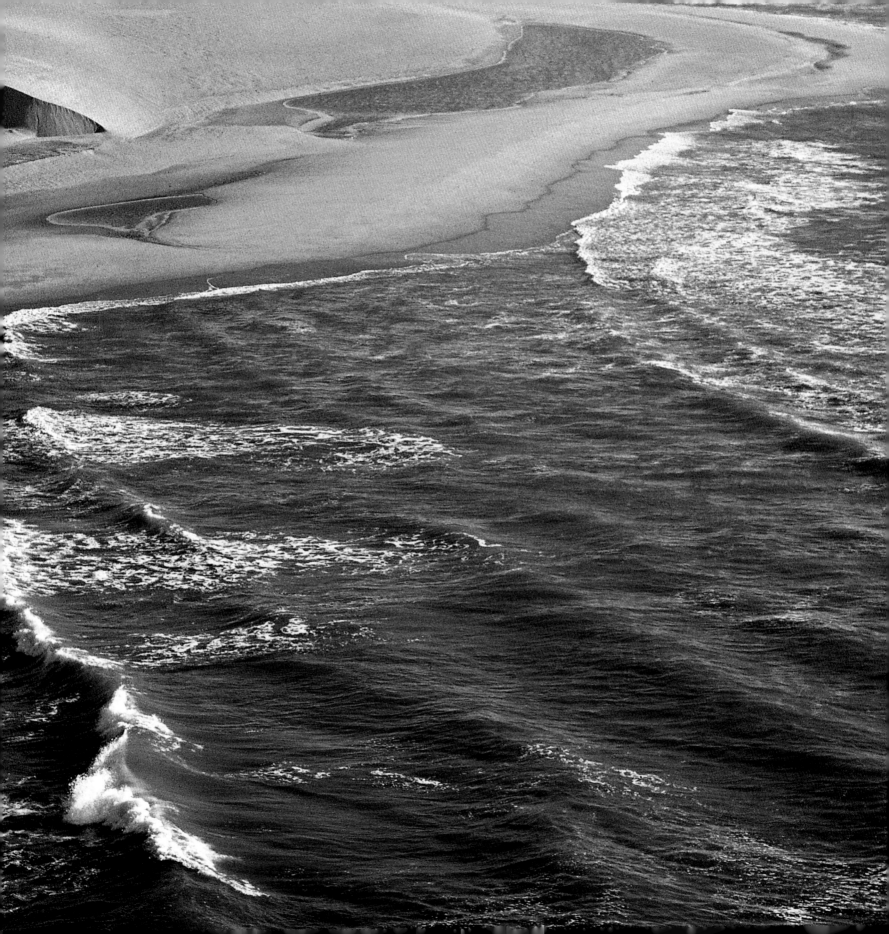

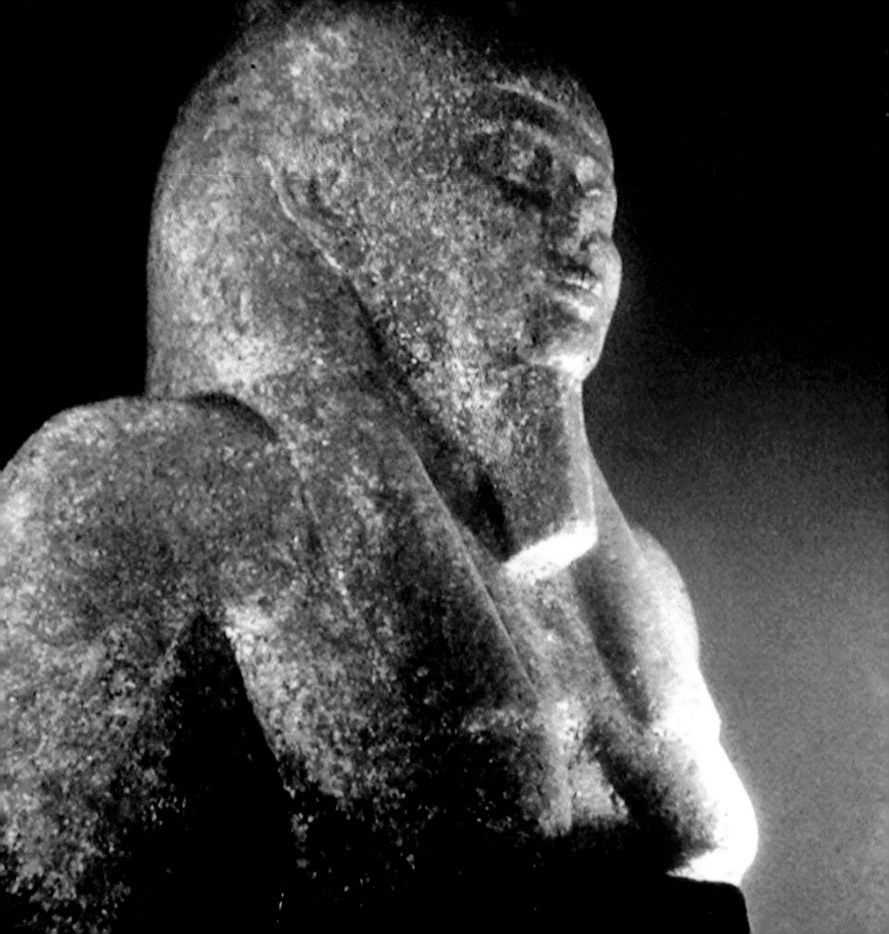

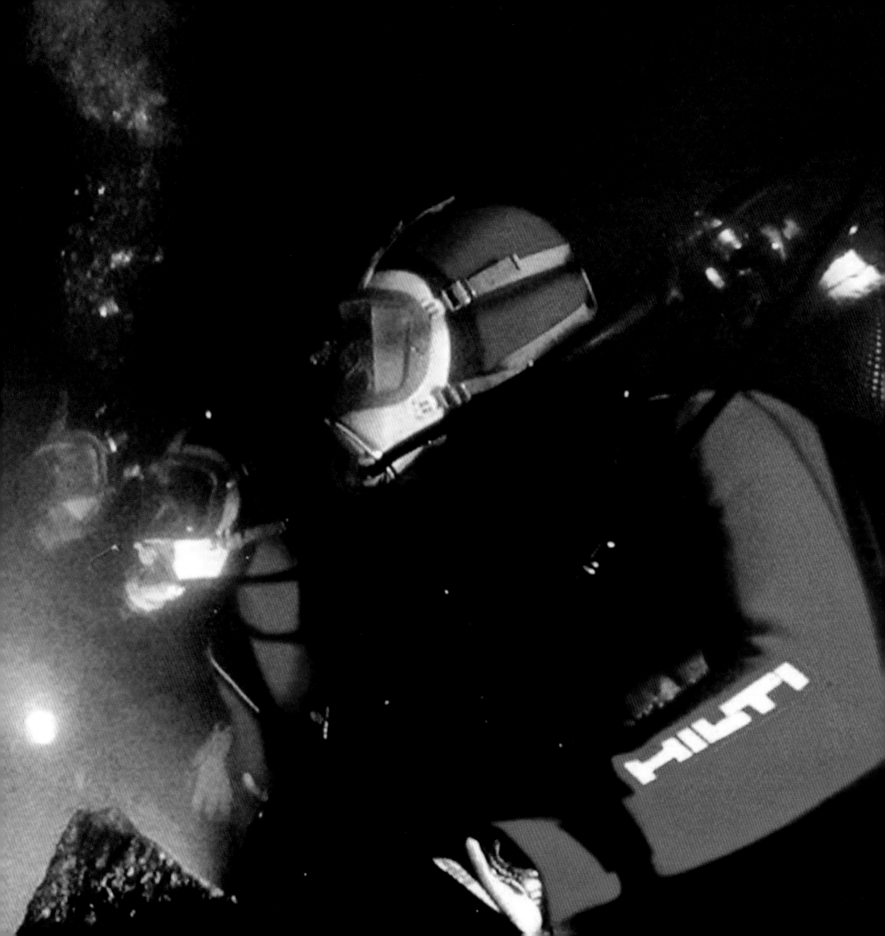

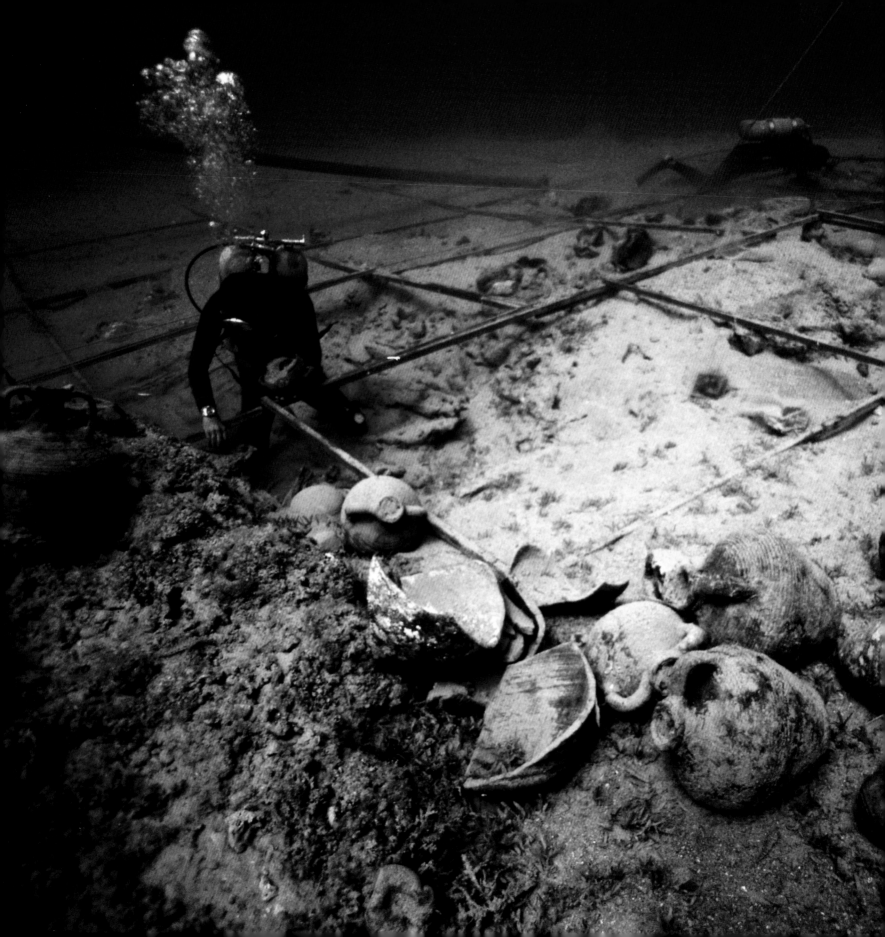

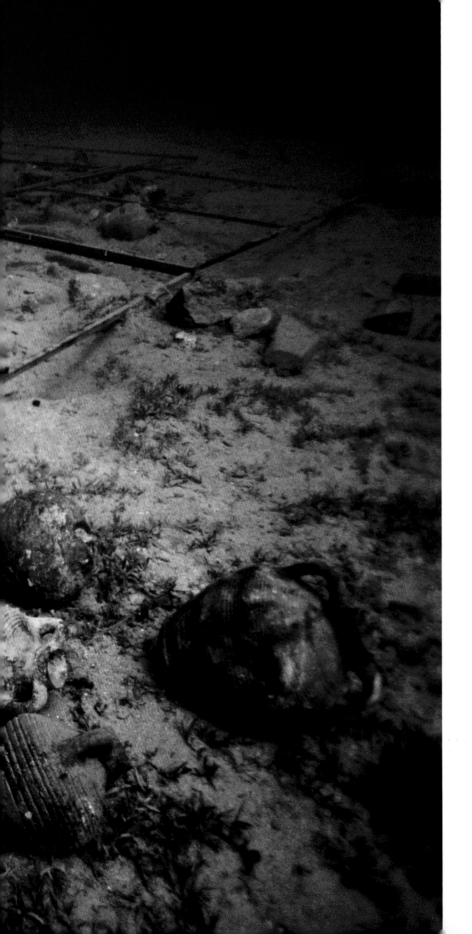

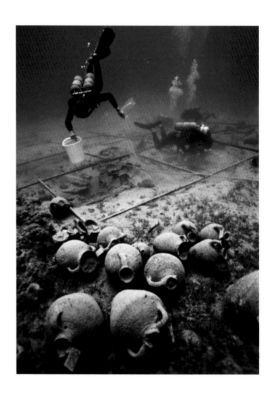

612-613 ● Mediterranean Sea, Alexandria (Egypt) - Port of Heraklion, statue of Hapi.

614-615 and 615 ● Aegean Sea, Serce Limani Bay (Turkey) - The wreck of an ancient ship carrying storage jars, now named the *Glass Wreck*.

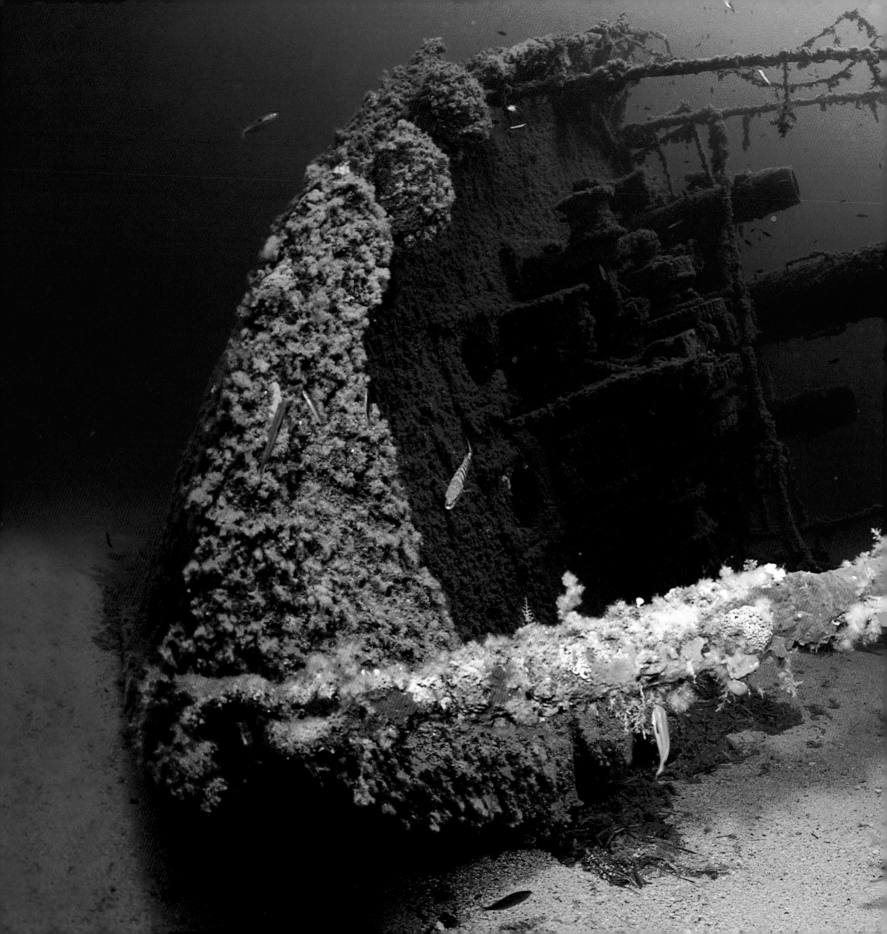

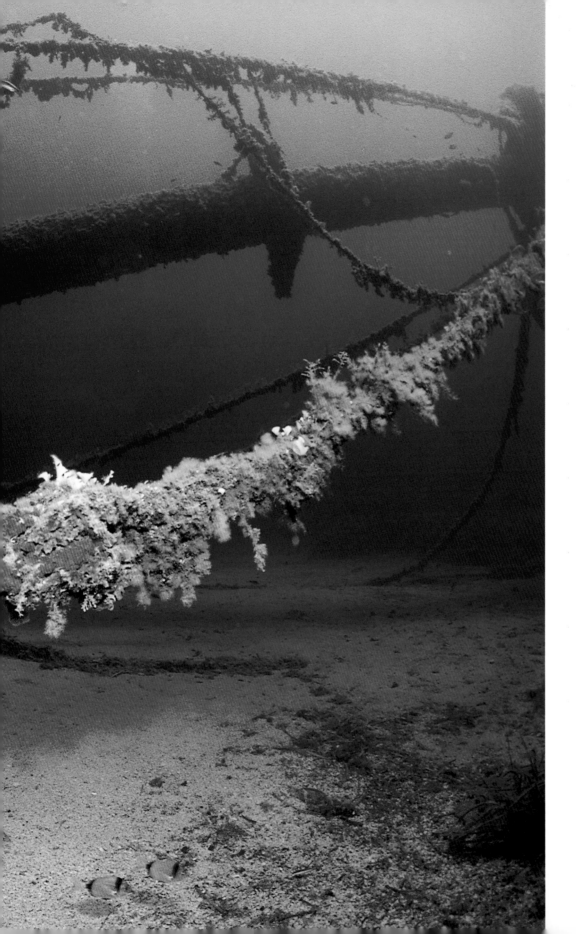

616-617 ● Mediterranean Sea, Capo Teulada, Sardinia (Italy) - The motorship *Dino*.

618-619 ● Mediterranean Sea, Mortoli, Corsica (France) - a British Vickers Viking airliner.

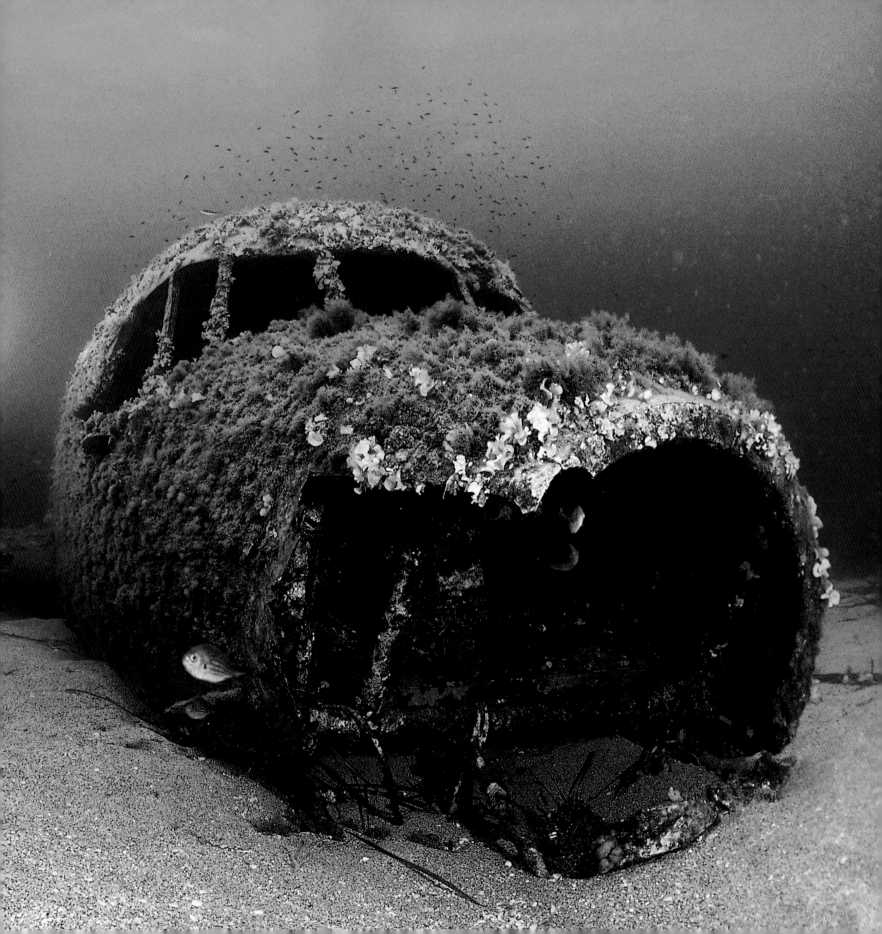

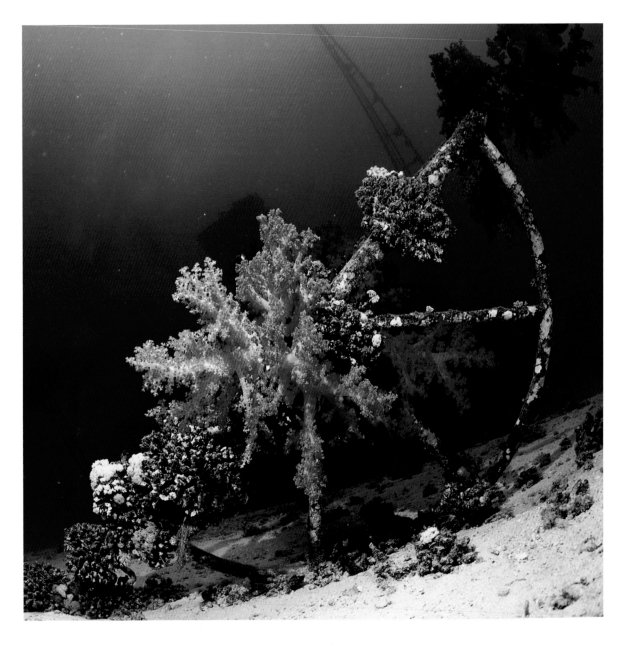

620 and 621 ● Red Sea, Abu Nuas (Egypt) - The merchant ship *Ghiannis D.*

622-623 ● Red Sea, Abu Galawa Reef (Egypt) - The wreck known as the *Tug.*

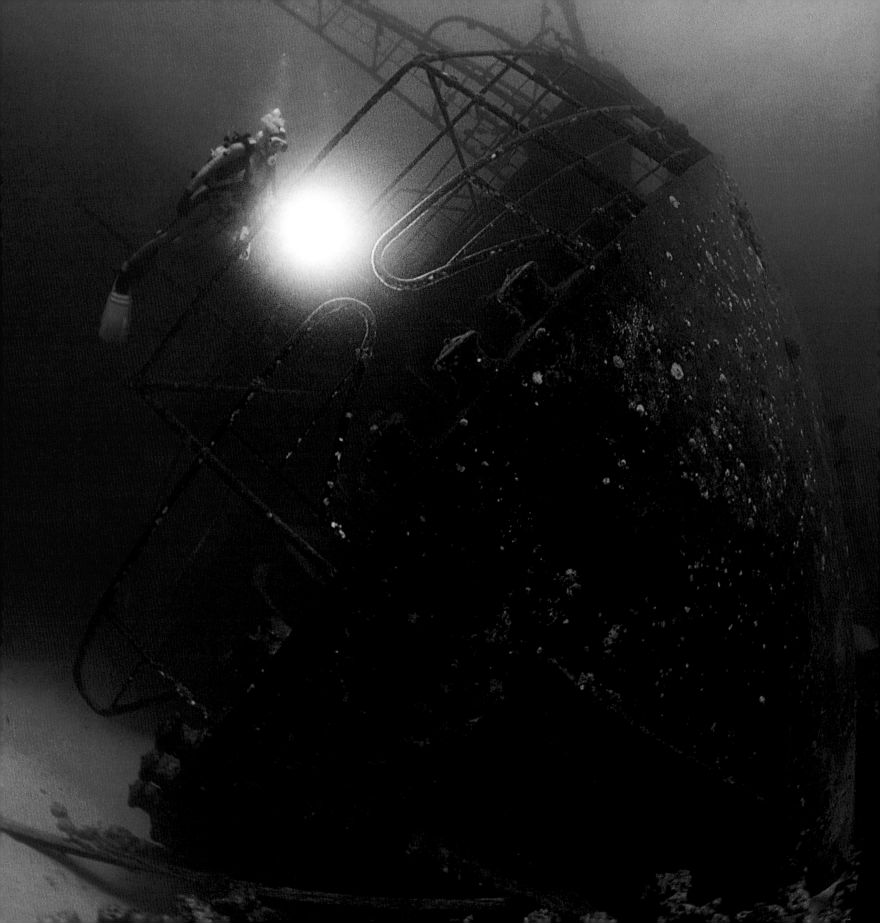

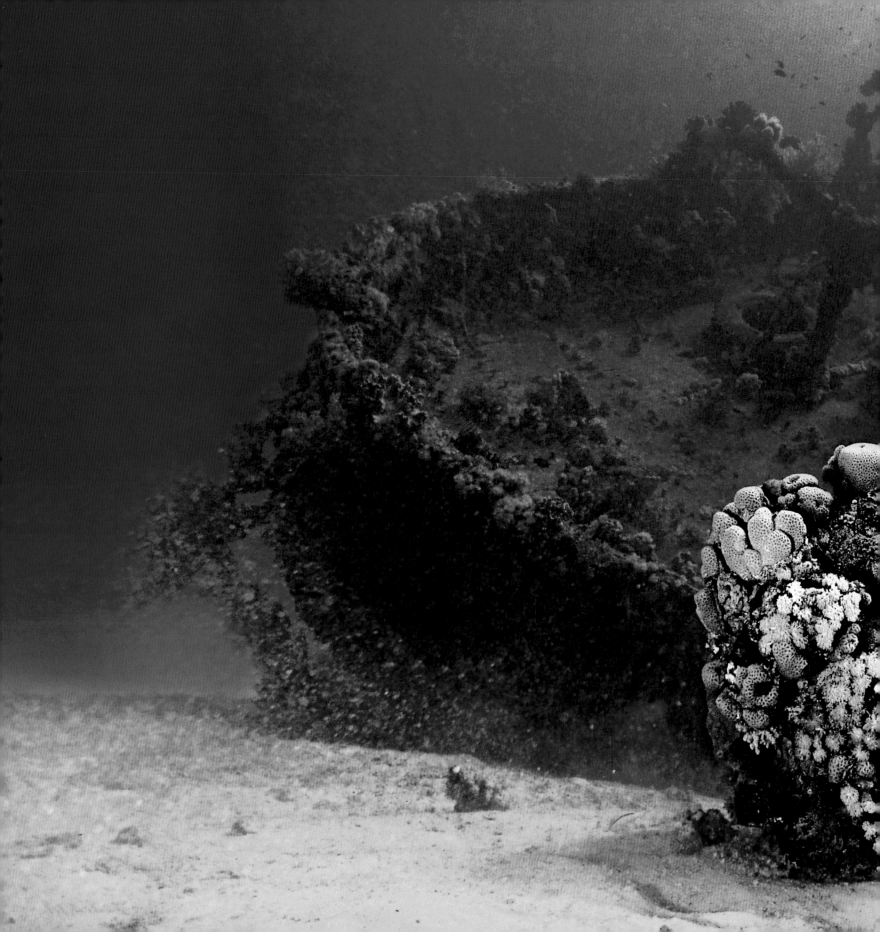

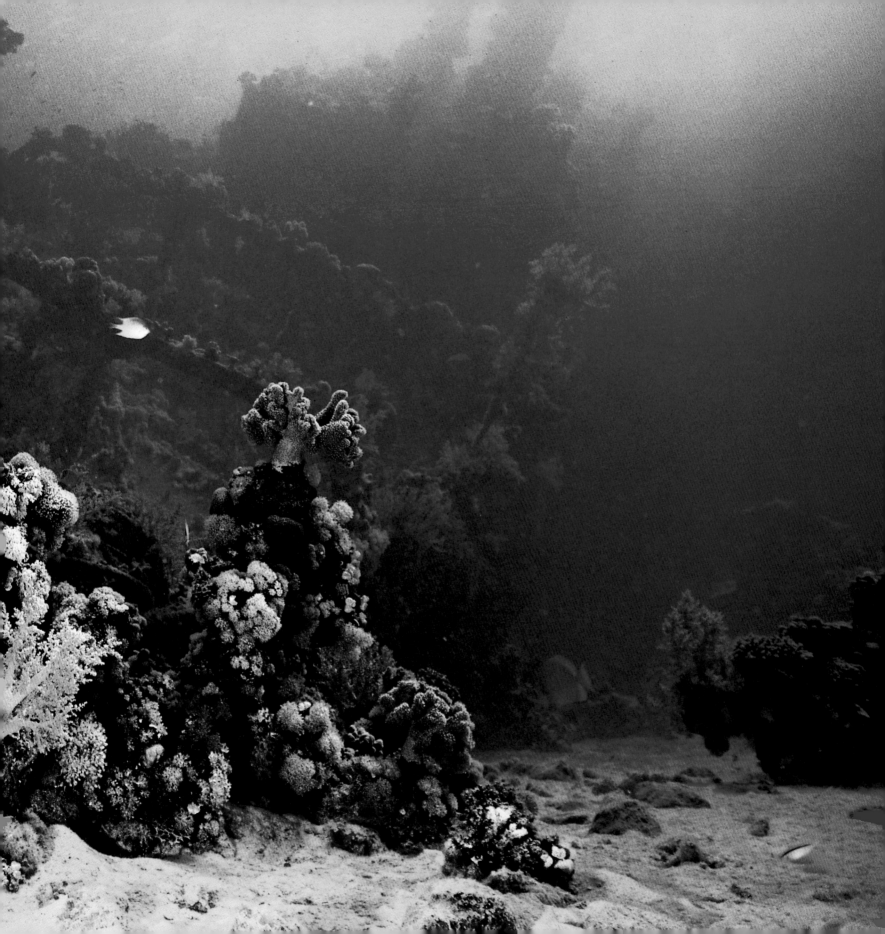

" Over the years, I have dived in submarines to visit the *LUSITANIA* and the *BRITANNIA* and every other sort of wreck. Each of these experiences has strengthened the conviction in me that the sea bed is an immense and intact museum. "

from ADVENTURES IN OCEAN EXPLORATION
by Robert D. Ballard

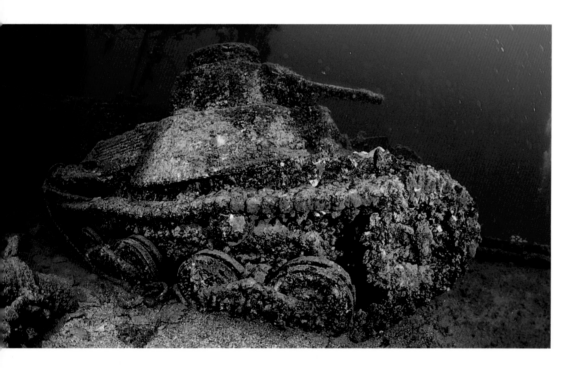

● Pacific Ocean, Truk Bay (Micronesia) - A tank found in the hold and the bows of the military cargo ship *San Francisco Maru*.

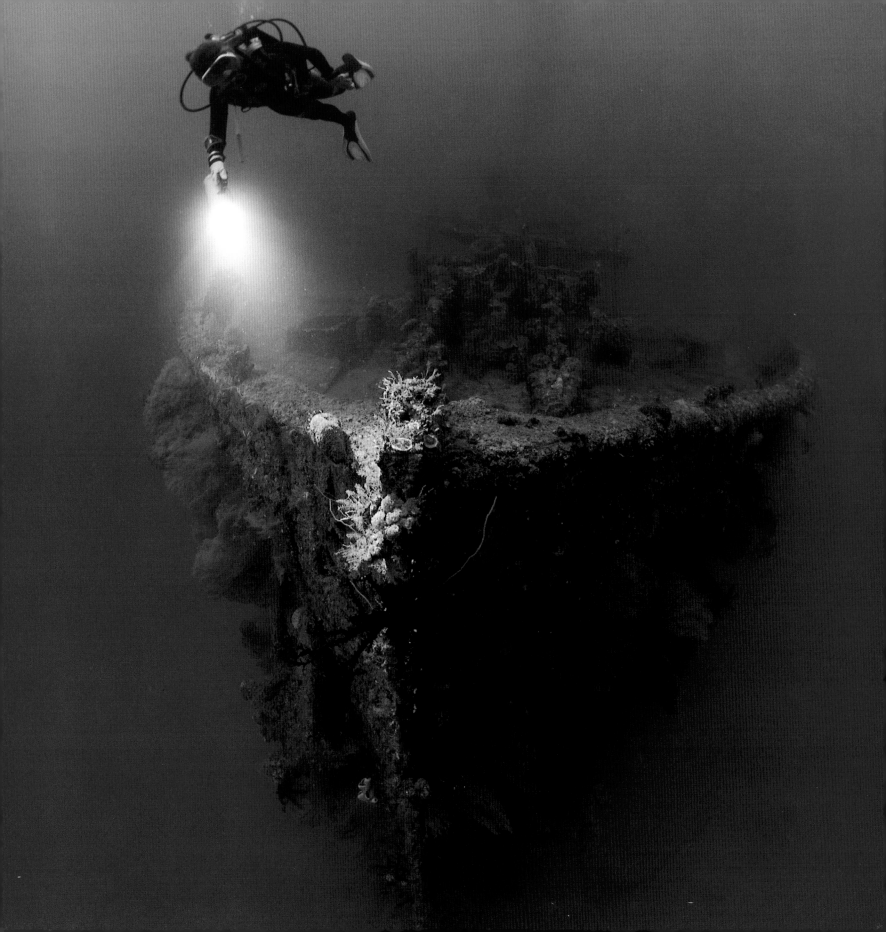

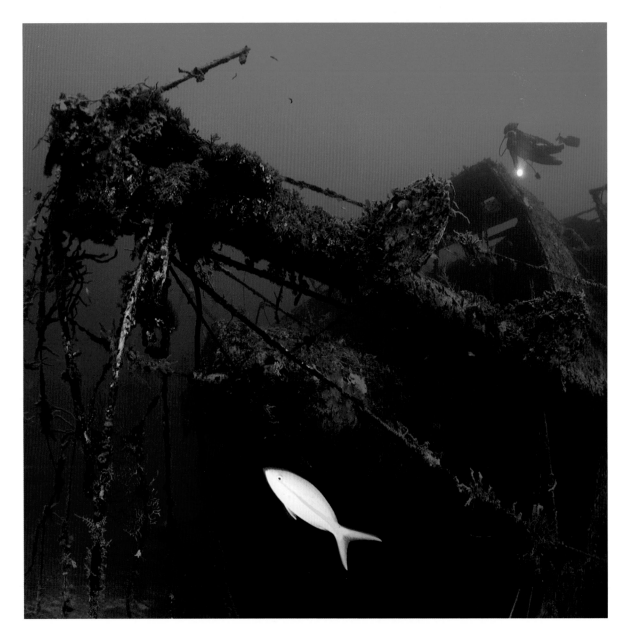

626 ● Atlantic Ocean, Guanaja (Honduras) - The merchant ship *Jado Trader*.

627 ● OAtlantic Ocean, Bermuda - The war steamship *Montana*.

628-629 ● Pacific Ocean, Rabaul (Papua New Guinea) - A Mitsubishi A6 M2 fighter-bomber.

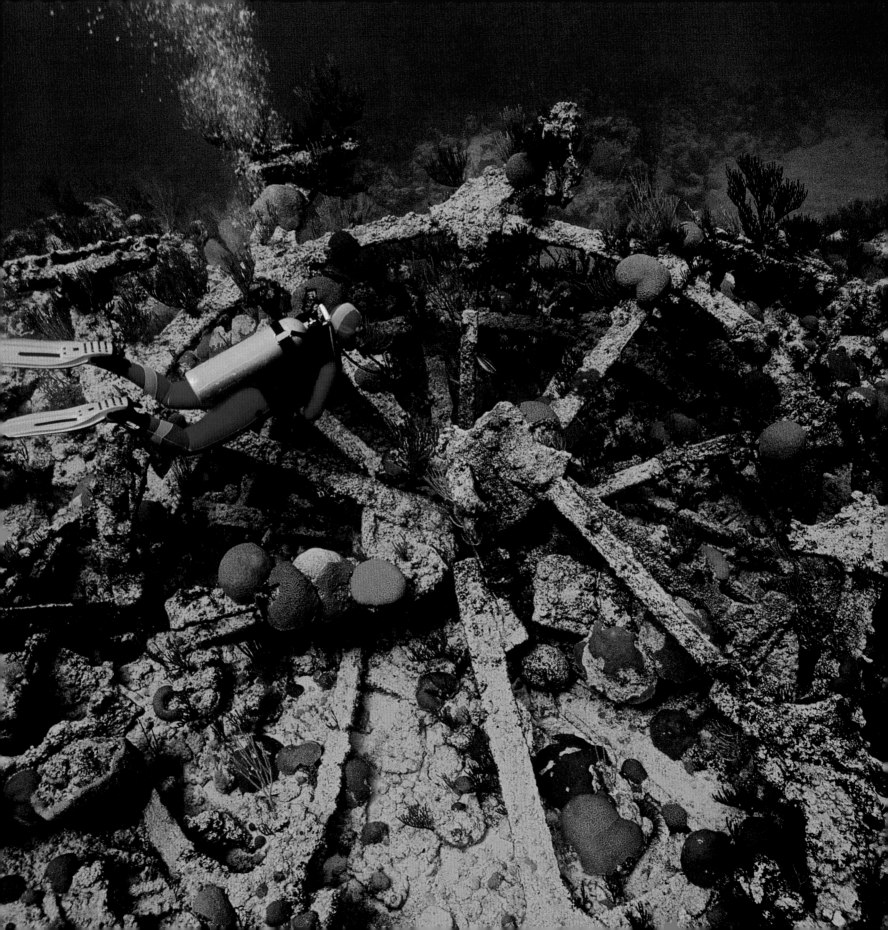

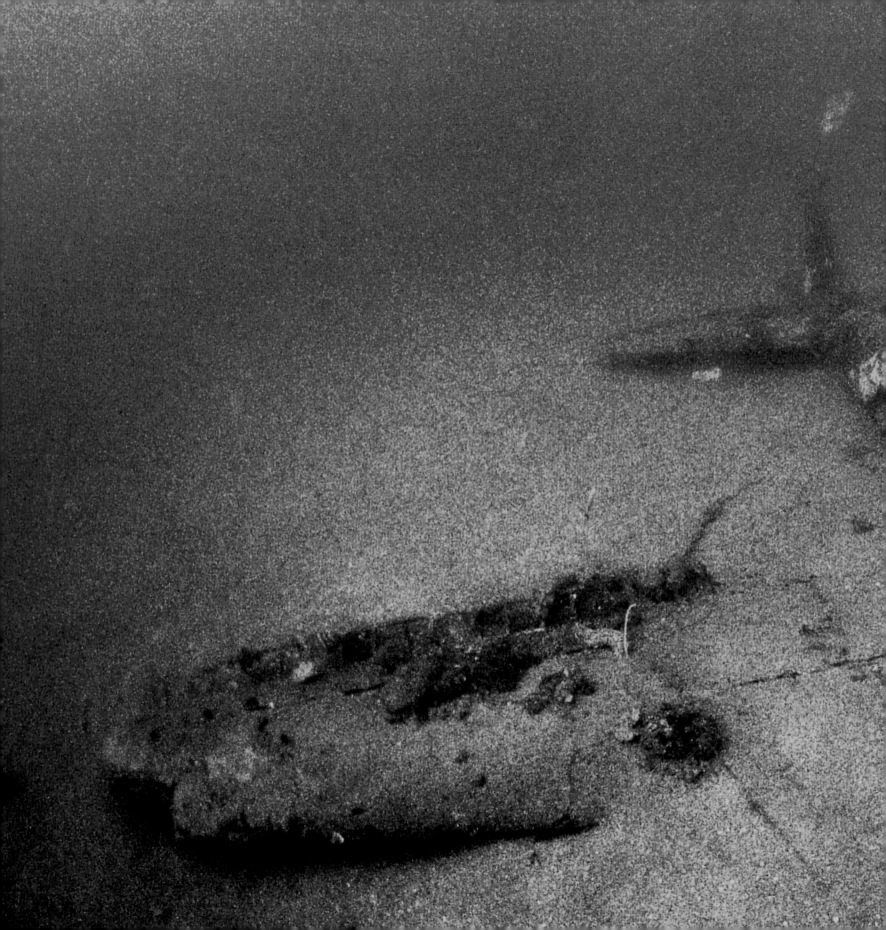

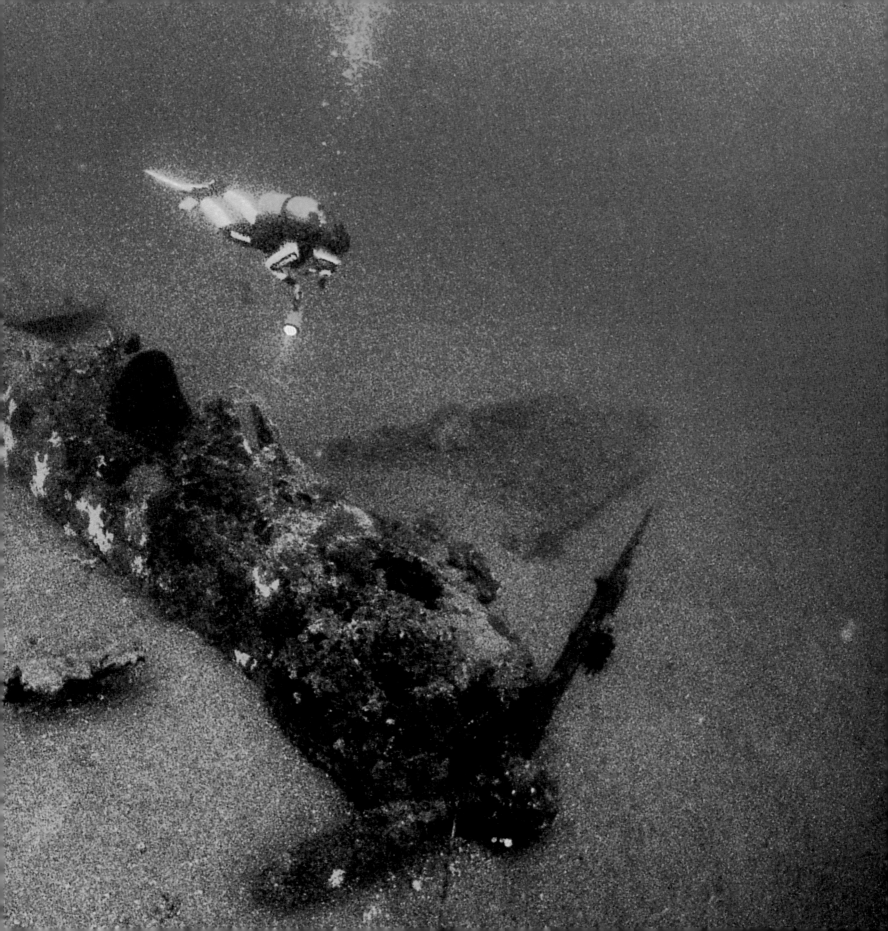

WATER and FIRE

GAETANO CAFIERO

● Pacific Ocean, Kalapana (Hawaii) - Kilauea.

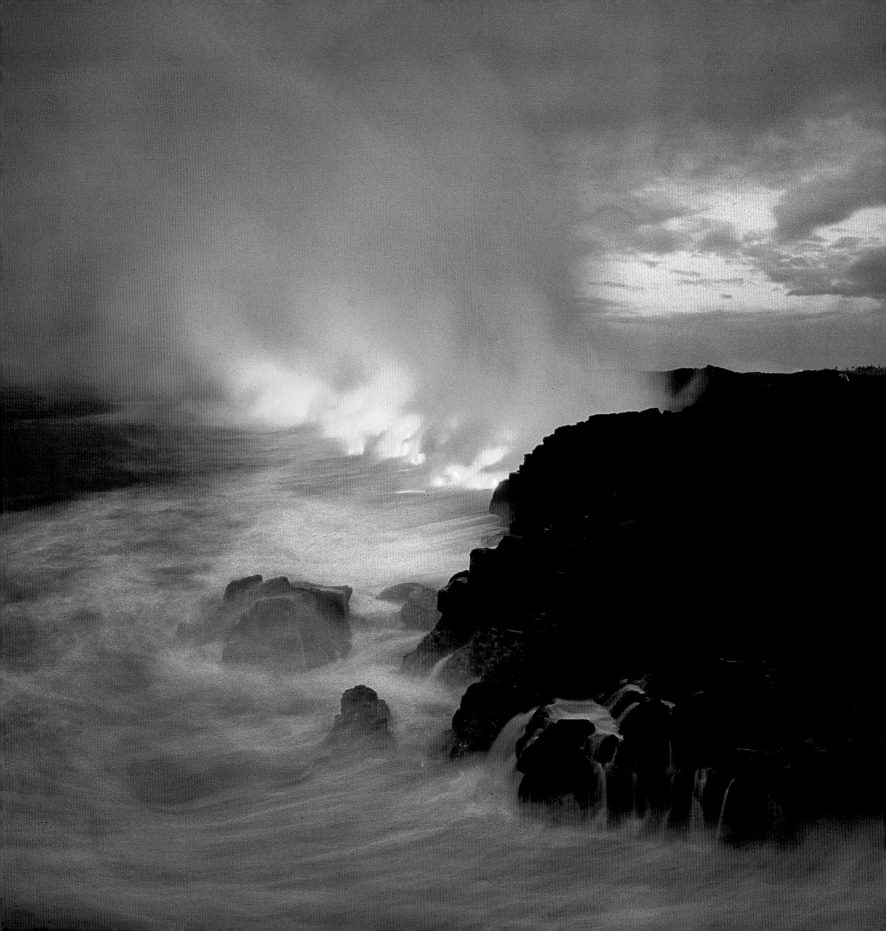

INTRODUCTION Water and Fire

Water and fire: only in the sea do these two primordial and contrasting forces (or, as was believed in antiquity, two elements) meet and combine positively. On the ocean floor, fire is belched from beneath the Earth's crust to create an oasis of life tens of thousands of feet down where the permanent darkness and lack of oxygen render the bed more empty of life than a stone desert. The water forces up gases and mineral compounds from the burning viscera of the Earth to form the first ring in the food chain that ends with the great predators. Immersed in eternal darkness, deprived of all plant life, these oases fertilized by volcanic sources are a

INTRODUCTION Water and Fire

RARE DEMONSTRATION OF BASIC BIOLOGICAL ELEMENTS IN ACTION. THE

VITAL ENERGY CREATED DOES NOT COME FROM THE SUN BY MEANS OF

PHOTOSYNTHESIS, BUT DIRECTLY FROM THE FIRE OF CREATION, WHICH

THE EARTH STILL PRESERVES AT THE BOTTOM OF THE OCEANS. EVEN

THE LARGE VOLCANOES OF MUD PERMEATED BY METHANE – THE MOST

ELEMENTARY OF THE HYDROCARBONS – ARE ABLE TO SUPPORT AN

ABUNDANCE OF ANIMAL LIFE THANKS TO THE CHEMO-SYNTHETIC BAC-

TERIA. OTHER OASES NOURISHED BY UNDERWATER VOLCANOES, WHICH

FORM THE RIDGES OF UNDERWATER MOUNTAIN CHAINS, PROVIDE AMAZ-

ING AND LUXURIANT HABITATS FOR LIFE CREATED BY THE CLOSELY-KNIT

SYMBIOSIS OF THE SEA WITH THE LAND, AND WATER WITH FIRE. ON THE

Water and Fire
Introduction

SURFACE OF THE LAND, THE ENERGY OF MAGMA IS CLEARLY APPARENT WHEN AN ERUPTION THROWS UP INCANDESCENT, MOLTEN ROCK, CREATING COLUMNS OF STEAM AS HIGH AS A MOUNTAIN. IT IS AN UNDERESTIMATED SOURCE OF IMMENSE ENERGY THAT COULD CHANGE OUR FUTURE. IN THE PAST SCIENTISTS SOUGHT FOR THE ORIGIN OF LIFE IN A PRIMORDIAL BROTH ON THE OCEAN'S SURFACE. TODAY, HOWEVER, KNOWLEDGE OF THE SEABED SPRINGS HAS CAUSED THEM TO CHANGE THEIR IDEAS AND THEY ARE NOW GIVING GREATER CREDENCE TO THE HYPOTHESIS THAT ORIGINALLY THERE WAS NOTHING MORE THAN THE TWO MOST ANCIENT OF ELEMENTS: FIRE AND WATER.

635 ● Pacific Ocean, Luzon Island (Philippines) - Mayon

636-637 ● Caribbean Sea, Monserrat Island - Soufrière Hills.

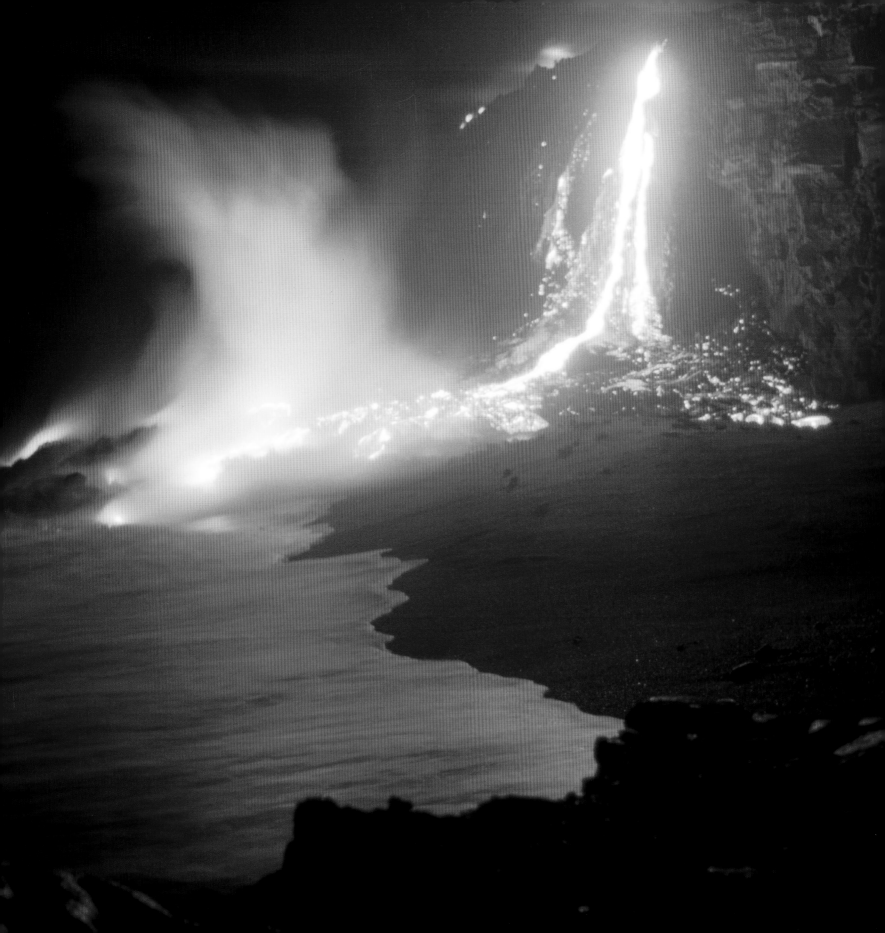

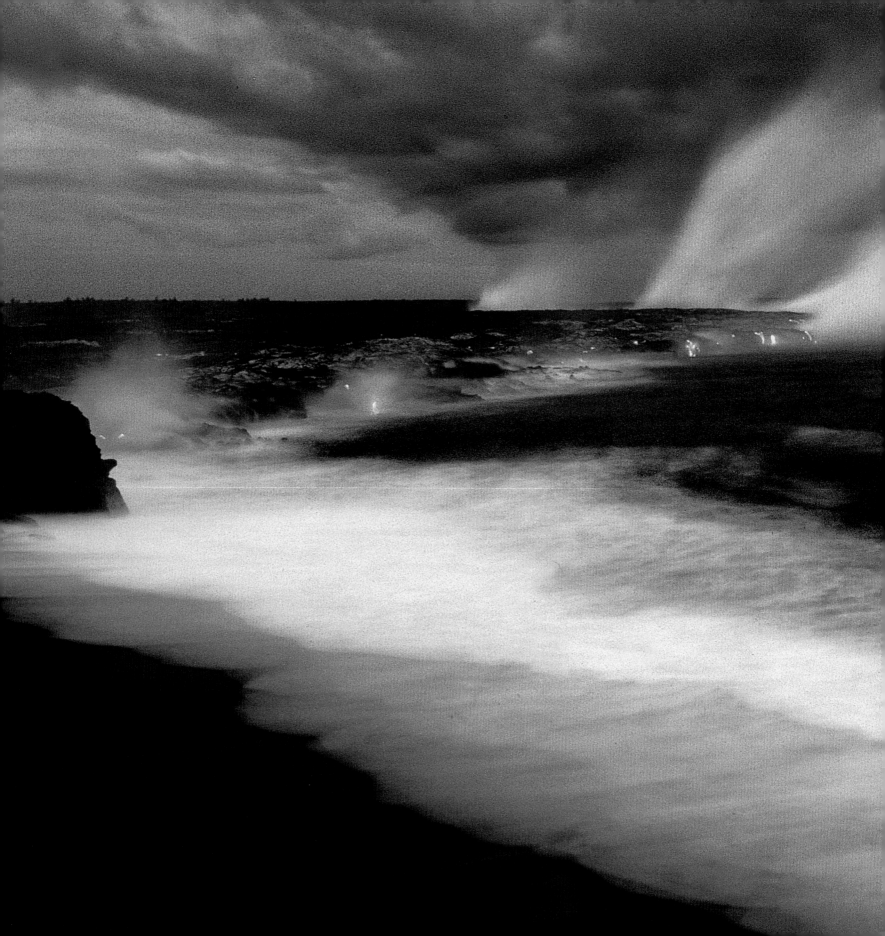

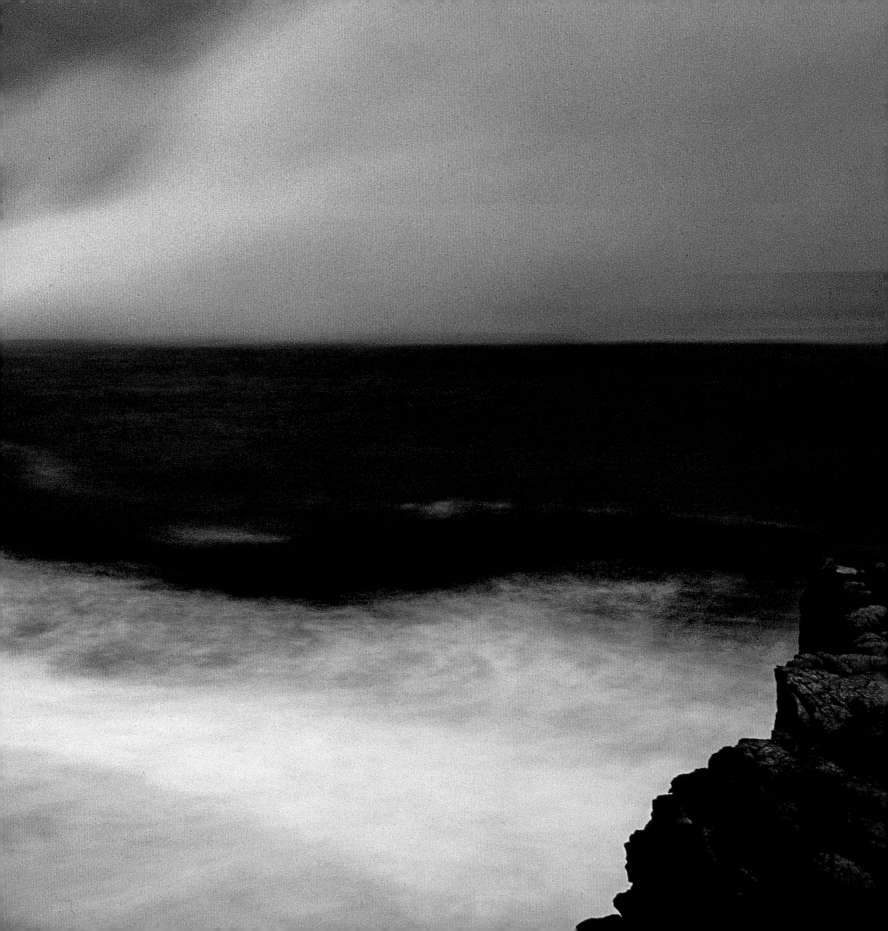

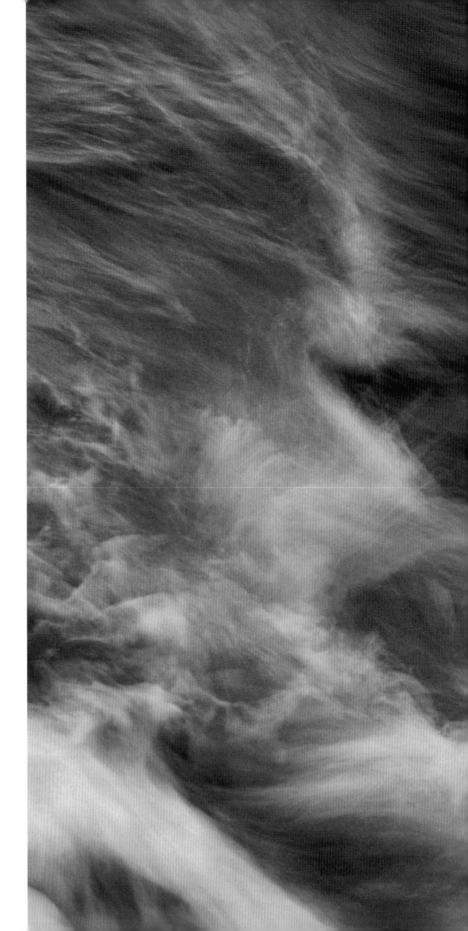

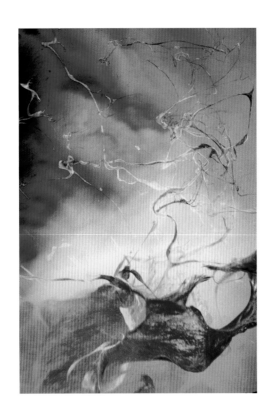

638 and 638-639 ● Indian Ocean, Réunion Island - the Piton de la Fornaise.

640-641 ● Mediterranean Sea, Sicily (Italy) - Stromboli.

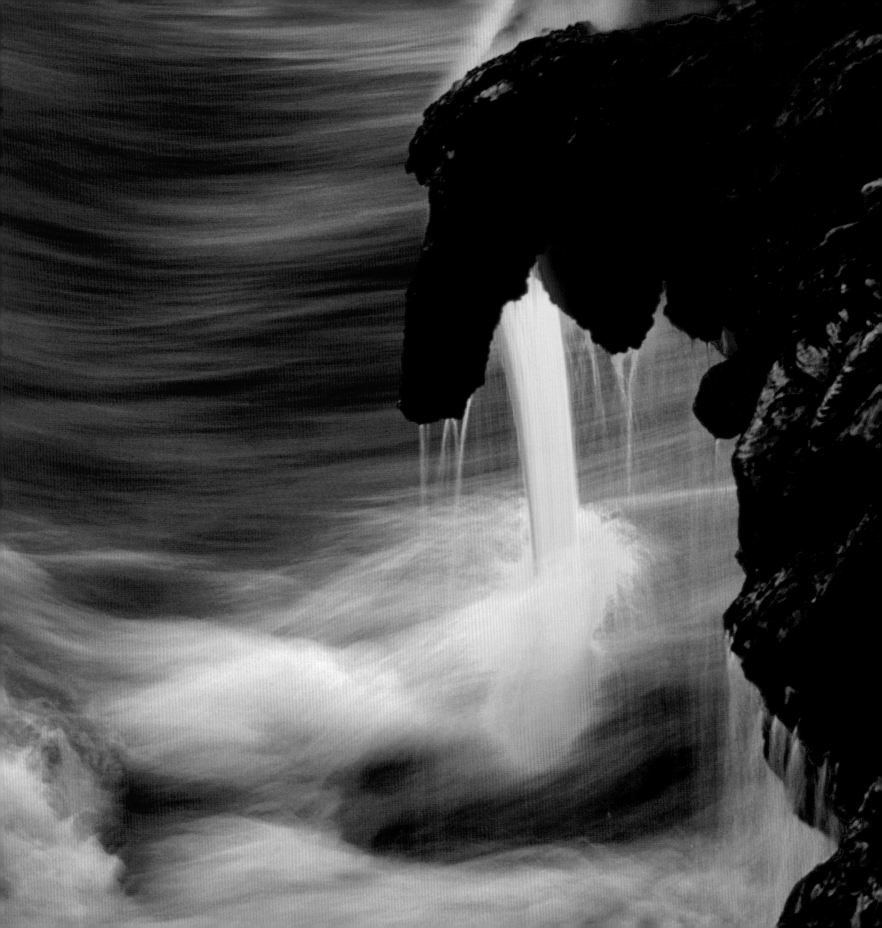

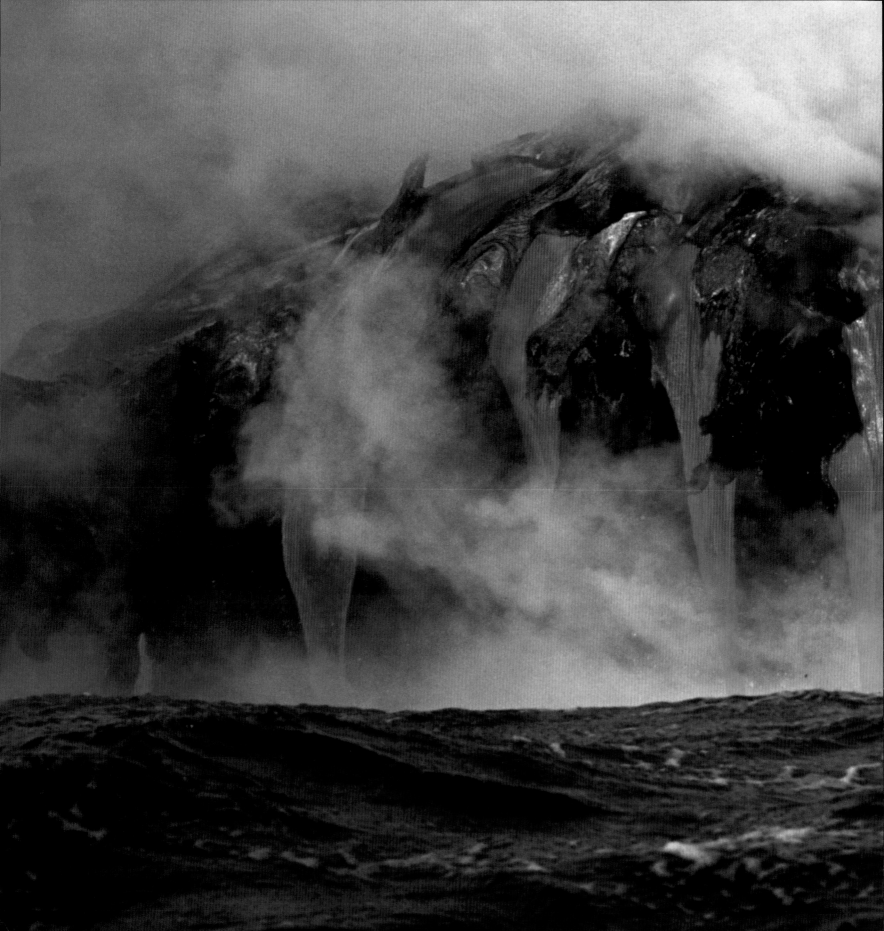

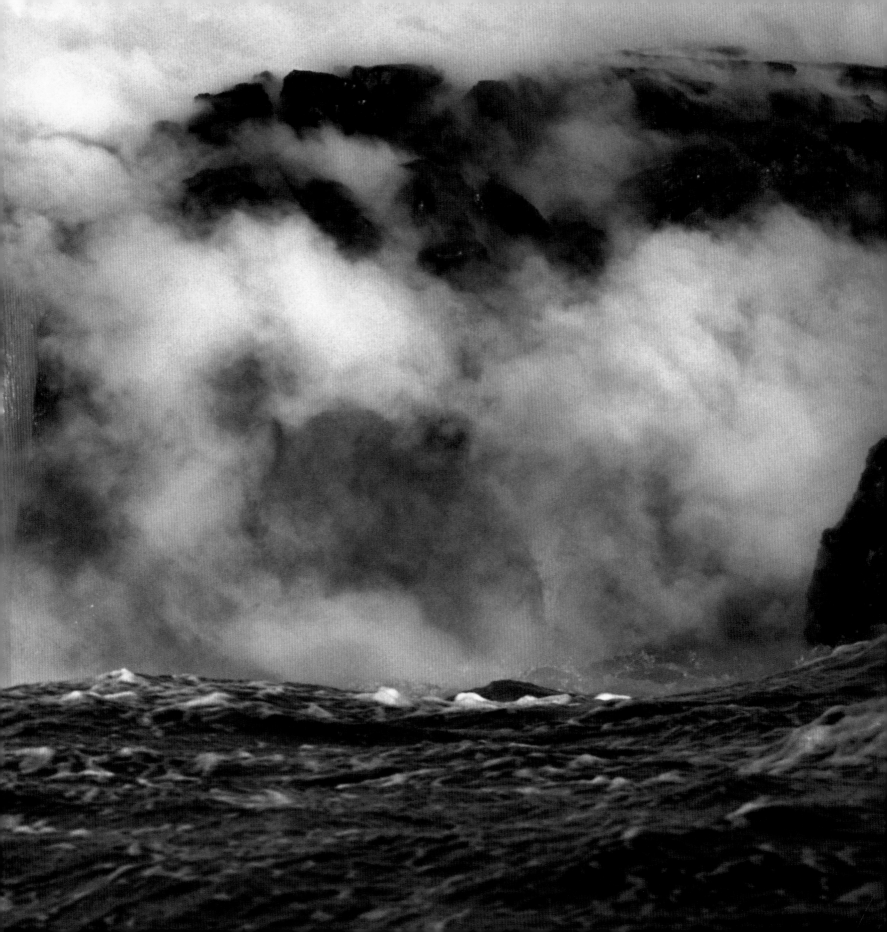

The roar
of Pu'u O'o

642-643 and 644-645
● Pacific Ocean,
Kalapana (Hawaii) -
Kilauea.

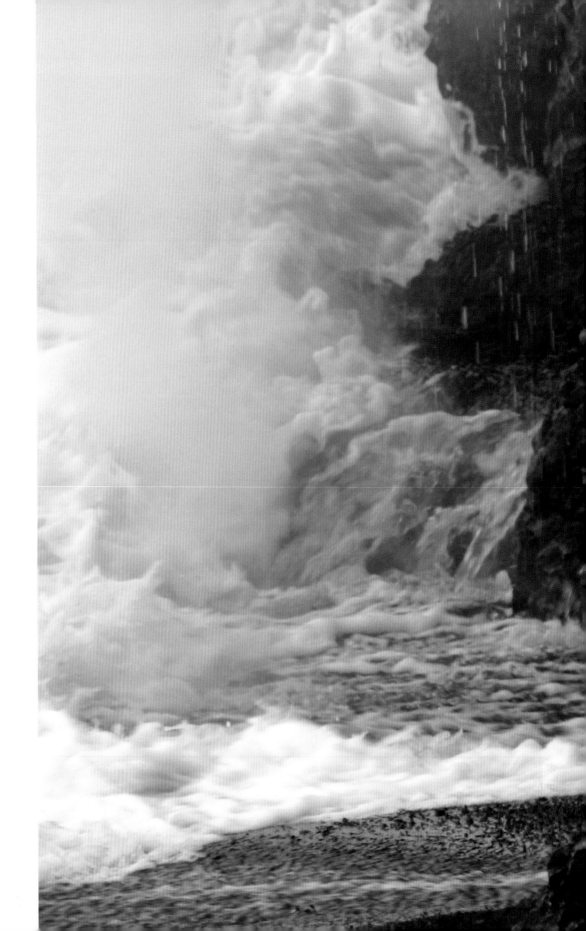

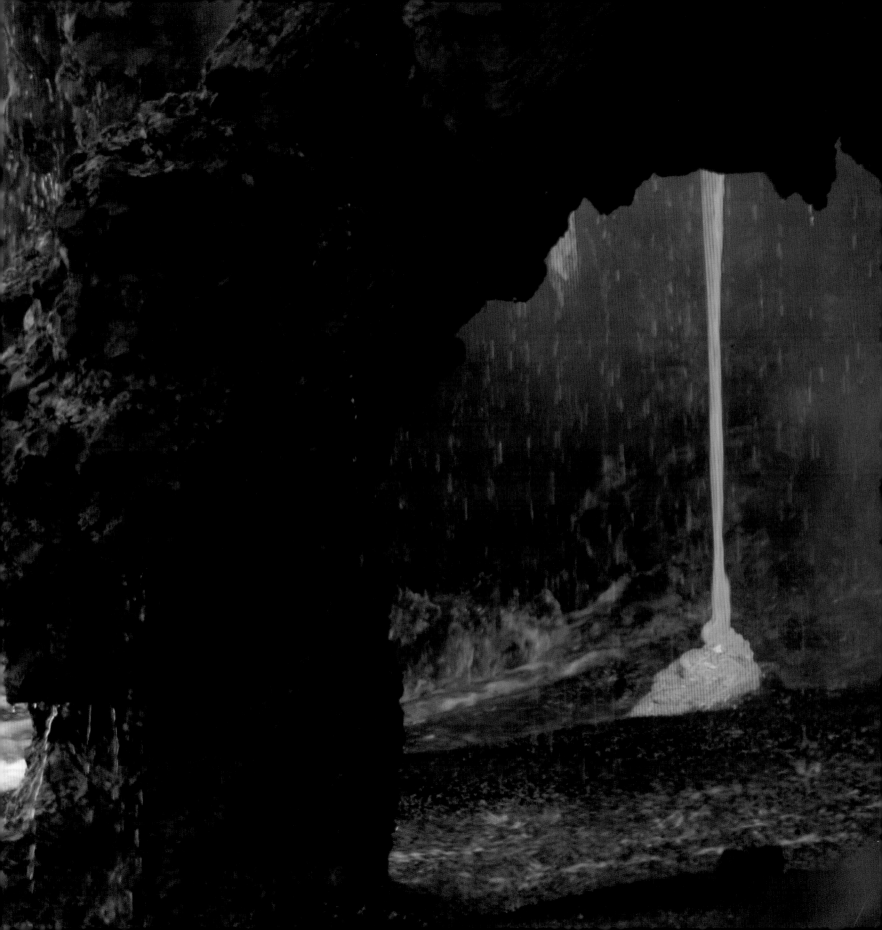

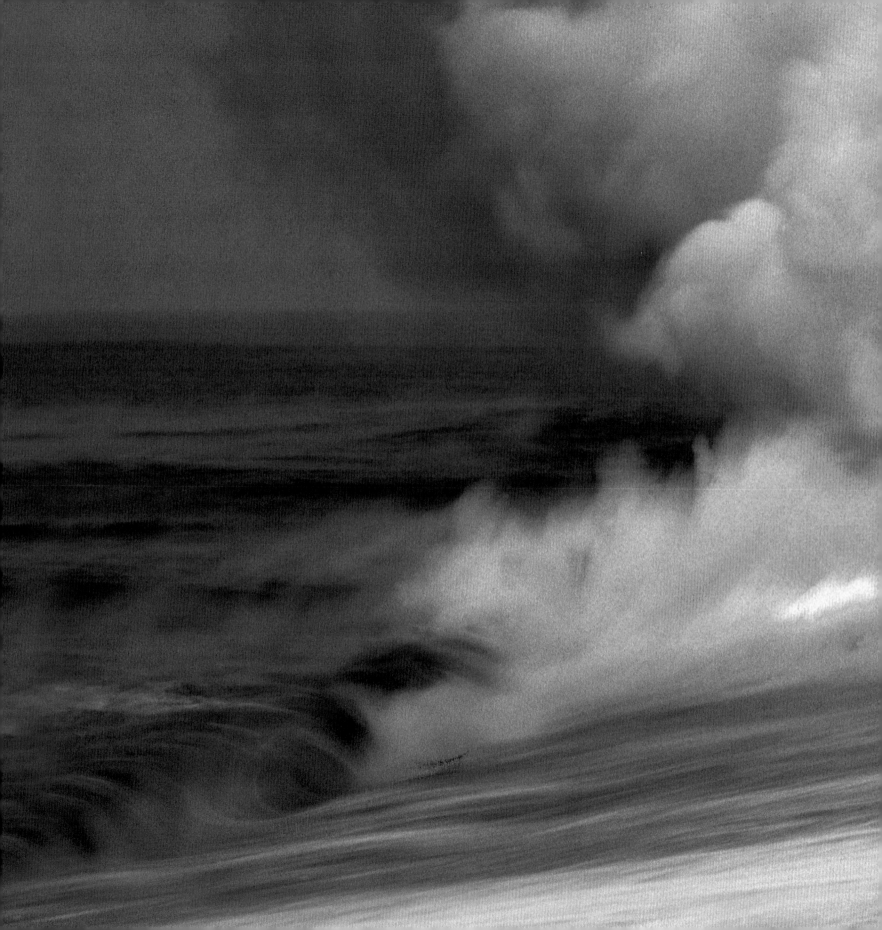

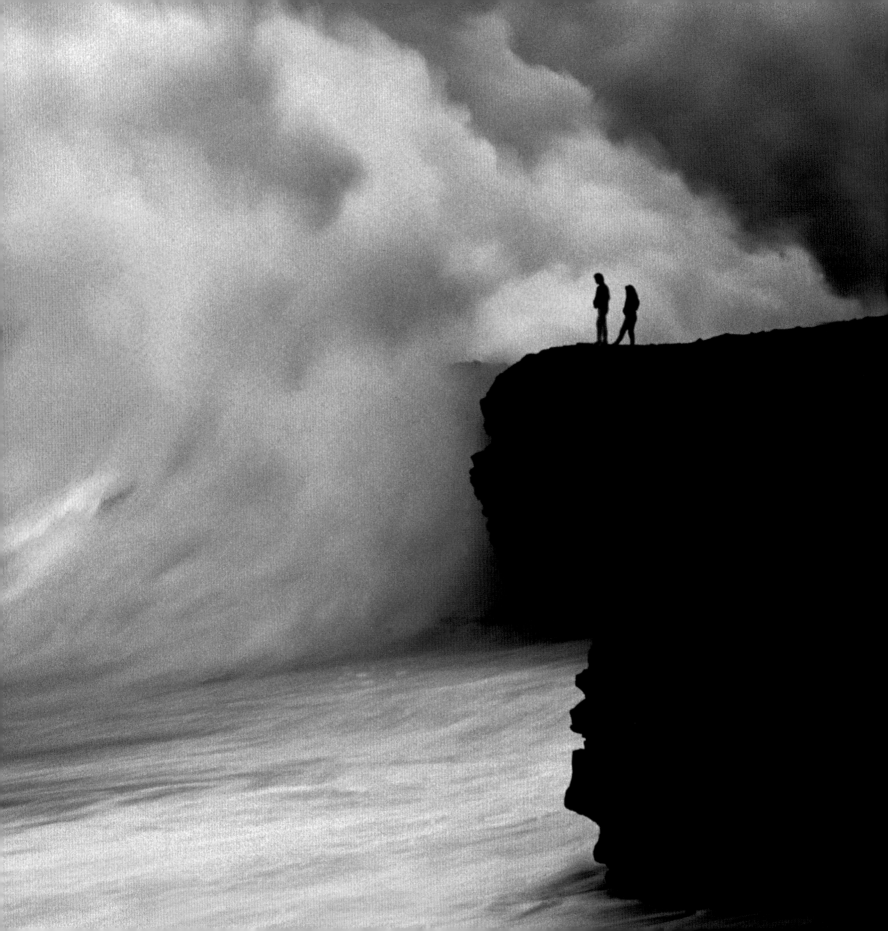

All

SHADES

of

BLUE

CORNELIA LAUF

● Mediterranean Sea - Highlights created by backwash.

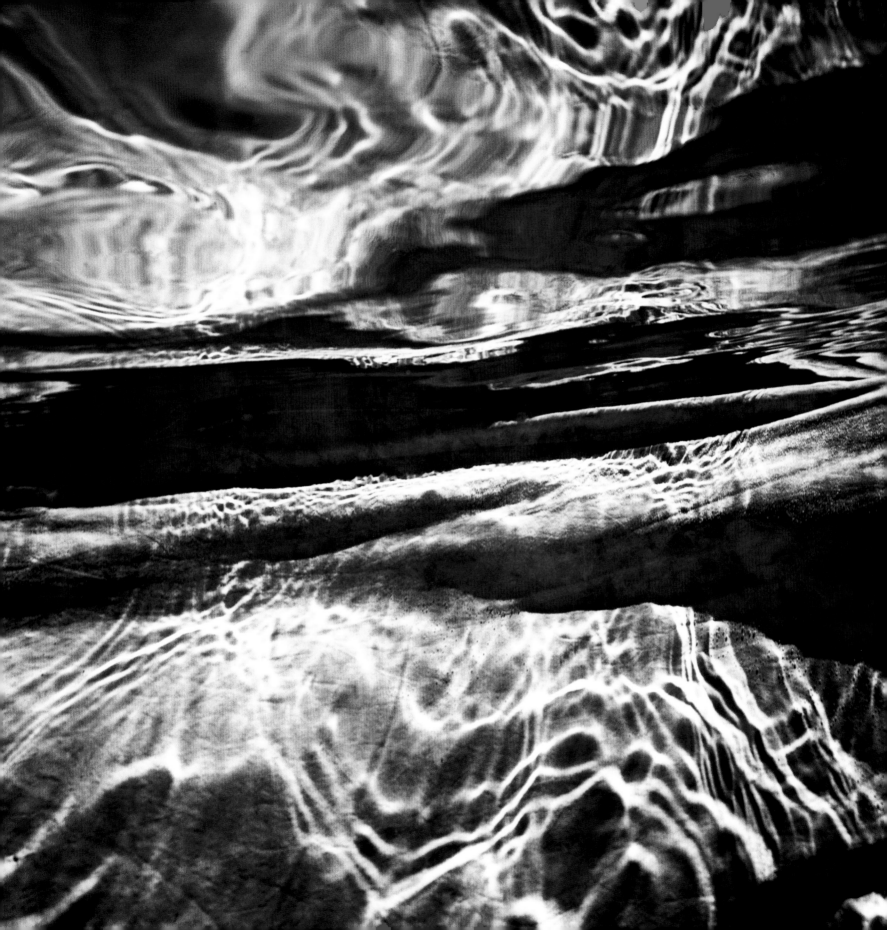

INTRODUCTION All Shades of Blue

HOMER SANG OF THE 'THE WINE-DARK SEA,' AND MANY CEN-

TURIES LATER CASPAR DAVID FRIEDRICH DREAMED OF BLUE ICEBERGS.

AND THE SPECTER OF THE BLUES AND BROWNS OF THE LARGE

BAROQUE-ERA NAVIES, WHOSE SHIPS, ALLEGORIES OF THE HUMAN SPIR-

IT, SANK IN THE TREACHEROUS WATERS OF THE OCEAN OF LIFE … OVER

THE AGES, THE EGYPTIANS, GREEKS, ROMANS, VIKINGS, PORTUGUESE,

DUTCH, FRENCH, AND BRITISH HAVE TRAVERSED THE SEVEN SEAS;

TODAY THE MODERN NAVAL POWERS CEASELESSLY PATROL THEM.

EVERY CULTURE HAS DEPICTED THE SEA WITH A DIFFERENT PALETTE OF

COLORS AND IN WIDE-RANGING MATERIALS AND FORMS. THERE ARE

IVORIES CARVED BY THE INUIT, AND PRINTS BY HOKUSAI IN WHICH A

INTRODUCTION All Shades of Blue

TSUNAMI FILLS THE SHEET WITH TERRIFYING BLUE. THEN THERE ARE THE

HURRICANES PAINTED BY WINSLOW HOMER IN THE BASALT TONES OF

THE FIRST AMERICAN REALISTS, WHO ILLUSTRATED THE ORIGINAL CON-

FLICT THAT EXISTED BETWEEN MAN, THE SEA AND THE ELEMENTS. AS

MONET SHOWED US, THE COLORS OF WATER CAN CHANGE CONTINU-

OUSLY, DEPENDING ON THE MOMENT OF THE DAY, FROM A DELICATE

PALLID PINK AT SUNRISE TO DEEPEST INDIGO AT NIGHT. IT IS ART'S

SUPREME POWER TO RECREATE THE IMPRESSIONS OF NATURE IN

COLOR. IN THE HANDS OF ARTISTS AND PHOTOGRAPHERS, NATURAL

PHENOMENA THAT CAN BE MEASURED AND DESCRIBED WITH PRECISION

SCIENTIFICALLY AND OPTICALLY ARE RENDERED ABSTRACTLY, THOUGH

All Shades of Blue

Introduction

RECOGNIZABLY, IN A SORT OF NEW LANGUAGE THAT CAN IMMORTALIZE AN ATMOSPHERE, A CLIMATE OR A COMBINATION OF COLORS BETTER THAN SCIENCE. EXAMPLES ARE THE ATMOSPHERIC STORMS OF TURNER, THE TURQUOISE VEILS OF BOUDIN, THE PRISMATIC BLUES OF LIONEL FEININGER, AND THE MARINE PHOTOGRAPHS OF HIROSHI SUGIMOTO, PHILIPPE THOMAS, AND BAS JAN ADER. IN THE TIME OF GOETHE, WHEN ART AND SCIENCE WERE STILL SISTERS, A POET COULD DABBLE WITH EXPERIMENTS WITHOUT LOSING HIS 'AURA.' TODAY IT IS NO LONGER THE SAME. WE MUST BE CONTENT WITH READING THE FORMS OF COLORS OF THE SEA THROUGH ART, AND WITH BEING ITS WITNESSES OURSELVES.

651 ● Red Sea - White and turquoise highlights.

652-653 ● Caribbean Sea, Cuba - Coralline hues on a beach in Matanzas.

654-655 ● Red Sea - Detail of the vivid livery of a parrotfish.

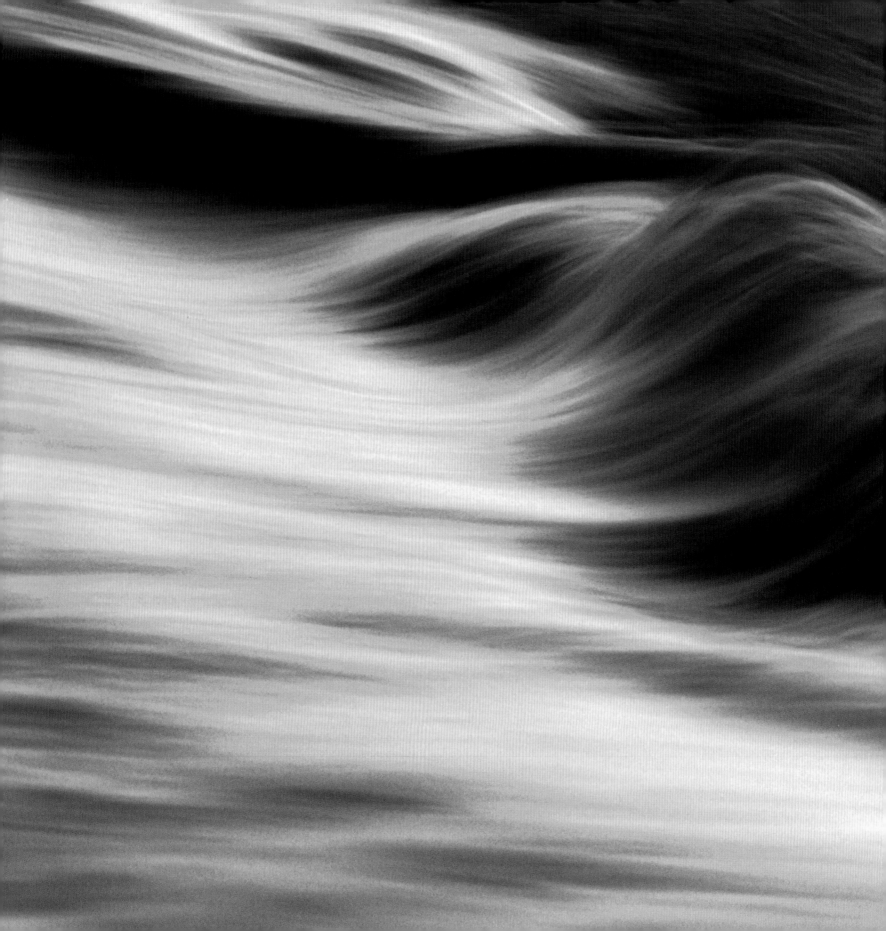

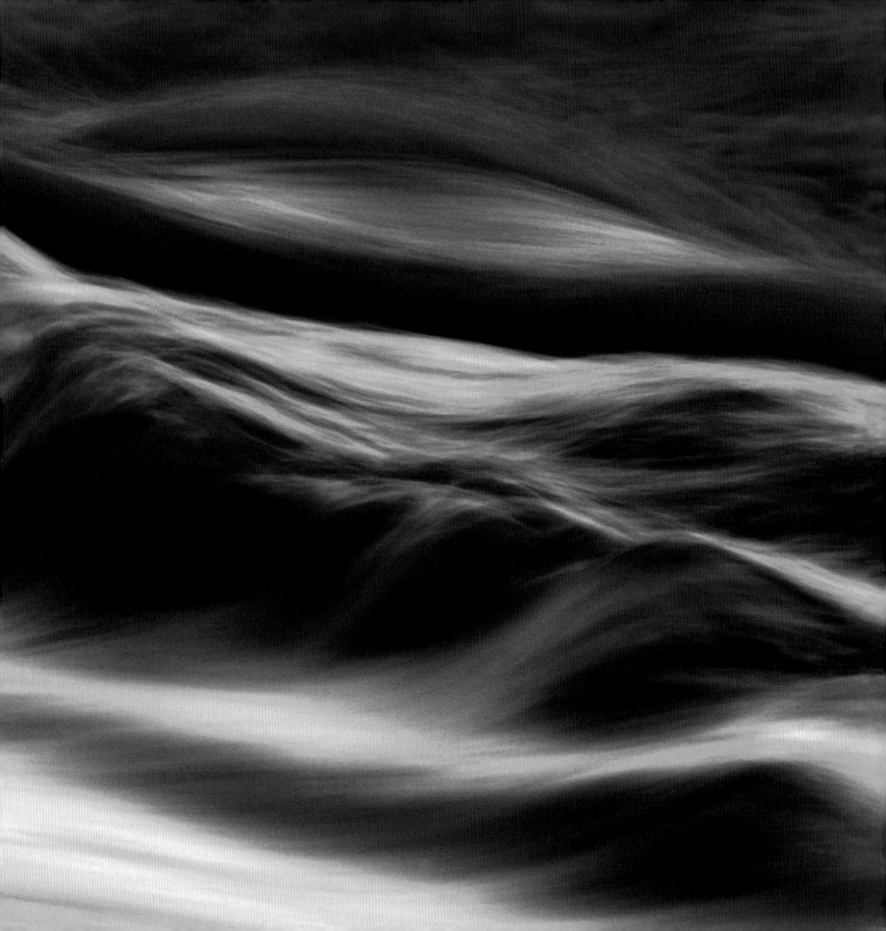

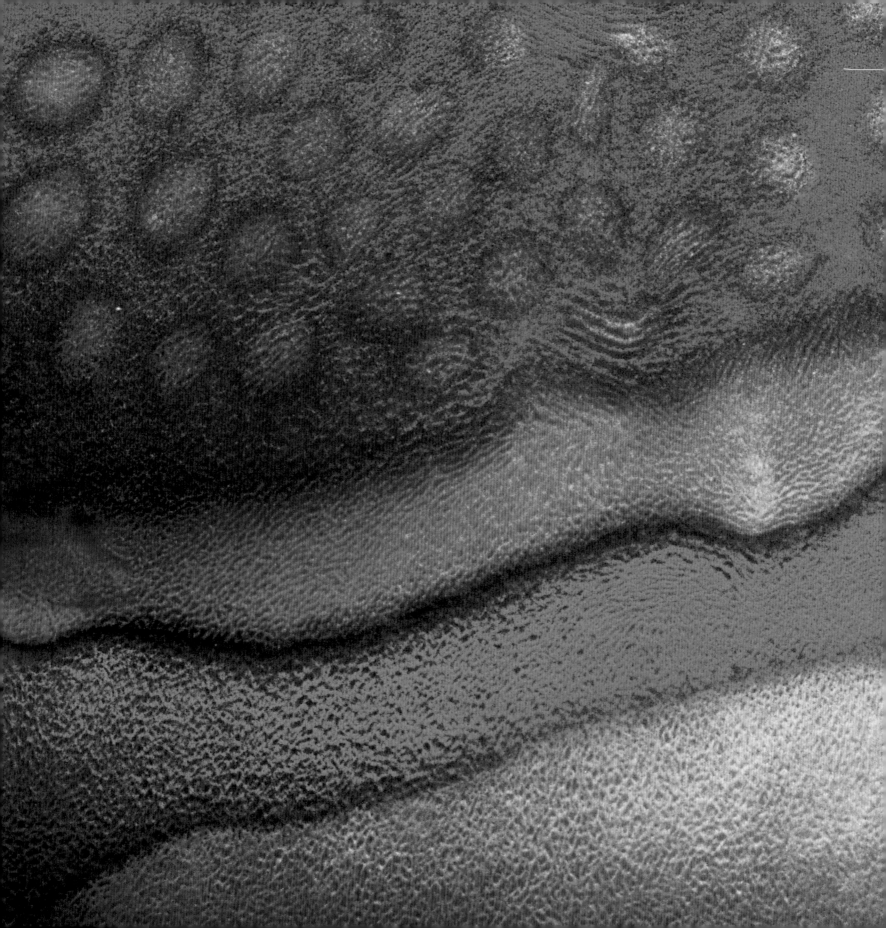

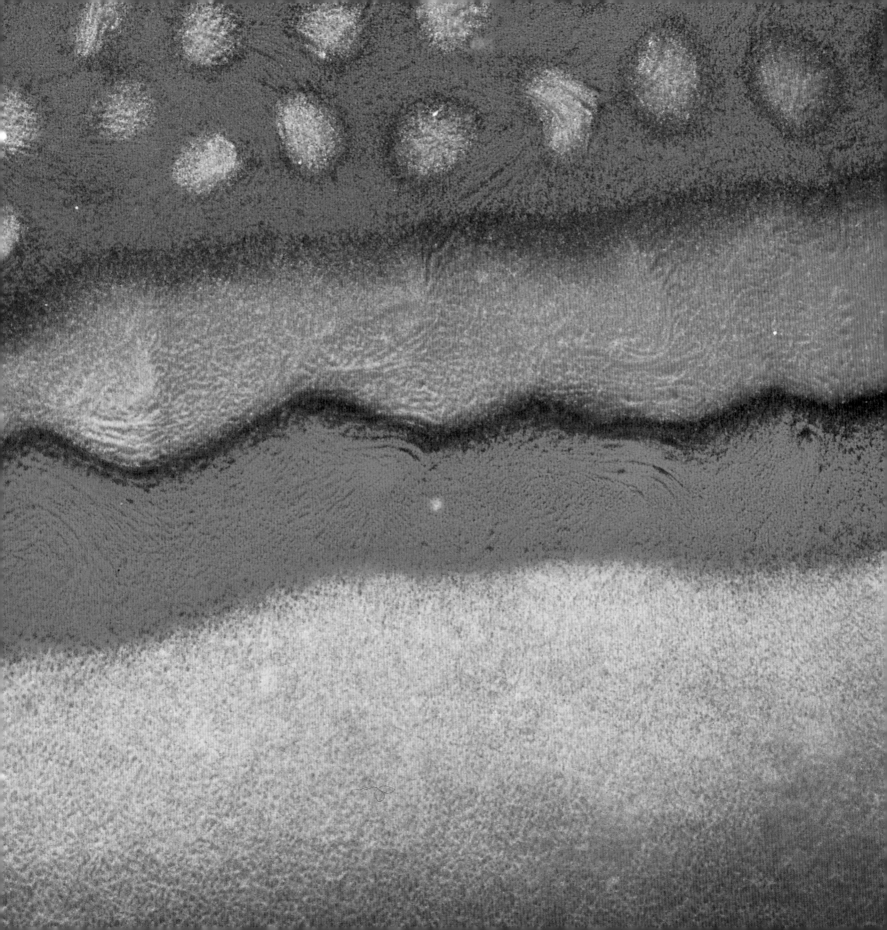

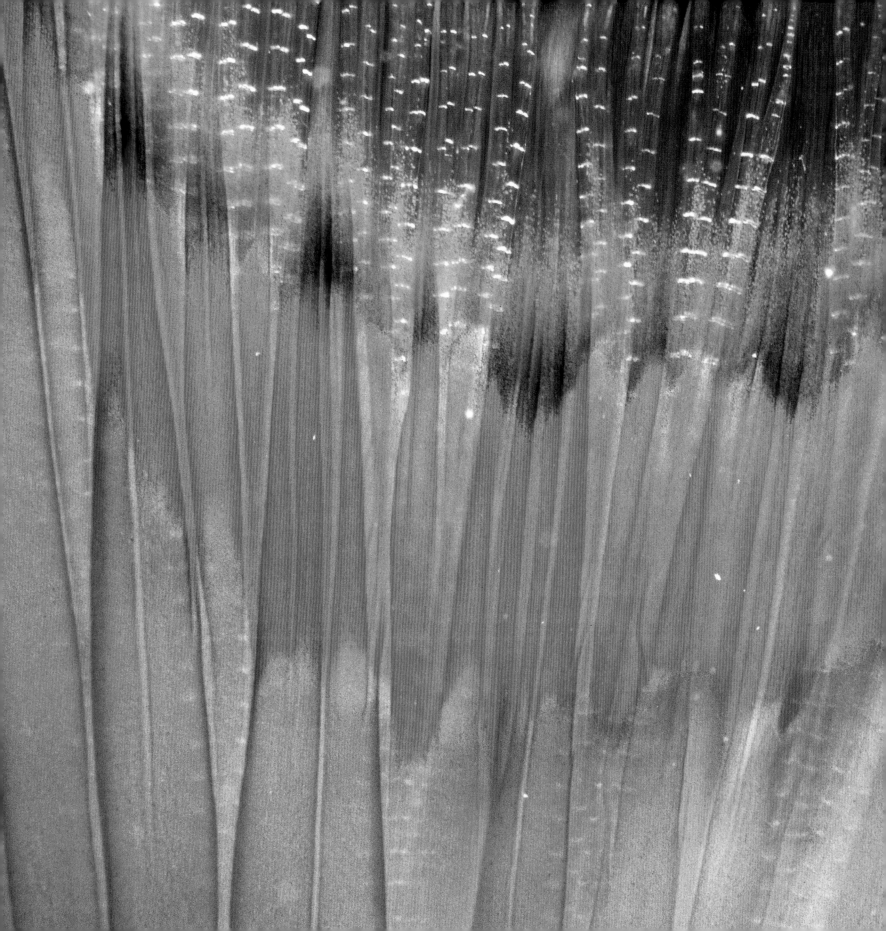

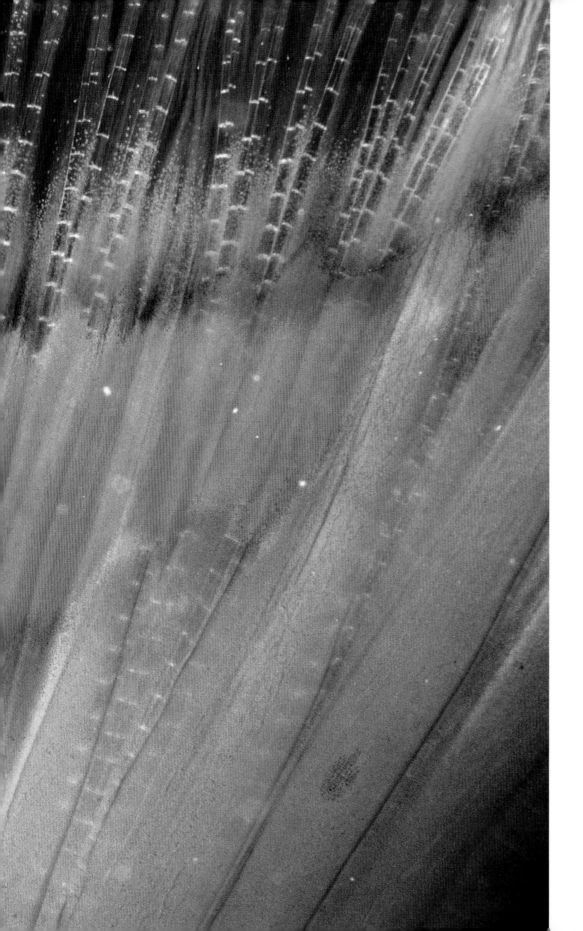

656-657 ● Red Sea - Tail of a parrotfish.

658-659 ● Mediterranean Sea, Egypt - Light and shadow on the coast at Marsa Matruh.

660-661 ● Mediterranean Sea, Egypt - Gentle brushstrokes of white, turquoise and blue paint the water over the reef and sea bottom.

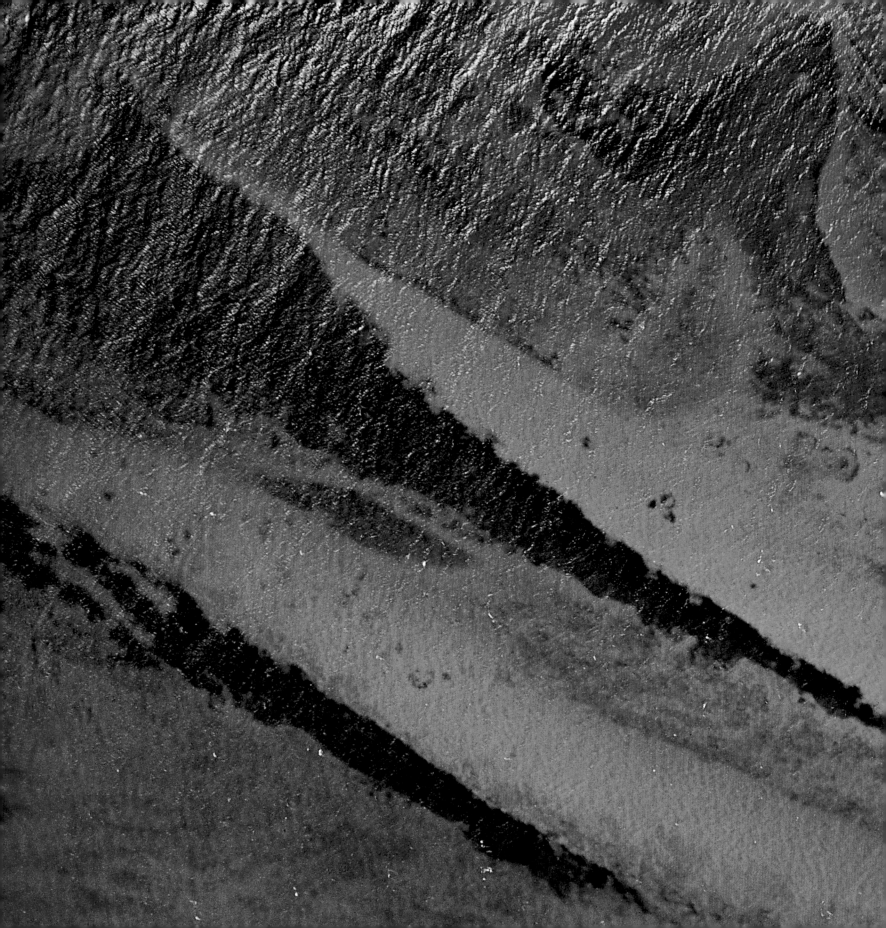

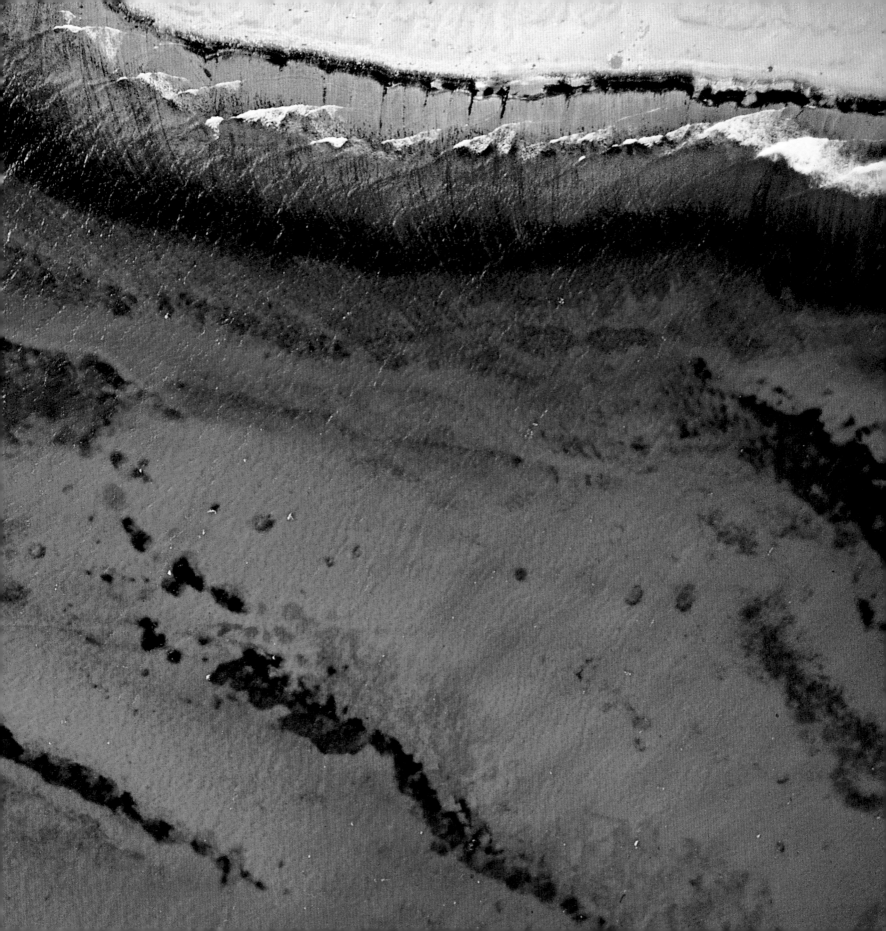

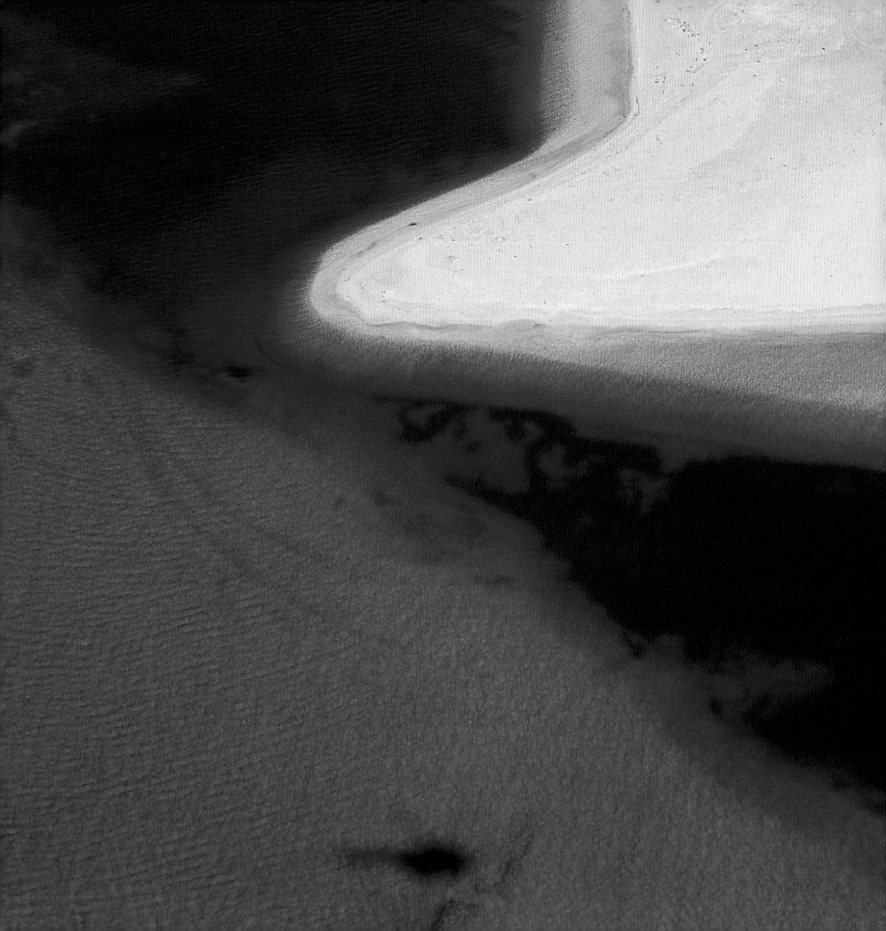

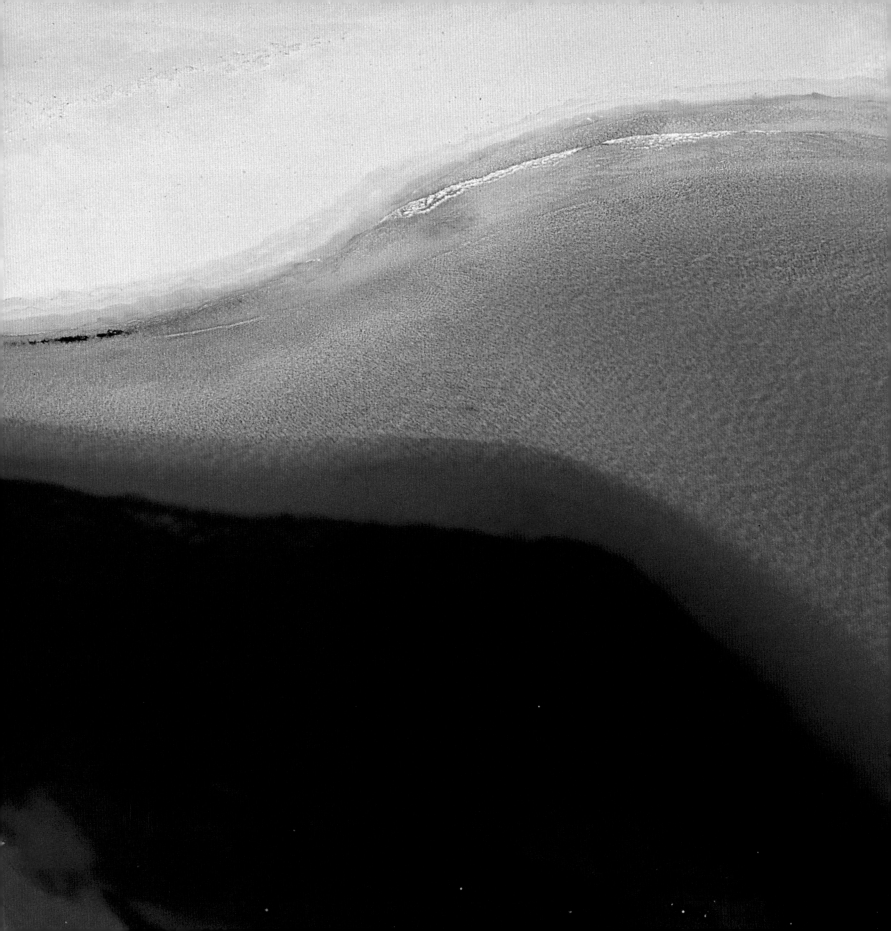

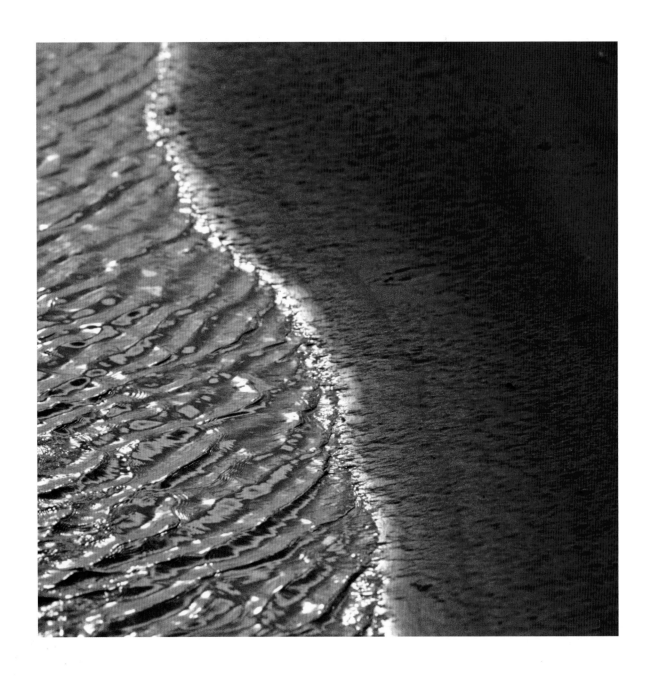

Atlantic Ocean - From long waves to a flat calm.

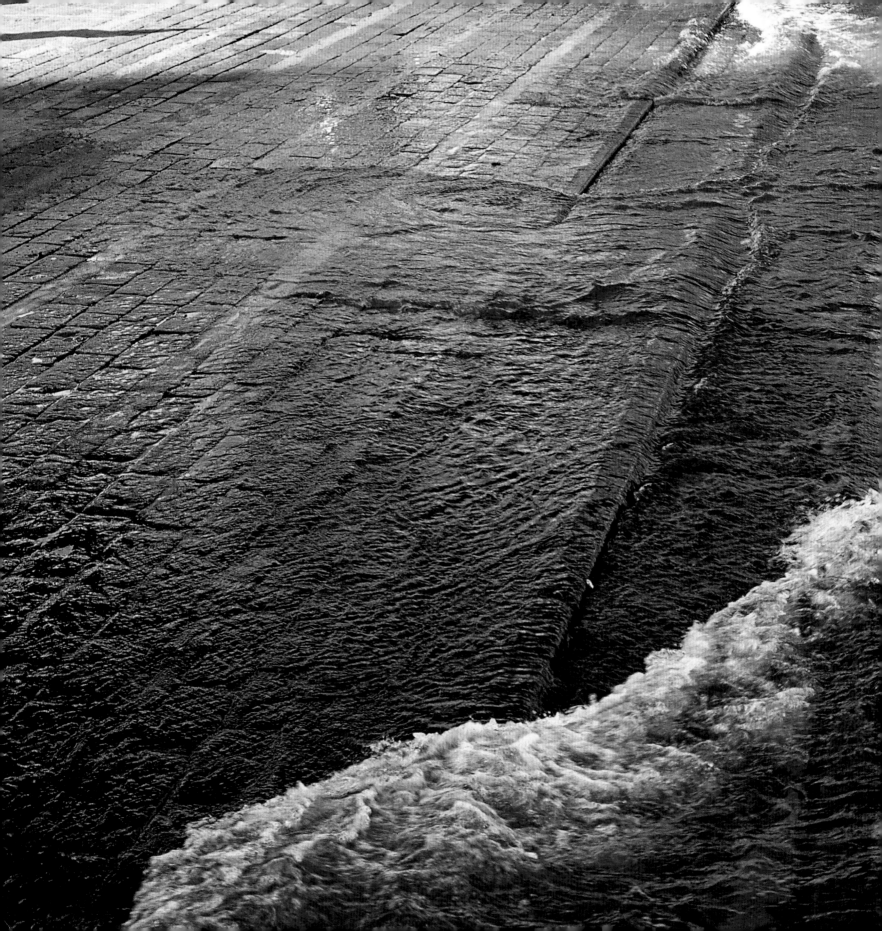

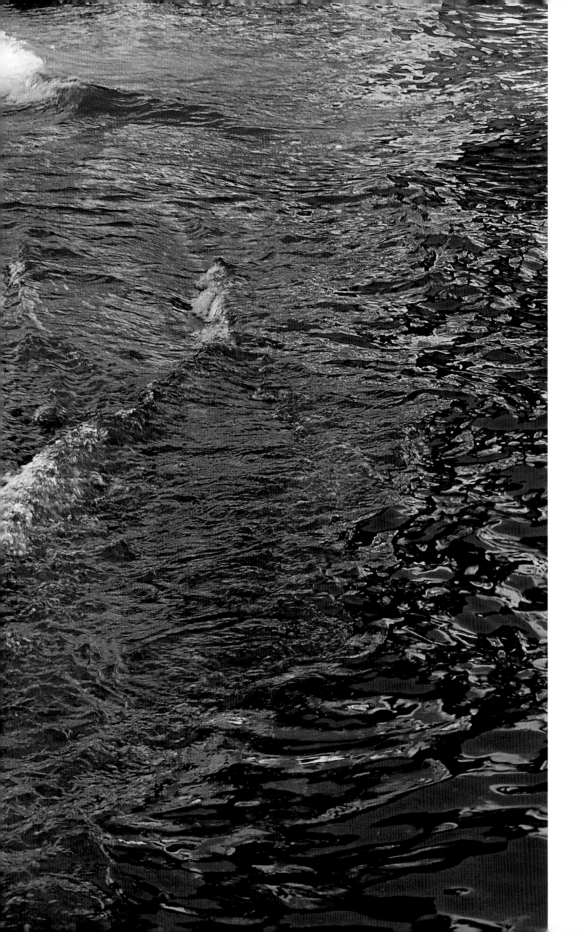

Color palette

664-665 ● Mediterranean Sea, Liguria (Italy) - Light plays over the port at Portofino.

666-667 ● Mediterranean Sea, Egypt - Reflections on a beach off Alexandria.

668-669 ● Caribbean Sea, Belize - All the shades of green and blue along the coast.

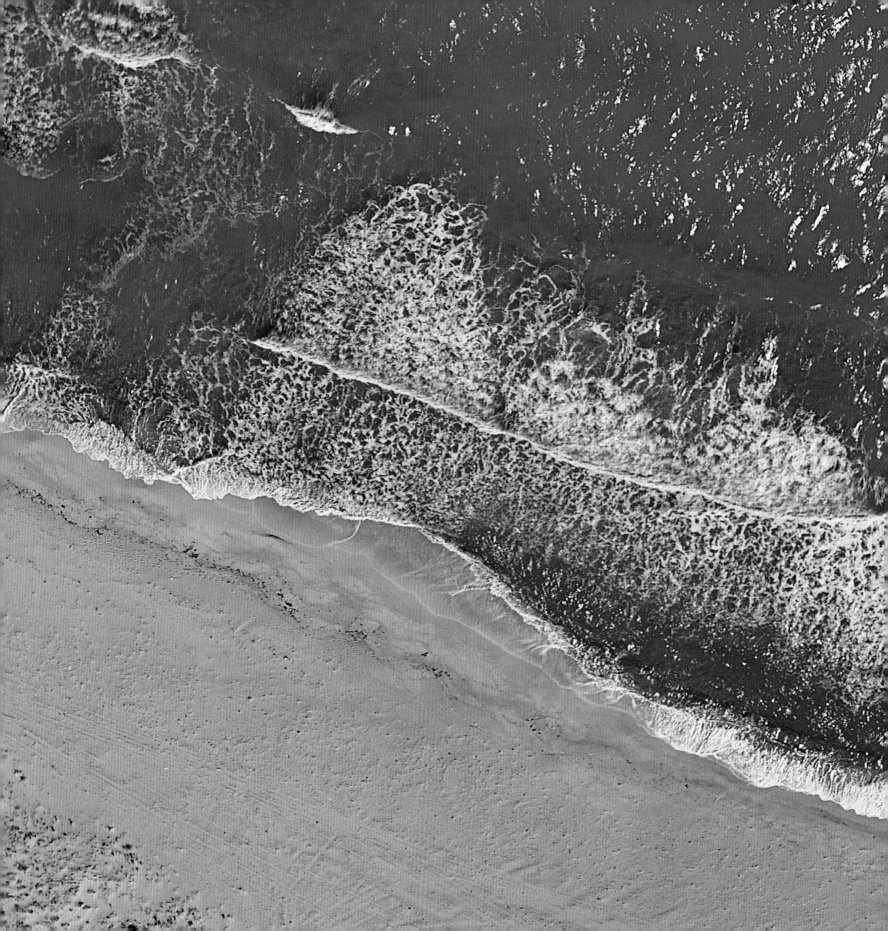

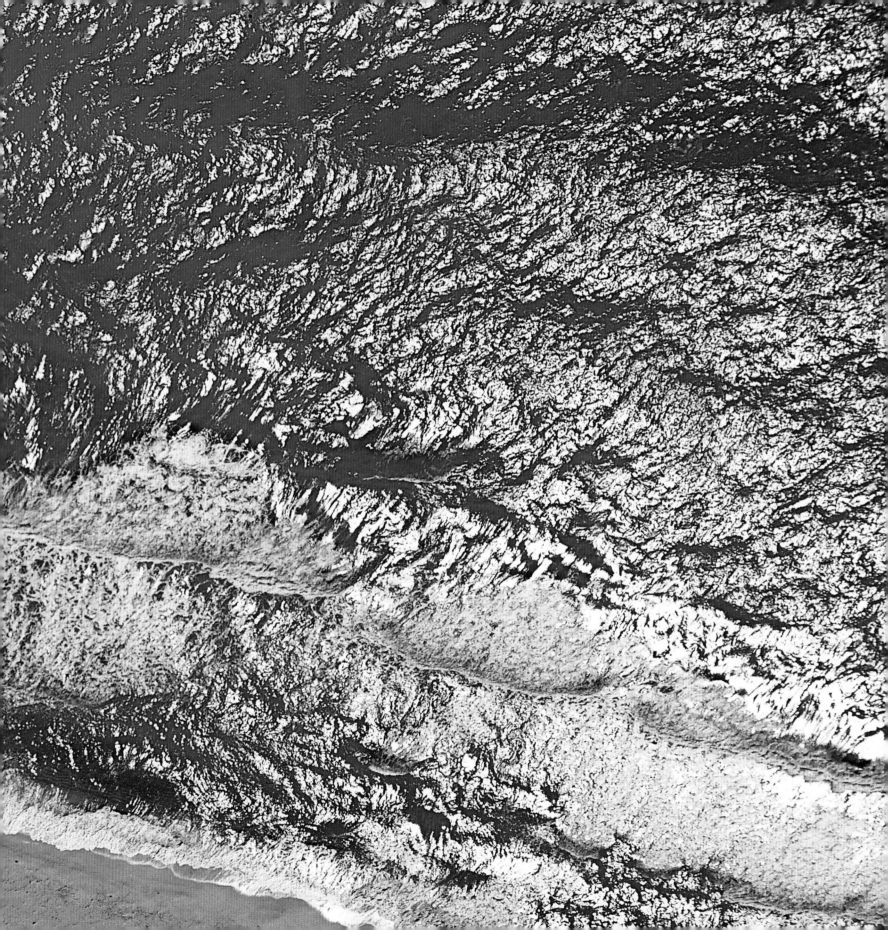

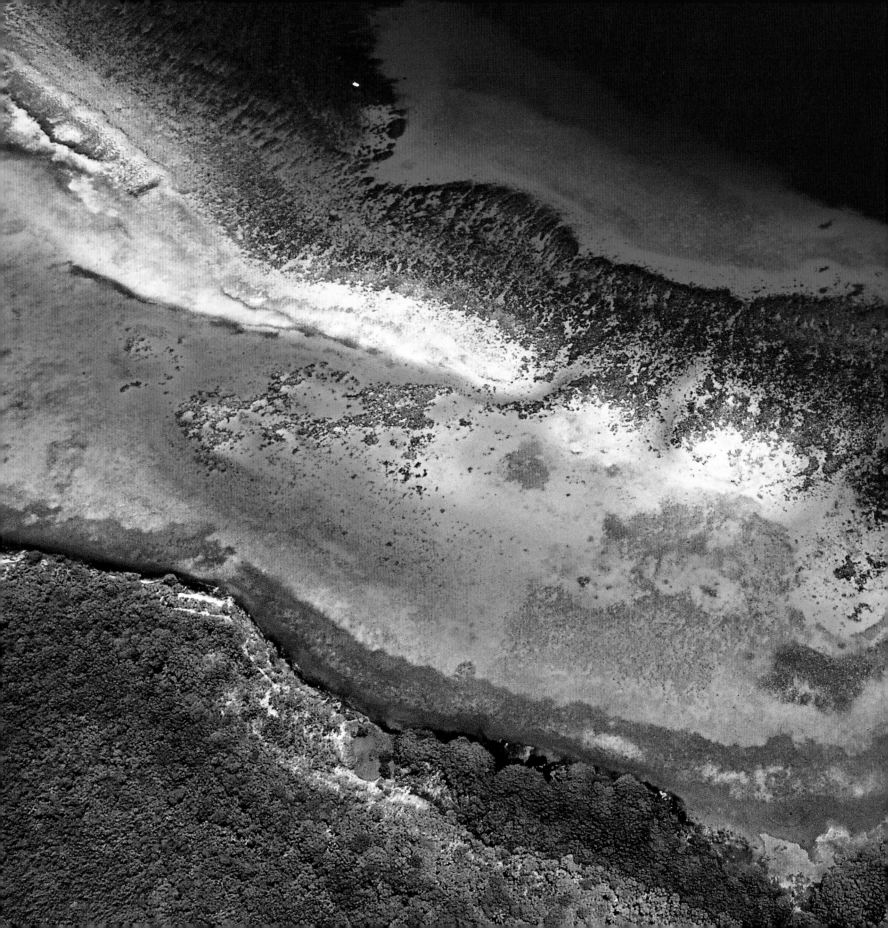

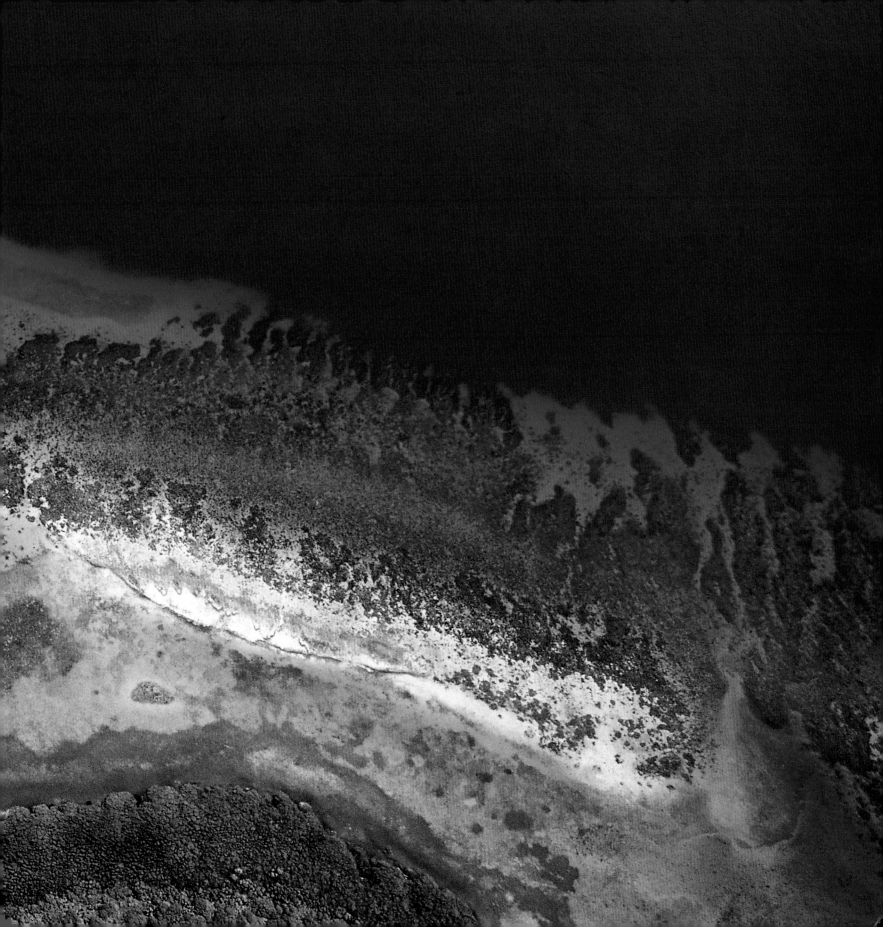

LOW TIDE

THIERRY JIGOUREL

• Pacific Ocean, Whitehaven Beach (Australia) - Effects created by the current.

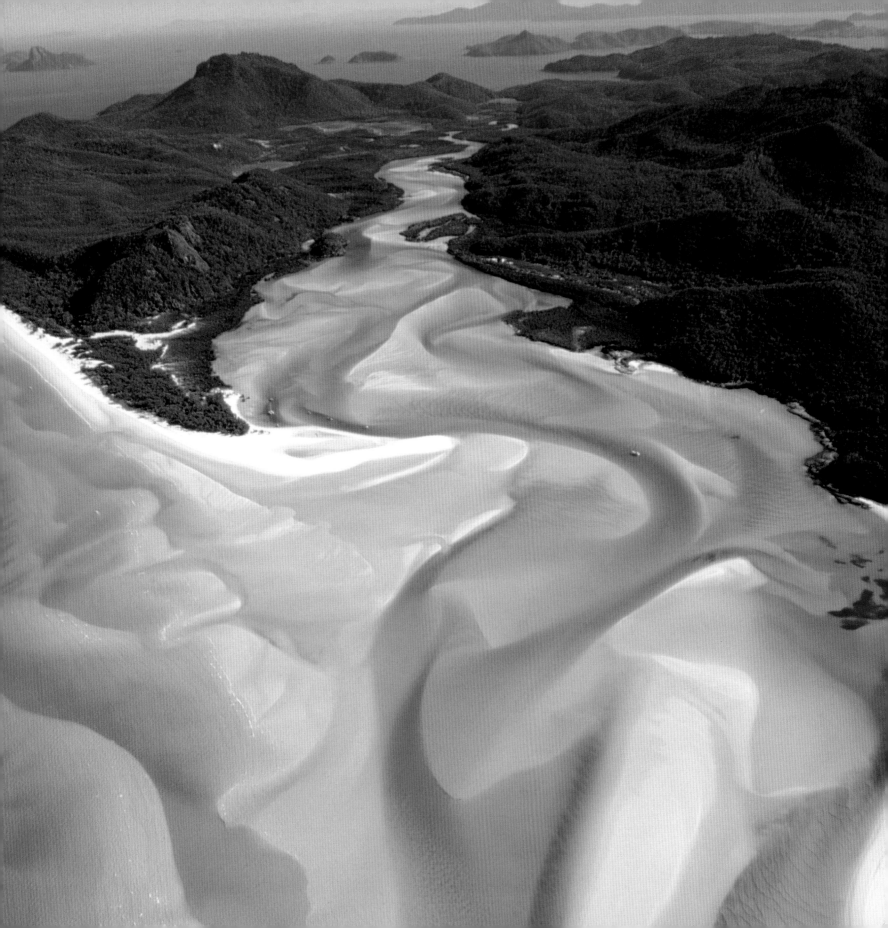

INTRODUCTION Low Tide

A POINT OF DEPARTURE FOR THE BEYOND,' SAID PLUTARCH.

THE IMMENSE OCEANS HAVE ALWAYS NOURISHED THE DAYDREAMS OF

THE PEOPLES WHO LIVE ON THEIR SHORES. THESE BROAD, DEEP AND

VAST PULSING ENTITIES HAVE ALWAYS IMPRESSED THEMSELVES ON US

MERE MORTALS. THE SEAS AND THEIR TIDES ARE THE LUNGS OF THE

WORLD. SINCE MAN BEGAN TO CONSIDER THEM, HE HAS SAID EVERY-

THING THAT THERE IS TO SAY ON THE TIDES, THAT SLOW AND INEX-

ORABLE SWELLING OF THE WATERS, AS POWERFUL AS A SEA MONSTER

AND AS REGULAR AS A SWISS WATCH. IF THERE IS ONE PLACE WHERE

THIS ETERNAL FORCE IS SEEN IN FULL, IT IS ON THE VAST SANDY

BEACHES OF THE NORTHWEST RIM OF THE OLD WORLD. ACCUS-

Red Sea, Ras Gharib (Egypt).

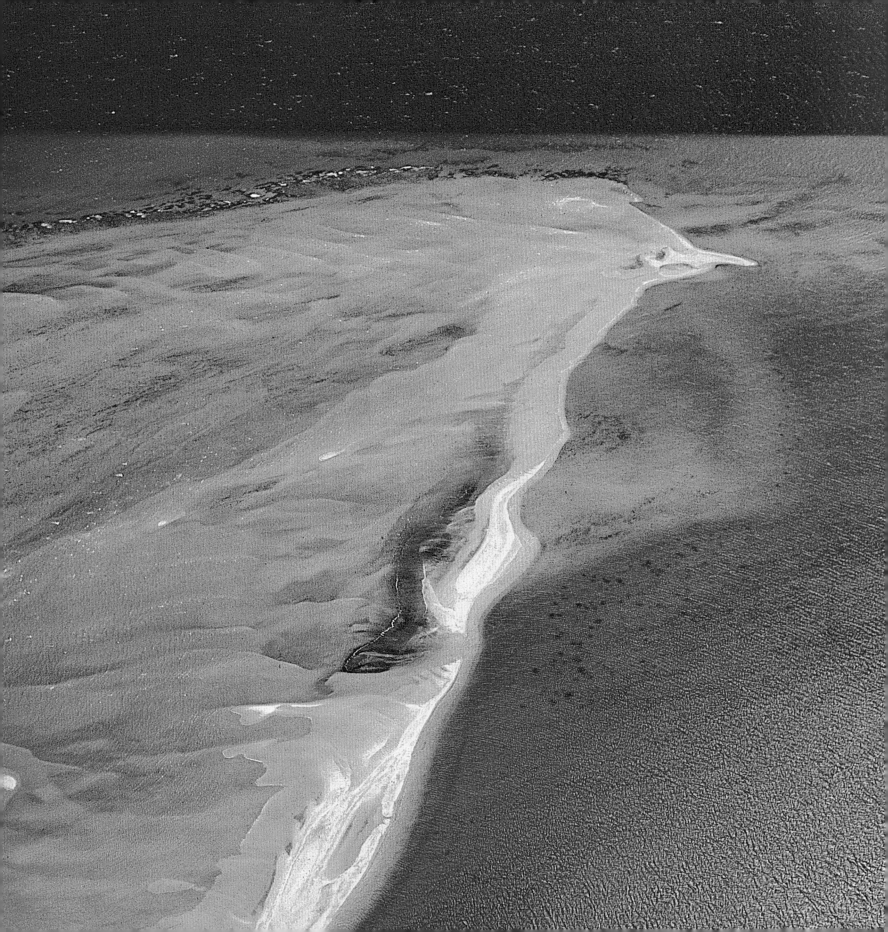

INTRODUCTION Low Tide

TOMED TO THE GENTLE MOVEMENT OF THE MEDITERRANEAN, JULIUS

CAESAR WAS AMAZED WHEN HE CAME UPON THIS PHENOMENON: 'IT

IS VERY DIFFICULT,' HE WROTE IN *DE BELLO GALLICO,* 'TO SAIL IN SUCH

AN IMMENSE AND BOUNDLESS SEA, SUBJECTED TO STRONG TIDES,

AND WITH FEW OR NO PORTS.' WHEN HE WROTE THOSE WORDS, CAE-

SAR HAD NOT YET COME INTO CONTACT WITH THE MOR BREIZH – THE

FEARSOME ENGLISH CHANNEL – WHERE THE WATER AT TIMES

RETREATS FOR MILES BEFORE RETURNING TO THE ATTACK. 'LA MER

CONTESTE LA RIVE' (THE SEA THREATENS THE SHORE) EXCLAIMED THE

POET XAVIER GRALL IN THE PRESENCE OF THE SEA, THAT CELTIC SEA

GOD MANANNAN MAC LIR, COVERED WITH SEAWEED, HIS POWERFUL

SHOULDERS DRIPPING WITH FOAM AND HIS BREATH SMELLING OF

INTRODUCTION Low Tide

IODINE. HERE, OFF NORTHERN FRANCE, THE DIFFERENCE IN TIDAL LEV-

ELS IS THE GREATEST IN THE WORLD: ANYWHERE BETWEEN 35 AND 50

FEET DIFFERENCE IN THE BAY OF MONT-SAINT-MICHEL! AND FUNDY

BAY IN EASTERN CANADA HAS THE STRONGEST TIDAL PULL. IT SHOULD

COME AS NO SURPRISE, THEREFORE, IF THOSE WHOSE LIVELIHOODS

WERE PROVIDED BY THE SEA SHOULD TAKE FEAR AT ITS UNFATH-

OMABLE MYSTERIES AND ATTEMPT TO EXPLAIN THEM WITH THEIR WILD

IMAGININGS. THE SHORE SWEPT BY BREAKERS, A PITILESS AND UNFOR-

GIVING ENVIRONMENT TEEMING WITH TINY CRAWLING CREATURES,

THAT MARKS THE BORDERLINE BETWEEN THE LAND AND SEA BECAME

THE THEATER OF THEIR DREAMS, A KINGDOM OF SUBMERGED CITIES.

FIRST AND FOREMOST REMAINS YS, THE MAGNIFICENT CAPITAL OF

INTRODUCTION Low Tide

PRINCESS AHÈS-DAHUD, WHO WAS TRANSFORMED INTO A MERMAID

AS A DIVINE PUNISHMENT. IN LANNION BAY BY SAINT-MICHEL, WHERE

THE TIDE SOMETIMES RETREATS NEARLY THREE MILES, SOMEONE

SWORE HE SAW THE CROSS OF THE CATHEDRAL OF A CURSED CITY ON

THE SEABED. AND UNTIL NOT SO LONG AGO THE ELDERLY CLAIMED,

SCREWING UP THEIR EYES TO SCAN THE HORIZON, THAT WHEN THE

SEA WITHDREW SO FAR AT SEPT-ÎLES, FABULOUS GARDENS COULD BE

SEEN. SURELY THIS BORDER ZONE, INTERLACED BY SANDY PATHS

SOON TO BE SWEPT AWAY BY THE ADVANCE OF THE SEA, MUST BE THE

OUTLYING REGION OF ANOTHER WORLD?

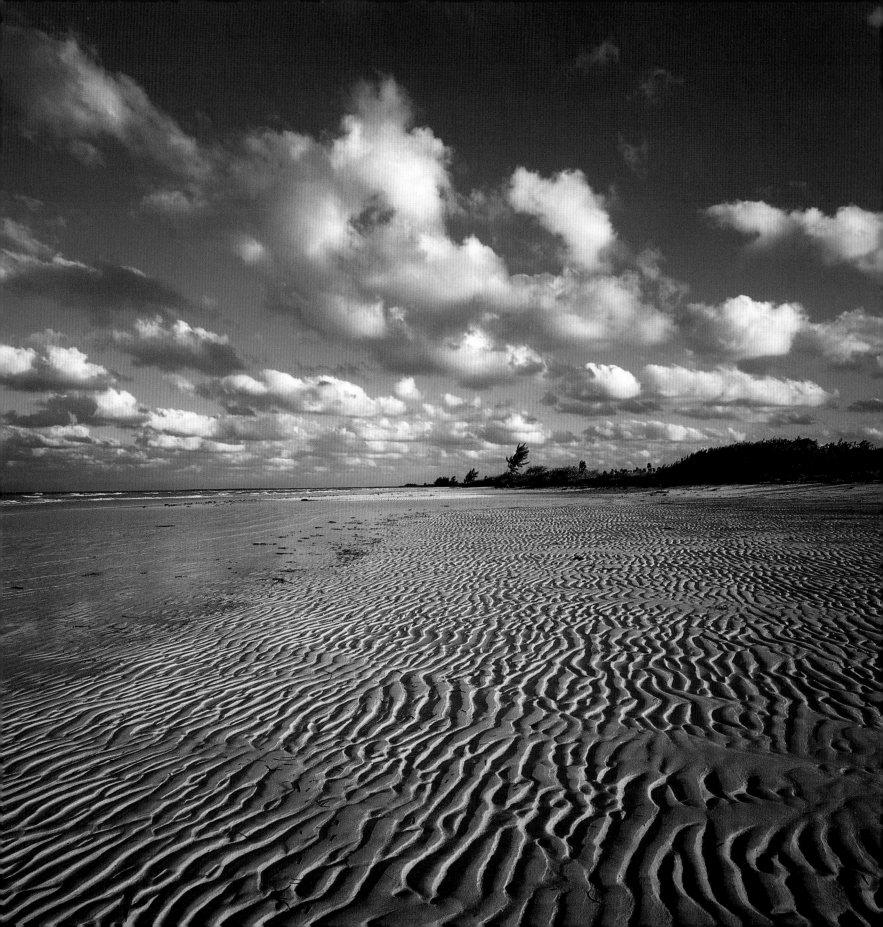

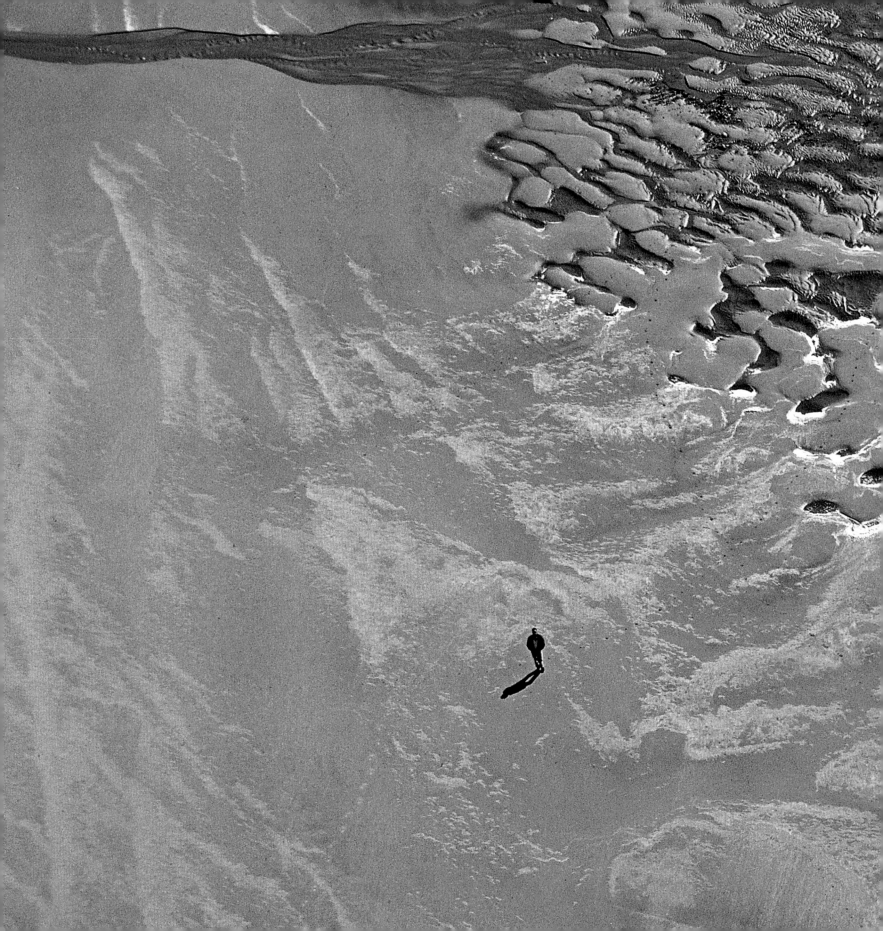

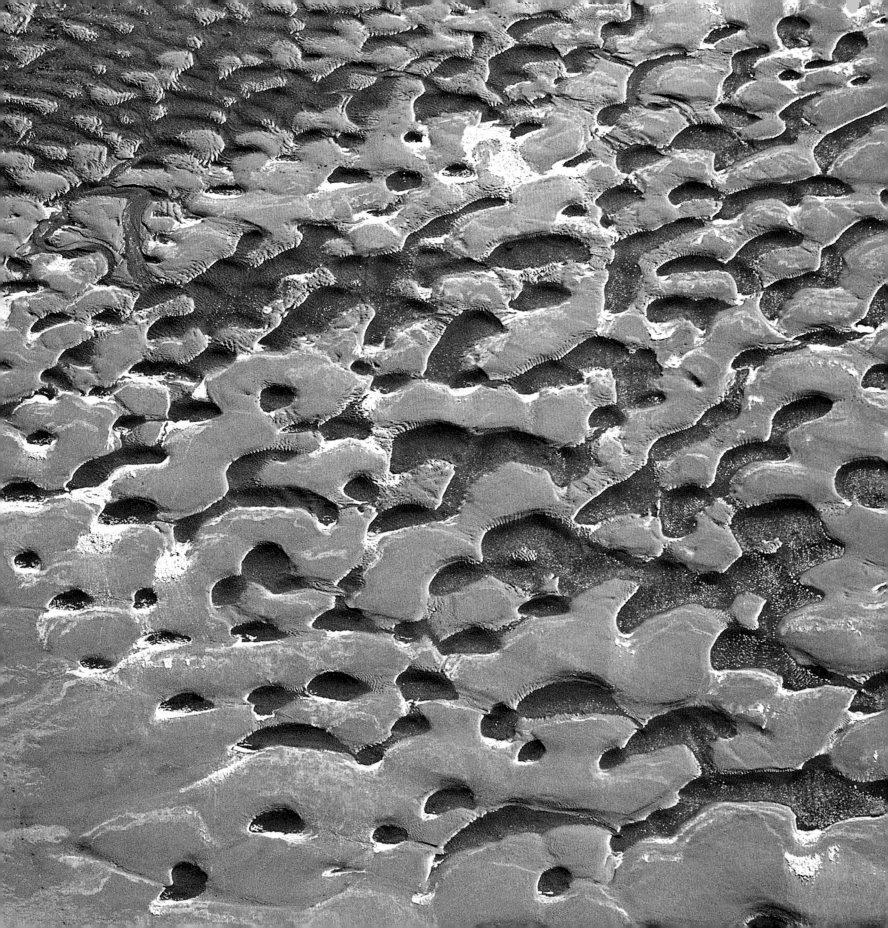

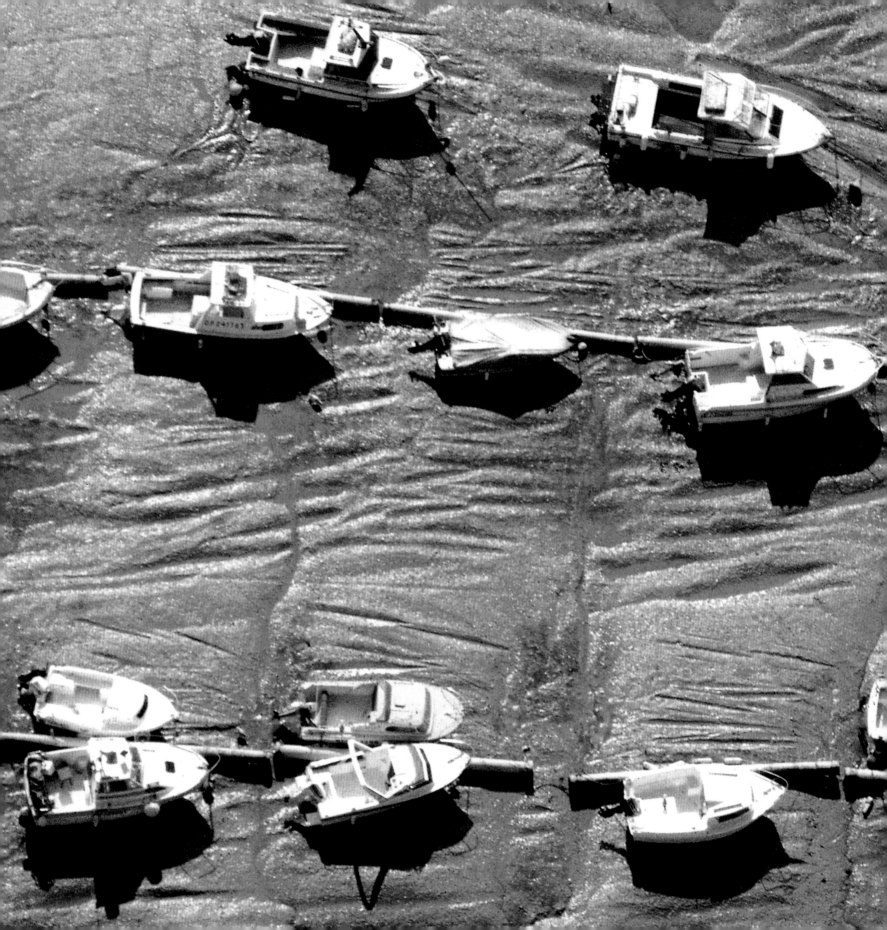

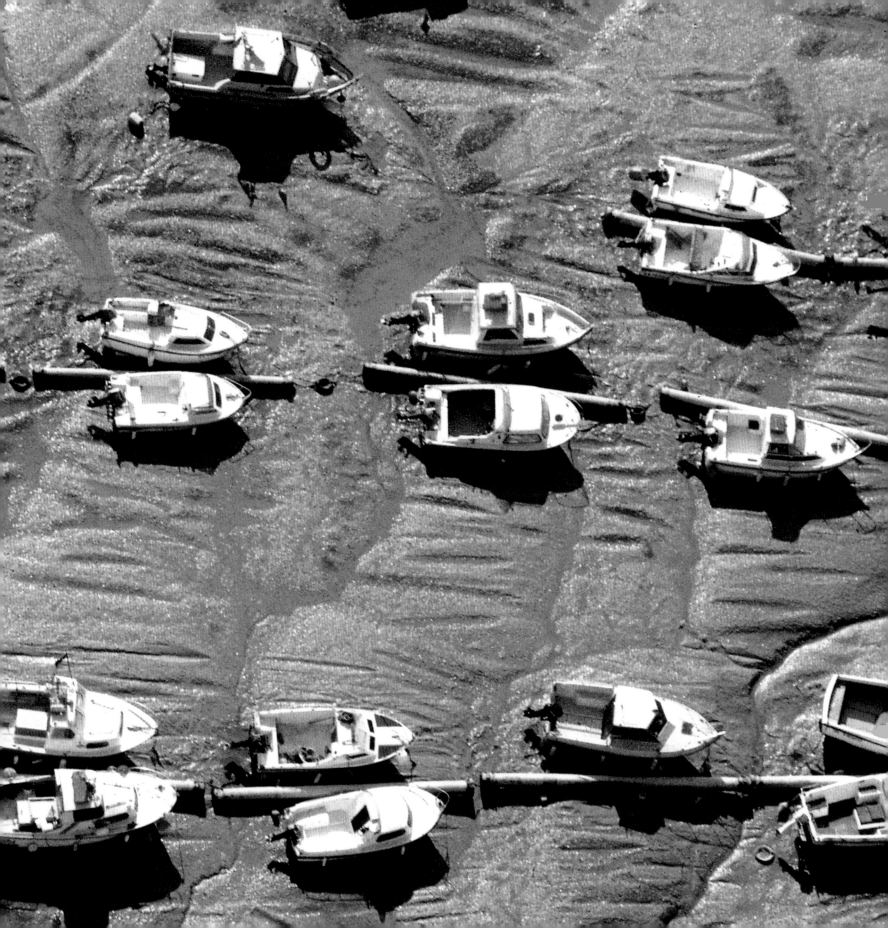

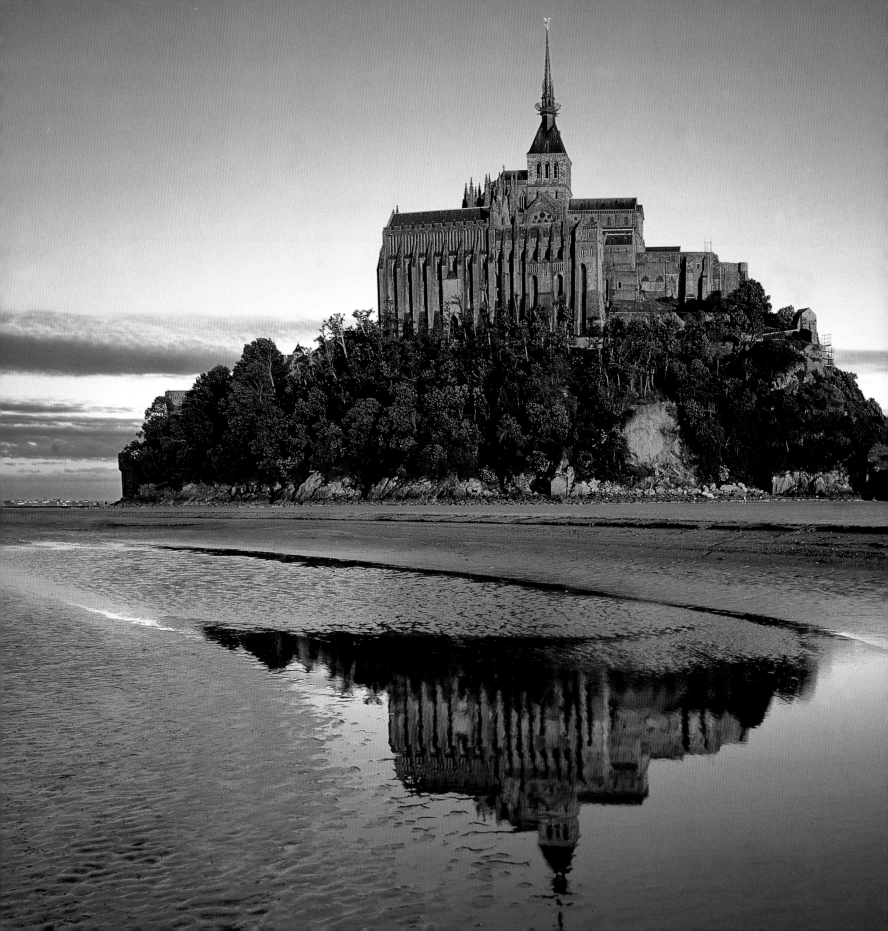

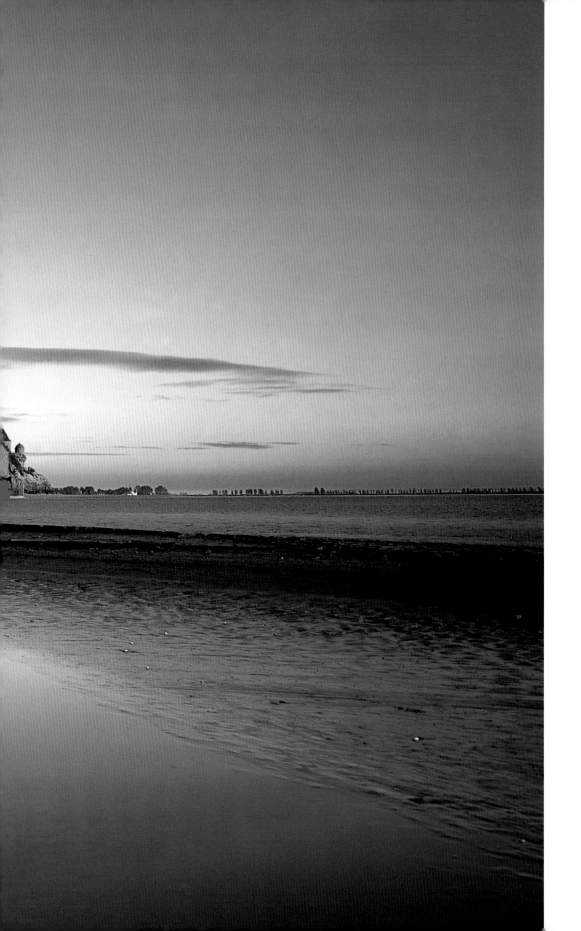

Suspended between land and sea

682-683 ● Atlantic Ocean, Normandy (France) - Abbey and island of Mont-St. Michel.

684-685 ● Pacific Ocean, Oregon (USA) - Haystack Rock and Cape Kiwanda.

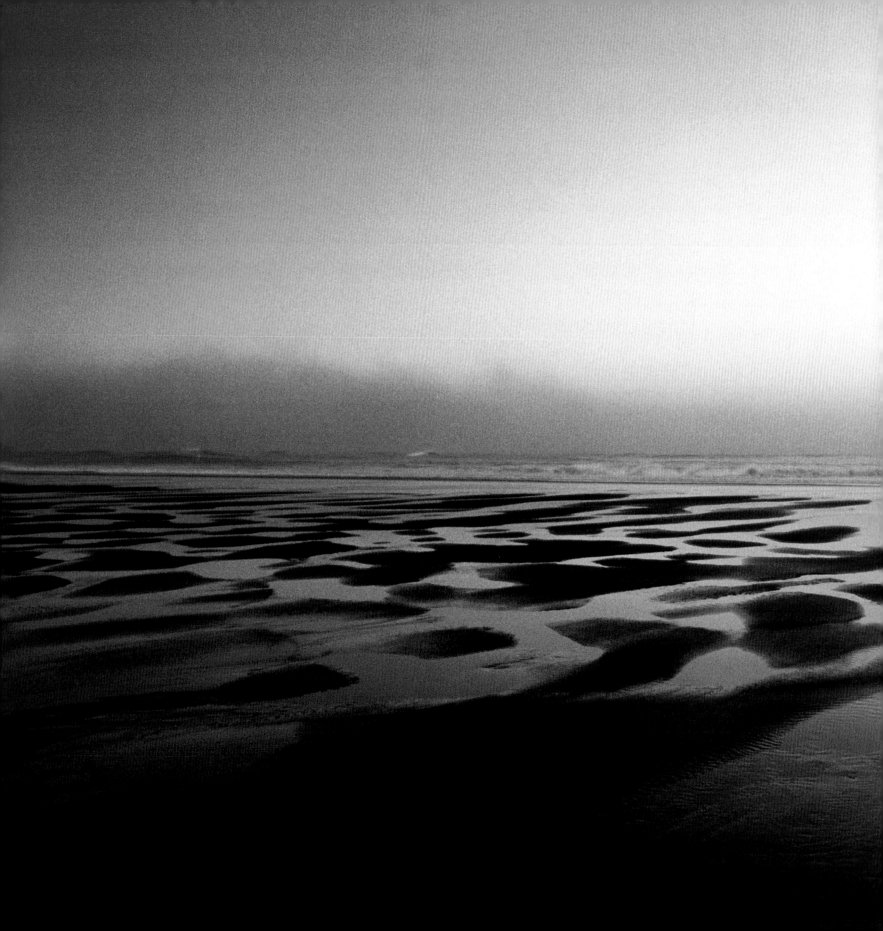

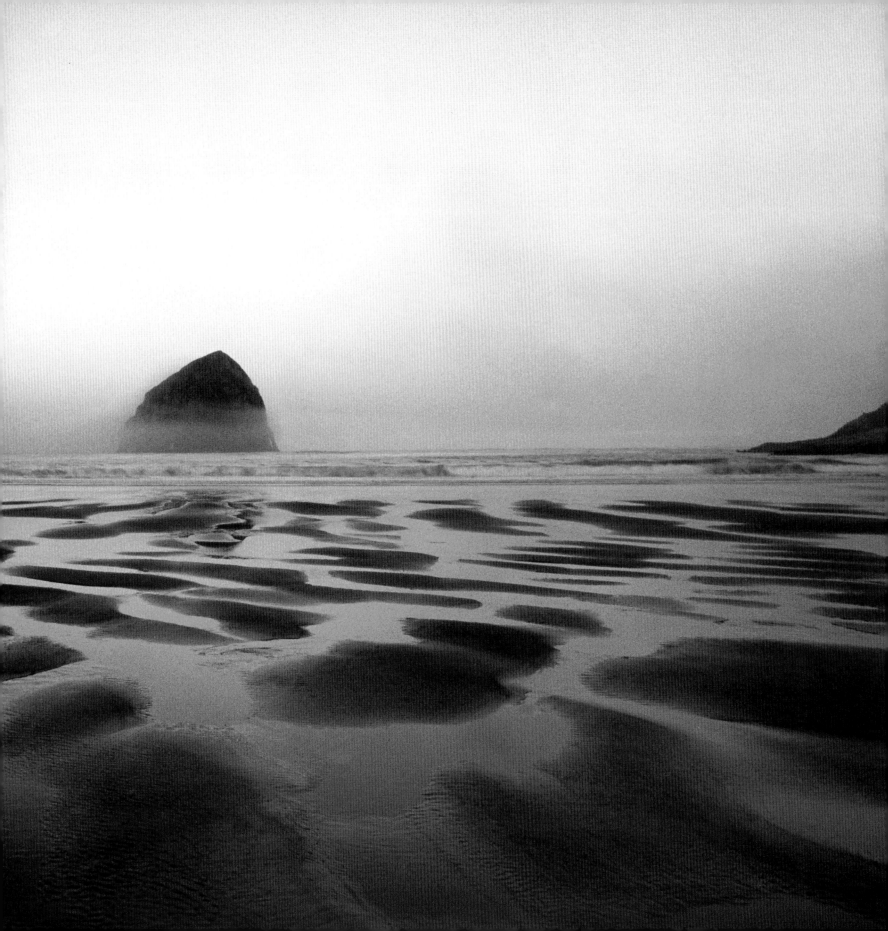

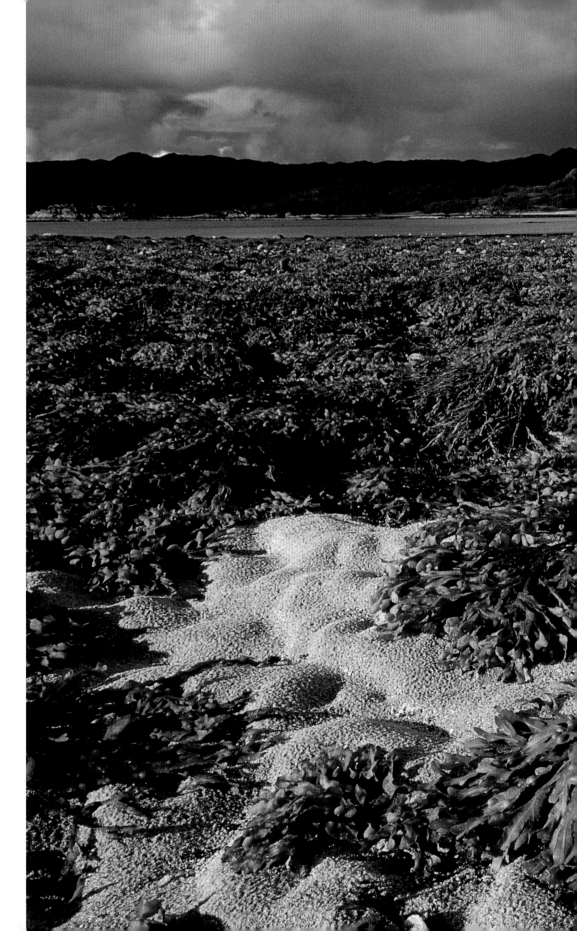

On the beach

- North Sea, Scotland - Thalassophyte seaweed on Lochailort beach.

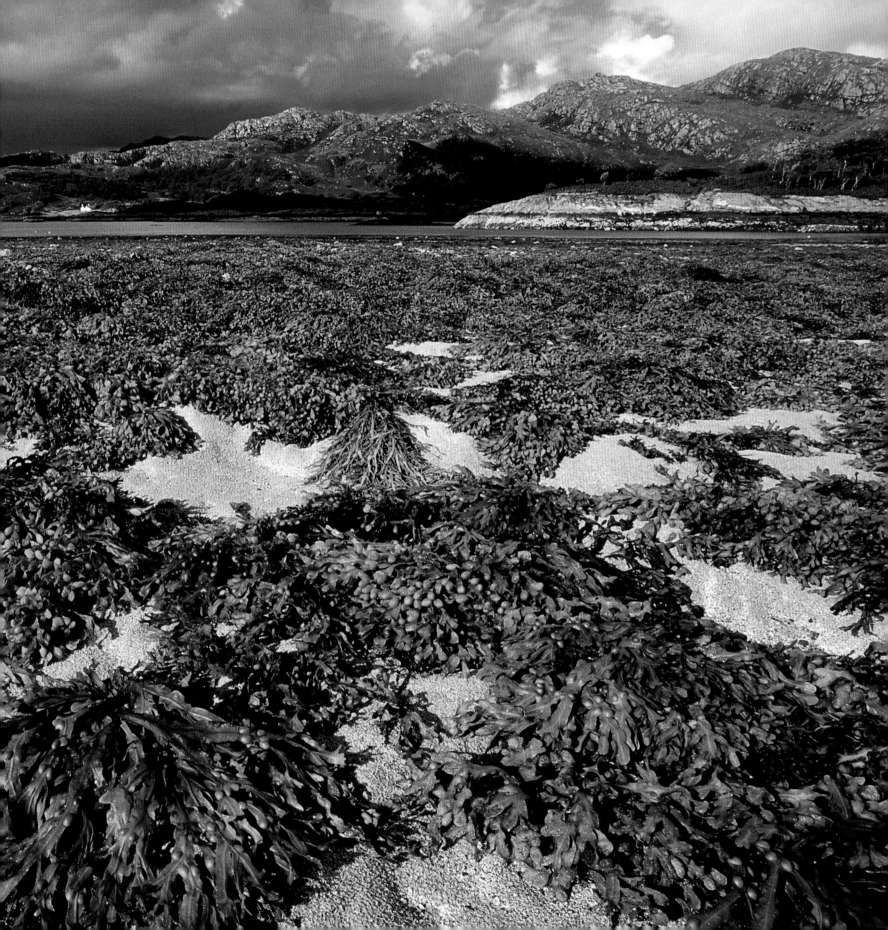

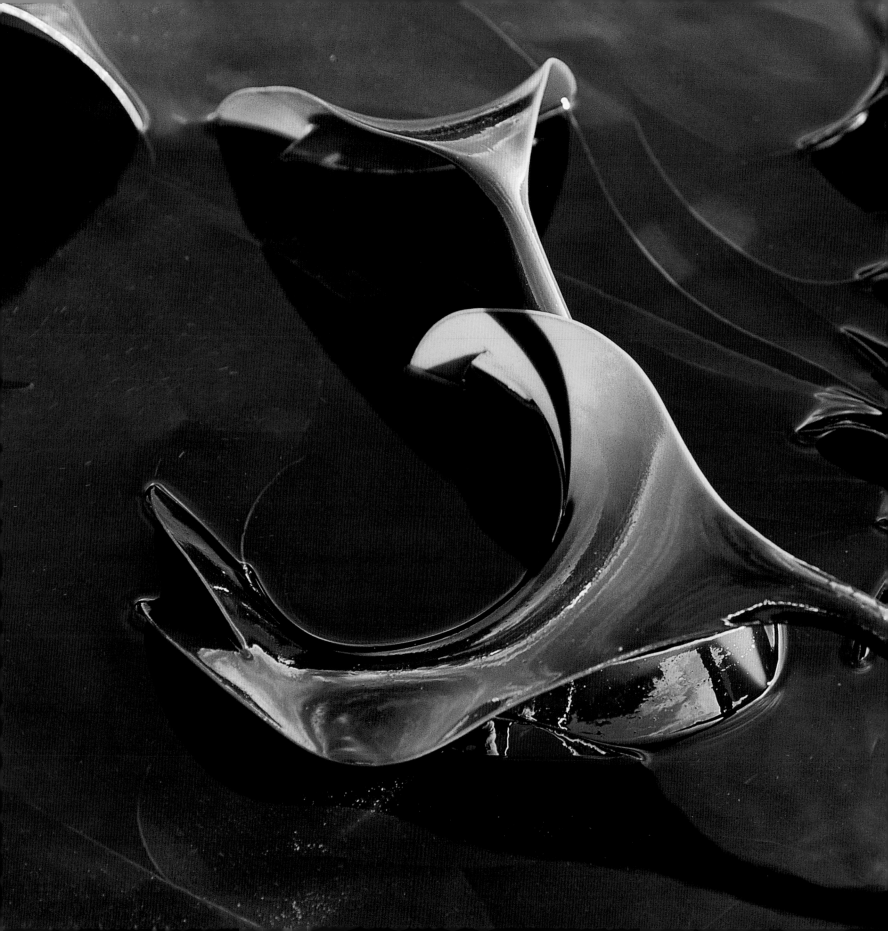

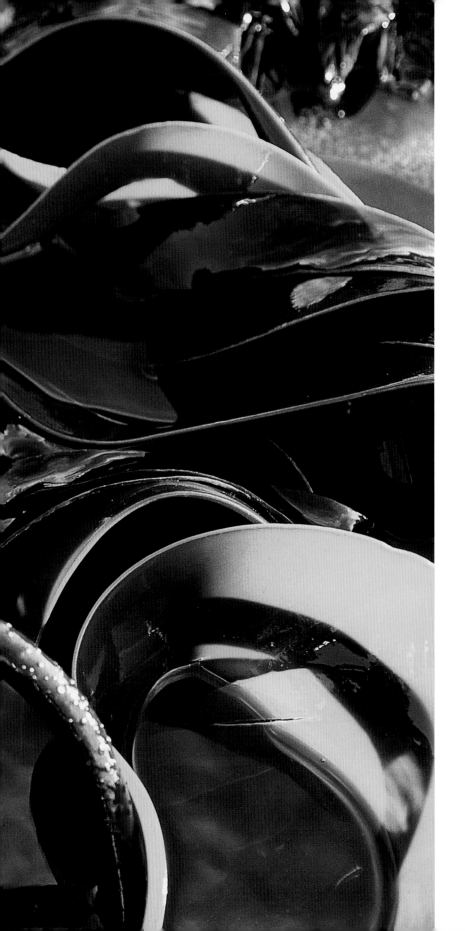

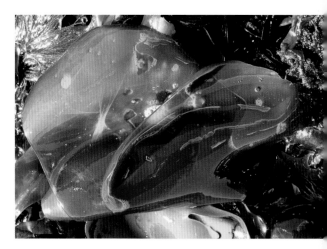

Atlantic Ocean, Western Cape (South Africa) - Tide pool with seaweed.

Sea
anemones
and starfish

Pacific Ocean, Australia -
A territorial struggle
in a tide pool.

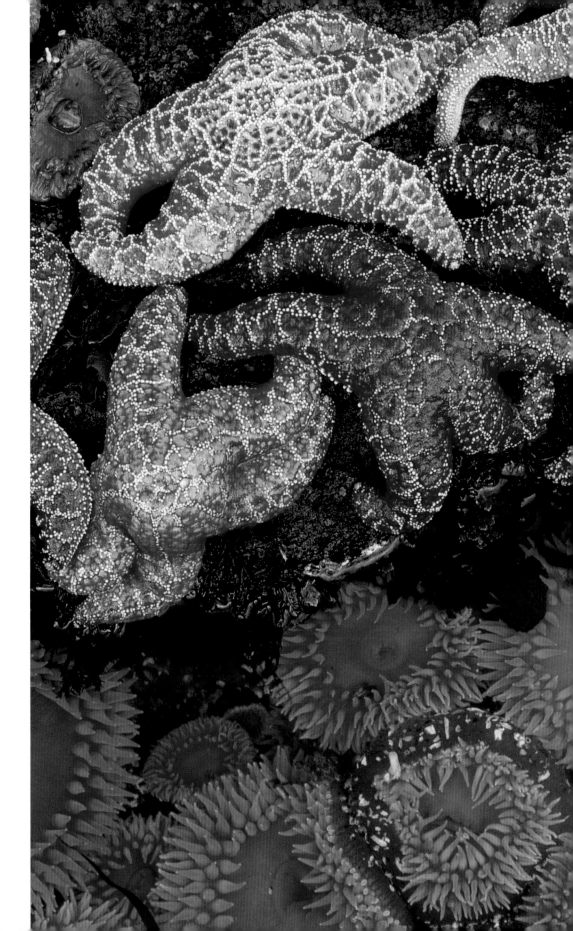

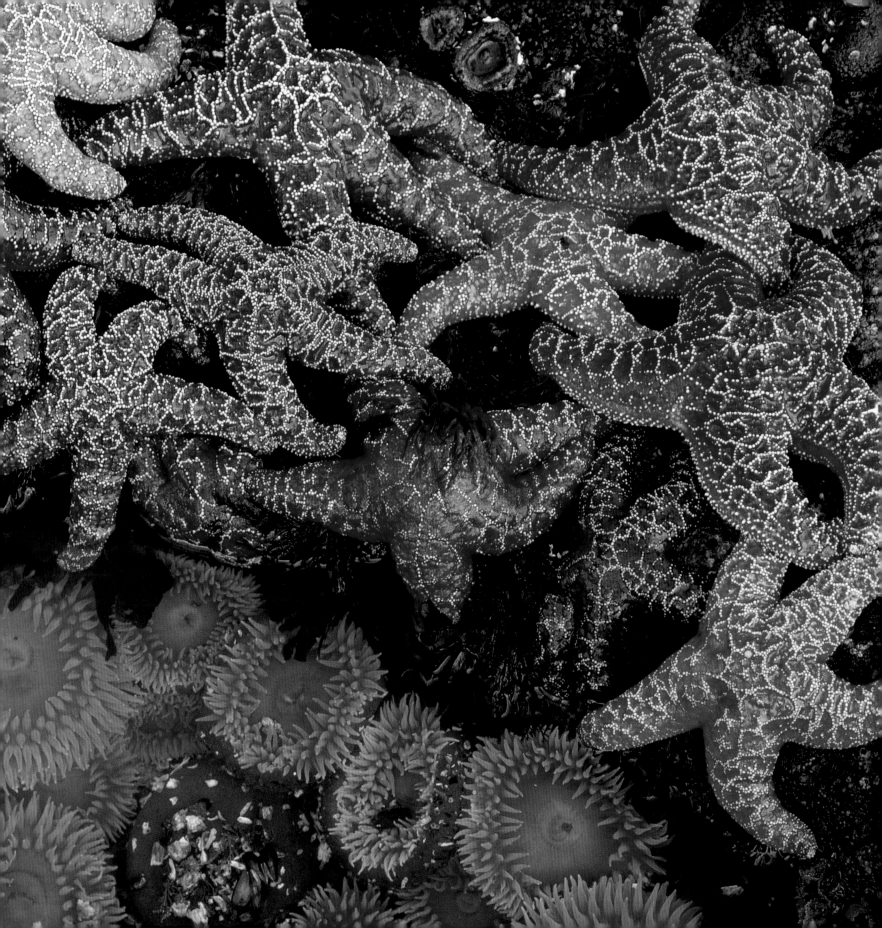

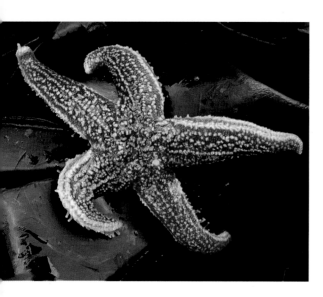

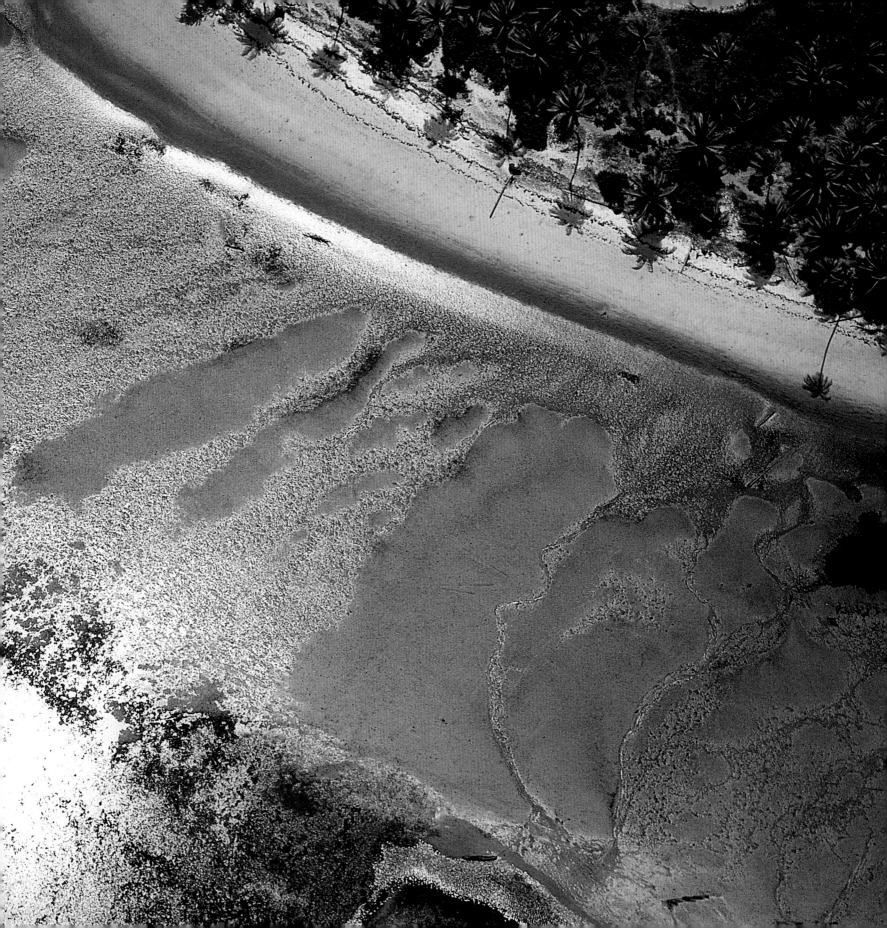

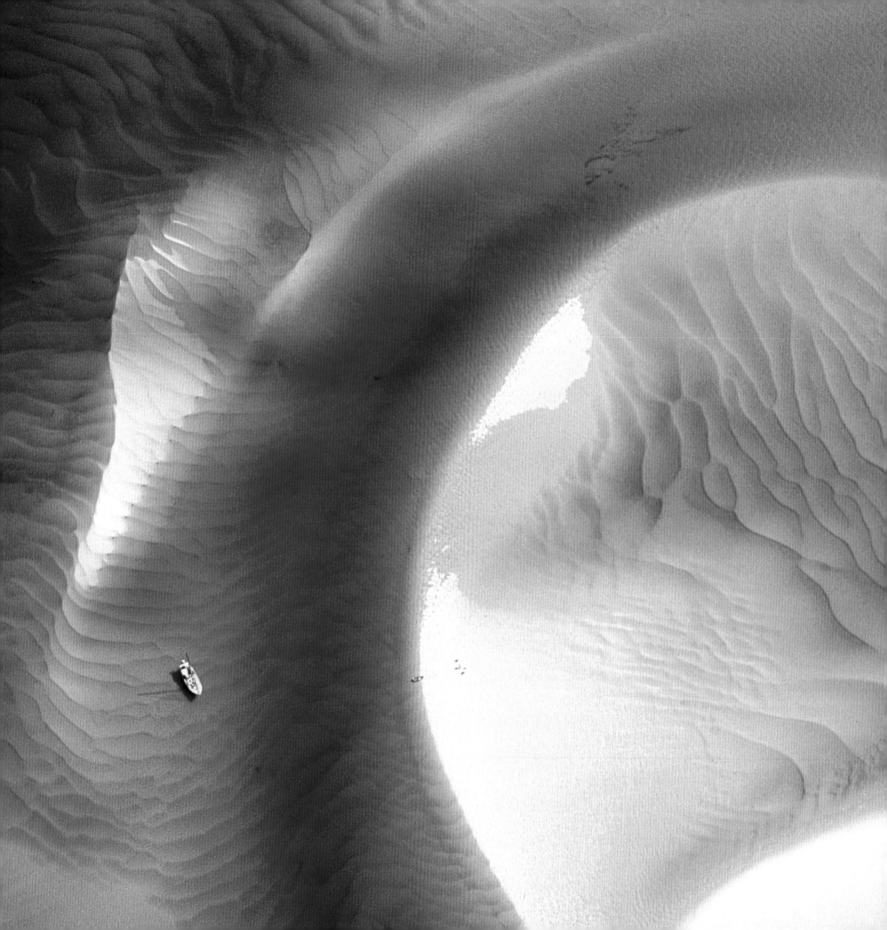

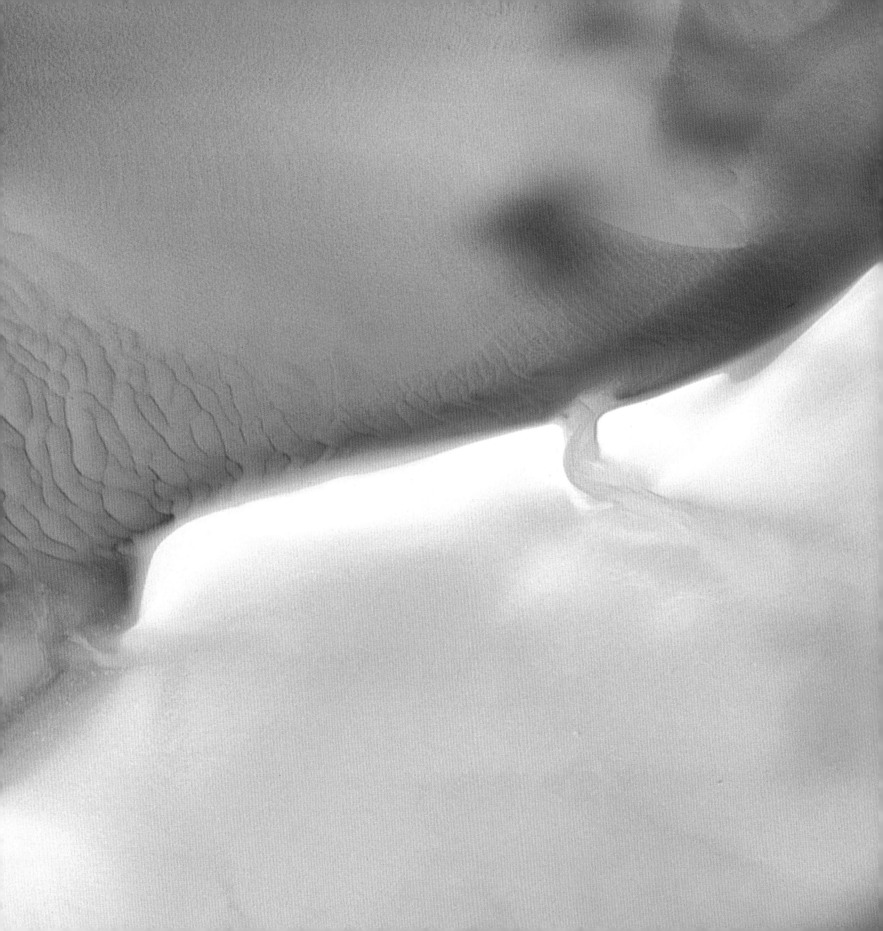

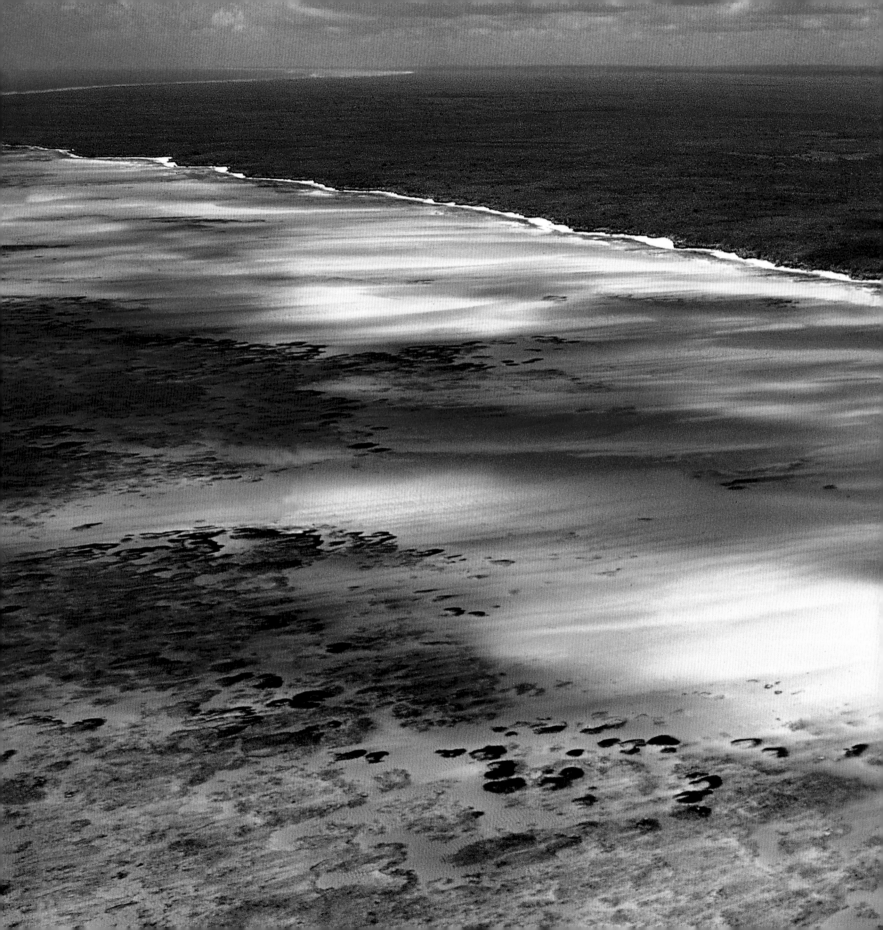

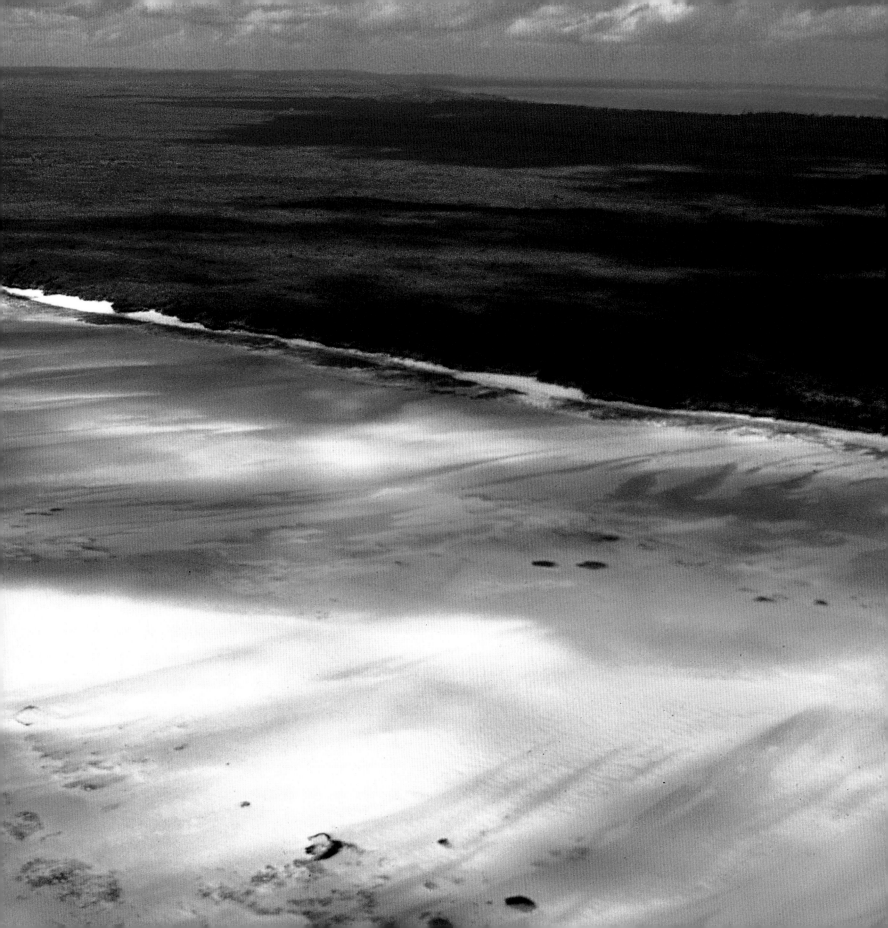

At the END of the DAY

GAETANO CAFIERO

• Pacific Ocean, French Polynesia - Rangiroa.

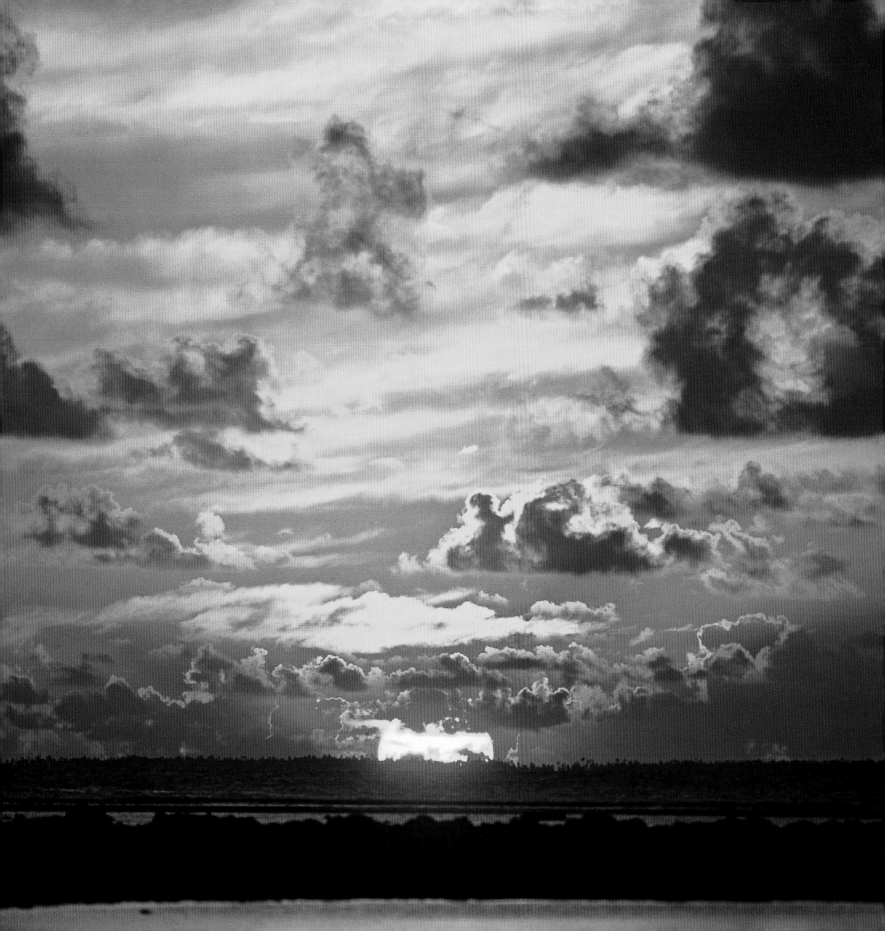

INTRODUCTION At the End of the Day

'Now was the hour which longing backward bends, in those that sail and melt their heart ... over the day that dies.' The hour of nostalgia – not just for Dante – occurs as the sun sets, when the last of the day's rays are about to slip away and the colors of the sea, whether they are dazzling, bright, clear, flat or lifeless, depending on the quantity and quality of the light, fade to darkness. The different brushstrokes of sunshine on the water and rocks are capable of producing the full range of the rainbow, a blazing kaleidoscope of color or just a single tone. What colors does the sun paint the sea? The trans-

INTRODUCTION At the End of the Day

PARENT NATURE OF WATER MEANS THAT IT APPEARS WHITE WHEN

IT FOAMS AND BLACK ON MOONLESS AND STARLESS NIGHTS. THE

WATER REFLECTS GREENS OF ALL HUES WHEN THE SEABED IS RICH

IN ALGAE, SEEMS PINKISH WHEN IT WASHES OVER CORAL SANDS,

AND OFFERS EVERY SHADE AND TINT OF BLUE AS THE DISTANCE

BETWEEN SURFACE AND SEABED INCREASES OUT AT SEA. BUT

THERE IS A TIME OF DAY WHEN ALL THESE COLORS TAKE ON A SIN-

GLE HUE: WHEN THE WARM AFTERNOON AIR BEGINS TO COOL AND

THE SEA BREEZE CHANGES DIRECTION, CARRYING THE SMELLS OF

THE SEA TO THE SHORE. THESE ARE THE HOURS IN WHICH THE SUN

SENDS OUT LONG GOLDEN DARTS THAT FIRST FLUSH BLOOD-RED,

At the End of the Day

Introduction

THEN ARE STAINED WITH MAUVE AND PURPLE. LIKE TEMPERA PAINT

IN A FRESCO, THE SUN'S LIQUID RAYS FALL ON THE WATER, REEFS,

AND CLIFFS AND PLAY WITH OBJECTS LEFT LYING ON THE BEACH: A

SUNSHADE, A CHILD'S BUCKET, A BEACH BALL … ORANGE WAVES

BREAK ON THE SHORE WHILE THE SILHOUETTES OF CAWING GULLS

GLIDE AND SWOOP AGAINST THE LAST QUARTER OF THE SUN ABOVE

THE HORIZON. THEN, SUDDENLY, THE FIRE OF SUNSET IS DOUSED,

THE SKY TURNS PALE AND SLOWLY THE SEA APPEARS TO BE TRANS-

FORMED INTO LIQUID LEAD, BEFORE PUTTING ON ITS TRANSLUCENT

NIGHT-TIME SHAWL OF REFLECTED MOONLIGHT.

703 ● Mediterranean Sea, Greece - Zakynthos.

704-705 ● Atlantic Ocean, Florida (USA) - A bridge between sky and sea.

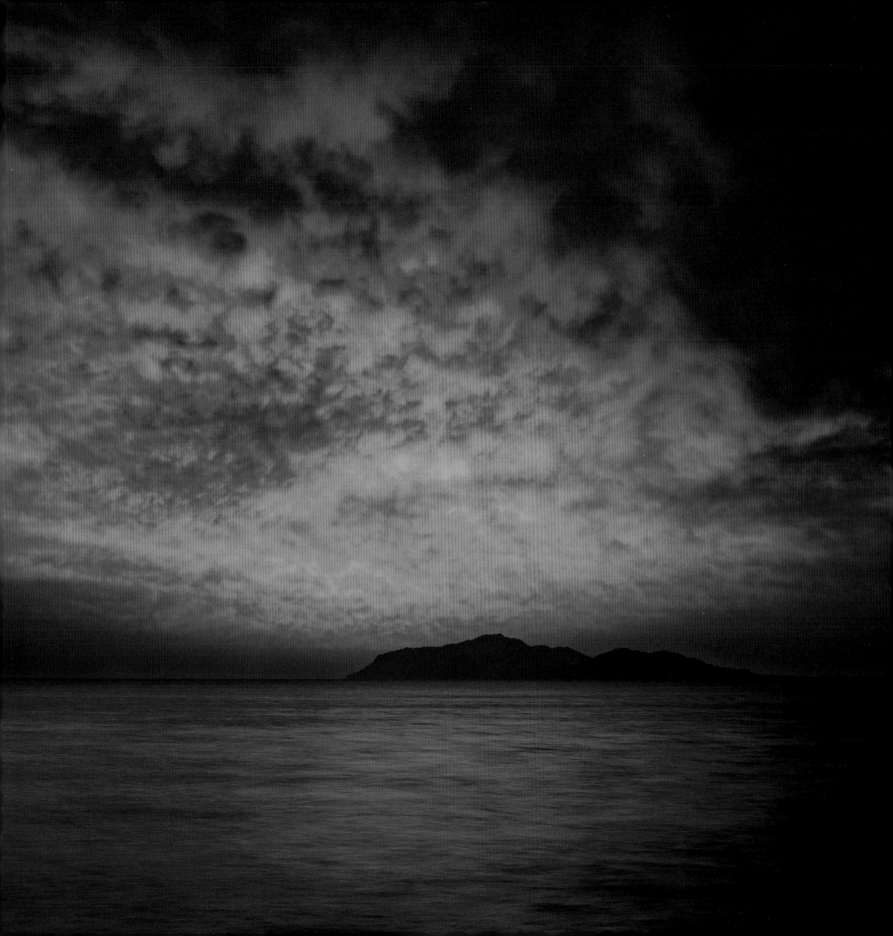

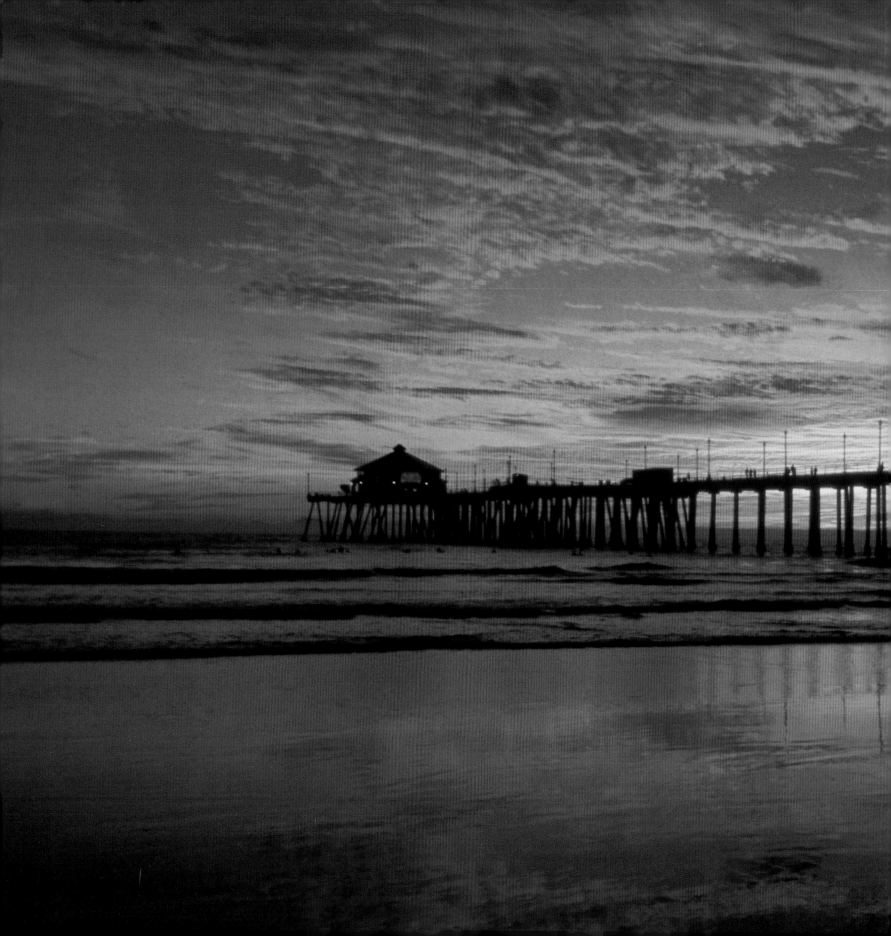

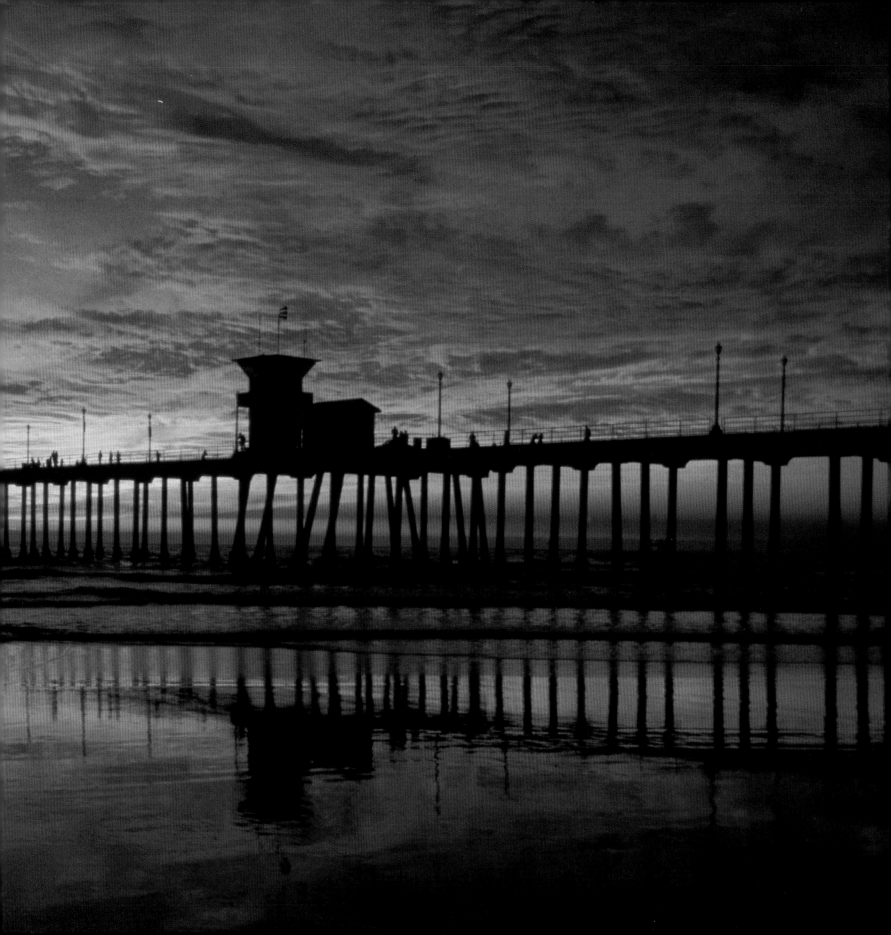

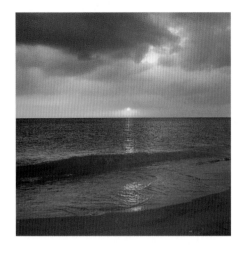 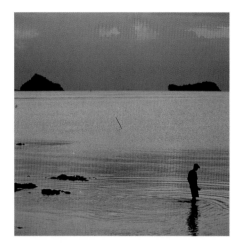 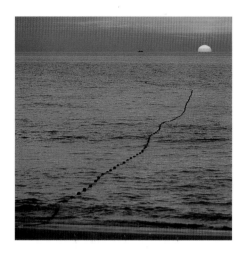

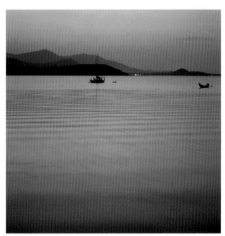 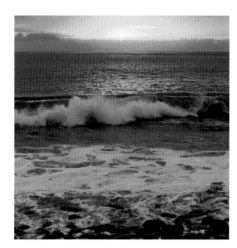 

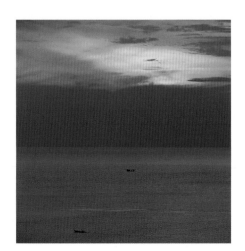

706 left to right, top to bottom:
- Atlantic Ocean, Florida (USA) - Key West.
- Indian Ocean, Thailand - Surat Thani.
- Indian Ocean, Sri Lanka - Trinkomalee.
- Indian Ocean, Thailand – Bay of Laem Mai Kaen.
- Pacific Ocean, Marquesas Islands - Fatu Hiva.
- Indian Ocean, Thailand - Phuket.

707 ● Caribbean Sea, Cuba - Capo San Antonio.

706

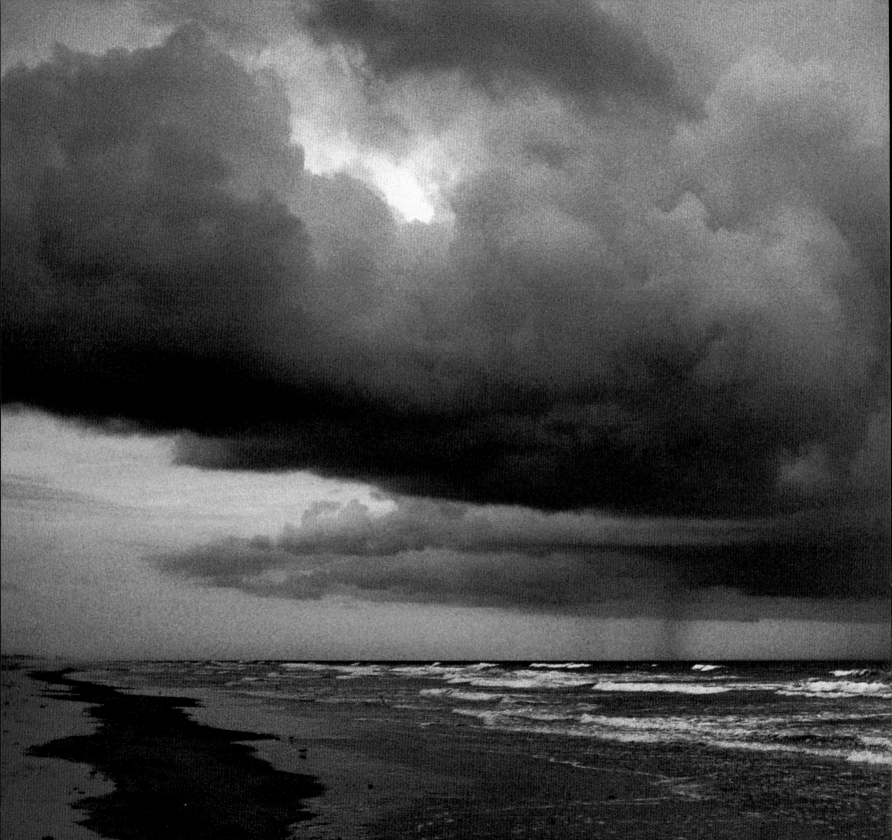

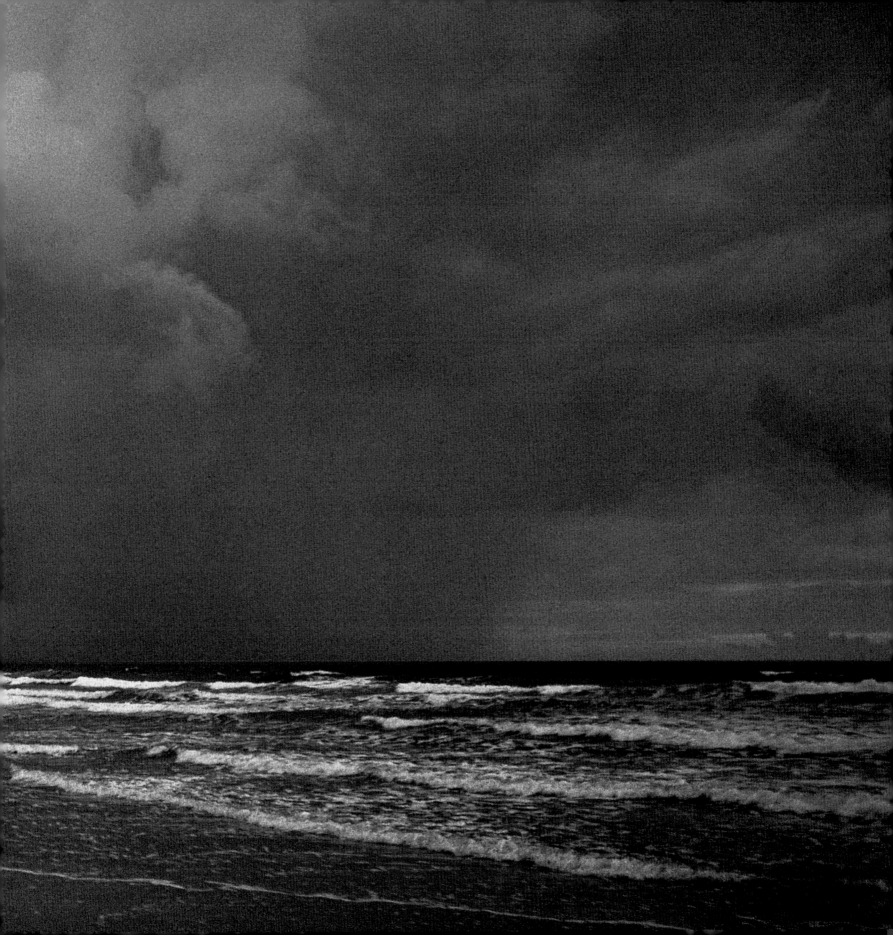

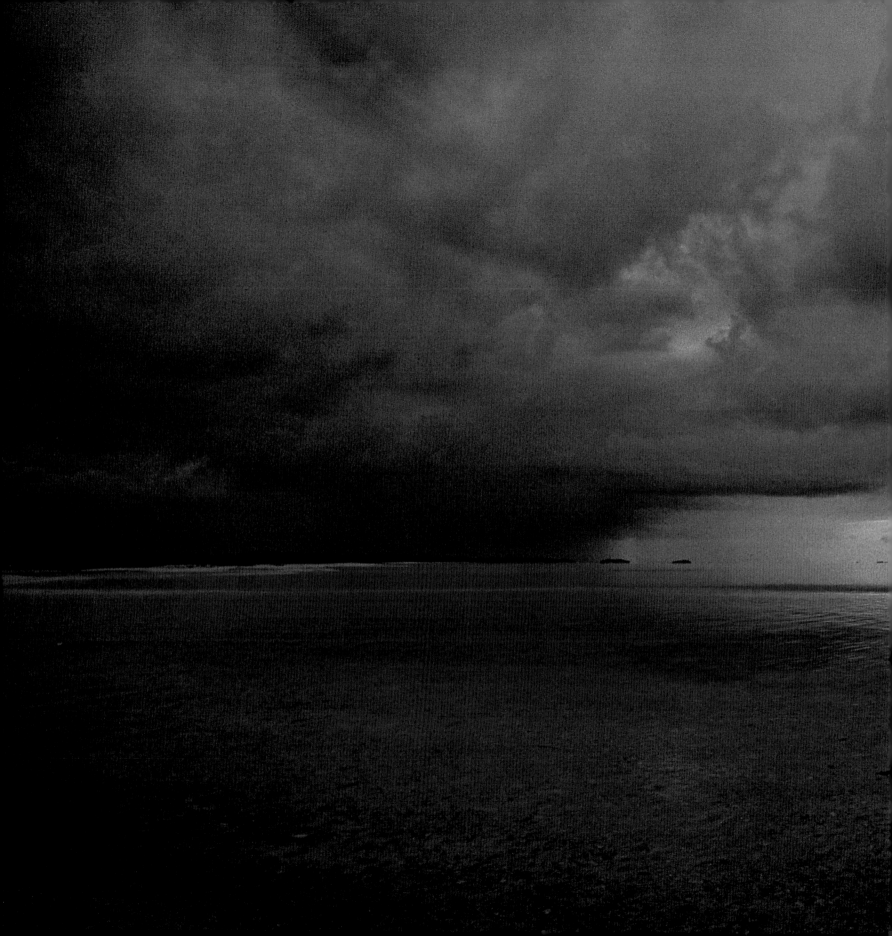

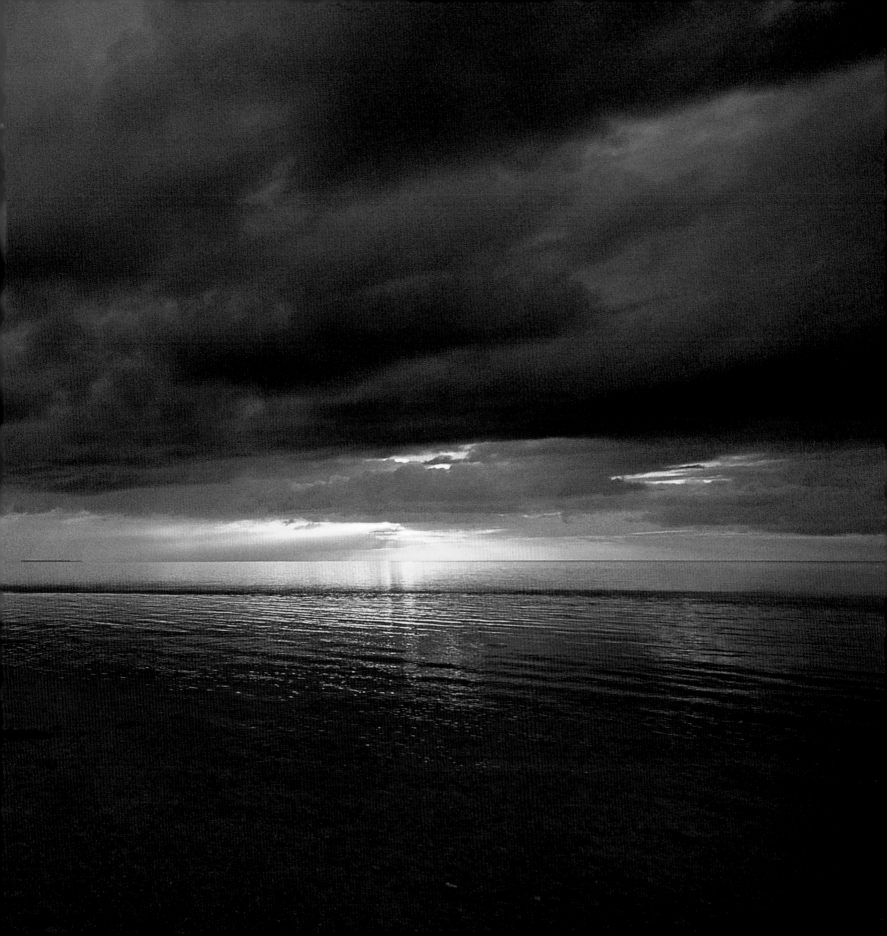

"THE DAY WAS ENDING IN A SERENITY OF STILL AND EXQUISITE BRILLIANCE. THE WATER SHONE PACIFICALLY; THE SKY, WITHOUT A SPECK, WAS A BENIGN IMMENSITY OF UNSTAINED LIGHT … IN ITS CURVED AND IMPERCEPTIBLE FALL, THE SUN SANK LOW, AND FROM GLOWING WHITE CHANGED TO A DULL RED WITHOUT RAYS AND WITHOUT HEAT."

from HEART OF DARKNESS
by Joseph Conrad

708-709 ● Atlantic Ocean, Florida (USA) - Canaveral National Seashore.

710-711 ● Pacific Ocean, French Polynesia - Fakarava.

712-713 ● Mediterranean Sea, Liguria (Italy) - Cinque Terre.

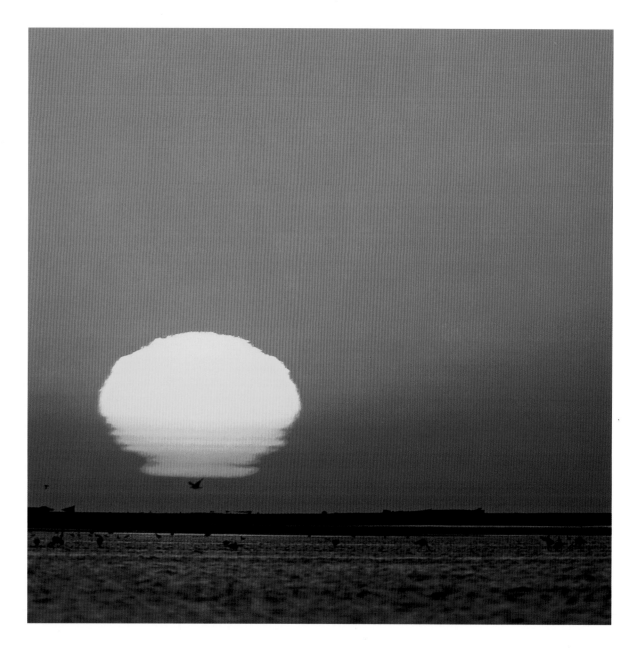

714 ● Atlantic Ocean, Namibia - Walvis Bay.

715 ● Atlantic Ocean, Florida (USA) - Egret near Naples.

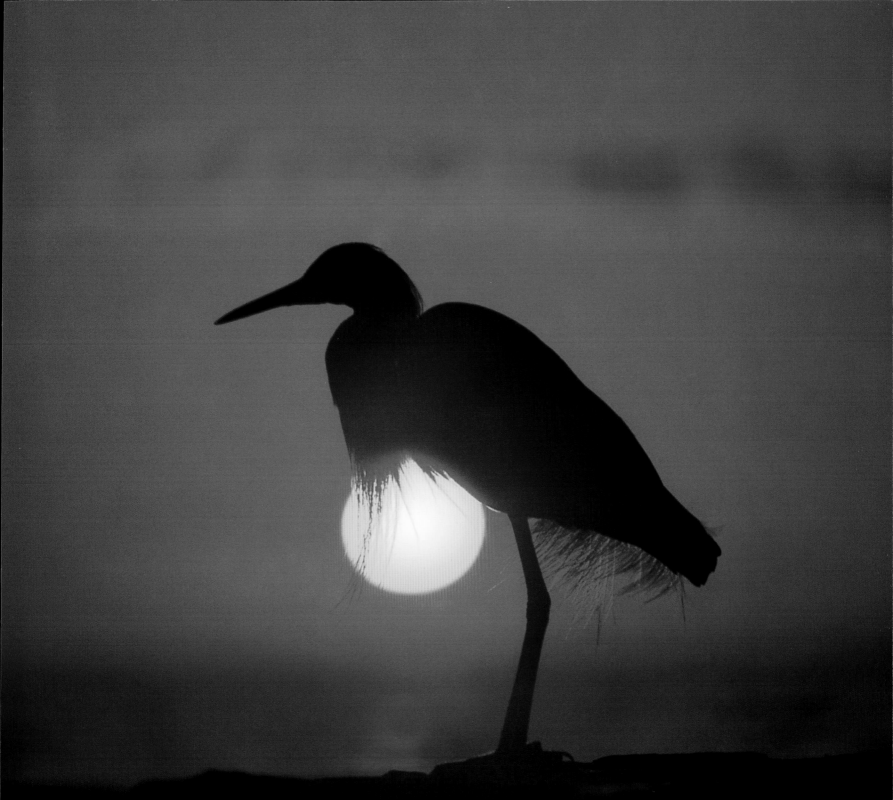

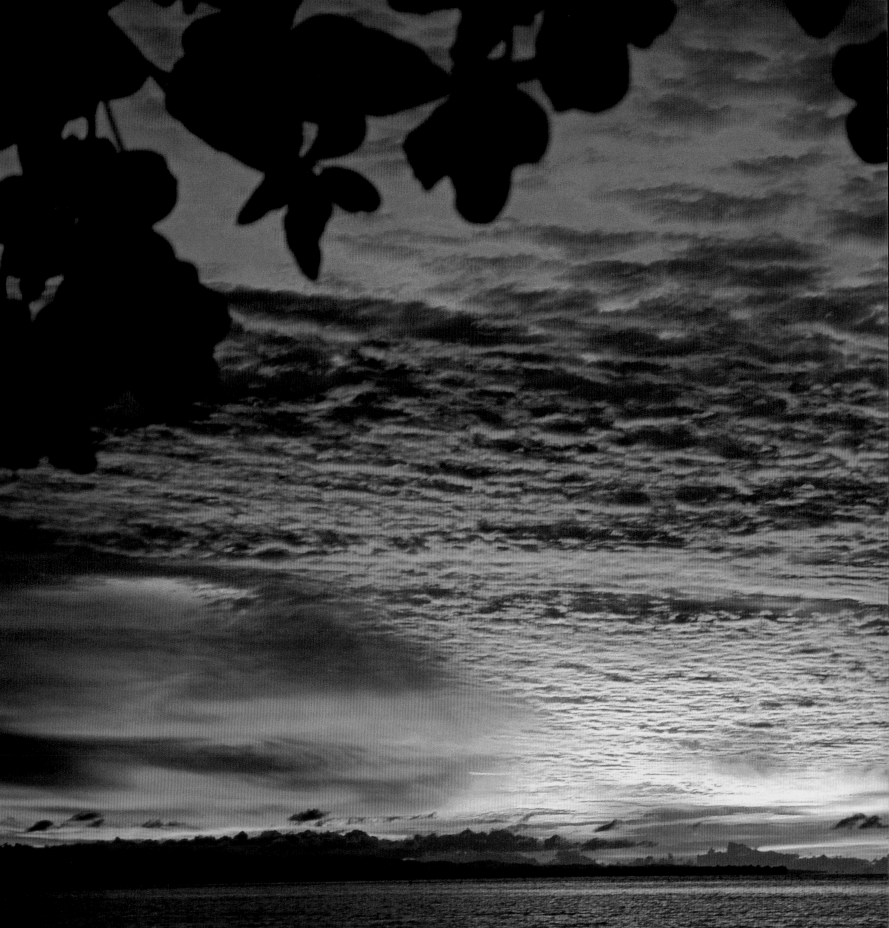

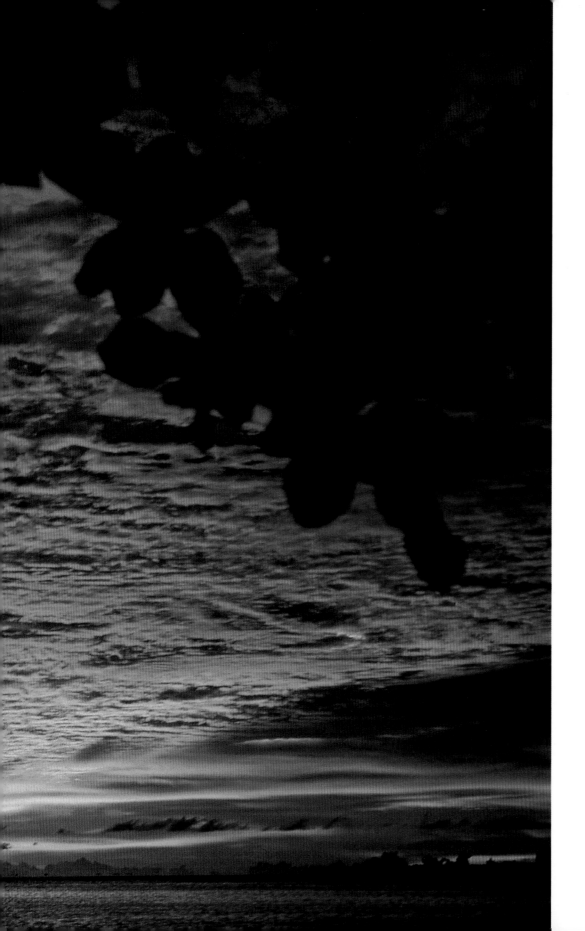

Tropical palettes

● Indian Ocean,
Thailand - Phuket.

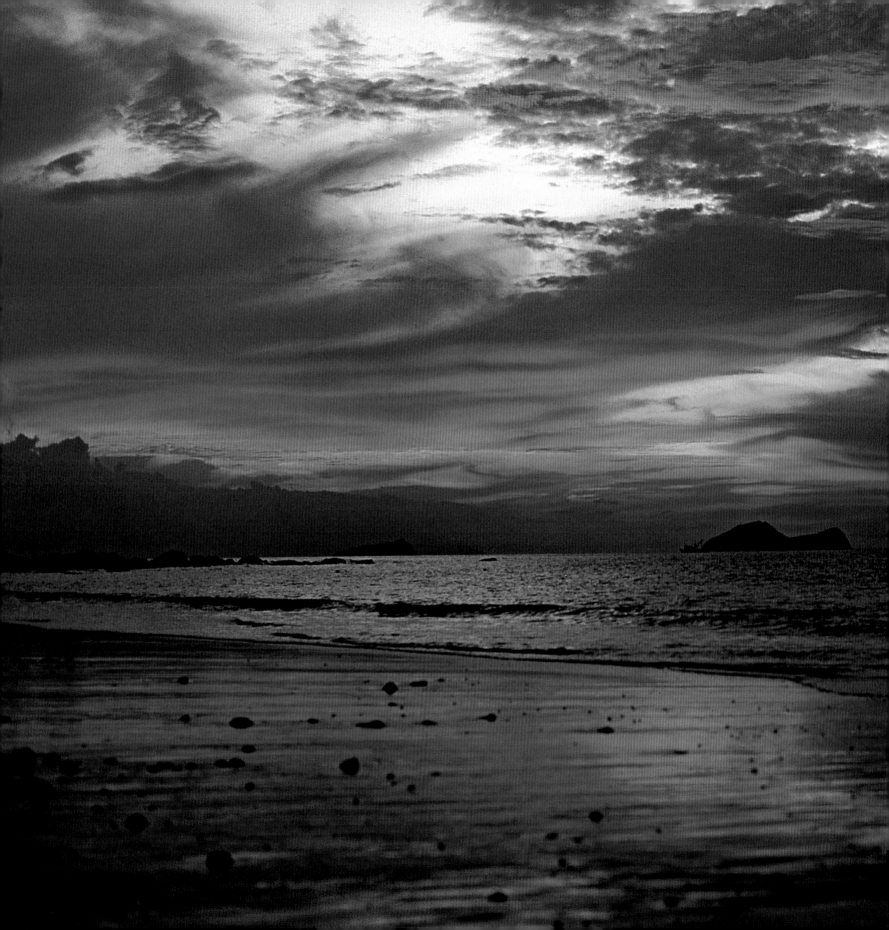

Indian Ocean,
Indonesia - Borneo.

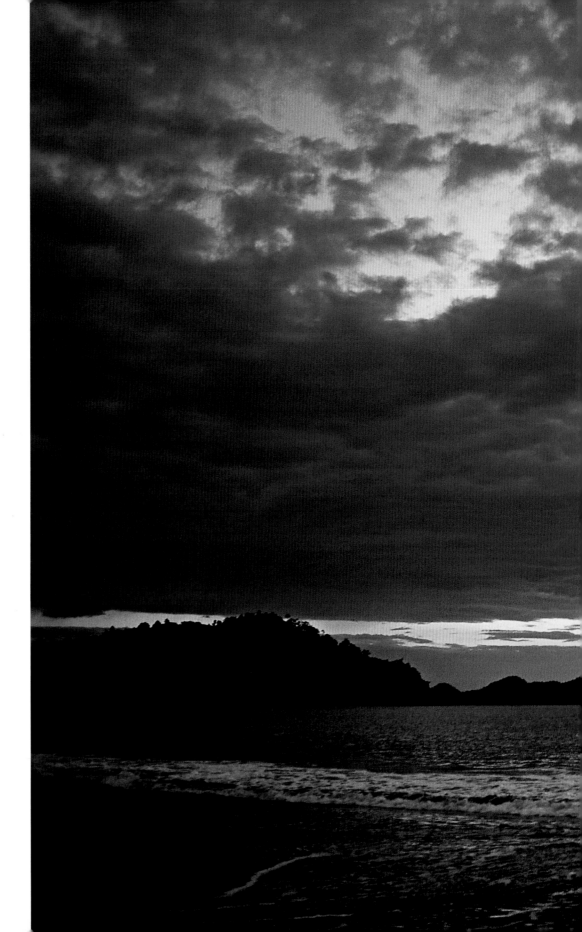

720-721 ● Indian Ocean, Thailand - Phuket.

722-723 ● Pacific Ocean, Hawaii (USA) - Keanae peninsula Maui.

724-725 ● Mediterranean Sea, France - Côte d'Azur.

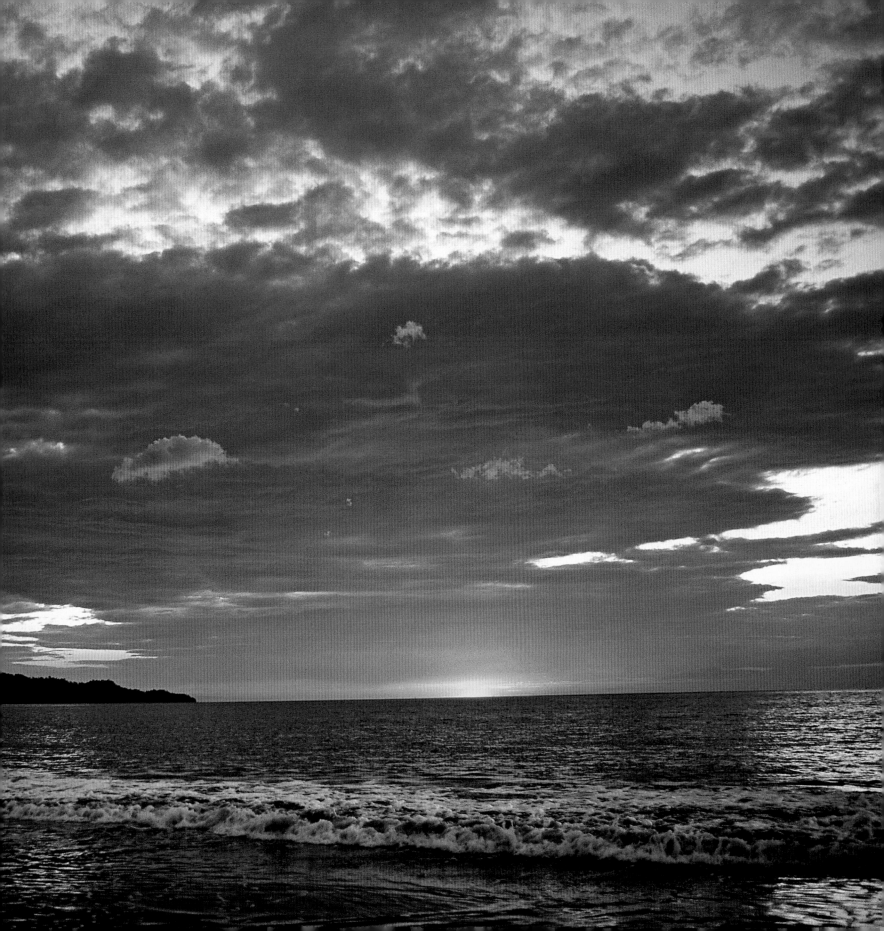

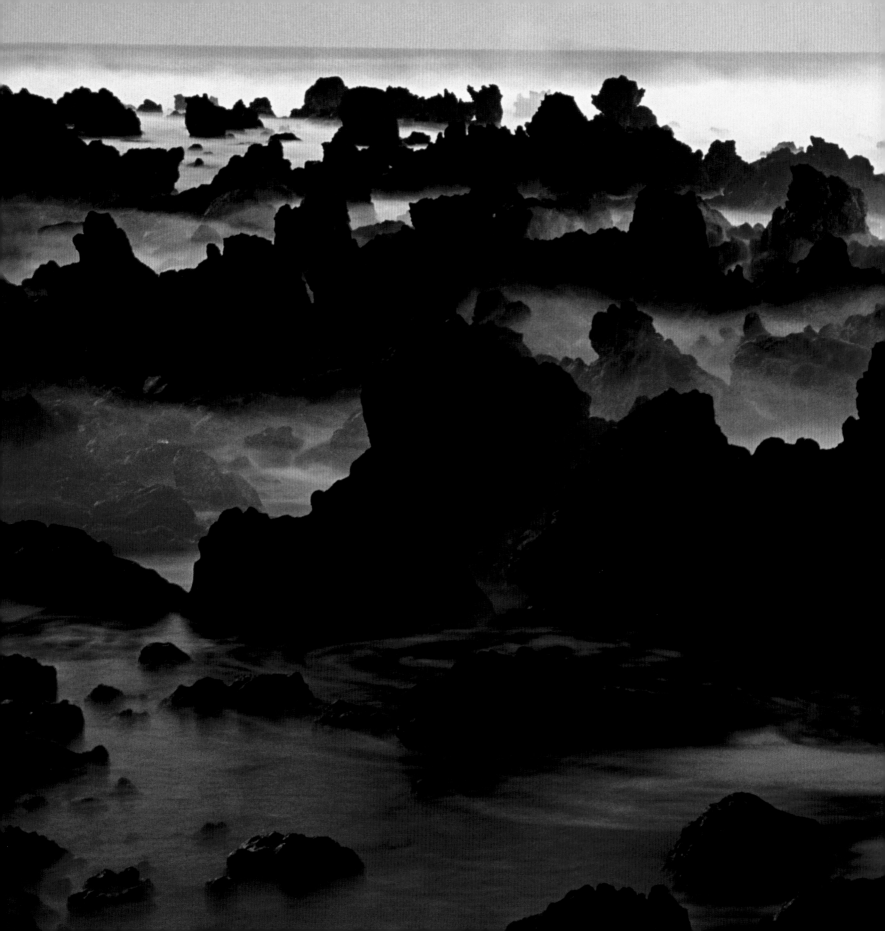

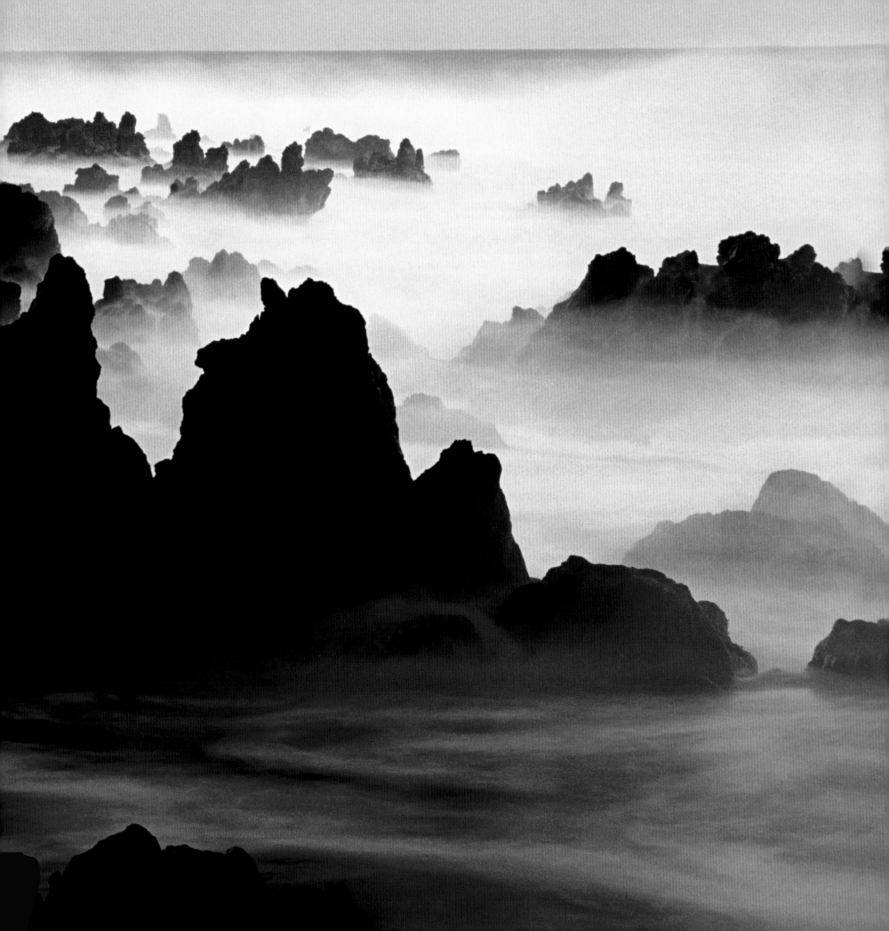

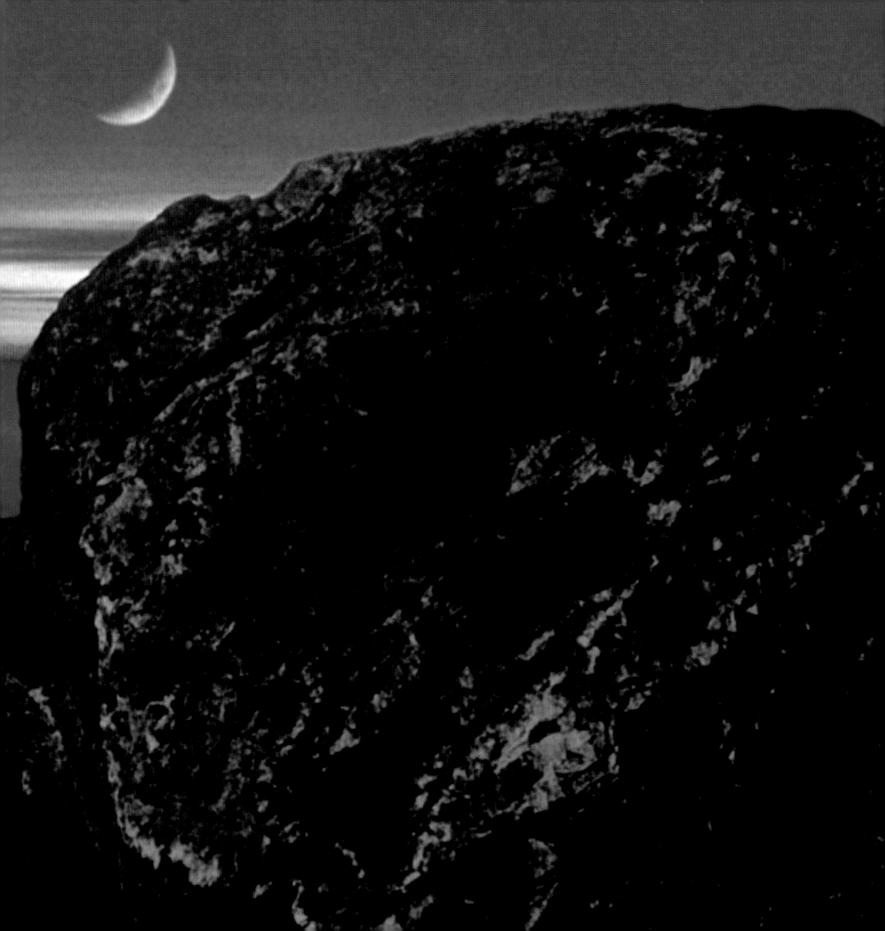

AUTHORS Biographies

GAETANO CAFIERO

Gaetano "Nini" Cafiero was born in Naples in 1937. A professional journalist he has published a dozen or so books on the sea, some with White Star. He is a member of the International Academy of Underwater Sciences and Technologies of Ustica, the Underwater Technologies and Scientific Research Group of Florence and the Historical Diving Society.

NORA L. DEANS

A graduate of Michigan University, Nora Deans writes about natural history and has been a writing consultant to many American aquaria, including those in Monterey, California and New Jersey State Aquarium. She currently works with the Alaska Natural History Association.

GIANNI GUADALUPI

Born in 1943, he has worked for thirty years as a writer, translator and editor of anthologies, with emphasis on the literature of real or fictitious journeys. He has written many successful books, some published by White Star. He is the editor of FMR and assistant editor of *Le Vie del Mondo*. He edits the series *Impossible Guides, Ancient States* and *Grand Tour* for Franco Maria Ricci.

THIERRY JIGOUREL

An expert on the geography, history and myths of Brittany, Thierry Jigourel is a journalist and author of books on this part of France. He has written for many years for magazines such as *Artus, Armor Magazine, Nouvel Ouest* and, more recently, *Ar Men*.

CORNELIA LAUF

An art critic and historian, Cornelia Lauf is also an exhibition curator and the author of many specialized publications. She is a researcher at Columbia University, New York, and spends her time between Rome and several American cities.

CARLO MARINCOVICH

Carlo Marincovich began sailing in 1950 in the Jole Olimpica class and has since been Italian champion in the Finn class. As a journalist he has covered the most important sailing races in the world, including the Whitbread, Admiral's Cup, Around Alone and America's Cup. He is the editor of the sailing magazines Nautica and Forza 7. Since 1978 he has been the sailing and Formula 1 correspondent for the newspaper La Repubblica.

GIULIO MELEGARI MAZZONI

A geologist and marine biologist, Giulio Melegari Mazzoni manages Underwater Operations and Technologies at SAIPEM, a company that builds off-shore platforms for ENI. For White Star he has written the chapter "*Egypt from Space*" in the book *Eyes of Horus*.

ANGELO MOJETTA

Angelo Mojetta is a marine biologist and diver. Having worked in laboratories and research institutes, he now divides his time between teaching and popularizing the marine sciences through articles, books and manuals. He is president of the Scientific and Environmental Committee of Assosub and the scientific consultant of the magazine *Sub*.

COLIN MONTEATH

Colin Monteath is a photographer, writer and climber. He has made more than 100 trips to the Antarctic since 1973 and even lived there for a period. Since 1983 he has been a member of many expeditions to the poles and world's highest mountains. Today he is considered one of the best of the "extreme reporters" in the world.

ALESSANDRA SENSINI

Born in 1970 in Grosseto, Italy, she entered windsurf competitions very young. After taking the Junior Championships in Italy, she began to win at all levels. She is gold medalist at the 2000 Sydney Olympics and bronze medalist at the 2004 Athens Olympics.

GIOVANNI SOLDINI

Giovanni Soldini was born in Milan in 1966 and has become one of the world's most famous sailors. He has participated in many sailing competitions, winning the *Roma x2* in 1996 (with Isabelle Autissier), the *Europe 1 Star* and the *Quebec-St. Malo* in 1997, and the *Atlantic Alone* in 1998. His voyage – and victory – in the 1998-99 *Around Alone* was a memorable event, during which he saved Isabelle Autissier whose boat had sunk in the South Pacific. Among his most recent exploits was his qualification, in the trimaran Tim, in the seventh *Route du Rhum*, considered the most glamorous of the single-handed transatlantic races.

INDEX

INDEX

PHOTO CREDITS

Cover Ron Dahlquist

Page 1 Onne van der Wal/Bluegreen Pictures

Pages 2-3 Marcello Bertinetti/Archivio White Star

Pages 4-5 Kurt Amsler

Pages 6-7 A. Conway/Archivio White Star

Pages 9, 11, back cover Marcello Bertinetti/Archivio White Star

Pages 12-13 R. Sanford/Corbis/Contrasto

Pages 14-15 Ron Dahlquist

Page 17 Marcello Bertinetti/Archivio White Star

Page 21 N. Rabinowitz/Corbis/Contrasto

Pages 22-23 Ron Dahlquist

Pages 24-25 B.S.P.I./Corbis/Contrasto

Pages 27, 31, 32-33, 33, 34, 35, 36, 37, 38-39, 40, 40-41 Archive NASA

Page 42 Original image courtesy of NASA/Corbis/Contrasto

Pages 43, 44-45 Archive NASA

Page 47 Gilles Martin Raget

Page 51 Marcello Bertinetti/Archivio White Star

Pages 52-53 R. Schmid/Simephoto

Pages 54-55 Antonio Attini/Archivio White Star

Pages 56-57, 58, 59 Guido Alberto Rossi/Image Bank

Pages 60-61 G. Simeone/Simephoto

Pages 62-63, 64-65 Anne Conway/Archivio White Star

Pages 66-67, 68-69, 69, 70-71 Marcello Bertinetti/Archivio White Star

Pages 72-73 Giulio Veggi/Archivio White Star

Pages 74-75 Airdata/Archivio De Agostini

Pages 76-77 Giulio Veggi/Archivio White Star

Pages 78-79 G. Simeone/Simephoto

Pages 80-81 J. Huber/Simephoto

Pages 82-83 Giulio Veggi/Archivio White Star

Pages 84-85 Guido Alberto Rossi/Image Bank

Pages 86, 87, 88-89 Antonio Attini/Archivio White Star

Pages 90-91 M. Borchi/Archivio White Star

Pages 92-93, 94-95 Antonio Attini/Archivio White Star

Pages 96-97 M. Borchi/Archivio White Star

Pages 98-99 Marcello Bertinetti/Archivio White Star

Pages 100-101 Antonio Attini/Archivio White Star

Pages 102-103 Gunter Ziesler

Pages 104-105 Tui De Roi/Hedgehog House

Pages 106-107 Marcello Bertinetti/Archivio White Star

Pages 108-109 G. Cubitt/Bruce Coleman

Pages 110-111 M. Melodia/Panda Photo

Pages 112-113, 114, 115 Antonio Attini/Archivio White Star

Pages 116-117 Marcello Bertinetti/Archivio White Star

Pages 118-119 Antonio Attini/Archivio White Star

Pages 120-121. 122. 123. 124-125. 126-127 Marcello Bertinetti/Archivio White Star

Pages 128, 129 J.P. Ferrero/Ardea London

Pages 130-131 R. Woldendorp/ Panda Photo

Pages 132-133 J. Huber/Simephoto

Pages 134-135 Y. Arthus-Bertrand/Corbis/Contrasto

Pages 136-137 Kurt Amsler

Pages 138-139 Livio Bourbon/Archivio White Star

Pages 140-141 M. Allwood-Coppin/Africaimagery.com

Pages 142-143 Marcello Bertinetti/Archivio White Star

Pages 144-145 Antonio Attini/Archivio White Star

Pages 146-147, 148-149, 149, 150-151 Marcello Bertinetti/Archivio White Star

Page 153 D. Parer & E. Parer Cook/Ardea London Ltd.

Page 157 Y. Arthus-Bertrand/Corbis/Contrasto

Pages 158-159 T. Mckenna/Corbis/Contrasto

Pages 160-161 Marco Moretti

Pages 162-163 J. Amos/Robertstock

Pages 164-165 M. T. Sedam/Corbis/Contrasto

Pages 166-167 K. Aitken/Panda Photo

Pages 168-169 I. Vissen/Hedgehog House

Pages 170-171 Y. Arthus-Bertrand/Corbis/Contrasto

Pages 172-173 Michael Yamashita

Pages 174-175 Kurt Amsler

Pages 176-177, 178-179 Marcello Bertinetti/Archivio White Star

Pages 180-181 Y. Arthus-Bertrand/Corbis/Contrasto

Pages 182-183 A. Conway/Archivio White Star

Pages 184-185 Airdata/Archivio De Agostini

Pages 186-187 Egidio Trainito

Page 188 Guido Alberto Rossi/Image Bank

Pages 189, 190-191 Y. Arthus-Bertrand/Corbis/Contrasto

Pages 192-193. 193 Antonio Attini/Archivio White Star

Pages 194-195 Fr. Jourdan/Explorer/Hoa-Qui

Pages 196-197 Jim Wark/Airphoto

Pages 198-199 Marcello Bertinetti/Archivio White Star

PHOTO CREDITS

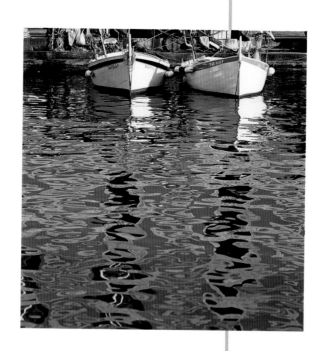

Mediterranean Sea, Liguria (Italy): Port in Camogli